THE GREAT SHIFT

ALSO BY JAMES L. KUGEL

The Idea of Biblical Poetry

Early Biblical Interpretation

In Potiphar's House

On Being a Jew

The Bible as It Was

Traditions of the Bible

The Great Poems of the Bible

The God of Old

How to Read the Bible

The Ladder of Jacob

In the Valley of the Shadow

A Walk Through Jubilees

The Assemblyman

The Kingly Sanctuary

The GREAT SHIFT

Encountering God in Biblical Times

JAMES L. KUGEL

Houghton Mifflin Harcourt
Boston New York
2017

www.hmhco.com

Library of Congress Cataloging-in-Publication Data is available.
ISBN 978-0-544-52055-4

Book design by Chloe Foster

Printed in the United States of America
DOC 10 9 8 7 6 5 4 3 2 1

To R., as always

CONTENTS

Part III. Transformations

Part IV. In Search of God

TIMELINE OF MAJOR FIGURES AND EVENTS

* Israel's Remote Ancestors

Abraham and Sarah, Isaac and Rebekah, Jacob and his wives	(dates uncertain)
Moses and the Exodus	13th–12th centuries BCE*
Joshua and the entrance into Canaan; Deborah, Samson, and the other Judges	13th–11th centuries BCE

* First Temple Period, ca. 1000 to 586 BCE

Saul becomes king of Israel	late 11th century BCE
King David (founder of the United Monarchy)	ruled ca. 1010–ca. 970 BCE
King Solomon	ruled United Monarchy ca. 970–ca. 930 BCE
King Rehoboam succeeds Solomon; breakup of the United Monarchy	late 10th century BCE

* Separate kingdoms of Judah (in the south) and Israel (in the north)

The prophets Elijah and Elisha	9th century BCE
The prophet Amos	early to mid 8th century BCE
Hosea, Isaiah, and Micah prophesy; Assyria threatening	latter half of 8th century BCE
Fall of Israel (Northern Kingdom) to Assyria	722–721 BCE

* Henceforth, Bible's focus is on Judah (Southern Kingdom)

Josiah becomes king of Judah	641–640 BCE
Jeremiah begins prophesying	627–626 BCE

---

* BCE stands for "before the Common Era," that is, BC

King Josiah dies; Neo-Babylonian Empire begins actively threatening	609 BCE
Babylonians deport King Jehoiachin and many prominent Jerusalemites (including the prophet Ezekiel) to Babylon	597 BCE
Fall of Jerusalem to Babylonians; mass deportation of Judeans to Babylon; Jeremiah and Ezekiel major prophets	587–586 BCE

* Babylonian exile and aftermath

After Cyrus's Persian Empire takes over Babylon, exiled Judeans begin to return to their homeland	late 6th century BCE

* Second Temple period, ca. 530 BCE to 70 CE

Persians rule province of Judah until decisive Battle of Issus, when Alexander the Great conquers entire region	333 BCE
Judah/Judea ruled by Egyptian Ptolemies	from 323 BCE
1 Enoch; Book of Jubilees	late third, early second century BCE
Syrian Seleucids take over Judea from Ptolemies	198 BCE
Book of Ben Sira written	ca. 180 BCE
Revolt of the Maccabees ousts Seleucids, leading to Jewish self-rule	166–63 BCE
Origins of Dead Sea Scrolls community	second half of second century BCE
Pompey conquers Jerusalem to start Roman rule	63 BCE
Jewish revolt against Romans ends in defeat	66–70 CE

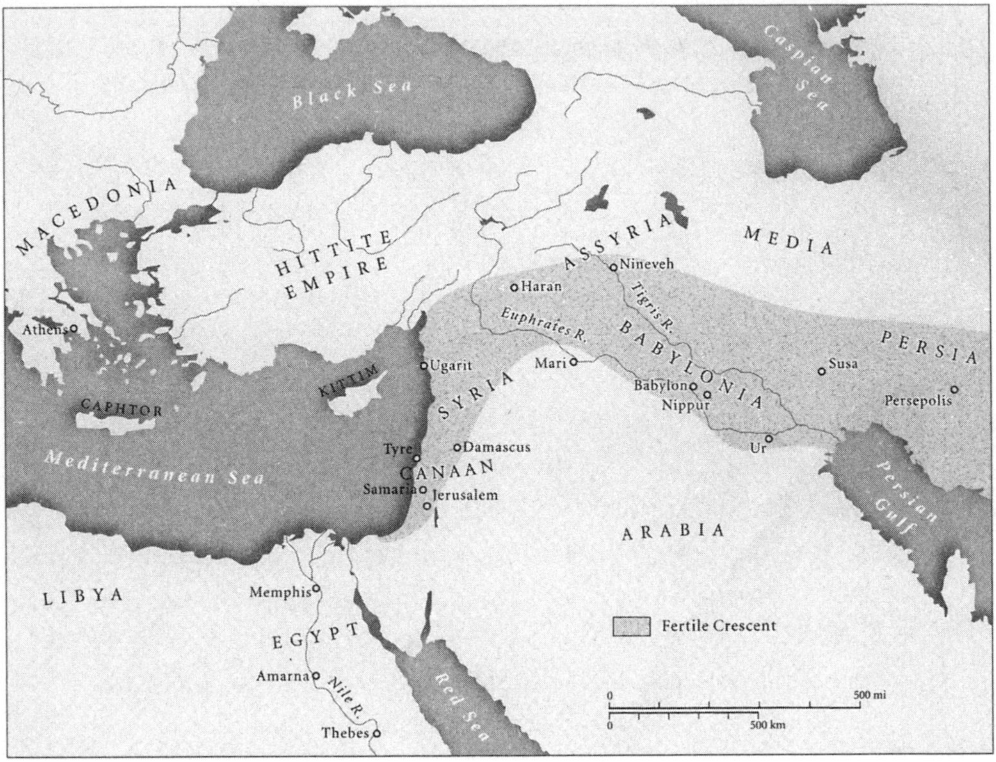

The Ancient Near East

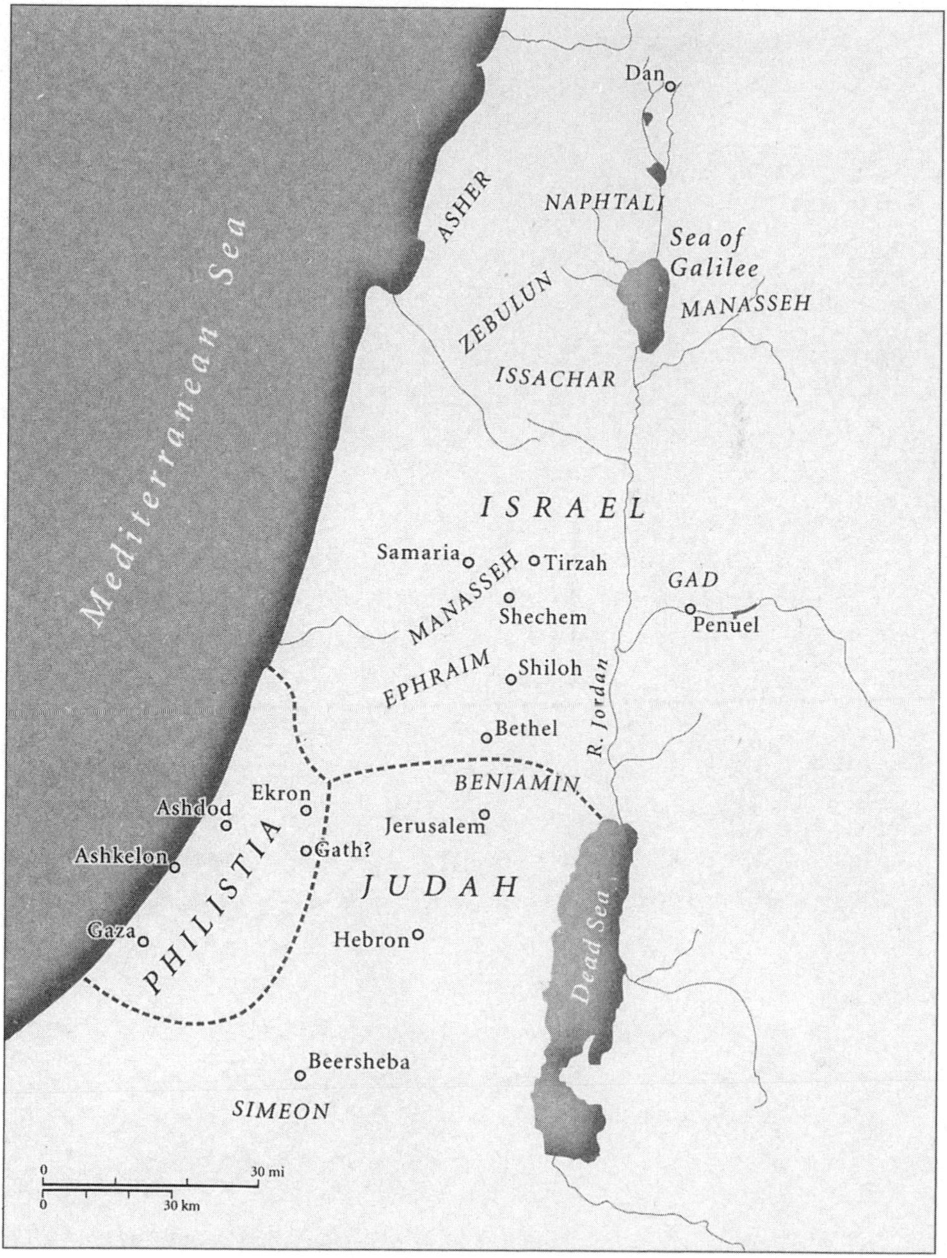

Israel and Judah

FOREWORD

I have spent most of my adult life researching and teaching the Hebrew Bible. For more than twenty years I taught at Yale and Harvard Universities, and another ten years at Bar-Ilan University in Israel. It has been a real pleasure teaching the students in these places, but I've never lost sight of my main purpose in going into this field. I wanted, as much as possible, to get inside the biblical world and see what ancient Israelites saw, to enter their minds in order to understand what the Bible is really saying. Over the years, I've written books on various topics, but I've saved for this last one what seems to me the most important question of all:

Modern scholars know that in biblical times, people did not "believe" in God in the way they do now. In truth, there is not a single verse in the Hebrew Bible that suggests that God's *existence* was a matter of belief or faith, and it certainly was not the subject of debate or questioning. (True, biblical figures are sometimes said to believe *in* God in the sense that they put their trust or faith in God's readiness to intervene on their behalf, believing that He will help them. But it was not God's existence that was believed in; that was simply obvious.)[1] Sometimes it is asserted that people back then simply *assumed* that God exists because they lacked today's knowledge of science and so had to conclude that some sort of divine being was in charge of life on earth. But if biblical stories are any kind of guide, people in ancient times sometimes *encountered* God, or at least thought they did.[2] Moreover, the whole way in which these encounters took place seems quite foreign to the experience of most of us today. My aim in the present study is to try to understand why this is so. The question I wish to answer, using all that we now know about biblical Israel and its neighbors, is: What was the actual, lived reality of God in biblical times, and why have most people lost it today?

A word of caution to begin with: this book is not for everyone. Many of the things that modern scholars have discovered about the Bible go against the established religious doctrines of Judaism and Christianity. This can be quite disturbing for some readers. Even among university researchers, there are those who try to put their own spin on recent discoveries, consciously or otherwise seeking to salvage what they can of traditional teachings. On the other extreme, there are certainly some contemporary scholars who see their mission as debunking everything people used to believe about the Bible. My own program here is to avoid either approach. What I wish to do is to make use of everything modern scholars have discovered about the Bible and the ancient Near East (as well as a few other topics) and to try to use these insights, along with a little imagination, in order to enter the world of the Bible as fully and truly as possible, to see things as they were seen then.

To do this, however, is to pursue a moving target, because even within the biblical period (roughly a thousand years long), things changed. If you go back far enough in biblical history, you find yourself in a very different world. How can someone make sense, realistic sense, of the things that people say and do in the Bible? One of the most common features in the writings of ancient Israel's prophets and sages is the assertion that God *speaks,* indeed, speaks to them: "The word of the LORD came to me, saying . . ."; "Thus says the LORD . . ."; "And the LORD spoke to Moses, saying . . ." What did they mean by this — did a voice just pop into their heads? God does not seem to speak in this way to people today. True, some people seek divine guidance or advice in prayer or meditation, and an answer sometimes emerges in their minds. But this is rather different from divine speech in the Bible, where the people involved are not usually seeking to hear from God; often, in fact, they flee at the very prospect. When God addresses Moses out of the burning bush, "Moses hid his face, because he was afraid to look at God." He tries to turn down the mission that God has reserved for him: "Please," he begs, "send someone else." Later, when God reveals Himself to the Israelites assembled at Mount Sinai, "all the people saw it and fell back and stood at a distance; 'You be the one to speak to us,' they said to Moses, 'and we will obey, but do not let God speak to us, lest we die'" (Exod 20:15–16; some Bibles, 20:18–19). Prophets summoned by God similarly react by saying, "Please find someone else": this is basically what Jeremiah says when God first calls him, and other prophets are likewise reluctant. In fact, the prophet Jonah didn't say anything; when God called him, he hopped the next ship to faraway Tarshish, hoping God would simply forget about him.

Moreover, what God has to say to these prophets, as well as to virtually all others, does not come in response to some request from the human beings involved. He* simply speaks to people unprompted, demanding that they do something or announce things to come. Amos describes transmitting God's message as a kind of knee-jerk reaction: "If a lion roars, who isn't afraid? And if God speaks, who doesn't prophesy?" What could have been the lived reality behind such assertions?

In fact, it is not just a matter of divine speech. Many biblical texts report that God actually appeared to people. Some modern theologians have sought to downplay these passages, since most people nowadays hold that God has no physical form, nothing that the eye can perceive. But that does not appear to have been the case with Abraham or Sarah or Jacob or Moses or Isaiah; all these, along with numerous other biblical figures, are said to have actually seen God, once or even several times. "The LORD appeared to him by the oak trees of Mamre," the book of Genesis reports matter-of-factly about Abraham. Jacob tells his son Joseph, "God Almighty appeared to me at Luz, in the land of Canaan, and He blessed me." "I saw the LORD standing next to the altar," Amos recounts. "Woe is me, I am lost," says Isaiah, "for my own eyes have beheld the King, the LORD of Hosts." "In the thirtieth year, on the fifth day of the fourth month . . . the heavens opened and I saw the appearance of God," Ezekiel says. Were they all lying? It seems to me more likely that these people (or more precisely, the people telling their stories) must have felt that they were telling the truth, at least in some sense; it was altogether plausible for a person to hear and see God in a way that is quite distant from us today. But to say this is virtually to admit that human beings today seem to have lost this vital capacity. Of course, one might just say, "Ancient people had a different understanding of reality," and leave it at that. But this doesn't really answer the question. Why do these biblical texts say what they say, and if there was any reality to them, why has it mostly disappeared?

Finding an answer is no simple undertaking; it involves getting into the nitty-gritty of modern biblical scholarship and its investigation of various biblical narratives and prophecies, the songs and psalms of the Bible, its laws and its proverbs — as well as borrowing some insights from neuroscience and anthropology. Before we are done, we will have looked at much of the Hebrew Bible, because almost all of it has something to tell us about the great

* Throughout this book, I have referred to God using the pronouns "He," "Him," "His," etc., since for the most part God was represented as a specifically male deity in biblical times. By the same token, the capital letter *H* is intended to convey the respect for the various forms of divine reference current in the Hebrew Bible itself.

subject at the core of this book: the reality of God in ancient times—and in our own.

A few technicalities before we begin:
Most of the translations of biblical texts are my own, but I have drawn here and there on two excellent modern translations, the New Jewish Publication Society (NJPS) and the New Revised Standard Version (NRSV) translations. For proper names from the Bible I have generally used the standard English forms rather than transcriptions of the Hebrew, thus: Jacob and not Ya'akov, Jerusalem and not Yerushalayim. In transcribing Hebrew words, I have used the rough English equivalents rather than "scientific" transcription, thus: *le-David* rather than *lĕdāwid.* The only exception is that cleaning-your-glasses sound represented by the letter *ḥ* (with an underdot), as distinct from our ordinary *h* sound.

The numbering of biblical verses poses a great problem, particularly in the book of Psalms. A surprising variety in the numbering of Psalms verses exists. Many modern translations do not include the various psalm headings in their numbering, so that a one-verse difference exists between such numberings and the traditional numbering of the Hebrew text. A similar gap appears here and there in other biblical books as well. After some deliberation I have decided to list the traditional Hebrew numbering alone in cases where there is only a one-verse difference, trusting that curious readers will easily be able to find the verse in question adjacent to the one listed in their own translations. In cases of more than a one-verse difference, I have listed the Hebrew numbering first, followed by "some Bibles, such-and-such."

PART I

"A Thousand Ages in Thy Sight . . ."

The Bible consists of texts composed at different times — by most accounts, over the course of nearly a thousand years. Within this period, people are sometimes said to meet God face-to-face. At other times God seems to be more remote and abstract; sometimes people don't actually encounter God at all. Which picture is the right one?

I

SEEING BIBLICALLY

Encounters with angels; Hidden behind the curtain; Waking dreams; A different kind of mind

The Bible sometimes seems to stress that when people encountered God, either directly or in the form of an angel, they "saw" in a special way, quite different from ordinary seeing. And yet what they saw was usually just another ordinary human being or some object from daily life.

In the book of Genesis, Hagar is the maidservant of Abraham's wife, Sarah. At a certain point she and Sarah have a falling out, and Sarah orders her to be banished — in fact, sent off into the bleak wilderness along with her young son Ishmael. This cruel decree is carried out, and poor Hagar wanders about with her son for a time. Eventually they run out of drinking water, and it seems they will both die of thirst. Hagar, despairing, leaves her son under one of the nearby bushes and sits down some distance away. "I don't want to have to watch the boy die," she says, and bursts into tears. But help is on the way:

> God heard the boy's cry, and an angel of God called to Hagar from heaven and said to her, "What is the matter, Hagar? Do not be afraid: God has heard the boy's cry from where he is. Get up, pick up the boy and hold him tight in your arms, for I intend him to become a great nation." And God opened her eyes and she saw a well of water, so she went and filled the water-skin with water and gave the boy to drink. (Gen 21:17–19)

This is one of those passages that biblical scholars call a "name etiology":[1] Ishmael's name means "God hears," or "May God hear," so the passage suggests — not once but twice — that Ishmael was so named because God *heard*

Ishmael's cry. Beyond this, there is a larger, national issue lurking beneath the narrative. Ishmael's descendants would indeed become a great nation, as later history was to show. This section of Genesis thus seeks to point out that, on the one hand, those Ishmaelites are actually the Israelites' cousins, both peoples descended from Abraham; but on the other hand, it was equally important to assert that they were Israel's inferiors, the descendants of a mere maidservant who had been unceremoniously booted out of Abraham's camp.

Two Kinds of Seeing

For our subject, however, what is most important is the beginning of the last sentence, "God opened her eyes and she saw a well of water." Why should the narrative have said that God *opened her eyes*? Minutes earlier, she seemed to be wandering around in the wasteland with nothing to drink. Now an angel calls to Hagar from heaven and tells her that everything will be all right and that, in fact, God has destined her son for greatness. Then God Himself opens her eyes and she suddenly sees a well that will save her life along with that of her son. Why didn't she see it before? Nothing in the text implies that she then had to *dig* the well, or that God led her to some previously hidden opening in the ground. Apparently the well was in plain sight all along. In fact, the text had earlier mentioned that Hagar put her son "under one of the bushes" because she couldn't stand to witness his death. But didn't she know that bushes, especially bushes in the scorched wilderness, must have some source of water to survive, and that such a source must therefore be somewhere very close by? If so, why did God have to open her eyes? And by the way, were they really closed?

The answer to all these questions has to do with the act of seeing itself. In numerous places in the Bible, the text seems to go out of its way to assert that there is a special kind of seeing associated with divine encounters. It is as if the normal faculty of sight is shut down, replaced by something else: at first, people *think* that their eyes are perceiving things, but this is just an optical illusion. That is why, in a divine vision, people often seem to be in some kind of fog (as Hagar apparently is here): the most obvious things seem to escape their attention. After a while, however, they catch on; suddenly they realize that this is a divine encounter, that their eyes are really not functioning normally, and what they think they are *seeing* they are not seeing at all. That is why God has to "open" Hagar's eyes afterwards; He has to switch her vision from the special to the regular sort of seeing in order for her to perceive what was right in front of her all along.*

This special kind of seeing is often marked as such in the Bible. One day, sitting outside his tent, Abraham sees three men approaching. Notice, however, the Bible's wording:

> Now the LORD appeared to him by the terebinths of Mamre, while he was sitting at the door of his tent in the heat of the day. And *he lifted up his eyes* and *he saw,* and *behold!* Three men were standing near him and *he saw;* and he ran from the tent door toward them and bowed down low." (Gen 18:1–2)

The first sentence describes to the reader what really happened: the LORD appeared to Abraham. But that isn't what Abraham saw, so the text stresses the fact that he was seeing in a different mode: "He *lifted up his eyes* and *he saw,* and *behold!* . . . and *he saw* . . ."[2] This vision carries on for a while: Abraham prepares an elaborate meal for his three guests, then watches them eat, or at least thinks that that is what he is seeing. (But every ancient Israelite knew that angels cannot eat.)[3] "Where is your wife Sarah?" they ask — but how do these strangers know his wife's name? The whole thing is like a dream, except that Abraham seems to be wide awake.

> Then He said, "I will return in a year's time, and your wife Sarah will have a son." Sarah had been listening at the door of the tent, which was in back of him. Now Abraham and Sarah were old, well advanced in years; Sarah had stopped having the periods that women have. So Sarah laughed to herself: "After I am all worn out, will I still have relations — not to mention that my husband is old too!" Then the LORD said to Abraham, "Why did Sarah laugh and say, 'Can I really give birth, old as I am?' Is anything too much for the LORD? In a year's time I will be back, and Sarah will have a son." (Gen 18:10–14)

It is important to pay close attention to the words. This whole section is being told to *us* from the point of view of the narrative: the *text* is saying that this

---

* A similar switch back to regular sight is specially marked in Gen 22:13, "And Abraham lifted up his eyes and he saw and behold! a ram caught in a thicket by its horns." This was a real ram, the one that Abraham goes on to sacrifice. But before that, apparently, his eyes were working in the "vision" mode. It is noteworthy, however, that the specially marked act of seeing usually *introduces* the vision rather than following it; see below.

is really God speaking to Abraham. But Abraham and Sarah don't know this; they are still in a fog—as they will be until the end.

Beyond this specific observation, what is remarkable about the whole incident is what it seems to be saying about human encounters with God. They do take place. A person could just be sitting in front of his tent on a hot afternoon, and suddenly God might appear to him. But the person could never really be sure of what he was seeing, because his eyes seemed to be telling him that this was just an ordinary human being.[4] (One might say this was his brain's way of representing to itself something that was not visual at all.) Then God begins to speak, and in the present example, even though Abraham doesn't know it is God speaking, the words enter his mind, "I will return to you in a year's time, and Sarah will have a son" (verse 14). The words turn out to be true: Sarah does indeed give birth to Isaac. But the accompanying visual part, the things that Abraham's eyes had been seeing, remain a kind of waking dream. Even after those true words coming from God had been spoken, the waking dream can continue, as is it does in this case. The passage thus ends: "Then the men set out from there and looked down toward Sodom, *and Abraham went along with them to see them off.*" He's still in a fog.[5]

A much briefer, but similar, case is the appearance of an angel to Moses. Tending his father-in-law's flocks, Moses arrives at Horeb, the site of the "mountain of God [or: the gods]."* Again, it is important to notice the wording:

> And the angel of the LORD appeared to him in a flaming fire from the midst of the bush, and *he saw* and *behold!* The bush was burning with fire, but the bush was not burnt up. Moses said, "I have to take a closer look at this *sight:* why isn't that bush burning up?" Once the LORD saw that he had come to take a look, God called to him from the middle of the bush, "Moses, Moses!" He answered, "Here I am." (Exod 3:2–4)

What is the text seeking to say? To *us,* the readers/listeners, it is saying that God appeared to Moses. But this is not what Moses saw. All he saw was a bush that somehow kept burning and burning, so much so that he was eventually persuaded to go off the beaten path to take a closer look. Was it a real bush? Real bushes don't keep burning like that. But once this vision had drawn Moses close enough to where God was,** God could begin to speak

* The Hebrew word *elohim* can mean either God or "the gods."

** Through most of the biblical period, there was no reason *not* to believe that God did not to him, and the visual part could disappear. Thus, when the text describes what Moses *saw* in this narrative — the thing that he calls "this sight"[6] — it is speaking strictly from Moses's point of view and talking about that other kind of seeing. As with Abraham, one might say that this was the brain's way of processing a nonvisual encounter in visual terms. Later, however, Moses hears God's *voice* and the "angel" disappears. Now Moses is out of the visionary mode of seeing. Actually, he sees nothing; all he is doing is listening to God speak.

Why was this plausible? By this I do not mean to ask if Moses or Abraham really had such an encounter; there is no way to know that, or even to know if such a person as Moses or Abraham ever really existed. Rather, my question is: What did the first audience of these stories assume — about God, and about seeing — that made these accounts seem plausible and even realistic? If one considers as a whole the Bible's various narrations of people's encounters with the divine, a definite pattern emerges — not in every case, to be sure, but in quite a few.[7] The people involved suddenly meet up with God, but this is not normal seeing. Indeed, the text sometimes enters into a kind of double narration, telling *us* that this was God while at the same time seeking to duplicate what the person involved saw, "three men" or "a bush that kept burning." At the same time, the narrative makes sure we know that the people are in a kind of fog: what they think they see (often referred to as an "angel") is not what they are really seeing, but the brain's way of processing this encounter. Eventually, however, God starts to speak to them; at this point they may or may not realize that what they had been seeing was a vision, but in any case, what they *hear* is the voice of God. So this is the pattern in many biblical narratives: what they see is an illusion, but what God says is real. The question is: Why? A few further examples may clarify the point.

The Moment of Confusion

Gideon ended up as a chieftain of the Israelites, one of the "judges" (the word *shofet* really means "leader" in early Hebrew) in the book of Judges. His rise to leadership began at a low point in his tribe's fortunes. The marauding Midianites keep attacking his kinsmen to seize their grain; in fact, the story opens

---

have some sort of physical form, and in this account, that physical form was in a specific place, on or near "the mountain of God/the gods."

with Gideon "beating out grains of wheat in the winepress to keep them safe from the Midianites." But then:

> The angel of the Lord appeared to him and said, "The Lord is with you, O mighty warrior." Gideon said to him, "Excuse me, sir, but if the Lord is with us, why are we having all this trouble? Where are all the miracles that our ancestors recorded for us, saying, 'Truly, the Lord took us up out of Egypt'? But now the Lord has abandoned us and left us in the power of the Midianites." Then the Lord turned to him and said, "Go in this strength of yours and save Israel yourself from the Midianites — am I not the one who is sending you?" But he said, "Please, sir, how should I be the one to save Israel?" (Judg 6:12–15)

The text says that what Gideon sees is an "angel of the Lord" in order to tell *us* that this was a vision. But all that Gideon sees is an ordinary man, whose greeting, "The Lord is with you," was apparently just a kind of pious hello in those days.* If he had realized that this was a divine vision and that what his eyes were *seeing* was not seeing in the usual sense, he would no doubt have fallen to his knees in reverence. But he is in one of those moments of confusion that are the mark of a divine encounter. So instead he uses the stranger's greeting to make his own, somewhat disrespectful retort: "Oh yeah? Well if God is with us, why are things so bad?" The visitor's referring to him as a "mighty warrior" must likewise have rung hollow in Gideon's ears: the mighty warrior was just now hiding his precious wheat grains in a winepress in case some Midianites should show up and take them from him by force!

Then "the Lord turned to him and said" — again, "the Lord" is what we readers are being told about Gideon's interlocutor. But Gideon still thinks this is an ordinary human being; that is what he "sees." Even when God says, "Go in this strength of yours and save Israel yourself from the Midianites — *am I not the one who is sending you?*" — Gideon somehow fails to catch the significance of these last words. Who would say such a thing if not God? But Gideon is in a fog; he thinks he is talking to a real person. "Please, sir," he says, "how should I be the one to save Israel?" He is still utterly confused.

It might seem in such passages that the distinction between an angel and God Himself is altogether blurred, as many scholars (including me)[8] have maintained. This is true, but it's not quite the whole story. Rather, the visual

---

* See Ruth 2:4. Note that our word "goodbye" is somewhat similar; it comes from the contracted phrase "God be with you," used as a pious farewell in Middle English.

part that constitutes the "angel" is altogether an illusion, a visual representation of something that is not visible; but what God says is quite real. So at first Gideon *sees* an angel (that is, the illusory vision), but then begins the true, audible part, "the LORD turned to him and said." This was true as well of the passage cited earlier about Moses and the burning bush: at first "the angel of the LORD *appeared* to him," but then "God called to him from the middle of the bush." In reality, it is *always* God who is speaking, but the angel in these ancient narratives is best understood as "God unrecognized," a visual representation of the nonvisual. (The Hebrew word *mal'akh,* translated as "angel," is rather more noncommittal than the English word. It means someone or something that is sent, an envoy or messenger, like Jacob's altogether human envoys in Gen 32:4.) In these visions, angels bear no external, physical signs of being anything other than human (because they are mirages in any case). They are nothing like the easily recognized angels of Renaissance painting, robed all in white, with a nice golden halo floating just above their heads. Rather, they look like ordinary people, at least to the person involved, because that person is always *in a fog,* as we have seen. It is only after a while that the person realizes the truth, and then his or her first reaction is fear: "I have actually encountered God Himself."

In the case of Gideon, the fog now starts to lift, at least partially, in the continuation of this passage:

> Then the LORD said, "But I will be with you, and you will defeat the Midianites to a man." He said to him, "If you will, sir, please *give me some sign* that it is you who are speaking to me. Do not leave here until I come back to you with an offering of mine and set it down in front of you." And he said: "I will stay here until you return."

What "the LORD" *says* are indeed God's words, but Gideon is still unsure who is speaking. True, asking for a sign is something one might request of God, but it could also be asked of a prophet of some kind.[9] In any case, asking for a sign is always a way of asking for proof *when one is in doubt.* And certainly what Gideon says next undercuts any notion that he understands that his interlocutor is a divine vision: every ancient Israelite knew that real angels neither eat nor drink, so placing an offering in front of this stranger (it seems to be just an ordinary meal of meat and unleavened bread) seems to indicate that Gideon still takes him for an ordinary human, or is testing him to see. It is only when the angel touches this offering with his staff that the visionary nature of this encounter becomes clear:

> A fire sprang up and engulfed the meat and the unleavened bread, and with that, the angel of the LORD disappeared from sight. When Gideon realized that it was indeed an angel of the LORD, he said, "Oh no! Oh Lord GOD—this means that I have seen the 'angel' of the LORD face to face." And the LORD said to him: "It is all right, do not be afraid, you will not die."

This is the final moment of recognition, ending in the appropriately panicky reverence. And it is certainly significant that while the optical illusion, the angel, has disappeared from sight, "the LORD" is still there talking to Gideon.

The "moment of confusion" seen in this brief encounter is duplicated in other biblical narratives as well. The famous account of Jacob's fight with an angel fits the same pattern:

> And Jacob was left alone, and a man wrestled with him until the break of day. When he saw that he could not overcome him, he wrenched Jacob's hip in its socket, so that the socket of Jacob's hip was strained in the fight with him. Then he said, "Let go of me, since it is getting to be dawn." But Jacob said, "I will not let go of you unless you bless me." He said, "Your name will not be Jacob any longer, but Israel, since you have struggled with God and with men and have prevailed." Then Jacob said to him, "Please now, tell me your name." He answered: "Why should you be asking for my name?" and blessed him there. Jacob named the place Peniel, saying, "I have seen God face to face and yet my life has been spared." (Gen 32:24–30)

Jacob thinks he is wrestling with a "man."[10] The fight with this stranger goes on, or seems to, the whole night long. (But who wrestles for an entire night?) Jacob appears in the end to get the better of his opponent, who asks to be released because it is getting to be dawn. Jacob's demand that his opponent bless him might seem to modern readers to indicate that Jacob is catching on, but in the Bible, the act of blessing is not as unusual as in modern times: human beings frequently bless each other. Here, in fact, Jacob seems to be asking for a blessing in the same sense that victorious schoolboys demand of their opponents, "Say 'uncle.'" The "blessing" that Jacob is demanding will be a sign of his fighting partner's utter submission. In other words, after a whole night of supposed wrestling, Jacob is still in a fog. Even the unexpected content of this "blessing"—that Jacob's name is to be exchanged for a new one, Israel—does not tip him off. The proof is that he then asks the "man" to tell him *his* name; any ancient Israelite knew that angels don't have names.[11]

Another moment of confusion occurs when an angel appears to the wife of Manoah (otherwise unnamed), the future mother of the biblical hero Samson. The story begins when "the angel of the LORD appeared to the woman" and told her that her frustrating period of infertility was about to end. She thinks he is a prophet, although she isn't sure: she later says that he looked "very frightening, like an angel/emissary of God." The things that this apparition *says* are altogether true: he gives her instructions for making her future son a Nazirite* from birth. But Manoah's wife hasn't caught on yet. When the stranger comes back for a return visit, she and her husband continue to act as if he is a human being.

> Manoah said to the angel of the LORD, "Permit us to detain you and kill a goat for you [for dinner]." The angel of the LORD said to Manoah, "Though you detain me I will not be able to eat your food; but if you wish to make a burnt offering to the LORD, then send it up"—because Manoah did not realize that he was an angel of the LORD. Then Manoah said to the angel of the LORD, "What is your name? For when what you said comes true, we will want to honor you." The angel replied, "Why should you be asking about my name, since it cannot be known?" Then Manoah took the goat and the grain offering, and offered them up to the LORD on a rock, and something wondrous happened while Manoah and his wife were watching. As the flames were rising up from the altar toward the sky, the angel of the LORD rose up in the flames of the altar. And Manoah and his wife saw this and they fell on their faces to the ground. The angel of the LORD never again appeared to Manoah and his wife; thus, Manoah understood that it was an angel of the LORD. And Manoah said to his wife, "We will surely die, because we have seen God." (Judg 13:15–22)

Here are most of the elements already seen.[12] Manoah and his wife offer their visitor a meal (just as Gideon did)—proof that they don't yet know that he is an angel. In fact, they are in such a fog that his weird answer, "Though you detain me I will not be able to eat your food," doesn't seem to strike them as weird at all. Then they make that other mistake (just seen in the case of Jacob and the angel) of asking an angel his name, when everyone knows that angels don't have names. Again, the angel's strange reply—"Why should you be asking about my name, since it cannot be known?"—doesn't tip them off in the slightest. It is only when the angel suddenly disappears in the altar's flames that they finally catch on and then, as in the previous instances,

---

* A special sort of devotee to God (cf. Numbers ch. 6).

their words reveal that "angels" have no independent reality, even in a waking dream. Rather, as Manoah says, "We will surely die, because *we have seen God.*"

The God of Old

This God does not seem to have much in common with the God of later theologians. Here, God is not everywhere, omnipresent; as already mentioned, modern scholars know that throughout the Bible, God is conceived — even in an optical hallucination — as having some actual form, a body.[13] In these narratives, God is just *elsewhere,* at least most of the time, hidden behind the curtain of ordinary reality and the usual way of seeing. Sometimes, however, He crosses that curtain to speak to human beings. When this happens, the people involved don't actually see *Him*: what they see, or think they see, is an "angel/envoy" or a "man" (an *apparition* might be the best way to say it) who looks like an ordinary human being.[14] They interact with this apparition for a time, sometimes a long time, and all the while they are in a kind of fog: they think they are seeing, but they are wrong.

Even when Moses and the leaders of Israel ascend Mount Sinai and are said to *see* God, it is striking that the narrative lowers its gaze just at the crucial moment:

> Then Moses and Aaron, Nadab and Abihu, and seventy elders of Israel went up [Mount Sinai]. And they saw the God of Israel: *under His feet* there was the likeness of a pavement of sapphire, like the very sky for purity. Yet He did not harm the leaders of the Israelites: they beheld God, and they ate and drank. (Exod 24:9–11)

They may actually have beheld God, their real partner in this covenant-sealing ceremony. But the narrative is at a loss to say anything about God's appearance: all it can describe is what was underneath His feet.

The state of mind that people have in these divine encounters seems quite similar to that of someone having a dream. When the dreamer wakes up, he says things like, "In my dream I saw someone approaching me; he was wearing a gray sharkskin suit and a black hat. He started talking to me, and I recognized the voice, as if we knew each other, but then suddenly I noticed that he had a pearl-handled revolver in his right hand. There was a loud bang, so loud that I woke up." Of course, the dreamer didn't really see any of the things he mentioned. In fact, his eyes did not *see* a thing: they were closed tight throughout the dream.[15] By the same token, that bang that he heard was an auditory illusion. In the biblical stories seen thus far, the people encountering God are not asleep, but they are in a fog, which is a lot like dreaming. As in a dream, the most illogical things seem to make sense to them, or else they are just ignored; it is only later that all or part of what was seen turns out to have been an illusion. But these are not useless illusions. They might be better described as a kind of theatrical setting that allows this auditory encounter with God to take place. Now, the *voice* of God might also be described as an illusion, a way for God to communicate with us through our sound software. But whatever the means, what God *says*, these texts are telling us, turns out to be true. Even in this, the similarity to dreams is striking. Consider, for example, Jacob's actual dream at Bethel:

> Jacob left Beer Sheba and went on toward Haran. He chanced upon a certain place and spent the night there, because the sun had set. Taking one of the stones of the place, he put it under his head and lay down in the place. And he dreamed there was a ladder stuck into the earth, whose top reached to heaven, and the angels of God were going up and down on it. The LORD stood over him and said, "I am the LORD, the God of Abraham your father and the God of Isaac; the land on which you are lying I will give to you and your offspring; and your offspring will be like the dust of the earth, and you will spread out to the west and to the east and the north and the south; and all the families of the earth will be blessed in you and in your offspring. Know that I will be with you and will keep you wherever you go and will bring you back to this land; for I will not leave you until I have done what I have promised you." Then Jacob woke from his sleep and said, "Surely the LORD is in this place, and I did not know it!" And he was afraid and he said, "How fearsome is this place! This is the very house of God and this is the gate of heaven." (Gen 28:10–17)

What Jacob *hears* is the voice of God, and what the voice says is altogether true: God will grant the land to Jacob and his descendants will spread out in all directions. But what is the significance of the *vision*, the ladder and the angels? This was a question that fascinated ancient biblical interpreters,[16] but in fact this visual part of Jacob's dream seems altogether parallel to the man-like "angels" and other visual effects that make up the waking dreams seen already. In other words, there was no particular *message* in the ladder and the angels, other than to signify that this place, which Jacob had just happened upon, was by its very nature a sacred spot connecting earth to heaven and thus destined to be the site of an earthly sanctuary, as Jacob goes on to vow (verse 22).[17]

Surprised, but Not Flabbergasted

All these encounters follow a similar pattern, but sometimes one of the elements is omitted or modified. For example, the story of the prophet Samuel's first encounter with God lacks any visual component. According to the narrative, Samuel had been given by his mother to serve Eli, a priest in the temple at Shiloh. Then, one night:

> The lamp of God had not yet burnt out, and Samuel was lying down in the temple of the Lord, where the ark of God was. Then the Lord called, "Samuel! Samuel!" and he said, "Here I am!" and ran to Eli, and said, "Here I am. You called me?" But he said, "I did not call you; go back to bed." So he went and lay down. The Lord called again, "Samuel!" Samuel got up and went to Eli, and said, "Here I am. You called me?" But he said, "I did not call, my son; go back to bed." Now Samuel did not yet know the Lord; the word of the Lord had not yet been revealed to him. Then the Lord called Samuel again, a third time. And he got up and went to Eli, and said, "Here I am. You called me?" Then Eli understood that the Lord was calling the boy. Therefore Eli said to Samuel, "Go, lie down; and if He calls you, you shall say, 'Speak, Lord, for Your servant is listening.'" So Samuel went and lay down in his place. Now the Lord came and stood there, calling as before, "Samuel! Samuel!" And Samuel said, "Speak, for Your servant is listening." Then the Lord said to Samuel, "See, I am about to do something in Israel that will set the ears of anyone who hears of it to tingling." (1 Sam 3:3–11)

Samuel is a novice, never having been addressed by God before. All this back and forth between him and Eli seems thus designed to tell us that Samuel's call to prophecy was no vague inner prompting, and certainly not a case of self-promotion. The voice that called him was so real that not once but three times Samuel mistook it for a perfectly human voice—in fact, that of his master. It is only on the fourth time that he is ready to hear God's words. So this, in a way, is parallel to the angel stories we have seen; here as well, the hearer of God's voice is also in a fog of sorts, but this time there is no accompanying vision.

The story of Samuel's call embodies another strange aspect of these narratives. In almost all of them, the people encountering God at first suspect nothing. This is the moment of confusion. But after a while they do catch on, and then their reaction is almost as striking as the encounter itself: they are surprised, but not exactly bowled over. So Eli, after Samuel comes to him for the third time, "understands" that it's God calling; in other words, he realizes that this was one of those manifestations of the divine that sometimes do occur. So he informs Samuel, who likewise seems to know about such things; summoned the next time, Samuel calmly replies, "Speak, for Your servant is listening." In the same way, Moses, once he has understood that this vision of a burning bush was meant to bring him to where God was, calmly answers the voice from the bush: "God called to him from the middle of the bush, 'Moses, Moses!' He answered, 'Here I am.'" No "What—a talking bush?!" Apparently, Moses likewise knows that such things occur.

True, Moses goes on to manifest his fear at this encounter: "And Moses hid his face, since he was afraid to look at God" (Exod 3:6). The same is true of nearly all the other cases mentioned: Sarah (see Gen 18:15), Gideon, Manoah and his wife, and Jacob (twice! Gen 28:17, 32:31) are all apparently in fear of their lives after having "seen" God, even if in this visionary mode. But this only reinforces the impression that, once the fog has lifted, they are no longer in unknown territory; encountering God *is* dangerous, and clearly, that is what has just happened. Here is one more example to add to the previous ones:

> And it came to pass, when Joshua was in Jericho, that he *lifted up his eyes* and *saw,* and *behold!* A man was standing across from him with his sword drawn in his hand. So Joshua went up to him and asked, "Are you one of us or one of our enemies?" And he answered, "Neither. I am the chief of the LORD's army; I have just arrived." Then Joshua fell facedown to the ground in prostration and said to him, "What does my lord wish to say to his servant?" And the chief of the LORD's army said to Joshua, "Take your shoe from off your foot, for the place on which you are standing is holy"—and Joshua did so. (Josh 5:13–15)

Here in compact form are nearly all the elements previously seen: the emphatic phrasing indicating a vision ("he *lifted up his eyes* and *saw,* and *behold!*"), the initial moment of confusion ("Are you one of us or one of our enemies?"), and the curious reaction to this divine encounter ("Then Joshua fell facedown to the ground in prostration and said to him, "What does my lord wish to say . . . ?"). Joshua, too, is surprised but not flabbergasted.

The Revelatory State of Mind

One might conclude that the resemblance of all these different accounts simply proves that later ones were based on the earlier accounts.[18] And this is probably true, for at least some of these texts. After all, every literature has its conventions, and the recurrence of the same basic pattern in these divine encounters suggests the existence of some such literary tradition. Even slight deviations from the pattern, as in the example of Samuel, are altogether within the usual bounds of established literary conventions.

But conventions have to have a starting point as well as a reason for becoming conventional, and these are the matters of interest here. Was there something in this combination of elements—the illusory appearance, the fog, the divine words spoken, the relatively mild surprise—that seemed to ring true in the minds of ancient readers/listeners? An answer of sorts comes from an unexpected source, the writings of ancient Greece and Rome. The religions of Greco-Roman civilization were in many ways strikingly different from those of the ancient Near East in general[19] and ancient Israel in particular. The Greeks had nothing corresponding to angels, for example; moreover, their myths are full of stories of gods who are frequently unfair and immoral, who feud with one another and sometimes take revenge on mortals, transforming themselves into animals or transforming humans into animals or plants.

It is all the more striking, therefore, that they sometimes describe divine encounters in a manner quite similar to the ones that we have seen. In Homer's *Iliad,* for example, gods and goddesses sometimes come down to earth disguised as ordinary humans; the person they encounter fails to recognize them—very much as Abraham or Gideon failed to recognize their divine interlocutors:

> Then the goddess [Aphrodite] spoke to her [Helen] in the likeness of an old woman, a wool-comber who used to card wool for her when she lived in Lacedaemon . . . "Come here," [Aphrodite said]. "Alexander [i.e., Helen's seducer, Paris] is calling you home. He's in his room on his inlaid bed, gleaming in his beautiful attire. You wouldn't think that he had just finished

> fighting an enemy! He looks as if he were going to a dance, or rather as if he had just finished dancing and sat down."
>
> So she spoke, and stirred Helen's heart in her breast. But when she [Helen] caught a glimpse of the goddess's beautiful neck, of her lovely breast and flashing eyes, she was shocked. Then she spoke to her, saying, "Strange goddess, why are you determined to fool me like this . . ." (*Iliad* 3:385–400)[20]

A similar instance occurs in Virgil's *Aeneid.* Shipwrecked with his men on the Libyan shore, Aeneas is despairing of his fate when he suddenly encounters a young girl; at least that's what he thinks. But it turns out—just as with Jacob's wrestling partner, or the "man" who visits Manoah and his wife—that the human being is an illusion: in this case, the young girl turns out to be none other than his divine mother Venus. Of course, she does not look like Venus: "She had a girl's face and clothes, and even carried the weapons of a girl from Sparta . . . Like a hunting-girl, she had a bow hanging handily from her shoulder, and she let her hair blow loose in the wind." The disguise fools Aeneas, and he asks her to tell him where they have landed and what sort of a place it is. Her answer goes on for nearly a hundred lines; at the end, she tells Aeneas to take heart and go on his way:

> She spoke, but as she turned away, a glint of rose shone forth from her neck and her heavenly hair exhaled its godly perfume. Her garment now flowed down to her very feet, and by her demeanor she was revealed to be a true goddess. Now he recognized his mother and pursued her with these words as she vanished: "Why do you cruelly delude your own son with disguises? Why not have our hands clasp each other and have our voices speak and reply in truth?" With such words he reproved her, then headed off toward the walls of the city. (*Aeneid* 1:402–10)

The resemblance of these passages to the earlier biblical ones is certainly remarkable. It is important to note, however, that while there were some contacts between biblical Israel and ancient Greece, there is little here to suggest any sort of direct literary borrowing. Rather, the common elements seen might point toward a different, and somewhat eerier, conclusion. Perhaps these literary resemblances reflect something deeper that ancient Greeks and ancient Israelites shared, an underlying set of assumptions about their own minds and how they interact with the divine. Both civilizations thus conceived of the possibility of *encountering* a deity in a way that is quite foreign to our own world of ideas and experience. For one reason or another, these encounters were held to start with something like a hallucination,[21] a waking dream of an uncanny meeting with a stranger and a conversation that, on later reflection, sounded quite illogical at points; ultimately this was followed by the stunning, auditory revelation of the deity's true identity and the true message that he/she had come down to transmit. In some of the texts that we possess, these elements may have already become conventional, but behind them may stand a once-common picture of the human mind and its encountering the divine that is altogether unfamiliar nowadays.

But if these things did, in some sense, "really happen" in the distant past, what was it that caused them to cease happening? Did God, or the gods, just lose interest in direct encounters with human beings? In his exhaustive catalogue of the phenomena of prophecy in the Hebrew Bible, the Swedish biblicist Johannes Lindblom asked a similar question: What was it that allowed some ancient Israelites to become prophets, that is, spokesmen and intermediaries between God and humans? Although he described at length various biblical accounts of spiritual possession and trance-like states, he ultimately pointed to what he called the "revelatory state of mind" as crucial for Israel's prophets, an openness to God addressing them directly:

> Typical of the revelatory state of mind is the feeling of being under an influence external to the self, a divine power, the consciousness of hearing words and seeing visions which do not come from the self, but from the invisible divine world, into which, in the moment of revelation, an entrance has been granted. This feeling of being subject to an external influence is perhaps the most constant element in the revelatory state of mind.[22]

In other words, the prophet's state of mind is such that he or she is open to a divine being or beings quite "external to the self," who could somehow penetrate their brains and make them see and hear things that come from elsewhere. But this was hardly the only way that God was understood in biblical times. In other parts of the Bible, God is conceived in terms closer to our own: He controls everything that happens, but from a distance.

2

JOSEPH AND HIS BROTHERS

Divine causality; The operating instructions of the world; Wisdom's ideology; Superstitious fools

The biblical story of Joseph and his brothers presents a picture of God's way with the world that is strikingly different from that of the narratives examined in the previous chapter. Here God is a long-range planner who arranges everything in advance and then sits back to watch the events unfold. He scarcely intervenes in human affairs, if at all; He is generally remote from the events themselves.

In the world of the Bible, things do not just happen: God is the great Unseen Causer of everything that humans do not cause on their own. This was true throughout the biblical period and manifested itself in different ways[1]—including prominently the way in which people thought about the weather. From time immemorial, inhabitants of the land of Canaan had looked skyward (for a long while to the Canaanite storm god Haddad/Ba'al, and later to the God of Israel) to "open the treasure-houses of the heavens" and bring down the precious raindrops needed for survival in that water-poor environment. The weather was so capricious there that it was sometimes obviously the product of divine manipulation. As God tells the prophet Amos, "I was the one who stopped the rain from falling three months before harvest-time. Or sometimes I would rain on one town, but on another I wouldn't let it rain; or one *field* would get rain, but another field, where I didn't make it rain, would just dry up" (Amos 4:7). The weather was thus not simply bad or good, and certainly not the simple product of high or low pressure areas moving about; neither did the rain come because of a cold front coming in from the north, although everyone knew that a north wind brings rain (Prov 25:23).

But the *ultimate* cause of good or bad weather was God; in fact, unusual weather was often intended as a divine warning or divine punishment.

Of course, God's control of life was still more obvious in the case of certain onetime interventions. When the Hebrews were enslaved by a wicked pharaoh, it was God who afflicted the Egyptians with ten plagues and then led them out of Egypt "with a mighty arm and an outstretched hand." Likewise, it was God who bequeathed the land of Canaan to the descendants of Abraham, Isaac, and Jacob — and then saw to it that Joshua was successful in the war to capture it. It was also God who unstopped the stopped-up wombs of Sarah, Rebekah, Rachel, and Hannah. But understanding these onetime interventions in this way belongs to a much larger mentality. In the biblical world — at least judging by the evidence we have — *anything* that did not have an evident human cause (and even some things that might seem as if they did) was caused by the divine. Indeed, even to say this falls somewhat short of the ancient Israelite sense of God's overwhelming, overbearing presence, at least according to the Bible's testimony. It may be difficult for people nowadays to conceive of God's utter mastery in this ancient way, but with some imagination this sense can be recaptured.

Judah and Tamar

The story of Judah and Tamar (Genesis 38) is a brief and somewhat embarrassing tale. Judah is a wealthy sheep-owner who ends up sleeping with his daughter-in-law, Tamar. Judah, as the eponym of the Kingdom of Judah, homeland of the Jewish people, ought to be an altogether positive character. But sleeping with your daughter-in-law is certainly not an acceptable thing to do. It was therefore necessary to explain how this positive character ended up doing such an altogether bad deed.

There were extenuating circumstances, as the Bible relates. Tamar had first been married to Judah's son Er, but he died. Then, in keeping with ancient custom, Judah married her off to his second son, Onan; but he died as well. At this point Judah, in keeping with the same custom, ought to have passed Tamar on to his third son. But he was afraid that she might somehow bring about the death of that son as well, so he kept Tamar unmarried in his household for a long time. As the years passed, she became increasingly desperate to have a child, in or out of wedlock, and finally fixed on a stratagem that worked. She knew her father-in-law was going off to Timnah with his flocks; since Judah had now been a widower for some time, she correctly supposed that he might be tempted to seek out some female companionship of the most fleeting kind. So Tamar dressed up as a prostitute, veiling her face with thick cloth, and hurried off to arrive at the entrance of the city before Judah. When he saw her, Judah indeed took her for a prostitute and ended up sleeping with her—without ever recognizing who she was. These were the extenuating circumstances: truly, neither of the two was blameworthy. When Judah subsequently found out that his daughter-in-law was pregnant, at first he was incensed. "Take her out and burn her!" he said. But when she explained to him how it all had happened, and that *he* was the father, he had to relent. "She was right," he conceded.

The biblical account is a bit more detailed, but this is the essential story. There is, however, one tiny difference between my account above and that of the book of Genesis—an altogether negligible detail, really—which nevertheless is quite telling. I said that Judah's two sons, Er and Onan, "died." In my version of the story, that was certainly enough. People do die, after all—some at a ripe old age, but some not, especially in ancient times. Yet in the world of divine causality, simply saying "they died" would have sounded a bit like Ronald Reagan's famous "mistakes were made." Some further clarification was necessary, one that explained how these premature deaths had come about:

> Er, Judah's firstborn, was evil in the LORD's eyes, so the LORD killed him. Then Judah said to Onan, "Go into your brother's wife and do your duty toward your dead brother: provide offspring on his behalf." But Onan knew that the offspring would not be considered his, so every time he had relations with his brother's wife, he would waste his seed on the ground without giving it on his brother's behalf. What he did displeased the LORD, so He killed him as well. (Gen 38:7–10)

Of the two deaths, the more interesting one is actually the first. Why did God kill Er? He was "evil." What he actually did or didn't do is apparently not important, but it was crucial for the narrative to assert that his death did not just happen. *God* killed him. The reason that this had to be said has already been given: God must be the causer of anything conspicuously lacking a cause, so it had to be said that He had, for whatever reason, brought about Er's premature death. The same assertion could have explained Onan's death, but in his case a more elaborate justification is offered: Onan's sin (not, apparently, what used to be called "onanism," i.e., masturbation, but coitus interruptus) was what angered God, so much so that He killed him too. But whatever the particulars, it was crucial for the narrative to say that the two brothers didn't just "pass away." As Amos asks (quite rhetorically), "Can misfortune befall a town if the LORD has not caused it?"

The Story of Joseph

It is against this background that I wish to consider another biblical story, one that could not be more different from that of Judah and Tamar despite their close proximity in the book of Genesis: the story of Joseph and his brothers, which stretches from Genesis 37 to 45. In particular, I want to focus on three separate verses in the story, verses which, although taken from different parts of the narrative, share a common theme:

> "What is this that the LORD has done to us?" (Gen 42:28)
>
> "Your God, and the God of your fathers, must have put a hidden treasure in your grain sacks." (Gen 43:23)
>
> "God has uncovered the crime of your servants." (Gen 44:16)

As will be seen, each of these verses reveals something crucial not only about the Joseph story, but more generally about Israel's different understandings of the role of its God in the world. In order to explain them, however, it is necessary first to say something about the narrative as a whole.

The biblical tale of Joseph is an extraordinarily moving story, with a series of dramatic ups and downs for its central figure and a very happy ending. Joseph, the favorite son of his father, Jacob, is seized by his jealous brothers and sold as a slave to a passing caravan. He ends up in Egypt, where he is bought by a high Egyptian official. The official's wife tries to seduce the handsome boy, but when he resists, she charges him with attempted rape and he is sent to prison. Eventually, the Egyptian king summons Joseph because of his reputation as a dream interpreter: the king has had a disturbing dream that needs deciphering. Joseph explains the king's dream, which foretells seven years of plenty followed by seven years of famine. The king then appoints Joseph to oversee the food rationing that will allow Egypt to survive the coming seven lean years.

When famine does indeed strike the whole region, Joseph's brothers in Canaan journey to Egypt, the only place where it is still possible to buy grain.

Joseph recognizes his brothers at once, but they, seeing someone dressed in the garb of an Egyptian official and speaking through an interpreter, simply take him for some senior Egyptian administrator. Deciding to go on with the masquerade, Joseph puts his brothers through a series of hardships — at first accusing them of spying, then freeing them, then, on their return visit, charging the youngest of them with the theft of his expensive drinking goblet. At the height of this last crisis, and with his brothers despairing of their fate, Joseph suddenly empties the room of his attendants and aides and announces the truth (in Hebrew) to his astonished siblings: "I am your brother Joseph, whom you sold into Egypt." A tearful reunion follows, ending with Joseph's father, who had long believed his son dead, traveling to Egypt to be united with his beloved offspring.

What is the overall message of this story? At first glance it might seem to be: *nil desperandum,* "Don't ever lose hope." Joseph, after all, suffered more than one setback — sold as a slave, later falsely accused of attempted rape, then stuck for years in a dismal Egyptian prison — yet he never despaired. His pluck and his willingness to overlook present difficulties in the hope for a better day are clearly what helped him through all his trials. Yet in the world of Israelite wisdom, to which this story belongs,[2] this optimistic outlook in turn derives from a still greater lesson of life, and that is the existence of a great, divine plan underlying all of reality. Whatever happens in this world, Israelite sages came to believe, happens in keeping with such a plan, a set of principles established long ago by God.

These principles, only some of which we humans can discover, are nothing less than the operating instructions of the world. In fact, the entirety of these principles is sometimes referred to by the word "wisdom," a kind of code word for the preprogrammed instructions that have forever governed life on earth. "How great are Your works!" a biblical psalm exclaims. "You have made them all *with wisdom*" (Ps 104:24). This doesn't mean, "Good job, God!" It is an assertion that there is an order to all of reality, that all things are governed by "wisdom," the world's great, underlying plan. Similarly: "*By wisdom* the LORD founded the earth, by understanding He established the heavens" (Prov 3:19). Moreover: "How great are Your works, *so very deep are Your plans:* a simpleton cannot know, nor a foolish man understand this" (Ps 92:6–7).

What are the operating instructions that biblical sages called *wisdom*? The most basic one has already been mentioned. The very idea that there are rules, that things don't happen at random or spontaneously but obey long-established principles — this is the central tenet of wisdom. As the above-cited verses indicate, this set of plans was held to be of divine origin; God had established them from the beginning of time to govern all that happens.[3] For this reason, biblical texts often contrast the vanity of human plan-making with the all-inclusive *divine* plan:

> The LORD overthrows the plans of nations, undoes peoples' designs; the LORD's plan stands forever, the designs of His heart for every age. (Ps 33:10–11)

> The LORD knows a person's plans — that they are futile. (Ps 94:11)

> To humans belong the plans of the mind, but from the LORD comes the spoken reply [that is, the last word]. (Prov 16:1)

> Many are the plans in a man's mind, but the LORD's plan — that is what will stand. (Prov 19:21)

Certainly some of the rules that make up this underlying set of plans belong to what might be described as early "science": thus, it was simply a rule that the light of the moon waxes and wanes according to a fixed design, and that the movements of the sun and stars are similarly patterned. Israelite wisdom also included such things as botany or ornithology: age-old experience had taught, for example, that if you cut down a tree, it can regenerate itself; even if it looks like a dead stump, "at the scent of water" it will bud anew (Job 14:9). Ostriches lay their eggs on the ground, "letting them warm in the dirt" and apparently caring little for their survival (Job 39:14–16), while storks build their nests in the highest fir trees (Ps 104:17–18). But other rules apply to human behavior. There is a proper way to behave in the royal court (Eccles 10:20), a proper way for parents to behave toward their children (Prov 13:24), and a proper way for the young to treat their elders (Sir 3:1–16). In general, modesty and the *via media* are the right path: "Better a dry piece of bread eaten in peace than a houseful of abundance that is consumed in strife" (Prov 17:1).

While such truths may have emerged from sustained observation, wisdom also had an idealistic side that did not always match appearances. It held, for example, that the righteous will ultimately get their reward in this world, while the wicked will inevitably be punished. For this reason, patience was *the* cardinal virtue of the wisdom outlook: wait long enough and everything turns out all right. Indeed, Joseph's patience in the face of adversity — which was ultimately rewarded — is a perfect illustration of this rule. Beyond these are dozens and dozens of other specific insights about life that make up the corpus of wisdom writings — a genre well known throughout the ancient Near East.

One might rightly ask here: Hadn't these rules always been the basic message of the Bible as a whole? The answer, modern biblical scholars say, is: yes and no. In many other parts of the Bible, there is no apparent prior plan. God's management of reality is a hands-on job, requiring constant adjustment to changing circumstances. Indeed, the God of Old follows no set of invariable, eternal principles; some biblical texts even glorify His capacity to shake things up and do the exact opposite of what we expect:

> The bows of the mighty may snap, while weaklings brim with power.
> The formerly fat are hired out for bread, while those who were hungry are feasting.
> A barren woman gives birth to seven, but the mother of many is bereft.
> The LORD can kill or bring back to life, send down to Sheol or raise up again.
> The LORD makes poor or makes rich, He humbles as well as exalts.
> He lifts up the poor from the dirt, and the needy from a pile of dung,
> He sits them next to the nobles and grants them the place of honor. (1 Sam 2:4–8)

In most of the book of Genesis, God follows no particular set of rules. He acts, or reacts, quite spontaneously. He discovers that Cain has murdered Abel and then sentences him to exile. After seeing that the human race, which He created, has turned out to be fundamentally flawed, God decides to bring a great flood to punish mankind. He decides to destroy the tower of Babel only after He has realized what the people are doing. And of course in all of these episodes and others, He personally *intervenes* in human doings in some hands-on, physical way.

The story of Joseph has a different quality. After Joseph has revealed his true identity to his brothers, he explains what has really happened — and why:

> "And now, don't be upset and don't blame yourselves for selling me here: it was to keep [people] alive that God sent me ahead of you. For the famine has already lasted for two years in the midst of this land, and for five years more there will be no plowing or harvest. But God sent me ahead of you to assure your survival in this land, and along with you to keep alive many other survivors. So *it was not you who sent me here, but God.*" (Gen 45:5–8)

If that is not enough, he goes on to reiterate the lesson later on. After their father's death, Joseph's brothers are afraid that he will at last take some revenge upon them, a revenge they know they justly deserve. But Joseph reassures them:

> Joseph said to them: "Do not be afraid—am I in God's stead? You planned evil against me, but God had planned it for the good, in order to keep a great number of people alive, as [He is] doing today." (Gen 50:19-20)

This is the whole point: humans may think what they think, but ultimately, they are merely part of a much larger game. As a verse cited earlier puts it, "Many are the plans in a man's mind, but the LORD's plan—that is what will stand" (Prov 19:21).

The Divine Travel Agent

It all reminds me of the story about the fellow who has a vivid dream one night, in which he is on a Greek ferryboat that suddenly overturns in the middle of the sea, and he and all the other passengers are drowned. "Repent before it is too late," a voice cries out at the end of the dream. Waking up, the man doesn't repent, but he does resolve never to find himself anywhere near Greece or Greek ferries, just in case this dream was some sort of warning. Several years pass, however, and one day he decides he needs a vacation: the French Riviera seems like the ideal spot. When he goes to make reservations, however, the travel agent tells him that the prices for France are particularly high this year: "You would do better to go somewhere like Greece," the agent says. The very word strikes fear into the man's heart, but the travel agent assures him that flights to Greece are quite safe—and of course involve no Greek ferries.

On the day of his flight everything begins well, but there is a problem at the Athens airport and the plane is forced to make an emergency landing on the Greek island of Santorini. The man then tries in vain to arrange a flight to the mainland, but all the flights are booked solid. "Why not take the ferry?" the airline official suggests. Now, the man is extremely reluctant, but a dream is just a dream, after all, and the ticket agent at the ferry's pier dismisses his misgivings: "The trip lasts only a couple of hours, and it's completely safe: in fact, this particular boat itself is brand-new, the weather forecast is for calm seas, and besides, we have never had the slightest emergency in over fifty years in the business." Reassured, the man agrees. As soon as the ferry is in open waters, however, the sea suddenly turns stormy, the ferry begins to list badly, and it now appears quite possible that the vessel will overturn. The man, in a panic, lifts his voice to heaven: "O Lord," he says, eyeing the other passengers on the boat, "I know I am a terrible sinner and did not repent as You said. But will You sacrifice all these other people just to punish me?" From heaven immediately comes the response: "Do you know how much planning and arranging it took for Me to get all you people together on the same boat?"

This is the God of the "wisdom" strand of Scripture, the divine travel agent who arranges things from afar and well in advance—in fact, a God who is Himself to some extent subject to the preexisting rules. If the righteous *must* ultimately be rewarded, then in a sense God has no choice but to reward them. It is almost as if wisdom, the great plan created by God (Prov 8:22), is a kind of independent, divine force. The book of Job at one point asks:

> Where does wisdom come from? And what is the source of understanding?
> It is hidden from the eyes of the living, concealed from the birds of the heavens.
> The Underworld and Death say, "We have only heard tell of it."
> But God understands the way to it; He knows its source. (Job 28:20–23)

Here it seems that wisdom is not only altogether remote and inaccessible—God alone knows where she comes from—but she is apparently quite distinct from Him. He knows how to find His way to her dwelling place, but she, the great set of eternal principles, is apparently an autonomous being. (By the way, she's a she, both in Hebrew and in Greek.)

This, in short, is a somewhat different notion of God's way with the world from that seen earlier. He still rules over all and is the owner of everything, but He has a very different management style, one that, in turn, bespeaks an altogether different notion of God's very nature. He is not the God of Old, lurking just beyond the curtain of ordinary reality, ready at any moment to cross over and intervene in human affairs. Nor, on the other hand, is He what post-biblical religion would make of Him: omnipresent, omniscient, all-powerful. Rather, He is a bit like the God depicted in the latter third of the book of Isaiah, a huge and remote deity whose control of the world can hardly be fathomed by human minds:

> Who has measured the oceans in the hollow of his hand [as God has], or
> marked off the skies with a yardstick?

> Or put the earth's soil in his bushel, weighed the mountains on a hand-scale and the hills in a balance? . . .
> The nations themselves are a drop from the bucket [to Him], they weigh as much as the dust on a scale.
> He can flick off islands like a mote; all the Lebanon will not provide His kindling, its animals do not equal one lone offering.
> The nations all together are nothing for Him, insignificance itself and less than zero. So to whom will you compare God? (Isa 40:12, 15–18)

Some biblical scholars connect the emergence of this great, world-bestriding, universal deity in Isaiah to political events in the history of Israel — in particular, the conquest of Jerusalem by the Babylonians in 587 BCE and their sack of God's holiest site, the Jerusalem temple. Once the shock had passed, the nature of God's dominion over His world had to be conceived anew. The fact that half a century later, the Babylonians would in turn be supplanted — not by tiny Israel, but by the mighty Persian Empire — itself suggested a huge deity, moving whole nations around like pieces on a chessboard. In fact, at one point God refers to Nebuchadnezzar, the Babylonian king and Israel's archenemy, as "My servant" (Jer 25:9); he's just another pawn in a much bigger game. But this is not necessarily a view imposed by later history; it is what we have seen in the story of Joseph.

Three Verses

The three interesting verses from the Joseph story listed earlier seem designed to tell us how *not* to conceive of God. The first, "What is this that the LORD has done to us?" comes as the brothers are heading home after their first visit to Egypt. Freed from prison, they depart with their grain sacks loaded with provisions. Unbeknownst to them, however, Joseph had ordered that the silver they paid for the grain be returned to them in full, each man's in his own sack. Stopping on the way, one of the brothers opens his sack to feed his donkey and is shocked to see that the silver he paid is now sitting in the mouth of the sack. "My payment's been returned!" he shouts. "Here it is in my grain sack." The brothers, far from rejoicing at this development, are immediately afraid of what it might mean. "Their hearts sank, and with trembling they said one to another: '*What is this that the LORD has done to us?*'" Of course, *we* know that it isn't the LORD who has done this to them, but their own brother Joseph.

The second verse cited comes under related circumstances. The brothers soon discover that *all* of them have had their payments returned, and their father Jacob is as disturbed by this news as they are. What could it mean? Jacob steadfastly refuses to let his sons return to Egypt, despite the family's dwindling grain supplies, because he is afraid of what might happen to the youngest brother, Benjamin, whom Joseph has demanded to see. Perhaps the "missing" money will be used as a pretext for harming them. As time goes on, however, their food situation only grows worse, until Jacob is forced to relent and entrust Benjamin to his older siblings for another trip down to Egypt. To make sure that the returned silver is not used against them, however, Jacob insists that they give it back to the Egyptians when they get there: "Perhaps it was all a mistake," he says. But when the brothers arrive in Egypt and with trepidation seek to hand over the money to Joseph's steward, the steward replies: "Everything's fine — don't worry! *Your God, and the God of your fathers, must have put a hidden treasure in your grain-sacks.* I already received your payment." Once again, we know the truth. It was not "your God, and the God of your fathers" who stuck the money in their grain sacks, but the steward himself.

It seems to me that both of these sentences are highly significant, precisely because neither of them was at all necessary. Why should the brothers, upon discovering along the way that one of them has had his payment returned, attribute this apparently inexplicable development to God? They could simply have asked, "What could this mean?" or even say what Jacob later says, "Perhaps it is all a mistake." Why bring God into it — or, to put the question more precisely, why should the narrative have gone to the trouble of inserting this mention of God when it serves no purpose? It has no role in the subsequent events; it is not what writers call "plot-related." The only thing it seems to accomplish is to make the brothers out to be superstitious fools; in fact, having them suppose that it was God almost seems, under the circumstances, to be making fun of the whole phenomenon of religious belief.

The same is true of the sentence spoken by Joseph's steward, which, if anything, seems more blasphemous: he uses the phrase "your God and the God of your fathers," so characteristic of pious biblical rhetoric (Deut 1:21, 6:3, 12:1, 26:7, 27:3, etc.; cf. Exod 3:13; 3:15, 16), in such a way as to put it to shame. And this is nearly my point. However, it is not religious belief as such that is being mocked, but rather the simple-minded sort of religious belief that the Joseph narrative is out to correct. The true God, this narrative seems to be saying, is not the one who suddenly appears to people or crosses over the curtain into our world in order to destroy or instruct or promise — He is not the

God of Old. The true God *doesn't* do such things, the narrative asserts, and He certainly didn't stick something into people's grain sacks! Rather, the true God is the long-range planner, the manipulator of great swaths of territory and human history. This is exactly the lesson Joseph seeks to impart to his brothers at the end: "You planned evil against me, but God had planned it for the good." You are only part of a much bigger plan. So the old way of apprehending the divine, that is, the God of Old, is quite consciously mocked here.

The third verse comes just before the end of the story. Joseph's expensive goblet has been "discovered" in Benjamin's grain sack (where the steward had put it!). The steward looks at them harshly: "Did you really expect to get away with stealing my master's goblet?" he asks. Judah, as leader of the brothers, replies: "What can we say to my lord — what can we plead, how can we claim to be innocent? *God has uncovered the crime of your servants.*" Now this is a particularly significant sentence. Judah seems to be saying that indeed, they have committed a crime, stealing Joseph's goblet. Of course he knows that this is not true; as far as he can figure out, the goblet must have found its way into Benjamin's sack in the same way that the silver found its way into *all* their sacks after the previous visit. But Judah confesses to the crime anyway; it would seem that he is less worried about what will happen in Egypt than what will happen in Canaan when he shows up at his father's door without Benjamin, whom he swore to look after. But once again, from the narrative's point of view, Judah's mention of God seems completely unnecessary — after all, why bring God into it? — and, in the sense that we have seen, to do so is once again to evoke — and to mock — a certain kind of religious belief, the old kind.

At the same time, what Judah says is actually quite true. God has indeed "uncovered" the brothers' crime — not the phony one that Judah is confessing to, but their real crime, selling their brother as a slave to be brought down to Egypt.[4] This is altogether parallel to Joseph's assertion to his brothers that they really didn't understand what they were doing, but that unwittingly, they were carrying out God's plan. Here, Judah really doesn't understand what he is *saying,* but in spite of what he thinks is a false confession, he is unwittingly telling the truth.[5]

Counting the Jubilees

After the Babylonians conquered Jerusalem and exiled its inhabitants to Babylon, God apparently did nothing to save the remnant of His people; off to Babylon they went, apparently starting with the Judean leadership in 597 BCE, and then more massively after the destruction of the Jerusalem temple a decade later. No doubt many at the time despaired: the musicians who were taken captive hung their harps in the trees and wept: "How can we sing a song of the LORD in a foreign land?" (Ps 137:4). But meanwhile, the great divine plan was slowly unfolding. According to the book of Jeremiah, God had told His prophet:

> "This whole land [of Judea] will be a desolate ruin. And these people will serve the Babylonian king for seventy years. But at the end of seventy years, I will punish the king of Babylon, and that nation of his, and the whole land of the Chaldeans for their sins, and I will turn them into an eternal ruin." (Jer 25:11–12)

Help was thus on the way, but it would take 70 years — and 70 years it turned out to be (or perhaps 60, depending on where one starts the counting or stops it). The Persian emperor Cyrus, having defeated the Babylonians in 539 BCE, issued an edict the next year allowing the Judeans to return to Jerusalem — and many of them did return, starting with a trickle in 520 or so. The prediction seemed to have been fulfilled.

Interestingly, however, that is not how the book of Daniel (written some four centuries later than Jeremiah) sees things. Its hero, Daniel, is said to be living during the Babylonian exile and thereafter, and at a certain point he finds himself studying Jeremiah's prediction of the 70 years:

> While I was praying, the man [= angel] Gabriel, whom I had seen before in a vision, came flying toward me at the time of the evening offering. He gave me understanding when he spoke to me and said: "Daniel! Now I have come to give you knowledge and understanding . . . Seventy *units of seven* years were decreed for your people and your holy city — to put an end to transgression, and finish with sin, and atone for wrongdoing, and bring eternal justice, to carry out the prophet's vision and to reanoint the Holy of Holies . . ." (Dan 9:21–24)

The book of Jeremiah had spoken of 70 years, but now it turns out that the divine plan was actually much longer, 70 "units of seven" years, or 490 years in total.[6] This truly was a God of long-range planning; Joseph's prediction of 7 years of coming famine seems paltry by comparison. Note also that here God does not even speak directly with Daniel: He sends a messenger (the angel Gabriel) as any mighty king would do. And the message he delivers is one of "knowledge and understanding," two key words in the wisdom tradition.

Indeed, earlier in the book, Daniel had uttered a prayer that presents a similar big-picture vision of God's workings:

> Blessed be the name of God from age to age, for wisdom and power are His. He changes times and seasons, deposes kings and sets up kings; He gives wisdom to the wise, and knowledge to those who have understanding. He reveals deep and hidden things; He knows what is in the darkness, and light dwells with Him. (Dan 2:20–22)

Nearly every word here is significant for our subject. God is praised "from age to age" because that is His true time frame, eons and eons. Consequently, true wisdom — that set of unshakable rules and long-range plans that *ultimately* always prove to be true — belongs only to Him, as does the "power," which likewise will reveal itself only ultimately, when everything works out. Earthly rulers, the kings who seem to govern our lives, are merely His pawns; He moves them around and replaces them in the same way that He changes the seasons, replacing winter with spring. Then: "He gives wisdom to the wise" — is that really fair? Oughtn't He to give wisdom to the stupid? But "the wise" here are the sages who alone can seek to attain divine knowledge, those "deep and hidden things" that most people miss. They miss it because it is "in the darkness," but light does indeed exist, and it is with Him.

The 490 years spoken of in the book of Daniel may seem like an oddly shaped chunk of time, but actually it makes great sense. Biblical law stipulates that the jubilee year is to come around once every 49 years (Lev 25:8);* 490 is just that unit of time multiplied by 10 (which comes out to be the same as Daniel's 70 "units of seven"). So it was that 490 years appears here and there as a mega-unit of time in the Dead Sea Scrolls (some of them contemporaneous with the book of Daniel).[7]

But even that unit of time pales before the vision of an anonymous Jewish text written around 200 BCE, the *Book of Jubilees.* It recounts in its own words much of the book of Genesis and the first half of Exodus, mentioning in many cases the precise year in which this or that event took place. The years are calculated from the time of the creation, but the author does not just say,

---

* There was some dispute in Second Temple times about the length of a jubilee; because of the apparent disagreement of this verse with the mention of the "fiftieth year" in Lev 25:10, some held that a jubilee lasts 50 years.

"1,870 years after the creation such-and-such happened." Instead, each date is calculated in multiples of 49 years (that is, the length of a single jubilee). So, to arrive at the year "1,870 years after the creation," he first counted the total number of complete jubilees preceding the event in question, in this case, 38 jubilees; if each jubilee lasts 49 years, then 38 jubilees brings us to a total of 1,862 years. This left him just 8 years short of the desired total. He could have just said "38 jubilees plus 8 years," but conventionally, each jubilee subdivides into 7 "weeks" of 7 years apiece. So "38 jubilees plus one 'week'" would bring him almost home; to this he only had to add a single year borrowed from the second week of that jubilee. In his book, he thus dated the event to the first year of the second week of the 39th jubilee, since (38 x 49) + (1 x 7) + 1 = 1,870.

This was certainly a clumsy way of keeping track of time! But the author did it for one reason. In the Bible itself, the 49-year jubilee was the longest unit of time, but for the *Book of Jubilees,* it was practically the shortest. God, this book seemed to say, sees history in multiples of jubilees and plans accordingly. The thunderous proof that the author offered for this assertion comes at the very end of the book, when the Israelites enter the Promised Land of Canaan exactly 50 jubilees after the time when Adam, the first human being, was created. *Fifty jubilees exactly?* Such a round number could not be the result of chance—obviously, it was God who had arranged things so as to fit this perfect number, which also meant that He had arranged the date of every single event between the creation and the entrance into Canaan so as to arrive at a total of 50 jubilees exactly. Now, 50 jubilees equals 2,450 years. If God is calculating things to fit such huge patterns, the book seemed to say, no wonder that we mere humans lose track of divine time and fail to see God's great hand behind all the events of our everyday world. Just like the poor fellow who is about to drown on the Greek ferry, we have no grasp of the great, divine plan underlying all of earthly life and human history.

Joseph Versus Abraham

We have not quite finished with Joseph, however. It is important to consider what sort of contact he has with God in this story. The answer is surprising: none. He is kicked around a lot—by his brothers, by his master's wife, by his cellmates, by life itself—yet not once does he lift his voice in prayer to the Almighty. Nor, for that matter, does he offer thanks to God when he is saved (from his brothers, who first planned to kill him, Gen 37:18–20; from execution, which probably ought to have been his punishment for attempted rape;[8]

from prison after his reputation as a dream interpreter reaches Pharaoh). He does say, when Pharaoh first tells him that he has heard of Joseph's abilities as a dream interpreter, "It is not I, but God who will give Pharaoh the proper answer." A nice sentiment,[9] but actually, there is no indication in the text that God ever supplies Joseph with the interpretation of Pharaoh's dreams: Joseph does it all on his own, without even praying for God's help (contrast Dan 2:19). After that, when Pharaoh decides to put Joseph in charge of food rationing in preparation for the coming famine, he asks rhetorically: "Can we find anyone like this man, who has the spirit of God in him?" (Gen 41:38). Here is a revealing turn of phrase. God's *spirit* dwells in Joseph, apparently on a permanent basis;[10] but given the utter lack of interaction between God and Joseph, what could that phrase really mean? It sounds more like a trait of Joseph's character than an assertion that God actually intervenes on Joseph's behalf or even *enters* Joseph's mind; His spirit is just permanently there.

Joseph is the only figure in the book of Genesis described as "wise" (twice, in fact: Gen 41:33 and 39). Enosh, Enoch, Noah, Melchizedek, Abraham, Isaac, Jacob — none of these distinguished ancestors is ever so described. Now, we have seen that "wise" is a kind of code word: *wisdom* is the great set of divine rules and plans, and someone who is wise necessarily understands this and acts accordingly. Joseph's wisdom is thus expressed not only in his ability to interpret dreams (a wise function in the ancient Near East), but in his character: patient, optimistic, modest, and of good disposition (he never takes revenge on his brothers). But to say this much is to say something important about Joseph. He does *have* these traits; he has a "self" very much like our own, with his own thoughts and emotions. He is forgiving and generous (42:25); at one point he turns aside and weeps (42:24); in the end he "cannot restrain himself" (45:1) and falls into his brother Benjamin's embrace and weeps again (45:14). His own ideas and assessments are never interrupted by God's; he could hardly be said to have what the previous chapter called the "revelatory state of mind."

Joseph thus stands in sharp contrast to earlier figures in Genesis — to Abraham, for example. Abraham is all about that revelatory state of mind. The first thing we know about him, reported in Genesis 12:1, is that God told him to leave his homeland: "The Lord said to Abraham, 'Depart from your homeland, your kindred, and your father's house, to go to the land that I will show you.'" This will obviously make for a momentous change in Abraham's life, as this sentence itself makes clear: leaving his homeland meant severing the connection to his larger clan (here called his "kindred"; this subtribe constituted a person's principal source of protection in the ancient world), as well as to his immediate family. Leaving them meant becoming a sojourner, an alien with no official status. Yet Abraham does not hesitate: he "went forth as the LORD had commanded him" (Gen 12:4). In fact, there is no mention of Abraham even considering the consequences, no indication that he *thought* anything on his own. He moves about like an automaton.

The same sort of automaton-like Abraham appears in what is a still more momentous act in his life, his willingness to offer his son Isaac as a human sacrifice to God:

> After these things, God put Abraham to the test and said to him, "Abraham, Abraham!" And he said, "Here I am." He said: "Now take your son, your only one, whom you love, Isaac, and go off to the land of Moriah: offer him up as a burnt offering there, on one of the mountains that I will show you." Abraham got up early in the morning and saddled his donkey and took two of his servants with him along with his son Isaac. He split the wood for the burnt offering and set out for the place that God had mentioned. (Gen 22:1–3)

Once again, Abraham does not seem to have any sort of inner life—one might even say, any sort of mind at all. He is not, as a famous essay once described him, "fraught with background."[11] God speaks to him (how or under what circumstances is not explained: this is apparently unnecessary), and off he goes, prepared to sacrifice his beloved son.

What do we know of Abraham as a human being? He is not "wise" like Joseph, with all the character traits that go along with that quality—patient, modest, and the rest. Later tradition repeatedly described Abraham as "faithful" (*ne'eman*), that is, someone trusted by God,[12] but he is never called even that in Genesis. The most that is said of him there is that he is "one who fears God"; that is, he was willing to kill his own son rather than face the consequences of disobedience. Much of the time, there does not seem to be a real "self" there; at least half his brain, it appears, is ruled by God.

This difference between the selves of Abraham and Joseph, I wish to suggest, is paralleled by the difference between the way God acts, or doesn't, in their two sagas. Joseph, with his fairly modern self, knows of God only as the remote, long-range planner, a God whose universe runs on automatic pilot, obeying rules established long ago. Abraham's God is altogether unpredictable, threatening at every turn to intervene, telling Abraham what to do, demanding, commanding, intruding at will. Both men of course believe that God is the great Unseen Causer, as mentioned at the beginning of this chapter; but they differ as to how this causality is expressed. For Abraham, God's control is immediate: just as Er and Onan could not simply die, but had to be "killed" by God, so nothing simply happens in Abraham's universe, and there are no rules: a ninety-year-old woman can give birth to a baby; a son granted by God's beneficence can be snatched away (or threatened to be) by God's whim. For both Abraham and Joseph, the differing depictions of God and of self seem to correspond to each other, and, as we shall see, this equation continues on in other ways elsewhere in the Bible.

3

THE LAST WILLS OF JACOB'S SONS

WHAT MAKES US SIN?; AN INNER STRUGGLE; AN ANCIENT SENSE OF SELF; ABRAHAM AND THE DINKA

The difference between the Joseph story and the other narratives of Genesis seems to have something to do with what modern-day researchers call the human "sense of self." Tracing its development may prove crucial in understanding not only how we differ from biblical man, but how people of the modern West also differ from people elsewhere in the world.

A strange book appeared sometime around the start of the first century BCE. Nowadays it is not a part of anyone's Bible, but for a time ancient Jews and Christians considered it altogether sacred. The *Testaments of the Twelve Patriarchs* is just what the title says, a set of twelve last will and testaments, allegedly composed by the twelve sons of the biblical Jacob (traditionally known as "the patriarchs").* These are not last wills in our sense: they do not talk about distributing money or property to one's heirs. Rather, they are "spiritual" testaments. In keeping with ancient custom, each patriarch here summons his children shortly before his death and transmits to them some of the lessons he has learned in his own life, along with some advice for their own future.

The book's a fake, of course. These testaments weren't really written by the biblical Reuben, Simeon, and Jacob's other sons. Instead, an anonymous au-

---

* The Greek word "patriarch" (πατριάρχης) originally referred to the founder or father of a nation; since each of Jacob's sons was considered to be the founder of a different tribe, they were collectively known as "the patriarchs."

thor apparently dreamed up the idea of having each of these biblical figures transmit his spiritual testament to his children. In this way, the real author could pass on his own beliefs about what is important in life; putting his beliefs in the mouths of Jacob's sons would give his ideas an authority, and a cachet, that they certainly would not have had if the author had signed his own name to them.

Marauding Spirits

The reason this book is of interest here is that its author (or perhaps its *authors,* since this seems to be a composite work) could not resolve the issue answered in two different ways in the two previous chapters: Who's in charge here? Are we the sole proprietors of our own brains, or are our minds penetrated from time to time by God or some other external power? More generally, as we shall see, this issue is connected to a subtler question: What exactly do we mean by "I"—and is this "I" the same concept that existed two or three thousand years ago?

For the author of the *Testaments of the Twelve Patriarchs,* the question "Who's in charge here?" presented itself most directly with a central concern of his book, the cause of human sinfulness. Most people, at least in some sense, want to do the right thing, and yet they often end up not doing it. What makes them go wrong? This was a pressing question in the first century BCE (as it is today), and to answer it, the *Testaments* and other, roughly contemporaneous writings propose two quite different alternatives.

The first answer is that of Outside Powers. We do wrong because something outside ourselves burrows into our minds and causes us to go astray. In these ancient texts, this outside force is typically identified as Satan or another evil angel* who dispatches his minions to attack human beings. These lesser demons are usually simply called "spirits" in Hebrew and Greek;** they quickly take over people's minds and cause them to lose control. In fact, they're a bit like bacteria: they can't be seen, but somehow they get inside

* The word "satan" was originally a common noun in Hebrew meaning "accuser" or "adversary." Later, angels with various names—Mastema, Sammael, Gadreel, Satanel, Belial, etc.—came to be considered the *chief* wicked angel. Eventually, "Satan" came to be a proper noun, referring to the embodiment and sponsor of all evil.

** Greek is mentioned because many first-century Jewish texts originally written in Hebrew have survived only in Greek translation, while other texts from this period were originally composed in Greek by their Jewish authors.

you, and once they do, you're in trouble. (The customary way to counteract their power is to pray to God with special "apotropaic" prayers, designed to turn aside their evil powers; sometimes these prayers worked, but sometimes they didn't.)[1] In the *Testaments of the Twelve Patriarchs,* each of these spirits is identified with a particular kind of sin: there is the Spirit of Licentiousness, the Spirit of Contentiousness, the Spirits of Arrogance, of Flattery, Injustice, and so forth. All of them are in the employ of the great Angel of Deceit,[2] another name for Satan in use at the time.

In his testament, Simeon (one of Jacob's twelve sons) confesses that he actually wanted to kill his brother Joseph, "because the Angel of Deceit had sent the Spirit of Jealousy to blind my mind, so that I would not treat him in brotherly fashion" (T. Sim. 2:7). Consequently, he warns his children:

> Beware of the Spirits of Deceit and Jealousy, for Jealousy takes over a person's whole mind and will not allow him to eat or drink or do anything good. Rather, it is always pushing him to kill the person of whom he is jealous. (T. Sim. 3:1–3)

Simeon's brother Dan has a different besetting sin, anger. Accordingly, he warns his children:

> For the Spirit of Anger traps [a person] in nets of deceit and blinds his natural eyes, and by lying makes his mind go dark, and [then] transmits to him his own way of seeing. And what does he [i.e., the Spirit of Anger] trap his eyes with? With hatred [in] the heart,[3] so that he [the spirit] gives him his [the spirit's] own heart against his brother, so that he [the person] will envy him [his brother]. [The Spirit of] Anger is evil, my children, for he becomes a soul to the soul. For he takes over the body of the angry person, then gains dominion over the soul, then grants to the body his own power, so that it will perform any transgression. (T. Dan 2:4–3:2)

This view of the cause of sin was hardly the invention of the *Testaments'* author; it is found in many texts of the same period. For example, the author of the *Book of Jubilees* (early second century BCE), writes of Noah's descendants:

> *Impure demons* began to mislead Noah's grandchildren, to make them act foolishly, and to destroy them. Then Noah's sons came to their father Noah and told him about the *demons who were misleading, blinding, and killing*

> his grandchildren. He prayed before the Lord his God and said: "God of the spirits which are in all animate beings . . . may Your mercy be lifted over the children of Your children; and may the *wicked spirits* not rule them in order to destroy them from the earth. (*Jub* 10:1–3)[4]

Later, in recounting the story of Abraham, the author of *Jubilees* has Abraham pray using rather similar language:[5]

> That night he prayed and said: My God, my God, God Most High, You alone are my God. You have created everything: Everything that was and has been is the product of Your hands. You and Your lordship I have chosen. *Save me from the power of the evil spirits who rule the thoughts of people's minds.* May they not mislead me from following You, my God. Do establish me and my posterity forever. May we not go astray from now until eternity. (*Jub* 12:19–20)

The fierce monotheism professed by Abraham in this prayer does not stop him from worrying about the "power of the evil spirits who rule the thoughts of people's minds." He knows what they can do if left unchecked; they can even cause a person to fall away from God, "from following You."[6]

A similar prayer was discovered among the Dead Sea Scrolls* seventy years ago:

> Forgive my sin, O Lord, and cleanse me of my iniquity. Favor me with the spirit of faithfulness and knowledge; let me not be caught in transgression. *Do not let any satan** or impure spirit rule over me;*[7] let no pain or an evil inclination take over me/my bones. (11Q5 [11QPs^a] col 19 "Plea for Deliverance" 14–16)[8]

Evil Comes from Within

The other explanation for human evil is quite the opposite of the Outside Powers answer, and it is basically what most people in the modern West be-

---

* A collection of ancient Jewish manuscripts discovered on the shores of the Dead Sea, starting in 1947. Most of the texts are dated to the end of the biblical period; that is, to the third, second, and first centuries BCE.

** The word "satan" here is not our Satan, but a general term for an evil spirit.

lieve. Evil comes from within us. More precisely, we are all given the capacity to choose what we do and to face the consequences. These two answers may be opposites, but, strange to tell, this second explanation for evil's origin is also found within the *Testaments of the Twelve Patriarchs.* For example, the "Testament of Asher" begins by asserting that "There are two ways, of good and of evil, and along with them *two impulses within our breasts* that differentiate them" (T. Ash. 1:5). What we do is thus the result of what we choose to do:

> If the soul *chooses the good,* everything it does will be in righteousness, and [even] if it sins, it will repent right away . . . But if it *opts for the [evil] impulse,* then its every action will be in wickedness, and, having driven away the good, it will take hold of the bad. (T. Ash. 1:6–8)

In other words, it's all up to the individual soul to set its own course.

This view seems to concur with a passage from the Book of Ben Sira, a second-century BCE Jewish text found in the Apocrypha section of many Christian Bibles (and known there as Ecclesiasticus, or Sirach):

> God created mankind in the beginning, and gave him over to the power of his own disposition.
> If you wish, you will keep a commandment, and faithfully do God's will.
> If you trust in Him, you too may live.
> Fire and water are set before you; extend your hand to whichever you choose.
> Life and death are before a person: whichever he chooses will be given to him. (Sir 15:14–17)[9]

Similarly, in the *Psalms of Solomon,* another apocryphal work from the same period:

> Our deeds are [done] by choice and [are] in the power of our souls.
> Doing right or wrong is the work of our own hands, and in Your righteousness You survey the sons of men. (*Pss. Sol.* 9:4)

Here, God is clearly a bystander; His "righteousness" is apparently mentioned because in the end God will *judge* the people for their actions, but their choices are their own.

"I Can't Decide"

These two poles, the external and internal explanations for the source of human evil, seem clear enough.[10] But as many scholars have noted, a number of authors (including some of those cited above) seem to hesitate between the two answers, sometimes even evoking both simultaneously, as if trying to settle somewhere in the middle. This may be the most interesting thing about the *Testaments of the Twelve Patriarchs* and other compositions from the same period. It is as if their authors had both possibilities in front of them, but all they keep saying is: "I just can't make up my mind!"

Take, for example, Moses's opening prayer in the *Book of Jubilees:*

> Then Moses fell prostrate and prayed and said: "Lord my God, do not allow your people and your heritage to go along *in the error of their minds* . . . Create for them a just spirit. *May the spirit of Belial not rule over them so as to bring charges against them before You and to trap them away from every proper path so that they may be destroyed from your presence.* They are your people and your heritage whom You have rescued from Egyptian control by your great power. Create for them a pure mind and a holy spirit. May they not be trapped in their sins from now to eternity." (*Jub* 1:19–21)

We saw above that *Jubilees* elsewhere seems to endorse the "outside" source of human evil—and indeed, it does so here as well: don't let Belial* rule over Israel, the author says—this is clearly the external understanding of evil's origin. If Belial does take over, he goes on to say, the consequences will be dire: Belial will be able to bring charges against the people before God (since accusing people before God is the satanic task par excellence), leading to the severest punishment.[11] But the author also asks God to prevent Israel from "go[ing] along in the error of their minds," and this seems to be talking about something *internal.*[12] The author also evokes a verse from the Psalms twice in this same passage, "Create for them a just spirit" and "Create for them a pure mind and a holy spirit" (for both, see Ps 51:12; some Bibles, 51:10). Here it is hard to know if this is to be accomplished externally or internally. That is, does God create a "just spirit" and a "pure mind" through an act of cleansing that presumably takes place entirely inside? Or is it more like (excuse the analogy!) changing a flat tire, where the old spirit is somehow exchanged for

---

* Or *Beliar,* yet another name for Satan or a similar demonic power.

a brand-new spirit from the outside, which is attached in the discarded one's place? It is not even clear that the author of *Jubilees* himself knew for sure.

Another example of hesitating between two explanations for human evil is in the already-cited "Plea for Deliverance" from the Dead Sea Scrolls:

> Forgive my sin, O Lord, and *cleanse me of my iniquity.* Favor me with the spirit of faithfulness and knowledge; let me not be caught in transgression. *Do not let any satan or impure spirit rule over me;* let no pain or *an evil inclination* take over me/my bones. (11Q5 [11QPs^{a}] col 19 "Plea for Deliverance" 14–16)[13]

Here again the author seems to have combined the external-source rhetoric *(Do not let any satan or impure spirit rule over me)* with the internal-source theme, "Cleanse me of my iniquity." Even more striking is the juxtaposition of "Do not let any satan or impure spirit rule over me" with "let no pain or *an evil inclination* take over me/my bones." Obviously, "any satan or impure spirit" is going to be invading the human being from the outside, whereas "evil inclination" (in Hebrew, *yetzer [ha]-ra*) was a kind of code word during this period for something *inside,* an internal urge that is part of every human's makeup.[14]

I should add that the fact that Satan's minions are sometimes called "spirits" only adds a further layer of ambiguity, since in both Hebrew and Greek this word can refer equally to an external *spirit* flying around and then entering the human mind, and to a person's own, internal *spirit,* what might elsewhere be called his or her "soul" or "heart" or indeed whole being.[15] In the *Testaments* and elsewhere, it is sometimes difficult to decide which sense is being evoked, the internal or external.[16]

The Semipermeable Mind

Despite the ambiguous evidence seen above, some students of these ancient Jewish and Christian texts have a tendency to dismiss the Outside Powers explanation as a mere metaphor. Everyone knows that there are no *real* evil spirits flying around out there, and even if there were, how could they get from the outside atmosphere to the inside of a human brain and take it over?

But to say this is to ignore a whole area of research that is currently being pursued by scholars in a variety of other fields — neuroscientists, evolutionary biologists, psychologists, and anthropologists (though somewhat less by historians, especially historians of ancient times). The object of their research is sometimes referred to as the "sense of self." Since this turns out to be a fairly important concept in this book, and one that is sometimes used in different ways, I ought to define what I mean by this term:[17]

> **sense of self:** the mental picture that people have of what a person consists of and does, as distinct from everything that is not that person (namely, the rest of the world). Or, to put it slightly differently: the assumptions about what a person *is* that a defined group of people carry around in their heads.[18]

This mental picture of our selves can be extremely significant in the way our brains process visual or auditory stimuli in daily life. However, the interesting thing that scholars have observed is that this "sense of self" actually varies greatly from civilization to civilization. People construe their selves differently, depending on where and when they happen to live. The apparent reason for this variety is that there is no "default" position when it comes to our sense of self, nothing that all people are born with; moreover, unlike other phenomena, our picture of who "I" am and how my brain functions does not seem to be explained by anything we know about the physiology of the brain.[19]

Some characteristics of the human mind do seem to be universal and hence, apparently hardwired into our sense of self. (All human beings, for example, exhibit what is called "psychic continuity," the feeling that we continue to be the same person minute after minute and year after year[20] — though it is not at all clear *how* we all come equipped with such a sense of things.) But there are other attributes of a given sense of self that are characteristic of only some human beings. What is more, when it comes to the self, it is far from clear if (and if so, where) there is a central, *physical* clearinghouse in the brain, a single spot where all the incoming sensory data and stored memories are synthesized into an ongoing picture experienced by that theoretical entity, "I myself."[21] The problem posed by this fact has been clearly stated by one writer:

> When the self is considered from the standpoint of neuroscience, one primary concern is how awareness is integrated and organized into a coherent whole, since the *whole* is what is emphasized when we refer to "the self" or "the mind." Here the emphasis is not upon any single, momentary act of perception or motor response, but rather upon the totality of the brain's functions into unified experience and action. Indeed, one major reason why

> the self seems so difficult to explain on a purely neurobiological basis is that, while we experience a unified consciousness, there appears to be an essential difference between the unified mind and the divisible brain. We know the nervous system is composed of millions of neurons grouped into numerous larger structures [or "systems"]. The question is, how [do] all these physically connected but materially separable structures function as a seamless whole that we experience as our unified selves?[22]

The answer to this question is far from simple, but most scholars agree that our self is in any case some sort of mental *construct,* a way our brains make sense of the ever-changing flow of data inside us.[23] What does this construct stipulate? When it comes down to details, our modern, Western "self" turns out to be only one sort of construct among many, and not, it turns out, a particularly popular one. In the words of another writer:

> No scholar has yet written the definitive history of the modern self, but we know now that it does have a history—and a geography. Although all human beings *construct* a self, most people in the past were probably not individual selves in the modern Western sense, and people in some parts of the world probably are not now. That is, they do not experience themselves as clearly bounded, but rather as seamlessly embedding in their tribes and their ecosystems; they do not think of themselves as unique, but rather as more or less identical to others of their kind; and they do not think of themselves as neatly integrated, but rather as invaded by strange spirits and forces that may pull them in many different directions.[24]

The only problem with this excellent summary is the word "probably" used twice in the second sentence. Anthropologists and other scholars have shown *for sure* that people outside of the modern West (which is to say most of humanity even today) are not individuals in the modern Western sense, nor did *any* segment of humanity construct a self like ours until quite recently. As a pair of researchers recently wrote:

> In the Western view, the individual is a separate, autonomous entity that comprises distinct attributes (e.g., abilities, traits, motives, and values), and it is these attributes that are assumed to cause behavior. Further, there is a belief in the inherent separateness of distinct individuals. People seek to maintain *independence* from others and to discover and express their unique configuration. A great deal of what is known [to Western scientists]

> about "human" nature is rooted in this model of the person. Yet a growing volume of research by psychological and cultural anthropologists indicates that over three quarters of the world — the part of the world typically considered non-Western — does not share this view of the person.[25]

This might then lead one to ask: if the world today offers evidence of widely varying "senses of self," what sort of *self* was carried about in the brains of people in biblical times, or even the somewhat later writers cited earlier in this chapter? For example, possession by deities or spirits is a common occurrence in many non-Western societies, and one that is in some ways reminiscent of the understanding of sin as presented in parts of the *Testaments of the Twelve Patriarchs* and other, contemporaneous writers.[26] The anthropologist Michael Lambek has studied extensively the phenomenon of spirit possession among inhabitants of the island of Mayotte (off Madagascar). There,

> Spirits enter the bodies of human beings and rise to their heads, taking temporary control of all bodily and mental functions . . . Despite the fact that the body remains the same, it is now occupied by a different person.[27]

One particularly widespread form of possession in our own day is the cult of *zar* spirits, witnessed across a broad swath of territory including parts of the Middle East and East Africa, particularly the Horn of Africa. After a person has been possessed by a *zar* spirit,

> everyone in the culture knows the procedure that follows. The patient will be interrogated in the house of the doctor. There the doctor will lure his own *zar* into possessing him in a trance, and through his intercession try to lure the unknown *zar* of the patient (his "horse") into public possession. Then the spirit will be led to reveal his identity by means of adroit cajolery, promises, and threats. The demands of the *zar* will be negotiated through a lengthy process of financial dickering. Finally, the patient will be enrolled, for the rest of his life, in the "*zar* society" of fellow sufferers, renting, as it were, his temporary freedom from relapse through regular donations and by means of participation in the worship of the spirit.[28]

Zar possession is more common among women than among men — and among married women more than the unmarried.[29] The spirit enters the woman's body and, once admitted, takes over:

> *Zar* spirits may be acquired or inherited, usually passing from mother to daughter or daughter-in-law, if there are no daughters. Everyone is potentially exposed to possession by a *zar* spirit. A state of possession is described as if the possessed is a horse and the *zar* is the rider . . . A *zar* may attack when someone is alone, especially at night, or perhaps standing under a large tree, or near a river, or in a cave, or when someone is playing an instrument or singing. Most of the conducive conditions are related to psychological pressures, and weak or melancholy people are most susceptible. Yet often those chosen have attractive qualities that provoke jealousy, as does a beautiful woman who is often praised for her beauty.[30]

In the light of such evidence, there does not seem to be any reason *not* to take quite literally the Outside Powers explanation of sin and evil as found in the *Testaments* and other writings of that period. Possession by malign spirits has been going on since time immemorial, and it continues to this day.[31]

A Different Sort of "I"

What does all this have to do with the Bible? Here one must proceed with caution, since little can be said for sure about the sense of self that characterized people in biblical times (all the more so because those "times" stretch out over nearly a millennium). Moreover, no matter which part of the Bible one is examining, there is no escaping the fact that biblical *texts* are not to be confused with biblical *people.* The former have been transmitted through the work of scribes and other figures; how they represent heroes and ancestors, kings and prophets and sages, may tell us little about what these various figures actually did, and perhaps even less — or nothing at all — about how they conceived of the functioning and limits of their own minds.

On the other hand, there is still less reason simply to assume that biblical man and modern man shared the same, or even a similar, sense of self. Too many of the above-cited neurological and anthropological studies suggest that this is not likely to be the case, and too many of the biblical texts themselves seem to back them up: these texts bear witness to a strange world, in which people's minds were sometimes penetrated from the outside — a world that seemed to assume that God or spirits or demons could quite naturally infiltrate people's brains, planting pictures in their minds or sticking words inside their mouths.

Many contemporary biblical scholars might react to such observations with a learned ho-hum: *of course* ancient Israelites believed such things. They also believed in magic; they thought that a person could be physically harmed if someone inscribed his name on an execration bowl or on a statue representing him and then smashed the bowl or statue to smithereens. (We know this because the smithereens, along with ancient documents explaining their function, are nowadays on display in numerous museums as well as a few private collections.) Ancient Israelites, along with other peoples around the globe, also believed in the efficacy of curses: speak these words over here and somehow they will fly through the air and attack someone over there, causing him or her to become sick or die. Demons? Some of the oldest texts we have from Mesopotamia are incantations or rituals aimed at protecting people from demons or the evil eye.[32]

Moving westward to the sphere of the otherwise philosophical Greeks or rational Romans, we find that a man could inscribe on a strip of lead the name of a young woman he was interested in — including in the inscription his request that she return his interest while throwing over her present suitor — and then drop this metal strip into a fountain, a bath, or a well; this, people apparently thought, actually worked. (You could also write the name of an enemy on a strip of lead and then drive a nail through it; deposit this in a public fountain or elsewhere and then sit back and wait for the victim to drop dead.)[33] Indeed, people have always used similar sorts of inscriptions to heal or harm[34] — these practices continued to be used by Jews well into the Middle Ages and beyond; in fact, on to the present day.[35] Throughout the ancient Near East, people knew that a great, heavenly god could somehow also inhabit a foot-and-a-half-high statue in a temple,[36] or that the same god could simultaneously exist (that is, actually, physically, be located) in two or ten different temples on earth.[37] The statue was, or was claimed to be, the god himself.

So: a different sense of self as well? Why not?

I am not sure, however, that such a reaction takes the full measure of what is meant by "sense of self" or how deep it goes. (In fact, it seems to me likely that *all* the aforementioned phenomena are somehow possible only if one has a sense of self very different from our own; if so, such a sense is not merely an additional oddity, but the essential base upon which all the other phenomena stand.) In any case, the fact that contemporary biblical scholars may be open to the *idea* of a different sense of self existing in biblical times does not necessarily affect how they — how *we* — read and understand actual passages from the Hebrew Bible. The fact is that we all are immersed in the Western and modern sense of self; as a result, we all tend to read the words of these ancient texts in a way that is probably quite different from that of their original audience. It is as if we are separated from the world of those words by a thick wall of Plexiglas that prevents us from ever truly crossing over and entering their world, even though we are staring right at it. So we read biblical accounts of people directly encountering God—the stories of Hagar, Abraham and Sarah, Jacob, Moses, Gideon, and the other narratives seen in chapter 1—without ever truly being able to enter into their reality. (Again: I am not speaking about a real person named Hagar or Abraham, but of the world in which these narratives made sense.) The most we can say is that those sorts of things may have happened "back then,"[38] or may *seem* to have happened back then, but whichever the case, they don't happen anymore. Nor is this incomprehension limited to ancient biblical narratives. Indeed, its most important manifestation comes with the whole matter of biblical prophets, people who consistently report that God spoke to them one day and gave them a message to transmit to the people as a whole, or to the king, or to some foreign nation (see chapter 7). How is a modern person to relate to this claim? Or, moving toward the end of the biblical period, how are we to understand the explanation for sin's origins in the passages seen in the *Testaments* and other texts, or even Philo of Alexandria's views on angels or on prophecy?[39]

Godfrey Lienhardt, a student of the anthropologist E. E. Evans-Pritchard in the mid-twentieth century, at one point studied the Dinka, a people of southeastern Sudan. The Dinka, Lienhardt wrote, have a different sense of self from that familiar to us, one that, he somewhat mournfully concluded, "I can discuss only inadequately":

> The Dinka have no conception which at all closely corresponds to our popular, modern conception of the "mind" as mediating and, as it were, storing up the experiences of the self. There is, for them, no such interior entity to . . . stand between the experiencing self at any given moment and what is or has been an exterior influence upon the self.

(Here, I should note, the distinction between inside and outside seems to be as blurry among the Dinka as it sometimes appears to be in the Dead Sea Scrolls or the *Testaments.*)

Lienhardt continues:

> So it seems that what we should call the *memories* of experiences, and regard therefore as in some way intrinsic and *interior* to the remembering person and modified in their effect upon him by their [very] interiority, appear to the Dinka as *exteriorly* acting upon him [and, therefore, potentially continuing to act upon him].
>
> A man who had been imprisoned in Khartoum called one of his children "Khartoum" in memory of that place, but also to turn aside any possible harmful influence of that place upon him in later life . . . It is Khartoum which is regarded as an *agent,* the subject which acts, and not as with us the remembering mind which recalls a place. The man is the *object* acted upon.[40]

Summing up his own years of research on this "sense of self" in different cultures, the anthropologist Clifford Geertz wrote in a well-known essay:

> The concept of person is, in fact, an excellent vehicle by means of which to examine this whole question of how to go about poking into another people's turn of mind. In the first place, some sort of concept of this kind, [that is, a "sense of self"] . . . exists in recognizable form among all social groups. The notions of what persons *are* may be, from our point of view, sometimes more than a little odd. They may be conceived to dart about nervously at night shaped like fireflies. Essential elements of their psyches, like hatred, may be thought to be lodged in granular black bodies within their livers, discoverable upon autopsy. They may share their fates with *Doppelgänger* beasts, so that when the beast sickens or dies they sicken or die too. But at least some conception of what a human individual is, as opposed to a rock, an animal, a rainstorm, or a god, is, so far as I can see, universal.
>
> Yet, at the same time, as these offhand examples suggest, the actual conceptions involved vary from one group to the next, and often quite sharply. *The Western conception of the person as a bounded, unique, more or less integrated motivational and cognitive universe, a dynamic center of awareness, emotion, judgment, and action organized into a distinctive whole and set contrastively both against other such wholes and against its social and natural background, is, however incorrigible* [i.e., irrefutable — JK] *it may seem to us, a rather peculiar idea within the context of the world's cultures.* Rather than attempting to place the experience of others within the framework of such a conception, which is what the extolled "empathy" in fact usually comes down to, *understanding them demands setting that conception aside* and seeing their experiences within the framework of their own idea of what self-

> hood is. And for Java, Bali, and Morocco, at least, that idea differs markedly not only from our own but, no less dramatically and no less instructively, from one to the other.[41]

Actually, there is nothing particularly elusive about the idea that people outside of what has been called the "WEIRD* world" have a different sense of their own minds. The Canadian philosopher Charles Taylor — not a biblical scholar nor, for that matter, an anthropologist or neuroscientist — has written insightfully about two kinds of "self," the premodern one, which he describes as "porous" (that is, semipermeable, open in some degree to the outside),[42] and the modern, closed-off one, the "buffered" self. The old kind of mind was *porous* in the sense that it was open to external influences:

> Once meanings are not necessarily *in* the mind, once we can fall under the spell [and] enter the zone of exogenous meaning, then we think of this meaning as including us, or perhaps penetrating us . . . This porousness is most clearly in evidence in the fear of possession. Demons can take us over. And indeed, five centuries ago, many of the more spectacular manifestations of mental illness, what we would classify as psychotic behavior, were laid at the door of possession . . .
>
> Here is the contrast between the modern, bounded self — I want to say "buffered" self — and the "porous" self of the earlier enchanted world . . . For the modern, buffered self, the possibility exists of taking a distance from, disengaging from, everything outside the mind. My ultimate purposes are those which arise within me, the crucial meanings of things are those defined in my responses to them . . . This is not to say that the buffered understanding necessitates your taking this stance. It is just that it allows it as a possibility, whereas the porous one does not. By definition for the porous self, the source of its most powerful and important emotions [is] outside the "mind"; or better put, the very notion that there is a clear boundary, allowing us to define an inner base area, grounded in which we can disengage from the rest, has no sense.[43]

---

* I am not sure of the origin of this acronym (Western, Educated, Industrialized, Rich, and Democratic) for our own societies, nor do these traits characterize all of the countries involved; on its own, however, this name does have one thing in its favor, the suggestion that, in the broad perspective of three or four millennia of human history, as well as in comparison to the great bulk of the world's population today, the way in which we denizens of the modern West view ourselves and the outside world must appear rather unique and, on reflection, altogether strange.

Homer and Abraham

Similar observations have been made about ancient Greek ideas of the mind or soul, bringing us considerably closer in space and time to biblical Israel. A little more than half a century ago, the German classicist Bruno Snell published a study entitled *The Discovery of the Mind in Greek Philosophy and Literature.* In it, Snell sought to trace the emergence of what we might call the modern "sense of self" by examining different stages of ancient Greek writing. Examining the very earliest stage — represented by the poetry of Homer and other ancient texts — Snell argued that we are still in the world of outside causes, gods and goddesses who intervene in human thought. A later writer, he said, might speak of Achilles or some other hero arriving at an assessment and plan of action on his own:

> Homer, however, could not do without the deity. We might substitute a *decision* on the part of Achilles, his own reflection and his own incentive. But Homer's man does not yet regard himself as the source of his own decisions . . . When the Homeric hero, after duly weighing his alternatives, comes to a final conclusion, he nonetheless feels that his course has been shaped by the gods. Even nowadays, when we try to recapture the past, we may lose sight of our own share in an event in which we were once implicated and ask ourselves: how did this plan, or that thought, ever come to me? If we take this notion, that a thought "came" to us, and give it a religious twist, we come fairly close to the Homeric attitude . . . Homer lacks a knowledge of the spontaneity of the human mind; he does not realize that decisions of the will, or any impulses or emotions, have their origin in man himself.[44]

This view of things is rather similar to that underlying the "malign spirits" explanation found in the *Testaments of the Twelve Patriarchs* (and in the religions that preceded it, in both ancient Israel and Greece). Things come from the outside. This includes, prominently, *words* that come from the outside. The "invocation of the muse" may have become a mere convention in later times, but in ancient Greece it was dead serious. You, mere human, weren't going to get anywhere in your epic poem on your own; what you needed was nothing less than divine dictation, so "Sing, O Goddess, of the wrath of Achilles . . ." (*Iliad* 1:1) was the request with which you had to begin. And such outside help was called for not just at the start of the poem, but at crucial points thereafter:

> Tell me now, Muses who dwell on Olympus—
> Since you, as divine, are present and know
> All things (while we have just hearsay, knowing
> Nothing firsthand)—Then who were the chieftains
> Who led the Danaans? Their numbers myself
> I could never relate, not if I had
> Ten tongues and ten mouths, a voice never ceasing
> And a heart made of bronze; unless you Muses,
> Heavenly daughters of shield-wielding Zeus,
> Should name for me all who came to Ilios. (*Iliad* 2:484–488)

True knowledge belonged to the gods, who could choose to impart it to humans, or choose not to.[45] This was true of all sorts of knowledge, not only poetry but history and philosophy and mathematics and yet other things. Humans could, of course, speculate about such matters on their own, but they could never know for sure if they were right. Snell quotes Xenophanes (late fifth–early fourth centuries BCE):

> Accordingly, there has not been a man, nor will there ever be, who knows for certain what I am saying about the gods, *or for that matter in regard to all things,* for even if one happens to say what is for the most part true, still he would not *know,* since [the expression] "it seems" has been established with regard to all things. (frag 34)

Similarly, Alcmaeon of Croton (fifth century): "Concerning things unseen the gods have certainty, whereas to us as men conjecture [alone is possible]." One can sense the frustration that stands behind these assertions. We can know for sure only that which has been revealed by the gods.

A later echo of this same mentality is found in hymns included among the Dead Sea Scrolls:

> What can I say unless You open my mouth? And what can I reply, unless You give me insight? . . . Without You, nothing can be done, and nothing can be known without You willing it. (1QH[a] *Thanksgiving Hymns* col 18:9–11)

> You prepared in the wisdom of Your mind the course [of things] before they existed, and everything is in accordance with Your will, and nothing can be done without You. *These things I know through Your knowledge*, since You opened my ears to [i.e., gave me to understand] wondrous mysteries . . .

> *What can I speak that is not known* [i.e., by You], *or say that has not been told* [by You]? Everything has been engraved before You with the memory's stylus for all the periods of eternity and uncounted times . . . (1QH[a] *Thanksgiving Hymns* col 9:21–26)

What Snell says about Homer brings to mind a number of passages from the Bible that seem to share the Homeric view. Take, for example, the previously mentioned departure of Israel's ancestor Abraham from his native land (Gen 11:34[some Bibles, 11:31]–12:6). According to the biblical account, Abraham first traveled from Ur northward to the city of Haran, and then continued on to Canaan. What caused Abraham to go that long way, leaving behind all but his immediate family, braving the hazards of travel in the ancient world to settle as a stranger in a place unknown? Simple: God told him to do it. "And the Lord said to Abram, 'Depart from your homeland, and your clan, and your kin, to the land that I will show you'" (Gen 12:1).

Here we seem to be in the land of Snell's Homer. Abraham doesn't *decide* to do what he is about to do; he is ordered to do so by God—for no apparent reason. Indeed, the very wording of this command is clearly intended to tell us how little Abraham's rational mind could have had to do with this turn of events: God tells him to leave everything familiar, including all those in his native land who might defend him in a dispute or take his side in actual combat, in order to go to some place that God does not even choose to name, "to the land that I will show you." Commanded, Abraham obeys. (Just as, later in his biography, he will bow to God's horrific order that he offer his beloved son Isaac as a human sacrifice on an altar "on one of the mountains that I will show you"—another destination undefined!)

At the same time, it seems to me that Snell may have overstated things a bit in the passage cited earlier, at least if his analysis is to be applied to Abraham. The biblical Abraham is not consistently an automaton. One could not say of the Genesis narrative (as Snell says of Homeric narrative) that it demonstrates no awareness "that decisions of the will, or any impulses or emotions, have their origin in man himself"—far from it! Elsewhere in Genesis, Abraham thinks for himself, weighs alternatives, and takes the initiative on his own: he *decides* to go to war, to divide the land of Canaan with his nephew Lot, to deceive the Egyptians ("Say you're my sister," he tells his wife Sarah), to bargain with the Hittites for a burial plot—God has no role in any of these events. In fact, Homer's heroes are not automatons either (as Snell certainly knew). Surely it is not their every thought that just "comes to them." Achilles, Agamemnon, Hector, and the rest likewise make plans, trick people, and exhibit all the mental capacities that we ourselves have. Rather, what might be more truly said is that *sometimes* in the Bible, as in the *Iliad* and the *Odyssey*, an ordinary, otherwise rational person hears a divine voice telling him or her what to do. But a lot hangs on that "sometimes." Clearly there was a time when such things happened, and just as clearly there came a moment when such a way of conceiving of human beings seemed somehow wrong, old-fashioned, and was eventually dropped.

When was that moment? No doubt it arose at different times in different places, and certainly not at a snap of history's fingers. But in the Greek-Jewish orbit, if one takes the evidence of the *Testaments* and contemporaneous texts as an indication, there seems to have been a period of coexistence of two different "senses of self," the one still quite open to external intruders, the other moving closer to our modern, Western selves, which for the most part deny the very possibility of such intrusion.[46]

The *Testaments* were begun roughly two centuries before the Jewish historian Josephus Flavius undertook to write the *Jewish Antiquities,* retelling his people's history to a Greek-speaking audience, including the narrative of Abraham's departure from Ur seen above. In recounting this departure, Josephus repeats what the biblical text had said, that Abraham left Ur "after God had ordered him to proceed to Canaan." But then, Josephus seeks to connect Abraham's departure to another cause entirely: his being the first monotheist.[47] The fact that Abraham believed in one God alone, Josephus explains, came to upset some of his non-monotheistic neighbors in Ur:

> It was in fact owing to these opinions that the Chaldeans [inhabitants of Ur] and the other peoples of Mesopotamia rose up against him, and he, *thinking fit to change his dwelling-place, at the will and with the aid of God,* settled in the land of Canaan. (*Ant.* 1:157)

Here is a marvelous bit of hedging on Josephus's part. As we have seen, the biblical text, which Josephus certainly knew by heart, clearly has God *command* Abraham: "Depart from your homeland . . ." But Josephus feels impelled to turn this into Abraham's *decision:* "thinking fit to change his dwelling-place . . ." That's why Abraham left: he had an internally generated idea: "The Chaldeans are angry at me — I better get out of here." And yet Josephus knows full well that the biblical account attributes Abraham's departure from Ur to God, "Depart from your homeland," so he adds, as if an afterthought, the words "at the will and with the aid of God." Of course, this falls far short of what Josephus had said earlier, that God had "ordered" Abraham to leave; here, in fact, Abraham is not even being directly addressed by God.[48]

In short, it seems that texts like this one by Josephus, or the earlier Qumran documents and the *Testaments of the Twelve Patriarchs,* bear witness to a true hesitation or even confusion, one that may well tell us a great deal about the evolving "sense of self" in that period. Of course, one can always say that such hesitation is merely conventional, the result of conflicting Persian- and Greek-inspired *ideas.* But what I have tried to suggest is that the conflict goes much deeper, to the very "sense of self" that these various authors carried about in their own heads. To put this question directly: Isn't it possible that the Abraham of Genesis was a little more like the Dinka than we usually think? And, centuries later, weren't the authors of *Jubilees,* the *Testaments,* and the Qumran "Plea for Deliverance" still holding on to a sense of self entirely different from our own?

I have intended these first three chapters to introduce the basic theme and scope of this book, namely, the human encounter with the divine as reflected in different writings during and just after the biblical period. In all, this study is intended to cover some ten centuries of human history in one part of the globe, and even if an ancient psalmist could write that "a thousand years are like yesterday in Your sight" (Ps 90:3), for this book's subject those centuries are hugely important, bearing witness to a fundamental change that can tell us much about the reality of God, both then and now. In the chapters that follow I intend to explore a number of specific aspects of this change, starting with the earliest evidence of religious beliefs and going on to such specifics as ancient priests and prophets, the biblical soul (and how it changed), ancient and not-so-ancient prayers, and ending in the period just preceding the dawn of Christianity and rabbinic Judaism.

PART II

Divine Encounters

In the ancient Near East, people were said to have actually encountered God/the gods. Biblical narratives as well as external evidence leave little doubt that this is how people understood things. But what lay behind such a construal, and was it really true? These questions are not easily answered; they bring us to the heart of our inquiry.

4

ADAM AND EVE AND THE UNDIFFERENTIATED OUTSIDE

HUMANITY'S ANCESTORS; *HOMO RELIGIOSUS;* A SENSE OF SMALLNESS; THE ENCHANTED WORLD

Adam and Eve left the Garden of Eden with more than a new set of clothes. They carried along with them an understanding of the world, which they later passed on to their descendants, the human race.

Scholars are divided about the story of Adam and Eve. Although it begins by telling about humanity's earliest origins, some argue that its real focus is not on the creation itself, but on a moment that comes much later in human development, the time when people first learn the secrets of agriculture. Human beings are not born farmers; somehow they have to figure out that if you take some vegetable seeds or grains of wheat and stick them into the ground — a seemingly wasteful and senseless act — in a few months the seeds will have sprouted into edible plants, repaying your investment a hundredfold. This is a lesson that has to be discovered and passed on. Scholars nowadays believe that agriculture sprang up more or less simultaneously in three or four different locations around the globe (including the Middle East), starting around twelve thousand years ago.

Before that time, one might indeed say that human beings lived like Adam and Eve; they inhabited a marvelous garden (or jungle), where all the food they consumed grew on trees or sprang up unbidden from the ground. An anthropologist, however, might characterize the same state somewhat differently. Preagricultural societies were often harsh; in some, people had to forage daily for their food, and the threat of starvation was an everyday concern.

In any event, Adam and Eve lived for a time in their Garden — we are not told how long; when God said to Adam that "you may eat from all the trees in the Garden" (except, of course, for the forbidden one), He was describing what was the ordinary way of life followed by early humans for countless millennia. Adam and Eve had no clothes; the pair walked around in the Garden naked "and were not ashamed," just as our ancestors did, and some peoples still do today.

At a certain point, however, Eve encountered a talking snake. Later interpreters of the biblical story saw this snake as a figure of Satan,[1] but there was nothing corresponding to Satan at the time of this story's composition — and nothing in the story to suggest it. Actually, snakes in the ancient Near East were sometimes associated with wisdom,[2] and this seems more to the point here: as it says in Genesis, "Now the serpent was cleverer than any other animal that the Lord God had made." This snake encouraged Eve to eat from the forbidden tree that imparted knowledge, and she and Adam did so. Their disobedience was promptly punished: "By the sweat of your brow," God tells Adam, "you shall eat your food" — in other words, Adam's newly acquired wisdom resulted in his becoming . . . a farmer. It was not a painless transition: from that point on, Adam and his descendants would have to toil long hours in seedtime and harvest time, but the rewards were great. Humanity now gained a measure of control over its food supply and could settle down, no longer needing to wander about in search of its next meal.

At roughly the same time that humans first understood the secret of agriculture, another, related insight emerged. Women's bellies, it now appeared, do not swell up and deliver babies at random, but as a result of a different sort of planting that took place nine months earlier. Here was a theory that at first must have seemed as unlikely as the idea of agriculture; eventually, however, experimentation demonstrated its truth, and life was changed forever. Now children were understood to have *two* parents, and sometimes a whole new social organization resulted. As the biblical account notes, henceforth the man would "cling to his wife and they shall be one flesh" (Gen 2:24); moreover, just as Adam was condemned to toil by the sweat of his brow for food, so Eve was told that "in pain you will bring forth children," the one painful harvest corresponding to the other.

Scholars doubt that this biblical story could be based on any collective, historical memory of the transition to agriculture. Rather, it seems to be more like a nostalgic reconstruction, perhaps reflecting reported encounters with still-existing, preagricultural societies. This notwithstanding, considering a few specific details in the biblical story—and taking them seriously—may help us to enter more fully into an early sense of self.

Life in the Garden

To begin with, it is most significant that God in this story exists *inside* the Garden. Adam and Eve "heard the sound of the LORD God walking about in the Garden at the breezy time of day" (Gen 3:8). He is not the remote, heavenly God of later times, nor a deity who inhabits a special temple or shrine reserved for Him, along with a specially trained cadre of priests who serve Him in a state of ritual purity. He is not even the God of Old as depicted in other Genesis stories, the God who is generally just *elsewhere* and only on occasion crosses over into the world of human beings. He never *enters* in this story because He is always already there, strolling about in the same garden inhabited by the naked human beings whom He has made. Their very nakedness ought to have been, as in other circumstances, quite incompatible with God's presence[3]—and this detail in the story certainly shocked ancient Israelites.[4] So what is this picture of divine and human cohabitation seeking to tell us?

No one knows when religions first began. It used to be argued that religion is a universal phenomenon—every known civilization has one, it was said, or at least *had* one at some point—and this fact was held to prove the truth of every religion's basic claim, that God (or the gods) must exist. But such a claim is wrong on several counts. To begin with, not every religion is *theistic,* that is, centered on God or the gods; more broadly, there certainly are now (and have been in the past) civilizations that lack anything corresponding to what we term, even in the most general sense, a religion.[5] Perhaps most basic of all, everything we now know about evolution indicates that human beings came into existence through a long process of development from earlier hominins.* *Homo habilis*[6] first appeared somewhat less than three million years ago; then came *Homo erectus/Homo ergaster*[7] (less than two million years ago). Fossil evidence of *Homo erectus* demonstrates that he was a traveler, apparently the first hominin to leave the African continent and settle widely in Europe and Asia. He may also have been the first hominin to control fire.[8] After this there appears a remarkable predecessor of the first Nean-

---

* A relatively new term designating creatures that paleoanthropologists now agree were either humans themselves or in the line of human ancestors.

dertals* and *Homo sapiens,* a species known as *Homo heidelbergensis,* dating back perhaps six hundred thousand years ago.[9] Evidence of this species' existence has been found in various parts of western Europe, including Spain, France, Germany, and England. A later representative of *Homo heidelbergensis,* going back almost four hundred thousand years ago, was discovered in Germany in 1994; he was the presumed manufacturer of an impressive collection of four hunting spears, wooden shafts sharpened at both ends with stone tools, which had apparently been used to kill wild horses — "the oldest reliably identified hunting weapons ever discovered."[10]

Could any of these early humans also be called *Homo religiosus,*[11] the first species to worship supernatural beings, or sacred places or animals or inanimate objects from the natural world, or in some other way manifest what could be considered religious behavior? It is sometimes argued that the practice of burying dead bodies (as Neandertals apparently did) indicates the existence of some sort of religious belief, but this is not necessarily so. After a few days, a dead body begins to stink; what is more, it can become a dangerous carrier of disease. Something must be done with it. A corpse can, of course, be disposed of in various ways: tossed into a bonfire, dropped into the sea, or simply carried to a remote location (where, however, its flesh will soon be consumed by animals and insects). Faced with such alternatives, early human beings (apparently starting with Neandertals) came to practice burial as a thoughtful and caring way of disposing of a former member of the family or clan.[12] But this does not indicate any hypothesizing of a present or future encounter of the departed with anything divine, or his or her coming back to life at some later date.

However, the practice at ancient burial sites of placing *grave goods* — a favorite tool, or perhaps a weapon of some sort — next to a dead person's body tells a different story. To do so seems to attest to the belief that the lifeless corpse will somehow make use of the buried item sometime in the future (otherwise, why throw away a perfectly good animal jawbone, or a carefully sharpened stone?). Scholars continue to debate the age of the earliest grave goods, but some date them back to more than one hundred thousand years ago. From a later period (forty thousand years ago) come meticulous drawings of game animals; while the evidence is far from conclusive, one hypothesis is that these drawings were intended to evoke spirits or deities connected

---

* This is the modern spelling of Neanderthal, whose name derives from the Neander Valley (German: *Tal,* "valley," used to be spelled *Thal*) near Düsseldorf, Germany, where parts of an ancient human skeleton were excavated in 1856.

with the hunt and in this way to gain the favor or aid of such spirits in the endless search for food.

Our Puny Selves

What, then, is the significance of this snapshot of God walking about among the humans in the Garden of Eden? In a sense, this image takes us back to the schematic beginnings of human contemplation, to the time when, one might imagine, the little men and women first began to consider themselves and the world in which they lived. This act of contemplation is crucial, going back to a time when humans saw themselves surrounded on all sides, endlessly being acted upon by all that was beyond their control or even comprehension. So in the biblical story, God walks among the naked humans in the Garden simply because His continued presence is necessary for nearly everything that the story narrates. That is why He never enters or appears; He is just always there, the principal actor. He makes the earth and the sky. He shapes Adam out of dirt: first He makes a kind of muddy statue, then He breathes His breath into the statue's nostrils, and Adam comes to life. After this He plants the plants in the Garden, and still later anesthetizes Adam into a deep sleep, which enables Him to take part of Adam's side or ribcage and turn it into Eve.[13] This God *does* everything, even making the animal hides to clothe the first humans after their sin (Gen 3:21, presumably after the crude fig-leaf garment they themselves had fashioned [3:7] had fallen apart). And even their sin, it should be remembered, was not the result of any human initiative; Adam and Eve were manipulated by the snake into violating God's orders (3:13).

In short, this is a world in which very little is done *by* the humans. Everything happens *to* them, and while an anthropologist would rightly object that this biblical picture of human passivity telescopes a lot of what we now know about the development of early man, for our purposes it is most suggestive about the sense of self that a hypothetical Adam and Eve must have had, inherited as it was from still earlier times and then passed on into far later periods. In a word, as soon as early humans were capable of contemplating themselves and their surroundings, they could not but have an overwhelming sense of their own *smallness*. The world around them was so obviously big and active. It impinged on them at every turn; it was always taking the initiative and making things happen. In their emerging consciousness, this surrounding world might best be described as a vague, great Outside. It was not personified, of course; we are still far from that. The Outside was just everywhere, endlessly doing; it was huge and they were very little. At times, the Outside's being must have seemed as palpable, and as accessible, to the humans as their own, filling up all of what we would think of as the empty spaces in their world, pulsing in the nighttime darkness or shining through the thick branches at noon. Its great hand, gloved in sky or sea or soil, was sometimes kind, sometimes cruel. And its presence was *heard* everywhere, in the rustling of the wind through the leaves or the croaking of the forest at night; all these sounds were part of a single chorus, "the sound of the LORD God walking about in the Garden." Since the Outside was not any kind of person, it was not given to any sort of characterization; it was the *undifferentiated* Outside, a hugeness not yet analyzed into discrete beings or functions, but just the "not-us" (or, more accurately, the "mostly not us") that was everywhere and left the little people full of awe.[14] Humans will develop and change, but this fundamental sense of their own little selves and how they fit into the larger, active world will not. Hardwired into the brain over eons and eons, it will only begin to leave them much later, and then not fully until modern times.

The Discovery of Agriculture

The wise snake causes Adam and Eve to understand. At his urging, they eat the fruit of the Tree-of-Knowing-Everything* and "the eyes of both of them were opened." If the knowledge that the tree imparted included an understanding of agriculture, then we are indeed at a very late point in human history (roughly twelve thousand years ago),[15] virtually yesterday. But returning to the preceding stages is important for our understanding of the developing *Homo religiosus* in his larger environment.

It all began about two and a half million years ago; there emerged a certain bipedal ape with a slightly larger brain than his fellows. "Bipedal" means that he could walk around erect on two legs, which he often did; like other apes, however, he also spent a lot of time in trees, sleeping in constructed nests for safety. His larger-than-average brain actually presented an evolutionary disadvantage, since babies with larger heads are more difficult to deliver, and

* The biblical text literally says "the tree of knowing good and bad," but *good and bad* here is what is called a *merism*, namely, mentioning two extremes in order to include everything in between, such as "night and day" (meaning "all the time"), "high and low" (everywhere), "man and beast" (all creatures), and so on.

also because big brains consume significantly more energy. To help with the former problem, the thickness and shape of the head gradually changed, but what is more, much of the brain's development was postponed until after the baby's birth. This meant that humans bear young that are *altricial*—utterly helpless, because in a sense they are born too soon. But if it were otherwise, the baby's head would be just too big to come out. (On the other hand, once out of the womb, the brains of newborn humans develop at a much faster pace in the first year than those of other primates. As Steven Pinker has noted, if our bodies grew proportionally to our brains in that first year, we would all be ten feet tall and weigh half a ton.)[16] As for the high energy demanded by bigger brains, this man-ape solved the problem by developing an energy-rich (carnivorous) diet along with a reduction in his own digestive tissue.[17]

As time went on, further adaptations led him to live at ground level much of the time, opening up new feeding opportunities and gradually separating him from other primates, until he became a distinct species, *Homo habilis* (starting ca. 2.6 million years ago), so named for his primitive toolmaking abilities.[18] *Homo erectus,* considered by some to be the first truly human species, emerged around 1.8 million years ago, standing and walking on his hind legs alone. This posture was not without problems, but it had distinct advantages, freeing up the hands to carry things while walking and providing a higher perspective on the surroundings. Over the next million years, *Homo erectus* gave way to *Homo heidelbergensis* (mentioned above) and thence evolved, according to many paleoanthropologists, into both *Homo neandertalis* and *Homo sapiens.* The African continent was humanity's birthplace, but our ancestors left it in stages[19] and migrated to other continents, until ultimately they were able to "fill the earth and subdue it" (Gen 1:28).

What were their ancestors, those early hominins, thinking? If the great Outside had been undifferentiated at first, doing virtually everything, filling land and sea and sky and utterly overshadowing the little people, gradually this quality began to recede just a bit. From approximately 2.6 million years ago is the first evidence of hominins' *knapping*—banging two stones together to break off sharp, thin flakes. The flakes could then be used for the purpose of cutting up meat and other foods—in fact, cutting almost anything that a modern knife can cut. By around 1.7 million years ago, symmetrically chipped-off stones were being used for hand axes; then, mastery of fire allowed early humans to cook their food, evidenced at least around 790,000 years ago,[20] if not earlier. Hunting large animals for food was the apparent purpose of the already-mentioned spears of *Homo heidelbergensis* (400,000 years ago).

Banging one stone against another to chip off flakes is certainly *doing* something. Does it require thinking? This is a more complicated question. To begin with, scholars distinguish two kinds of stone-flake production. The first involves banging the "hammerstone" against the "core" stone to produce a flake sharp enough to cut up some meat or open a nut. This is a fairly straightforward act, a necessary part of the sequenced task of cutting or opening something which, scholars say, merely requires "procedural memory." The second kind aims at shaping both faces of the stone chip so as to produce a more or less symmetrical blade, such as that of the above-mentioned hand axes. The mental abilities necessary to produce such bifaces are more complicated, demanding multiple levels of intentional organization. (In fact, some scholars have sought out a physical connection between the neurological requirements of these carving skills and those needed for the emergence of language.)[21] What is more, the biface itself was probably a different kind of object from the simple stone flake in the minds of its producers. It had an independent existence, a tool in its own right,[22] whereas the simple stone chip was merely part of a larger and oft-repeated procedure. As a result, the biface was probably carried about even when no specific task was in sight, especially since it was a multipurpose tool, butchering animals, cutting or shaving wood, digging into the ground, and perhaps even being thrown at animals for defensive or offensive purposes.[23]

Worshiping Bears

Archaeologists sometimes quote a saying (attributed to the cosmologist Martin Rees): "Absence of evidence is not evidence of absence." In other words: just because we haven't found something doesn't mean it didn't exist back then. So, for example, with regard to the stone tools mentioned above: it is convenient to use them to chart human development, since bifaces and other stone tools stay around forever, just waiting to be unearthed by archaeologists. But their discovery tells us very little about the actual way of life of the humans who made them, since those same humans probably manufactured all sorts of other things that don't stay around for millennia—baskets, baby carriers, bows and arrows, blowguns, boomerangs, and much more (these are only a few perishable things that begin with the letter *B*).[24]

The same is true when it comes to early evidence of what we like to call "religion." All we have is what we have: those grave goods, cave drawings, and the like. They tell us nothing of the thinking that preceded them—perhaps by millennia — nor, on the other hand, can we always be sure of things that are claimed to give evidence of the "religious." A recent example is instructive.

After prehistoric bear bones were discovered in caves in various parts of western and central Europe, some scholars argued for the existence of an ancient bear cult in Neandertal times. Neandertals did generally inhabit caves, and the position of the bones in some of these caves seemed suggestive of some deliberate arrangement: the longer bones (tibia, femur, humerus) appeared to have been laid along the sides of the cave and the bear heads in the corners. This apparently deliberate disposition, it was thought, might have been made for religious reasons. Such a conclusion had been encouraged by an early find of the Swiss scholar Emil Bächler, who excavated the Drachenloch ("Dragon Lair," so named for the mass of bear bones unearthed there) in the eastern Swiss Alps during the period 1919–1923. Especially intriguing to Bächler was a bear skull he uncovered with a femur stuck into the area of the cheekbone. He argued that the femur could only have ended up in this position if it was deliberately turned as it was moved behind the cheekbone — suggesting direct contact between a Neandertal inhabitant and the bear skull.

The idea of a prehistoric bear cult in Europe was, and still is, thrilling. It bespeaks a time when we humans were still closely connected to the rest of the animal kingdom — still frightened by the power and predations of these huge fellow-mammals, perhaps seeking symbolically to harness that power or overcome it, or even in some way identifying ourselves with them as, for example, the totem of our group. Those big bones and skulls neatly arranged in caves seemed light-years away from what we normally think of as religion today, and yet there they were, mute testimony to a world of emotions and ideas that we can scarcely imagine. These Swiss discoveries also linked up with evidence of bear cults (if that is what they were) from later times in the colder regions of Asia, Europe, and North America; it was tempting to think that the roots of this animal's numinous quality for humans were far more ancient, perhaps instinctive, or an ancient meme that never died. And indeed, a certain fascination with bears may go back very far.[25]

At the same time, however, these findings have been vigorously challenged. To begin with, Neandertals were not the only inhabitants of caves; bears themselves were finding refuge in caves for their months of hibernation. In fact, bears and humans seem to have occupied caves at different periods, so the coexistence of bear bones and evidence of humans in caves was not an indication in itself of any Neandertal interest in bears. What is more, some Neandertals lived in open-air settlements, but no bear bones were found there.[26] As for the position of the bones in caves, other factors — water seepage in the caves, or even strong winds — might have produced the same results. In short, many scholars today doubt that the hypothetical bear cult ever existed, and these doubts now extend to the very existence of something resembling religion among Neandertals.[27] It could have existed; we just don't have the evidence.

Humans Contemplating

More fundamentally, one might say that looking for material remains to confirm the existence of religious ideas or practices inevitably puts the cart before the horse. Long before humans made any *object* that gave evidence of such things, they were looking at, and fitting into, the world around them in a certain way, conceiving of their own existence in some form or other in their own minds. When did this begin, and what did it consist of? Scholars can make a start by comparing the cranium capacities of chimpanzees (whose mental abilities have been pretty well explored by contemporary scientists) with those of various early humans: chimpanzee brains average about 400 cubic centimeters (gorilla brains go slightly higher, to an average 500 cc or so); the brains of *Homo habilis* already exceeded these, rising up to 500–800 cc; *Homo erectus* to 750–1250 cc; early *Homo sapiens* to 1200–1700 cc; and modern man to an average of about 1350 cc. Somewhere along this continuum, our ancestors began to contemplate themselves and their surroundings, but there is little light that fossil remains or the material culture can shed on when this first occurred. It certainly did occur, however; about this there can be no doubt.

At first, as suggested above, this must have been of the vaguest sort of contemplation: the great Outside kept doing almost everything, so that the little humans could hardly think of themselves as separate from its huge, overshadowing presence. It flowed around and through them by day and by night, bringing good or ill fortune, making them see this or that in their dreams, smell this smell or think this thought, so that it was often hard to know where the Outside left off and their insides began.

Little by little, however, they were able to step back just a few centimeters, and a new kind of contemplation emerged: the formerly undifferentiated Outside came to be examined piece by piece, and with this the relationship of one piece of the outside world with another. Such relationships could involve actors of any sort — the waves at a bend in the river could be connected to the newborn black cormorants and both of these to the leaves of a certain grayish bush, since all belong to the "enchanted world,"[28] in which almost anything is possible: rocks, trees, or ordinary-looking plots of ground are all potentially extraordinary, potentially numinous. But the magical was actually a close friend of primitive science, the "science of the concrete," and if the work of modern anthropologists is any guide, investigating the slight similarities and differences of various plants and animals was an activity of potentially great complexity and sophistication.[29]

One particular sort of relationship was that of causality — apparently it had been there even before humanity's emergence.[30] It starts with a basic awareness of what psychologists call "launching events": first this happens, and then that happens as a result. To move from this to more complicated forms of causality requires a cognitive leap, but when it took place is not obvious, since, once again, such a change was probably not immediately documented in stones or pigments; in fact, "leap" is misleading, since it likely did not happen all at once, and certainly not as a generalized, all-purpose ability. At some point, however, speculation about causality must inevitably have led to noticing (or hypothesizing) temporally or physically remote launching events: the thing that happened five minutes ago, or last week, is responsible for what just happened now. In the enchanted world, of course, this was one possibility among many. It might also be that some happenings were simply mysterious, magical, or altogether causeless; or their causes might somehow be hidden from view.

To be sure, there was a lot for early humans to think about besides launching events, but it is equally important to recognize that speculating about causality was not exactly an idle pastime. How could one *not* seek to understand those things on which life itself most depends — especially those things that had no evident cause, like the sudden availability or disappearance of edible foods; abundant rain or sustained drought; the sudden death of one or perhaps many members of the group; and similar mysteries. Surely something was making these things happen. Moreover, there were all those observable events that seem to follow a regular pattern: the path of the sun moving through the sky, the seasons that succeed each other in an established sequence. So long as such things were, if even contemplated, simply chalked up to that huge, uninvestigated cause — the great Outside — further speculation was not a concern. With time, however, thinking about hidden causes offered a different perspective. Things such as these cannot keep happening on their own: there must be some invisible cause behind them — in fact, the very multiplicity and diversity of these different events suggested a multiplicity of causes, or rather, *causers*, animate beings, who were making these things happen.[31]

At first they were not remote at all; they were those human-sized, human-like, shadowy figures glimpsed now and again at the back of the forest, flitting in and out of the light under the trees. *They* must be the ones who were responsible. Here was a potentially troubling thought, precisely since these causers *were* hidden, and their influence might thus extend well beyond the obvious; paranoia reigned. At the same time, however, the existence of hidden causers explained virtually everything for which the human beings could not identify an evident cause. Humanity was now ready to meet the gods.

An Obvious Conclusion

Before we leave the Garden and the great Outside, however, one further observation imposes itself—indeed, it is an observation that should be obvious by now.

It was said earlier that there is no default sense of self, no one, natural way of conceiving of what a person's *I* consists of and how it fits into the rest of the world. This is undeniably true today: people in Philadelphia or Paris share this planet with the Dinka of south Sudan, but their senses of self could not be more different, and this is true as well of the Yąnomamö[32] of the Amazon and the Mbuti[33] of the Congo, as well as of millions of others who belong neither with the Philadelphians nor the Forest dwellers, the Pashtun tribes of western Pakistan or the Marathi of neighboring India. The anthropologist Clifford Geertz was cited earlier as saying that for the inhabitants of "Java, Bali, and Morocco, at least, [the sense of self] differs markedly not only from our own but, no less dramatically and no less instructively, from one to the other."

And yet, if one were to look for a common origin of all these different ways of construing the self, the search would seem inevitably to lead back to the Garden. The great "not-us" that surrounded the first humans, this undifferentiated Outside that did almost everything, overshadowing the little band of people, rustling all around them and through them, left an (almost) indelible mark on humanity. It is clearly visible in the semipermeable mind of biblical times, along with the fundamentally *small* sense of self on which it is postulated. The selves that developed elsewhere in different locations across the globe were all variations on this basic theme; indeed, the theme's continuation is visible even with us modern, Western humans, although the harsh cultural conditions into which we have been born have for the most part turned our originally open, semipermeable selves into oddly stunted and closed-off organs, which today are scarcely aware of their tiny opening to the Outside.

5

THE FOG OF DIVINE BEINGS

Worshiping Ba'al; A two-tiered world; Scientific approaches to religion; Ancient demons; The fluidity of divine beings

The existence of the gods brings us close to historic times, and the gap between idea and artifact necessarily shrinks. Still, it is difficult to fill in the blanks between then and now. The "absence of evidence" problem prevents us from knowing anything which may have existed in the minds of our early ancestors but which left no material remains. We can, however, discover something more about the divine-human encounter in what we do have — ancient artifacts and texts from Mesopotamia and ancient Canaan in which the gods were manifest, and the various reflections of this reality in a number of biblical texts.

The prophet Hosea lived in the eighth century BCE, a time of political upheaval. The kingdom of Israel was under threat from the mighty Assyrian Empire, and Hosea, as God's earthly spokesman (that is what a prophet in Israel was), was charged with reporting to the Israelites God's words of warning:

> Rebuke your mother, rebuke her (since she's no longer My wife, and I'm her husband no more),
> To get her to stop her whoring and push her lovers from off of her breasts.
> Or else I'll strip her naked, show her just as she was
> on the day that she was born;
> I'll turn her into a desert, a parched land, dying of thirst. (Hos 2:4–5; some Bibles 2:2–3)

The image was certainly meant to shock. God here is presented as an outraged husband, or rather, ex-husband, and He is saying to the Israelites that their current difficulties are not His fault, but their mother's (that is, the female embodiment of the people of Israel): she's a whore. This, in the broader context, is a reference to the Israelites' worship of other gods. She should have been faithful, Hosea says, to her true husband, the God called YHWH* — but instead she's been keeping company with other deities. If she doesn't stop, this God says, she will be stripped naked and humiliated.

Hosea Versus Ba'al

To Hosea's listeners, the message was clear: the prophet was reproving them for offering sacrifices and prayers to another god well known in Canaan, Ba'al, whose particular responsibility in Canaanite religion was agriculture. He was the storm god who came riding in on the clouds to fertilize the parched ground. In fact, that is the reason for the name Ba'al. Officially, his name was Hadad, but he is usually referred to by the Hebrew word *Ba'al,* which meant "master" or "lord," but also "husband"; he was the earth's spouse, whose rainwater fertilized the soil and made the crops grow.

In this context, God's threat to strip Israel's mother naked acquires a more concrete, and ominous, meaning. It is made explicit in the last words quoted: "I'll turn her into a desert, a parched land, dying of thirst." Stripping Israel's mother naked meant taking away her green and yellow dress, the ripening plants and grains that usually covered her "body," Israel's land. When this happened, as it sometimes did in Canaan's chronically water-short climate, the crops couldn't ripen and people went hungry.

This was a striking image, but in a sense, Israel's mistake was understandable. After all, Ba'al was known everywhere in Canaan for his role as the storm god. This fact was brought home in a hoard of ancient texts discovered by archaeologists at a site in northern coastal Syria, nowadays called Ras Shamra. These texts, part of the royal library of the ancient city-state of Ugarit that went back to the fourteenth century BCE, included lengthy passages of the epic poetry of northern Canaan, in which Ba'al prominently figures as a dynamic, youthful deity, deferred to by lesser powers:

---

* Traditionally spelled with its consonants only, as the precise vowel sounds connecting them have been lost since biblical times. In most Bibles, this name is rendered "the LORD."

I tell you, O Prince Ba'al, and I repeat, O rider of clouds!
Crush your enemy, Ba'al, crush him now and defeat your foe!
Then take on unending kingship, your everlasting dominion.

Ba'al was indeed the "rider of clouds,"[1] and as such worthy of ruling on high. Among the gods he was specifically "Mr. Rain," the go-to deity to put an end to drought. If so, and if rain was once again an issue of survival, who could blame Israel's embodiment, its "mother," for turning worshipfully to the powerful rainfall specialist? Nevertheless, Hosea is unsparing in his indictment of Israel's female persona:

So their mother went a-whoring, she who bore them went astray.
She said, "I'll go after my lovers, who gave me my bread and my water,
my wool and my flax, my oil and my drink."
But however hard she pursued them, she never caught up with a one;
however much she tried, she never took hold of her lovers.[2]
Then she said, "I'll go back to my husband; I was better off then than now."
But she still had no idea: it was I who gave her the grain;
the wine and the oil [were from Me];
I gave her bountiful silver — and the gold that they then gave to Ba'al.
So now I'm taking My grain back, and My new wine that's just now in season.
I'll take back My wool and My flax, which before used to cover her shame.
(Hos 2:7–10; some Bibles 5–9)

Modern scholars are not sure how much, if any, of our current book of Hosea was actually spoken by a prophet bearing that name, or even if there ever was such a prophet. But if one takes Hosea's words at face value, his message here is an indictment of Israel for turning to Ba'al for help. The reason is not, according to what he says, because the Israelites have failed to be faithful monotheists, adhering to the belief that there is only one true God. (Monotheism is still a few centuries away.) Rather, it seems that their fault lies in their failure to recognize that the bounty they attributed to Ba'al had actually come from another deity, YHWH (that is, the Lord) — that's why they were being punished. In fact, perhaps the most interesting part of Hosea's speech comes at the end, when he looks forward to a time when Mother Israel will finally realize her mistake:

And it shall be at that time — says the Lord — that you [Israel] will call [Me] "my husband" and no longer call Me "my Ba'al." (Hos 2:18; some Bibles, 16)

As already mentioned, the Hebrew word *ba'al* itself means "husband." But here God is telling the Israelites not to keep calling Him *ba'ali,* "my *ba'al,*" but to use another word, *ishi* (literally, "my man") instead. What this suggests to scholars is a rejection of a classic case of *syncretism,* the practice of identifying one god with another (just as Greek Zeus and Hera came to be identified by Romans with their own deities Jupiter and Juno). Much as Hosea didn't approve, some Israelites were still in the habit of referring to the God YHWH as "my Ba'al," as if the two names belonged to the same divine person.[3]

The Upper Shelf

All this should help us to consider what it meant to live in the world of the gods. They were "up there," existing on a kind of upper shelf, while we humans were "down here," on earth.[4] They controlled almost all the things that were vital to our existence—the grain, the wine, and the oil, in fact, how long we live, how many children we have, and what our lives are actually like: prosperity or hardship, peace or war, feast or famine. All these things were in the hands of those mysterious beings on the upper shelf. By the time ancient Israel came along, people had been perceiving reality in terms of these beings for so many millennia that they were simply an irrefutable fact of life. The ones "up there" were as real as the "down here" things that they controlled, as real as the fruit in the trees or the rainwater in the cisterns.

The most basic aspect of this arrangement was clearly left over from the undifferentiated Outside: humans were still very small. It was just that now, in this second phase, the great, looming Outside had been divided up: the multiplicity of things that happen on earth was now attributed to a multiplicity of unseen causers. We little humans were in the hands of powerful beings whom we couldn't really see, but who were obviously doing the things that had the greatest impact on our lives. The question this poses is: How did all this come about? How did humans move from contemplating the undifferentiated Outside to worshiping the sacred beings known to us from later times?

As suggested in the previous chapter, the early human interest in causality seems to form part of the overall picture. It may be that anthropomorphic statues and paintings from Upper Paleolithic times (starting perhaps thirty thousand years ago) give evidence of such a belief in divine causers, supernatural beings in human form. It seems unlikely to most scholars that these humanlike representations are the work of an ancient Grandma Moses or

Norman Rockwell bent simply on memorializing their friends and neighbors or the humdrum details of daily life in their societies. Similarly, carved representations of big-breasted, wide-hipped women, such as the Venus of Dolní Věstonice (ca. 29,000–25,000 BCE) or the Venus of Willendorf (ca. 24,000–22,000 BCE), may well have been worshiped as Great Mother goddesses or the bringers of fertility (although, once again, the evidence is not unequivocal).[5] The cave paintings at Lascaux (seventeen thousand years ago) include some strange creatures — half man, half bird, or half man, half lion — which are obviously not representations from nature; these have been more confidently connected to the early worship of divine beings. But these still leave unanswered the fundamental question: What was it in people's *minds* that moved them to do the sorts of things that seem to characterize the earliest stages of religious behavior — not only bringing offerings to divine causers connected to the natural world,[6] but perhaps even earlier, revering certain places and objects identified as *special*, numinous or sacred; worshiping an animal totem or "spirit being" associated with a particular tribe or group; venerating dead ancestors; and perhaps yet other forms of ancient religious behavior?

Until recently, the earliest worship of such divine beings was frequently connected to the practical needs of civilization:[7] people had to be coerced into behaving in ways that ensured their collective survival, and to that end gods were invented to establish the rules ("Thou shalt not kill," "Thou shalt not steal," etc.) and demand that they be obeyed. (Presumably, societies that failed to invent gods were at an evolutionary disadvantage and did not survive.) The trouble with such an explanation is the absence of any evidence that this is how things began; in fact, this explanation seems to derive from the projection of later reality — the rule-giving gods or God from the religions that we *do* know — onto religion's unknown, oldest ancestor.[8] What is more, this picture is rather slanted toward the religions that are closest to us in thought; anthropologists have studied societies that have nothing resembling divine rule-givers or even deities of any recognizable kind. Along with such "social good" explanations, it was also sometimes alleged that religions were first invented in order to provide answers to mankind's great, unanswerable questions, or to allay the common human fear of death, or of the unknown. Here again, however, the problem is the absence of any evidence to support these contentions, as well as another recognizable tilt toward things that are still on our mind today: great, unanswerable questions, the fear of death, and so forth.

Neuroscience and Hidden Causers

Starting two or three decades ago, neuroscientists, evolutionary biologists, psychologists, and philosophers began reexamining the question of religion's origins, seeking new answers through the insights of their own disciplines.[9] Probably the best known of these are the "learned naysayers," scholars who have tacitly or openly denied any reality to religious phenomena and have therefore sought to explain religion's existence as the result of some other feature of early human development.

One such feature is the human brain's built-in hyperactive agent detection device (HADD), which causes us to react automatically to unexplained sights or sounds as if they might be caused by *agents*, someone or something capable of initiating action—even though most of the time the imagined agent will prove to be a false alarm. Since it does produce false alarms, this brain feature is described as *hyperactive* or *hypersensitive*[10]—and it is found in nonhuman brains as well. It is the reason why your dog barks at almost anything, including the sound of snow sliding off the roof, and why a sudden creaking sound coming from a closet may suggest to you that *someone* is in there. But a thousand false alarms are worth it if one time our HADD gives us early warning of what turns out to be a real threat—there really *is* a burglar in the closet.

The HADD, it has been argued, combines with another basic feature of cognition, the human "theory of mind" (ToM)[11]—our attribution of mental activity to a perceived agent (usually another human being). Thus, if we see someone coming toward us, we assume that he (or it) has a mind like ours, and that this mind is what is directing him toward us. As a result, we seek to put ourselves in his shoes, trying to figure out what he is thinking and intending to do. All this, it was argued, is fine when it comes to other human beings, and maybe even some animals—it protects us and guides us in social interactions. But when ancient humans' HADD caused them to imagine an unknown creature rustling through the grass or sailing across the nighttime sky, they not only attributed the perceived activity to an unknown agent, but they further supposed that this agent had a mind that was causing it to move (hence the name "theory of mind"). From there, this approach holds, it was only a small step to imagining unseen deities piloting the sun or driving the rain clouds in off the sea. Even if offering prayers or sacrifices to the imagined deity did not work every time, the small material loss was far outweighed by the potential gain if it did.

Religion is thus sometimes presented as an ancient human example of *exaptation*,[12] or else it is seen as a mental *spandrel*,[13] both terms referring to a feature originally evolved to fulfill one purpose but which ultimately came to fulfill another. A HADD was great for detecting potential enemies, and a theory of mind could help you figure out what to do when confronted with one. But once developed, these brain features ultimately led to the creation of religion—a mixed blessing in the eyes of some neuroscientists. Along with this, however, other scholars have sought to claim that the religious impulse is not a behavioral exaptation, but the expression of a built-in, physical part of the human brain, branded by critics as the "God spot,"[14] an inborn predisposition to religious feelings and thoughts.[15] In addition, scholars of varying approaches have highlighted a somewhat surprising characteristic of religion, the apparent *necessity* of including counterintuitive elements in religious beliefs—supernatural beings, reports of happenings that contradict experience or the laws of nature, and so forth.[16]

These various attempts to put things on a more scientific basis are certainly suggestive, though a number of basic shortcomings emerge from the scholarship so far.[17] In general, the somewhat polemical character of the research (as mentioned, they basically all start from the assumption that religious consciousness is some sort of accidental byproduct of human evolution or an evolutionarily favored delusion), as well as the very multiplicity of their proposed conclusions, has done little to settle the matter of religion's origins; although individual insights are promising, the work overall has been highly speculative, if not to say scattershot. My own point of departure is the belief that religious behavior is indeed rooted in reality, but a reality predicated on a mode of being quite different from our own, of which the semipermeability of the mind is only one representative aspect.

While neuroscientists and evolutionary biologists have been approaching religion through their disciplines, ethnographers and anthropologists have continued the study of specific religious rituals and worship in various non-Western civilizations. This undertaking has yielded a vast array of individual studies—indeed, charting the various practices and beliefs that might fall under the general heading of religion is now a steady feature of ethnographic fieldwork, widely recognized as a central concern of the whole discipline of anthropology. It would be difficult to name all the distinguished field anthropologists whose work has focused on religion over the last century, but certainly such a list would include such outstanding scholars as Bronislaw Malinowski,[18] Franz Boas,[19] E. E. Evans-Pritchard,[20] Godfrey Lienhardt,[21] Claude Lévi-Strauss,[22] and Clifford Geertz.[23]

It should be stressed, however, that the work of these scholars has not been aimed at uncovering religion's beginnings. Its major achievement has been in the development of new approaches and forms of analysis: the study of witchcraft and magic; the structural analysis of myth; religion as a symbolic system;[24] and much more. These certainly have helped in broadening the very notion of what "religion" consists of, as well as how we might best go about trying to understand it as a phenomenon. But it is simply a fact that the religious ideas and behavior of the non-Westerners today are altogether the contemporaries of our own, Western religions. Only the notion that these non-Westerners are "primitive" and thus theoretically closer to religion's origins might lead one to identify what they think and do as representing the beginning of it all—and such an assumption is methodologically suspect.*

Another approach to trying to understand how humans came to worship divine beings like Ba'al is to go back to the earliest evidence of their existence. As far as the Bible is concerned, this means staying in the Bible's own geographic and cultural orbit, since evidence from Mesoamerican religion or sub-Saharan Africa may provide some interesting parallels, but it will offer no direct, genetic connection to biblical Israel and environs.

The problem with this approach, as scholars themselves readily admit, is that such evidence does not go back particularly far.[25] Walter Burkert, an outstanding historian of ancient Greek religion, has stated the problem clearly:

> Ancient religion is a tradition as old, perhaps, as mankind itself; but its tracks are lost in prehistory as time scales expand. The measurement of epochs from the eighth century BC onwards is made in centuries or even decades, but before this lie four "dark centuries," and then [before these] some eight centuries of Bronze Age high civilization. The Early Bronze Age stretches back over an additional thousand years, and [before these,] the Neolithic [Age] extends over more than three millennia. The Upper Paleolithic, which then spans more than 25,000 years, still leaves the beginnings of human history almost as remote as ever; there are indications of religi[on] stretching from the Lower Paleolithic.[26]

---

* An analogy with language might make the point more clearly. Linguists have studied the speech of contemporary civilizations that are, in some respects, rather similar to that of our Stone Age ancestors, yet their languages are every bit as sophisticated and complicated as English or Japanese. As Steven Pinker has noted: "The universality of complex language is a discovery that fills linguists with awe . . . There are Stone Age societies, but there is no such thing as a Stone Age language" (*The Language Instinct,* New York: Harper Collins, 2000, p. 14). Nor, one might add, is there a contemporary Stone Age religion.

The problem is the same with regard to Israel's religion(s),[27] or more broadly, the religions of the ancient Near East to which Israel belonged. Considering the ever-widening periods of time past, the specific evidence of religious practices and beliefs that can be gathered will always fall hopelessly short of religion's theoretical starting point and tell us little about the earliest gods and their worship.

Yet this *is* the evidence that we possess, and if it comes eons too late to give us the whole story, it can at least offer us a glimpse of times far distant from our own. Indeed, the ruins of ancient temples and related structures, and even the (somewhat later) remains of the earliest writings from the ancient Near East, can tell us a great deal about how divine beings were conceived long before the time of the human encounter with God as presented in the Hebrew Bible. Particularly crucial for this endeavor is the historical evidence of ancient Mesopotamia, starting with Sumer, where evidence of writing appears as early as the late fourth millennium BCE. From only slightly later times comes the adaptation of the Sumerian pictographs to a system of signs made by a wedge-shaped tool sunk into wet clay: these are the cuneiform signs used by the ancient Babylonians and Assyrians, ancient Canaan's neighbors to the east.

The Enchanted World

One thing we know from the oldest writings of Mesopotamia is that associating "religion" only with gods and goddesses is far too narrow. (This is one way in which the neuroscientists' focus on the HADD and the like falls far short of the whole picture.) To borrow a phrase from the philosopher Charles Taylor, this was the "enchanted world," vibrant and alive and brimming with the unknown. It was enchanted *in general*, since what I mean to describe above all is an attitude, a way of looking out at, and conceiving of, reality. So people slogged along in their usual, scruffy, human activities, but always up ahead loomed the possibility of something wholly different, the sudden realization that things are not at all as they seem, that the upper shelf was at it again; one could never really know for sure what was going on up there. "Enchanted" here is also meant to suggest this word's connection to *incantations* and magic, since this was a world in which all sorts of spiritual entities held sway, known and unknown, visible and invisible, animate and inanimate (such as sky and wind): these were the different agents responsible for all that happens on earth. Perhaps one of them had cast some sort of spell.

Some of the oldest evidence of religious ritual that we possess is concerned with demonic powers, invisible creatures who brought disease and death to humans. In Mesopotamia, as elsewhere, their malign influence was not easily countered; all people had were certain rituals, including sacrifices, incantations, and apotropaic prayers, any of which might help to get rid of them.[28] One of the relatively few "religious" texts surviving in Akkadian from the Archaic period (2300–2000 BCE) describes a ritual performed to protect someone who has been afflicted by the evil eye. It required bringing a sheep into the victim's house, holding it up at each of the house's four corners, and then slaughtering it:

> One black virgin ewe: In (each of) the corners of the house he will lift it up (?). He will drive out the Evil Eye and the [ ] . . . In the garden he will slaughter it and flay its hide. He proceeds to fill it with pieces of . . . plant. As he fills it, he should watch. The evil man [ ] his skin. Let [him] car[ry (it) to the river], (and) seven (pieces of) date palm, seven (pieces of) oak, and seven (pieces of . . .) let him submerge.[29]

Surely no one would waste a whole sheep and these other edibles if he did not believe, or at least hope, that this might work in getting rid of the evil eye —which is to say that being attacked by the evil eye was a part of a feared reality toward the end of the third millennium BCE. Moreover, the very fact that this ceremony was written down suggests that it was believed to be effective, perhaps even that it had worked in the past—if not every time, then at least sometimes.

In ancient Mesopotamia, fighting off curses uttered by humans was also a real concern: the curses often called upon a specific demon to attack the victim, making him sick or even killing him. The terror inspired by such demons was, at least for some, a real aspect of daily life. Here is a description of the malevolent spirit Lamashtu in another Akkadian text from the same Archaic period:

> She is singular, she is uncanny.
> She is a child born late in life (?), she is a will-o'-the-wisp,
> She is a haunt, she is malicious,
> Offspring of a god, daughter of [the god] Anu.
> For her malevolent will, her base counsel,
> Anu her father dashed her down from heaven to earth,
> For her malevolent will, her inflammatory counsel.

> Her hair is askew, her loincloth is torn away.
> She makes her way straight to the person without a (protective) god.
> She can benumb the sinews of a lion,
> She can . . . the sinews of a youngster or infant.[30]

If we now fast-forward to ancient Israel, many things will be seen to have changed, but much of the enchanted world remains. King Saul is thus reported to have gone to a medium for advice, a woman who knew how to rouse the dead. The medium succeeds in summoning the dead prophet Samuel from his sleep in the grave (1 Sam 28): Samuel is angry at being disturbed, but then he tells Saul that his death is imminent—a piece of information from the "other side" which, it turns out, was altogether true. In other words, the dead continue to exist somewhere "down there," and a medium can force them to come up to the surface and reveal what they know.

Biblical laws forbade consulting mediums and other things that never would have been forbidden if people were not still doing them:

> You shall not let a witch live. (Exod 22:17)

> Let there not be found among you anyone who passes his son or daughter through fire, or someone who casts magic spells, or a soothsayer, or a diviner, or a magician, or a sorcerer, or someone who consults ghosts or informing spirits, or one who summons up the dead. (Deut 18:10–11)

> Do not consult ghosts, and as for the informing spirits, do not seek to be defiled by them . . . Anyone who consults informing spirits and goes astray after them—I will set My face against that person and cut him off from among his people . . . A man or woman who has a ghost or an informing spirit shall be put to death. (Lev 19:31, 20:6, 27)

> [God says:] I will destroy the sorcery you practice, and you shall have no more soothsayers. (Mic 5:11)

> Do not curse the deaf or put a stumbling-block in the path of a blind person. (Lev 19:14)

Why should cursing the deaf be forbidden, but cursing other people apparently permitted? The obvious answer is that curses were believed to work actual harm; someone who hears himself being cursed, or hears *about* his being cursed, can try to ward off the curse's effects — with prayers and sacrifices, or by counter-cursing — but a deaf person is defenseless, just as defenseless as a blind person who trips over a stumbling-block.*

A Fishy Plural

Looking back at Hosea's battle against Ba'al worship, it is clear that he is still very much in the enchanted world. Those powers that are on the upper shelf are still dealing out weal and woe; the matter of who really is "Mr. Rain," Ba'al or YHWH — or even if the two names were sometimes deemed to belong to a single, syncretized deity — was probably far less important to the ordinary Israelite than the much-needed help that invoking one or both of them could bring.

But one aspect of Hosea's speech has yet to be mentioned. What does the prophet mean by telling Mother Israel to get rid of her "lovers," in the plural? If her crime is pursuing Ba'al instead of YHWH, isn't that just one lover? Why does Hosea have her say, "I'll go after *my lovers,* who gave me my bread and my water, my wool and my flax, my oil and my drink"? And a few verses later, God says:

> I'll destroy her vines and her fig trees, which she thought were payments for
> service, given to her by her lovers,
> And I'll turn them into a forest, where beasts gobble up their prey.
> That is how she'll be punished for the days of the Be'alim,
> when she used to bring offerings to them. (Hos 2:12–13)

"Be'alim" is the plural of "Ba'al," so there can be little doubt that these Be'alim are her lovers.[31] But how can there be more than one god named Ba'al?

Hosea is not the only one to refer to this god in the plural. Elsewhere, in the book of Judges, it says: "The Israelites did what was wrong in the eyes of the Lord, and they worshiped the *Be'alim*" (Jud 2:11). And a little later: "And the Israelites did what was wrong in the eyes of the Lord and they forgot

* Deafness from birth had no remedy; the deaf could not be taught to speak or understand as nowadays.

their God YHWH, and they worshiped the *Beʿalim* and the *Asherot*."*[32] After Gideon's death, according to Judges 8:33, "the Israelites went back to whoring after the *Beʿalim*." "We worshiped the *Beʿalim*," the Israelites confess in Judges 10:10 and in 1 Samuel 12:10. Elijah reproves King Ahab: "You have forsaken the commandments of the LORD and gone after the *Beʿalim*" (1 Kings 18:18). Why do these texts keep referring to a singular god in the plural?

A Basic Misconception

Here the evidence from the ancient Near East has proven particularly enlightening, since recent research has revealed a basic misconception that has long existed about the way in which ancient divinities were actually conceived. We tend to think of the gods as divine humanoids, equipped with bodies that look very much like our own — rather like those statues of gods and goddesses familiar to us from classical Greece and Rome. But there was always something rather fluid about the very idea of divine beings in the ancient world. Even those human-looking gods and goddesses portrayed in Greek statuary were, in ancient myths, sometimes said to change their shapes: Zeus could become a swan or a bull, Callisto was turned into a bear and later put up in the heavens, and Aphrodite could become an old lady wool-comber, while her Roman equivalent, Venus, could take on the disguise of a teenage huntress. Go back into the ancient Near East and the whole idea of reducing a god to a single, humanoid being is sharply refuted by the evidence. Gods were many things at once.

Thus, according to the Egyptologist Hans Bonnet, gods in ancient Egypt could take up residence inside various things or people — or even other gods:

> Just as any god can take up his abode in a fetish or in an animal, or even in the king, so he can inhabit the body of another deity. The formula "Amon-Re" does not signify that [the god] Amun is the same as [the god] Re or that one god has merged into the other. It simply notes that Re is in Amun — but not in such a way that both would be indissociably attached to each other and could continue to exist only in partnership. No inhabiting is permanent. The partners can separate again and be manifest independently; they can also form unions with other deities. So it is not a contradiction for there to

---

* Asherah was a goddess, the concubine of the Sumerian god Anu and, in Canaan, that of the supreme deity El. The form *Asherot* is, like *Beʿalim*, plural.

exist, alongside Amon-Re, such figures as Min-Re, Khnum-Re, Re-Atum, or simply Re.[33]

The same sort of fluidity is attested in Mesopotamia. A hymn to the Mesopotamian god Marduk, written toward the end of the second millennium BCE, presents him as manifesting various other divinities in himself:

> Sin (the moon god) is your divinity, Anu (the sky god) your sovereignty,
> Dagan is your lordship, Enlil your kingship
> Adad is your might, wise Ea your perceptions,
> Nabu, holder of the tablet stylus, is your skill.
> Your leadership (in battle) is Ninurta, your might Nergal . . .[34]

All the names mentioned belong to different gods; they are all, at least in this hymn, deemed to be present in the single deity Marduk.

Ancient treaties between two states often listed divine witnesses as potential enforcers of the treaties. This did not involve theological speculation or divine braggadocio; listing the witnessing gods was a down-to-earth matter, since properly identifying them was needed to ensure credible enforcement of the treaty. It is significant, therefore, that in some ancient Near Eastern texts, the same deity is sometimes mentioned more than once and connected to two or more geographic sites. In one case, for example, the treaty witnesses include "Ishtar of Arbela" but also "Ishtar of Nineveh," as well as the planet Venus, which was generally equated with the goddess Ishtar. How many separate Ishtars existed in the eyes of the treaty makers?

A similar array of multiple manifestations of a single god—this time, of Ba'al—are found in a treaty of King Esarhaddon of Assyria:

> May Ba'al-Shamēm, Ba'al-Malagē, and Ba'al-Ṣaphon raise an evil wind against your ships, to undo their moorings, tear out their mooring pole . . .[35]

Such multiple manifestations of deities in the ancient Near East are so much the rule that the Assyriologist Barbara Nevling Porter has suggested that the Akkadian word *ilu*—heretofore always translated as "god"—should really be redefined:

> Like "gods," *ilus* are usually represented in Mesopotamian texts in anthropomorphic form, as divine persons who could eat, take trips, marry, and have adventures (the *ilu* Ea as king, for example). In addition, however, each

> *ilu* was also imagined as a force of nature or a human power (the *ilu* Ea represented fresh water, for example, and the *ilu* Adad, storm) and by extension, as the power in such phenomena (Ea was understood to be the power for life in water, for example, and Adad, the violent and destructive energy in storms). *Ilus* were further identified with an array of objects and abstract entities, including for most great gods a number, a semi-precious stone, a mineral, an animal or emblem, a star, constellation, or other celestial entity. Ishtar, for example was not only a divine person and the embodiment of love, war, and a variety of other activities and forces, but was also identified with the number fifteen, the semi-precious stone lapis lazuli, the mineral lead, and . . . the planet Venus — equations made explicit in god-lists, but also clearly reflected in hymns, royal inscriptions, mystical commentaries, and other types of texts, as well as in visual imagery . . .[36]

After having further illustrated the fluidity of these Mesopotamian deities,[37] Porter concludes:

> An Assyrian *ilu,* in short, was not a "god" in our sense, but a set of related but not completely congruent phenomena and qualities, *only one of which was imagined as a divine person.* Including in itself this array of aspects, a Mesopotamian *ilu* (and its Assyrian counterpart) thus had greater fluidity of manifestation and greater potential for identification with other *ilus* who shared similar qualities or powers than *the more strongly personified — and thus bounded* — God of Judaism, Christianity, or Islam, or than the anthropomorphically conceived gods of Greek mythology.[38]

All this is of great importance to the present study. The very fluidity of the ancient *ilu* suggests that these divine beings occupied a kind of intermediate position between the ever-changing manifestations of the undifferentiated Outside and what Porter calls the "more strongly personified" (that is, person-like) sort of god that we know from the Bible, later Greco-Roman depictions, and other sources. The gods of Mesopotamia simultaneously existed in different places and different forms. Here is part of an oft-cited hymn[39] of the late second millennium in praise of the warrior god Ninurta:

> O lord, your face is Shamash (the sun god), your hair . . . ;
> Your eyes, lord, Enlil and [Ninlin] (the wind god and his consort, who move across a set path in the sky),

> Your eyeballs are Gula and Belet-il[i] (both of them mother goddesses and stars),
> Your eyelids, O lord, are the twins Sin (the moon) [and Shamash (the sun)],
> Your eyebrows are the corona of Shamash, which [. . .]
> Your mouth's shape, O lord, is Ishtar-of-the-stars,
> Anu and Antu (the sky and his consort) are your lips, your speech [. . .]
> Your discoursing tongue (?) is Pabilsag (a storm god), who [ ] on high,
> The roof of your mouth, lord, is the circumference of heaven and earth.

It would certainly be misleading simply to say that Ninurta is *a* heavenly deity: in this hymn he is all the gods of heaven at once, indeed, as the last cited line asserts, he encompasses heaven and earth together.[40] (Has the great Outside truly been differentiated, even here?)

The plural Be'alim, Mother Israel's lovers, thus seem to hark back to a conception of the gods that existed for centuries in Mesopotamia and ancient Canaan. The same god can exist in two or more places at once, or can be manifest in different forms simultaneously, in a star or planet, in a little statue, in an animal, an emblem, and so forth. Indeed, the Bible itself speaks of Ba'al existing at different sites: Ba'al Saphon (Exod 14:2) but also Ba'al Pe'or (Num 25:3). Other texts from this region invoke "Ba'al of the Lebanon," "Ba'al of Ugarit," and "Ba'al of Sidon."

The biblical scholar Benjamin Sommer has suggested that the best way to understand this fluidity in ancient gods might be to appropriate a concept from elsewhere:

> We might borrow a phrase from Indian culture to describe these local Ishtars as something like avatars of Ishtar. This term is appropriate, because it "implies a certain diminution of the deity when he or she assumes the form of an *avatāra. Avatāras* usually are understood to be only partial manifestations of the deity who assumes them."[41]

In other words, the *ilu*s of Mesopotamia, as well as the various Be'alim located here and there in ancient Canaan, were not the sum total of the god or goddess. Rather, they were fluid manifestations, genetically connected with other manifestations of the same deity elsewhere on earth or in the heavens, in stars and in statues. Perhaps, as with the Indian avatars, you could worship a god in one place and connect thereby to *all* that comprised his or her being, down here or on high.

This may also have been true of Israel's own deity, YHWH. He is mentioned as "YHWH of Teman (the southland, that is, Edom) and his Asherah"* on a clay water jar discovered in the eastern part of the Sinai desert, at a site called Kuntillat Ajrud ("[isolated] hill of wells"), not far from the current Israeli-Egyptian border.[42] The writing has been dated to the eighth century BCE. Another water jar there mentions "YHWH of Samaria and his Asherah," and an inscription on a bench at the site likewise reads "YHWH of Teman." It seems as if one element of the basic fog of a god's being — namely, the ability of a god to be manifest simultaneously in two different locations — was shared, at least for a time, in the religion of Israel. Indeed, what may have been at stake in Hosea's anti-Ba'al polemic was not just the matter of calling the rain-bringing deity by the right name, but two rather different ways of conceiving of a god: the old, fluid way of the Be'alim, or the apparently newer way of thinking of a god or goddess as equal to its sole, humanoid manifestation, what Barbara N. Porter described above as "the more strongly personified — and thus bounded — God of Judaism, Christianity, or Islam."[43]

Asking About Marduk

If I could buttonhole an ancient Mesopotamian and ask him the question of this book, "How do you and the gods interact? Have you ever met one face-to-face?" I think I know what his answer would probably be. Certainly he *has* seen Marduk/Enlil face-to-face, in that indescribably sacred presence of the god who is condensed into a small, wood-and-metal being, the one that is carried out of the Esagila temple during the annual Akitu festival and paraded before the people — "Yes, I have *seen* Marduk." But if he were asked: "Fine, but apart from that, what does Marduk, or any of the gods and goddesses, actually have to do with your life and the life of your family?" he would probably react with incomprehension, motioning skyward with a gesture that you can still see in the modern Middle East and which means, simply, "God." "What do the gods have to do with me and my family? Everything! They are in my city, protecting its interests. They are in other cities as well, simultaneously in this shrine and that shrine and that one. Of course they are up in the skies, in the stars and planets that I can see with my eyes. So what are you asking about? Tell me how you can begin to make sense of

* Asherah was the name of both a goddess and a sacred grove; probably the latter is intended. See also the brief discussion in Kugel (2003), 232–34.

the world without realizing that the gods control everything and we humans are almost nothing, their little servants subject to their will."

This is, I believe, what an ancient Mesopotamian would say, and the answer of an ancient Canaanite or an early Israelite would probably not differ in kind. But there is one location in particular where the meeting between humans and deities was particularly revealing, a meeting whose character can thus shed further light on the reality of encounters with God as depicted in the Bible.

6

ETERNITY IN ANCIENT TEMPLES

CONTAGIOUS HOLINESS; SACRIFICING ANIMALS;
A TABERNACLE IN THE WILDERNESS;
CEREMONIES THAT DENY THE OBVIOUS

In the last chapter we caught a glimpse of who the gods were and what they were like. It remains to see where they lived, and how humans — not all humans, only those who were specially trained and prepared — could actually meet the gods face-to-face.

All manner of peoples in different places around the globe have reported actually encountering this or that deity. In fact, ancient societies have often devoted much of their precious resources to enabling such encounters to take place, creating a physical spot where gods and humans can meet in some close physical proximity. Some of the earliest material evidence of religions that we possess consists of the physical remains or accoutrements of ancient temples, or rooms in houses or other structures that were apparently intended as a meeting point for humans and gods.[1]

The very idea of such a meeting was fraught with danger. After all, gods and goddesses existed on the upper shelf of reality, infinitely superior to mere humans; why should humans have thought that the gods could be encountered at all? And even if that were possible, wouldn't the humans be scared to death of such a meeting? The gods had all the power; one false move in their presence and they might kill you — so the best course no doubt would be to let the gods go about their business undisturbed. In fact, just touching a deity's accoutrement — such as the large box (the "ark of the covenant") identified with God's presence[2] — killed a man named Uzzah in the time of King David:

> When they came to the threshing floor of Nachon, Uzzah reached out his hand to the ark of God and took hold of it, since the oxen [pulling its cart] were stumbling. The anger of the LORD was kindled against Uzzah, and God struck him down because he had laid his hand on the ark, and he died there, next to the ark of God. And David was greatly troubled because the LORD had burst forth in that way; he named the place Perez Uzzah ["the bursting forth against Uzzah"] [as it is known] to this day. Fright of the LORD seized David that day; he said, "How can the ark of the LORD ever be brought to me?" (2 Sam 6:6–9; 1 Chron 13:9–12)

All Uzzah wanted to do was prevent the ark from slipping off the cart. But the ark was permeated with holiness (just as emblems and statues were so permeated, as we saw in the previous chapter); touching it was like touching a high-tension wire. So no matter how noble his purpose, Uzzah's uninvited touch cost him his life; dealing with deities was undeniably dangerous. And yet, as far as we can go back in history, people ran the risk: they *met* gods and goddesses (as well as dead ancestors, indwelling spirits, and the like), not only through chance encounters but at special, prearranged meeting points. Why did this happen, and when did it start?

The "why" part is easier to answer. Ancient humans were certainly aware of the dangers involved in encountering the powerful divinities, but they were also inevitably drawn to seek out such meetings. This attraction was due not only to what the German theologian Rudolf Otto termed the *mysterium tremendum et fascinans* (the mystery that both frightens and fascinates)[3] of the divine, but also because of the simple fact that these divine beings ran the world. Evidence of their ceaseless activity was visible everywhere in what we would call natural phenomena. They were responsible for specific places and people and events—the tightening death-grip of a drought, for example, as well as the sudden, inrushing storm clouds that put an end to it—but also for the steady rhythms of the seasons and the skies, the waxing and waning of the moon (*someone* must be doing that), the ripening and withering of the fruits and grains, life and death itself. Everywhere was a buzzing, vibrant presence of gods or angels: "the sound of them goes throughout the earth, and their words to the edge of the world" (Ps 19:5).[4] To actually meet these controllers afforded the precious opportunity to win their favor and, sometimes, to save one's group from destruction. True, such meetings had sometimes ended in disaster, but this was hardly a reason to abandon them: on the contrary, the humans could seek to design the physical circumstances in which meetings with the gods would take place in such a way as to minimize the danger and maximize the possibility of a favorable reception.

Out of these considerations arose *all* of the characteristics of the ancient Near Eastern temple. A word of caution here: the very word "temple" may confuse modern readers, since most people nowadays think of a temple principally as a place where human beings gather together to worship.[5] But the "house of prayer" type of temple is a relatively late idea; Christianity and Islam inherited it from Judaism's synagogue, which first made its appearance sometime in the late biblical period.[6] Long, long before that, however, was a different sort of temple in the ancient Near East, a grand house or palace that had one overriding purpose: to be the earthly residence of a god or goddess. As such, its every feature was designed to please the deity whose "house" it was while minimizing the potential danger inherent in encountering a supernatural being at close quarters.

Cadres of specially trained personnel ("priests") officiated in the temple; their entrance was predicated on, among other things, their strict maintenance of ritual purity, so that no uncleanness, nor the slightest flaw, could repel the god or goddess.[7] Inside the temple, all that was desirable in the world was offered to the deity—animal and vegetable sacrifices, some of them burned on an altar and thereby apparently vaporized for divine consumption; wine or beer libations of similar purpose; songs of praise and flattery sung to the divine beings in order to win them over. The inner part of the temple was the most sacred place, normally entered only by high officials of the priesthood and the royal court, since it was here that the god himself resided, inhabiting a small statue of wood, metal, and fabric and shimmering with divine power.[8] Indeed, save for this statue, the items mentioned are all paralleled by the prescriptions and descriptions of temple worship in the Bible, particularly in the making of the desert tabernacle (Exod 25–40) and the laws of sacrifices and ritual purity found in the book of Leviticus (especially chapters 1–10) and elsewhere.

Holiness

People are somewhat stymied by the word "holiness." Modern dictionaries fall back on synonyms, "the quality of being sacred" and the like, which really don't tell us anything. In a way, this is all to the good; the indefinability of this word reflects our own, stuttering, human response to something that seems, if we try to take it seriously, overwhelming, inexpressible. But in the context of the Hebrew Bible, the dimensions of this quality can at least be set out schematically, in a widening set of concentric circles.

Holy is, first and foremost, what God is. This is, in fact, God's primary characteristic, *the* adjective that describes Him. Thus, the seraphim surrounding God's throne proclaim in unison, "Holy, holy, holy is the Lord of Hosts" (Isa. 6:3). This is His essence. But holiness is contagious. Anything that comes into close proximity to God becomes holy by dint of this proximity: a quality, or some sort of energy, jumps from Him to whatever is nearest, rather like the spark from a Van de Graaff generator. So God's holiness sticks to the angels surrounding His heavenly throne; they are referred to simply as *kedoshim,* "holy ones." In God's earthly temple in Jerusalem[9] was a small enclosure set off from the rest. It was known as the holy of holies (a kind of superlative meaning "the holiest place"). This was where God was deemed to appear, enthroned above the outstretched wings of the two cherubim atop the ark of the covenant. According to Leviticus 16, only one human being, the high priest, was ever permitted to enter this enclosure, and this only for a few moments on the holiest day of the year, the Day of Atonement. Anyone else would be overcome by the holiness and die.

The next concentric circle of holiness was that of the temple as a whole, which was also touched by God's contagious holiness.[10] It was called, among other names, the *mikdash,* "the holy place," while its appurtenances are called *kelei kodesh,* vessels of holiness. Most of the temple compound was closed to all but the priests, the *kohanim.* They were the holiest people in Israel, having been appointed to mediate between God and ordinary Israelites. Priests could touch things in the temple, or *see* things there, that ordinary people could not—if non-priests did, they would probably go the way of Uzzah. In fact, in one historical incident, the people of the town of Beit Shemesh are said to have met a similar fate for merely *seeing* the ark:

> [The people of] Beit Shemesh were harvesting wheat in the valley, when they lifted up their eyes and they saw the ark. They rejoiced at *seeing:* the ark was entering the field of Joshua of Beit Shemesh and it stopped there. A large stone was there, so they split the wood of the wagon and offered up the cows [drawing the wagon] as a whole burnt offering to the Lord. And the Levites took down the ark of the Lord and the chest that held its gold utensils, and they placed it on the large stone; then the people of Beit Shemesh offered burnt offerings and other sacrifices to the Lord that day . . . And He [God] struck down the people of Beit Shemesh *because they had seen the ark of the Lord;* and He killed 50,070 people. The people mourned, because

> He had struck such a blow upon the people. The people of Beit Shemesh asked: "Who can survive in the presence of the Lord, this *holy* God?" (1 Sam 6:13–15, 19–20)

Touching, or merely coming close to, or, in fact, just seeing the sacred ark and similarly holy things could result in sudden death.[11] The reason is that, as this text specifies, Israel's God is a *holy* God, and contagious holiness spells danger.[12]

This fact reflects another fundamental difference between the ancient Near Eastern temple and the later "house of prayer." The temple really wasn't for everyone.[13] In Mesopotamia, gods and goddesses were identified with a "main city" that housed their own temple; by the middle of the third millennium if not before, each city had its patron deity, although temples dedicated to other gods might also exist within the city.[14] But ordinary citizens had little contact with the temple itself; they stood as outside spectators for festivals and other occasions. The temple's main purpose was, in the pungent phrase of the Assyriologist Leo Oppenheim, "the care and feeding of the gods."[15] Only trained specialists could perform the various duties involved; others, for the most part, stayed away.

Feeding the Gods

As to what the "the care and feeding of the gods" consisted of, in much of the ancient world gods and goddesses wanted one thing in particular: fresh meat. Animal sacrifices have been, from most ancient times, the principal form of communication with the divine in much of the world, *the* gesture that humans could make toward the powerful causers. Naturally, this circumstance has aroused the curiosity of scholars, who have proposed a variety of reasons for it, for example: (1) animal sacrifices were a primitive form of feeding the deity and so gaining his/her favor;[16] (2) along with this, to give up a healthy, living animal was to give up something very valuable — in some cultures, the most valuable possession people had; it was intended to impress the deity with the sacrificer's devotion and largesse;[17] (3) since some sacrifices were "shared" between the deity and the humans offering it, this sacrament had originated as a means of blunting the human horror at taking an animal's life for food;[18] (4) at bottom, sacrifices were a way for the humans involved to have a meat meal together — an essentially communal act that reinforced the social order;[19] (5) humans had always, and happily, been a violent species, often beating and killing fellow-humans over a trifle: animal sacrifices were a way of channeling mankind's love of bloodshed in a positive, harmless direction;[20] (6) animal sacrifices were intended as a substitute for the sacrificer's own life, a way of saying to the deity, "Take Bossie's life and spare mine";[21] or perhaps (7) the very spectacle of a fellow mammal passing from life into death at a god's altar spoke to some primal instinct in the human onlookers, a moment of heightened reality shared with the divine. The simple truth is that no one knows which, if any, of these considerations was responsible for the widespread adoption of animal sacrifices across the world, but whichever the reason, animal sacrifices had an unchallenged place in ancient worship. Wrestling with relatively new norms of divine behavior, ancient interpreters of the Bible wondered why Abel's sacrifice gained divine favor while his brother Cain's did not (Gen 4:4–5).[22] Shouldn't anyone who seeks to please God be rewarded? To an earlier generation of Israelites, however, the answer must have been perfectly obvious. Abel offered the "firstlings of his flocks" to God; Cain brought some vegetables. Meat was the ideal sacrifice, and it always spoke louder than a vegetable offering, and certainly louder than good intentions or heartfelt prayers. Much later, Sallust (Platonus Sallustius), the fourth-century CE Roman philosopher and author of *On the Gods and the World,* could still opine: "Prayer without sacrifice is just words."[23]

The Death of Aaron's Sons

According to the Pentateuch, the first sanctuary in which the Israelites as a whole people offered sacrifices to God was not a solid stone structure at all, but a large, portable tent, known as the *tabernacle* (the Hebrew term *mishkan* more properly means "dwelling place") of God, which they carried with them during forty years of wandering in the wilderness before their entry into Canaan. Scholars have generally believed that the very existence of such a tabernacle, along with its particular dimensions, was a projection of later reality onto this formative period in the wilderness.[24] Since temple worship was a central feature of Israelite religion in later times, so this argument went, priestly writers sought to claim that some sort of mini-sanctuary must have existed during all those early years of wandering. But precisely because these were years of *wandering,* the sanctuary must have been easily taken apart and reassembled—hence the retrospective invention of a portable tabernacle. Some scholars have recently taken issue with this reconstruction, however, arguing that in fact the theme of a tent shrine is an ancient Canaanite notion, embodying concepts and motifs now familiar from the writings of Ugarit.[25]

Whichever the case, the Pentateuch recounts at length how the tabernacle was constructed and made ready for Israel's regular sacrifices to God. The cloth hangings that constituted the sanctuary's "walls" were put into place, the priests were clothed in their ritual garments in a state of ritual purity, the altars were readied, and then — tragedy struck:

> Moses and Aaron went into the Tent of Meeting. When they came out again they blessed the people, and the glory of the LORD appeared before the whole people. Fire came forth from in front of the LORD and consumed the burnt offering and the fats on the altar. When the people saw it, they exulted and fell down on their faces.
>
> Now Aaron's sons, Nadab and Abihu, each took his censer, put fire in it, and laid incense on top; but they offered unholy fire before the LORD, such as He had not commanded them. Fire came forth from the LORD and consumed them, so that they died in front of the LORD. (Lev 9:23–10:2)

The first of these two paragraphs is almost as important as the second; in fact, they form a kind of pair. In the first paragraph, everything goes right, and God actually appeared in some visible form in front of the whole people — just as Moses had earlier told them He would (Lev 9:4, 6). Along with this, some sort of fire came shooting forth from the place where God was, and it burned up everything on the altar. Seeing these miraculous things, the people roared their approval and fell to the ground in reverence.

This was not the sort of thing that happened every day; in fact, it corresponded to nothing that usually went on in temples. But clearly it was important to say that it had happened once. Like certain other occurrences in the Bible — the time that a select group of Israelites was allowed to see God face-to-face on Mount Sinai (Exod 24:9–11), or the time that Moses was permitted to see God physically pass by while he was sheltered in a cleft in the rock (Exod 33:17–23) — this was an assertion that God does have an actual, visible being, his "glory" *(kavod)* or "substance." Even if we do not get to see it, some people have.

Then, what had been going so right suddenly went all wrong. Aaron's two sons made a mistake, rather like Uzzah's mistake in touching the ark or the mistake of the men of Beit Shemesh in looking at it — and they paid the same price. In fact, the very thing that had a moment earlier been the reason for rejoicing — namely, the fire that "came forth from in front of the LORD" — now came forth again, this time costing the lives of two young priests. What was their mistake? Apparently they brought ordinary censers into the *mishkan* (this is the meaning of the "unholy fire" here, incense burners that did not belong to the private world of the sanctuary but had been obtained from the outside), or perhaps they had prepared the incense in the wrong manner, or set it down in the wrong place, or had made some other error. As in the case of Uzzah, one might have thought that God would give Aaron's sons some leeway: after all, this was their very first day on the job! But just as with Uzzah, the reaction was automatic: cross this boundary and you are done for.

Denying the Obvious

A larger question hangs over these "electrocution" narratives—in fact, over the whole phenomenon of worshiping the gods in the temples of the ancient Near East: What did the people who entered these temples actually think was going on? We have already seen that the very notion of a god in the ancient Near East was different from what one might expect. A Babylonian or Assyrian *ilu* could be in two places or more simultaneously and take different forms: the goddess Ishtar was located in the star Venus, but also in the earthly cities of Arbela (the modern Arbil in northern Iraq), Nineveh (the site of modern Mosul, also in northern Iraq), Carchemish (now on the Turkish-Syrian border), and apparently others. A hymn attributed to the Assyrian emperor Assurbanipal illustrates the same point: in it, the king seems to be speaking about two different Ishtars simultaneously—in the plural, but as if they were one goddess:

> Exalt and glorify the Lady of Nineveh,
> magnify and praise the Lady of Arbela,
> who have no equal among the great gods.
> Their names are most precious among the goddesses!
> Their cultic centers have no equal among all the shrines! . . .
> I am Assurbanipal, their favorite . . .
> I grew up in the lap of my goddesses . . .[26]

Reading such things, one has to wonder: Did the people—perhaps not the common people, who had little to do with temples and sacrifices (or with fire coming forth from the Lord, for that matter), but the priests and the king and his servants—did these people really believe that any of this was true?

Much of this particular way of thinking has become clearer since the discovery and translation of a number of ancient texts written in Sumerian and Akkadian.* The texts describe the ceremony by which a divine statue was completed and set in its place in a temple, a ceremony that involved the "mouth opening" *(pīt-pî)* and "mouth washing" *(mīs-pî)* rituals.[27] The purpose of these rituals was to pave the way for the statue to become a full-fledged deity. For this to happen, the mouth of the statue was symbolically opened. The reason is explained in an incantation that was part of the *pīt-pî* ceremony: "This statue, without its mouth opened, cannot smell incense, cannot eat food nor drink water"[28]—all things that a god was expected to do. In other words, it was just a statue until its mouth was ritually opened. In fact, while throughout the manufacturing process, the image (say, a statuette of the god Marduk) was referred to as the "image," after the process was completed, it was no longer an image—it was now simply called Marduk. By the same token, a newly minted god or goddess was also, upon completion, described as having been "born in heaven," and not, apparently, fashioned on earth. "You are counted with the gods, your brothers," as one text puts it.[29]

Perhaps most surprising is what happened to the craftsmen who fashioned the image. After the statue had been completed—that is, after it had been clothed, given weapons and a crown, and last of all, after its *melammu,* a kind of halo of power, had begun to radiate outward to the beholder—the artisans who made it were, according to some texts, required to hold out their hands, which were then symbolically cut off with a sword. This was a way of asserting that they had nothing to do with the statue's creation. Indeed, in one Babylonian mouth-washing ritual, the artisans were made to recite: "I did not make him [the statue]; Ninagal [who is] Ea, [god] of the smith, made him."[30]

At this point, an obvious question arises: Who did these people think they were fooling? The craftsmen knew perfectly well that they had just finished making this spindly little statue with their own hands; they likewise saw what their fellow artisans had done. Yet here they were all denying the obvious and holding out their hands to be ritually severed as if to say that they had no role in the statue's creation.

A related case of denying the obvious: during the spring and fall New Year's festivals in Babylon, the statue of Marduk/Enlil, the supreme deity, was carried from the silent peace of his temple out into the bustling streets of the capital. This was a rare occasion for the townspeople to come close to the

---

* An extinct language of Mesopotamia, now used as a general name for various dialects of ancient Babylonian and Assyrian.

god, and they eagerly crowded around him. At the same time, priests or sages would study the statue's face, because they knew that the real god inhabited his statue, so that any slight changes in the statue's expression might be a sign of what the god was thinking and planning for the future:

> When Marduk, leaving the Esagila temple at the beginning of the year, has an open mouth — Enlil will raise his voice in anger against the land.
> When Marduk has his eyes closed — the land's inhabitants will feel sadness.
> When Marduk has a somber face — famine will take hold of the countries.
> When Marduk has a face that shines — Enlil will make the land shine forever.

Once again, these human beings seem to be denying the obvious. A statue is a statue; its expression never changes.

Footsteps of the Divine

One must be careful with broad, cross-cultural comparisons. Still, this "denying the obvious" with regard to a Mesopotamian temple's deity is somewhat similar to another sort of denial, embodied in some steps leading up to the entrance of an ancient temple excavated at 'Ain Dara in northern Syria.[31] The temple resembles others located in that part of the world (including, incidentally, Solomon's temple in Jerusalem, according to the biblical description) — except for one striking feature. On the steps leading up to this temple's doorway, the builders made a set of huge footprints, symbolically representing the god's entrance into his sanctuary. The footprints are sunk into the temple's steps in the same way that human footprints might be sunk into mud or wet cement — but the feet themselves are many times bigger than human feet, and the length of the stride they mark off is far greater than a human stride. Archaeologists estimate that, on the basis of this stride, the god or goddess of that temple would have been some sixty-five feet tall! How could the builders have imagined such a huge deity ever making its way through the rather normal-sized entrance of the temple? This, apparently, did not trouble the temple's otherwise careful planners.

Not unrelated to the foregoing: the late Assyriologist William Hallo once described what he saw as a hierarchy of ongoing offerings that the Mesopotamian worshiper could present to the god in his temple. As already mentioned, the common folk had little to do with what went on inside the temple. But some people could afford to submit to the god a written text, a "letter prayer" that would be deposited in the sanctuary and perhaps taken into consideration by the god or goddess concerned. Of course, things get lost in the mail or overlooked in an Oriental bureaucracy. Some wealthier petitioners would therefore submit a gift to accompany their request: a votive stone carving or a replica of a bowl, a mace head, a seal, or some other object taken from daily life. These would be inscribed with a standard formula, "for the sake of the long life of the donor," or "for the life of the king," "for the donor's family," and so forth. Alternately (or in addition), a more specific prayer, such as a petition for success in a given venture or thanks for favors previously asked and now granted, might be joined to this basic dedicatory inscription.

But at the very top of this hierarchy of gifts was what Hallo called the "optimal dedicatory, or votive offering, the statue of a worshiper set up in the cella of the deity and inscribed with his prayer, which was conceived thereby as proffered perpetually by the statue of the worship to the statue of the deity, both statues serving as images or surrogate of their originals."[32] At first blush, this seems like a strange sort of gift. If I were the deity, I'd take the bowl or the mace head; what pleasure could I derive from having a statue of the king or other high official crouching before me day after day?

A Foreign Embassy

The common thread that seems to run through the various phenomena treated so far in this chapter reveals something basic about the ancient Near Eastern temple and the holiness of the deity inside. Did Uzzah, the people of Beit Shemesh, and Aaron's two sons actually meet the sudden death described in the Bible? Whatever really happened, these three narratives all seem to be imparting the same lesson. The boundary between what is God's and what is man's is absolute: if an ordinary human crosses that border, even with the best of intentions, destruction will usually follow. The reason is that, at bottom, *the gods don't belong down here,* among us, at least not in a space continuous with our own. Their essence is entirely different from ours. As the artisans asserted once the little statue of the god was completed, "this god was born in heaven." That was where divine beings were from, axiomatically, so no matter who created the outer shell, the *god* was an emissary from "up there" to down here. For this reason, we humans have to create a little island in our midst, a temple or some other sacred precinct whose borders are inviolable, in order for the divine ones to sojourn among us. One might thus think of the temple as a kind of foreign embassy. It is right in the middle of our town, but normally we cannot enter it; its border guards will open fire automatically on anyone who tries.

To say this is to approach the real point: the border is inviolable because the reality inside the temple is necessarily discontinuous from that which is outside. The normal rules do not hold. Gods *can* simultaneously be up there, in a planet or star, and down here in a temple, because their *down here* is not part of the surroundings. So can the mighty Marduk really be inside this little statue? No problem—and truly, no need to build a bigger statue; this little one will do just fine, because size inside the temple is utterly different from size outside. And his lips might move or his expression might change; the *real* god was inside looking out. What more striking demonstration of the disjunction between a temple's "inside" world and its physical surroundings than those huge, divine strides leading up to the normal-sized door of the temple at 'Ain Dara? Something happens as soon as the huge god crosses the threshold into the interior world of the temple: the ordinary norms of size collapse. As for the priests who officiate inside, they are a bit like the local workers hired by the foreign embassy personnel: no matter what their ordinary citizenship may be, once they are on embassy grounds, their loyalty does a complete about-face. Now they will shoot down their fellow citizens rather than allow even one of them to breach the embassy's borders.

As for the statue of the suppliant as described by William Hallo: facing the god, humbly pleading his case and that of his people, the suppliant inside the temple is likewise in a realm altogether disconnected from the outside; his inside body and his outside one exist in two different realities. One might wish to describe the inside realm as a kind of symbolic world, but "symbolic" does not capture the essence of it. (As the Catholic writer Flannery O'Connor once wrote about the Eucharist, "If it's a symbol, to hell with it.")[33] Inside the temple is a time-stopped, sealed-off place of another reality, a sort of concentrated eternity. There the god—the actual *causer* of great events, who is normally hidden from view—is present in a kind of frozen timelessness of being, and the suppliant (or, rather, his statue) is in the god's real presence in exactly the same form as the god, frozen in the same timeless world.

The Tower of Babel

Does this all sound like a bunch of mumbo jumbo? It certainly must have appeared that way to some ancient Israelites. The story of the Tower of Babel is recounted in a few sentences in the book of Genesis:

> Now everyone in the whole land spoke the same language and the same words. And as they traveled from the east, they found a plain in the land of Shinar and settled there. Then they said to one another, "Let us make bricks, and burn them," so that they could use the bricks for stones and bitumen for mortar. Then they said, "Come, let us build ourselves a city with a tower reaching up to the sky, and [thereby] make a name for ourselves, so that we will not be scattered across the whole earth." But the Lord came down to see the city and the tower that the humans had built. And the Lord said, "If, as one people with one language, they have undertaken to do this, then nothing will stop them from doing whatever they please to do. Come, let us go down, and mix up their language, so that they will not understand one another's speaking." So it was that the Lord scattered them from there across the whole land, and they left off building the city. That is why it was called Babel, because there the Lord mixed up the whole land's language; from there the Lord scattered them from there across the whole land. (Gen 11:1–9)

Like many stories in Genesis, this one presents a mixture of themes. To begin with, it relates a disparaging explanation of the name of Israel's mighty neighbor (and frequent enemy), Babel/Babylon. Why was their great city known as Babel? Not—as the folk etymology had it—because it was the gateway of the god (*Bab-ilu*), but because God had once punished the people of that land by confusing (*balal*) their speech.

A second theme is the story's explanation for the existence of different but clearly related Semitic languages in the region. In the beginning, the story says, everyone could understand everyone else; it was only because of the builders' misbehavior that peoples drifted apart, and suddenly speakers of Akkadian could not understand speakers of Aramaic, who could not understand speakers of Hebrew or Arabic (although the words often did sound quite similar). And why did this building project offend our God? Here is yet another theme in the story, Babylonian hubris: apparently, the builders' fault was their intention to build a huge metropolis such as those that did in fact exist in Mesopotamia ("so that we will not be scattered across the whole earth"). God takes no pleasure in such human agglomerations, the story says, since they can only lead to arrogance and overreaching ("Come, let us build ourselves a city with a tower reaching up to the sky, and [thereby] make a name for ourselves").

Mixed in with all this, however, is a critique aimed specifically at Babylon's religious institutions, and in particular the emblematic *ziggurat* (or, more correctly, *ziqqurat*), a kind of stepped pyramid that the Sumerians, Babylonians, and Assyrians built to honor their gods. (What its precise function was is unknown.) Ziqqurats had become an essential feature of temple complexes in Mesopotamia as early as the third millennium BCE. In all, archaeologists have uncovered the remains of some twenty-eight of them in present-day Iraq and another four in Iran. Since the area of the Tigris and Euphrates valleys did not feature large stone formations for people to quarry, the massive ziqqurats had to be built—just as the Bible reports—out of mud bricks (at first only sun-dried ones, but later they came to be fired in specially constructed kilns); the bricks were often stuck together with bitumen (a kind of asphalt-like substance). Because these materials are far less durable than actual stone, most of these ancient structures eventually fell into heaps of rubble—some of them probably collapsed in biblical times, so that the biblical story of the Tower of Babel may indeed be based on the ruins that travelers to Mesopotamia would have likely seen with their own eyes.

All these different elements have been combined into one short narrative, the biblical account of the Tower of Babel. If this tale seems to highlight the Mesopotamian ziqqurat, lurking in the background is something else that distinguished Israelite worship from that of its Mesopotamian neighbors, something far more important. True, Israelites and Mesopotamians both had temples, and much of what went on inside both—the animal sacrifices, libations, enforcement of purity laws, singing of prayers and hymns, and so forth—was indeed comparable. What is more, the Israelites apparently had multiple sanctuaries and sacred "high places" where sacrifices were offered to a God who must have been deemed present, or potentially present, in two places at once—very much like the Beʿalim of whom Hosea spoke.[34] But the Israelites, as best we know, did not have that little cultic figure of the deity that was all-important in the worship of Mesopotamians and others. Though the prohibition of making such images may have become codified only later on,[35] the evidence uncovered by archaeologists so far suggests that ancient Israelites simply did not have cultic statues of the God YHWH.[36]

What is one to make of this fact? It used to be alleged that aniconic (imageless) worship represents an older stratum of religion, one that was ultimately displaced (perhaps in stages) by the emergence of skillfully wrought statuary.[37] The truth appears to be somewhat more complicated, skewed even in ancient times by various writers on the subject,[38] as well as by modern scholars who have continued to evoke the iconic/aniconic dichotomy, as if it were always one or the other. (The Nabateans,* often cited as aniconic worshipers, actually demonstrate a variety of different forms in their religious art: geometric, semifigural, and fully figural shapes coexist. Thus, the god Dusares/Dushara was sometimes represented by a simple pillar or standing stone, but sometimes by a *slightly* iconic figure that depicted the deities' eyes but nothing more.)[39]

In fact, the very word "aniconic" itself seems to be too broad. In the case of the ancient Israelite temple, scholars speak of a specific phenomenon, "empty-space aniconism,"[40] whereby a throne or platform was created for the deity, but it was left empty. The deity was, as it were, invited to come and occupy the space specially designated for him (perhaps as he was held to occupy the nonfigural or semifigural objects mentioned above). This form of aniconism is apparently evidenced in the Israelite sanctuary as described in the book of Exodus: inside the *Holy of Holies* was the ark of the covenant, a box of acacia wood that had been overlaid with gold and topped with a golden cover. On each side stood the carved statue of a cherub—a large, winged figure (perhaps with an animal body, though this is not certain):

> The cherubim will have their wings outstretched above. They will thus overspread the ark-cover with their wings, while their faces will be turned toward one another; toward the ark-cover will the faces of the cherubim be set [from either side] . . . *That is where I [God] will meet with you [Moses].* There, above the ark-cover, between the two cherubim that are on top of the ark of the covenant, I will speak with you of whatever I have to command you concerning the people of Israel. (Exod 25:20, 22)

God is not represented here in the form of a statue or image. Rather, a special space was set off for Him, "above" or "on" the outstretched wings of the cherubim. (Indeed, this particular space was so connected to His nature that God is sometimes referred to as "the one who sits/is enthroned atop the cherubim"—1 Sam 4:4; 2 Sam 6:2; 2 Kings 19:15; Isa 37:16; Ps 80:1, 99:1; 1 Chron 13:6.)

Although scholars disagree as to the implications of this posture, it certainly seems to imply that God was *not* permanently present, at least not physically, in his temple; rather, the space above the cherubim was the place

---

* An Arab people from northern Arabia and the inland Levant; remains of Nabatean settlements have been found at Petra (in modern Jordan), Avdat and Halutzah (in the Negev region of southern Israel), and elsewhere.

"where I [God] will meet with you [Moses]" when such a meeting is necessary, the spot from which "I will speak with you of whatever I have to command you." But God was not embodied there in any form. Indeed, the very flimsiness of this perch, poised above the outstretched wings of the cherubim, seems best suited to a God who appears there, speaks, and then disappears again, like some sort of sacred hologram.[41] This bit of iconography is thus of a piece with the same basic conception of God seen in the angel narratives as well as in various prophetic books. He is a God who appears and disappears, stepping across the curtain that separates ordinary from extraordinary reality. This is so even in the Jerusalem temple, with its fixed location for divine encounters: God appears there, but He hardly seems to be there permanently.[42]

An Elusive Presence

Aniconic worship was thus more than just the absence of cultic images, of idols. It went along with a thoroughly un-Mesopotamian conception of how divinity worked. In a Babylonian or Assyrian temple, the god was simply there, present in the temple itself (though also simultaneously present in the heavens, as well as in sacred objects and symbols and at other cultic sites, as we have seen). In the ancient Israelite conception of things, the temple had a different role: inside it, a place was prepared for God's appearance, but He would appear or disappear as He wished.[43] My aim in stressing this point is not to argue that Israel was altogether different from its Mesopotamian neighbors; given all the common elements in Mesopotamian and Israelite worship, as well as the centuries of cultural (though not always friendly) contacts, it would be foolish to suggest that these two civilizations were worlds apart, even in religion. Nor, save for a misguided desire to "defend" biblical Israel's absolute uniqueness in all things, is there any reason to understate the many things it shared with surrounding civilizations.

Nevertheless, the particular sort of aniconism practiced in the Israelite sanctuary (at least as it is depicted in the Bible and, thus far, the archaeological record) suggests a rather different idea not just of what a temple is, but of what a deity is. Throughout the Hebrew Bible, Israel's God comes and goes, appears or is heard and then vanishes — even when there is a sanctuary with a special place permanently available for His presence.[44]

Earlier it was suggested that some of these appearances might be described as a "waking dream." This description may be apt, but it somehow falls short of the reality it seeks to name. We all know what a dream is, and saying a dream can also occur when someone is awake is simply to tame the uncanny, transferring the thing that we do know into a setting in which it is unknown but nonetheless sounds plausible. The truth, I think, is more elusive and so probably should be expressed differently. Given a very different sense of self (with its semipermeable mind, as we have seen presumed in so many biblical texts), *seeing* God is indeed how to describe what took place, albeit in a different register — not once, but frequently enough for this description of what happened to remain conventional for quite a while, until, as we will also see, it eventually began to fade.[45]

How did this other sort of self perceive its place in the world? Part of this outlook has already been summarized by the representative Mesopotamian cited at the end of the previous chapter: "Tell me how you can begin to make sense of the world without realizing that the gods control everything and we humans are almost nothing, their little servants subject to their will." In other words, how he conceived of himself and his fitting into the world was crucial for what he perceived as reality; this is, indeed, the whole theme of this book.

Such things were crucial for the ancient Israelite as well, and yet one would not be wrong in supposing that he might be a little less emphatic about actually catching sight of the deity than the Mesopotamian was. To be sure, he was glad to know that God's "house" — the temple — was in the midst of his city, a physical connection with the divine that perhaps, though not necessarily, meant that Israel's God would look after its interests. In fact, he could (and did) go to God's temple to offer a sacrifice, atoning sin or paying off a vow, or simply seeking to participate in one of the annual festivals in what he conceived to be God's earthly home. What is more, he might pray to God from any location: throughout the biblical period ordinary people are represented as praying in time of need by holding up their hands in the air (the conventional posture of prayer) and seeking to gain His attention. All this notwithstanding, Israel's God was fundamentally a coming-and-going deity. The very fact of His appearing suggests *His* willful crossing of a boundary; we may have entered His temple or sacred spot, but it was ultimately God who crossed over into our world. In so doing, He came to address humans directly — not only in the biblical representations of Abraham and Sarah, Jacob, and all the rest, but also speaking directly to prophets, penetrating their semipermeable minds with a message to pass along to others.

7

IMAGINING PROPHECY

Prophets and poets; Jeremiah's prophecies; Modern voice hearers; Colors in the brain

We have just seen that the God of Israel was depicted as inhabiting, or at least in some sense present in, an ancient Near Eastern–style temple. But this was hardly the only way in which God was encountered. The whole phenomenon of prophecy presumes that God (or the gods) can speak to human beings. This presumption is perhaps the most dramatic evidence that people in biblical times had a sense of self different from our own. But what else can be discovered about biblical prophets and the voices that they heard?

Biblical prophecy presents the most striking, but also the most puzzling, model of human encounters with God. Time and again, prophets report their having been addressed personally by God, or their having seen some divinely sent vision (and sometimes both). What can this really mean? Did a voice just suddenly pop into their ears, and/or a picture suddenly come before their eyes?

The beginning of an answer has already been suggested: in the encounters with angels narrated in Genesis and other books, various people in the Bible seem simply to assume that their own minds are subject to outside intervention. It is most significant that Abraham, Joshua, Gideon, Manoah and his wife, and the others are surprised, *but not flabbergasted,* to encounter God. (The same was seen to be true of Homer's Achilles and Virgil's Aeneas.) Once they understand that it is a deity who is speaking to them, they do not faint or stare in utter disbelief. Instead, they drop to the ground in reverent obedience. Apparently, in reality or at least in its literary reflections, such things were thought to just happen from time to time. And this is true as well of prophets called by God.

The Pentateuch uses the phrase "And the LORD said to Moses" some 64 times. The similar phrase "And the LORD spoke to Moses, saying . . ." appears even more frequently, 89 times in all. The words following either of these assertions are thus presented as having been communicated by God directly to Moses. Various other prophets similarly introduce their prophecies with the words "Thus said the LORD"—in fact, prophets say this more than 300 times in the Hebrew Bible. The book of Jeremiah, one of the Bible's longest prophetic books, has its own favorite equivalent, "So says [*ne'um*] the LORD"; this phrase was used some 162 times, in addition to reporting that "the word of the LORD came to Jeremiah" or similar formulations another 44 times.[1]

What is one to make of such written testimony? Was the assertion that *God* spoke these words merely a conventional way of introducing the prophet's own pronouncements or ideas?[2] It certainly may have become conventional at some point, in the same way that the ancient Greek "invocation of the muse" came to be conventional (more or less).* But, as scholars have suggested with regard to Homer,[3] the assertion of divinely given speech started off as a lived reality—and continued to be so for some time.[4] Indeed, just as the ancient Greek poet experienced an external muse helping him to come up with ordered, poetic lines of dactylic hexameter, so the ancient Israelite prophet seems to have believed that what he was saying had come from the outside, from God, and like the Greek poet, the biblical prophet often expressed this divinely granted message in poetic form—that is, in the balanced, connecting clauses that were the mark of elevated speech in ancient Hebrew.

Were the Prophets Poets?

The similarity between ancient Greek bards and Israelite prophets has thus suggested to some scholars that the men and women whom ancient Israelites called prophets were basically the same sort of figures whom other nations called poets.[5] This is a comparison worth taking seriously. After all, poets in classical Greece and Rome claimed to have been *inspired* (quite literally): a god or divine muse breathed something into their minds, and out came a

---

* See chapter 3.

poem. And it was not just poets who believed this. In Plato's *Ion,* Socrates presents his own idea of inspiration:

> All good poets, epic as well as lyric, compose their beautiful poems not by art, but because they are *inspired or possessed* . . . For the poet is a light and winged and holy thing, and there is no invention in him until he has been inspired and is out of his senses, and the mind is no more in him. When he has not attained to this state he is powerless and unable to utter his oracles . . . And therefore, *God takes away the minds of the poets and uses them as his ministers, as he also uses diviners and holy prophets,* in order that we who hear them may know them to be speaking not of themselves who utter these priceless words in a state of unconsciousness, but that God himself is the speaker, and that through them he is conversing with us.[6]

Any Israelite in biblical times would probably have had no difficulty in concluding that what this Greek philosopher is talking about is indeed the figure that "we" call a *nabi* (prophet) or *ḥozeh* (visionary) or *ish ha-Elohim* ("man of God"). Socrates continues with a concrete example:

> Tynnichus the Chalcidian affords a striking instance of what I am saying: he wrote nothing that anyone would care to remember but the famous paean that is in everyone's mouth, one of the finest poems ever written, simply an invention of the Muses, as he himself says. For in this way the God would seem to indicate to us and not allow us to doubt that these beautiful poems are not human or the work of man, but divine and the work of God; and that the poets are only intermediaries of the gods by whom they were severally possessed.[7]

All this may help us imagine the reality of biblical prophecy. Perhaps the prophets were indeed very much like poets in our own day. Prophets started out, as best we know, without any formal initiation or anyone having appointed them — other than God.[8] Poets, too, generally start writing without any formal approval or confirmation ("nothing to authenticate the mission imposed," wrote Basil Bunting). And just as modern poets often say that the beginning of a poem, or a whole poem, just "came to them," so the prophet's words were placed by God "in their mouth," that is, ready to be spoken, or sometimes simply "were found" (Jer 15:16), apparently without effort. Perhaps because many prophets had a gift for speaking in verse — and a gift for speaking in general — people were fascinated and gathered to hear them, just as they might for a poet; some people even bothered to commit the prophets' memorable sayings to writing. The Bible also reports that prophets, like ancient poets, sometimes used musical instruments, "lyres, timbrels, flutes and harps," to accompany their prophesying (1 Sam 10:5), rather like ancient Greek bards. Elisha, when asked to prophesy, called for a musician: "And as the musician played, the hand of the LORD came upon him and he said, 'Thus says the LORD . . .'" (2 Kings 3:15–16). Moreover, a passage in the book of Ezekiel presents God as telling the prophet not to be disturbed by the fact that some of his listeners seem to regard him as a kind of entertainer:

> [God said to Ezekiel:] "As for you, son of man, your countrymen talk together about you by the walls and in the doorways of their houses; they say to one another, 'Let's go hear what word is coming forth from the LORD.' So they go to you like an audience, and they sit in front of you, My people do, and they listen to what you have to say—but they won't do what you tell them. Lust is what's on their lips, and getting money is in their hearts. As far as you are concerned, you are to them like a love song sung with a beautiful voice and musical accompaniment; they hear what you say to do, but they do not do it. Yet when this thing comes—and come it will—then they will know that a prophet has been among them." (Ezek 33:30–33)

Of course, there are also significant differences between biblical prophets and inspired Greek poets. To begin with, prophets are not generally praised for the beauty of their words;[9] in fact, they are not much praised at all. Rather, they are usually presented as merely repeating what God has told them to say,[10] starting off with the stock messenger formula, "Thus says the LORD" (this was in fact an aspect of prophecy proudly stressed in later times).[11] Commissioned by God to pass along a specific communication from Him concerning matters at hand, they prophesied about such things as Israel's affairs of state; Israel's neighbors, particularly in time of crisis; the king and the royal court, or other individual Israelites; and the people as a whole. In this sense, biblical prophets could be described as political figures, functioning somewhat differently from most classical poets.[12] They also advised (and often rebuked) the king or prominent members of society. They cursed Israel's enemies (their curses were deemed to be effective, backed with divine power), and not infrequently also excoriated the people of Israel and their leaders on God's behalf. Some performed symbolic acts in addition to speaking (1 Kings 11:29–31, 22:11; Ezek 37:16; Hos 1:1–8), something not attested in classical poets.[13] Indeed, some prophets are said to have performed miracles.[14] Considered together, these various manifestations of prophetic activity in the Bible seem to put it somewhat outside of what we normally associate with ancient poets.[15] Yet these must be balanced against the other, rather compelling, similarities of poets and prophets. Perhaps it would be best to say that biblical prophets represent a special kind of poet-like figure, with their own way of functioning and their own special role in society. Beyond saying this, generalizations will not be particularly useful; it might be better to examine two rather different prophets from Israel's history.

Balaam's Couplets

The story of the pagan prophet Balaam is told in the book of Numbers.[16] Balaam's particular specialty was cursing people. (In biblical times, curses were believed capable of hurting people, even causing their death; some prophets were prodigious cursers.)[17] As such, Balaam was hired by the king of Moab to curse the Israelites, whom the king feared might be planning to encroach on his territory. Balaam traveled all the way from northern Syria to Moab to do the job, but God ultimately frustrated his plans. Every time Balaam tried to curse the Israelites, all that would come out of his mouth were blessings.

> [After Balaam arrived in Moab,] God came to Balaam, and Balaam said to Him, "I have arranged the seven altars [as You demanded], and I have placed a bull and a ram on each altar." Then the LORD *put a word in Balaam's mouth,* and He said, "Go back to Balak [the Moabite king], and speak to him thus." So he returned to Balak, who was standing beside his burnt-offerings with all the officials of Moab. Then *he spoke his couplets,* saying:
>
> "From Aram Balak brought me here, called me forth from the eastern mountains:
> 'Come, curse this Jacob for me; Come, damn the people of Israel!'
> Can I damn those whom God has not, or doom those not doomed by the LORD?
> From the tops of these crags I can see them, I glimpse them beneath these hills:
> a people who'll live on its own, not reckoned as part of another.
> Who can count Jacob's descendants, or number Israel's seed?
> Let me die a righteous man's death, so my offspring will end up like them."
> (Num 23:4–10)

The passage begins by saying that God *put a word in Balaam's mouth,* an utterly straightforward attribution of Balaam's words to God. Indeed, by Balaam's own account, God was forcing him to say what he didn't want to say: he wanted to curse Israel and get his promised fee.[18] But the phrase used just before Balaam begins his speech, "Then *he spoke his couplets,*" is more equivocal. The word "couplets" is my attempt to render the Hebrew *mashal,* which means something like "poetic speech," since such speech consisted of passages of successive two-part lines, like Balaam's above. Poetic couplets were often (though not always) used by prophets, but they were also employed by ordinary people with a gift for rhetoric, people who made no claim to divine inspiration. In fact, the book of Job uses the same phrase used here, "Then *he spoke his couplets,*" to introduce Job's altogether human complaints (27:1, 29:1).

So: were Balaam's couplets an exact quote of God's words to him, or were they his own rewording of the general message that God had just "put in Balaam's mouth," making him a bit more like a poet? A passage later on in the story suggests that at some point, the prophet was indeed free to formulate his words on his own. After two attempts at cursing the Israelites,

> Balaam saw that it pleased the LORD to bless Israel, *so he stopped going time and again after divine oracles* and set his gaze toward the wilderness. Lifting up his eyes, he saw Israel encamped tribe by tribe; the spirit of God came upon him, and he *spoke his couplets* and said . . . (Num 24:1–3)

Here, unlike the previous times, Balaam doesn't have to go off in search of a direct oracle from God — apparently, he has gotten the general idea and he can now go it on his own. (True, the passage says that "the spirit of God came upon him," but this assertion may be added to make clear that the poetic message that he is about to proclaim, even if it is not the result of a divine oracle, nevertheless has divine approval.)

What happens after this only strengthens the idea. The Moabite king, frustrated by Balaam's inability to curse the Israelites, informs him that his promised fee will not be paid; he is to return home without an honorarium. Then Balaam — without any mention of God dictating his words — announces that he has foreseen Moab's destruction:

> The words of Balaam, son of Beor; the words of a man whose eye sees true;
> the words of one who hears God speak and knows the Most High's mind,
> who sees what God Almighty sees, bowing low but with open eyes:

> I glimpse it, but it is not yet; I behold what is not close;
> A star rising up from Jacob, from Israel comes forth a king,
> crushing the Moabites' skulls, smashing the heads of the Sethites;
> Edom falls into his hands, Seir becomes his possession, and Israel is
> triumphant. (Num 24:15–19)

One might thus conclude, at least on the basis of this one case, that prophets sometimes were thought to have had a good bit of latitude. They couldn't change the overall message (despite his trying, Balaam could not curse Israel), but perhaps when prophets said, "Thus said the LORD," they did not mean that He spoke these very words. On the other hand, this may be too rational a view of prophecy. Perhaps "Thus said the LORD" meant precisely that.

Jeremiah of Anathoth

Jeremiah, son of Hilkiah, was a relatively late biblical prophet. He was born in the town of Anathoth, about three miles northeast of Jerusalem, sometime toward the end of the first half of the seventh century BCE. He apparently began his life of prophecy at a relatively early age and lived through good times and bad, the former associated with the heyday of King Josiah's thirty-year reign (640–609 BCE), which then quickly degenerated into the political and strategic blunders of Josiah's successors, ultimately leading to the fall of the Kingdom of Judah to the Babylonians in the early sixth century BCE. The first phase of this national catastrophe—of which Jeremiah warned unrelentingly—climaxed in 597 BCE, with the Babylonian conquest of Judah and the deportation of much of its aristocracy to exile in Babylon. This was certainly bad enough, but a bungled attempt at revolt in Judah led to renewed suffering: a prolonged siege of Jerusalem ended in 587 BCE with the destruction of the city and the desecration of the holiest spot on earth, the Jerusalem temple, God's earthly residence. Jeremiah himself sought refuge in Egypt, where he apparently died.

Jeremiah came toward the end of a long line of prophets. There were his immediate predecessors, the famous prophetic figures of the eighth and seventh centuries: Amos, Hosea, Isaiah, and Micah, followed by Nahum, Habakkuk, and Zephaniah. Before these "writing prophets"—so called because actual collections of their words are included in the Bible—were earlier prophets such as Elijah and Elisha, whose messages and miraculous deeds are recounted in 1 and 2 Kings, but whose words were never gathered into collections. Still earlier were the prophet-like figures mentioned in texts from ancient Mesopotamia, the *āpilu/āpiltu* (male/female "spokesperson" for the deity),[19] *muḫḫû/muḫḫûtu* ("ecstatic")—both known to us from Akkadian texts of the eighteenth century BCE—as well as *raggimu/raggimtu* ("proclaimer") and others found in later writings from the Neo-Assyrian period.[20] All this is to say that, long before Jeremiah's time, the existence of prophets and the phenomenon of prophecy were simply a fact of life, apparently taken for granted by ordinary Israelites.

The book of Jeremiah[21] begins with the prophet recounting how—apparently as a young man, perhaps only a teenager—he discovered that he was born to be a prophet:

> The word of the LORD came to me, saying: "I knew you even before I formed you in the womb, and before you came out, I had already set you apart: I appointed you to be a prophet regarding the nations." I said, "Oh no! Sir, LORD, I can't make speeches—I'm just a boy." But the LORD said to me, "Do not say, 'I'm just a boy.' You will go to whomever I send you and say whatever I tell you to say. And do not worry about them, because I will be there to save you—declares the LORD."
>
> Then the LORD put out His hand and touched me on the mouth, and the LORD said to me, "Now I have put My word in your mouth. As of today I am commissioning you to speak concerning the nations and the kingdoms—the uprooting and pulling down, the destruction and devastation, the rebuilding and the replanting." (Jer 1:4–10)

So later on, when Jeremiah repeatedly stood in front of his townsmen and said, "This is what God told me to say," he was—if this account is true—simply fulfilling a role that God had assigned him from birth (or, as a matter of fact, "even before I formed you in the womb"). But in saying the sort of things that he said, was Jeremiah literally transmitting God's own words? Had God, to borrow Socrates's description, "taken away the prophet's mind" and replaced it with His own? As noted, prophets often ended up criticizing the reigning king of Israel, and one such passage in the book of Jeremiah poses the question of "Is God speaking?" rather clearly. Here, Jeremiah is denouncing King Jehoiakim for his corrupt ways:

> A man builds his house through injustice, unfairness from bottom to top,
> He makes someone work for no wages, or hires but then doesn't pay;
> "I'll build me a palace," he says, "equipped with the finest of rooms,

windows and panels of cedar, and painted inside with vermilion" —
Do you think that's what makes someone kingly, a house with the best cedar panels?
Wasn't your father content to eat and drink without frills,
While acting with justice and fairness — wasn't that what seemed to him good?
He gave the poor man his due; for him that was true satisfaction.
Isn't that what it means to obey[22] Me? — so says the LORD.
But your eyes look only for profit, your heart's always out for more gain,
Shedding the innocents' blood, oppressing and crushing at will.
Therefore, thus says the LORD concerning Jehoiakim son of Josiah, king of Judah:
No one will go around mourning, crying "Ah my brother! My sister!"
No one will go around mourning, "Your majesty! Oh my lord!"
You'll be buried like a dead donkey, dragged and dumped outside the gates of Jerusalem. (Jer 22:13–19)

This brief passage puts the problem squarely, since scholars disagree on which parts of it are being claimed to be God's own words to Jeremiah. Perhaps the whole passage, with its ringing indictment of a corrupt king, is being presented here as God's actual words; or perhaps only the words following *Therefore, thus says the LORD* are said to have come from God, announcing God's verdict after Jeremiah had presented the indictment on his own. Or perhaps this passage is implying that none of these words actually flew into the brain of the prophet; all that Jeremiah* may have gotten was some sort of indication of what to say, which he *assumed* to have come from God — a flash of insight that he then elaborated on his own, rather like an inspired poet in modern times. The question is important not only in regard to the prophet-as-poet, but more significantly, in our overall effort to understand just how far the ancient sense of self, with its semipermeable mind, could go.

Hearing Voices

Psychologists and other researchers know that some people still hear voices. The voice that they hear, according to some subjects interviewed, can be clearly male or female, although for others it can be without gen-

* I should stress throughout that I am not talking about the historical person named Jeremiah, if such a person ever existed, but about the prophet Jeremiah as presented in a biblical book by that name — an important distinction. See also note 12 of this chapter.

der. Sometimes the voice is recognized as belonging to a person the hearer knows — a friend or relative (alive or dead), but other voice hearers report that the voice seems to come from an anonymous, disembodied speaker.[23] In any case, hearing voices is often symptomatic of some deep mental disturbance: psychotic disorders of various sorts, including schizophrenia, are often associated with hearing voices, as are dissociative identity disorder and related problems. Most dramatically, hearing voices is sometimes connected to the crimes committed by serial killers, who report that they were "instructed" by a voice to seek out their victims. Perhaps the most famous such instance was that of the "Son of Sam" murders of the 1970s in New York City, whose perpetrator claimed to have been told to kill by a demon who had taken possession of his neighbor's (Sam's) dog. (The killer, David Berkowitz, later retracted his story, claiming it was a hoax.) Other, recent voice-hearing murderers may be less well known but no less deadly (Herbert Mullin, Priscilla Joyce Ford, James Huberty, Joseph Hunter Parker, and many more). Beyond these are just ordinary voice hearers, thousands of patients diagnosed with symptoms of psychosis who need a daily cocktail of antipsychotic, antidepressant, and antianxiety medications to silence the sounds in their heads.

But not all people who hear voices can be described as mentally ill. Some early studies concluded that between 2 and 4 percent of the general population report hearing voices; most of these subjects did not present any other symptoms associated with mental disorders. Other researchers have put the figure considerably higher. One study of 150 male students in England found that more than 15 percent of the subjects surveyed endorsed the statement, "In the past I have had the experience of hearing a person's voice and then found that no one was there." The same study added that "no less than 17.5% of the [subjects] were prepared to score the item 'I often hear a voice speaking my thoughts aloud' as 'Certainly applies.'"[24] Another, more recent study of 103 "healthy individuals with auditory verbal hallucinations" — that is, ordinary voice hearers — suggests the same overall assessment: "Auditory verbal hallucinations (AVH) occur in approximately 10%–15% of the general population, of whom only a small proportion has a clinically relevant psychotic disorder."[25] Indeed, a 2011 review of recent scholarly literature dealing with voice hearing in the general population likewise proposed the overall figure of 15 percent.[26]

Starting in the 1980s, the Dutch social psychiatrist Marius Romme and colleagues created the Hearing Voices Movement, which has sought to bring together researchers and people who report hearing voices in order to better understand the phenomenon. This movement's point of departure has been the belief that treating voice hearing as a disability is often counterproductive, and that such auditory experiences might sometimes be better approached as a potentially helpful, and even meaningful, phenomenon. The Hearing Voices Movement has spread rapidly over the last three decades in Europe and elsewhere; apart from inspiring the creation of a number of local and national organizations, it sponsors an annual world congress attended by hundreds of delegates.[27]

The existence of apparently sane people nowadays reporting that they hear voices (when all we know about the brain asserts that such hearing must be impossible) is certainly striking in the present context. The question that it raises is this: obviously, most of these sane, Western voice hearers are not operating with a "sense of self" that is different from ours. They apparently think of their minds as self-enclosed entities, just as most people do: "If there is a God, well, He's out there and I'm in here." So the fact that they nonetheless hear voices is a paradox: most of them can only conclude that they suffer from some abnormality of the brain (albeit a harmless one)—they don't really think that someone "outside" is talking to them. But what if they lived in a world with a different, *enabling* sense of self, one in which people's minds in general were conceived to be semipermeable, open to the outside? Would not such an environment cause them to view themselves, and the voices that they hear, rather differently?

An investigation bearing on this question was undertaken in a recent study[28] that focused not on otherwise normal voice hearers, but on three sample groups of twenty adults each, all of whom "met the inclusion criteria of schizophrenia" and all of whom reported hearing voices. The three groups came from three very different locales and cultures: San Mateo, California, USA; Accra, Ghana; and Chennai, India.

In each group, interviewees were asked about a range of subjects, including their own impressions of voice hearing. "We asked people what they found most distressing about the voices, whether they had any positive experiences of voices and whether the voice spoke about sex or God. We asked what caused the voices and what caused their illness." The results were quite interesting.

> Broadly speaking the voice-hearing experience was similar in all three settings. Many of those interviewed reported good and bad voices; many

> reported conversations with their voices, and many reported whispering, hissing or voices they could not quite hear. In all settings there were people who reported that God had spoken to them and in all settings there were people who hated their voices and experienced them as an assault.
>
> Nevertheless, there were striking differences in the quality of the voice-hearing experience, and particularly in the quality of relationship with the speaker of the voice. Many participants in the Chennai and Accra samples insisted that their predominant or even only experience of the voices was positive — a report supported by chart review and clinical observation. Not one American did so. Many in the Chennai and Accra samples seemed to experience their voices as people: the voice was that of a human the participant knew, such as a brother or a neighbor, or a human-like spirit whom the participant also knew. These respondents seemed to have real human relationships with the voices — sometimes even when they did not like them. This was less typical of the San Mateo sample, whose reported experiences were markedly more violent, harsher and more hated.

Certainly these results would suggest that a society's "givens" have a lot to do with how voice hearing is interpreted, and even the extent to which a voice hearer is likely to identify himself/herself as the recipient of a divine communication.[29] A lot depends on the society in which the voice hearer lives. And this was as likely to be true in Jeremiah's time as in modern-day Chennai and Accra.[30] In other words, hearing voices in itself is probably not enough to make someone a prophet. In ancient Israel, there may have been dozens, or hundreds, of people who regularly heard voices — but this in itself probably did not mean that they were prophets; it all depended on what the voices were saying.

Prophets Outside the Bible

For some time, biblical scholars have turned to studies of prophecy in various non-Western societies for help in understanding prophecy in ancient Israel. One thing that these non-Western studies demonstrated was the utter commonness of prophets, shamans, miracle workers, and other sorts of divine intermediaries in African, Pacific Islander, Indian, Native American, and other societies; indeed, in many places, such divine intermediaries continue to exist and thrive (sometimes in tandem with modern medicine, modern technology, and modern terminology, all of which are otherwise identified with the modern West). In the light of these studies, it would seem that to remark on the *existence* of prophecy and related phenomena in these societies is, in the broad perspective, as trivial as remarking on the existence in them of marriage or burial rites, or ceremonies marking initiation into adulthood, or customs surrounding hunting and fishing. Prophet-like figures have always existed, and some continue to exist in numerous places around the globe. The acceptance of such intermediaries seems to have a lot to do with, first of all, the sense of self prevalent in a given society and, related to this, the society's own predisposition to legitimize prophecy as an institution.

Among biblical scholars, one pioneering study using these data was Robert R. Wilson's *Prophecy and Society in Ancient Israel* (1980), in which the author reviewed the anthropological evidence for various sorts of intermediaries across a broad range of modern societies along with what scholars know of prophecy in the ancient Near East outside of Israel; he then compared this material to what we know of prophecy from various biblical texts.[31] His work led to a number of further studies by Thomas Overholt, in particular the 1986 book, *Prophecy in Cross-Cultural Perspective,* and *Channels of Prophecy* (1989). Starting with the fieldwork of such early scholars as E. E. Evans-Pritchard and Franz Boas, Overholt followed Wilson in tracking numerous subsequent anthropological studies in a varied range of locales. Both scholars sought to highlight connections between biblical prophets and these nonbiblical figures.

An important subject for both Wilson and Overholt was the one evoked above, the crucial importance of the prophet's potential audience in his surrounding society in confirming and shaping his role as a prophet. As Wilson put it:

> Throughout our discussion of the creation of intermediaries [in African societies], we have referred to the role that society plays in the process . . . In addition to supplying the general social matrix that allows intermediaries to exist, societies also validate incipient intermediaries, provide guidance to aid their development, and ultimately support their vocation by believing in their powers.[32]

Overholt similarly asserted that prophecy always involves a "set of three actors — a supernatural entity, a prophet, and an audience — and a pattern of interrelationship among them."[33] This pattern, he argued, is more multidirectional than might first appear:

> The focus on interrelationships . . . calls for some enlargement of traditional notions concerning a prophet's authority. Because prophets, generally speaking, function as messengers of a god, viewing their revelatory experiences as the primary source of their authority seems justifiable. In all instances of which I am aware, a person who is actually functioning as a prophet is assumed to have been the recipient of some such communication. [While] these essentially private experiences form the theological justification for prophetic activity, inevitably, they are also culturally conditioned, because both the perception and later articulation of these experiences are affected by the prophets' social and historical context.

In other words, prophecy may start with a private revelation, but the role of its audience is crucial from the beginning: both the prophet's self-understanding as such, as well as his articulation of his "private" revelation to a public audience, depend on the society's own receptivity to prophets and the conventions surrounding the prophets' function. Moreover:

> Because the act of prophecy must necessarily take place in a social context, [the] reactions [of listeners] are critically important. Prophets seek to move their audiences to action, and audiences may be said to attribute authority to prophets, insofar as they acknowledge and are prepared to act upon the "truth" of their message. In their response, audiences in effect judge the acceptability of prophets . . .[34]

At this point, one might well ask why, given the important role of the prophet's audience in the whole process, Jeremiah was ever accepted as a true prophet. According to his book's portrait of him, Jeremiah's speeches were often met with great hostility. He was physically attacked by his fellow Judeans at various points in his life, put in the stocks (Jer 20:2), thrown into prison (32:2, 37:15), charged with treason (37:13), beaten (37:15), at one time dropped into a cistern and left to die (38:6), and otherwise generally mistreated. His listeners certainly did not seem to be "validating" what Jeremiah said or providing him with guidance of any kind.

But in a larger perspective, Wilson's and Overholt's descriptions of society's validating the prophet's role seem altogether accurate. Not only had Jeremiah apparently been recognized as a true prophet early on, but even those who eventually tried to silence him were, in the clearest terms, accepting his standing as a true divine spokesman — otherwise, why not dismiss him as a madman lacking any connection to Israel's God? This fact was dramatically illustrated in one famous incident, Jeremiah's speech at the gates of the Jerusalem temple (Jeremiah 7). There he told his listeners that, far from being a guarantee that God would not allow any enemy to enter Jerusalem, the temple itself could and would be destroyed, just as the old temple at Shiloh was, if they did not reform their ways. The reaction of the people was immediate:

> The priests and the prophets and all the people heard Jeremiah speaking these words in the temple of the LORD, and when Jeremiah had finished saying all the things that the LORD had told him to say to all the people, then the priests and prophets and all the people seized him and said, "You will die for this! Why have you prophesied in the name of the LORD, saying 'This temple will be like Shiloh, and this city will be destroyed, with no one living here'?" And all the people gathered around Jeremiah in the LORD's temple. (Jer 26:7–9)[35]

If they did not think that Jeremiah was indeed a true prophet, saying what he claimed God had told him to say would be of no weight.[36] Surely nowadays someone who claimed to have received a message from God might easily be dismissed as some sort of crank or the victim of mental illness; and just as surely, ancient Israel had its share of psychotic and schizophrenic voice hearers. Yet apparently, dismissing Jeremiah as one such person did not occur to anyone at the Jerusalem temple that day, nor in the days that followed. Why not? Clearly, people believed he was a true prophet, whether what came out of his mouth was a verbatim quote of God's speech or a poetic elaboration.

An Unhappy Man

Jeremiah was hardly indifferent to the hostility he encountered, and one of the unique things about the book of Jeremiah is its inclusion of passages in which the prophet reflects on his own frustrations:

> Is there anyone whom I can talk to — to warn them, so that they'll heed?
> But everyone's ears are stopped up, they're unable to take in my words.
> The word of the LORD has become: an embarrassment, which they don't need.
> But I'm full of the wrath of the LORD; I can't hold it inside any more.
> (Jer 6:10–11)

Particularly suggestive are those passages labeled as Jeremiah's "confessions" or "laments" (Jer 11:18–12.6, 15:10–21, 17:14–18, 18:18–23, and 20:7–18), in which he addresses God and bemoans his fate as a prophet *malgré lui*. These passages are much studied by scholars,[37] in part because they give us a glimpse (Jeremiah's and/or a later writer's) of what a prophet's mind and his innermost feelings might be. In this respect as well, Jeremiah's book is strikingly different from that of other prophets:

You know me, O LORD, so remember; think of me, grant me revenge—
on the people wishing me harm!
Don't lead me on with Your patience; look at the insults I've borne—
because of You!
When Your words first came I devoured them:[38] Your words were a joy,
a delight to my heart;
Your name was joined to mine, "the LORD God of Hosts."
I avoided the revelers' parties; my joy was Your hand placed upon me.
So I sat by myself, all alone, brimming with Your righteous anger.
Then why is it now I have unending pain, a wound that will never be healed?
Will it turn out that what You have been is a fountain whose waters have failed?
(Jer 15:15–18)[39]

Some scholars have asked (quite rightly, to my mind) why such thoughts would have been recorded at all; they only seem to cast doubt on Jeremiah's credentials as a true prophet. "I did everything You said," Jeremiah keeps saying, "I held up my end of the bargain." Yet God, apparently, has not. True, at first "Your hand was upon me" (apparently meaning: I was possessed by Your speaking to me), and this was a source of great joy, a living confirmation of his mission. But now, it seems that the voice has dried up, "a fountain whose waters have failed." Does this describe a prophet whose words are not confirmed by events—or even a prophet who can no longer hear God's voice? (And, on the positive side, does it not give us a glimpse of what it was like to be a prophet at his high point, when "Your words first came" and "Your hand [was] upon me"?)

Look at how they are saying, "So, where's the word of the LORD?
Let's see it come to pass!"
I haven't shied from [predicting] evil, an ill day I didn't wish for.[40]
You know the things that I said; they were spoken in Your very presence.

> Don't now become my downfall! You're my shelter in time of trouble.
> (Jer 17:15–18)

Once again, what Jeremiah has said would happen hasn't happened yet, and this has played right into his enemies' hands: "Let's see it come to pass!" they say mockingly. He protests that God knows exactly the words that Jeremiah spoke, adding, "I personally didn't wish for an ill day to come—I was just saying the things that You told me." Later, his tone becomes more accusing:

> You tricked me, O Lord, I was tricked; You led me on to defeat.
> Now I'm the butt of their jokes; all day long, everyone mocks me.
> Whenever I speak I get angry, "You thieves! You robbers!" I yell.
> Yes, "the word of the Lord came upon me"—for shame and dishonor all day.
> But if I say, "I'll stop talking—I won't speak His name anymore,"
> Then a fire burns deep in my heart, it rages inside my bones,
> And I'm too tired to hold it inside; I just can't. (Jer 20:7–9)

Here is Jeremiah at war with something deep inside, which, however, he says came to him from the Outside: "the Lord's wrath," "the word of the Lord." This capacity for something to pass from outside the prophet's mind to inside is, apparently, just a given. In one of his most revealing sentences, Jeremiah himself reflects on this divine prerogative: "The mind," he says, "is full of twists and very deep—who can know it? I, the Lord, probe the mind and inspect its inmost parts, to give each person his due, according to what he has done" (Jer 17:9–10).[41]

"What Do You See?"

One last facet of Jeremiah the prophet is worth mentioning, even in this brief survey. It was not always God's voice alone that led to his prophesying: sometimes the divine message was introduced by a vision of some sort, accompanied by the question "What do you see?"

> The word of the Lord came to me: "What do you see, Jeremiah?" and I said, "I see an almond branch (*shaqed*)." And the Lord said to me, "You have seen right, since I will make sure (*shoqed*) to carry out My word." (Jer 1:11–12)[42]

> Then the word of the LORD came to me a second time: "What do you see?" And I said, "I see a bubbling pot tipped away from the north." And the LORD said to me: "The evil will pour out from the north against all the land's inhabitants." (Jer 1:13–14)

> And the LORD said to me, "What do you see, Jeremiah?" And I said, "Figs. The good figs are very good, but the bad figs are so bad that they cannot be eaten." And the word of the LORD came to me: "Thus says the LORD, the God of Israel: Just as with these good figs, I will single out favorably the exiles of Judah whom I have sent off from this place to the land of the Chaldeans, and I will look after them . . . But as for those bad figs, so bad that they cannot be eaten, thus says the LORD: so will I treat King Zedekiah of Judah and his officials and the remnant of Jerusalem that is left in this land, along with those who are living in the land of Egypt, and I will make them a horror to all the kingdoms of the earth . . ." (Jer 24:3–9)

These instances are particularly interesting because the question that God asks, "What do you see?," seems to *presume* that the prophet is having some sort of vision, one that will then serve as an opening to God's spoken message, like the word *shaqed* or the image of the good and bad figs.[43] Incidentally, Jeremiah was not the first to be asked this sort of question, nor the first to get this sort of answer:

> This is what He showed me: He was standing on a wall [built] plumb, and He had a plumb line in His hand. And the LORD said to me, "What do you see, Amos?" And I said, "A plumb line." And my Lord said, "I hereby set a plumb line in the midst of My people Israel—I am through with pardoning them." (Amos 7:7–8)

> This is what my Lord GOD showed me: There was a basket of summer fruit (*qayiṣ*).[44] He said, "What do you see, Amos?" And I said, "A basket of summer fruit." And the LORD said: "The end (*qeṣ*) is coming to My people Israel; I will not pardon them again." (Amos 8:1–2)

What is striking about the things that prophets "see" is that their visions function in a way that is not very different from the visions of Hagar, Abraham, Jacob, and the others discussed above. As in those cases, so here too, what the person's eyes seem to be capturing *is not normal seeing*—it is that other kind of seeing, what was called earlier an "enabling vision," which then led to God speaking. His speech, while not actually auditory, turns out to be true; in the case of the prophets, God gives the prophet a message that He wishes to transmit to someone else.

In fact, such enabling visions are not an infrequent opening for the verbal message received by the prophet. Here, for example, is the prophet Isaiah's famous vision of God in His heavenly temple:

> In the year that King Uzziah died, I saw my Master sitting on a throne, high and lofty; and the hem of his robe filled the temple. Seraphs were perched above Him, and each had six wings: with two they covered their faces, with two they covered their feet, and with two they flew. And one called to another and said: "Holy, holy, holy is the LORD of hosts; the whole earth is full of His glory."
>
> The doorposts shook at the sound of the one who called, and the temple filled up with smoke. And I said: "Woe is me! I am lost, for I am a man of unclean lips, and I live among a people of unclean lips; yet my eyes have seen the King, the LORD of hosts!" Then one of the seraphs flew to me, holding a live coal that had been taken from the altar with a pair of tongs. The seraph touched my mouth with it and said: "Now that this has touched your lips, your guilt has departed and your sin is erased." Then I heard the voice of my Master saying, "Whom shall I send? Who will go for us?" And I said, "Here I am. Send me." (Isa 6:1–8)

This too is a vision; the passage certainly does not say that Isaiah has been physically transported to heaven to see God enthroned there.[45] Rather, what he sees has the same sort of enabling function glimpsed earlier. The vision transforms Isaiah into a worthy carrier of God's words and so leads into the auditory message, the divine speech that follows:[46]

> Then He said, "Go and say to this people:
> 'Listen, but don't comprehend; stare, but don't understand;
> Make the minds of this people dull, their ears undiscerning, and their eyes unable to see,
> Lest with eyes that can see and ears that can hear, their minds may indeed comprehend,
> and then they may turn and be healed.'"
> And I said, "Until when, my Master?" And He said: "Until towns are laid waste, with no one inside, houses empty of people, and farmland left to lie fallow.

> For the LORD will banish the people, and much land will be forfeit and lost."
> (Isa 6:9–12)

Similar enabling visions characterize the accounts of numerous prophets, right down to Zechariah, arguably the last of the canonical prophets (see Zech chapters 1–6).

One striking aspect of the divine question "What are you seeing?" deserves mention here. The fact that God is said to ask this question in the first place is significant, since it seems to presume that the prophet is indeed seeing *something,* and seeing not in the ordinary way, but in a prophetic vision. It is certainly remarkable that this sort of seeing functions in a way quite comparable to the visual hallucinations that preceded God's words in the stories of Hagar, Abraham and Sarah, Jacob, and the others. In other words, for all their differences, those Genesis narratives and these prophetic ones share the same basic scenario: first the person sees, or thinks he sees, something or someone, and this ultimately leads to direct address from God; then the thing seen — three strangers, a burning bush, or a basket of summer fruit — fades away; it was just a means to opening a channel of direct address from God. Of course, the fact of this shared scenario proves nothing in itself, but the common elements are nonetheless striking for their being unnecessary. There was no apparent need for a visual hallucination to precede God's words to any of His prophets, nor, for that matter, was there any need for the visionary encounters that Israel's ancient ancestors experienced just before God spoke to them. And yet, this seems to have been a common scenario for both groups. In this sense, Abraham might truly be said to be a prophet, as he was at one point (Gen 20:7); his visions, like those of Amos, Isaiah, Jeremiah, and later prophets, led into a verbal message sent from God.

The Unanswerable Question

What, in the end, do we really know about biblical prophets? They say they hear voices, and in the light of recent research, this claim seems altogether plausible: a lot of people do, even today. Of course, this does not mean that the voice they hear is of divine origin, and the very fact that diagnosed schizophrenics also claim to be in touch with God hardly strengthens the case.*[47] On the other hand, anthropologists report the existence of prophets

---

* Jeremiah and his fellow prophets were probably not schizophrenics, although they did do

and other sorts of intermediaries in a wide variety of societies; the very fact of their existence — and particularly in view of similar figures documented in Mesopotamian societies preceding or contemporary to biblical Israel — suggests that their existence in ancient Israel was unremarkable.

At the same time, we have seen that reported visions or voice hearing alone are apparently not enough to make someone a prophet. A lot depends on the preconceptions of the voice hearer's own society; prophecy seems to flourish where it is part of the cultural landscape, and the prophet's own self-understanding depends in large measure on his ongoing relationship with his society. Does this mean that Jeremiah and the others were playing on their countrymen's predispositions in order to present themselves as communicating with higher powers? Such a conclusion is not to be ruled out. But this hardly eliminates the opposite supposition. Perhaps it was his society's own assumptions — about the reality of prophecy itself, and along with this, the very sense of self that Jeremiah and his fellow citizens shared — that enabled him to hear a voice to which, in other circumstances, his ears might have been altogether deaf.

The biblicist Johannes Lindblom was cited earlier in connection with what he called a prophet's "revelatory state of mind," and his words are perhaps worth repeating in the present context:

> Typical of the revelatory state of mind is the feeling of being under an influence external to the self, a divine power, the consciousness of hearing words and seeing visions which do not come from the self, but from the invisible divine world, into which, in the moment of revelation, an entrance has been granted. This feeling of being subject to an external influence is perhaps the most constant element in the revelatory state of mind.[48]

This certainly sounds like Jeremiah — and not him alone. It may not have been his hearing of an actual voice, nor yet society's willingness to accept

---

some pretty strange things. On God's instructions Hosea married a prostitute (Hos 1:2), then named their daughter "Unloved" ("for I will no longer love the house of Israel"), while the son born after her was called "Not My People," in keeping with God's condemnation, "for you are not My people") (Hos 1:6–8). Somewhat more dramatically, on God's instructions Isaiah took off his clothes and sandals and walked around naked for the next three years (Isa 20:2–3); his contemporary, the prophet Micah, similarly stripped himself naked for an undisclosed period (Mic 1:8). God told Ezekiel to eat a scroll made out of parchment (Ezek 3:1–3), lie on his left side for 390 days, followed by 40 days on his right side (Ezek 4:5–6), shave his hair and beard (5:1–4) and perform all manner of other symbolic acts.

someone in the prepared niche of "prophet," that made Jeremiah a prophet. These were certainly necessary, but along with them came the particular sense of self described by Lindblom's "revelatory state of mind."

Ultimately, the answer to *the* question about biblical prophecy — was there any reality to it all? — depends on whether the questioner attributes any reality to an external God who can nonetheless enter a prophet's mind. Certainly if this is an illusion, then so is the basic premise of prophecy, and everything collapses. And the fact that some of the voice hearers mentioned above were indeed schizophrenics or sufferers of other mental disorders might indeed support such a conclusion — although there are also those sane voice hearers, who, we have seen, actually constitute a significant part (10 percent? 15 percent?) of even modern, Western populations. But perhaps, in considering what has been seen above, one might frame the question a bit differently. After all, whether sane or otherwise, voice hearing is something that *happens in the brain:* someone standing next to a voice hearer hears nothing, so we are not talking about a voice traveling on sound waves into the voice hearer's ear. Rather, whatever is happening in the brain is being *construed* by the brain as a voice — indeed, a voice speaking words. So the question is really: Is it construed out of nothing, or out of something?

Seeing Colors

Perhaps an analogy from a quite different area of neuroscience might frame the question with a bit more sophistication. According to the way we normally conceive of seeing, our eyes capture a picture of whatever is going on outside and then send that picture on to the inside, the brain, where it can be used. The crossing from outside to inside ought therefore to take place at the obvious border-point, the eyes themselves. But this is not at all how we really see: here, as elsewhere, the line separating outside from inside is a lot fuzzier than our own, modern self-image would have it.

To begin with, there's a lot of the outside that is truly "out there" but which we don't see at all, simply because it is beyond the normal range of human perception. The reason is that our eyes come equipped with receptors capable of processing only part of the larger electromagnetic spectrum. (Other species can "see" things we can't; for example, bees can detect some ultraviolet light, which helps them to locate nectar in flowers.) When we see, our eyes pick up only the light waves that they are designed to pick up — from sunlight or some other, artificial source, like a light bulb — as those waves are reflected off the objects around us. The different ranges of wavelengths are ultimately processed as colors: this is how our brains sort them out into usable information. But the colors aren't really "out there"; a brain is required to convert those different wavelengths into different colors.

Various species, including human beings, have evolved brains with this capacity, because it turns out to be a good way of making sense of those perceived wavelengths, using them to create a picture of the outside. Imagine if, instead of being processed as colors, the reflected light off of each object we perceive was represented by a little flashing sign that displayed the object's wavelength: we would see nothing but various shades of gray along with a lot of twinkling numbers telling us the wavelengths of what we were seeing. Surely, this would not be a very useful way of identifying the ear and part of the neck of a tiger otherwise hidden by some tall grass next to that tree! Colors allow us, quickly and effortlessly, to use information supplied by different wavelengths of light in order to sort out and identify everything in our visible range, an obvious help in every aspect of daily life. But those colors are generated *inside*, and they represent only one possible way of sorting out the reflected light. (Nowadays, we can program a computer to sort out wavelengths differently, so that, for example, what our eyes perceive as two indistinguishably close shades of black can be converted into, say, red and blue.)

How, then, does seeing happen? In the human retina, two kinds of photoreceptor cells, called rods and cones, react to the different wavelengths: the rods are especially active in low light, since they are far more sensitive to light overall than the cones; but it is the cones that are responsible for color perception. (There are actually three different types of cone cells in our retinas, each sensitive to a different range of wavelengths that are ultimately processed into what we see as colors — but as already implied, this happens at the end of a long series of steps.) The light's data thus pass from the eyes themselves to the optic nerve, and from there to the optic chiasm, at the base of the hypothalamus; there the information from both eyes is combined and eventually passed on to something else called the LGN (lateral geniculate nucleus), which in humans is a six-layered sensory relay nucleus that further processes and sorts the information until it is forwarded to the visual cortex, way at the back of the brain above the cerebellum. The visual cortex is actually the largest system in our brain and the one responsible for ultimately making sense of all the input deriving from the previous stages. In this sense, what we think we *see* is really a projection of what's going on deep inside the visual cortex onto something we like to think of as the outside. But what, more generally, truly is "out there"—and how different is it from what we perceive "in here"? Here is a matter of great theological import. The world *is* full of reflected light, but what turns it all into a lush, multicolored image?

8

THE BOOK OF PSALMS AND SPEAKING TO GOD

Psalms, then and now; God "just beyond the curtain" and the presumption of divine proximity; Neuroscience and the question of consciousness

This chapter may seem to reverse our subject, since it deals not with "God speaks to man," but with "Man speaks (or, rather, prays) to God," principally, but not exclusively, in the book of Psalms. But approaching the encounter between God and human beings from the opposite side will reveal something crucial (and usually overlooked) about the whole subject.

The book of Psalms has always been a favorite part of the Hebrew Bible. Of course the Pentateuch (Torah) was, for various reasons, read and studied from ancient times: it became, as we shall see, the focus of Judaism and, though to a lesser extent, of early Christianity as well. But the book of Psalms was turned to less in study than in loving devotion.[1] Traditionally attributed to the authorship of King David, the Psalms put into words what any worshiper might wish to say — to cry out for God's help; to express the cautious hope, but sometimes also the despair, that followed; to give thanks for all of God's blessings; most of all, perhaps, simply to address God in the Bible's own words, letting the Psalms' "I" become one's own — these are the things that have always made the book of Psalms a uniquely loved part of the Bible.

The Psalms of King David

As with many other parts of the Bible, modern biblical scholarship has changed perceptions about the Psalms.[2] Compositions that were, until the late nineteenth century, regarded as the "occasional [that is, inspired by a particular event or occasion], personal lyrics of King David" have come to be thought of by scholars as neither occasional, nor personal, nor the lyrics of King David. Instead, careful study has revealed that the Psalms were written by different hands over the course of many centuries. (To mention only the most obvious case of a relatively late psalm, the opening words of Ps 137, "By the rivers of Babylon, there we sat down and wept," clearly refer to the Babylonian exile, which took place some four centuries after the time of King David.) Moreover, while most of the Psalms were composed, or at least have reached us, in the "Jerusalem dialect" used in the Southern Kingdom (Judah), others are written in a different dialect, apparently native to the Northern Kingdom (Israel); some of these psalms also mention various sites located in the North.[3] This has led scholars to suppose that these psalms might have been associated with sanctuaries or "high places" at various Northern locales, perhaps brought to Jerusalem by priests fleeing the Assyrian conquest of the North in the eighth century.[4]

Then how did the tradition of Davidic authorship get started? About half of the canonical psalms in Hebrew have headings that refer to David, such as *mizmor ledavid,* a phrase usually translated as "a psalm of David."[5] This might seem (and after a while did seem) to attribute the psalm's authorship to David. But scholars know that this phrase could equally well mean "a psalm about David," "a psalm belonging to David," "a psalm belonging to the Davidic king [that is, one of David's dynastic descendants]," or—perhaps most likely—"a psalm belonging to the Davidic kings' collection of psalms." In short, the old idea of David as the author of the whole book of Psalms is no longer accepted by most modern scholars.

But if King David did not write most (or any) of them, who did? As the literature of Israel's neighboring states came to be deciphered and translated over the course of the nineteenth and early twentieth centuries, scholars began to compare Israel's psalms to those of ancient Egypt or Mesopotamia. They soon came to an obvious conclusion: just as these nations' hymnic compositions apparently had a role in public worship, so too did many of the Hebrew psalms. They seem to have been intended for recitation at one or another of Israel's ancient sanctuaries, either by a choir or an individual, and in either case presumably as a complement or accompaniment to the offering of sacrifices.[6] As we have seen, ancient Near Eastern sanctuaries were deemed to be the earthly residence of the deity. Scholars were therefore quick to notice that many of the biblical psalms refer explicitly to temples or other holy sites where sacrifices were offered to God:[7]

> But I, through Your abundant love, enter *Your house;* I bow down in awe at *Your holy temple.* (Ps 5:8*)

> Sing to the LORD, all those on earth; worship the LORD in joy; *enter into His presence* [i.e., at the sanctuary] with rejoicing. (100:1–2)

> With a freewill offering *I will sacrifice to You;* I will greatly praise Your name, O LORD. (54:8; some Bibles 54:6)

> Let me offer You a *sacrifice of thanksgiving,* and call on the name of the LORD.
> Let me pay off my vows to the LORD in the presence of all His people, in the courts of the *LORD's house,* in your very midst, O Jerusalem. (116:17–18)

> Bless the LORD, O you servants of the LORD, who stand *in the LORD's temple* by night. (134:1)

> I bow down to *Your holy temple* and give thanks to Your name. (138:2)

In short, the psalms appear to be, for the most part, liturgical compositions, written to be sung or recited in any one of various Israelite temples or holy places. They weren't David's "occasional, personal lyrics" at all; they were

---

* The numbering of verses in the Psalms sometimes differs among different translations; here, for example, the traditional Hebrew numbering (5:8) appears in the widely used New Revised Standard Version (NRSV) as 5:7: the reason is that the NRSV regularly does not count a psalm's heading as a separate verse. (Another modern translation, the New English Bible, omits the psalm headings altogether!) Throughout I have followed the traditional Hebrew numbering of verses. Note also that the numbering of the psalms themselves in the Old Greek Psalter (and modern versions based on it) is different from the traditional Hebrew numbering and, hence, differs as well from most modern Jewish and Protestant translations: in the Old Greek, Psalms 9 and 10 appear as a single Psalm 9. As a result, through most of the Psalter, the Old Greek numbering is one less than the Hebrew. The discrepancy disappears after Psalm 147, which appears in the Old Greek as two psalms, 146 and 147.

somebody's (or several somebodies') accompaniment to the offering of sacrifices.

As to the authors of these compositions, scholars have little to go on. Jerusalem court figures or officials, learned Levites (who otherwise served in sanctuaries), members of a guild of northern psalmists,[8] perhaps even some prophets[9]—whoever they were, these authors clearly do not share a single profile. Many of them in all probability had been *commissioned* to write what they wrote—to put together words of praise or thanksgiving to be uttered by or on behalf of the king, or to create some sort of national hymnal for festivals and other occasions. But the precise circumstances of their activity remain altogether unknown.

Another unknown is when the psalms were written. It used to be thought that psalms must have entered temple worship at a relatively late date, since there is no mention of psalms or hymns being part of the temple service as it was described (in painstaking detail) in the book of Leviticus. By contrast, temple singers *are* mentioned prominently in the books of 1 and 2 Chronicles, which most scholars date to sometime toward the middle of the Persian period (539–332 BCE). This suggested to scholars that the psalms were written sometime in the fifth century BCE or so, presumably too late to have been mentioned in Leviticus. But this whole approach to the question has now been abandoned. To begin with, the discovery of the cache of ancient Canaanite writings at Ugarit (the city was destroyed around 1180 BCE, so its writings must go back to before that date) has turned up parallels to elements in a number of biblical psalms.[10] Thus, dating the psalms as a whole to the Persian period seems most unlikely. If—to cite another argument—the language and syntax of various psalms suggest that they were originally written in northern Israel, this would imply that they were composed before the Assyrian conquest of the North in 722–721 BCE—again, a relatively early date.[11] On the other hand, Psalm 137 is clearly a look back at the Babylonian exile; it likely was written sometime in the late sixth or early fifth century BCE. Scholars suggest that the alphabetical acrostic Psalm 119, along with other acrostics as well as Psalm 1, which functions as an introduction to the Psalter, have been dated even later, perhaps as late as the fourth or third century BCE.[12] But this still leaves most of the Psalms undatable; commentators generally are content to label a psalm as "probably post-exilic" or "arguably pre-exilic" and leave it at that.

One thing that has struck scholars in this connection is the "one size fits all" character of a great many of the psalms.[13] For example, numerous compositions ask for God's help in fighting "the wicked," "my enemies," "my foes," and "those who rise against me," but they never get around to saying who those enemies are. Wouldn't specificity be desirable if one truly wanted God's help, or revenge? But the enemies are usually described in vague metaphors: they are "lions," "jackals," and "serpents," bloodthirsty hunters who have "set a trap for me" or "dug a pit." This seems to suggest that such psalms were intended to be used again and again by a variety of different speakers whose circumstances in some general way fit the words. On the other hand, the very fact that there are 150 psalms in our canonical book of Psalms—rather than just a single, formulaic sentence or two to fit any circumstance—has led scholars to suppose that in biblical times, officials at different temples and sacred sites must at least have been trying to give worshipers the impression of *some* specificity. "Let's see, you're making good on a vow?" a priest might say. "All right, repeat after me . . ." "Recovery from illness? Let the choir sing this hymn of thanksgiving on your behalf . . ."

Beyond compositions that were intended for individual worshipers, some of the psalms were clearly meant to mark communal festivals and other regularly occurring events. The three pilgrimage festivals, Passover, the Feast of Weeks, and the Feast of Booths, would especially have been marked by joyful singing. It may also have been the case that individual communities celebrated the (real or mythical) founding of their particular sanctuary with songs of praise. In addition, the book of Psalms also contains communal requests for help in imminent danger, as well as hymns of praise not connected with any particular occasion. And then there are other psalms that commentators find difficult to characterize, like the ever-popular Psalm 23 ("The Lord is my shepherd . . ."), which seems quite sui generis.[14] In sum, the book of Psalms is a collection (or more precisely, a collection of collections) written by different people and assembled from different sources and periods.[15] What can be learned from these disparate writings?

Cry of the Victim

The psalms that seem most relevant to the human encounter with God are the ones that request some form of divine help. These requests constitute a significant part of the biblical book of Psalms, and while they contain little concrete information about their authors or date of composition, they do offer one kind of testimony that is uniquely valuable. On the face of things, these psalms were all intended to be spoken by people in need. Whether composed by such people themselves or by temple personnel is immaterial:

their words are a cry for help, and the terms in which that cry is phrased can tell us a lot about how their speakers conceived of their interaction with God.[16] "Hear me," the psalmist says to God. "Here is what I am asking You to do."

Of course, for much of the biblical period Israel's God, YHWH, was one deity among many; "pure monotheism," the belief that there exists only one true God and that all others are simply an illusion, cannot be demonstrated to have existed in Israel before about the seventh century BCE. Prior to that time, some Israelites may have limited their worship to a single God, but probably without denying the existence of other deities (this is the phenomenon sometimes called *monolatry,* "serving One").[17] Others went further, worshiping YHWH along with other gods; indeed, we have already seen evidence of Northerners whose religion combined the worship of YHWH with that of Ba'al — the Be'alim against whose worship Hosea and other prophets intoned.

Thus, when the authors of the book of Psalms called out to God for help, they were addressing a specific God — for much of the biblical period, one among many. They turned to Him because He was *their* God (even if there were others), a deity associated specifically with the land in which they dwelled and the people of whom they were a part. He was naturally assumed to have a physical body, indeed, one rather human-sized and humanlike. To modern readers brought up on an omnipresent deity, this way of conceiving of things may seem to detract from the reality of God, but I suspect that if ancient Israelites ever heard of a bodiless, omnipresent deity (but of course they didn't), they would at first have been profoundly disturbed. How could one imagine a God without a body, a God who was everywhere at once? It would have been like praying to oxygen. Their God, by contrast, had a definite, identifiable presence: He was just over there, on the divine side of the divine-human divide, a powerful being who normally resided among those powerful ones who dwelt in heaven. (To be sure, God had an earthly presence as well; He could appear in His temple or temples. As was seen earlier, however, the presence of deities in multiple locations presented, for a very long time, no contradiction. They were here, but they also were elsewhere.)

Of course, an ordinary Israelite never saw God, and as far as he or she was concerned, this was all to the good. God's presence in Israel's midst was a bit like that of the government in a modern Middle Eastern state. You're glad that it exists and, to the extent possible, makes things run properly; but the last thing you want is to come individually to its attention, since this might have the most dire consequences in taxation or even personal life and liberty.

So too with Israel's God. It was comforting to know that His earthly home base was in your very midst, since that meant, or could mean, that He would fight to protect His lands (and you as well) from foreign invaders and other catastrophes. Moreover, as a God of justice and right, He would no doubt punish the wicked for their crimes and in general see to the orderly operation of at least those close to His home base. But you yourself normally had no interest in His taking notice of you as an individual.

The exception, of course, was when you as an individual desperately needed divine help — when you or your loved ones were gravely ill or otherwise in danger. Then, in contrast to the way such things were contemplated elsewhere in Scripture, ancient Israelites pulled out all the stops, describing their suffering in painful detail:

> My life's ebbing out like water, all my bones are coming apart;
> My heart is like wax, melting in my insides.
> My strength is as dried out as clay, and my tongue is stuck to my mouth;
> You're setting me down to lie in the dirt and the dust of the grave. (Ps 22:15–16)

> My wounds stink and fester, because of my folly.
> I'm bowed down and crooked, in darkness all day.
> My muscles ache with the fever; nothing's straight in my flesh.
> I'm numb and completely crushed down; I groan to my heart's inner crying. (38:5–8)

Ancient Israelites normally conceived of God as existing *elsewhere,* on the other side of the curtain that separated ordinary from extraordinary reality. (This was true even when He was held to inhabit this or that temple.)[18] From the other side of that curtain, He could hear human beings asking for divine aid, but He was not exactly on call: you could cry out, but He wouldn't always answer or do anything for you. Even bringing lavish offerings to His sanctuary wouldn't necessarily attract His attention.* What did often work, however, was "the cry of the victim."[19] God was by definition fair,[20] and nothing was conceived to spur Him to action more than the pitiful moan of someone who was suffering unjustly.

> Have mercy on me, LORD; I am in such pain! My eyes are wasting away with sorrow, my body and spirit too.

---

* Though it sometimes did; for example, Solomon's copious sacrifices in 1 Kings 3:4–5.

> My life is ending in pain, my years in groaning; in my misery my strength has left me; my bones are wasting away. (Ps 31:10–11)

Although these psalms of request are unique in their directness, the theme of the "cry of the victim" plays a role in a few biblical laws as well:

> If you should take your fellow's garment in pledge [for a loan], you must give it back to him before the sun sets. After all, it is his only clothing, all that he has to cover his bare skin—what else can he sleep in? Consequently, *if he cries out to Me,* I will hear him, for I am compassionate. (Exod 22:26–27)

Loans throughout most of the biblical period were basically a form of charity. A person was not to demand interest on a loan or to discount it (as the verse just preceding the above passage says): money had to be loaned to one's countryman for free—mostly to poor farmers who needed something to tide them over until the harvest. But what if the farmer couldn't pay even after his crop came in?

The usual practice in loaning money was to secure the loan with a pledged item: the borrower would temporarily give the lender some valued possession that would be returned to him only after the loan was repaid. But in the above passage, it is clear that the borrower is extremely poor: he has nothing to give in pledge, no prized family heirloom or bit of jewelry, only the shirt off his back. So that is what he offers. In such a case (similar to someone who gives a millstone in pledge, Deut 24:6) the lender is not to accept the pledged item, or at least he must return it before sunset, since keeping it would be grossly unfair.

What is striking, however, is the precise wording of this law. The text could have limited itself to pointing out the obvious: the borrower has offered the only thing he has to offer, his own garment. Clearly, he would not have done so if he were not desperately poor; as the passage says, he has nothing else to warm his body in the nighttime cold. This certainly ought to have been justification enough for requiring the lender to return the garment as soon as it was offered. "Give it back at once," the law could have concluded. But the passage mentions one further element, the cry of the victim: "Consequently, if he cries out to Me, I will listen to him, for I am compassionate." Other sorts of prayers and petitions were no doubt deemed to reach God, but it is the cry of those who suffer injustice or great pain that are said here to spur Him into action.

Similarly, another law in the book of Exodus states:

> Do not abuse any widow or orphan. Because if you should abuse them, then *they will certainly cry out to Me,* and I will just as certainly hear them. Then I will become angry and kill you at sword-point, so that *your* wives will become widows and your children orphans. (Exod 22:21–23)

Once again, it is not the simple facts of the case — the actual abusing of a widow or an orphan — that guarantee divine intervention.* God may or may not be aware of these abuses on His own, but it is the cry of these easily victimized members of society (widows and orphans were proverbially helpless) that will always trigger His intervention: "they will certainly cry out to Me, and I will just as certainly hear them."

Indeed, the cry of the victim is mentioned as the decisive element in various biblical narratives of the Israelites' exodus in Egypt:

> [God tells Moses:] I have indeed seen the suffering of My people who are in Egypt, and *I have heard their cry* at the hands of their taskmasters; indeed, I know their plight full well . . . But now listen! The *cry of the Israelites* is coming to Me; indeed, I have seen the misfortune that the Egyptians are inflicting upon them. (Exod 3:7–9)

> We cried out to the Lord and He heard us, and He sent an envoy to take us out of Egypt. (Num 20:16)

> We cried to the Lord, the God of our fathers, and He listened to us and saw our suffering, our plight, and our misfortune. (Deut 26:7)

So also with other piteous cries:

> When the poor are being robbed *and the needy cry out,* "Now I will act," says the Lord. "I will come to the rescue and help." (Ps 12:6)

> When they cried out, the Lord heard and saved them from all their troubles. (Ps 34:18)

---

* In fact, it is noteworthy that neither of these laws is stated in a neutral formulation, such as "If a person should do such-and-such to another person . . ." Rather, they are addressed to the potential victimizer, as if God were somehow closer to him than to the victim: "Under normal circumstances," God is saying, "I'd like to help you out, but if I hear the cry of the victim, I'll have no choice but to intervene."

Here then is one important thing to be learned from these psalms of request: God is thought to react to the prayers and cries of human beings who are suffering (rather than reacting to the injustice itself, or to the oppressors' bad behavior). This is as much as to say that prayer had an acknowledged role in the divine machinery by which God managed the world; *in extremis* people prayed to God for help, and it was their cry that (sometimes) moved God to act.[21]

A Cold and Impersonal Deity

Would it be possible for someone to believe in a God who doesn't hear people's prayers? It certainly would. One has only to look back at the story of Joseph to see a deity who is not prayed to (the hero, Joseph, never asks God for help, not even in the direst of straits). Instead, the God of this narrative is, as we have seen, the great long-range planner who has everything plotted out in advance. In such an arrangement, prayer by definition can have no role, since nothing can change what has already been decided.

Somewhat similarly, scholars have noticed that those sections of the Pentateuch found among the priestly instructions ("P") present a strikingly different picture of God from that underlying the Psalms.[22] In these P passages — which actually constitute a hefty part of the Pentateuch as a whole — God seems to be an altogether cold and impersonal deity. He never speaks to humans in the first person, "I will do this" or "I have ordered that," not even to Moses. Apparently, to do so would imply a closeness, and a personhood, that these passages sought to avoid. So similarly, God here does not forgive; instead, these parts of the Pentateuch say about penitent sinners that "it will be forgiven to them." Perhaps most strikingly, people never pray to God in these passages. Clearly, the priesthood was deeply implicated in whatever went on in the temple (or the tabernacle that preceded it during Israel's wanderings in the wilderness) — what sorts of sacrifices were offered to God, the layout of the tabernacle/temple, the laws of ritual purity, and so forth. But there is not a word about the psalms of request that we have been examining, even though some of them seem explicitly connected to worship in the temple. In fact, the whole idea of humans praying in the temple or outside of it is basically absent. What counted, apparently, were the sacrificial offerings that people brought to the temple; words of any kind were just words.

Against this background, the passages from the Psalms cited above take on a greater significance. They present a vivid picture of human beings who pray to God in the hope, one might even say in the expectation, that their words are not uttered in vain: somehow, God will, or at least may, hear them. As the Joseph story and these P passages demonstrate, a belief in the efficacy of prayer is not a necessary element in a theistic religion; one can certainly believe in God without imagining that He attends to, or even hears, people's prayers. And yet people do believe this, not only in the book of Psalms, but in later Judaism and Christianity and Islam — in fact, as scholars have documented, people in the most disparate parts of the globe are known to pray to various deities, not only in ancient times, but in all periods up to and including the present day.[23] This may seem an obvious point about human behavior, but in the long view, it is nonetheless striking.

The Great King

If this first point seems obvious, the second is even more so — but still worth stating. The basic situation in these psalms of request is always the same: a meek and humble supplicant[24] calls out to God, who has all the power. He is the great king,[25] and this very idea deserves a further word of explanation. Nowadays we tend to think of the conditions in which we live as ever-changing, the product of interacting forces that operate on both the personal and worldwide stage. With regard to the latter, for example, those shifting forces (the world economy, the alignment of various military powers, the existence of persistent "trouble spots," and so forth) are conceived to combine — sometimes quite irrationally — to bring about war or peace, prosperity or famine, a brilliant future or an outlook of the darkest gloom. In the ancient Near East, things were simpler; everything that happened was deemed to be generated from the top down, starting with God/the gods who, like an earthly king, sat enthroned at the very apex of the power pyramid and controlled all that happened below.[26]

In the book of Psalms, God is thus explicitly the King, ruler of the world (see in particular Pss 29, 47, 93–99, 145). He is addressed as "O King!" (20:10, 98:6, 145:1), "my King" (5:3, 44:5, 68:25, 74:12, 84:4), and "our King" (47:7, 89:19) and is also explicitly referred to as the "eternal King" (10:16, 29:10, cf. 145:13, 146:10), "King of the earth" (47:3, 8), "the glorious King" (24:7, 8, 9, 10), and so forth, before whom earthly kings tremble in fear and acknowledge as their master (102:16, 138:4, 148:11). One adjective closely associated with this picture is the word "great." God is frequently praised with the Hebrew term *gadol* (Pss 47:3, 48:2, 76:2, 77:14, 86:10, 95:3, 96:4, 99:2–3, 135:5, 138:5, 145:3,

147:5), which, like its common English equivalent, can mean great in degree or quality (that is, important, outstanding, and the like) or simply *big*, great in size or reach or power:

> Great is the Lord, and much to be praised; His greatness is beyond measure. (Ps 145:3)

It is probably impossible to sort out which of these meanings is intended in this or most of the Psalms' assertions that God is *gadol*, since they are all closely connected, but together with "king," "great" suggests suggests the gap that separates the little supplicant from the divine addressee.

Yet, despite the overwhelming power of the divine king, the supplicants in these psalms are *not* overwhelmed, and this very fact seems to belong to the theme of the "cry of the victim" examined above. In other circumstances, he or she might be a polite, reserved human being, but coming before God in the psalms of request, the supplicant is axiomatically desperate. People who are starving or fleeing an assailant are never polite. They need help right away. So too — whatever the particulars of the individual speaker's needs — the psalmist is never bashful about addressing God in the imperative and *demanding* relief, sometimes implying along the way that He is actually a rather sluggish deity:

> Rise up, Lord! Lift up Your hand! Don't forget the downtrodden!
> How can the wicked man scorn God, supposing that You won't react?
> But You have seen! You've observed the trouble, the grief;
> You have the power to help the helpless; surely You should aid an orphan. (Ps 10:12–14)

> How long, O Lord? Or will You just forget me forever? How long will You hide Your face from me?
> How long will I ache in my soul and keep suffering in my heart all day?
> How long will my enemy be exalted over me? (Ps 13:2–3)

> I am crying out to You, Lord. O my Rock, don't keep silent toward me,
> because if You hold back from me, I'll be as good as dead. (Ps 28:1–2)

> How long, my Lord, will You just look on? Save me from their ravages,
> [save] my life from those lions!

> Don't let my lying enemies rejoice over my fate. [Don't let] those who have no reason to hate me wink their eye . . .
> You have seen, O Lord, don't sit still; my Lord, do not stay far from me! Wake up! Get up and take my side, my God and Master of my case. (Ps 35:17–23)

Sound Times Distance

In addition to the role of the victim's cry and the theme of God's kingship and greatness throughout the Bible, a third aspect of biblical prayers is to be mentioned here. While many of the psalms of request seem to have been specifically crafted for recitation in a temple or sanctuary, God's earthly home, other passages seem to suggest that human cries for help can be uttered from anywhere; they will reach God no matter what. Clearly, this undercuts the very idea of physically going to a special sanctuary to seek help. A few biblical texts thus seem to suggest a compromise solution: while presence in God's own sanctuary is indeed the ideal place from which to pray for God's help, prayers from elsewhere will somehow reach the sanctuary and be heard by God Himself:[27]

> In my distress I cry out to the Lord, appealing to my God;
> In His temple He hears my voice, my cry to Him reaches His ears. (Ps 18:7)

In fact, prayers are sometimes said to travel great distances. God promises to hear the prayers of Israel's scattered exiles coming to him "from there," faraway Babylon or other places of their exile (Deut 4:29). Jonah is said to have cried out to God from the belly of a "great fish," and his prayer seems to have reached Him (Jonah 2:2, 11). The account of Solomon's inauguration of the Jerusalem temple is quite explicit about the temple's role: God is in any case in heaven, but the temple will act as a kind of launching pad from which people's words may ascend to God's attention (1 Kings 8:32, 34, 42–43, etc.).*

---

* A heavenly God would of course have easy access to the words of humans down below, since sound was conceived to travel upward. Thus God says, "The outcry of Sodom and Gomorrah is so great! . . . I will go down and see if they have gone astray, as their cry *that has reached Me* [indicates]" (Gen 18:21–22). In the Babylonian *Atra-ḫasīs* epic, the gods resolve to destroy the world because the noise that the humans below are making is so great, and it reaches the gods so clearly in heaven that it is preventing them from sleeping (frag 1, col 1, 2–8).

Strikingly, however, Solomon's speech also asserts that merely praying *in the direction* of the temple will have the same effect as being inside it:

> [Solomon says:] May Your eyes be open day and night toward this house, the place of which You said, "My name shall be there," so that You may heed the prayer that Your servant prays *toward this place.* Then, when You hear the supplications of Your servant, or of Your people Israel as they pray *toward this place,* heed [them] in Your heavenly dwelling-place; heed and forgive . . .
>
> Any prayer or supplication that is from any individual or from all Your people Israel, each of whom knows his own afflictions, when they stretch out their hands *toward this house,* then hear in Your heavenly dwelling-place . . .
>
> Or if a foreigner, who is not of Your people Israel, comes from a distant land . . . and *prays toward this house,* then may You hear in heaven, Your dwelling-place, and do according to all that the foreigner cries out to You . . .
>
> If Your people go out to battle against their enemy, wherever You may send them, and they pray to the LORD *via the city* that You have chosen and *the house* that I have built for Your name, then may You hear in heaven their prayer and their plea, and take up their cause. (1 Kings 8:29–30, 38–39, 41–43, 44–45)

In this view of things, geography didn't count for much: prayers will axiomatically be heard from wherever they are uttered, and distance was no barrier. In later times Daniel, a resident of Babylon, "had had windows made in his upper chamber facing toward Jerusalem, and three times a day he knelt down, prayed, and made confession to his God" (Dan 6:11).

A related belief is attested in the story of Hannah (1 Sam 1). Hannah is, to her great distress, childless, and on one occasion she goes to the great temple at Shiloh to seek God's help:

> The priest Eli was sitting on a seat near the doorpost of the temple of the LORD. In the bitterness of her heart, she prayed to the LORD and wept. She made a vow and said: "O LORD of Hosts, if You take note of Your maidservant's distress, and if You keep me in mind and do not neglect Your maidservant and grant Your maidservant a male offspring, I will give him to the LORD for all the days of his life; and no razor shall ever touch his head."*

* This was the distinctive mark of the Nazirite, who was vowed to God (see Num 6:5).

> Now as she was speaking her prayer before the LORD, Eli was watching her mouth. Hannah was praying in her heart [i.e., silently]; her lips were moving, but her voice could not be heard, so Eli thought she was drunk. Eli said to her: "How long are you going to keep up this drunkenness? Cut out the boozing!" But Hannah answered: "Oh no, sir, I am a woman of saddened spirit. I have drunk no wine or strong drink, but I have been pouring out my heart to the LORD. Don't take your maidservant for an ill-behaved woman! I have been praying this long because of my great distress." Eli answered her: "Then go in peace, and may the God of Israel grant you what you have asked of Him." (1 Sam 1:9–17)

If Eli couldn't hear her, how did Hannah ever expect God to hear her? But she did. Somehow, even though no sound was coming out of her mouth, she apparently believed that God would hear her vow and, she hoped, act accordingly. (Which He did; "at the turn of the year she bore a son," 1 Sam 1:20.) This too seemed to defy the laws of physics, just as much as Jonah's prayer from the belly of the fish, or any prayer uttered at some distance from God's presumed locale, a temple or other sacred spot.

Many other things could be said about the Psalms, or about biblical prayers in general, but the foregoing three points have been chosen for what they imply for the overall theme of this book. We have already seen a great deal of evidence indicating that people in biblical times believed the mind to be semipermeable, capable of being infiltrated from the outside. This is attested not only in the biblical narratives examined earlier, but it is the very premise on which all of Israel's prophetic corpus stands. The semipermeable mind is prominent in the Psalms as well; in a telling phrase, God is repeatedly said to penetrate people's "kidneys and heart" (Pss 7:10, 26:2, 139:13; also Jer 11:20, 17:10, 20:12), entering these messy internal organs[28] where thoughts were believed to dwell and reading — as if from a book — all of people's hidden ideas and intentions. God just enters and looks around:

> You have examined my heart, visited [me] at night;
> You have tested me and found no wickedness; my mouth has not transgressed.
> (Ps 17:3)

> Examine me, O LORD, and test me; try my kidneys and my heart. (26:2)

Indeed God is so close that inside and outside are sometimes fused:

> Let me bless the LORD who has given me counsel; my kidneys have been instructing me at night.
> I keep the LORD before me at all times, just at my right hand, so I will not stumble. (Ps 16:7–8)

(Who's giving this person advice, an external God or an internal organ?)

Such is God's passage into a person's semipermeable mind. But the flip side of all this is prayer, when a person's words, devised on the inside, in the human mind, leave his or her lips in order to reach — somehow — God on the outside. As we have seen, those words were indeed believed to make their way to God; in fact, it was the cry of the victim that in some sense made the world *work,* causing God to notice and take up the cause of justice and right. Now, the God who did so was also, we have seen, a mighty King, who presumably ranged over all of heaven and earth:

> He mounted on a cherub and flew off, gliding on the wings of the wind. (Ps 18:11)

> He makes the clouds His chariot, He goes about on the wings of the wind. (Ps 104:3)

Yet somehow, no matter where His travels might take Him, God is also *right there,* just on the other side of the curtain that separates ordinary from extraordinary reality, allowing Him to hear the sometimes geographically distant cry of the victim or even to hear an inaudible, silent prayer like Hannah's. The doctrine of divine omnipresence was still centuries away and was in fact implicitly denied in many biblical texts,[29] yet something akin to omnipresence seems to be implied in God's ability to hear and answer prayers uttered from anywhere, no matter where He is. In fact, this seems implied as well in the impatient, recurrent question seen above, "How long, O LORD?"; the psalmist seems to be saying, "I *know* You've heard me, so when will You answer?"

Perhaps the most striking thing suggested by all this is the extent to which the Psalms' depiction of God seems to conform to the general contours of the great Outside as described in an earlier chapter. God is huge and powerful, but also all-enfolding and, hence, just a whisper away. Somehow, people in biblical times seem to have just *assumed* that God, on the other side of that curtain, could hear their prayers, no matter where they were. All this again suggests a sense of self quite different from our own — a self that could not only be permeated by a great, external God, but whose thoughts and prayers could float outward and reach a God who was somehow never far, His domain beginning precisely where the humans' left off.

One might thus say that, in this and in other ways, the psalmists' underlying assumptions constitute a kind of biblical translation of a basic way of perceiving that had started many, many millennia earlier, a rephrasing of that fundamental reality in the particular terms of the religion of Israel. That other, primeval sense of reality and this later, more specific version of it found in these psalms present the same basic outline, which is ultimately a way of fitting into the world: the little human (more specifically in the Psalms, the little supplicant) faced with a huge enfolding Outside (in the Psalms, the mighty King) who overshadows everything and has all the power: sometimes kind and sometimes cruel (in the Psalms, sometimes heeding one's request, but at other times oddly inattentive or sluggish), the Outside is so close as to move in and out of the little human (in the Psalms as elsewhere, penetrating a person's insides, but also, able to pick up the supplicant's request no matter where or how uttered).[30]

Mysterians

Thinking about the very idea of prayer — and how, as was just suggested, its roots may go back to earlier centuries of human consciousness — ultimately leads us to the most basic question of all that scholars in various disciplines ask about the sense of self (whether the ancient or modern one): Where does the picture of ourselves that we carry around in our heads come from? Is our "I" — the "I" that, among other things, prays to God — something that really exists? *Of course it does!* we think. But neuroscientists who study the matter are not so sure.

All human minds, despite their differences, do seem to share certain things. We all have a sense that we are alive; in fact (as mentioned previously), we all feel that we continue to be the same person over time.[31] What is more, we do not identify ourselves as *being* our brains or our bodies; somehow we think of ourselves as the owners of those brains and bodies — our "I" seems to be some sort of being distinct from these body parts. But is there any physical evidence of its existence? Or is it just what the British philosopher Gilbert Ryle derisively called the "ghost in the machine"? The neuroscientist Patricia Churchland has posed the problem in these terms:

> I think I am *something*, yet my self is not anything that I can actually observe —at least not in the way I can observe pains or fatigue or my hands or my heart. So if my self is not something I can observe, what is it? If the "self" is a mental construction—a mode of thinking about my experiences—what are the properties of this construction, and where does this construction come from?[32]

This is the great problem of thinking about the self and its peculiar way of perceiving things. Neuroscientists have studied individual brain functions and know how many of them work: over recent decades they have mapped different areas of the brain and identified their functions with sometimes surprising precision.[33] But putting this information together has not led to the discovery of anything resembling the human sense of self; what scholars have investigated about the brain's functioning can be fully described without recourse to its postulated owner, the person himself/herself. In short, science doesn't need any "I." But apparently we do.

Philosophers have long debated this conundrum, known as the "mind-body" problem, and its ramifications sharply divide today's researchers. Some hold that our "I" will eventually be explained, located somewhere in the brain's own complicated, overlapping circuitry, while others hold that our mind is necessarily an ultimately unknowable entity.[34] Why is this important to our present subject? We have seen that the basic premise of the book of Psalms is that God is "out there" and, among other things, hears the desperate cries of human beings. It is certainly possible that this is a piece of mental baggage left over from the great Outside and the dawn of human consciousness. But how are we to judge it when we know so little about the other half of this interaction, the "I" who is asking this question? This "I's" very existence may *itself* be the product of a slowly evolved combination of different systems of neurons and synapses, systems that came together to create the illusory world that is human consciousness—an entity no less potentially mythical than the Supreme Being, but one that has persisted simply because it has served to keep us going as a species.[35]

Scholars today are quite divided on our ability to find an answer to the problem of consciousness. Some are rather optimistic about finding a purely physical solution, searching for its components in different brain systems;[36] others (sometimes called *mysterians*) maintain that the question is, for one reason or another, unsolvable;[37] yet others say that "consciousness" is an impossibly vague term that must be broken down into its components, some (or possibly all) of which can be explained in terms of neural systems.[38] Who's right?

Trapped in Our Humanity

Part of the problem is that we humans are not exactly objective observers. We all seem to have a particularly human sort of consciousness, but this may not be the only kind of consciousness around. It certainly might be possible that other sorts of creatures — a man from Mars, for example, or even some undeniably conscious beings who already exist right here on earth — have a form of consciousness that we can never fathom, precisely because our consciousness *is* so human and thus incapable of entering into another sort of consciousness entirely different from our own.[39]

The philosopher Thomas Nagel has posed the problem in a provocative essay entitled "What's It Like to Be a Bat?"[40] Consciousness, he asserts, is what makes the mind-body problem inevitably intractable. If someone were to ask, "What's it like to be a rock?" the answer would be quite straightforward. It's not *like* being anything, because — at least as far as we can guess — a rock doesn't perceive its own existence or anything else, which is to say, it has no consciousness. But could one say the same for a fellow mammal of ours, say, a bat? Surely bats have brains; they perceive the outside world, find food, mate, nurse their young, and do many of the other things that mammals do. It seems likely that, given all this, bats are in some sense aware of their own existing (as perhaps are dogs and lions and pigeons and all sorts of other creatures).[41] But are human beings capable of understanding what it's like to be a bat? Bats are not reading this book, and the minute you begin to attribute to bats your own mental processes, you're not talking about real bats. They do have brains, but what goes on in them is clearly very different from what goes on in ours. Among other things, bats' nighttime vision is very different from ours; they perceive the outside world by issuing high-pitched little shrieks and then "seeing" their surroundings (or seeing as much of their surroundings as is important to them) by a process called echolocation, gauging the distances embodied in the echoes of those shrieks as they come back to the bats' ears. They are different from us in other ways too: they spend the daylight hours sleeping, hanging upside down from the branches of trees or other perches. Is there any significant way in which we can be said to know what their existence is *like?* Nagel argued that our consciousness inevitably has a subjective character: we don't just experience things, but we experience them in a certain, human way. We can generally understand the character of each other's experiencing precisely because we are all humans.[42] But we really have no access to an objective account of consciousness, if such a thing can even be said to exist.

Homo Orans

All this suggests that we may know a lot less than we think about what happens when humans turn to God in their prayers. By this I do not mean what happens *to people,* whether their pulse rates go up or down, or if various areas on a brain scan suddenly light up or go dark.[43] Rather, I am speaking about the reality of this interaction as our human consciousness perceives it, and the certainty that our consciousness is as subjective in this respect as in all others. Perhaps an *objective* consciousness, or a Martian's consciousness, would reveal this interaction with God (and God Himself) to be as different from what is really taking place as our colorful picture of a sunny afternoon is different from what we now know about those different wavelengths being reflected off objects and our brain's step-by-step transformation of them into colors. We certainly know that all sorts of humans, equipped with very different senses of self, have prayed in the past to all manner of divinities, and that millions, nay billions, of people also pray now. In this sense, our species might well be called—modern naysayers notwithstanding—*Homo orans* (the praying human). But what is implied about the reality underlying this praying, and who the praying "I" truly is, seem to be matters likely to remain unfathomable for some time.[44]

PART III

Transformations

Thus far we have seen some of the ways in which humans encountered God in biblical times. The texts themselves seem to describe these as real events: there is a real God "out there" who, on this or that occasion, somehow crossed over into our world to speak with patriarchs and prophets. All this suggests that these biblical accounts presume a different sense of self from ours today. God could penetrate the minds of human beings and cause them to see or hear things in a way that we no longer can.

But not all biblical texts presume the same sort of human self. Alongside Abraham's encounters with God are Joseph's non-encounters. Indeed, sometimes we can see how a particular practice or institution changed within the biblical period. Old ways of encountering God turned into new ways, or sometimes ceased to be encounters at all.

9

TO MONOTHEISM . . . AND BEYOND

Monotheism and monolatry; The quest for one God; Divine omnipresence?

We have seen that God is depicted in Scripture in various ways, but for later generations, His enduring depiction was that of the Supreme Being, the one true God in the world. Biblical scholars know that this depiction is accurate only to a certain extent. Not only is this representation not how He was first understood, but it is also not, on closer inspection, a very accurate reflection of the God of later times.

As everyone knows, biblical Israel's great gift to the world was monotheism, the belief that there exists only one God and that all other gods are simply an illusion, a mistake. As of today, there are an estimated 2.18 billion Christians and 1.7 billion Muslims, all of whom profess to believe in one God alone. As "daughter" religions of ancient Israel and the teaching of its reputed spiritual leaders, Abraham and Moses in particular, these nearly 4 billion people — more than one out of every two people on earth — all owe this central tenet to a tiny nation that once inhabited a small strip of territory on the eastern Mediterranean, a people whose population probably never went beyond that of a medium-sized modern city, that is, 2 or 3 million souls at the most. Quite an achievement!

No Other Gods

There is little agreement, however, as to when, why, and under what circumstances Israel came to this belief. To some, the answer seems obvious. Did not

God order Israel to be monotheists in the Ten Commandments promulgated at Mount Sinai?

> You shall have no other gods beside Me.* You shall not make any statue or representation of what is in the skies above or on the earth beneath or in the waters under the earth — you shall not bow down to these or worship them, since I, the Lord your God, am a particularly zealous deity, one who punishes children for the sins of their fathers, in fact, up to the third or fourth generations of those who reject Me, while showing kindness to the thousands of those who love Me and keep My commandments. (Exod 20:3–6)

For many centuries the first sentence above was indeed taken to mean something like "there are no other gods except Me." But scholars know that this isn't quite what the words are saying. To begin with, the Hebrew phrase *'al-panai* doesn't mean "except for Me." This phrase generally has a spatial sense; it means "in front of Me" or "in My presence," and it is really this that God is outlawing in the Ten Commandments. "You can't worship Me and some other deity in the same sanctuary," or perhaps more generally (although even this is a bit of a stretch), "You can't worship Me and also worship some other god or gods," in a sanctuary or anywhere else. Apparently in connection with this,[1] God goes on to forbid worshiping statues or likenesses, since that form of worship was indeed common to other gods, but apparently not to Him.[2]

In any event, this commandment is *not* saying what it has often been taken to say, that there is only one true God in the world, the God whose name in Hebrew letters is YHWH.** If that were its intention, the text could have easily, and far more clearly, said, "You are to have no other gods besides Me, because *I am the only God* — thinking that there are any other gods is just stupid!" What God is really saying — that He does not permit people

---

* This is considered to be the first of the Ten Commandments by most Christians, but the second commandment according to traditional Jewish interpreters, the first being the previous sentence, "I am your God, the Lord, who brought you out of the land of Egypt, the place of [your] servitude." This is interpreted by Jews as a requirement to believe in God's existence and intervention in human history. The second commandment, according to Jewish interpreters, consists of what Christians generally hold to be the first and second, namely, the prohibition of worshiping any other god and the prohibition of worshiping a sculpted image.

** As already mentioned, Jews at an early stage ceased pronouncing this name, substituting for it "my Lord." As a result no one knows for sure which vowels originally joined these consonant sounds together. YHWH is the usual transcription of the four Hebrew consonants, and the all-capitals Lord is their usual rendition in English Bibles.

to worship Him along with any other god—seems to be an endorsement of what scholars call *monolatry*, worshiping one deity principally or exclusively while not denying the existence or efficacy of other deities. To this demand God adds a none-too-subtle warning: "I, the LORD your God, am a particularly zealous deity," punishing not only the sinner himself but his or her descendants, down to the fourth generation. God's declaration that He is an *el qanna* (a zealous deity) thus has the ring of a concession, "Okay, I *am* an unusually demanding deity," He says, since He is asking of His worshipers something that most gods would never think of requiring: exclusive loyalty.

Elijah at Mount Carmel

Monolatry is a pretty good description of what the Bible presents as God's demand for most of the biblical period: "Worship Me exclusively, and let other people worship their own gods." This falls short of monotheism, strictly speaking. Certainly Abraham,[3] Isaac, and Jacob nowhere proclaim that theirs is the one, true God; moreover, as we have just seen, the Ten Commandments don't do so either. A bit later, in the ninth century BCE, the prophet Elijah is represented as rebuking the people for not giving their exclusive loyalty to the God YHWH: pure monotheism is not even on the table. In fact, all Elijah demands is that people stop "hopping from one branch to another" like birds, sometimes worshiping YHWH and sometimes Ba'al. He wants King Ahab, and all his Israelite subjects, to come out unambiguously in favor of YHWH as *their* deity, but even this was apparently asking too much of the king. In fact, their encounter is quite revealing:

> When Ahab caught sight of Elijah, Ahab said to him, "Is that you, you trouble-maker of Israel?" He answered, "I'm not the one who's troubling Israel—it's you and your family; you're the ones who have disobeyed the LORD's commandments and followed the *Be'alim.* Now therefore have all Israel come together for me at Mount Carmel, with the four hundred and fifty prophets of Ba'al and the four hundred prophets of Asherah, who eat at the table of Jezebel [Ahab's wife]."
>
> So Ahab sent orders to all the Israelites, and assembled the prophets [of Ba'al] at Mount Carmel. Then Elijah came up to all the people and said, "How long will you keep hopping from one branch to another? If the LORD

> [that is, YHWH] is God, follow him; but if it's Ba'al, then go and follow him." But the people did not answer him a word. (1 Kgs 18:17–21)

What ensues is a theological contest between Elijah and the prophets of Ba'al. Each side is to prepare an altar along with a sacrificial bull as an offering. But of course, an animal sacrifice has to be burned, so each side is further required to call upon its deity to send down the fire from heaven. The god who does so will be the winner.

At first, this test must have seemed rigged. As we have seen, Ba'al was the storm god who rode the rain clouds and thereby fertilized the arid farmlands of Canaan. The "fire" that was to come down from heaven was obviously a bolt of lightning, Ba'al's trademark; clearly, he should win this contest. But according to this biblical account, he didn't. Ba'al's prophets certainly tried; they danced around the altar and gyrated and cried aloud—all to no avail. They also slashed their bodies with swords and lances "until the blood gushed out over them," but this too was of no use. Meanwhile Elijah watched from the sidelines, occasionally mocking their efforts, until late in the afternoon. Then, finally, he went into action:

> At the time of the offering of the [afternoon] sacrifice, the prophet Elijah came near and said, "O Lord, God of Abraham, Isaac, and Israel, let it be known this day that You are God in Israel, that I am your servant, and that I have done all these things at your bidding. Answer me, O Lord, answer me, so that this people may know that You, O Lord, are God, and that You have turned their hearts back."
>
> Then the fire of the Lord came down and consumed the sacrifice, the wood, the stones, and the dust, and even licked up the water that was in the trench [around the altar]. When all the people saw it, they fell on their faces and said, "The Lord is indeed God; the Lord is indeed God." (1 Kgs 18:36–39)

It is hard to know how to take this last sentence. No one, I think, really doubted that YHWH was *a* god. The issue at hand was rather if He was the only god worthy of worship by the people of Israel, or if, on the contrary, the worship of Ba'al could coexist with His. In the first sentence of the paragraph cited above, Elijah asks of God that this test prove that "You are God *in Israel,*" apparently without denying that other peoples might perfectly well worship Ba'al. In light of this, even the closing affirmation, "the Lord is indeed God," seems intended to assert that God is the deity of this land and its people, the only god that Israel should worship.

A century later, the prophet Hosea was, as we have seen, still trying to get the Northerners to stop worshiping Ba'al, but without any notable success. Many of Israel's later prophets similarly denounced the worship of "foreign" gods; they too seemed to be aiming at a single-minded devotion to Israel's God without necessarily denying the efficacy of placing an offering to Ba'al or Asherah on their altars. Apparently, professing monotheism only became a requirement in Israel at some later point. But when, and why, did this happen?[4]

To answer this question, it is necessary to reconsider monolatry itself, which, in the larger perspective, must appear to be a rather strange form of worship. After all, if Ba'al was the go-to god for rain, why would anyone limit his or her worship to another God, YHWH, especially since His original specialty seems to have been warfare, not precipitation?[5] (It was precisely this that must have made monolatry a particularly hard sell for Elijah, Hosea, and others to transmit to a skeptical Israelite public.) Why should anyone espouse monolatry—and how did the whole idea get started?

Various explanations have been proposed. Perhaps limiting Israel's worship to a single deity was necessary to distinguish the Israelites from their Canaanite neighbors—worshipers of El, Ba'al, Asherah, and other deities—especially if, as some scholars have proposed, some of those Canaanite neighbors ended up constituting a good part of early Israel's population.[6] Indeed, aspects of both El and Ba'al seem to have preceded and played a role in the characterization of Israel's God—in a sense, they *merged* into YHWH.[7] Monolatry would thus be a kind of line in the sand, a way of saying, "our God of Israel had nothing to do with the Canaanites and their religion." A bit later on, the need for political unification may have also worked in favor of monolatry. David's mighty empire was, in the view of many scholars, cobbled together from disparate peoples or "tribes," some of them having been persuaded to join with David under threat, if not at actual sword-point. (This rambunctious federation lasted scarcely two generations before breaking apart into northern and southern halves, Israel and Judah, but even the composition of these two entities was more likely based on coalitions of convenience than on tribal groupings of longstanding.) Under these circumstances, devotion to a single God, YHWH, may also have served as the religious glue binding Israel and Judah, first jointly and then severally.[8]

The Anxiety of Multiplicity

All this may be so, but there is another aspect of monolatry that may have played a crucial role — and which in any case is, from the standpoint of the present study, the most interesting phenomenon connected to it. To understand this side of monolatry, we must move from the mundane domain of politics to the realm of the divine, since this is, after all, what monolatry is all about.

In the human heart, something there is that loves the One. Perhaps it had always been so.[9] No one knows who the first deity was, or if such a deity started off alone or as part of a whole group of divine beings, a company that might have included deified ancestors, all the wandering stars of heaven, plus marauding evil spirits and goblins and sprites, the inhabitants of this sacred tree or that stone. But it is not hard to imagine that the very first *personification* of what had previously been the great, undifferentiated Outside was barely even that: some sort of lone divine *being* who could be thought of as such, a usually hidden, human-like causer of all things whose cause was unknown. Whether or not this is so (and of course we shall never know), the fact is that — at least with regard to the ancient Near East — scholars have demonstrated that any sharp differentiation between a primordial polytheism and a much later monotheism is not altogether descriptive of what really existed.[10] Here and there, in ancient Egypt,[11] Assyria,[12] Greece,[13] and elsewhere, "the gods" often had a way of sliding into "the god," the One whose shimmering unity encompassed all the manifestations of specific deities and their personal domains and functions.

The very existence of a pantheon, in which a given society's various divinities are considered to make up an established collectivity, also bears witness to a certain hesitation between the One and the many. A collectivity obviously bespeaks a polytheistic inclusiveness; but a pantheon usually also features one supreme deity, whose existence makes (or once made) possible the collective functioning of the other gods and goddesses. In theory, of course, conceiving of such a divine company was not logically necessary: indeed, the phenomena to which its gods and goddesses were connected — a fruitful harvest, success on the battlefield, human fertility, various heavenly bodies — did not *seem* to be working in any coordinated fashion. If not, then wasn't the existence of a supreme deity ruling over the others a kind of quest for unity in the midst of diversity, for the One over all the others?[14] It is striking, in any case, that in the Semitic lands, specific deities named El, Il, Ilu, Elohim, Allah — all derived from the basic word for "god" — seem to head (or to have headed) the pantheon, as if to say that this "generic" deity, who lords it over all those other ones beneath him, is somehow the very essence of divinity. Noteworthy as well is the pedigree and distribution of a similarly generic "god" name in the Indo-European world, beginning with the hypothetical proto-Indo-European deity Dyeus, as in Sanskrit *Dyàuṣpítaḥ* (the *pítaḥ* part means "father"), whose form is paralleled in Latin *Jupiter;* meanwhile the same root is reflected in the Greek *Zeus,* Latin *deus,* "god," Germanic *Tues*day, and perhaps even Greek *eudia,* "fair weather" (presumably, for sailing the Aegean).[15]

At Ugarit, a council of gods held sway; it was known as the "assembly of the gods" or "assembly of *El,*" who headed it. Strikingly, the same phrase occurs in Psalm 82, which relates how Israel's God long ago dissolved this assembly and took over as the reigning One:[16]

> God stands in the divine assembly, He rules among the gods.
> "How long will you [gods] judge falsely, showing favor to the guilty party?
> Give justice to the poor, the orphan; find in favor of the needy, the wretched.
> Rescue the poor and the lowly, save them from the wicked."
> (But they* did not know or understand, walking about in darkness; the earth's foundations tottered.)
> "I used to think that you all were gods, sons of the Almighty;
> and yet you will die like humans, and fall like the falling stars."
> Arise, O God, rule over the earth, since all the nations are Yours.

Here is a scenario designed to explain how the many became the One; it all came about because the lesser gods were not doing their job, specifically, not joining together in the fair administration of justice. As a result, the very foundations on which the earth rests were in danger of collapse. So God condemned his former subalterns to oblivion and took over all their previous functions for Himself. (But these "previous functions," as we shall see shortly, presented a sharp challenge to any such deity.)

True Monotheism, But . . .

So when, finally, can one speak of *pure* monotheism in Israel? A number of biblical passages that scholars date to the sixth and later centuries BCE are

---

* That is, the other gods.

frequently cited as evidence of Israel's espousal of monotheism in its purest form, for example:

> So you shall realize today and keep ever in mind that the LORD is God in the heavens above and on the earth below: *there is no other.* (Deut 4:39)

> I am the first and I am the last, and *there is no God but Me.* (Isa 44:6)

> I am the LORD and there is no other; there are *no gods save for Me.* (Isa 45:5)

All this seems quite unambiguous: there is only one God, ours. Nevertheless, passages just adjacent to these seem to endorse the idea that other, lesser divinities do exist:

> And when you look up at the sky and see the sun and the moon and the stars and the whole host [i.e., army] of heaven, do not be led astray into bowing down before them and worshiping them. These the LORD your God has assigned to all the [other] peoples under the heavens, but the LORD took you and brought you out of Egypt—that iron smelting pot!—to be His own people, as [you are] this day. (Deut 4:19–20)

The "whole army of heaven" had, from time immemorial, been considered to be gods. Thus the sun, the moon, and the stars were, as we have seen, identified with various Babylonian and Assyrian deities. In the above passage, God is said to have arranged for other peoples to worship these heavenly bodies. Was He just tricking them? Rather, it would seem that these heavenly bodies are indeed real beings with real powers, something like demigods or "godlings." As such, they were put in charge of the other peoples, and it is altogether legitimate for these other peoples to worship them. But God adopted Israel as His own people (this is basically a restatement of Deut 32:8–9), as demonstrated by His intervention in the exodus from Egypt. So it is wrong *for Israel* to worship those lesser deities; they should worship God directly. Similarly:[17]

> Lift up your eyes on high and look! Who created these [heavenly bodies]?
> He [God] summons their hosts [i.e., armies] by [a specific] number, He calls all of them by name,
> Because of His great strength and power, not one of them fails to appear.
> (Isa. 40:26)

Here too, those heavenly bodies are real, active beings. God is of course their superior, indeed, He created them, so that they are utterly submissive to His power; but they are nonetheless heavenly beings. This may be a kind of monotheism, but it is not one that denies the category of divinity to all but one God.

It was not easy to deny that those heavenly bodies, however inferior to God they might be, were nonetheless something like minor deities. After all, the sun goes across the sky day after day. In an era when machines were not yet dreamt of, it must have seemed obvious that the sun had some sort of animate being inside it or behind it who was driving it through its daily course. So the most one could say was that God had ordered the sun's driver to do what he does — but this hardly negated his existence as a heavenly power in his own right. The same was true of the moon and its nightly waxing and waning, as well as of the planets and stars, whose sometimes irregular movements through the sky had long been studied. Sure, God was in charge, but these other powers were nonetheless undeniably up there, lesser divine beings who obeyed His orders.

Another argument in favor of the existence of multiple, albeit lesser, deities was simply the matter of efficiency. If there was only one God — who, as we have seen, was deemed to have a body very much like our own — how could He do absolutely everything at the same time? He had not only to move all those heavenly bodies through the sky (in different directions), but also to cause the rain to fall or not to fall (or to fall here and at the same time fall there, hundreds of miles away); indeed, the one true God had to run everything on land and sea, control rivers and streams, forests and deserts and all their animal inhabitants, and in addition to all this, observe the actions of human beings, each and every one of them at the same time, so as to be able to punish the guilty and reward the virtuous? It was fine to say that God *did* see everything, as some late biblical texts maintained:

> These seven [branches of a lampstand represent] the eyes of the Lord, which range throughout the whole earth. (Zech 4:10)

> The eyes of the Lord range throughout the whole earth, to strengthen those whose heart is true to Him. (2 Chron 16:9)

But in practice this was hard to imagine. How could one God have anything resembling our own, physical eyes and still be looking at everything all the time and all at once?

God's Helpers

One obvious answer was to imagine that God really didn't do all this personally, but that He delegated the responsibility to others. He might be the only true deity, but He could nonetheless have created invisible helpers — angels or spirits — who would faithfully carry out His orders. So it was that the late biblical period saw the emergence of a cadre of independent angels, the first angels to have names, such as Gabriel (Dan 8:16), Michael (Dan 12:1), Raphael (Tobit 12:15), and a host of others (for some bad angels, see, for example, those named in *1 Enoch* 6).[18] On reflection, however, this again is not far from polytheism. By the common understanding, angels were themselves divine creatures. But then, what was the difference between a monotheistic God ordering His angels to do this or that and a polytheistic El ordering various lesser deities to take on their regular tasks?[19]

The existence of such semi-independent, heavenly operators might also answer what was a fundamental problem with the whole idea of monotheism. A verse in the book of Isaiah posed the problem succinctly, describing a God who "forms light and creates of darkness, who makes well-being and creates evil — I, the LORD, make all of these" (Isa 45:7). This is monotheism at its most severe: everything bad that you can think of, the bubonic plague, devastating earthquakes, and famine-induced mass starvation, as well as humanity behaving at its most sadistic, murderous worst — all these, God says, come from Me alone. (Indeed, this same verse's evocation of light and darkness is certainly not irrelevant. Whatever a world that consisted solely of light might be like, it is nothing like our world; the mixture of light and dark is the essence of our existence "down here." So too with well-being and evil.)

Yet how can one conceive of such a God as "good," or even as "ours"? If He is responsible for everything, indiscriminately alternating the bad with the good, He might as well just be a personification of randomness, Lady Luck, or the "way of the world." There must be some other way of understanding reality. Zoroastrianism is often credited with the creation of the first theological dualism, whereby two divine beings, one good and one evil, are locked in eternal combat — a conception that is said to have influenced later Judaism and Christianity.[20] Indeed, the demonic "spirits" sent out by Satan in the *Testaments of the Twelve Patriarchs* may be one reflection of this belief. But whether God's opponent was a single divine being (known eventually as Satan, but also called by other names in late biblical times: Satanel, Gadreel, Beliar, Sammael, and others)[21] or consisted of an entire army of evil spirits (as in such Second Temple period Jewish books as *1 Enoch* and *Jubilees*),[22] the result was the same: good and evil both came from heaven, but from different divine beings. So in various ways, what was identified above as Isaiah's "severe" monotheism was in practice modified by the theoretical presence of other heavenly causers, the makers of evil who might ultimately (and repeatedly) be defeated by God, but not before causing a lot of human misery. So this, too, brings us back to an only slightly disguised form of polytheism. In theory, God was in charge of everything, including good and bad angels. But how different was this from saying that He was the head of a polytheistic pantheon?

Considering all of the foregoing, it would seem that Israelite monotheism per se was really not such an innovation after all. The hesitation between the One and the many had existed long before Israel itself existed, and while some biblical texts proclaim Israel's God to be the only true God, those same texts assert in the same breath that other gods were created to take care of all nations other than Israel. Then, in the late biblical period, there appeared a profusion of angels who sometimes seem to be semi-autonomous agents, actors with a will of their own; in fact, some of them are downright evil, like Satan and his army of evil spirits, found in such late texts as *1 Enoch, Jubilees*, and the *Testaments of the Twelve Patriarchs*. The existence of independent angels came so close to polytheism in this period that still later texts are at pains to say that no, they really are not independent at all, but were doing exactly what God tells them to do, "obedient," "tireless" in performing their various tasks, and "never deviating from the path which He commanded them."[23] All this attests to what might rightly be called the weakening of biblical monotheism—and just at the very moment when, as a slogan, "one God alone" was being championed by Jews and Christians in the strongest terms.

A Physical Body

Monotheism had two sides to it. The first, the idea that a single God is responsible for everything in the world, was contradicted by the very existence of those lesser divine creatures, the good and wicked angels who, as we have just seen, accompanied monotheism in all but its purest form, a form rarely espoused in practice. In this sense, there really wasn't any difference between monotheism and monolatry; in fact, not much difference between monotheism and polytheism.

But monotheism's other aspect was indeed significant and ultimately, over the course of centuries, helped lead to a most significant change in the whole way humans came to perceive God. This change did not have to do with God's singleness as such, but with a different way in which human beings gradually came to conceive of His actual being. (In fact, "conceive" does not tell the whole story. It was not only that people began to think about Him in a new way; they eventually report that they came to perceive Him, *encounter* Him, in a whole new register.) This all-important change had to do with a subject already discussed in passing, the fact that a great many biblical texts seem to presume that God had a physical existence, an actual body.

As we have seen, some parts of the Bible depict God's body as not much bigger than an ordinary human's. God "walked about" in the Garden of Eden (Gen 3:8), spoke with Moses and others "face to face" (Exod 33:11, cf. Deut 34:10, Jdg 6:22) and even "mouth to mouth" (Num 12:8). In fact, God's physical body was, according to some texts, altogether visible, so that *seeing* God, even if it was not something that happened every day, was sometimes presented as the hallmark of any true encounter with Him. Thus, Moses worries that people won't believe he truly encountered God, which meant *seeing* Him: "But suppose they don't believe me or pay me mind, but say: 'The LORD did not *appear** to you'" (Exod 4:1). Perhaps for the same reason, other biblical figures take care to assert that they actually did see God. Jacob tells his son Joseph, "God Almighty *appeared to me* at Luz, in the land of Canaan, and He blessed me" (Gen 48:3). On Mount Sinai, Moses, Aaron, and others "saw the God of Israel . . . they beheld God, and they ate and drank [to seal their covenant with Him]," Exod 24:10–11). "I saw the LORD standing next to the altar," Amos recounts (9:1). For a time at least, encountering God meant, or could mean, actually seeing Him, and He apparently had a body that was basically the same size as that of a human being.

Of course, it is hard to know what this *seeing* meant. Was it some sort of vision or waking dream, such as those described above in chapter 1? Was *seeing* sometimes used as a sort of metaphor or shorthand for "truly encountering the presence of God"? This may have been the case with a God presumed to reside in one or more sanctuaries or temples. Thus, the psalmist asks, "When will I enter [the Temple] and see the face of God?" (Ps 42:3). This may mean merely, "When will I get to the place where God resides and truly be in His presence?" Similarly, God decrees in the book of Exodus, "Three times a year, all your males will see the face of the lord, YHWH" (Exod 23:17), that

* In Hebrew, this phrase is literally "was not seen by you."

is, be in His actual presence.* But however it was understood (and probably it was understood differently in different contexts), seeing God was for some time the hallmark of a true encounter.

Along with such statements, however, others suggest that seeing God's body was profoundly dangerous. "Woe is me, I am lost," says Isaiah, "for my own eyes have beheld the King, the LORD of Hosts" (6:5). Manoah says to his wife, "We will surely die, because we have seen God" (Judg 13:22). At Mount Sinai, God "went down in a cloud," where He "stood with him [Moses]" and then "passed in front of him" (Exod 34:5–6). Presumably, God's human-sized body ought to have been altogether visible, but if He "went down in a cloud" in this passage, it seems that the cloud was there to protect Moses from actually catching sight of Him. Later, Moses's appearance was physically affected (perhaps disfigured) by speaking with God (Exod 34:29–35).[24] On another occasion, Moses's ability to actually see God's face became the subject of a respectful disagreement between the two.[25] Moses asks to see God outright, but God turns him down:

> [God said:] "You cannot see My face, since no one can see Me and live." [Moses accepts this news with a stony silence.] But then the LORD said, "Look, over there is a place near Me; stand up on that rock, and while My being** passes by, I will put you in the cleft of that rock and shield you with My hand until I have passed by. Then I will take My hand away, so that you can see Me from behind, but My face will not be visible. (Exod 33:20–23)

In other words — and despite all that was said above — this text says that while you can't see God face-to-face, the greatest of prophets, Moses, came as close as anyone could: he caught a glimpse of God from behind.

With time, however, even this attenuated sort of seeing disappeared. Ezekiel begins his book by saying that "In the thirtieth year, on the fifth day of the fourth month . . . the heavens opened and I saw *the appearance*[26] of God" (1:1). Isn't the "appearance of God" a kind of undercutting reservation? Continuing on, the prophet says he beheld the "semblance of a throne."

---

* In these last two examples, the pronunciation of the verb has apparently been altered by ancient scribes, so that "see the face of God" became "be seen [before] the face of God," and "all your males will see" became "all your males *will be seen*" — in both cases because of what was later a scandalous idea, seeing God.

** Hebrew *kabod* is used to designate God's physical being; sometimes this word is translated as God's "presence" or "glory."

> And above this semblance of the throne was the semblance of the appearance of Someone upon it . . . Like the appearance of the rainbow in the cloud[s] on a rainy day, such was the appearance of the radiance all around. This was the appearance of the semblance of the LORD's substance, and when I saw it, I fell on my face. (Ezek 1:26–28)

Whatever else may be learned from this passage, the profusion of "semblances" and "appearances" seems to be stressing that this was really not seeing God's body directly, not even from behind or below.[27]

When Moses recounts the events at Mount Sinai in the book of Deuteronomy, he stresses what the Exodus account did not, that at the great revelation at Sinai the Israelites actually *saw* nothing:

> You [Israelites] came near and stood at the foot of the mountain, and the mountain was burning bright to the very midst of heaven—darkness, cloud, and deep shadow. And the LORD spoke to you from the midst of the fire. You heard the sound of words *but you saw no shape—nothing but a voice.* (Deut 4:11–12)

> From the heavens He caused you [the people of Israel] to hear His voice, in order to discipline you.* On earth He made you see *His great fire*; and from the midst of that fire you heard His words. (Deut 4:36)

God was in heaven. He called down to the Israelites and they could hear His voice, and when they came closer they could also see a great fire burning on top of the mountain. The fire appears to have been some sort of earthly outpost from which God's words were heard, but the Israelites did not *see* anything of God Himself during this whole revelation.

The Still, Small Voice

Ultimately, *all* biblical texts are the product of scribes and scribal culture,[28] and they come down to us through chains of editors and rewriters, so it is often difficult to attach a particular passage to even an approximate date. With this word of caution, however, it is worth considering what is certainly one

---

* This act of hearing was "in order to discipline you" because it was painful, designed to "put the fear of Him upon you, so that you not sin" (Exod 20:20).

important landmark that belongs somewhere in the gradual change we are tracing. It comes in an encounter with God that took place just after a scene examined above, when the prophet Elijah challenged the prophets of Ba'al on Mount Carmel. Immediately after, the Bible relates that Elijah was threatened with death by Ba'al's champion, Queen Jezebel (1 Kgs 19:1–2), so the prophet wisely fled southward to Horeb/Sinai, where he went into a cave to spend the night. The next day, God ordered Elijah to come out:

> He [God] said, "Go out and stand on the mountain before the LORD, for the LORD is about to pass by." Then a great strong wind split the mountains and shattered the crags before the LORD, but the LORD was not in the wind. After the wind—a shaking [or "earthquake"], but the LORD was not in the shaking. After the shaking—a fire, but the LORD was not in the fire. And after the fire: the *sound of the thinnest stillness.* When Elijah heard it, he covered his face in his cloak and went out and stood at the entrance of the cave. Then there came a voice to him that said, "What are you doing here, Elijah?" (1 Kgs 19:11–13)

The oxymoron translated above as "the sound of the thinnest silence" was rendered in the King James Version of the Bible as "a still, small voice," and as such it has enjoyed a rich afterlife in the English language. Endless sermons have been preached about it, usually taking the phrase to refer to a person's own inner promptings, "the voice of conscience." A nice thought, but this doesn't fit the context at all. Rather, scholars connect this narrative to the previous encounter between Elijah and the prophets of Ba'al. Ba'al, after all, is the god of storm clouds and the fertilizing rain that they bring—in short, a god connected with natural phenomena such as those that characterize other nature deities the world over, gods of fertility and the harvest and of the great natural cycles that they control. But this biblical narrative is at pains to assert the very opposite, that the LORD, YHWH, does not inhabit these natural manifestations of divine power. The wind passes by, but He is not in the wind; the earth rumbles as if an earthquake is taking place, but God is not in the rumbling either, nor in the fire that appears next (perhaps intended to mean lightning). And interestingly, Elijah is not fooled by any of these outward manifestations of divine power. It is only when he hears this sound-that-is-barely-a-sound that Elijah knows that the LORD has come, and he covers his face and comes out of the cave; then God begins to address him.

We are probably still far from those explicit professions of monotheism seen earlier, "There is no God but Me" and the like. Nevertheless, a certain trend is observable in the different sorts of divine encounters described so far: from a God with a human-sized body that can be seen, to one whose body can be seen only obliquely, glimpsed from behind; to one who cannot be seen at all, but only heard,* apparently because God resides in far-off heaven; along with a God whose voice is not the booming, almost unbearably loud sound that accompanies natural phenomena like thunder and earthquakes, but something altogether *un*-natural, a sound so thin it can hardly be heard at all (but this, our last passage seems to be saying, is what the voice of God really sounds like — it is not *in* natural phenomena, but separate from them).

It should be said again that this apparent trend is in no sense a straight-line progression. The history of divine encounters as reported in the Bible is not one step forward and then the next, but includes lateral jumps, idiosyncratic depictions that become traditional for a time, followed by later imitations and slight modifications, then fresh starts and various subsequent resumptions and reiterations. It would not be wrong to think of all these biblical representations as *models,* perhaps comparable to those of modern-day scientists in their attempts to explain the invisible in terms of things seen, leading to the arcane world of string theory and the like.** In biblical Israel too, there were different models, different ways of depicting what truly occurred by trying to connect the world of the senses with what is merely sensed.

To continue this search for the proper model: the God in the first chapter of Genesis is also a disembodied voice (similar in this respect to the God at Sinai as described in Deuteronomy). He issues commands that are mysteriously carried out. "Let there be light," He says, and then "there was light." Who made the light? We are not told. Its creation seems to have just been ordered into existence, and the result is subsequently inspected by God Himself, who, the Bible reports, "was pleased,"[29] as if observing from the sidelines. The same pattern is repeated for the rest of creation, the earth and the sky, the sun and the moon and stars, and so forth — God is never depicted,

* Rather like the angel narratives examined in chapter 1, wherein God appears as an ordinary human being, until the appearance evaporates and God begins to speak true words to the human being(s) involved.

** In another way, such attempts might be compared to contemporary physicists' pursuit of the "Theory of Everything," namely, the attempt to unify the three nongravitational basic forces of particle physics — weak, strong, and electromagnetic forces — with the role of gravitational force as the basis of the theory of general relativity. The overall goal, thus far not achieved, is to arrive at a single explanation that will account for all four.

never has a body, but just speaks, after which things happen. This description would fit to some extent with the deity who inhabits the priestly sanctuary described above (that is, the desert tabernacle or *mishkan,* and the Jerusalem temple that followed in its wake). God is said to "meet with" select human beings inside this sanctuary; in fact, He is inside the closed-off Holy of Holies within the sanctuary, in the special place where He is said to "dwell" —namely, above the wings of the cherubim stretched out above the Holy Ark. This flimsy perch does not seem suited to any sort of real body;[30] once again, God's presence seems to consist of some sort of disembodied voice, a spiritual presence that has no physical manifestation. His being exists in, or perhaps as, an empty space.

The Three Omni's

These conflicting models for representing God's being are all to be found in the Hebrew Bible. But for all their differences, a definite process of abstraction is observable. If monolatry or monotheism was a cause of this process or its result is hard to say. But one thing is clear: the national deity of a tiny people settled in the highlands of Canaan might quite conceivably appear in the form of a man-sized divine being who has just stepped over from the other side of the curtain. But a deity who rules over entire nations and peoples (even with the help of underlings) could hardly be thought to exist in a body the size of an ordinary human being. He must be as huge as the book of Isaiah says, His throne itself consisting of the whole sky, and for whom the whole earth is just a convenient footstool (Isa 66:1).[31] And after all,

> Who has measured the oceans in the hollow of his hand [as God has], or marked off the skies with a yardstick?
> Or put the earth's soil in his bushel, weighed the mountains on a hand-scale and the hills in a balance? . . .
> The nations themselves are [to Him] a drop from the bucket, they weigh as much as the dust on a scale. (Isa 40:12, 15)

Could such a huge being even be said to have a body at all?

What happened next, the thing that was to be the most important development in the human encounter with God for later centuries and centuries, may have been anticipated within the Hebrew Bible, but it was not stated explicitly until the period just following the biblical period. God came to be characterized by the three omni's: omnipotent, omniscient, and omnipresent, that is, all-powerful, all-knowing, and existing everywhere all at once. This understanding had the most profound effect on Judaism and Christianity.

Of the three omni's, one was really not much of an innovation at all: divine omnipotence. After all, this is how Israel's God is consistently presented in the Bible, even if, in strictly literal terms, He is never actually defined as omnipotent. Nowhere in the Bible is God ever overcome by any other deity or even engaged in any theomachy,[32] a conflict of deities such as is found in Greek, Babylonian, and Egyptian mythologies.[33] Despite what some scholars have identified as the recrudescence of ancient mythological motifs in the Bible,[34] such as the identification of *tehom* ("abyss" in Gen 1:2) with the Mesopotamian sea monster Tiamat, or the crossing of the Red Sea evoking the divine conflict with the sea god Canaanite Yamm, there is nothing that challenges God's position in the Bible as more powerful than any other divinity. He is simply "greater than all the other gods" (Exod 18:11); He "does whatever He wishes, in heaven and on earth" (Ps 135:6, 115:3). Even when human armies appear to defeat Israel, these defeats are no defeat of God, but rather manifestations of God's use of foreign nations to punish His people. Those foreign armies are the "stick of His wrath" (Isa 10:5), which once used can be thrown away. The "problem of the stone"* may have troubled medieval philosophers, but such questions had no role in divine omnipotence in biblical times.

But the other two omni's are a somewhat different case. To begin with, divine omniscience and omnipresence are potentially related. A deity who is everywhere all at once also knows, thanks to his omnipresence, everything that is going on every minute of the day. (This may not be the most ethereal definition of omniscience, but it does cover at least most of what early post-biblical sources might have meant by the term.) As mentioned, neither of these omni's is stated as such in the Hebrew Bible. There is no assertion that God is omniscient, nor that He is everywhere always, without interruption.[35] True, a passage in Psalm 139 is sometimes used as evidence of the latter:

---

* If God is all-powerful, then can He create a rock so huge that He Himself cannot pick it up? (If yes, then there is something that God cannot pick up, which means He is not all-powerful; if no, then there is something that God cannot create, so He is not all-powerful.)

> If I could go up to the sky, there You would be; or down to Sheol, You are there as well.
> If I took up the wings of a gull to settle at the far end of the sea,
> Even there Your hand would be leading me on, holding me in its grip.
> (Ps 139:8–9)

This may be read as omnipresence, but it seems to be more an answer to the question just preceding it, "Where can I go from Your spirit, or how can I get away from You?" (verse 7). In other words, try as I may to escape from You, You somehow manage to be there, no matter how far I travel. True, in this and other verses in the same psalm, the psalmist attests to the feeling of God's overbearing presence. Yet he never quite says what he easily could have, "Where can I go from Your spirit, since You are everywhere?" Divine omnipresence is not yet a general principle. And indeed, numerous earlier biblical texts had explicitly presented God as *not* omnipresent. Likewise, God is never described in the Hebrew Bible as omniscient. He can penetrate people's insides to discover their secret thoughts, but this is different from saying He automatically knows everything at all times.

Little by little, however, the presumption that God is both everywhere and all-knowing began to be articulated as such,[36] since if God is everywhere, then He obviously sees everything that is going on. In *1 Enoch*, an apocryphal work whose earliest parts go back to the third or fourth century BCE, the angels say to God "You see all things, and there is nothing that can be hidden from you" (*1 En* 9:5). Indeed,

> "You know all things before they happen, and You see these things and You permit them, yet You do not tell us [angels] what we ought to do to them with regard to these things" (*1 En* 9:11)

Similarly, the Jewish sage Ben Sira* says of the godless man:

> He does not realize that the eyes of the LORD are ten thousand times brighter than the sun;
> They see all the things a man does, observing the things that are most hidden.

* He lived in the early second century BCE; his book, called "The Wisdom of Ben Sirach" (or "The Wisdom of Jesus the Son of Sirach") is included in some Bibles in the Apocrypha or under "Deuterocanonical writings."

> Before anything exists, it is known to Him, and He sees what will be after everything ceases. (Sir 23:9–20; cf. 16:17)

The opening line above is rather close to those passages seen earlier (Zech 4:10, 2 Chron 16:9) that claim that God's eyes "range throughout the whole earth." But Ben Sira goes significantly farther, asserting that God simply knows *everything*, and knows it even before it exists; correspondingly, He also knows what will happen after it ceases to be.

Ben Sira lived more than a century after the Greek conquest of Judea, when Greek ideas and institutions had already begun to leave their mark on Jewish religious thought, and an all-knowing, omnipresent deity was certainly a notion that resonated with Stoic philosophy.[37] It should not be surprising, then, that other Jewish texts from a slightly later period repeat the same claim:

> For the ways of men are known by Him always, and He knows the secrets of the heart before they happen. ([Apocryphal] *Psalms of Solomon* 14:8)

Similarly, from the "Testament of Naphtali," *Testaments of the Twelve Patriarchs*:

> For there is no creature and there is no thought that the Lord does not know, since He created every person in His image. (T. Naph. 2:6)

As mentioned, divine omniscience went in tandem with omnipresence. The first-century Jewish philosopher Philo of Alexandria, who lived in a Greek-speaking city and wrote his commentaries on the Torah and other treatises in mellifluous Greek, espoused a sweeping picture of divine omnipresence:

> God is everywhere, because He has stretched out His powers through earth and water, air and heaven, and left no part of the universe empty of His presence.[38]

A peculiarity in the Old Greek (Septuagint) version of the book of Exodus provided Philo with what he considered biblical proof of the doctrine of divine omnipresence. A certain verse, Exod 17:6, was rendered into Greek as having God say to Moses, "*Here* I am standing in front of you *there,* on the rock in Horeb."* From this apparent contradiction Philo concluded that "He [God] who is here, is also there and elsewhere and everywhere, since He has filled everything through and through and left nothing empty of Himself."[39]

But such sweeping claims that God is everywhere and knows everything sometimes ran into trouble with the Bible itself. True, numerous passages referred to God's capacity to penetrate the human mind and *find out* anything —but this is not the same as just automatically, effortlessly, *knowing*. And besides, there were a number of biblical narratives that seemed patently to deny that God knows all. One instance was the brief biblical tale of Cain and Abel, whereby Cain kills his brother Abel in a fit of rage:

> Cain said to his brother Abel, ["Let us go out to the field"].** And when they were in the field, Cain rose up against his brother Abel and killed him. Then the LORD said to Cain, "Where is your brother Abel?" He said, "I do not know; am I my brother's keeper?" And the LORD said, "What have you done? Listen! Your brother's blood is crying out to Me from the ground! [As of] now, cursed are you from the ground that opened its mouth to swallow your brother's blood at your hands. If you till this ground, it will no longer yield its riches to you. You will become a nomad, a wanderer on the earth." (Gen 4:8–12)

God asks Cain a straightforward question, "Where is your brother Abel?" Apparently God asks because He doesn't know, and at the time that these events were written down, there was no harm in this (any more than there was in His question to Adam in Gen 3:9, "Where are you?").[40] Then, as God draws closer to the scene of the murder, He discovers that Cain's answer—"I don't know"—was a deception: He hears Abel's blood crying out from the ground and immediately sentences Cain to a life of wandering.

If we fast-forward from the time in which this narrative was first written down to the time of the Bible's ancient interpreters, the discomfort of the latter with it is palpable. For example, the *Book of Jubilees* (probably composed at the start of the second century BCE) recounts the incident, but makes no mention of God's question "Where is your brother Abel?" Moreover, while *Jubilees* does say that Abel's blood *cried out*, in its retelling the blood does not cry out to God ("to Me" as in the biblical text), but somewhat more vaguely "to the heavens." In short, in the *Jubilees* version God did not need to ask

* Modern translators: "Behold [Heb *hinneni*] I will stand in front of you . . ."
** The bracketed phrase is not in the traditional Hebrew text.

Cain where Abel was or even to hear Abel's blood crying out in order to know what happened. He just knew.

Two and a half centuries after *Jubilees,* Philo of Alexandria again takes divine omniscience for granted. He asks:

> Why does *He who knows everything* ask the brother-murderer, "Where is Abel your brother?" He wishes that the man himself should confess of his own free will . . . since he who kills through necessity will confess . . . but he who sins of his own free will will deny it. (*Questions and Answers on Genesis* 1:68)

A generation later, the Jewish historian Josephus recounts the story of Cain and Abel in some detail—and with a few significant additions:

> Abel, the younger one, was concerned with justice, and believing that God was *present at every action* that he himself undertook, he made a practice of virtue . . . [Later on,] Cain, incensed at God's preference for Abel, slew his brother and hid his corpse, since he thought that the matter might thus remain a secret. But God, *aware of the deed,* came to Cain and asked him where his brother had gone, since He had not seen him for many days, although previously He had always seen him together with Cain. Cain was thus cast into difficulty and, having nothing to reply to God, at first said that he was likewise surprised at not seeing his brother. But then, exasperated by God's persistent, inquisitive meddling, he finally said that he was not his brother's baby-sitter or body-guard responsible for whatever happened to him. At this, God accused Cain of being his brother's murderer. (*Jewish Antiquities* 1:55–57)

Here Josephus goes out of his way to say what the biblical text clearly does not, that God knew all along that Cain had murdered Abel. In fact, Josephus prepares the ground for this assertion of divine knowledge even in his description of Abel. He says that Abel believed that God was indeed "*present* at his every action"—hence, it would seem, omnipresent.* Of course, the biblical story contains no evidence of Abel entertaining such a belief, but Josephus, troubled as all ancient interpreters were by God's question "Where

* Cain, by contrast, does not understand that God is present even when unseen: according to Josephus, he buries Abel's corpse "since he thought that the matter might thus remain a secret."

is your brother Abel?" has resolved to make a virtue of a necessity and turn divine omniscience into the whole point of the story. So he goes on to assert — again, without any support from the biblical text — that God was "aware of the deed" even before He asked Cain where Abel was.

But if so, why did God ask this question at all? Josephus's answer is that God wanted to rattle Cain with "persistent, inquisitive meddling" until Cain blurted out his true feelings, that he was not his brother's "babysitter" (in Josephus's Greek, his *paidagōgos* — the household slave charged with taking the master's children to school), nor his *phulax,* a guardian or protector. A reader of Josephus might object that there is no "persistent, inquisitive meddling" in the story, but Josephus has a clever explanation for this as well. He understands Cain's answer to God's question, "I do not know; am I my brother's keeper?" to be two answers, the second quite separate in time from the first. He theorizes that God *must* have followed up Cain's first answer, "I do not know," with further questions: "Come on, Cain. You must have some idea where he is! I mean, I always used to see you two guys together, Cain and Abel, Cain and Abel. And now: just Cain. Where did Abel go?" Josephus reasons that this must have been what happened, since Cain would never have had to give the second answer unless the first had proved insufficient. So finally, unable to stand up to God's "persistent, inquisitive meddling," he blurted out his true disdain for Abel — and God then charged him with the murder.

A New Remoteness

If omniscience and omnipresence seemed to go together, it was ultimately the latter that proved the more important. In essence, God could no longer be conceived as having a body, or indeed as having any sort of physical being at all. He was just everywhere all the time.[41] And this was to have the most profound effect on how people encountered God from this point on.

The new model of a bodiless, omnipresent deity might seem to be a kind of return to the great Outside, that all-embracing, all-powerful Being who had dwarfed the little humans back in the Garden — but one ought not to be too hasty. There is certainly no evidence that the existence of such a being is hardwired into the human brain (as some recent, misguided writers have claimed),[42] and in any case, the new, three-omnied model was significantly different from the great Outside. The undifferentiated Outside was just what its name implied, with everything lumped together: all that we mean by God, plus cricket-song and cold snaps, lakeside sunrise and gnawing hunger and the warm west wind, all of these undifferentiated and endlessly moving in and through the little human beings. By contrast, the three-omnied God had no physical existence at all, hence no confusion of being; He was always right there, but on an altogether different plane. And since He was everywhere, He was also nowhere, at least not in the old way, poised on the other side of the curtain. Of course He still spoke to prophets and sages, and humans still spoke to Him — no longer as real interlocutors, but as humans conversing with a living Being who was absolutely everywhere all around, as close as the little humans' own lips or the tips of their fingers, but stretching to the farthest outreaches of the world. Here the divine Outside existed in a wholly new register, endlessly present but truly inconceivable.

This may sound like the answer, however schematic in form, to the question with which we began this book, namely: What happened to the God of Old and His direct encounters? But there are still some things missing, things that are of the most vital importance to our theme.

10

A SACRED AGREEMENT AT SINAI

Laws that come from God; Prerogatives of a divine sovereign; Laws in Israel's early history

In the biblical account, the covenant at Mount Sinai marked the beginning of God's connection to one particular people, Israel. But why did it take the particular form that it did — and how did that form come to represent an entirely different sort of encounter with God?

We saw in the previous chapter some of the changes that took place in Israel's encounter with God, as He went from being the people's main God to being its only God, and then to being the God of the whole world, indeed, the three-omnied God of post-biblical times. But an important element in this story is missing. In the account of God's meeting with the people of Israel at Mount Sinai, something happened that went on to define the nature of His future connection with them. This encounter took place, according to the book of Exodus, three months after the Israelites had left Egypt and crossed the Red Sea on their way into Canaan. They came to Mount Sinai (location unknown to this day) and there God, enfolded "in a thick cloud," proclaimed the Ten Commandments. The question is: Why would He do that?

A Divine Lawgiver

To be sure, this was the beginning of God's connection to the people of Israel, and of Israel's acceptance of Him as its God. But why should this event have involved the Ten Commandments, or commandments of any kind? God could have just said: "From now on, you're my people and I'm your God."

Why make this new reality conditioned on a set of laws (and these ten laws in particular)? This is not an idle question, and the answer seems to reveal something basic about the very nature of God in ancient Israelite religion. He is of course represented as a heavenly king,[1] but more particularly, as a divine lawgiver. Elsewhere in the ancient Near East, the gods were champions of justice, but the actual laws were typically promulgated by a human king: the laws of King Ur-Namma in ancient Sumer (who ruled from 2112 to 2095 BCE), the laws of Hammurabi in Babylon (ca. 1750 BCE), and so forth.[2] In ancient Israel, it was God who created the laws, communicating them (according to the Pentateuch) to Moses, who then passed them on to the people. As a lawgiver, He was quite alone: there is no instance in the whole Hebrew Bible of a flesh-and-blood Israelite king issuing laws on his own initiative.[3] Examining the moment in the biblical narrative when God's kingship over Israel first began can thus reveal something important about the original significance of His first laws, the Ten Commandments:

> The LORD called to him [Moses] from the mountain, saying, "You have seen what I did to the Egyptians, how I carried you on eagle's wings and brought you to Me. And now, if you obey Me and keep [the laws of] My covenant, then you will become My treasured possession from among all peoples, for the whole land is Mine. And you shall be to Me a kingdom of priests and a holy nation. These are the words that you shall speak to the Israelites. (Exod 19:3–6)[4]

A "covenant" is just a bit of English legalese for a binding agreement of some sort. What God is saying to Moses here is that if the people of Israel agree to abide by the provisions of this covenant, then He will adopt them as His "treasured possession."[5] He certainly had other choices, He goes on to imply: Israel is being singled out "from among all peoples, *since the whole land is Mine.*" But this still leaves unexplained the necessity for concluding a formal agreement along with its attached laws, the Ten Commandments. Why was there a covenant at all?

Vassal Treaties

Part of the answer, according to many scholars, has been provided by archaeological finds from the ancient Hittite capital city of Hattuša, now located in the town of Bogazköy in north central Turkey. In the Bronze Age, the Hittites ruled over a vast empire that reached southward to include much of the territory of present-day Syria. In this empire's ancient capital archaeologists unearthed a huge library of some ten thousand inscribed clay tablets, many of them dealing with foreign relations and other matters of state. Starting in the 1930s, a number of Hittite treaties were published, and it was not long before these attracted the attention of biblical scholars. The reason was that they had a familiar ring.

The Hittite treaties are known as *suzerainty treaties* or *vassal treaties* because they cover relations between the emperor (or suzerain) and his various vassal states.[6] Like all sorts of other documents — wedding invitations, business letters, UN resolutions — the treaties acquired a fairly standard format. They begin with the self-identification of the suzerain: "These are the words of the Sun-god [that is, the monarch], King So-and-so." This is followed by a lengthy historical prologue,[7] in which the suzerain reviews all he has done for the vassal (sometimes starting with his or his forebears having conquered the vassal's land and put a puppet on the vassal state's throne). The next section contains the treaty's stipulations, prominently including the requirement that the vassals pledge their undying loyalty to the suzerain and vice versa. This was extremely important to the suzerain: his main concern was that the vassal state remain faithful to him and not try to strike a better deal with another emperor down the road. The suzerain would thus say things like this to his vassal:

> I have now made you swear an oath to (me,) the King of Hatti, and to the land of Hatti, and to my sons and grandsons. Observe the oath and the authority of the King. I . . . will protect you, Tuppi-Teššub . . . [But if] you commit [. . .] and at a time when the King of Egypt [is hostile to me, you] secretly [send] your messenger to him [or you otherwise become hostile] to the King of Hatti [and cast] off the authority of the King of Hatti *and become a subject of the King of Egypt,* you, Tuppi-Teššub, will have transgressed this oath . . . Whoever is [my] enemy shall be your enemy. [Whoever is my friend] shall be your friend.[8]

Another treaty similarly demands:

> You shall be at peace with my friend and hostile to my enemy. If the King of Hatti goes [to war] against the land of Ḫanigalbat,* or Egypt, or Babylonia,

* The Assyrian name for Mittani, a Hurrian-speaking state in northern Syria and southeast

> or the land of Alshi—whatever lands that are located near the borders of [your] land which are hostile to the King of Hatti . . . [when the King] goes out to attack them, [if you] do not mobilize wholeheartedly with infantry [and chariotry] and do not fight [wholeheartedly], you will have violated the oath.[9]

In short, these treaties almost always specified that the vassal state's leader will never leave the suzerain's "protection" or otherwise break faith with him.[10] There were further demands: payment of annual tribute, refraining from attacking another vassal of the suzerain, and so forth. The treaty also included the requirement that the text of the agreement be placed in the vassal's sanctuary and that it be read out in public at regular intervals. The treaty then ended with a long list of the gods and goddesses who acted as witnesses to its enactment, followed by a detailing of the (divinely authorized) curses that would befall any vassal state that failed to uphold the treaty's conditions, as well as the blessings that would accompany its faithful adherence.

When biblical scholars became aware of the ancient suzerainty treaties, starting in the 1950s, they were struck by some of the resemblances between them and the Ten Commandments.[11] Thus, the fact that the Ten Commandments start with the brief sentence "I am the LORD your God, who took you out of the land of Egypt, the place of bondage" seemed to tally with the first two elements of the Hittite treaty formula, the "self-identification of the speaker" and the "historical prologue" (though this prologue is considerably shorter than in the Hittite treaties). More important, however, was the first commandment per se, "You shall have no other gods beside Me,"* which seemed to parallel the demand in Hittite (and later, Assyrian) suzerainty treaties that the vassal remain faithful to the suzerain and not form any alliance with another nation. We have seen that exclusive worship of one deity was a rather unusual requirement for an ancient Near Eastern god to make. But this very fact may help explain why the treaty form was used: it was a way of presenting God as a kind of divine suzerain who was simply demanding what any suzerain regularly demanded of his subjects, *exclusive* loyalty.

Other provisions of the treaty format are lacking in the Ten Commandments as presented in Exodus chapter 20, but they are found elsewhere. In particular, scholars pointed out that the overall format of the book of Deu-

---

Anatolia from around 1500 BCE–1300 BCE. Alshi, mentioned here, was a territory north of Assyria.

* On this wording, see chapter 9.

teronomy seems to match closely that of the suzerain treaty, starting with the self-identification of the suzerain (Deut 1:1–5), a lengthy historical prologue (1:6–3:29), and treaty stipulations (all the laws of Deut 4:1–26:19, including, of course, the demand not to worship "the sun, the moon, and the stars, all the host of heaven" in 4:19 and following); these are followed by the provision for the deposit of the document (Deut 27:1–26), and a section of blessings and curses (Deut 28:1–68). (Since Deuteronomy is a "treaty" between God and Israel, there is no section of divine witnesses). An equally remarkable set of resemblances is found in a third biblical text, chapter 24 of the book of Joshua, where virtually all of the Hittite treaty elements appear to be present, even the "divine witnesses" provision, which is hinted at when, at the very end, Joshua points to a certain stone, "which, since it heard all the words that the LORD spoke to us, it will be a witness against you if you break faith with the LORD your God" (Josh 24:27).

A Religion of Laws?

Given all this, it is difficult not to accept the idea that there is some connection between these ancient suzerainty treaties and the various biblical texts cited, though some intermediate channels of influence may remain undiscovered.[12] Israel's God was indeed like a conquering suzerain—first and foremost because He demanded absolute loyalty and the avoidance of any foreign entanglements; but He was also a bit like a conquistador in the sense that, while originally connected to southern and/or eastern sites like Sinai,[13] He now "annexed" the people of Israel and the far-off territory of Canaan to which they were headed. In fact, He moved there Himself. True, He didn't intend to do so at first. It was only Moses' pleading that persuaded him to abandon the "mountain of God" [or: "of the gods"] and accompany His newly acquired favorite all the way into Canaan.*

> Moses said to the LORD, "Look, You are telling me to take this people up [to Canaan], but You haven't told me who You are going to send along with me. And You [just] said that You know me by name, and [said to me] "You have found favor in My eyes." So now, if I indeed have found favor in Your eyes, let me know Your ways so that I may obey You—so that I will [continue to] find favor in Your eyes, and You will consider this nation as Your people."

---

* Note that this passage was cited in chapter 9 in somewhat abbreviated form.

> And He said: "I will send my Presence [literally, "My Face," apparently, some kind of angel or divine hypostasis]* with you, but I Myself will be leaving you." And he said to Him: "If Your Presence is not going, please do not make us leave this place. But how can it truly be demonstrated that I have found favor in Your eyes — I and Your people — unless You Yourself go along with us? In this way I and Your people will be clearly differentiated from all the other people on this earth." And the LORD said to Moses, "I will do even this thing that you have said, because you have indeed found favor in My eyes, and I know you by name." (Exod 33:12–17)

So it was that the deity named YHWH followed the Israelites from His former home to take up residence in Canaan.[14] Thus, in both its aspects (the demand of exclusive loyalty as well as God's suzerain-like act of annexation), the suzerainty treaty form well captured the precise nature of Israel's relationship with its God. And, while the prohibition of worshiping other deities was foremost, the other laws of this covenant would go on to shape the life of every Israelite — keeping the Sabbath, honoring parents, and all the other commandments of the Decalogue.

Interestingly, however, this does not seem to have happened all at once. In fact, quite the opposite appears to have been the case: for a long time, keeping divinely established laws was a notion hardly mentioned. Noah, Abraham, Isaac, and other early figures all offered sacrifices to God, but there is no indication that there were any rules governing how or what to sacrifice. The same is true of other things,[15] indeed, of most of the Ten Commandments. To be sure, there were *some* biblical rules: Cain is punished for murdering his brother; Joseph knows that sleeping with his master's wife would be "a sin against God" (Gen 39:9). But these and other rules are of the sort found in almost every society. There is little hint in these early narratives of what Israel's religion would later become.

One might say that this is just the point: these narratives describe the state of things before the great revelation of divine law at Mount Sinai. But things don't seem to have changed much after that episode. Who in the period of the Judges, which followed the great Sinai revelation, ever mentions those laws? Not Gideon or Deborah or Samson or any other Israelite leader in the period of the Judges. Did any of these people keep the Sabbath? King David lived even after their time,[16] yet he seems to have gone about his life without

---

* Note that God had previously said He would send an "angel" to lead the Israelites into Canaan (Exod 23:20, 23, cf. 27; 33:2).

ever referring to the laws of Sinai or showing any awareness of them. Even when he commits his great sin—having relations with another man's wife and then arranging for the man to be killed in battle—neither he nor the biblical narrator make any reference to the Ten Commandments' prohibition of adultery and murder, though these are hardly obscure. Indeed, when the prophet Nathan comes to rebuke David after this incident, he presents his rebuke in the form of a parable, as if he had to convince David that what he had done was wrong. Why didn't Nathan just say: "David, you have violated two of the most important laws in Israel, enshrined in the Ten Commandments; God will surely punish you for this"?

For some scholars, these bare facts have suggested that adherence to divine law did not play a particularly important role in Israel's religion, at least not at first. There may be good arguments to explain the relative absence of reference to God's covenant and its laws in early prophetic writings (save for one apparent, though sometimes contested, reference to the Decalogue in Hos 4:2), as well as the more generalized absence of reference to divine laws, such as in the narrative instances cited above.[17] Still, looking at the larger picture it is clear that adherence to God's laws only gradually became a central feature of Israel's religion. But with time, observing those laws did indeed come to be (to the extent that our biblical texts can be said to reflect the lived reality of at least part of the population) a crucial element in Israelite piety. This, then, is another important transformation, and one with great ramifications for our understanding of the divine-human encounter.[18]

One interesting manifestation of this change is described in the biblical book of 2 Kings, where the high priest Hilkiah is said to have discovered a previously unknown scroll of laws in the Jerusalem Temple. After the contents of the scroll are read to King Josiah, he immediately tears his clothes (a sign of great distress) and says to the High Priest:

> "Go inquire of the Lord on my behalf, and on behalf of the people, and on behalf of all of Judah, concerning the words of this scroll that has been found. For great indeed must be the wrath of the Lord that has been kindled against us, because our fathers did not obey the words of this scroll to do all that has been prescribed for us." (2 Kgs 22:13)

The scroll is described as one of legal instruction (*torah*), which modern scholars have identified as (roughly) the central legal core of the book of Deuteronomy. Thus Josiah, according to this account, understood at once that his people's failure to adhere to this legal code may have already spelled disaster for "all of Judah" and its people. In other words, failure to adhere to a written text may on its own condemn a people to destruction, even if its contents had been quite unknown.

But this incident goes on to represent a certain hesitation on the king's part. Should he rely solely on the words of this newly discovered (and presumably divinely given) text, or should he recruit an authoritative human to validate its message? Josiah chooses the latter. He orders Hilkiah to "inquire of the LORD on my behalf," and the priest forthwith goes and consults the prophetess Huldah, who confirms this grim diagnosis (2 Kgs 22:15–17). What clearer symbolic representation could there be of this intermediate state, whereby a sacred text must vie with the mantic revelation of a prophetess?

Not long after this incident, the prophet Jeremiah is represented[19] as reproving his countrymen for their disregard of various biblical prohibitions, ending with at least five of the Ten Commandments:

> If you put your ways and your deeds aright, if you *judge disputes fairly* between one man and another [Exod 23:1–3; cf. Lev 19:15, Deut 16:18–19]; if you do not *oppress the stranger, the orphan, and the widow* [Exod 22:20–23, 23:6–9, etc.], nor *shed innocent blood* [Exod 21:12 etc.] in this place; if you do not go after *other gods* to your own harm [Exod 22:19, 22:13, etc.], then I will [continue to] dwell with you in this place, in the land that I gave to your forefathers forever . . . But will you *steal* and *murder* and *commit adultery* and swear *false oaths* and sacrifice incense to Ba'al and *follow other gods* whom you did not know? (Jer 7:6–8)

Here, clearly, the provisions set forth in the Ten Commandments are now the index of the people's loyalty to God. These ten laws themselves were altogether simple and straightforward — hardly the stuff of profound contemplation — nor did keeping them, on the face of things, require constant vigilance or effort.[20] Moreover, as we have just seen, the Bible never mentions Gideon or Deborah or Samson or David or any other early Israelite leader doing something (or not doing something) because of some divine law. But surely Moses did not need to stay on Mount Sinai for "forty days and forty nights" (Exod 24:18) in order to memorize ten simple commandments. In the book of Exodus, the Ten Commandments are followed by a multitude of others statutes (Exodus chapters 21–23) governing such criminal offenses as assault and battery, theft, kidnapping, rape, and so forth; acts of negligence that carry legal liability (your ox gores my slave); commercial transactions of various sorts (I hire you to take care of my ox when I'm out of town); gap loans to poor farmers and the permissible forms of collateral that can be demanded of them; the prohibition of anything smacking of the worship of other gods; laws of the Sabbath and various festivals; dietary restrictions; and much more. These are presented in the text as further stipulations binding God to Israel, since the ceremony (actually, two ceremonies) that sealed God's covenant is narrated in Exodus 24:1–9, *after* all these other laws have been mentioned.

Even this, however, did not mark the end of lawgiving presented in the Torah. The rest of the book of Exodus and the three books that follow (Leviticus, Numbers, and Deuteronomy) are in fact full of further laws: rules governing the construction of the desert tabernacle and the offering of sacrifices inside it; priestly purification, and other things connected to the sanctuary; miscellaneous laws concerning, for example, a husband who suspects his wife of unfaithfulness but has no proof; a child who refuses to obey his parents; the proper way to besiege a city; a man who divorces his wife but then wants to take her back; and many, many more. It is because of this profusion of laws that the Pentateuch as a whole came to be known in Hebrew as the Torah (in this word's sense of "law" or "legal procedure"), and similarly as the *nomos* (law) in Greek.[21]

Apart from such specific laws, there came the frequent theme of Deuteronomy (but found elsewhere as well) that *serving* God — which is to say, both worshiping Him and showing Him one's devotion — was accomplished not only through the sort of sacrificial offerings found throughout the ancient Near East, but through keeping God's "laws/statutes/commandments (Deut 4:40, 45; 5:10, 26; 6:17; 8:11; 11:13; 13:5, 19; 26:17, 18; 27:10; 28:1, 15, 45; 30:10, 16, etc.). Here, then, is a striking transformation of the connection between the people of Israel and their God, one that would be repeatedly ratcheted upward until, toward the end of the Second Temple period, God's aspect as divine lawgiver would be unsurpassed. In His Torah He had given Israel 613 commandments to live by, day after day.[22] Thus was born something theretofore quite unheard of, a religion that consisted of keeping divine laws.

In sum: Go back far enough in biblical history and divine laws seem to play a minor part at best. Indeed, the altogether static nature of a written legal code must seem somewhat at odds with the God of Old, who generally acted or reacted spontaneously and by His own judgments. But God's role as divine lawgiver became increasingly important as time went on, until — as we shall see — in late- and post-biblical times, divinely given law became a, perhaps *the,* meeting-place of God and humans. Saying this, however, still leaves open the larger question. Had something changed in people's minds — specifically, in the way they conceived of themselves and of the way their minds worked — that caused them now to seek out God's laws and keep them as a religious act? What was happening to Israel and its God?

11

THE EMERGENCE OF THE BIBLICAL SOUL

Ancient expressions for oneself; A growing interiority; Bodily resurrection and the immortal soul

The biblical "soul" was not originally thought to be immortal; in fact, the whole idea that human beings have some sort of sacred or holy entity inside them did not exist in early biblical times. But the soul as we conceive of it did eventually come into existence, and how this transformation came about is an important part of the history that we are tracing.

The biblical book of Proverbs is one of the least favorites of ordinary readers. To put the matter bluntly, Proverbs can be pretty monotonous: verse after verse tells you how much better the "righteous" are than the "wicked": that the righteous tread the strait and narrow, control their appetites, avoid the company of loose women, save their money for a rainy day, and so forth, while the "wicked" always do quite the opposite. In spite of the way the book hammers away at these basic themes, a careful look at specific verses sometimes reveals something quite striking.[1] Here, for example, is what one verse has to say about the overall subject of the present study:

> A person's soul is the lamp of the Lord, who searches out all the innermost chambers. (Prov 20:27)

At first glance, this looks like the old theme of the semipermeable mind, whose innermost chambers are accessible to an inquisitive God. But in this verse, God does not just enter as we have seen Him do so often in previous chapters, when He appeared (apparently in some kind of waking dream) to Abraham or Moses, or put His words in the mouth of Amos or Jeremiah, or in general was held to "inspect the kidneys and heart" (that is, the innermost thoughts) of people. Here, suddenly, God seems to have an ally on the inside: the person's own soul.

This point was put forward in rather pungent form by an ancient Jewish commentator, Rabbi Aḥa (fourth century CE). He cited this verse to suggest that the human soul is actually a kind of secret agent, a mole planted by God inside all human beings. The soul's job is to report to God (who is apparently at some remove) on everything that a person does or thinks:

> "A person's soul is the lamp of the LORD, who searches out all the innermost chambers": Just as kings have their secret agents* who report to the king on each and every thing, so does the Holy One have secret agents who report on everything that a person does in secret . . . The matter may be compared to a man who married the daughter of a king. The man gets up early each morning to greet the king, and the king says, "You did such-and-such a thing in your house [yesterday], then you got angry and you beat your slave . . ." and so on for each and every thing that occurred. The man leaves and says to the people of the palace, "Which of you told the king that I did such-and-so? How does he know?" They reply to him, "Don't be foolish! You're married to his daughter and you want to know how he finds out? His own daughter tells him!" So likewise, a person can do whatever he wants, but his soul reports everything back to God.[2]

The soul, in other words, is like God's own "daughter": she dwells inside a human body, but she reports regularly to her divine "father." Or, to put this in somewhat more schematic terms: God, who is on the outside, has something that is related or connected to Him on the inside, namely, "a person's soul." But wasn't it always that way?

Before getting to an answer, it will be worthwhile to review in brief something basic that was seen in the preceding chapters. Over a period of centuries, the basic model of God's interaction with human beings came to be reconceived. After a time, He no longer stepped across the curtain separating

---

* The Hebrew text uses a word borrowed from Latin, *curiosus,* which means "spy" or "informant," especially as a member of the emperor's secret police. The Jews under Roman occupation were of course quite familiar with the term.

ordinary from extraordinary reality. Now He was not seen at all—at first because any sort of visual sighting was held to be lethal, and later because it was difficult to conceive of. God's voice was still heard, but He Himself was an increasingly immense being, filling the heavens; and then finally (moving ahead to post-biblical times), He was just axiomatically everywhere all at once. This of course clashed with the old idea of the sanctuary (a notion amply demonstrated in ancient Mesopotamian religion as well), according to which wherever else He was, God was physically present in his earthly "house," that is, His temple. But this ancient notion as well came to be reconfigured in Israel; perched like a divine hologram above the outstretched wings of the cherubim in the Holy of Holies, God was virtually bodiless, issuing orders (like "Let there be light") that were mysteriously carried out.[3]

If conceiving of such a God's being was difficult, His continued ability to penetrate the minds of humans ought to have been, if anything, somewhat easier to account for. He was incorporeal and omnipresent;[4] what could stand in the way of His penetrating a person's mind, or being there already? Yet precisely for this reason, Proverbs 20:27 is interesting. It suggests that God does not manage this search unaided: there is something *inside* the human being that plays an active role in this process, the person's own self or soul.

Three Hebrew Words

Most people nowadays, if they think about the soul at all, think of it as a kind of spiritual entity, the body's opposite and complement. Souls are often deemed to be immortal, as opposed to bodies, which perish and disintegrate. But this was not the soul as it was conceived throughout much of the biblical period. In fact, asking what the soul was in biblical times is really putting the question backwards. What should really be asked is the meaning—and the history—of three different words in Hebrew, each of which ended up being translated as "soul" in most Bibles. What exactly did these words designate at first, and how did their meaning change?

The word for soul used in Proverbs 20:27 is *neshamah*. It is clearly related to the verbal root meaning "to breathe," so much so that most modern Bibles translate it here and there as "breathing" or "breath." Thus, for example, *neshamah* in Genesis 2:7 is usually rendered as the "breath" or "life-breath" that God breathes into the lifeless body of Adam—essentially an act of divine mouth-to-mouth respiration.[5] (Interestingly, "breath" or "breathing" is connected to different words for soul or spirit in various Indo-European languages: Latin *spiritus,* Greek *psuchē* [often spelled in English as "psyche"], German *Geist* [and English "ghost"], Slavic *dusha,* Sanskrit *atmān,* and so forth.) *Neshamah* is not an especially common biblical term—it is the least common of the three terms translated as "soul." When it does not actually mean breath itself, it is usually a kind of shorthand for "all things that breathe," that is, all living things (e.g., Ps 150:6). In fact, its use in Proverbs 20:27 is rather unique—here, "soul" is actually a good translation—and its use in this verse is therefore potentially significant: it says that there is something *inside* people (permanently, not the breath that comes and goes) whose role it is to light the path for God as He inspects "all the innermost chambers." It is also noteworthy that this verse marks the only appearance of *neshamah* in the whole book of Proverbs. While the word does appear in other books, making for a total of 24 uses of the word in all, this is still a relatively small number; it pales before the most common word translated as soul in the Hebrew Bible, *nefesh.*

Nefesh appears some 753 times in the Hebrew Bible, making it one of the most common nouns in the language as a whole. The trouble is, *nefesh* means quite a few things besides soul. Like its cognates in other Semitic languages, it can sometimes mean "neck" or "throat."[6] Thus, when the psalmist says that "the water has reached my *nefesh*" (Ps 69:2), he means it has risen up to his neck and he is about to drown. The Israelites, grown tired of subsisting on manna in the wilderness, say to Moses, "Our *nefesh* is sick of eating this second-rate food" (Num 21:5); in this and other usages, *nefesh* seems to mean something like "throat," or perhaps "appetite." More commonly, *nefesh* designates the human being as a whole, a person—rather like *soul* in English in such expressions as "some poor soul is likely to touch that wire," or "a town of some 100,000 souls." Along with this, however, *nefesh* is occasionally used for *any* animate being (*nefesh ḥayyah*), such as the fish in the sea or the birds in the sky, indeed, "cattle and creeping things and wild animals of all kinds" (Gen 1:20, 21, 24, etc.). Probably the word's most common meaning is something like "self," especially "myself" (*nafshi*). Most of the time, *nafshi* does not seem to refer to anything especially holy or spiritual. "My soul" is just "me."

The third Hebrew word that is often translated as "soul" is *ruaḥ,* and its root meaning is very much like those of *nefesh* and *neshamah*: "wind," "breath," hence "inclination," "disposition," "spirit," and yet more. It often designates a temporary state, a mood (sometimes in combination with another word, "bitter of spirit," "lowly of spirit," "shortness of spirit" [= impatience], and so forth). But as with *nefesh* and *neshamah,* if one examines the use of *ruaḥ* without assuming beforehand that our concept of soul *must* have existed somewhere in biblical Hebrew, then there is little reason to consider "soul" as one of its meanings. In truth, there are very few biblical verses in which any of these three terms *must* be translated as "soul" in the sense that this word has now, something spiritual that all people "have" and that constitutes their immaterial essence.[7]

The conclusion to which this leads is, at least at first, somewhat shocking. It is not, as some have argued, that biblical souls were simply conceived to be *different* from ancient Greek souls or more modern souls. Rather, for much of the biblical period, there simply were no souls. People were people. They had breath that came into their lungs and went out again, and so long as this happened they were alive; it is this that *neshamah* mostly refers to. Similarly, when ancient Israelites talked about their *nefesh* or their *ruaḥ,* for the most part they meant nothing like "soul" in our sense; they mostly meant "me." People in biblical times certainly had minds (usually referred to in Hebrew as a person's "heart," since this was presumed to be the physical place of understanding),[8] and they seem to have had, as all people have, a sense of self, albeit one that was rather different from ours today. But it is only relatively late in the biblical period that people began to believe that they had something inside of them or attached to them that was their immaterial, spiritual essence. Thereafter, when readers encountered the words *neshamah, nefesh,* and *ruaḥ* in various biblical verses, they naturally understood them to be referring to this spiritual essence — and soon enough, to be referring to a person's *immortal* soul. Suddenly, the Bible was full of souls. But such readings are, for the most part, a later imposition.[9]

The Spiritual Projectile

The word *ruaḥ* had another use in biblical Hebrew. It referred to an immaterial and invisible spirit dispatched by God; the *ruaḥ* would travel from Him and enter a person, effecting some fundamental change in the process. (Clearly this was another way of expressing the basic phenomenon that we have been charting, the divine entry into the semipermeable mind.) This is rather similar to the picture observed in late- and post-biblical texts,* wherein an external *wicked* spirit — such as the Spirit of Licentiousness, the

---

* See chapter 3.

Spirit of Hate, of Anger, and so forth — is dispatched by Satan or some other archfiend to enter the victim's mind and lead him or her astray. But in earlier biblical texts, the "spirit" is sent by God and it usually serves to transform the person into God's servant or to grant him supernatural powers. The biblical story of Samson, for example, is full of such transforming spirits:

> The woman bore a son, and she named him Samson. The boy grew up, and the LORD blessed him. The spirit [*ruaḥ*] of the LORD began to stir him in the encampment of [the tribe of] Dan . . .
>
> [One time,] he went down to Timnah, and when they entered the Timnah vineyards, a lion came roaring at him. Then the spirit of the LORD rushed upon him and he tore the lion apart with his bare hands, as one might tear apart a little goat. But he didn't say a word to his father and mother of what he had done . . .
>
> [Later,] the spirit of the LORD rushed upon him, and he went down to Ashkelon and killed thirty of its men . . .
>
> When he reached Lehi, the Philistines came shouting toward him, but the spirit of the LORD rushed upon him and the ropes that were [binding] his arms became like flax when it's on fire, and the bonds melted off his arms. (Jdg 13:24–15:14)

In these incidents, God's *ruaḥ* "rushes upon"[10] Samson and suddenly he can tear apart an attacking lion with his bare hands, or kill thirty men unaided, or rip off the ropes holding him as if they were mere flax. God sent a similar sort of *ruaḥ* to other figures in those early days:[11]

> [About the judge Othniel:] The spirit of the LORD came upon him, and he ruled Israel, and the LORD gave King Cushan-rishathaim of Aram into his hand. (Jdg 3:10)

> [About Jephthah the Gileadite:] Then the spirit of the LORD came upon Jephthah, and he passed through Gilead and Manasseh . . . He inflicted massive defeat on them. (Jdg 11:29–33)

> [About King Saul:] As he turned away to leave Samuel, God gave him [Saul] another heart, and all these signs were fulfilled that day. When they were going from there to Gibeah, a band of prophets met him, and the *spirit of God* rushed upon him, and he began to act like a prophet amongst them. (1 Sam 10:9–11)

The list goes on, but these examples should make clear that a *ruaḥ* was something like a spiritual projectile, sent by God to enter or land upon an individual and change his behavior or abilities in some significant way. In fact, just as Satan sent evil spirits in later writings such as the *Testaments of the Twelve Patriarchs,* so God in earlier times sometimes sent a *ruaḥ* to do harm or mislead:

> Now the spirit of the Lord departed from Saul, and *an evil spirit from the Lord* began tormenting him. And Saul's servants said to him, "An evil spirit from God is tormenting you. Let our lord now command the servants who attend you to look for someone who is skillful in playing the lyre; and when the evil spirit from God is upon you, he will play it, and you will feel better." (1 Sam 16:14–16)

> [God tells Isaiah about the Rabshakeh] "I will put a spirit in him, so that he will hear a rumor and return to his own country." (2 Kgs 19:7)

At least in one passage, an evil *ruaḥ* is said to have come before God and volunteered to mislead:

> [The prophet Micaiah reports to King Ahab:] "And the spirit came forth and stood before the Lord and said, 'I will lead him [Ahab] astray.' The Lord said, 'How?' And he [the spirit] said: 'I will go out and become a lying spirit in the mouths of all his prophets.' And He said, '[All right!] Lead him astray and get the better of him — go now and do it!' So it has come about that the Lord has put a lying spirit in the mouths of all these prophets of yours, since the Lord has decreed disaster upon you."[12] (2 Chron 18:20–22)

The very existence of this "projectile" spirit seems to have been a more explicit, and convincing, way of imagining *how* God (or later, wicked angels or Satan) attached Himself to the human being. It was like a midair refueling. God did not personally slip inside people or, on the other extreme, simply whisper something in Samson's ear. Instead, He sent an invisible intermediary to come upon Samson and equip him with those special abilities.*

---

* Sending a *ruaḥ* to do the job is altogether appropriate. After all, "wind," "breath," and "spirit" all have something in common: they refer to something immaterial and invisible, something you can't point to or hold in your hands or put in a box, but at the same time something that is active and the *result* of whose doings can indeed be observed. Because this something is invisible and immaterial, the book of Ecclesiastes repeatedly describes a

Clearly, the divine projectile sort of *ruaḥ* is quite different from the *ruaḥ* that was inside the human being — the breath in his lungs or, metaphorically, his state of mind.[13] But the tradition of these divine projectiles, these *ruḥot*, may have had something to do with the gradual transition that is the subject of this chapter.

A New Inwardness

Despite all that was said above, at some point ancient Israelites began thinking of themselves as having what we usually mean by "souls," and then began imposing this understanding on the three words mentioned.[14] The evidence for the later stages of this change is quite clear, as we shall see. But how it began, and why, are not so easy to determine. One possible source of evidence, however, is the book of Psalms.

For the most part, psalms have a straightforward agenda. "Help me, I'm in terrible danger," many of them say, or "Save Your people now, since our enemies are threatening." Others are psalms of praise to God or words of thanksgiving for divine intervention, either on the part of an individual or the people as a whole; a number of psalms also appear to have been composed for the celebration of a festival. In general, the psalms were, as we have seen, clearly connected to temple worship, intended to be recited as an accompaniment to an animal sacrifice, either one offered by the people as a whole or recited on the part of an individual, in payment of a vow or the like. These sorts of psalms hardly call for the psalmist to reflect on his inner state (other than saying such things as "I'm in deep trouble," or "You really saved me"), or even to acknowledge that he or she *has* an inner state. So the psalmists usually don't talk about what's *inside* them; this is just not part of the program. It's either "You," "You," "You," or else "He," "He," "He," where both these pronouns refer to God. It is against this background that one must consider the exceptions, such as the following:

> O God, You are my God, I search for You, my *nefesh* thirsts for You,
> My flesh faints for You, like a parched and thirsty land without water . . .

---

futile endeavor as a "chasing after the wind [*ruaḥ*]" (Eccles 1:14, 2:11, 17, 26, etc.). Elsewhere the same author observes, "No one controls the wind [*ruaḥ*], or can lock up the wind [again, *ruaḥ*]" (8:8).

> So I will bless You as long as I live, I will lift up my hands [in prayer] and call on Your name.
> My *nefesh* is sated with a rich feast, and my mouth praises You with joyful lips,
> when I turn my thoughts to You on my bed, calling You to mind in the watches of the night.
> For You have been my help, and in Your wings' protection I rejoice. My *nefesh* clings to You, Your right hand supports me. (Ps 63:1–9)

I have left the word *nefesh* in Hebrew, but "soul" would certainly seem to be the right translation here. The psalm is, rather exceptionally, concerned with the psalmist's inner feelings, his "thirst" for God* and his desire to come close to Him. Particularly remarkable is the mention of how he turns his thoughts to God "on my bed," "in the watches of the night," when apparently he is alone and not participating in any ceremonial or liturgical occasion.

All this strikes a rather different note from that of most psalms. But it is not entirely unique:

> At *night* my hand is stretched out [to God] without ceasing; my *nefesh* refuses to be comforted.
> When I call God to mind, I cry out; I think [of Him] and my *ruaḥ* falters.
> My eyes are held wide open,[15] I am so troubled I can't even speak.
> I think of days of old, times long gone by; *at night* I think and *commune with my heart,* I think and search my *ruaḥ*. (Ps 77:2–7)

Here again, the psalmist is apparently alone at night. The precise meaning of many of the expressions in this psalm is still debated by scholars, but the overall picture is clear. God is not present. Rather, He is called to mind, remembered, cried out to; and then, in going over past events, the psalmist (not God!) looks deep into his heart and searches his *ruaḥ*. I have again left *nefesh* and *ruaḥ* untranslated, though it seems to me the usual translations — "soul" and/or "spirit" — are altogether appropriate here.

These nighttime yearnings are not limited to the Psalms. A passage in the book of Isaiah — one that scholars date "late," to the period following the Babylonian exile — has the prophet say:

---

* Note also that "thirsting" and being "sated with a rich feast" both evoke that other meaning of *nefesh,* "throat" or "appetite."

O Lord, we cry out to Your name; and Your name is the soul's (*nefesh*) delight.
My soul (*nafshi*) longs for You at night, and the spirit (*ruaḥ*) inside me searches You out. (Isa 26:8–9)

Here again the psalmist is alone at night, longing for God. But the larger point is that in all these passages, it is the "spirit inside me" that longs for God and searches Him out. By the same token, the speaker in Psalm 77 clearly has an interior *something* that is causing him pain, a pain that arises specifically when he thinks of God or reaches out to Him; thinking of God causes his *ruaḥ* to fail, or later, brings him to search out his *ruaḥ*. So too:

My *ruaḥ* is fainting within me; inside me, my heart is numb.
I consider the days gone by and think about all You have done, mulling over the work of Your hands.
I stretch out my hands to You [in prayer], my *nefesh* longs for You like the thirsty earth.
Answer me soon, O Lord; my *ruaḥ* is giving out. (Ps 143:4–7)

As noted, this focus on what is going on "within me," on my *nefesh* or *ruaḥ*, is not typical of most psalms, but scholars are generally reluctant to assign such compositions to a particular movement or school, or even to point to a specific time when they emerged (though many of them are held to be "post-exilic"). Wherever and whenever they originated, however, their interiority is altogether exceptional. So too with these lines:

Make a pure heart for me, and put a new, steady spirit (*ruaḥ*) within me;
Don't send me away from Your presence, and do not take Your holy spirit (*ruaḥ*) away from me. (Ps 51:12–13)

It seems here that the *ruaḥ* is a permanent resident within a person, rather like his heart. If the old *ruaḥ* is no good, then, as the first line says, a new one will have to be substituted.[16] But the second line adds that this indwelling *ruaḥ* is *Your* holy spirit—that is, it somehow belongs to, or is connected, to God; indeed, it is "holy."* Later, this same psalm asserts:

---

* Of course, asking God not to "take it away" means, "Don't kill me." But that the *ruaḥ* itself is described as holy is certainly significant.

If You wished a sacrifice [from me] I would give it; but it is not an offering
You want:
The sacrifices of God are a broken spirit (*ruaḥ*), a broken and crushed heart
You will not turn away. (Ps 51:18–19)

This is the psalmist's spirit, deep inside him. Broken and crushed at the thought of his sins (mentioned earlier in this psalm, lines 4–7), it is like, or in fact better than, a sacrifice offered at the temple, since it is what will bring forgiveness from God.

Late Biblical Psalms

Biblical psalms were, for the most part, connected to temple worship, but scholars long ago noticed that a few seem to be placeless and occasionless, apparently designed to be recited anywhere, as an independent act of piety.[17] Perhaps the best known example is that of Psalm 119, an eightfold alphabetical acrostic[18] (making it by far the longest psalm in the Psalter, 176 verses in all). It certainly does not appear to have been designed for public recitation (doing so takes quite a while!).[19] Was it originally intended to serve as a kind of spiritual exercise, or some sort of litany, and/or a series of repeated requests for revelation?[20] No one can say for sure. Scholars have also wondered about the unceasing references to God's *torah,* His laws, statutes, ordinances, rules, and so forth (eight much-repeated synonyms in all); perhaps this was, as one recent essay has put it, a reflection of a new sort of piety, "seeking Torah as a substitute for seeking God."[21]

Whatever the case, one aspect of this psalm makes it stand out from others in the book of Psalms: it is all about the psalmist's inner "me." Endlessly, he refers to his own state of mind: "I am seized with rage," "my flesh creeps from the fear of You, I am in awe of your rulings," "My eyes pine away for Your salvation, for Your promise of victory," "My eyes shed streams of water because people do not keep Your Torah," and so on and so forth. In addition to his other bodily references—"my lips," "my mouth," "my eyes," "my tongue"—there is, of course, "my *nefesh.*"

We also learn about the psalmist's longing for God, what he has done to come closer to God, his devotion to God's precepts, his struggles with his enemies ("the wicked"), his resolutions for the future—but all this is filtered through the psalmist's own, very present self. I do not say this in disapproval,[22] and in any case some might explain this psalm's intense focus on the speaker as a natural consequence of the psalm's unique literary genre and/or intended setting and use, about which we know nothing. All this notwithstanding, I believe most readers will recognize that the striking difference between Psalm 119 and most other biblical psalms is not simply a matter of its length or unique literary genre, but of its steady gaze inward.

The Thanksgiving Hymns

If one asks where all this is headed, part of the answer is found in compositions that belong to the late- or early post-biblical period.[23] The Dead Sea Scrolls, for example, include a series of *Thanksgiving Hymns,* so named because many of them begin with the formulaic phrase "I thank you, my Lord." At first glance, these hymns might seem like biblical psalms, which, as we have seen, often addressed words of thanks to God, usually in some generalized, one-size-fits-all form.* But the *Thanksgiving Hymns* have an altogether different flavor from that of most biblical psalms.[24] Like Psalm 119, the speaker of the *Thanksgiving Hymns* is intensely concerned with his own inner self (which he refers to as his *ruaḥ*). He repeatedly stresses how unworthy he is, being by nature a filthy creature, a thing of "impurity," "made out of mud," "in sinfulness from [my mother's] womb," and so forth. At one point he wonders out loud how he could have attained the knowledge he has acquired, since he is certainly not worthy of it:

> These things I know through Your wisdom, since You have opened my ears to wondrous mysteries, though I am a creature of clay mixed with water, the essence of shamefulness and a fountain of impurity, a smelting pot of transgression and constructed of sin, a spirit of error and depravity without knowledge and terrified by [Your] proper judgments. (1QH[a] *Thanksgiving Hymns* col 9:23–25)[25]

For the most part, the "I" of these *Thanksgiving Hymns* is in an utterly spiritual world, the stark inside world of the soul—a place of great darkness and bright light, of human insignificance and divine splendor.[26] If one had to find something in the Bible comparable to the world of these hymns, it

---

* See chapter 8.

would not be in the Psalms, but in the book of Daniel (perhaps the last biblical book of the Hebrew Bible to be written, and thus completed around the time of the *Thanksgiving Hymns'* composition). Here God "reveals deep and hidden things, He knows what is in the darkness, and the light dwells with Him" (Dan 2:21–22).

Another of the *Thanksgiving Hymns* offers thanks to God for having

> saved my soul (*nafshi*) from the Pit and lifted me up from the Underworld of Abaddon to the eternal heights [that is, of heaven], where I can walk about on an endless expanse. [Thus] I know that there is hope for one whom You have created from dust to [join] the everlasting company [of angels]. You have purified the debased spirit (*ruaḥ*) of [its] grave misdeeds, to stand in assembly with the host of holy ones [that is, the angels]. (col 11:20–23)

Whatever else one might say about such passages, they do not describe anything from the outside world, the world of the sun.[27] This person is not describing any earthly journey, but the voyage of his soul on high, up to the home of the angels. Thanks to this voyage, he knows "that there is hope for one whom You have created from dust"; he will be able ultimately to "stand in assembly" with the angels for all eternity, because, however impure his physical being may be by nature, his soul has been purified and is now fit to join their company.

All this, it seems, is the endpoint of what began with the new interiority seen above. Now the *nefesh* or *ruaḥ* has become rather like what we mean by the human soul, which is, in fact, what the ancient Near Eastern temple was conceived to be, the meeting-place of heaven and earth. Now this meeting takes place inside the human being. The soul is thus nothing less than the carburetor where two unlikes, heaven and earth, commingle to power all that humans think and understand. As another *Thanksgiving Hymn* puts it:

> I have known You, my God, through the *ruaḥ* that You have put inside me, and I have listened faithfully to Your wondrous counsel through Your holy spirit (*ruaḥ*). You have opened up knowledge within me through Your hidden perception and the wellspring of Your strength. (col 20:14–16)

From the standpoint of the present study, these lines may be the most significant ones in all of the *Thanksgiving Hymns.* The speaker is saying that it is his soul, "the *ruaḥ* that You have put inside me," that enables him to know God. Here, as with classical prophecy, God "open[s] up knowledge" in a person — but not by penetrating his insides. The capacity to know God is, as it were, already *in* him, thanks to the soul that God has inserted into him (apparently from birth).[28] All he has to do is to "listen faithfully to Your wondrous counsel" emerging from this holy *ruaḥ,* because the soul is God's hidden source of understanding ("hidden" probably in the sense that the soul has no observable, physical being) and the "wellspring of Your strength."

The Inward Gaze

Anyone who has studied the history of ideas knows that human thought does not stop on a dime. Old ways of conceiving of things coexist with new ones, sometimes in open rivalry, but just as often in a forced harmony that is adopted despite its obvious internal contradictions. In chapter 3 we saw that two rival explanations for the origin of human evil coexisted in the *Testaments of the Twelve Patriarchs* and other texts. The "demonic possession" model was still strong in late- and post-biblical times: the wicked spirits unleashed by the Archfiend in the *Testaments of the Twelve Patriarchs* give ample evidence of the ongoing ability of these outside forces to penetrate a person's insides. But along with this there existed the "interior struggle" model, whereby two warring forces — the good and the bad — are *part of the person's insides,* each struggling to take control of the person's life. As Jacob's son Asher explains in the "Testament of Asher," "There are two ways, of good and of evil, and along with them *two impulses within our breasts* that differentiate them" (1:5). In other words, the soul is divided: there is a good part and a bad part, and the two are at war with each other. Similarly, the *Psalms of Solomon* (first century BCE) affirmed:

> Our deeds are [done] by choice and [are] *in the power of our souls.* Doing right or wrong is the work of our own hands, and in Your righteousness You survey the sons of men. (9:4)

It may not be obvious at first, but a dotted line connects this other view of human sinfulness to the verse with which we started, "A person's soul is the lamp of the LORD . . ." In that verse, the *neshamah* is a divine agent, something inside a person that acts on God's behalf; similarly, in the "interior struggle" model of the cause of human sinfulness, there is something *inside* a person that struggles against sin, seeking to overcome the person's inclination to do the wrong thing. Indeed, what was most interesting was how these two different models seem to overlap in the *Testaments* and other texts, the interior struggle sometimes being attributed to an earlier *invasion* of a person's insides by a demonic spirit. This is a good example of the "forced harmony" of two opposing conceptions mentioned above.

In view of subsequent history, however, it is clear that by late- and post-biblical times, the "inner struggle" view was on its way to victory.[29] And this reflects the new reality of the soul. In a sense, the great Outside had now established a permanent presence on the inside. Such was not the case in the representations of Abraham or Moses or Gideon: God was external and crossed over for a time, then went back behind the curtain. Nor was it the case with the "spiritual projectile," whether dispatched by God or by Satan. But now, a new interiority had taken over. A person's *nefesh* or *ruaḥ,* which used to be another way of referring to himself or herself, had become a foreign implant — inside, but belonging to God.

Greek Souls

In trying to understand what brought about this change, some scholars have pointed to the infiltration of Greek philosophical notions of the human soul into the land of Judea, particularly after Alexander's conquest of the area in the late fourth century BCE. Perhaps it was the entry of Greek ideas of the soul at this time that began to penetrate Jewish (and later, Christian) understandings of the Hebrew *nefesh* or *ruaḥ*. But the Greek soul was, no less than the Jewish one, a protean entity: what the human *psuchē** really was, *where* it was, and what happened to it when its owner stopped breathing were questions that had received a variety of answers in Greece by the time the last verses of the Hebrew Bible were being written (second century BCE).

For some time, the Greek *psuchē* was, a bit like the Hebrew *nefesh, ruaḥ,* or the lifebreath *neshamah,* terms that designated a person's self or inner feelings, sometimes specified as a kind of animating force; it is not far from other Greek terms, such Homer's *thumos* (spirit, strong feeling, strength, desire, inclination) or *noos* (mind, thought).[30] Moreover, as with a *ruaḥ* or *neshamah,* having a *psuchē* was a necessity of life; it was, for example, what a person risked losing in battle, life itself. As a consequence, *empsuchos* (having

* This is the common Greek word for soul; I have used the modern transcription of Greek ψυχή, otherwise spelled in English as "psyche."

a *psuchē*) came to be a synonym for "alive." While lacking any precise or commonly agreed-upon definition, the *psuchē* appears to have been conceived for some time as part of, or connected to, a person's physical existence. Thus, one scholar has observed:

> In fifth century Attic writers, as in their Ionian predecessors . . . the psyche is imagined as dwelling somewhere in the depths of the organism, and out of these depths it can speak to its owner with a voice of its own. In most of these respects it is again a successor of the Homeric *thumos.* Whether it be true or not that on the lips of an ordinary Athenian the word *psyche* had or might have a faint flavor of the uncanny, what it did not have was . . . any suggestion of metaphysical status. The "soul" was no reluctant prisoner of the body: it was the life or spirit of the body, and perfectly at home there.[31]

Meanwhile, however, the *psuchē* was sometimes distinguished from the physical body, so that eventually the two were often spoken of as opposite entities. It is difficult to fix when exactly this opposition began to emerge in Greek thought, but it may be attested as early as the sixth century.[32]

This opposition of soul and body achieved its classical expression in one of Plato's best known dialogues, *Phaedo* or "On the Soul," which centers on the death of Socrates. In this dialogue, Socrates unfolds his various arguments for the immortality of the soul, and the fundamental dualism of Socrates's argument — soul versus body, immortal versus mortal, spiritual versus physical — went on to influence Greek and Roman thinkers and their later Christian and Muslim inheritors.[33]

Did these themes, and in particular that of the separation of body and soul, find their way from Greece into Jewish writings as well, or were they already there? This is a somewhat more complicated issue.[34] Some relatively early biblical texts have been cited to support the idea that ancient Israel always had its own notion of the soul's independence from the body,[35] indeed, its immortality. It used to be thought, for example, that Abigail (Nabal's wife in 1 Sam 25) was referring to such immortality when she said to David:

> If someone should set out after you and try to kill you [literally, "seek your *nefesh*"], then may my lord's *nefesh* be bound up in the bundle of life thanks to the LORD your God, and let Him sling away the lives of your enemies in the pocket of His slingshot. (1 Sam 25:29)

But most scholars now agree that what Abigail was wishing David, albeit in rather elegant language, was that he go on being "bound up in the bundle of life,"* that is, continue living, while God took care of his enemies. Wishing someone an immortal soul was not only unlikely in the context of David's life and times, but it's also not exactly the kind of wish that a fighter like David would have wanted to get before going into battle. "May you remain alive" is more likely what Abigail meant.

On the other hand, the inward-looking biblical psalms examined above probably preceded Alexander's conquest by at least a century or two (nor did Greek philosophical influence instantly follow Alexander's conquest). Their outlook seems to be homegrown. The author of the book of Ecclesiastes, which some scholars date to the Persian period (meaning that it preceded Alexander's conquest by at least several decades),[36] seems to be aware of the claim that souls somehow survive death, though he himself is not particularly convinced:

> For the fate of people and the fate of an animal—they have the same fate! The way the latter dies, so does the former—they all have the same breath (*ruaḥ*), so a person is no different from an animal; all of them amount to nothing. Everyone goes to the same place: everyone came from the dust and everyone goes back to the dust. So who can really know** that the *ruaḥ* of humans goes up on high while the *ruaḥ* of an animal goes down to beneath the earth? (Eccles 3:19–21)

Later, however, in his poetic description of the last day of a person's life, he says something rather different. This is the time, he says,

> when a person goes off to his eternal home, and the mourners make their rounds in the square . . . and the dust returns to the earth as it was and the *ruaḥ* returns to God who gave it. (Eccles 12:5, 7)

Given such evidence, it seems unwise to chalk up the Jewish focus on the human soul to Greek influence alone. Perhaps the change in the understand-

---

* The same phrase might be translated as "the bundle of the living," which might be taken as a more explicit way of wishing someone continued life.

** Such apparently rhetorical questions are virtually negations in biblical Hebrew: Ecclesiastes means, "No one can know," implying that those who claim men and animals have different fates are just making it up.

ing of *nefesh* or *ruaḥ* was something that evolved in parallel to the Greek soul; it may also have been affected by the somewhat earlier influence of Persian demonology, or by some combination of Greek and Persian notions.[37] In addition, it may have had something to do with the interest in determinism attested in the Dead Sea Scrolls and earlier texts.[38]

But whatever the cause, the new interest in what makes people sin — attested in the *Testaments of the Twelve Patriarchs* and other late- and post-biblical writings — may have been, at least in part, a reflection of what had been happening on the Outside. The supreme God of monotheism, soon to be the omnipresent God, was different from the old deity who was just waiting in the wings, who could enter into our minds or our lives at will, in the enchanted world where strange things just sometimes happened. Now He was more like the God of the Joseph story, where there were *rules* that governed reality (even, as we have seen, rules that governed what God did or did not do). This God was, for all His grandeur, remote; Joseph doesn't pray to Him, nor does God noticeably intervene as the events of Joseph's life unfold. He is on the Outside, but having planned everything in advance, He need not play any active role in the story's unfolding. This may tell us something basic about the changing sense of self over the long haul.

After Joseph explains the meaning of Pharaoh's dreams, the Egyptian king decides to put him in charge of the royal court:

> Pharaoh said to his courtiers: "Could we ever find someone like this, a man who has the spirit of God inside him?" Then Pharaoh said to Joseph, "Since God has informed you of all this, there is no one as discerning and wise as you." (Gen 41:38–39)

Here, the divine has, as it were, moved inside: the "spirit of God" directs Joseph's actions from within, and it is this that makes him the perfect job applicant for head of the royal court: he is ipso facto "discerning and wise."

Not too long after this began the soul's internal battle with its own evil side, as here in the *Testament of the Twelve Patriarchs:*

> If the soul chooses the good, everything it does will be [done] in righteousness, and [even] if it sins, it will repent right away. For when a person's thoughts are set on righteous things and he rejects wickedness, he immediately overthrows what is evil and uproots the sin. But if [the person's soul]

> opts for the [evil] impulse, then its every action will be in wickedness, and, having driven away the good, [it] will take hold of the bad; it will [eventually] be ruled by Beliar (Satan). (T. Ash. 1:4–8)

More important even than this internal struggle, however, was the fact that the reality of God, which had always been "out there," was now explicitly connected to something deep in here. Whoever looked into his own soul—perhaps in the silence of a dark night, when everyone else was asleep—would find spread out in front of him a stark world of black and white, good and evil, and certain fateful choices which, once made, could never be retracted.

> So you, my children, do not become like those two-sided people, [people] of both goodness and wickedness; but cling solely to goodness, because *that is where God resides* and what men yearn for. Flee from wickedness, doing away with the [evil] impulse by your good deeds; for two-sided people serve not God, but [only] their own desires—in order to please Beliar and people like themselves . . .
>
> For, people's righteousness is shown by their end, whether they meet up with the angels of the Lord or of Satan. For when a troubled soul leaves [its body], it is tortured by the [same] evil Spirit it [once] served in its lusts and bad deeds. But if it leaves in a state of ease, it meets up [after death] with the angel of peace, who will summon it [back] to life. (T. Ash. 3:1–2; 6:4–6)

A Chorus of Voices

The *Testaments of the Twelve Patriarchs* is apparently a composite text, its beginnings going back to the first or second centuries BCE, but then supplemented by two or three later editors, the last of whom was clearly a Christian whose interpolations thus cannot be earlier than the late first century CE.[39] In this respect, the *Testaments* cannot help us to compose a chronology of the soul's development in late biblical times. But other texts can.

The oldest parts of *1 Enoch* go back to at least the late third century BCE. Here it is clearly stated that souls survive the death of their bodies. Thus:

> And now look: the spirits of the *souls of the men who have died* are making suit, and their groan has come up to the gates of heaven. (*1 En* 9:10)

> There I saw the spirit (*ruaḥ*) of a dead man making complaint, his lamentation [reaching] up to heaven . . . Then I asked [the angel] Raphael: . . . "This spirit who is making suit—who does it belong to, such that his lamentation is going up and making suit unto Heaven?" And he answered me and said, "This is the spirit that came forth from Abel, whom his brother Cain murdered. And Abel will make accusation against him until his posterity perishes from the face of the earth and his posterity is obliterated from the posterity of men." (22:5–7)

So is it as well in a first-century text called the *Testament of Abraham*. In a touching scene at the end of his life, Abraham has an extended conversation with personified Death, who has come to take his soul away.

> Abraham said to Death: "Leave me alone for a little while, so that I can rest on my bed, since my heart feels very weak. For from the time I first saw you with my own eyes, my strength has given way. All the limbs of my body seem to be like a lead weight, and my breathing is quite labored. So leave for a little while; as I said, I cannot stand to see your form." His son Isaac then came and fell upon his breast, weeping, and his wife Sarah came in as well and embraced his feet, wailing bitterly . . . and Abraham reached the brink of death. Now Death said to Abraham, "Come and kiss my right hand, and may cheerfulness and life and strength come [back] to you." But Death was deceiving Abraham: when he kissed his hand, his soul immediately stuck to Death's hand. And immediately the archangel Michael stood beside him with multitudes of angels, *and they bore his precious soul in their hands* . . . And they buried him in the Promised Land by the oak of Mamre, while the angels escorted his precious soul and ascended to heaven singing the thrice-holy hymn [Isa 6:3] to God. (*T. Abr.* 20:4–12)

Here, clearly, Abraham's soul separates from his body immediately after death: his body is buried in the land of Canaan, while his soul is carried up to heaven.

The Wisdom of Solomon is another first-century Jewish composition (now included among the biblical Apocrypha in Christian Bibles, sometimes referred to simply as "[the Book of] Wisdom"). Written from the start in Greek, it may have been composed for the Jewish community in the Greek-speaking city of Alexandria (Egypt). It says that the souls of the righteous, despite any suffering they may appear to have undergone in their final hours, are headed toward an immortal afterlife:

> But the souls of the righteous are in God's hand, and torment shall in no way touch them. In the eyes of the foolish they may seem to have died, and their departure [from life] may look like ill-treatment, as if their leaving us marks their downfall; yet [in truth] they are at peace. For even if in the sight of others they may seem to have been punished,* immortality is what they await; and following this slight bit of disciplining, they will be richly rewarded, since God, having now tested them, will have found them worthy of Himself. (Wis. 3:1–5)

A somewhat different scenario calls for the dead to be in a state of suspension until, after a time, they are resurrected.[40] The book of Daniel thus foretells:

> And at that time, the great angel Michael will arise, standing over your people's children — and it will be a time of trouble, such as has never come about since the nation has been until then. At that time, your people will be saved — each one who is found written in the book. *And many of those who are sleeping in the dust of the earth will awake, some to eternal life, and some to shame and eternal contempt.* But the knowing ones will shine as bright as the brightness of the firmament and like the stars forever and ever. (Dan 12:1–3)

A number of other texts further specify that there exists a kind of storehouse ("treasury")[41] that souls enter after death, presumably waiting there for their bodies to be resurrected so that they can return to their previous owners:

> [An angel says to Ezra:] Did not the souls of the righteous *in their treasuries* ask about these matters, saying, "How long are we to remain here? And when will we harvest our reward?"
>
> [Later, Ezra asks:] If I have found favor in Your sight, O Lord, show this as well to Your servant: after death, as soon as each of us yields up his soul, will we be kept in a state of rest until such time as You will renew creation,

* Presumably judging by the spectacle of a painful death.

or will we be tormented at once?" . . . [God's answer:] "Concerning death, the teaching is: When the decisive decree has gone forth from Most High that a man shall die, as the soul leaves the body to return again to Him who gave it, first of all it adores the glory of the Most High. But if it is one of those who have shown scorn and have not kept the ways of the Most High, and who have 'despised his law' [Num 15:31], and hated those who fear God, such souls will not enter into treasuries, but they will immediately wander about in torments. (4 *Ezra* 4:35, 7:75–80)

The post-biblical soul was sometimes depicted not only as separate from the rest of the human being, but not even belonging to its human host. Rather, it was conceived of as dwelling in its temporary, fleshly home, a little divine oasis amidst the human body. Since, according to Genesis 2:7, God breathed His *ruaḥ* into Adam's nostrils, so it must happen to all subsequent human beings:

> And I, Your servant, know, by the spirit that You placed in me [ ],
> that all Your works are righteous and Your word will not depart.
> And all Your ages are appointed [ord]ered in all their details.
> (1QH[a] *Thanksgiving Hymns* col 5:35–37)

And what God breathes in at the beginning of a person's life, He logically must take back at the end. Religious Jews recite this brief prayer upon awakening:

> My God, the soul (*neshamah*) that You have put inside me is pure. You created it, shaped it, and breathed it into me, and You are preserving it within me, and You will take it from me and return it to me in the Age to Come. So long as the soul is within me, I will thank You, O my Lord God and God of my fathers, Master of all beings, lord of all souls. Blessed are You, Lord, who restores souls to dead corpses.

Truth or Fiction?

Was this new kind of soul a discovery or an invention? This is ultimately the question raised by this chapter.

It was suggested above that the gradual emergence of the soul came about more or less in tandem with the gradual abstraction and re-understanding of God: He no longer stood just over there, behind the curtain separating ordinary from extraordinary reality. Now, He was *the* God, the only one, and of necessity, He became a huge, cosmic deity, looking down from the heights of heaven, until finally, He was simply everywhere all at once, like the air we breathe. But "everywhere" is a kind of nowhere, abstract and therefore remote; God needed to be sought out. Late at night, one could turn to this soul and feel what was truly real, in an entirely different register — not the variegated, inviting world of the sun, but the stark moonscape of the soul, where what is ultimate is also proximate, and the things of this world dissolve into a wholly different kind of being.

Was this merely self-delusion? A theme throughout this book has been that the "self" is itself a construct, and one whose nature (either utterly overshadowed, or semipermeable, or the battleground between good and evil, or a little door inside leading Outward) had been, from the very beginning, closely linked to the way human beings construed their encounter with the undifferentiated Outside. Western philosophy gradually abandoned the ethereal word "soul" in favor of "mind" or "self"; but today, thanks not only to neuroscience but to contemporary philosophy as well, the self is in trouble. "Its demise was gradual, but by the end of the twentieth century the unified self had died the death if not of a thousand qualifications, then of a thousand hyphenations."[42] In its place has come . . . well, nothing in particular. Our notions of ownership of, and identification with, a self are now widely considered the product of human evolution, created to serve the overall goal of survival. But whatever the self's lack of physiological reality may prove, our *sense* of self is certainly real; as one contemporary writer has comfortingly observed, "To have a sense of X doesn't necessarily entail that X exists."[43]

This brings us back to the particular construction of self which, as we have seen, began to emerge in later biblical times. Its stark inner landscape, a place of heightened reality, opened the way to God. It was thus a kind of ever-present, vital possibility: a little bit of enabling legislation. And surely it had cognates elsewhere in the world: Hinduism, Buddhism, are altogether focused on the inward gaze, their spiritual exercises (prominently meditation) aimed at its cultivation. But Judaism, and later Christianity, never went far in that direction. In both religions, the ultimate reality still lies outside the human being: God stands apart and away, as if to say that, in the end, man is not the whole point, but that the inward turn ultimately leads outward, to a divine reality beyond oneself.

This notwithstanding, the emergence of the late- and post-biblical soul marks a change of supreme importance, reflecting nothing less than a new way in which humans began to conceive of themselves. Did this new soul merely *reflect* a broader, emerging sense of self in Israel — or did it actually help bring it about? And if the latter is the case, wasn't the emergence of a new sense of self fundamentally tied to a new way of conceiving of God?

12

REMEMBERING GOD

Moses strikes the rock; Thanking the gods in ancient inscriptions; Thanksgiving becomes obligatory

People had gradually come to think of their insides differently. Now there was something "in here" that approximated the later Jewish and Christian concepts of the soul. Yet despite this internal presence, people still suffered from an ancient problem, perhaps more than ever before: they often failed to see God's hand in the events of this world. He did things, sometimes intervening in human affairs in the most obvious manner. But people still (indeed, proverbially) forgot.

The Bible recounts that, toward the end of their forty years of wandering in the wilderness, the Israelites ran out of water. They complained bitterly to their leaders, Moses and Aaron: "Why did you take us out of Egypt only to have us die here of thirst?" Thereupon, God instructed Moses to pick up his staff and go with Aaron to a certain rock. "Speak to the rock," God tells them, "so that it gives forth water, and there will be enough to drink for all the Israelites and their flocks." The two then proceed to carry out this instruction:

> Moses took the staff from before the Lord as He had commanded him. Then Moses and Aaron gathered the people in front of the rock, and he said to them: "Hear me now, you rebellious ones: can we get water for you from out of this rock?" Moses lifted up his hand and struck the rock twice with his staff, and abundant water flowed from the rock, so that the congregation and their flocks could drink. Then the Lord said to Moses and Aaron,

> "Since you did not show your trust in Me, sanctifying Me in the Israelites' sight, you will not lead this congregation to the land that I am giving them." (Num 20:9–12)

Moses's Mistake

That last sentence comes as a shock. Didn't Moses and Aaron do exactly as they were told? Then why should they now be prevented from finishing their mission of leading the Israelites into the Promised Land?

This passage has posed something of a challenge to biblical interpreters in every period.[1] Some have suggested that Moses had erred in *striking* the rock. After all, God had told Moses to *speak* to the rock, but He didn't say anything about Moses hitting it with his staff—so he was punished. But this explanation seems unlikely on two counts. First, this wasn't the first time that Moses was told to produce water from a rock. The same thing had happened years earlier, at the very start of the Israelites' wanderings in the wilderness.[2] On that occasion, too, there was not enough water for the people to drink; then as well, the people quarreled with Moses, and God instructed Moses to go to a certain rock with his staff.

> [God said:] "I will be present there, next to the rock at Horeb, and you will *strike the rock* with your staff and water will come out of it for the people to drink." And Moses did so in the sight of the elders of Israel. (Exod 17:6)

Here there was apparently no problem with striking the rock: it gave up its water and God said nothing to Moses in the way of a reproach. So if there was no problem the first time, what was wrong the second time?

Those who blame Moses for striking the rock instead of talking to it have another problem as well. In the incident with which we began, no less than in the one just cited, God orders Moses to *take his staff*. What would be the point of such an order if all that Moses had to do was speak to the rock? What is more, the Hebrew word for "speak" (here *dibbartem*) seems to be connected to the same root that appears elsewhere as a verb meaning "strike" or "smash." True, in the latter sense it is usually in the *hiph'il* ("causative") form, but some scholars have suggested that *dibbartem* here may simply be an alternative to that form with the same meaning—that is, "strike." After all, what sense does it make for Moses to *speak* to a rock? At least hitting it is an action that might conceivably open some crevice through which water could then flow, perhaps from an underground stream beneath it. What would talking accomplish?

Considering such evidence, other commentators have ventured that Moses's big mistake was striking the rock *twice*. After all, God had said nothing about striking it two times; if Moses had deviated from his instructions even in this one detail, wouldn't that be enough to merit punishment? But this, too, seems unlikely. God's instructions did not specify that Moses strike the rock any specific number of times; He certainly didn't say "once and no more." Even if Moses had struck it ten or twenty times, could that really be construed as disobeying God's order?

Actually, I have never understood why this passage should seem so mysterious to commentators. The Bible states the reason for Moses's and Aaron's subsequent punishment quite clearly: "Since you did not show your trust in Me,[3] sanctifying Me in the Israelites' sight, you will not lead this congregation to the land that I am giving them." What does this mean in context? It means that Moses should never have said what he said to the people: "Hear me now, you rebellious ones: *can we get water* for you from out of this rock?" The problem was the "can *we* get water." Through this little slip of the tongue, it seemed as if Moses and Aaron were actually taking credit for a miracle that God was about to perform and thereby not "sanctifying Me in the Israelites' sight."

The slip is somewhat understandable. After all, faced with the same situation some years earlier, Moses had been ordered by God to strike the rock and everything turned out fine. Moses was silent that first time; perhaps it was hard for him to believe that striking a rock would produce anything. But now, God gives Moses what looks like the same order, and Moses — having no reason to fear that the outcome will be any different this time — confidently uses the occasion to reprove the Israelites for their lack of faith: "Hear me now, you rebellious ones: can we get water for you from out of this rock?" Some Bible translations render God's subsequent rebuke of Moses as: "Since you did not trust in Me" or "Because you did not trust Me enough," but neither of these makes sense. Moses had plenty of trust that everything would turn out well; that's why he could give his swaggering challenge to the people, "Hear me now, you rebellious ones: can we get water for you from out of this rock?" Rather, it was precisely his overconfidence that led him to omit a crucial step, namely, his failure to declare publicly his reliance on God and thereby "sanctifying Me in the Israelites' sight."

In a word: Moses's mistake was forgetting God. And this, it turns out, was not an uncommon problem in the ancient Near East. People—including kings and other leaders—sometimes failed to give the gods proper credit for their beneficial interventions into the affairs of mankind.

Royal Braggadocio

Ancient Near Eastern kings were not famous for their self-effacing modesty. It was not uncommon for monarchs to commission monumental statues of themselves, sometimes accompanied by inscriptions detailing their glorious personal histories as well as their tremendous acts of beneficence to their own people and humanity in general. Generations of schoolchildren have memorized Shelley's famous sonnet "Ozymandias," in which a long-dead king boasts, "My name is Ozymandias, King of Kings. Look upon my works, ye Mighty, and despair!" Shelley's poem was inspired by a real inscription of Ramesses II of Egypt (then only recently published) which reads in part, "King of Kings am I, Osymandias [Ramesses's other, regnal name]. If anyone would know how great I am and where I lie, let him [try to] surpass even one of my works!" Surely here is no wavering or hovering: Ramesses II is virtually an all-powerful god himself.

The genre of the self-glorifying inscription was carried to especially great heights by various kings in Phoenicia and Asia Minor, whose inscriptional autobiographies have been rightly characterized by one scholar as "royal braggadocio."[4] Some of them are, indeed, little more than "How great am I!"

> I am Kilamuwa, the son of Hayya. [King] Gabar reigned over Ya'diya, but he d[id] nothing.
> Then there was Bamah, but he did nothing.
> Then there was my father Hayya, but he did nothing.
> Then there was my brother Sha'il, but he did nothing.
> But I, Kilamuwa, the son of *Tm-*[5]—what I did the ones who preceded [me] did not do.
> My father's kingdom was in the midst of mighty kings, and all of them stretched forth their hands to consume [it].
> And I [too] was in the hands of the kings—[but] like a fire! burning the[ir] beards and burning their hands . . .
> I Kilamuwa, son of Hayya, sat on the throne of my father.
> In the presence of the earlier kings, the *mškbm* had whined like dogs.

But I — to them I was a father and to them I was a mother and to them I was a brother.
Someone who had never even seen the face of a sheep, I would make him the owner of a flock;
someone who had never seen the face of an ox, I made him the owner of a herd, and the owner of silver and the owner of gold;
and someone who had never seen [even ordinary] linen in his youth, in my day he was covered in byssus.
I held the *mškbm* by the hand; I made their attitude [toward me] like the attitude of a fatherless child toward its mother.[6]

Apparently, it just didn't occur to King Kilamuwa (ninth century BCE, Anatolia) to share his glory with anyone else (at least not here); after all, propaganda — boasting, "royal braggadocio" — was what these inscriptions were all about.

And yet, even amidst this lavish self-praise, other kings did take the trouble to remember their divine sponsor(s). Here, for example, is the Karatepe Inscription from what is now southern Turkey, in which the eighth-century BCE king Azitawada sets out his accomplishments:

> I am Azitawada, *the blessed one of Ba'al, the servant of Ba'al,* who was placed in authority by Awrikku, the king of the Danunites. Ba'al made me a father and a mother to the Danunites. I gave life to the Danunites. I expanded the territory of the Adana Valley from east to west. In my days, the Danunites had everything pleasant, abundance and pleasure. And I filled the arsenals of Pa'ar, and I acquired horse after horse and shield after shield and army after army — *thanks to Ba'al and the [other] gods,* I shattered the rebellious ones.

The language is strikingly similar to the previous inscription — like Kilamuwa, Azitawada was "a father and a mother" to his people and the source of economic prosperity. But unlike the former, Azitawada starts off by identifying himself as Ba'al's servant and acknowledges the help of Ba'al and other deities. Indeed, a few lines further down, he announces:

> And I have built this city and named it Azitawadiya, for *Ba'al and Reshef of the stags* had dispatched me to build it. And I built it *thanks to Ba'al and thanks to Reshef of the stags,* with abundance and pleasantness and good living and peace of mind.

Azitawada actually claims to have been sent by Baʿal and Reshef to build the city that he inaugurated. And this sort of piety, even in the midst of self-promotion (after all, in the same breath he names the new city after himself!), seems rather more typical.

Why should this have been? If the whole point of these inscriptions was to catalogue the king's great accomplishments, why bring the gods into it? Kilamuwa certainly felt no necessity to do so. Perhaps, in the case of Azitawada, it was merely a formulaic gesture, like the clergyman's invocation at the start of some public event in which there will be no further need to refer to the deity. But I think not. Azitawada says that Baʿal and Reshef actually *sent him*, commissioned him, to build the new city; at some level, I think he must have believed this to be true. (And, on the other hand, he certainly doesn't seem to think of himself as a mere pawn: these are *his* mighty deeds as well as those of his divine patrons.)

Another inscription, that of Zakir, king of Hamath and Luash, goes a bit further, attributing nearly all his success to divine help. "I was oppressed," he begins, "but Baʿal Shameyn ("the Lord of Heaven") delivered me and stood by me, and Baʿal Shameyn made me king in Hadarik." He continues:

> Now Bar Hadad, the son of Hazael, king of Aram, united se[ven]teen kings against me . . .And all these kings set up a circumvallation* against Hadari[k], and they erected a wall higher than the wall of Hadarik, and they dug a moat deeper than [its] moa[t]. But I lifted up my hands to Baʿal Shameyn, and Baʿal Shameyn answered me. [And] Baʿal Shameyn spoke to me through seers and messengers. [And] Baʿal Shameyn [said to me:] Do not fear, for I have made [you] king, [and I] shall stand by you, and I shall deliver you from all [these kings who] have rammed a circumvallation against you." Thus spoke to me [Baʿal Shameyn and he drove away?] all those kings . . .

One thing that has fascinated scholars since this inscription was discovered in 1903 is its apparent reference to prophet-like intermediaries, "seers and messengers," who announce Baʿal Shameyn's support. Although the inscription breaks off at this point, it appears that this deity did indeed do as he promised and drove the enemy away. Apart from that aspect, however, we have here another king who—in a way that must have been, on some level,

---

* A line of fortifications—here presumably including a siege-tower enabling the attacker to look into the besieged city and/or eventually enter it.

sincere — attributes the defense of his reign to direct divine intervention. Note that this and the other inscriptions are not the writings of starry-eyed visionaries, but of down-to-earth, hardheaded kings proud to record for eternity their own achievements. Yet most of them are eager to split the credit — that seems to be the whole point. As the biblical scholar Maxwell Miller observed:

> In short, Zakir "killed two birds with one stone." He dedicated the stela to the gods because of the support which they had given him in the past and used it to convey his request for further blessings. But he also intended the statue to serve as a memorial to himself, inscribed on it a record of his mighty deeds, and attempted to insure that this record would not be removed in the years to come. These two motifs — dedication to the gods, memorial to the king — are often combined in the Assyrian inscriptions.[7]

I believe Miller's comment is important, since the combination it highlights well illustrates the overlapping mentalities described earlier: on the one hand, man is supreme — "Look at all the great things I've done!" On the other hand, I did almost nothing: everything came from the gods.

The Moabite Stone

That other reality, in which the gods loom large and even kings cower at their feet, was not just a matter of divine lip-service, of saying thank-you with words alone. Consider the case of King Mesha of Moab who, seeing that he was about to be defeated in battle, took his oldest son and killed him, offering his body as a gift to the Moabite god Chemosh. This is, at least, the biblical account of the reason for Mesha's surprising victory over his Israelite adversary:

> Now King Mesha of Moab was a sheep breeder, who used to deliver to the king of Israel [as tribute] one hundred thousand lambs, and the wool of one hundred thousand rams. But when Ahab died, the king of Moab rebelled against the king of Israel. So King Jehoram marched out of Samaria at that time and mustered all Israel . . .
>
> When the king of Moab saw that the battle was going against him, he took with him seven hundred swordsmen to break through, opposite the

> king of Edom; but they could not. Then he *took his firstborn son* who was to succeed him, and *offered him as a burnt-offering* on the wall. And great wrath came upon Israel, so they withdrew from him and returned to their own land. (2 Kgs 3:4–5, 26–27)

While we have no external confirmation of this incident of human sacrifice, there is no doubt that King Mesha did exist. He lived in the ninth century BCE and left behind one more of those pious-but-boasting inscriptions of the sort already seen:

> I am Mesha, son of Chemosh[-yatti], the king of Moab, the Dibonite.
> My father (had) reigned over Moab for thirty years, and I reigned
> after my father. And I made this high-place for [the god] Chemosh in
> Qarḥo . . .
> because he has delivered me from all kings, and because he has made me triumph over all my enemies. As for Omri, king of Israel, he humbled Moab for many days, for Chemosh was angry with his land.
> And his son reigned in his place; and he also said, "I will oppress Moab!" In my days he said so.
> But I triumphed over him and over his house, and Israel has perished; it has perished forever!

Forgetting God

What can be concluded from all this? In biblical times, God/the gods were held to intervene in daily life—this is evidenced not just in biblical stories, but in the Mesha stone and the Phoenician inscriptions examined above as well. Yet somehow, numerous biblical texts also say that people sometimes *forgot* these interventions. Such forgetting was not without consequences; in fact, it almost always is said to have led to disaster. This is the lesson imparted by the great hymn sung by Moses at the end of his life, in which he recounts *in nuce* the whole history of Israel (Deuteronomy 32). Things start off well enough: God chooses Israel to be His own portion and carries them "on eagles' wings" to the land that He had promised them. But soon the people go astray:

> Jeshurun [a poetic name for Israel] grew fat and rebelled: You grew fat and bloated and dull.

And he abandoned the God who made him, and scoffed at the Rock of his salvation . . .
You were unmindful of the Rock who bore you, and you *forgot* the God who gave birth to you. (Deut 32:15, 18)

Other summaries of biblical history likewise stress the role of forgetting God in bringing down disaster:

He made it a decree in Jacob, and established a statute in Israel . . .
That *they should not forget* God's deeds, but hold fast to His commandments,
And not be like their fathers, a rebellious generation . . .
But the Ephraimites . . . did not keep God's covenant; they refused to follow His instruction,
And they *forgot His deeds,* the miracles He had shown them . . .
If He killed [some among] them, then they would seek His favor and again beseech Him:
They would remember that God is their Rock, and the Most High God their redeemer . . .
[Yet] time and again they rebelled in the wilderness, in the wasteland they aroused His wrath.
Once again they tested God and vexed the Holy One of Israel.
They did not remember His power, how He had saved them from their foe. (Ps 78:5, 7–11, 34–35, 40–42)

Similarly:

He rebuked the Red Sea, and it dried up; He led them through the depths as through a desert.
He saved them from the hand of the foe; from the hand of the enemy He redeemed them.
The waters covered their adversaries; not one of them survived.
Then they believed His promises and sang His praise.
But *they soon forgot* what He had done and did not wait for His plan to unfold . . .
They forgot the God who saved them. (Ps 106:9–13, 21)

It is hardly surprising, therefore, that among the admonitions in Deuteronomy is the commandment not to forget God:

> Beware . . . lest your heart grow haughty and you *forget the Lord your God*, who took you out of the land of Egypt, the place of your enslavement, and who led you through the great and terrible wilderness . . . [Lest] you say to yourself, "My own strength and the force of my own hands are what got me all that I have acquired." (Deut 8:14–17)

A Biblical Trope

It would be tedious to survey every biblical passage that suggests that Israel at times "forgot" God,[8] but it may be worth pausing here to consider this whole idea of forgetting. It certainly does not refer to an actual lapse of memory.[9] Rather, it is a kind of trope or metaphor, one that was uniquely suited to the particular situation of Israel (and many other peoples) throughout much of the biblical period. They were no longer like those early humans, utterly buffeted by the great Outside all around them; nor were they yet like humans in more recent times, for whom God's very existence depends on an imaginative act of faith, if it is not altogether denied. Instead, they were (to judge by biblical and inscriptional texts themselves) somewhere between these two poles, convinced of God's active presence in the world while at the same time seeking to control in their own lives everything that humans can control. These two tendencies pull in opposite directions, and *forgetting*—the most passive sort of action, lacking any malice aforethought—was really the perfect expression of this in-between state. It was what happened when someone moved too far from the divine dependence pole.

So, at least after a certain point, it was necessary for people to remind themselves that, even when their presence was not obvious, the gods were watching. Indeed, some scholars have compared the language of the Zakir inscription to that of biblical psalms,[10] suggesting that the psalms of thanksgiving were in fact a kind of verbal monument-making, a public announcement of a person's indebtedness to God—often using expressions similar to those engraved on the stone steles erected by pious Near Eastern kings.[11] What the psalmist said was, in effect: "I hereby acknowledge that You have all the power. Alone, I am helpless." That is why the speakers of the biblical psalms of request so often describe themselves as "poor," "needy," "destitute," "wretched," and the like—sometimes two or three of these near synonyms lumped together:

> May it please the LORD to rescue me; O LORD, rush to my aid.
> Let those who are out to kill me be put to shame and contempt . . .
> For I am *poor* and *needy;* may my lord take me into account.
> You are my aid and my refuge; O my God, do not delay! (Ps. 40:14–15, 18)

> Let all kings bow down to Him, all the nations worship Him;
> For He rescues the *needy* when they cry out; and the *poor,* and the one who is helpless.
> He spares the *indigent* and *needy;* He saves the *needy* one's life. (Ps 72:10–13)

> Turn to me and have mercy on me, for I am *alone* and *poor.*
> My heart's distress only worsens — save me from my sufferings! (Ps 35:16–17)

Passages such as these once gave rise to a theory among scholars that the book of Psalms was originally intended for the lower classes: people who could not afford to offer an animal sacrifice could always go the temple and request that a psalm be said on their behalf. But subsequent investigation has found scant support for this theory. Rather, *any* supplicant presented himself/herself as poor and downtrodden; the idea was that "if you don't desperately need My help, don't bother Me." Asking for divine help was thus ipso facto an act of submission and humbling yourself.[12] This was something that even great kings did:

> Then the word of the LORD came to Elijah the Tishbite: "Have you seen how Ahab has humbled himself before Me? Because he has humbled himself before Me, I will not bring disaster in his lifetime." (1 Kgs 21:29)

> [God tells King Josiah:] "Because *you have been fearful and have humbled yourself* before the LORD when you heard what I have decreed against this place and its inhabitants — that it will become a desolation and a curse — and because you have *torn your clothes* [a sign of mourning] *and wept before Me,* I for My part have listened, says the LORD." (2 Kgs 22:19)

"Please God"

Muslims are famous for inserting the phrase *insh'allah* (if God wishes) in their everyday speech: "After I graduate, *insh'allah* . . ." "When I arrive in New

York, *insh'allah*" and so forth. Although this deference to the divine becomes automatic after a while and may not tell us too much about the inner mental state (or piety) of the speaker, its continued existence does, I think, give evidence of the old theme of *not forgetting*, but in a somewhat new form.

Muslims sometimes point to a certain passage in the Qur'an as the source for saying *insh'allah:*

> And never say of anything, "I will indeed do this tomorrow," except [when adding], "If God so wishes." And remember your Lord (should you forget) and say, "Perhaps my Lord will lead me to something that is closer than this to proper conduct." (*Al Kahf* 18:23–24)

In fact, however, such conversational evocation of the deity was hardly a Muslim innovation (nor does the above passage claim that it was). Long before Islam, pious Jews and Christians had done the same. An epistle in the New Testament gives precisely the same instruction:

> Humble yourselves before the Lord and he will exalt you . . . Come now, you who say, "Today or tomorrow we will go into such and such a town and spend a year there and trade and get gain," whereas you do not know about tomorrow. What is your life? For you are a mist that appears for a little time and then vanishes. Instead you ought to say, "If the Lord wills, we shall live and we shall do this or that." (James 4:10, 13–15)

Later Christians likewise took this advice to heart, at least for a time:

> After speaking many spiritual words, she said to them, "I have spoken to the emperor and he was a little displeased. But do not lose heart. For, *God willing,* I will not rest until you have fulfilled your mission."[13]

This raises an interesting point. If today's Muslims continue to insert this deferential phrase, "If God so wills," into their daily speech, what happened to the modern West? The phrase certainly did go on for some time. Sometimes people preferred the Latin *Deo volente* or *volente Deo*[14] (both meaning, "with God willing," "so long as God wills"), as did Cervantes, for example, in *Don Quixote:*

> With this answer I sent him away; and now I take my leave of your Excellency, first offering to your notice another work of mine, called "The La-

> bors of Persiles and Sigismunda," which, *Deo volente,* will be finished in the course of four months . . . (Part 2, "Dedication to Count de Lemos")

But with time, the practice died out in the West. Remarkably, the expression was already becoming scarce in Shakespeare's time, though not altogether absent:

> . . . So, gentlemen,
> With all my love I do commend me to you:
> And what so poor a man as Hamlet is
> May do, to express his love and friending to you,
> God willing, shall not lack. (*Hamlet,* act 1, scene 5, lines 182–86)

Eventually, "God willing" or its Latin incarnations (sometimes now abbreviated as D.V. or V.D.) disappeared entirely from the speech of most ordinary people in English, though it went on for a time to punctuate the speech and letters of clergymen, no doubt as a sign (sincere or otherwise) of their piety. A few other late users appear; the fierce abolitionist William Lloyd Garrison (1805–1879) still employed the expression in his correspondence:

> Though it will be very inconvenient for me to attend the annual meeting of your State society, yet I cannot find it in my heart again to disappoint you and some of my other New-Hampshire brethren. Therefore, I mean to be with you, *Deo volente,* on that interesting occasion.[15]

I should mention the existence of another, parallel expression in English, "please God." In an earlier day one might have said, "I shall take my belongings and, please God, leave this house forever." But like "God willing" and *Deo volente,* this one is no longer with us. It should be noted that the words "please God" are not a parenthetical aside, "Please, O God, make this happen," but are actually an old English subjunctive: "May it please God . . ." or "If it please God . . ." This usage seems to have been influenced by the parallel expression in French, *plaise à Dieu.*[16] Indeed, a small landmark in the fading of this expression appears in the work of François Rabelais, the bawdy French parodist, who mocked its use way back in the sixteenth century:

> "By no means," answered [Father] Hippothedee, "will you be cuckolded, if it please God."
>
> "O the Lord help us now," quoth Panurge; "whither are we driven to,

good folks? To the *conditionals,* which, according to the rules and precepts of the dialectic faculty, admit of all contradictions and impossibilities. If my Transalpine mule had wings, my Transalpine mule would fly, *if it please God.*"[17]

An Afterthought

The reflexive insertion of "If it please God" into daily speech has something of a parallel within the Bible itself: the insertion of words of thanksgiving into biblical narratives where previously there had been none.[18] That is, God performs all sorts of miraculous interventions in the Bible, but scholars have shown that, for a time, these gifts went without formal thanksgiving. It would seem that the narrative itself was deemed acknowledgment enough, rather like the psalmist's "I hereby acknowledge that You have all the power. Alone, I am helpless." Later editors, however, apparently saw the omission of words of praise and thanksgiving after the incident as a flaw; they therefore inserted passages (usually from existing songs) that might do as an expression of thanks on the part of the humans involved.[19] These passages might be interpreted as bearing witness to a growing piety within the biblical period, but I believe that this does not quite tell the whole story. Giving thanks for divine favors was becoming ritualized and routinized, rather like *insh'allah* or *Deo volente;* it had become a duty. Only after such a stage did the flagrant violation of this new requirement demand retroactive correction, as if, without it, God's role might indeed seem to have been forgotten.

The passages themselves give some evidence of having existed earlier as independent songs. Take, for example, Hannah, Elkana's barren wife in 1 Samuel 1. At length her barrenness is overcome; she prays to God for help and is rewarded with the birth of a son, Samuel. Thereupon, the Bible reports, Hannah sang the following hymn* to God:

My heart exults in the LORD; my strength is exalted in my God.
My mouth derides my enemies, because I rejoice in my victory.
There is no Holy One like the LORD, no one besides You;
  there is no Rock like our God.
Talk no more so very proudly; let no arrogance come from your mouth;

---

* Cited previously, chapter 2.

for the LORD is a God of knowledge, and by Him are actions weighed.

The bows of the mighty are broken, while the weak are girded with strength.
The formerly sated have hired themselves out for food, while those who were hungry are fat with spoil.
The barren woman has borne seven, but she who had many children is bereft.

The LORD kills and brings back to life; He sends down to Sheol and raises up.
The LORD makes poor and makes rich; He brings low, but He also exalts.
He raises up the poor from the dust; He lifts the needy from the ash heap,
to make them sit with princes and inherit a seat of honor.
For the foundations of the earth are the LORD's, and on them He has set the world. (1 Sam 2:1–8)

Even a casual inspection of the words reveals that they are not really appropriate to Hannah's situation. Instead, this song appears to be a celebration of some sort of military triumph. What would Hannah be referring to in mentioning her "enemies" and her "victory"? And what might "the bows of the mighty are broken" refer to? Perhaps the verse that most betrays the inappropriateness of this song is the only one that actually does refer to childbirth: "The barren woman has borne seven, but she who had many children is bereft." No doubt, this verse in particular suggested that the song in question might be Hannah's hymn of thanksgiving; she *was* a barren woman. But in the preceding narrative, it is clear that she has thus far given birth to only one child, not seven! Was she exaggerating? Considered as a whole, this song's real subject is not Hannah's (or anyone else's) giving birth, but God's unpredictable behavior in granting victory, or whatever else He should want, to whomever He sees fit. "The LORD kills and brings back to life; He sends down to Sheol and raises up. The LORD makes poor and makes rich; He brings low, but He also exalts."

Two possible explanations might account for the song's place in the narrative. It might simply have been a well-known song; Hannah felt that the overall theme of God's unpredictable power was altogether applicable to her situation, so she sang it—in which case it might well have been part of the original narrative. The other explanation, however, seems more likely in the light of other biblical passages: *someone else*, a later editor or copyist, inserted this song because it seemed improper for Hannah to have had her desperate prayer for children (1 Samuel 1) answered by God without her subsequently offering some words of thanks.

Such an explanation, while merely possible here, seems rather unassailable in other cases of songs in the midst of biblical narratives. For example, the book of Judges contains an account of the defeat of the foreign general Sisera and his subsequent murder at the hands of Jael (Judges 4). Following this, Deborah sings a long hymn of praise recounting the same events in poetic style. The problem is that the details in the song don't match the ones in the prose account: Deborah comes from a different tribe, the participants in the battle against Sisera are not the same, and in the song Jael kills Sisera in a way that differs sharply from that in the prose account.[20] If so, why was the song included at all? It seems that sometime after the prose account had been written, someone felt there was something missing: no one ever expressed thanks for God's help in this striking victory. So, apparently, an anonymous editor dug up the poetic victory song (which has probably inspired the prose version in the first place)[21] and stuck it in Deborah's mouth: at least now, he thought, thanks would properly be expressed, and no one could accuse Deborah of "forgetting" God.

The same is true, some scholars hold, of a song attributed to Moses, the "Song of the Sea" in Exodus 15. According to the preceding narrative, the Red Sea split in two, allowing the Israelites safe passage from one side to the opposite bank, but when the Egyptians sought to pursue them, the waters of the sea came crashing back and drowned the Egyptian army. But if so, how did the Israelites, just now arriving on the opposite shore, already know the words of this song? Were they all simultaneously inspired to know the lyrics, or did they merely (as one ancient interpretation maintained) repeat each verse after Moses? This is not the major problem, however. Once again, the words of the song don't seem truly to match the words of the prose narrative. In the latter, the sea splits in two for a time, allowing the Israelites to cross, and then returns to drown the Egyptians. But the song makes no mention of the sea splitting. Instead, what it describes seems to be more like a bad storm at sea, with huge waves crashing down: "At the blast of Your nostrils the waters piled up, the breakers stood up in a heap; the deeps congealed *in the heart of the sea.*" The last phrase cannot refer to anything close to shore in biblical Hebrew; it means *in the middle* of the sea. The song adds that the Egyptians "sank into the billows like a stone," "they sank like lead in the mighty waters." But how could they sink at all if they were pursuing the Israelites in the space of dry land that had opened up and then were overcome by the returning waters: they couldn't "sink"—their feet were already on the bottom![22] Still more problematic, the song ends by describing events which, according to the surrounding narrative, had not yet taken place:

In Your kindness You led the people whom You redeemed; You guided them by
Your strength to Your holy abode.
When the peoples [of Canaan] heard, they trembled; fright seized the
inhabitants of Philistia.
Then the chiefs of Edom were dismayed; trembling seized the leaders of Moab;
all the inhabitants of Canaan melted away.
Terror and dread fell upon them; by the might of Your arm they turned still as
a stone—
until Your people, O LORD, could go past them, until the people You created
went past.
You brought them in and planted them at the mountain of Your land,
the place, O LORD, that You made Your abode,
the sanctuary, O Lord, that Your hands have established. (Exod 15:13–17)

None of these things had happened at the time of the crossing of the Red Sea; indeed, according to the biblical narrative, it would be nearly forty years before the Israelites would "go past" the Edomites and Moabites and enter the land of Canaan, and considerably longer before God's "abode" or "sanctuary" would be permanently established in Canaan.

What, then, is this song doing in the book of Exodus? Scholars theorize that, as in the previous case, this song was inserted later on to fill a perceived gap: without it, there would be no thanksgiving hymn after this miraculous act of salvation—and that idea was, at a certain point in Israel's history, suddenly unthinkable.[23] So an already existing song was enlisted—in this case, probably a celebration of the events of the exodus connected to a particular local sanctuary, the one alluded to in the last verse above. Even though its words jangled somewhat with those of the prose account, the inserted song took care of the thanksgiving problem, and that was enough.

Scholars have identified other inserted songs of thanksgiving: David's song in 2 Samuel 22 (which also appears in slightly different form as Psalm 18), Hezekiah's song (apparently a psalm designed to be sung after recovery from illness) in Isaiah 38, and Asaph's song in 1 Chronicles 16 (apparently a compound of Pss 105:1–15, 96:1–13, and Ps 106:47–48), and others.[24] The reason for their insertion into the narrative is the same: at a certain point it seemed necessary that the biblical figures involved express their thanks—and so some preexisting material was enlisted to do the job. But why weren't these songs of thanksgiving there from the start—why weren't they expressly composed to fit precisely the events described in the surrounding prose? The answer appears to be that the convention of expressing thanks only became obligatory after the prose narratives were already in existence. It would seem that this convention emerged in response to the "forgetting" problem, a convention that was now an obligatory routine. An increasingly remote and distant God needed institutionalized thanks precisely because He was *there*, somewhere, but not obviously so. The days of His physically crossing over from behind the curtain were over.

Inserted Thank-Yous

Saying thank you to God gradually came to be thought of as an actual *duty*. A later rabbinic text expresses some astonishment at the fact that this had not always been the case, even among Israel's own ancestors:

> From the time God created the world until Israel stood at the [Red] Sea, we find no one who uttered thanksgiving to God, save for the [people of] Israel [as a whole]. He created Adam, but he did not offer thanksgiving. He saved Abraham from the furnace and from the kings, but he did not offer thanksgiving. Similarly, [He saved] Isaac from the knife, but he did not offer thanksgiving. And similarly, He saved Jacob from the angel and from Esau and from the men of Shechem, yet he did not offer thanksgiving [etc.]. (*Exodus Rabba* 23:4)

The absence of grateful acknowledgment for such kindnesses clearly was no problem at the time these biblical narratives were written down—but why not? Oughtn't Abraham, Isaac, and Jacob to have uttered heartfelt words of thanksgiving on the occasions mentioned? But they didn't. It was only toward the end of the biblical period that such thanks became a religious requirement.

Many people today "say grace"* before or after eating. This institution does go back to biblical times, but only late biblical times; there is no indication that it existed before the second or third century BCE. Thus, the book of Deuteronomy is lavish in its praise of the land of Canaan that the Israelites are about to enter:

> The LORD your God is taking you into a goodly land, a land with flowing

* The expression has nothing to do with the Pauline doctrine of divine grace, but derives from the Latin *habere* [or *referre*, etc.] *gratiam*, or in the plural *agere gratias*, "express thanks."

> streams, springs and fountains gushing forth from plain and hill; a land of wheat and barley, of vines, figs, and pomegranates; a land of olive trees and honey; a land where you may eat food without stinting, where you will lack nothing; a land whose rocks are of iron and from whose hills you can mine copper. *And you will eat and be satisfied and bless the Lord your God for the goodly land that He has given you.* (Deut 8:7–10)

The last sentence seems to describe a spontaneous act: given such abundance, the Israelites will naturally bless God for having given them this land.[25] (Note: what was given was the land, not a meal!) And actually, there is nothing resembling grace before or after meals in most of the Bible itself: Adam and Eve, Abraham and Sarah, Isaac and Abimelech, Jacob and Esau, Joseph and his brothers, the Israelites in the wilderness, David, Solomon, Elijah and Elisha — all these and more are said to eat and drink, sometimes under miraculous circumstances, but there is no blessing before or after their meals.

With time, however, such a blessing before and/or after eating seems to have become obligatory — indeed, the last sentence of the above passage came to be the biblical warrant that such acts of blessing were a divine commandment. The *Book of Jubilees* (early second century BCE) may suggest as much:

> Rebekah made fresh bread out of new wheat. She gave it to her son Jacob to bring to his father Abraham, some of the first fruits of the land, so that he would *eat (it) and bless the Creator* of everything before he died. Isaac, too, sent through Jacob [his] excellent peace offering [and wine to his father] Abraham for him to eat and drink. *He ate and drank. Then he blessed* the Most High God who created the heavens and the earth, who made all the fat things of the earth, and gave them to mankind to eat, drink, and bless their Creator. (*Jub* 22:4–6)[26]

The same act of offering thanks for food served is witnessed in the Dead Sea Scrolls,[27] and in the New Testament,[28] and rabbinic Judaism.[29] Saying thank you was now a sacred obligation. In retrospect, the emergence of this formulaic, obligatory acknowledgment might be seen as a model of things to come.

13

THE END OF PROPHECY?

HOW PROPHECY'S CHARACTER CHANGED; PREDICTIONS OF A DISTANT DAY; ANGELIC INTERLOCUTORS; PROPHECY BECOMES SCRIPTURE

There were prophets in Israel, and then, according to various sources, there weren't. Or were there? Prophet-like figures certainly did exist after the return from Babylonian exile; that is, in the late sixth century BCE. *But they were different from their predecessors, and the differences can tell us much about our overall theme.*

For some time, prophecy was an institution whose existence was simply taken for granted in ancient Israel. In the eighth century BCE, Amos and Isaiah presented themselves to people as spokesmen carrying a message from God, and as such they were apparently listened to (at least, this is what the books bearing their names report). Prophets sometimes recount how they happened to become prophets, but there was no apparent necessity for them to explain to their listeners what a prophet was; everyone already knew that. A century and a half later, some people found Jeremiah's prophesying troubling or even seditious, to the point of threatening his life, but they do not seem to have questioned his standing as a legitimate spokesman of Israel's God. On the contrary, if they hadn't believed that his words were, in one way or another, divinely dictated or sanctioned, why would they care what he said, or even bother to listen to him?

No More Prophets

But later on, after the Judeans had started streaming back to their homeland following their exile in Babylon, prophecy's status seems to have changed.[1] Three more prophets of the Hebrew Bible — Haggai, Zechariah, and Malachi — prophesied just after the return from exile, but after them . . . nothing. Indeed, the book of Zechariah itself reports that "prophet" had become something of a dirty word, referring in later times mostly to liars and charlatans:[2]

> And it will be that in that time — so says the LORD of Hosts — that I will remove the names of idols from the land, so that they will no longer be mentioned; and along with this, I will rid the land of the prophets and the spirit of impurity, so that if a man should act as a prophet, his father and mother — his own parents! — will say to him, "You must die, since you have spoken falsehood in the name of the LORD." And his parents, his father and mother, will put him to death even as he prophesies. Then the prophets will be put to shame because of the visions they have had in their prophesying, and no one will don the [prophet's] hairy mantle to deceive. (Zech 13:2–4)

Still later writings seem to take it for granted that prophecy had ceased some time before. For example, the book of 1 Maccabees asserts that after the death of Judah the Maccabee,

> There was great distress in Israel, such as had not existed since the time when prophets ceased to exist among them. (1 Macc 9:27)

Similarly:

> [Azariah prayed:] "For we, O lord, have become fewer than any other nation, indeed, we have now become the lowliest in all the land because of our sins. In these days we have no ruler or *prophet* or leader, no burnt offering or sacrifice or oblation or incense, no place in which to sacrifice before You and find mercy." (Prayer of Azariah 15)

> Know, then, that in former times and in former generations our fathers had righteous helpers and holy prophets . . . and the Mighty One heard their prayer and forgave us. But now the righteous have been gathered in [i.e., have died] and the prophets have gone to sleep [i.e., have died]. We too have

> left our land and Zion has been taken away from us. Now we have nothing left except the Mighty One and His Torah. (2 *Baruch* 85:1–3)[3]

Somewhat later, it became rabbinic doctrine that prophecy had simply ceased to exist:

> [In reference to Dan 8:21 and 11:3–4] Alexander the Macedonian [i.e., Alexander the Great] ruled for twelve years and then died. Until that time there were prophets who prophesied through the Holy Spirit; thereafter: "Incline your ear and attend to the words of sages."* (*Seder Olam* 30)[4]

> When Haggai, Zechariah, and Malachi, the last prophets, died, the Holy Spirit [*ruaḥ ha-Kodesh*] ceased in Israel; nevertheless, people had recourse to a *bat qol* [a voice from heaven]. (Tosefta *Soṭah* 13:3, b. *Yoma* 9:2, etc.)[5]

Prophets Galore

Numerous post-exilic sources thus seemed to agree that prophecy had ended sometime following the return from Babylonian exile, either shortly thereafter or perhaps as late as the time of Alexander. Particularly in light of the absence of any canonical prophets after Haggai, Zechariah, and Malachi, the cessation of prophecy must have seemed perfectly self-evident.

Eventually, however, the idea that prophecy had simply ceased was found to conflict with evidence from other sources.[6] For example, the author of the Wisdom of Solomon (first century BCE) had opined:

> Although she [Wisdom] is but one, she can do all things,
> and while remaining in herself, she renews all things.
> In every generation she passes into holy souls
> and makes them friends of God, and prophets. (Wis 7:27)

Likewise:

> The holy word vouchsafes the gift of prophecy *to any proper person*. For a prophet, being a spokesman, declares nothing on his own, but all he speaks

---

* Prov 22:17, cited here to mean that, without further prophets, our only recourse is the wisdom of rabbinical sages.

> belongs to Another, a resonance from Someone Else. (Philo, *Who Is the Heir?* 259)

Even if some would-be prophets were denounced as false prophets, their very existence seemed nonetheless to attest to the continued claimants of the prophetic mantle:

> But You, God, despise all the plans of Belial, and it is Your idea that will triumph, and Your heart's plan will stand forever. But [the wicked] come to inquire of You *out of the mouths of false prophets,* from deluded simpletons. (1QH[a] *Thanksgiving Hymns* col 12:13–17)

Josephus, the first-century CE historian, reports extensively on the existence of various prophets in his own time.[7] Prophecy now was frequently identified as the ability to foretell future events,* and Josephus devotes particular attention to John Hyrcanus, who ruled Judea as high priest in the first century BCE and whose predictive powers were apparently the stuff of legend.[8] What is more, Josephus himself claimed to have prophetic powers, having received nighttime visions in which "God foretold to him of the impending disasters of the Jews, as well as the fates of the Roman kings" (*Bellum judaicum* 3:351).[9] He also successfully predicted that the general who took him captive in the Great Revolt, Vespasian, would soon succeed Nero as the Roman emperor:

> Vespasian, however, ordered him to be guarded with every precaution, intending shortly to send him to Nero [presumably, then to be executed as a leader of the revolt]. Upon hearing this, Josephus expressed a desire for a private interview with him . . . and said to him thus: "You believe, Vespasian, that you have taken captive Josephus, just another prisoner of war. But I have come to you as a messenger of greater things. If I had not been sent on this mission by God, I certainly would respect the practice of the Jews and how it befits a [captured] general to die. But are you sending me to *Nero*? Why is that? Will any successor of Nero be around for long—until you? It is *you,* Vespasian, who will be Caesar, *you* will be the emperor, and your son after you. (*B.J.* 3:399–401)

* Unlike the prophets of earlier times, who were seen principally as intermediaries and spokesmen of God; see chapter 7.

Despite his being the bearer of good news (for Vespasian, at least), Josephus was kept as a prisoner for the next two years. But Nero committed suicide in 68 CE, and his death was followed by the "Year of the Four Emperors": Galba, Otho, and Vitellius all ruled briefly as emperors but all met their deaths in the single *annus mirabilis* of 69 CE. Then, in November of that year, Vespasian seized power and took over as emperor; Josephus was right! He was subsequently freed and adopted into Vespasian's family, and so became known as Flavius Josephus.[10]

Not only did Josephus attest to the ongoing existence of prophets, but references in Philo,[11] the Dead Sea Scrolls[12] the New Testament,[13] and other early Christian writings[14] likewise bear witness to the continued presence of prophetic figures. Indeed, the theme of the cessation of prophecy came to be taken up by some Christian writers as a polemical point against Judaism: prophecy had indeed been taken away from the Jews because they rejected Christ, but it then became a Christian possession.[15]

How then to explain this conflicting evidence? On the one hand, we have the flat assertion in various Second Temple period* sources that prophecy had ceased, an idea supported by some ancient writers as well as by the absence of prophetic writings in the Hebrew Bible after Haggai, Zechariah, and Malachi; and on the other, we have clear evidence of the existence of prophets continuing into the first century CE and perhaps beyond, long after its supposed cessation.

Scholars have proposed various solutions.[16] Some maintain that prophecy did effectively cease in Israel, for one or more reasons. Prophecy may have been a kind of zero-sum game, so that as the writings of pre-exilic prophets — not only preserved but revised lovingly throughout the Babylonian exile and thereafter — grew in stature, those of post-exilic prophets seemed to pale by comparison. Or perhaps there was a real difference in quality: after all, who among the post-exilic prophets could compare with Amos or Isaiah or Jeremiah?[17] Or perhaps it all had to do with the pre-exilic prophets' function in society. They were so often represented as rebuking the king or the royal court for malfeasance; once there was no king, what need was there for such a "reprover at the gates" (Amos 5:10)?[18]

---

* The Second Temple period technically covers the whole time from the rededication of the Jerusalem temple (according to some sources in or around 516 BCE) through to its destruction by the Romans in 70 CE. In this sense "Second Temple period" is nearly synonymous with the "post-exilic era," though in practice scholars have a tendency to use "Second Temple period" to refer specifically to the closing two or three centuries BCE through the first century CE.

Other scholars, however, maintain that the whole idea that prophecy ceased is a myth. After all, the writings of Philo, Josephus, and various New Testament texts give irrefutable proof of prophecy's continuation. If people maintained the opposite, this must have been because rabbinic Judaism (or its predecessors) championed the idea, for one reason or another.[19] Or perhaps what was called prophecy's "cessation" ought to be reconceived; prophecy did not so much cease as gradually transform itself. Second Temple visionaries lived in a different time with different concerns, including a sense of recent history and the divinely controlled future: naturally, these concerns created a new kind of prophecy scarcely identifiable as the continuation of the older kind.[20]

Certainly some of these explanations can help to account for the discordant assessments of prophecy in Second Temple times. But there are a few things missing in this summary that may not only round out our understanding of the subject but, more important, say something significant about how Israel's encounter with God was changing.

Prophets with Angels

One of the striking features of prophetic texts from the later parts of the Hebrew Bible is the central role played by angels. Earlier, "classical" prophets reported that God spoke to them (directly or through some sort of vision or dream) and told them what to say. This tradition continued into later times, but along with it sometimes came the stipulation that the prophet did not hear directly from God, but through an intermediary, an angel of some sort.[21] Upon consideration, this proves to be a highly significant development.

One relatively early instance of an angelic intermediary is found in the book of Ezekiel. Ezekiel is said to have prophesied in Babylon at the start of the exile (he was thus situated chronologically on the seam separating the earlier, "classical" prophets like Amos and Isaiah from those who prophesied after the return from Babylonian exile). Chapters 40–48 of Ezekiel include a detailed plan for the rebuilt temple in Jerusalem, a plan that in some striking ways differed from that of Solomon's temple. Ezekiel introduces this plan by saying that "the hand of the Lord was upon me" (his frequent way of introducing the account of a vision) and that God had brought him in this vision back to the land of Israel. But strangely, at this point another figure takes over:

> When He brought me there, I saw a man who looked as if [made] of bronze. He held a linen cord and a measuring rod in his hand while he stood by the gate. And the man spoke to me: "Mortal! See with your eyes and hear with your ears and turn your mind to everything that I am going to show you, since [this is what] you have been brought here to be shown. Report everything that you see here to the House of Israel." (Ezek 40:3–4)

It seems odd that God, who "brought me there," is replaced by this "man" (a term sometimes used for an angel),* who goes on to lead Ezekiel on a visionary tour of the rebuilt Jerusalem temple. Surely this tour must have been an important topic for later Israelites, especially the priests, since this plan of the new temple was to differ from that of its predecessor. "On whose authority are you saying these things?" a listener of Ezekiel's might have asked. Yet Ezekiel's intended answer was apparently not "God," at least not directly, but some humanlike intermediary, a kind of vision-within-a-vision.[22]

Later prophetic texts — not all, to be sure, but some — similarly feature an angel as the intermediate source of a vision. For example, the book of Zechariah begins:

> On the twenty-fourth day of the eleventh month, the month of Shebat, in the second year of [the Persian King] Darius [that is, 520 BCE],[23] the word of the LORD came to the prophet Zechariah son of Berechiah son of Iddo; and he [Zechariah] said, "This evening I saw a *man* mounted on a red horse. He was standing amidst some myrtle trees in a glen, and behind him were red, sorrel, and white horses. Then I said, "What are these, my lord?" The *angel* who was speaking with me said to me, "I will show you what they are." The *man* who was standing amidst the myrtle trees continued, "These are those whom the LORD has sent to go about the earth." (Zech 1:7–10)

As in the passage from Ezekiel, this one starts by attributing the prophet's vision to God ("the word of the LORD came to the prophet Zechariah"), but it is, like the previous passage, mediated through a humanlike figure ("I saw a man mounted on a red horse") who is sometimes referred to as a man and sometimes an angel. The passage continues:

> Then they [the horses, or more likely their heretofore unmentioned riders] spoke to the angel of the LORD who was standing amidst the myrtle trees

* For example, Gen 32:24–30, Dan 8:15.

> and they said: "We have been going about on the earth and have found the whole earth to be dwelling in tranquility." The angel of the LORD called out: "O LORD of Hosts! How long will You fail to have mercy on Jerusalem and the towns of Judah, with whom You have been angry for seventy years?" And the LORD answered the angel who was speaking with me with favorable words, words of consolation. Then the angel who was speaking with me exclaimed, "Thus said the LORD of Hosts . . ." (Zech 1:11–14)

I have cited this passage at length to underline its somewhat confusing hierarchy of speakers. There is, first of all, the prophet Zechariah, who is retelling a divinely granted vision that he had (and which came to him, according to the previous passage, as "the word of the LORD"). On the next level up are the variegated horses (or their riders) whose job apparently consists of roaming the earth and reporting on what they see (in this case, that the whole earth is "dwelling in tranquility"). Higher than them is the "man mounted on a red horse," who is also described as an angel of the LORD. Above him, apparently, is the "LORD of Hosts" Himself.

The obvious question is: Why doesn't God just speak directly with His prophet? It might seem that the answer is equally obvious, in fact, that it has already been given:* once the world had only one, true deity, Israel's universal God, He logically must, by dint of His very universality, have had to rely on lesser divine beings to report to Him up in heaven on the doings of little humans upon the earth. (In fact, this particular passage goes so far as to suggest that even the angel, "the man mounted on a red horse," is not in touch with what is happening down on earth: that's what those other multicolored horses are for, galloping around the entire land and reporting to an angel who reports to God.)

Such lesser divine beings notwithstanding, the question remains: Why didn't post-exilic prophets take the initiative and ask God directly about the issues dearest to Israel's heart at the time? But they didn't. Rather, it seems that Israel's evolving understanding of God must have made it increasingly difficult to countenance such a direct confrontation. An angelic intermediary — already part of the heavenly retinue — was a far more imaginable interlocutor.

In various writings from the late- and post-biblical period, angels assume a similar role, replacing the direct address of God and revealing hidden things to the visionary. Thus, in *1 Enoch,* the angel Uriel reveals the secrets

---

* In chapter 9, the section headed "God's Helpers."

of heaven to Enoch after his ascent on high.[24] Somewhat later, the biblical sage Ezra poses a series of theological questions to his angelic interlocutor (also Uriel) in *4 Ezra*;[25] in *2 Baruch,* the protagonist discourses with an angel named Ramael; in *4 Baruch,* Jeremiah "remained sitting in a tomb while the angels came to him and elaborated to him all the things that the Lord would *reveal to him through them*" (4:12).

The New Testament book of Revelation is likewise communicated from God to the book's speaker, John of Patmos, by means of an angelic intermediary: "God made it [the contents of the book] known by sending His angel to His servant John" (1:1). At the book's conclusion,

> And he [the angel] said to me, "These words are trustworthy and true, for the Lord, *the God of the spirits* [presumably, *ruḥot*] *of the prophets,* has *sent His angel* to show His servants what must soon take place. See, I am coming soon! Blessed is the one who keeps the words of the prophecy of this book."
>
> I, John [of Patmos], am the one who heard and saw these things. And when I heard and saw them, I fell down to worship at the feet of the angel who showed them to me, but he said to me, "You must not do that! I am a fellow servant with you and with *your brothers the prophets,* and with those who keep the words of this book. Worship God!" (Rev 22:6–9)

In all these works, angels act as go-betweens. This was apparently how God communicated with mere humans after a time—not directly, across impossibly great astronomical (and spiritual) distances—but through a human-sized angel who could communicate with prophets and sages by addressing them face-to-face.[26]

Angelus Interpres

The same angel who appears to Zechariah in the previously cited passages goes on to dominate the whole first part of the book:[27] Zechariah continuously refers to "the angel who was speaking with me" (in Zech 2:2, 2:7; 4:1, 4; 5:5, 10; 6:4). Interestingly, however, the angel not only converses with Zechariah, but sometimes exercises a more specific role: he explains to the prophet the significance of what he (Zechariah) has seen (see Zech 1:9; 2:4; 4:5, 11, 14; 5:6; and 6:5). In other words, the prophet alone may have received a vision from God, but he also needs some divine being to explain it to him.[28] Because of his interpretive function, this type of angel is sometimes called an *angelus interpres* ("interpreting angel"), and he appears in a number of biblical and post-biblical texts.[29] For example, Daniel encounters such a figure (in fact, probably two in the following passage):

> [Daniel reports after having his vision of the four beasts:] As I was looking on in this night vision, *someone* [who looked] *like a human* arrived with the clouds of heaven. He came up to the Ancient of Days [that is, God] and was presented to him . . . As for me, Daniel, my spirit was disturbed on account of this and the vision in my mind alarmed me. I came up to *one of those standing about* and I asked him the significance of all this, and he explained the meaning of these things. "As to these four mighty beasts, four kings will arise upon the earth . . . [etc.]" (Dan 7:13–17)

In the next chapter, Daniel encounters another *angelus interpres*, this time identified as the angel Gabriel:

> While I, Daniel, was having this vision and seeking an understanding [of it, suddenly] there stood in front of me someone who looked very much like a man. Then I heard a man's voice [coming] from [the River] Ulai, and it called out and said: "Gabriel, explain to this fellow what he has just seen." And he came next to me, but as he approached I became frightened and fell face-down. Then he said to me, "Mortal! Understand that this vision is about the time of the end." (Dan 8:15–17)

The angelic narrator of the *Book of Jubilees* (called the "Angel of the Presence") is likewise a kind of *angelus interpres*.[30] He recounts to Moses most of biblical history, from the creation of the world to just before the giving of the Torah in Exodus. But his is not merely a recounting: in the process he explains to Moses (and to us readers) the hidden sense of such familiar episodes as the creation of Eve, the causes of the Flood, the biblical calendar, and so forth.

In another apocryphal book, the *Testament of Abraham*, God dispatches the angel Michael to interpret a certain dream of Abraham's son Isaac:

> The Lord said: "Go down, O chief angel Michael, to My friend Abraham, and whatever he tells you to do, do it, and whatever he eats, eat with him as

> well.* Meanwhile, I will send My holy spirit upon his son Isaac. I will put the subject of his [Abraham's] death into Isaac's mind, so that he will see his father's death in a dream. [Then] Isaac will relate the dream, *and you will interpret it,* so that he [Abraham] will know his end." (*T. Abr.* 4:7–8)

The *angelus interpres* is, upon consideration, a further jump away from the direct encounter with God. God does not speak directly to the human; rather, He sends a vision, or a dream, or even, in the above passage, "My holy spirit" to plant a dream. But things do not end there; the human then needs the *angelus interpres* to explain what he has seen or heard.

Long-Range Predictors

Since the late nineteenth century, scholars have emphasized that a "prophet" in the Hebrew Bible was not principally a predictor of future events but a divine spokesman, someone who had been summoned by God to transmit a message to the people or the king or some other individual. This is certainly true in the case of Hosea, Amos, Jeremiah, and other prophets examined herein. What is more, Northern prophets like Elijah and Elisha sometimes personally interceded on the people's behalf with God, or performed miracles on God's behalf. This too was part of classical prophesying.

But this likewise changed in post-exilic times. Prophets now seemed to have acquired much the same function that the word "prophet" conveys in modern English: that is, they came to be associated in particular with foretelling the future.[31] This is true, for example, of the way classical prophecy itself was reinterpreted in the Dead Sea Scrolls: the things that God had told to pre-exilic prophets were actually long-range predictions of things that were coming to pass only now, in the time of the Dead Sea Scrolls community. "And God told Habakkuk to write down the things that were going to befall *the last generation,* although he did not make known to him when that period would be complete" (1QpHab *Pesher Habakkuk* 7:1–2). The task of revealing the connection between those ancient prophets' words and the present was left to the prophetic "Teacher of Righteousness" (better: "the Right Teacher" or "the True Teacher") of the Dead Sea Scrolls, "to whom He has made

---

* He probably means, "pretend to eat with him," because by a common convention, angels don't eat or drink.

known all the secrets of the words of his servants the prophets. 'For there is yet time for [the fulfillment of] the vision, but it will be fulfilled and will not disappoint'" (1QpHab col. 7:4–6, quoting *Hab* 2:3).

Similarly, an incident recounted in the book of Numbers, wherein the Israelites came across a well in the wilderness and sang a song of thanksgiving (Num 21:16–20), turned out to be, in the Dead Sea Scrolls interpretation, an allegorical prophecy written down by Moses but whose true, predictive meaning could only be understood many centuries later, in the light of the community's own recent history:

> The well [represents] the Torah, and those who dug it are those of Israel who returned [in penitence] and left the land of Judah to dwell in the land of Damascus. God called them "princes" [in Num 21:18] because they beseeched Him, and because their glory was never gainsaid by any man's mouth. The "Scepter" is the expounder of the Torah . . .and the "nobles of the people" are those who came to dig the well with the staves with which the "Scepter" had decreed to walk about. (*Damascus Document* 6:3–10)[32]

In this respect prophecy was conceived to be a far narrower activity than in pre-exilic times. It no longer meant advising or rebuking the king, or urging the people to do something or refrain from doing it. Now its frequent purpose was predicting the future, and the long-range future at that, since seeing something that was already on the horizon may not have required anything beyond ordinary perspicacity.[33] At the same time, however, all manner of sacred texts, such as the "Song of the Well" just seen, could turn out to be prophecies under a different name, presented in the form of narratives, or laws, or almost any kind of writing considered to be of sacred origin. Thus, the psalms of David might *seem* to be psalms, but in truth, they were the writings of an ancient prophet:

> David the son of Jesse was wise and enlightened as the light of the sun, and a scribe and wise and unblemished before God and men in all that he did. And the LORD gave him a wise and enlightened spirit and he wrote *psalms*, three thousand and six hundred, and *songs* to be sung before the altar . . . for all the days of the year, three hundred and sixty-four, and for the Sabbath offerings, fifty-two songs, and [other] *songs* . . . so that the total was four thousand and fifty. *All these he composed through prophecy, which had been granted to him by the Most High.* (11QPs[a] *David's Compositions* col 27:2–11)

David is never called a prophet in the Hebrew Bible, but here he has become one—indeed, a prophet of prodigious output. Nor is this text, found among the Dead Sea Scrolls, the only instance of "David the prophet." Philo of Alexandria similarly refers to the author of Psalm 84—presumably David—as "a certain prophetic man."[34] Little wonder, then, that the New Testament book of Acts observes, "David . . . *being thus a prophet,* knew that God had sworn with an oath to him that He would put one of his descendants on the throne . . ." (2:29–30). So Josephus could write about King Solomon:

> After this solemn appeal to God, he [Solomon] turned to address the multitude and made clear to them the power and providence of God, in that most of the *future events which He had revealed to David* his father, had actually come to pass, and the rest would also come about, and God Himself had given him his name even before he was born, and had foretold what he was to be called and that none but he should build Him a temple, on becoming king after his father's death. And now that they saw these things being fulfilled in accordance with David's prophecies, he asked them to praise God. (*Jewish Antiquities* 8:109–110)

Prophets with Pseudonyms

This new understanding of the prophet's function as *predicting* went hand in hand with another characteristic of Second Temple period visionaries, the belief in an approaching "time of the end," when life on earth would cease to exist as we know it. Such a belief inspired various writings in the late- and post-biblical periods: the book of Daniel in the Hebrew Bible and the book of Revelation in the New Testament are two good examples of this form of writing. (The unifying theme of such compositions has been described by scholars as "apocalyptic eschatology"—our word "apocalyptic" comes from the Greek word for "revelation," and "eschatology" is focused on the *eschaton,* Greek for "the last," as in the end of time.)

Revealing secrets about the time of the end—and often, asserting that the time of its unfolding is not far off—was what many Second Temple visionaries did. But often, they did not do so in their own names; rather, they adopted the names of figures from the ancient past. Thus, various compositions were attributed to Enoch, the antediluvian sage who was said to have ascended bodily into heaven while still alive;[35] he was said to have passed on some of the secrets of heaven to people on earth, who ultimately collected them into what is now known as *1 Enoch.* (There is also a second and a third *Enoch.*) The same period gave rise to the *Book of Jubilees* (allegedly dictated to Moses on Mount Sinai), the *Apocalypse of Abraham, 4 Ezra, 2 Baruch (Syriac Apocalypse),* the *Testaments of the Twelve Patriarchs,* and many more. Attributing such writings to figures from the ancient past was, of course, a way of appropriating their legitimacy as biblical figures;[36] but claiming that Enoch, Baruch, and the others had authored these texts also had the effect of making the books look like truly *long-range* predictions, since these alleged authors had lived hundreds and hundreds of years before these books were actually written.[37]

It should be noted that the biblical figures chosen to be the pseudonymous authors of these books were often *not* prophets: Enoch, Baruch, and Ezra, for example, were known principally as scribes and sages (in fact, "scribe" was simply a synonym of "sage" in this period). This has led some scholars to argue that the true antecedent of this Second Temple apocalyptic literature is the sage rather than the prophet—that, in fact, many of these compositions were written by people who belonged to schools of sages and scriptural interpreters. It may be, on the other hand, that the choice of other biblical pseudonyms—Abraham, Jacob, and others, and even prophets like Moses, Jeremiah, and Ezekiel—suggests that any figure from the biblical past would do, so long as he or she could be plausibly presented as the recipient of privileged knowledge.[38]

The Messiness of History

Part of these texts' concern with eschatology may have arisen, at least in part, as a reaction to what might be called the messiness of history.[39] A Jew living in, say, the second or third century BCE would certainly have been puzzled by developments in his country's recent past. Way back in the early days, history (at least as recounted in various ancient books) seemed to make sense to him. Genesis told how Israel's most ancient ancestors had found favor with God and were rewarded. Exodus recounted the people's miraculous escape from slavery and oppression, and how their God concluded a great covenant with them at Mount Sinai, choosing Israel as His own, special treasure. Israel's conquest of Canaan and its subsequent flourishing under King David and King Solomon seemed to offer direct proof of God's favor. If the northern tribes were subsequently conquered and exiled, surely this was a punishment for their sins—as was the Babylonian conquest of the southern Kingdom of

Judah and the exiling of much of its population to Babylon. But the Babylonians themselves were swiftly overcome by the Persians, presumably a divine demonstration that Israel's God had simply *used* them to discipline His own, favorite people. This ongoing divine favor was manifest in the fact that the Judeans did indeed return to their homeland as promised, and many of them likewise looked forward to a return of the northern tribes to their ancient homeland, a first step toward the establishment of David's old empire redivivus.

But as decades turned into centuries, any hope for such an outcome began to fade. Judea was now simply part of the huge Persian Empire, and a rather unimportant part at that. How could one possibly believe that Israel was the favorite of the world's one, true deity, the universal God, when that God did not seem to be doing anything to restore Israel to its former glory? Such doubts were only fueled by later events: the Persians were eventually expelled, but not by Israel's God; rather, the armies of Alexander the Great conquered the whole region, and Judea came under the thumb of new foreign leaders, first Ptolemaic, then Seleucid. During this time, the "remnant of Israel" seemed to fare neither well nor badly; to some onlookers, this very fact — neither punishment nor prosperity — must have made it seem as if the whole idea of Israel's God controlling their fate had been a mistake from the start.

From such a viewpoint, only some huge, momentous event, a Big Bang that would change everything, could redeem Israel's traditional belief in its God's special concern for its fate. We saw above how the chronology of the *Book of Jubilees* suggested that God's true control of history was expressed not in centuries, but in huge units of time, like the 2,450 years (exactly fifty jubilees) separating the creation of Adam from the entrance of the Israelites into Canaan after the exodus from Egypt. So too, other apocalyptic writings sought to reaffirm God's control of events by focusing on the *longue durée:* divine time was dealt out in chunks of centuries, so that the little ups and downs of any given period could only mislead people by having them fail to notice the larger, divinely created patterns.

One such pattern was the theme of the succession of empires in the biblical book of Daniel. It appears in different forms.[40] Thus, in chapter 2, when the Babylonian king Nebuchadnezzar has a troubling dream, he demands of his sages not only to interpret its meaning, but to start by relating to him the content of the dream that he dreamt — a seemingly impossible task. But Daniel, with divine help, is equal to it. He not only is granted a knowledge of *what* the king dreamt in a night vision of his own, but also recognizes that the dream is actually a long-range prophecy about what will happen "in the end of days" (2:28). Having stated this as its true subject, he turns to the details of his dream:

> O King . . . as you looked on, there appeared a great statue . . . The head of this statue was of fine gold; its chest and arms were of silver; its belly and thighs of bronze; its legs were of iron, and its feet part iron and part clay. Then, as you were watching, a stone was hewn out, but not by hands, and it hit [the] feet of iron and clay and crushed them. Then the iron, clay, bronze, silver, and gold were crushed, and . . . a wind carried them off until no trace of them was left. (Dan 2:31–35)

Such was the king's dream; having recounted it, Daniel then explains its significance to the king. The head of gold, he says, represents Nebuchadnezzar himself.

> But another kingdom will arise after you, inferior to yours [that is, a kingdom of silver]; then yet a third kingdom, of bronze, which will rule over the whole earth. Then the fourth kingdom will be as strong as iron: just as iron crushes and shatters everything . . . so will it crush and smash all these [others]. (Dan 2:39–40)

The very fact that there will be a series of four kingdoms is compared to the proverbial series of four metals: gold, silver, bronze, and iron (see Isa 60:17). This means that each kingdom will eventually be followed by one of lesser worth. Of course, living in their own particular time, people are usually so occupied with their daily affairs that they fail to see the larger patterns. But to Daniel, the divinely aided sage, it is clear that when the time of the fourth kingdom is over, everything will come to a dramatic end—and perhaps a new beginning.

In the latter part of the book of Daniel, it is Daniel himself who receives a prophetic vision, and its message is similar. He sees four "mighty beasts" coming up out of the sea: a lion with eagles' wings; a bear "with three fangs in its mouth amidst its teeth"; a four-winged leopard with four heads; and then "a fourth beast . . . fearsome dreadful, and very powerful, with great iron teeth," devouring, crushing, and stamping whatever was left (Dan 7:3–7). Now even Daniel needs an interpreter—and he gets one:

> One like a human being came with the clouds of heaven: He reached the Ancient of Days [i.e., God] and was presented to Him. To Him are attributed sovereignty and glory and kingship. All peoples and nations of every language must serve Him. His sovereignty is an everlasting sovereignty that will not pass away, and His kingship is one that will never be destroyed. (Dan 7:13–14)

The "one like a human being" is, once again, an angel, who goes on to reveal the vision's significance: "These great beasts, four in number, are four kingdoms that will arise out of the earth" (Dan 7:17).[41]

In short, the problem of the "messiness of history" was basically solved by kicking the can down the road. However inexplicable Israel's current situation may have appeared to the Judean remnant, its ultimate resolution had been planned out long in advance and revealed in such works as the biblical book of Daniel or extrabiblical compositions like *1 Enoch, Jubilees,* and *4 Ezra.*

The Flying Book

One more aspect of post-exilic prophecy and similar writings needs to be mentioned: its connection to a seemingly unrelated development in Israel's social history, the increasing importance, and prestige, of literacy in Second Temple times.[42] The rise of literacy in Second Temple times was simply one manifestation of the wider march of progress paralleled in other societies,[43] but in Judea it turned out to have particular significance for what prophets perceived—and wrote down. A prime example comes from the prophecies of Zechariah.

Chapters 1–8 of the book of Zechariah consist principally of a series of eight visions that the prophet had, all in a single night. Time and again, the prophet "lifts up his eyes"* and sees some symbolic object or vista; then "the angel who was speaking with me" explains to him the significance of the vision. Particularly important for our subject is Zechariah's report of his sixth vision:

> And I lifted my eyes again and saw, and behold, a flying scroll. And he [the angel] said to me, "What do you see?" And I said, "I see a flying scroll,

* On this phrase see chapter 1.

> twenty cubits long and ten cubits wide." And he said to me, "This is the curse that is going out across the whole land: Anyone who has stolen and gone unpunished on the one hand, or anyone who has sworn a [false] oath and gone unpunished on the other—I am sending it forth says the LORD of Hosts, and it will enter the house of the thief and the house of the person who has sworn falsely by My name, and it will lodge in their houses and destroy them, wood and stones alike. (Zech 5:1–4)

A biblical "cubit" is about a foot and a half long (that is, a little less than half a meter). The flying scroll that Zechariah saw was thus about 30 feet long and 15 feet wide (9 by 4.5 meters)—in a word: huge. But it is not the scroll's size alone that is important, but the mission that it has been sent to accomplish. It is to act as God's "enforcer," punishing thieves and those who have sworn a false oath.[44]

It is certainly significant both these particular crimes are among those mentioned in the Ten Commandments. Modern readers should remember that there was no police force in ancient Israel: victims of a crime and their families had to gather evidence on their own and then take the accused to court. In the case of theft, it certainly must have happened often that the thief was never found: it was relatively easy to conceal a stolen item or sell it even before the crime was discovered (Exod 22:7, cf. 21:37–22:1). Likewise, someone who swore a false oath (in court) had a good chance of going unpunished. Unless the judges managed to trap him in some inconsistency, his testimony would stand, and he (or perhaps his allies) would get whatever he was scheming for. By contrast, murder, adultery, and "coveting"—also mentioned in the Ten Commandments—usually had some background that made it easier to uncover the wrongdoer: simmering hatreds, semi-secret trysts and the like might more likely lead to a conviction. Hence the need for some divine intervention specifically to make unpunished thieves and perjurers pay for their crimes.

But why a giant flying *scroll*? Could not God Himself, or some avenging angel, strike down the guilty?[45]

An important message—beyond its prophetic content—seems to be contained in this vision. It is no longer God Himself, but His written word, that enacts justice. Thus, the flying scroll contains a "curse" (though "accusation" or "indictment" might be a better translation here)[46] that will physically attack the houses of the guilty and cause them to crumble "wood and stones alike." But that scroll is also apt to remind us of where these crimes are condemned, that is, in the Ten Commandments of sacred Scripture. In other words, God's mighty arm has now taken on the contours of a book: it is the book that indicts and the book that punishes. What greater literalization could there be of "the word of God in action"?[47]

For a long time, the written word had probably been accessible to only a privileged part of Israel's population. Exactly how large this privileged part was remains a much debated topic among scholars.[48] But whatever the actual extent of reading and writing, evidence shows that both enjoyed widespread prestige after the Babylonian exile. This situation might be compared to that of computers in the U.S. circa 1970: while relatively few people in the overall population had the ability to use, not to speak of program, a computer, these new machines were already well on their way to conquering the imaginations of everyone. Computers had the ability to store, and to call up, vast quantities of knowledge; they had a speed and reliability unmatched by the sharpest human mind; most important, they already had a kind of metaphorical quality as *the* way in which information would be entered and remembered for future generations. These same things could be said of literacy in ancient Israel: people increasingly "conceived authority as bound up with *writtenness*."[49]

Prophets on the Page

Reviewing all the above, one must conclude that prophecy did not exactly die in post-exilic times. The many neutral or positive references to living prophets in late Second Temple period texts, in the New Testament and early Christian literature, as well as in the writings of Josephus and still later figures, all give the lie to the notion that prophecy itself simply ceased after Haggai, Zechariah, and Malachi. On the other hand, something like a reconfiguration of prophecy and prophets *did* take place. Prophets now were sometimes addressed not by God but by the "angel who was speaking to me," and such angels not only answered the prophet's/sage's questions, but also acted as interpreters of visions and messages sent by God—in short, they were intermediaries between God and humans. Moreover, prophets were now long-range predictors, revealers of the great, divine plan. And along with all this, the growing cachet of the written word was having an effect. The very existence of written collections of pre-exilic prophets' words no doubt added to their prestige, showing them as both authentic and everlasting. The comparison of these "classic" prophets with their post-exilic homologues may have diminished somewhat the standing of the latter.

To make matters worse, later prophets themselves seemed increasingly to be looking over their shoulder at their predecessors,[50] borrowing specific expressions and motifs from earlier prophets. Thus, chapters 40–66 of the book of Isaiah are widely attributed today to an unknown prophet active during the Babylonian exile and the period of return that followed it. These chapters are among the most moving in the Hebrew Bible, informed with a Hebrew style unmatched elsewhere.[51] Yet, consciously or otherwise, their author seems to have been deeply influenced by the language of his predecessors, particularly by the prophet Jeremiah, but also here and there by the books of the Pentateuch, Psalms, Lamentations, and Isaiah 1–39.[52] Sometimes, indeed, this anonymous writer seems in virtual dialogue with his predecessors. Here Jeremiah asks a rhetorical question:

> Can a young girl forget her jewels, or a bride her adornments? Yet my people have forgotten Me for days without number. (Jer 2:32)

This accusation seems to be consciously answered by the anonymous prophet called Second Isaiah:

> Can a woman forget her baby, and not have compassion for the child of her womb? Even if she might forget, I [God] will not forget you. (Isa 49:15)

A similar instance: the book of Jeremiah included this prediction:

> As I live, says the LORD: If you, O King Coniah [i.e., Jehoiachin], son of Jehoiakim of Judah, were a *signet ring* on My right hand, I would tear you off and hand you over to the ones who are trying to kill you. (Jer 22:24–25)

It is probably no accident that his words were echoed by the prophet Haggai:

> On that day, says the LORD of Hosts, I will take you, O Zerubbabel, My servant, the son of Shealtiel, says the LORD, and make you *like a signet ring;* for I have chosen you, says the LORD of Hosts. (Hag 2:23)

Zechariah was clearly thinking of Second Isaiah when he uttered these words:

> The word of the LORD concerning Israel: Thus says the LORD, who *stretched out the heavens and founded the earth,* and *formed the human spirit within.*

> "See, I am about to make Jerusalem *a cup of reeling* for all the surrounding peoples." (Zech 12:1–2)

Each of the marked phrases has its equivalent in Second Isaiah. Thus, Zechariah's "stretched out the heavens and founded the earth" calls to mind Isa 42:5, "Thus says GOD, the Lord, who created the heavens and stretched them out, who spread out the earth and what comes from it . . ." Zechariah's additional phrase describing God, "who formed the human spirit/breath (*ruaḥ*) within," modifies the continuation of this verse in Second Isaiah, "who gives spirit/breath (*neshamah*) to the people upon it." Next, Zechariah's warning, "See, I am about to make Jerusalem a cup of reeling for all the surrounding peoples" evokes Isa 51:17, "Wake up, wake up! Stand up, Jerusalem! You who have drunk from the LORD's hand the cup of His wrath, you have drunk to the bottom the flagon cup of reeling."

There is scarcely a better example of this new sort of phrase-borrowing prophecy than the New Testament book of Revelation. Nearly every page contains allusions and echoes of earlier prophets, and sometimes Revelation's author, John of Patmos, seems quite consciously to be evoking a particular book or even a specific chapter from an earlier prophet, as if to say, "What he said back then is happening now." Such is certainly the case with the following:

> Then I saw *a new heaven and a new earth;* for the first heaven and first earth had *passed away*, and the sea was no more. And I saw the holy city, *the new Jerusalem*, coming down out of heaven from God, *prepared as a bride adorned* for her husband . . . And I heard a loud voice from the throne saying: "See, *the tabernacle of God is among men, He will dwell amidst them; He will wipe away every tear from their eyes; Death will be no more; mourning and crying and pain will be no more; for the former things have past away.* (Rev 21:1–4)

Every one of the indicated phrases is an allusion to a biblical verse, most of them from chapter 65 of the book of Isaiah. Thus, "I saw a new heaven and a new earth" in Rev 21:1 evokes a famous verse in Isa 65:17, "For behold! I am creating a new heaven and a new earth."[53] The "new Jerusalem" in the next verse echoes the promise of Isa 65:18, "I will [re]create Jerusalem as a joy, and her people as a delight." Jerusalem being "prepared as a bride adorned for her husband" echoes Isa 61:10, "Let me rejoice in the LORD, let me delight in my God, for He has clothed me in garments of triumph, wrapped me in a robe of victory, like a bridegroom adorned with a turban, like a bride bedecked with her finery." God's instruction to the Israelites to construct the wilderness tabernacle, "Let them build Me a sanctuary so that I may well in their midst" (Exod 25:8) is reprised in the next verse of Revelation, "See, the tabernacle of God is among men, He will dwell amidst them." "He will wipe away every tear from their eyes" in the next verse of Revelation is like Isa 25:8, "My lord God will wipe the tears away from every face" just as the next phrase, "Death will be no more," echoes the continuation of this same verse in Isaiah, "He will destroy death forever" (Isa 25:8). "Mourning and weeping and pain will be no more" alludes to Isa 65:19, "Never again will the sound of weeping or crying out be heard there," and, "for the former things have passed away" picks up Isa 65:17, "The former things will not be remembered, they will never come to mind."[54]

No one would say that these or the other echoes and allusions to earlier Scripture are the product of chance. Clearly, the words of earlier prophets are cited so as to connect them to the present day, as if the events of the day were nothing less than the fulfillment of ancient prophecy. But in citing them, latter-day prophets and visionaries may have unwittingly confirmed in some people the feeling that true, reliable prophecy had come to an end. References or allusions to the prophets of old may well have led at least some to conclude that the prophets of the past were the real thing, and their later successors a pale imitation.

Is it not often the case that tumultuous changes in society can make the very people who initiate those changes nostalgic for some of the things that were before? It is said that the leader of the Russian Revolution, V. I. Lenin, once attended a poetry reading being given by the best known poet of the Revolution, the modernist Vladimir Mayakovski—but Lenin suddenly walked out in the middle. When the reporters covering the event ran out after him to ask why he was leaving, Lenin said simply: "I prefer Pushkin."[55] If the various bits of evidence examined above are any indication, it is not hard to imagine how some Judeans must have reacted to the newfangled prophets and seers who arose in post-exilic times, with their weird, otherworldly concerns, including the apocalyptic "time of the end," their citations and allusions to earlier Scripture, along with their angelic intermediaries and interpreters. Certainly not all of the returnees declared prophecy to have ended, but no doubt more than one or two must have muttered the post-exilic Judean equivalent of "I prefer Pushkin."

Daniel the Re-interpreter

Certainly the best known biblical example of the tendency of later prophetic figures to reinterpret existing Scripture is found in the book of Daniel. Daniel relates that on one occasion he "consulted the books concerning the number of years that, according to the word of the LORD that had come to Jeremiah the prophet, were to be the end of Jerusalem's desolation, seventy years" (Dan 9:2). This introduction in itself is surprising. The book of Jeremiah does indeed report that the prophet had said that in seventy years, the Babylonians would be punished and Israel's fortunes would be restored (Jer 29:10; cf. 25:12) — and this, give or take a few years, is exactly what happened. So what was Daniel consulting the books for? Seventy years are seventy years. But then the angel Gabriel appears and informs Daniel of the real meaning of Jeremiah's promise: he didn't mean seventy years, but seventy *groups* of seven years apiece, making for a total of 490 years:

> While I was still speaking, praying, and confessing my sin and the sin of my people Israel, setting my supplication before the LORD my God on my God's holy mountain — while I was still in the midst of praying, the "man" Gabriel, whom I had seen in the earlier vision, was sent forth in flight and reached me at the time of the evening offering. He spoke to me enlighteningly and said: "Daniel, I have come to you now to give you insight and knowledge. At the start of your prayer, a word went out, and I have come to tell it . . . Seventy groups of seven years have been decreed for your people and your holy city. (Dan 9:20–24)

As was seen above, the notion of 490 years *exactly* was not unique in Second Temple Judaism, and the reason is not hard to find.[56] Biblical law stipulates that the jubilee year is to come around once every forty-nine years (Lev 25:8);[57] the number 490 is simply one jubilee multiplied by ten (which comes out to be the same as Daniel's seventy "weeks of years" that is, the seventy units of sevens in Dan 9:24). So it came about that 490 years also appears here and there as a mega-unit of time in the Dead Sea Scrolls[58] (some of them contemporaneous with the book of Daniel).

In any event, this last-cited passage from Daniel recalls a number of themes already seen above: (1) the prophets of old (in this case, Jeremiah) had prophesied, but they themselves didn't understand the hidden message of their prophecies; (2) this in turn reflects the fact that most prophets are actually long-range predictors, their predictions having to do with times far distant from their own; (3) an angel (here, Gabriel) is needed to explain the significance of an ancient prophet's (here, Jeremiah's) words. It should be mentioned, moreover, that the whole book of Daniel embodies another phenomenon already discussed, pseudepigraphy. "Dani[e]l" was the name of an ancient, perhaps legendary, sage (he is mentioned in passing in Ezek 14:14). An anonymous author in the middle of the second century BCE chose this ancient sage to be the central figure of the book of Daniel, situating him in the Babylonian exile — thereby also turning his book into yet another collection of long-range predictions, some of which had already occurred or were coming to pass in his own time.

A Widening Gap

What can these various characteristics of the Second Temple period prophet/visionary tell us about how God was encountered in Second Temple times?

Perhaps the most striking element is the great distance that now seems to separate God from even those human beings who are held to be closest to Him, His prophets. It is not only that in this period He is often conceived to speak indirectly, through an angelic intermediary; equally significant is the content of the message that prophets now heard, since it, too, bespoke a great gap between humans and God. Thus, in pre-exilic times, the voice that prophets heard spoke of the immediate: "This is what God told me to tell you. It all has to do with the Assyrians. (Or the Egyptians, or the Babylonians, or Edom, Aram, Ammon, or Moab. Or with you, O king.) If they/you don't do as God says, this or that terrible thing will occur." Now, the message was different: "I saw this amazing sight. An angel explained to me that it all had to do with what will happen in the time of the end; reality as we know it will change forever. God is in charge, even though it is not always obvious. So keep the faith."

Other developments likewise bespeak the growing distance between God and humanity. In pre-exilic times, there was usually nothing obscure in what God told His prophets to say. So, for example, Isaiah had stressed just how obvious things were, at one point somewhat sarcastically suggesting to God, "Make the minds of these people impenetrable, and their ears hard of hearing, and their eyes sealed up tight; otherwise, they will see with their eyes, and hear with their ears, and their minds will understand — and [they will] then change their path and be made right" (Isa 6:10). But in Second Temple times, nothing was obvious. The future was hidden even from the visionary himself: he needed to have it deciphered and explained to him. Joseph and Daniel were both dream interpreters—but consider the difference between them. Pharaoh tells Joseph his dream, and then Joseph explains what it means. King Nebuchadnezzar, by contrast, demands of his wise men first to tell him *what* he dreamt—and only Daniel, with divine help, can meet this challenge. The king's demand is actually paralleled by the "handwriting on the wall" incident in Daniel chapter 5. There, a human hand suddenly appears and writes something on the wall of King Belshazzar's palace, but none of his wise men can even read the letters—until Daniel is summoned. (He can indeed read the writing, but he still has to explain what the cryptic words mean.) In both these cases, it is not enough for Daniel to be a clever interpreter. He must first *supply the text* to be interpreted.*

In considering the foregoing, it would be easy for a modern naysayer to exclaim, "Aha! It was all a bluff. That's why these pseudo-prophets and sages had to keep invoking some future Big Bang that will turn everything around, and why in the meantime God was always claimed to have arranged things in incomprehensibly huge patterns, while prophetic visions and ordinary reality are glimmering with secret meanings that only the initiates can understand." But to say this is, I think, to utterly misconstrue the minds of the people involved. To begin with, they weren't modern Westerners. God, or His angels, regularly did all sorts of things on a daily basis that would otherwise be quite inexplicable. How could one begin to understand the operation of the world without recognizing God's role and ultimate control of everything beyond human reach, sun and moon and stars, wind and rain and dew? And then there were those wicked powers, the evil *ruḥot:* how could one account for the sudden death of a man or woman in the prime of life without referring to those evil spirits as the ultimate cause? Why were some people suddenly struck dumb, their faces contorted into a grotesque rictus, or made unable to walk or even roll over in bed? And who but those wicked angels could kill a newborn baby, exacting revenge for some unknown deed, or else just being evil? No, there was no denying the divine (benign or satanic) in everyday life. What the Second Temple sages sought to do was what sages *always* try to do, to understand, to fit one observed fact with another. In the meantime, their oft-repeated prayer was: "Do not let the evil spirits rule over me," "Do not let Beliar/a satan take over my mind." The semipermeable mind was alive and well.

But even if all this is so, why were so many of these sages patent liars, writ-

---

* See in this connection Daniel's prayer (2:20–22), discussed in chapter 2.

ing books in which they pretended to be Moses or Enoch or Ezra? Wouldn't any honest person start with the truth of who he or she was?

This too misconstrues the mental world of these ancient sages. To begin with, authorship is a modern concept, as many studies (some quite unrelated to the Bible) have shown.[59] To superimpose this later concept onto compositions in which the very idea of authorship is absent guarantees misunderstanding. However, what the author himself believed about his own text is a very different question, and its answer will certainly vary from text to text. To mention a specific case: I have often been asked what the author of the *Book of Jubilees* thought he was doing. Here he was, in the second century BCE, writing a text that claimed to have been written a thousand years earlier, and written by Moses at the dictation of the Angel of the Presence, who in turn had been commissioned by God to dictate the book to him — who did he think he was kidding? I believe that I have come to know this author rather well over the years, and so I think I am right in saying that he didn't think that he was kidding anyone. The setting of his book may have been a fiction (although, for the reason mentioned above, he himself wouldn't put it that way), but I think I know that he was quite convinced that every word of his book had come to him from God. And the same might be said of a great many Second Temple period prophecies.[60]

PART IV

In Search of God

The transformations explored in the preceding section all reflect a growing sense of God's distance from humanity, and along with this, an increasing focus on the inside, on what ultimately became the soul. The soul was not God but God's, the special part of a human's insides allied with and devoted to Him. These changes then took on new forms of expression and led to a new kind of divine encounter.

14

THE ELUSIVE INDIVIDUAL

Collective punishment; Self-reflection in late biblical texts; Telltale changes in retold stories

Biblical texts from post-exilic times attest to a gradual move away from what had existed in an earlier day. Considered together, do these suggest a new focus on the importance of a single human life and a person's own virtues and vices?

I have read quite a few studies that seek to date "the emergence of the individual." Depending on who you read, the individual first emerged in ancient Mesopotamia, or perhaps in classical Greek civilization, or, no, in post-exilic Israel, or else in imperial Rome; make that the early Church, the rise of Islamic science, in thirteenth-century western Europe, the Italian Renaissance, the Protestant Reformation, and so forth.[1] On balance, it seems unwise to approach this matter in terms of *the* individual; a closer look reveals that such an absolute creature does not exist even today, and as for its "emergence," it seems to come and go even within a single society in a single period.

A potentially more fruitful undertaking might be to look at a number of specific changes in belief or practice as evidenced in the Bible, which together may shed some light on the overall subject of the present study.[2]

Achan's Kin

One item related to this inquiry has repeatedly been the subject of scholarly scrutiny, ancient and modern: Who should be punished for committing an offense?[3] The Bible is notoriously inconsistent on punishment. On the one hand, a number of passages seem to presume that it is perfectly natural for people to be killed for something that they personally did not do. Take, for example, the story of Achan (Joshua 7):[4] After the Israelites entered the land of Canaan, they were mysteriously defeated in a confrontation with the men of Ai, whom they had expected easily to overcome. Upon investigation, the reason becomes apparent. One of the Israelites, a certain Achan, had secretly taken some of the spoils of battle for himself instead of leaving them to be destroyed as God had instructed. Confronted with his crime, Achan confessed: "It is true. I have sinned against the LORD, the God of Israel" (Josh 7:20). The punishment for his crime was not slow in coming:

> Joshua took Achan the [grand]son of Zerah, along with the silver and the cloak and the wedge of gold [which he had taken illegally] *and his sons and his daughters and his ox and his donkey and his flock and his tent and everything that was his.* He brought these, along with all the Israelites, to the Valley of Achor. And Joshua said: "Just as you have brought disaster [*'achor*] upon us, so will the LORD bring disaster upon you this day." Then all the Israelites stoned him. They then burned *them* in a fire and *stoned them* with stones. They then raised a great pile of stones over him [which remains] to this day. Then the anger of the LORD subsided. (Josh 7:24–26)

It does not matter if this incident ever took place (it seems to most scholars to be designed to explain why the Valley of Achor—"Disaster"—is so called).[5] But the narrator apparently saw no problem with Achan's sons and daughters and domestic animals being burned alive and stoned for something they did not do. In fact, what is so interesting for our subject is that "they" and "he" seem to be used interchangeably in the last three sentences. It is as if the narrator assumes that Achan's offspring and possessions are an extension of his own person—as if they are not *individuals* in our sense, but expressions of a single, collective existence.[6]

This is hardly an isolated case. In the story of Dinah (Genesis 34), Simeon and Levi avenge their sister's rape by tricking the men of Shechem into undergoing mass circumcision, which was apparently performed on all the males in a single day.[7]

> On the third day [after this], when they were all in great pain, Simeon and Levi, two of Jacob's sons and [full-]brothers of Dinah, each took his sword and came upon the city [Shechem] unawares, and *killed all the males.* They *killed Hamor* and his son Shechem [the rapist] at sword-point; then they

> took Dinah out of Shechem's house and went away. The other sons of Jacob then fell upon the corpses and plundered the town, since *they* had defiled their sister. They seized their flocks and herds and donkeys; everything that was inside the town and outside it they seized. All their wealth *and their children and their wives they took as prisoners—all that was in the houses they took as prisoners and booty.* (Gen 34:25–29)

Jacob later reproves his sons for creating strife between him and the neighboring Canaanites (Gen 34:30), but he says nothing about the unfairness of killing all the males of Shechem to avenge a single man's act of rape. As for Jacob's sons then seizing the Shechemite women (now widows) and children—no ancient reader needed to be told what this meant: the women would become household slaves, many of them no doubt raped at will, and the town's children would likewise be enslaved for life. But what were *they* guilty of? Again, however, the most interesting thing about this passage is its maintaining that the town was plundered "since *they* [the men of Shechem] had defiled their sister"—where "they" should really refer to a single individual. Was there any reason to believe that *all* the townsmen, or even any subgroup thereof, had participated in that crime? Or does this tale, like the Achan narrative, seem to presume that relatives and neighbors can quite naturally be assimilated into a single collective personality of the perpetrator and therefore suffer collective punishment?

In another famous incident, the wicked Jezebel, wife of King Ahab, arranges to have Naboth killed so that Ahab can expropriate Naboth's prized vineyard (1 Kings 21). Naboth is accordingly framed and stoned to death. This story has a moral lesson, however: Elijah informs Ahab that God is aware of his crime and has ordained his punishment: "In the place where dogs licked up the blood of Naboth, dogs will lick up your blood as well" (1 Kgs 21:19). Hearing this, Ahab "humbled himself," exchanging his regular clothing for sackcloth and fasting,[8] and God took notice:

> Then the word of the LORD came to Elijah the Tishbite: "Have you seen how Ahab has humbled himself before Me? Because he has humbled himself before Me, I will not bring disaster in his lifetime. *I will bring the disaster on his family in his son's time.*" (1 Kgs 21:29)

Clearly, there is some distinction here between Ahab and Ahab's son (Jehoram): God's promise to visit Ahab's punishment on his son is presented as a lightening of his sentence. But what did Jehoram do?! He is apparently considered something like a limb of his father's body, to be lopped off at some future date and thus punishing Ahab in such a way as to allow him to continue living. But wasn't Jehoram a separate person?[9]

The same question might be asked of God's punishment of David after his sin with Bathsheba (2 Samuel 11). David's act of adultery with her, and his subsequent arrangement for her husband to be murdered, were dastardly crimes for which the severest punishment was due (2 Sam 12:10–13). But then, perhaps prompted by Nathan the prophet, David fasts and prays and lies down on the ground in self-abasement:

> David said to Nathan: "I have sinned against the LORD." Then Nathan said to David, "The LORD has set aside your punishment; you will not die. However, since you have spurned . . . the LORD in this matter, *the son born to you* [by Bathsheba] shall die" . . . And the LORD afflicted the baby whom [Bathsheba,] the wife of Uriah, had borne to him, so that it became weakened to death. David entreated God on the baby's behalf, and he fasted and went in and lay down on the ground that night. When the senior servants of his palace arose and tried to get him up from the ground he refused, nor would he have any of the food they brought with them. Then, on the seventh day, the child died. (2 Sam 12:13–19)

Once again an innocent human being, the baby that Bathsheba had borne to David from their illicit union, is punished for someone else's guilt. True, the baby was, quite literally, the product of their sin; nonetheless, this is another clear case of vicarious punishment, as if the newborn baby was no real person but something more like a finger or a toe of the king, to be chopped off as a painful but survivable loss in consideration of David's ritual acts of appeal to God.

"Vicarious" and "transgenerational" punishment seem to be a regular feature in numerous passages in the Hebrew Bible.[10] In perhaps the best known of such cases, God is said in the Ten Commandments to "visit the punishment of the parents upon the children, to the third and fourth generations of those who reject Me" (Exod 20:5)*[11] The same principle is maintained in the list of divine attributes in Exodus 34:

---

* The phrase "of those who reject Me" (some translations: "of My enemies") is much debated; it has sometimes been interpreted to refer to those who *continue* to reject Me in the third and fourth generations, but the more straightforward meaning is that the descendants of "those who rejected Me in the first generation" will be punished to the third or fourth generations, even if these are altogether innocent. In the next verse, God promises to "save up kindnesses

> The LORD passed in front of him [Moses] and cried out: the LORD, a God merciful and compassionate, patient and of great kindness and faithfulness; keeping kindness for the thousands, forgiving transgression and iniquity and sin. *But He will not wipe away* [all guilt], but *will visit the transgression of the fathers upon their children and grandchildren, to the third and fourth generation.* (Exod 34:6–7)[12]

This is Achan all over again: a person's flesh and blood are ipso facto liable to be punished along with, or even instead of, the guilty person himself. Much later, the book of Lamentations still held by the same principle to explain the destruction of Jerusalem by the Babylonians:

> Our fathers sinned and are no more; but as for us, we are the ones to suffer their punishment. (Lam 5:7)

Nevertheless, this principle underwent evident modification in several places. The book of Deuteronomy, for example, quotes without modification the assertion in the Ten Commandments that God punishes children for their parents' sins (Deut 5:9–10). But then it goes on to contradict that statement outright:

> And you shall know that the LORD your God is *the* God, a God who may be trusted to uphold His covenant and loyalty to those who love Him and keep His commandments — for a thousand generations [to come]! But he requites *directly* anyone who rejects Him, destroying him; He accepts no delay for those who reject Him, but requites them *directly.* (Deut 7:9–10)

The Hebrew phrase translated as "directly" (*el panayv*) is sometimes rendered as "to their face," "in their own person," or "instantly." Each of these carries a somewhat different nuance, but the overall sense seems clear: God will not have to resort to transgenerational punishment but will punish sinners directly, "in their own person," without delay. Later in the same book, transgenerational punishment is once again clearly ruled out:

---

to the thousands of those who love Me and keep My commandments" (Exod 20:6). Taken on its own, this too is somewhat ambiguous. The word "thousands" is subsequently glossed in Deut 7:9 and elsewhere as "a thousand generations," but here it may simply have meant saving up kindnesses (or "covenant loyalty") for the thousands of people who are loyal to Me.

> Let fathers not be put to death because of [their] sons, nor sons be put to death because of their fathers; let each be put to death for his own offense. (Deut 24:16)[13]

Unripe Grapes

Along with these passages in Deuteronomy are equally striking ones in the book of Ezekiel. In fact these, even more clearly than those already seen, present transgenerational punishment as unacceptable:

> What is wrong with you, O you who apply this proverb to the Land of Israel: "The fathers eat unripe grapes, but it is the children's teeth that ache"? I swear, says the Lord God, you will no longer use this proverb against Israel. All lives belong to Me: as the life of the father, so is the life of the son—both are Mine. Whoever sins, that person will die. (Ezek 18:2–4)[14]

There follows a lengthy illustration of this principle: a righteous man who has led an exemplary life, "Such a man shall live, the Lord God says" (Ezek 18:9). But if such a man has a son who is quite his opposite—one who commits every sin in the book—"He [the son] shall not live! If he has committed any of these abominations, he shall be put to death; the responsibility is his" (Ezek 18:13). Now suppose the wicked son in turn has a son of his own, one who has "obeyed My statutes and observed My laws":

> He shall not die for the transgression[s] of his father—he shall surely live! His father, since he practiced oppression and robbed a brother and did no good [even] within his family—he died for his transgression[s]. And if you should ask, "But why isn't the son punished for the sin of the father, however much the son himself may have acted justly and fairly, keeping all My laws and putting them into practice—shall such a one 'surely live'?" [The answer:] The person who commits the sin is the one who shall die. The son will not bear the punishment of the father, nor will the father bear the punishment of the son. The righteous man's righteousness will stand by him, and the wicked man's wickedness will be upon him. (Ezek 18:18–20)

I have cited this repetitive set of examples precisely because it is so repetitive. Ezekiel sounds as if he's talking to an eight-year-old. *Now do you under-*

stand? Now do you get it? Clearly, even at this relatively late date, the idea of transgenerational or vicarious punishment was still deeply rooted. Ezekiel's patient explanation is apparently aimed at an audience for whom the idea of individual responsibility needed detailed illustration.

This passage in Ezekiel is explicit in its abandoning transgenerational punishment. But it goes further: even undoubted sinners, if they turn from their evil ways, need not pay the penalty for their former misdeeds:

> "But the wicked man, if he turns away[15] from the sin that he has done and [now] keeps all My laws and acts justly and fairly, he [too] shall surely live and not die. All the sins that he did will not be counted against him; he shall live by dint of the righteous acts that he has done. Do I delight in the death of the wicked? asks the LORD. Rather, do I not [delight] in his turning away from his former doings, so that he may live?" (Ezek 18:21–23)[16]

The Transgenerational Advantage

In view of this apparent evolution — from (1) punishing children for the sins of their fathers to (2) assigning responsibility for sins only to those who actually committed them, to (3) divine forgiveness even for the sinner himself, so long as he abandons his sinful ways — one might well ask why these changes took so long to work themselves out. Indeed, why should God ever have been represented as punishing later generations for the sins of earlier ones? But actually, it made good sense. Everyday life, as human beings have always observed, often seems unfair. Apparently virtuous people sometimes end up suffering terrible mishaps, while the notoriously sinful at times seem to be getting away scot-free. Even the most obvious candidates for reward or punishment are sometimes passed over. Gangsters and politicians ride around in chauffeur-driven limousines, while professors take the bus. Where is divine justice?

Vicarious punishment offered a kind of answer. The guilty may seem to get away with their crimes, but God is simply biding His time, perhaps even unto the third or fourth generation. As for the reward of the virtuous, this too may take time, but even if the virtuous person himself died unrewarded, somewhere down the line, one of his descendants will be receiving a reward all out of keeping with his own modest virtue: he's living off the good deeds of his departed ancestor. Moreover, if the divine bureaucracy thus appears sluggish or inscrutable, well, so does the human one. In either case, things seem eventually to work out, and that is the main thing; justice delayed may nonetheless be just.

This should in turn cause us to view the above-cited passages from Deuteronomy and Ezekiel in a somewhat different light. In rejecting the old, familiar argument of vicarious punishment, these passages were, in effect, throwing away God's best excuse. What could make these biblical authors take such a step? It is tempting, in the context of the present study, to say that somehow an ancient sense of self—one whose "I" included a person's whole family, indeed, whole tribe or people—had been slowly eroding. The truth now seemed far simpler: the only fair way to administer reward and punishment was directly, *el panayv*; the unripe grapes should affect only the teeth of him or her who ate them. As the French sociologist Marcel Mauss observed, "There has never existed a human being who has not been aware, not only of his own body, but also at the same time of his individuality, both spiritual and physical."[17] But what the human makes of this awareness—a person's sense of self—is always a construct.

At the same time, it is far from clear that anything as basic as a change in people's sense of self was involved in the matter of divine punishment. The shift from vicarious to direct punishment may have started off as some particular person's *idea*, an idea about justice that gradually gained widespread acceptance (at least in the Hebrew Bible); but such a change need not necessarily have been rooted in something quite so deep or widespread as a change in people's sense of self, a new way of conceiving of themselves as individuals. The fading out of transgenerational punishment *may* be symptomatic of something broader, but this remains to be seen.

In the meantime, it is also worth mentioning (though this hardly undermines the previous argument) that the rejection of vicarious punishment, like so many things in biblical thought, proceeded by two steps forward, one step back. Long after any of the above-cited texts was written came the book of Esther, whose stereotypical villain, Haman, received classical transgenerational punishment: not only was he killed, but his ten sons were executed after him (Esther 9:7–10)—what did they do, apart from having the wrong father? In fact, five hundred other people (Esther 9:6) were subsequently killed, then three hundred more (9:15), and finally an additional seventy-five thousand for good measure (9:16). True, these corpses may be the fantasy of a subject people eager to imagine that revenge had, at least on one occasion, been theirs; but whatever else these numbers prove, they seem to be saying that the idea of vicarious punishment was not altogether dead.

Thinking About Myself

The next item to be discussed is a bit harder to pin down than the straightforward acceptance or rejection of vicarious punishment; still it needs to be mentioned. A number of relatively late biblical texts present a person's thoughts about himself, reflecting on his life in general or recounting something that has happened to him — in short, something that might fit under the general heading of "thinking about myself." Clearly, this would seem to belong in a chapter about the elusive individual, precisely because such self-reflections are strikingly absent from the Hebrew Bible. But what exactly counts as self-reflection?[18]

It is sometimes said that King David is the most interesting "character" in the Bible (perhaps because his story is no literary invention at all, but a slightly airbrushed record of the real-life doings of a guerilla leader who robbed and murdered his way to the throne).[19] But it may be significant for our subject that there is not a lot of self-reflection in this story. David is defined by his actions; we are not privy to his inner thoughts in his relations with Saul or Jonathan or Bathsheba or anyone else, nor are we told what he was planning at various crucial turning points in his life — in short, there is very little "I" there, and apparently not because he was a particularly self-effacing personality. The same might be said of earlier heroes, such as Samson in the book of Judges. He performs all manner of amazing feats of strength in Judges 14–15, then carries on with Delilah for much of the next chapter — but what he was thinking about what was happening to him, at the time or even afterwards (when the Philistines gouge out his eyes before bringing him down to Gaza), is a total blank.

As mentioned, such things *may* be significant, but not necessarily. The absence of self-reflection from biblical biographies may simply be a matter of literary convention that tells us nothing about the biblical sense of self in Samson's time, or David's. To mention an analogous case: for centuries, Western historiography consisted mainly of recounting military conquests and defeats, as well as recording (and often distorting) the doings of kings and queens in court, sometimes degenerating into the grossest sort of royal boasting. (After all, who was paying the historians?) Social history — chronicling the way ordinary people lived and died — is essentially an invention of the twentieth century; a spinoff, women's history, emerged only toward the end of that century. Or, returning to the world of the Hebrew Bible, scant attention is paid to women there, even insofar as they affect men; there is thus almost no mention of affairs of the heart in the Bible, no face that launches a thousand ships. But this probably tells us nothing about the real-life role of women in biblical times—only about what was deemed significant, or seemly, to report. Another example of the influence of literary convention on our question may lie in those psalms of request examined earlier, in which the psalmist pulls out all the stops, relating in gruesome detail his physical suffering or the threats to his life. This too seems to be a matter of convention, reflecting an unspoken assumption concerning God's response to prayer: "If you want My help, you'd better need it!" (And of course none of this is accompanied by any account of the psalmist's inner life, of what he is thinking in these dire straits, apart from the fact that he is in mortal danger and needs help now.)

In short, rather than our considering the *absence* of self-reflection per se, it may be more promising to examine a shift from its absence to its presence—among prophets, for example. It would not be unfair to say that Israel's ninth- and eighth-century prophets do not dwell much on their inner selves.[20] Elijah and Elisha perform miracles, but we are told nothing about their inner thoughts at such moments—what they were thinking or what it took for them to do what they did.[21] The same could be said of the great eighth-century prophets: What do we know about the inner life of Amos or Isaiah? God tells Hosea to "get a wife of whoredom" (Hos 1:2), in other words, "Go marry a prostitute"—certainly an odd demand—but what Hosea himself thought about this is never related. What was said about Abraham earlier might indeed describe all these prophets. They are not "fraught with background" at all; rather, they are presented to us as ciphers, faceless communicators of the divine word.

But then there come the exceptions. As we have seen, the sixth-century prophet Jeremiah does not hesitate to tell us what is going on inside him, especially in his well-known "laments":

> Is there anyone whom I can talk to—to warn them, so that they'll heed?
> But everyone's ears are stopped up, they're unable to take in my words.
> The word of the LORD has become . . . an embarrassment, which they don't need.
> But I'm full of the wrath of the LORD; I can't hold it inside any more.
> (Jer 6:10–11)

His doubts, his disappointments, are displayed for all to see:

When Your words first came I devoured them: Your words were a joy,
a delight to my heart;
Your name was joined to mine, "the LORD God of Hosts."
I avoided the revelers' parties; my joy was Your hand placed upon me.
So I sat by myself, all alone, brimming with Your righteous anger.
Then why is it now I have unending pain, a wound that will never be healed?
Will it turn out You've been for me . . . a fountain whose waters gave out?
(Jer 15:16–18)

Perhaps a generation later, we encounter the anonymous prophet who authored chapters 40–66 of the book of Isaiah. He too reflects on his life. In fact, he sometimes sounds a bit like Jeremiah:[22]

My Lord GOD taught me to speak, with an eloquent word for the weary,
Rousing my ear every morning to utter an eloquent line;
Yes, my Lord GOD opened my ear, and I did not object or retreat.
I surrendered my back to the floggers, gave my cheeks for my beard to be plucked.
I did not protect my own face from their insults, their spit and abuse.
My Lord GOD gives me His help. That's why I won't be ashamed—
Why I harden my face like flint, since I know that I won't be disgraced.
Who dare try to take me on now? My Defense stands right at my side.
(Isa 50:4–8)

It would be nice to see in such passages the emergence of a new sense of self reflected in, among other things, the way these two prophets speak of themselves and their role.[23] But the prophets who followed them—Haggai, Zechariah, and Malachi—are as faceless as Jeremiah's predecessors, and the same is certainly true of the apocalyptists who came still later, submerging their own identities in the pseudepigraphic personae that they adopted. In short, Jeremiah and Second Isaiah may attest to a new sort of self-reflection, but, as the saying has it, one swallow (or even two) does not a summer make. They may just have been exceptional.

Job and Ecclesiastes

There are, however, two strikingly new selves in the Hebrew Bible that bear special mention here. The books of Job and Ecclesiastes (Hebrew *Koheleth*) are often grouped together, since the author of each expresses, in his own way, dissatisfaction with the overall ideology of "wisdom" (discussed above in chapter 2). Both books take issue with the notion that God's supreme control of reality guarantees that life is basically fair, that righteousness is rewarded and evildoing punished — and in so doing their authors disagree with the message repeatedly articulated in the story of Joseph in Genesis, as well as throughout the biblical book of Proverbs and later in the book of Ben Sira (Sirach), and, for that matter, in traditional wisdom collections from ancient Egypt and Mesopotamia dating back to the third millennium BCE.[24] Perhaps it is this oppositional stance that led the authors of Job and Koheleth to reflect on their own lives (at only a slight remove) as proof that wisdom's ideology is false. In any case, their lives and their thoughts are front and center in these books, and this sets them apart from traditional wisdom collections, whose speakers — wise sages who have mastered wisdom's truths — speak ex cathedra, faceless embodiments of an altogether predictable set of eternal verities.[25]

Job's biography is well known. He was originally a champion of traditional wisdom, respected by his fellow sages as one who not only espouses wisdom's teachings but exemplifies them in his daily life. Then catastrophe strikes. A wicked angel (called here a satan*) challenges God to allow him to put the righteous Job to the test: "Make him truly suffer and see if he remains faithful to You." God accepts the challenge and allows this heavenly challenger to do his worst; first the satan destroys Job's wealth, suddenly causing his flocks and herds to be seized by raiders, then kills Job's servants and all of his ten children, and finally afflicts Job's own body with terrible sores. At first Job bears his downfall bravely, as a traditional wisdom sage ought: "Should we accept only good from God," he asks his skeptical wife, "and not accept evil as well?" (Job 2:10).

But then Job's "comforters" arrive. The term "comforter" itself is somewhat misleading. It was traditional for someone who had suffered a personal loss to enter a ritual of mourning, tearing his own clothes (very costly) and/or covering his skin with sackcloth (very uncomfortable), putting ashes on his head and lamenting his fate. (This is, for example, precisely what Jacob does in reaction to the news that his son had been killed, Gen 37:34.) The job of comforters was not so much to make the mourner feel better as to enact a set ritual, one that, like all rituals, created a kind of familiar territory for people

* Not the Satan of later times, the embodiment of evil, but a heavenly accuser or adversary. See Zech 3:1–2, Ps 109:6, 1 Chron 21.1.

in moments of transition or stress.[26] As part of this ritual, the mourner at first had to "refuse to be comforted" (Gen 37:35), loudly lamenting or not speaking at all, while the comforters uttered the usual truths about disaster or death — that, however difficult this might seem, what had happened was part of the divine plan and therefore had to be accepted. (This is what was called, in later times, *tzidduk ha-din,* "justifying the decree.") When at last the mourner ritually surrendered and "accepted consolation" (*kibbel tanḥumin*), the comforters' job was done and they returned home.

That is what should have happened with Job, but his loss was so great that he just wasn't buying what his comforters said. Nothing like this *can* be accepted, he tells them: God has obviously set out to destroy me. It would have been better if I had never existed.

> "Let the day I was born not have been! Nor the night when they wished for a boy!
> Let that day be so covered in darkness, so black that no deity sees it; let no ray of light ever find it.
> With dark clouds hovering above it, let drear and gloom repossess it, their blackness covering all." (Job 3:3–5)

The comforters of course say what they have been trained to say: "Job! Get a hold of yourself! You've been a comforter yourself so many times. There must be a logic to what has happened to you. And if not — well, take your case straight to God. True, He sometimes punishes us — but He also binds up our wounds. Just accept it and move on" (chapters 5 and 6).

This may all seem like merely ritual behavior, and "Job" is in any case a fictional character. But no reader of the book can escape the feeling that behind this book stands a real (and rather modern) self, someone who is accustomed to thinking about his own life, indeed, watching it on the big screen, while God, for all His being God, is no longer the overwhelming Master to whom all must simply submit:

> "But I'm innocent — shouldn't I know? That's why I'm sick of my life.
> It's all the same, as I said: He kills both the good and the bad.
> If disaster should suddenly strike, He laughs as the innocents fall.
> A villain grabs somebody's land? He covers the magistrates' eyes.
> (If that's not Him, then where is He?)
> So my days run faster and faster, soon they're gone! But they gave me no pleasure.
> Now they're off like a swift-running boat, like an eagle after its prey.

If I say I'll forget my complaining, give up my heart's lamentation,
I still dread the suffering that's left, since I know I won't get off easy.
I'm 'in the wrong,' that's all; why waste the last of my strength?"
(Job 9:21–29)

Modern readers sometimes mistake Job's theological skepticism. He has no doubt about God's existence; in fact passages like the above (and there are many) only stress how much he feels God's heavy presence breathing down on him. But it is the notion that God is fair that he can no longer abide:

"Why do the wicked live on? Growing older, they only get richer.
They reproduce, smile on descendants, while they themselves live securely—
no rod of God's ever strikes them.
The bulls in their fields rut on demand, and their cows give birth without fail.
Their infants gambol like sheep; their children dance in a round,
playing on harp and on timbrel, singing to the sound of the pipe.
They spend out their days in comfort, then peacefully head to Sheol.
To God they say, 'Let me be. I have no need of religion.
Who's "Almighty," that we should revere Him? What good does it do to pray?'
Yet all that they have didn't come from themselves—the fate of the wicked is
too much for me!
How often is *their* light snuffed out, as their downfall at last overtakes them?
Let God in His anger rebuke them. Make them like a straw in the wind, like
chaff that the storm carries off.
'God saves His wrath for their children'? Let Him punish the source—so he'll
know!
Let his own eyes witness his downfall, let him taste the Almighty's
displeasure!
If not, why should he care if those who come after die young?
Should he be allowed to teach God or act like some heavenly judge?"
(Job 21:7–22)

Lest all this get a little abstract, Job keeps reminding us of his very real, physical condition:

"But now, my soul is exhausted; my suffering tightens its grip.
Nighttime snatches my strength, and my sweats refuse to let go.
With great effort I loosen my clothes or tug at the neck of my gown.

I've been thrown down to the mud — yes indeed, 'I am dirt and ashes.'*
If I bow to You, You don't answer; if I stand, You pay me no mind.**
You've become a bringer of torment, You hound me with all of Your force.
You whisk me up with the wind, until my senses all fail me.
Oh I know the end that awaits me; there's one place for all who have lived.
But must He attack a ruin? Must I cry out in pain to perish?
And have I not wept at my hardship, vexing my soul at my downfall?
I begged for the good but got evil; though I yearned for the light, all was black.
Now my insides are never at peace, days of pain are all that is left."
(Job 30:16–27)

The end of the book is altogether predictable. God always has the last word, so how dare a mere mortal call His justice into question?

"Who is this who demeans understanding with words that lack any insight?
Stand on your feet like a man! Now *I'll* ask, and you give the answers:
Were you there when I set earth's foundations? Tell me, if you're truly clever.
Who fixed its size — you must know! — or measured it out with a rule?
Into what were its bases inserted, and who put its cornerstone down,
as the morning stars droned in chorus, and the sons of God all gave song?"
(Job 38:2–7)

As suggested above, it is revealing to think about the man behind the man, the one who enjoys contemplating what it means to be a suffering human being in a world still controlled by God, but in which God's spokesmen can only answer in familiar clichés, while the author's own spokesman is vivid and strikingly *big,* a hero observed in detailed close-ups on the big screen. What ultimately makes the most sense to him in this world is not arriving at a conclusion, but playing both sides of the Ping-Pong table and then declaring the match a draw.

To one familiar with biblical Hebrew, Job is masterwork. His speech is full of vivid images enlisted in the service of densely argued speeches, for the most part in classical biblical Hebrew (bearing some similarity to the language of Isaiah and Jeremiah) but peppered with numerous learned borrowings from Aramaic and Akkadian. (These were apparently intended to support Job's identity as someone from "the land of Uz" [Job 1:1], one of those

---

* Cf. Gen 18:27.

** Bowing and standing (with arms extended upward) are both biblical postures of prayer.

places to the south and east of biblical Israel where wisdom was proverbially said to flourish [1 Kgs 5:10; some Bibles 4:30].)

The figure of Koheleth (in modern transcription: Qohelet) is altogether different: his speech is often colloquial and not particularly elegant. In fact, scholars are not quite sure what to make of his language; it seems to belong to a slightly different dialect from standard Hebrew, with some possible connections to what we know of Phoenician. As to its author, the first verse asserts that these are "the sayings of Koheleth, son of David, king in Jerusalem." The only son of David who was king in Jerusalem was Solomon, so this verse, along with Ecclesiastes 1:12, which mentions Koheleth being "king in Jerusalem over Israel," was always taken as an indication that "Koheleth" was just some sort of nickname of Solomon's, who had a reputation for wisdom (1 Kgs 5:9–14; some Bibles 4:29–34). As for the name "Koheleth," it seems to be derived from the Hebrew root meaning "assemble, collect." If this was Solomon, perhaps it was a reference to his assembling the various tribes and subtribes that his father David had ruled and gathering them into a truly unified state. He may thus have been nicknamed the "man of the assembly," the *koheleth,* a word that was ultimately translated into Greek as *ekklēsiastēs,* which is why his book is called Ecclesiastes in English and other languages.

But the attribution to King Solomon is generally rejected today by modern scholars. To begin with, it makes little sense for someone born in the royal court to have expressed himself in a non-Jerusalemite Hebrew, in fact, in a kind of otherwise unknown barbaric yawp.[27] Moreover, there are two loanwords in the book derived from ancient Persian, *pardes* (an enclosed garden or orchard) and *pitgam* (a royal decree). Even if Solomon himself was a master of foreign languages, what would he gain by slipping in these words if none of his readers could know what they meant? To say that Solomon wrote these words in his book would be the equivalent of a Shakespearean scholar claiming that a poem containing such words as "shampoo" or "juggernaut" or "pundit" had been penned by the Bard; any linguist could figure out that these are loanwords borrowed from Hindi as a result of Great Britain's prolonged colonization of India, long after Shakespeare's death. It is the same with *pardes* and *pitgam.* The period of prolonged contact between Judea and the Persian Empire was from the end of the sixth to the end of the fourth centuries BCE, when Judea was part of the empire, so this would seem to be the period in which the book was written.[28] Moreover, words designating a royal decree and a fancy sort of orchard are just the kind of things picked up by a native population from their distant foreign emperor or his minions. As for the name Koheleth, scholars now suggest that it reflects another Semitic root, rare in Hebrew but present in the Bible (Num 16:23, 20:2, Neh 5:7) as well as in Syriac, and meaning "to argue" or "reprove."[29] Putting all this together, it seems reasonable to assume that Koheleth was the real name, or nickname, of some sort of Persian-appointed Jewish official, the "Arguer," who ruled over "Israel" (that is, the Jews) in Jerusalem and environs, perhaps indeed someone who was a "son (that is, a descendant) of David," and therefore a likely candidate to be appointed by the Persians as a governor (*peḥa*), if not quite a "king" in the usual sense, over his countrymen.

Perhaps the most striking element in the book is that Koheleth the man (and here, I think, it is proper to identify the book's speaker with its flesh-and-blood author) is, even more than Job, a doubter of wisdom's clichés about God. There really doesn't seem to him to be any great ordering Hand in the world; taking the long view, life seems to this author to consist of a series of actions and opposite actions, so that everything cancels itself out:

> So futile, says Koheleth, everything's so futile.
> What does a person ever net from all the efforts he expends under the sun?
> One generation goes out and another comes in, but the earth stays the same forever.
> The sun rises and the sun sets, then rushing back to its place, it rises again.
> The wind blows to the south, then turns to the north; it turns and turns as it goes — the wind — and goes back again by its turning.
> All the rivers flow to the sea, but the sea is never full,
> [because] to the source of the river's flowing, there they flow back again.
> Though all words grow tiresome, people never stop speaking;
> the eye never takes in enough, nor is the ear filled up with hearing.
> What has been is what will be, and what has been done will be done again,
> for there's nothing new under the sun.
> Sometimes there's something about which it's said, "Look at this! This is new!"
> But long ago it existed, in the ages that came well before us.
> There's no remembrance of former things, just as, with regard to the things that come later, they will likewise have no remembrance with those who come after them. (Eccles 1:2–11)

Koheleth's ideas and affiliations have been much discussed, but what is of interest here (as with Job) is how he seems to conceive of himself and his fitting into the world. Perhaps the first point to be made is that *examining* his own life is important to him. This is something that one does not find earlier in biblical texts.[30] In fact, his book is a kind of intellectual autobiography, and he therefore spends not a little time telling the reader about himself. Of course, a great many scholars have suggested that this "autobiography" is pure fiction: this is the work of some philosophically inclined sage pretending that he is King Solomon, the better to investigate life from the standpoint of someone with unlimited access to wealth and power. This may be the case, though the book's strange language, the name Koheleth, and the absence of any overt attempt to connect this figure with Solomon (by saying, for example: "I am Solomon" instead of "I am Koheleth") might well lead one to believe that this is a Persian-period governor's first-person account of his own life. Whichever the case, however, what is striking is that the speaker of this book begins with a lengthy account of how he used his abundant resources to test whether it is better to be a "fool" (not an idiot so much as a hedonist) or "wise" (the opposite of a fool).

> I, Koheleth was a king in Jerusalem over Israel. So [being a king], I set my mind to searching out and examining through wisdom everything that is done under heaven. Oh, what a miserable task it is that God has given to human beings with which to busy themselves!
>
> I observed all the things that are done under the sun, and everything seemed futile and a chasing after the wind [that is, a fruitless waste of time].
>
> That which is twisted cannot become straight,
> just as that which is absent can never be counted.* [. . .]
>
> I said to myself, "Let me test you with pleasure and enjoyment" — but this as well proved futile . . . I acquired many possessions: I constructed houses for myself, I planted vineyards, I got gardens and orchards and planted in them all manner of fruit trees. I had pools of water made for me, to irrigate a forest burgeoning with trees. I acquired slaves and servant girls, and had home-born servants as well; likewise many herds of cattle and sheep were mine, more than any other's I had seen in Jerusalem. I stored up silver and gold, and with these the treasuries of the provincial rulers. I acquired male and female singers, and those delights of mankind, a concubine, nay many. I got more and more of all that was before me in Jerusalem — but all the while, my [pursuit of] wisdom was at my side. Anything that my eyes desired I did not withhold from them; I did not refuse them any sort of pleasure, and my heart rejoiced in all my wealth — for such was my lot from all

* In other words, you don't know what *isn't* there.

my wealth. Then I turned to assess all the possessions that I had acquired and all the wealth that I had gotten and kept. And I saw that everything was futile and a chasing after the wind, since there is no net gain under the sun. (Eccles 1:12–15, 2:1, 4–11)

As we have seen, there are many autobiographical monuments that Phoenician and other kings have set up to their own glory, some of them preceding by centuries the Persian period in which Koheleth's book was probably written. A lot of them actually turn out to be royal invention.[31] Koheleth, too, may be exaggerating his wealth, but to make a different point; he is not boasting but recounting a serious undertaking, his own search for the best way to live one's life. And so it is important to say how he intended to do this: *not* by asking for God's help or prophetic inspiration or anything of the kind, but through considering his own experiences, using all the great resources at his disposal to try things out, since "What can someone else do who comes after the king? Only that which has been done before." (Eccles 2:12)

> Then I turned to consider all the oppression that is done under the sun, and indeed, here are the tears of the oppressed, who have no one on their side. The oppressors have the power, but they [the oppressed] have no one on their side. So I rate the dead,[32] since they are already dead, higher than the living, because these still have to remain alive. But better off than both of these is the one who has not yet been, because he has not experienced the evil that is done under the sun. (Eccles 4:1–2)

This is not all there is to Koheleth, by any means. His concern with his own life continues throughout the book, extending even to the epitaph he creates for himself at the end of the last chapter. Apparently, he would like to be remembered most of all as a maker of wise sayings, someone who "weighed and studied and created many proverbs; Koheleth sought to find fitting words, written down squarely — truthful sayings" (Eccles 12:9–10). But as he scrutinizes his own life, what emerges is no great, single theme but a series of contradictory statements: "Wisdom's advantage over folly is like the advantage light has over darkness" (Eccles 2:13), yet, "What will befall the fool will befall me as well [i.e., death], so why should I seek to accrue more wisdom [than him]?" (2:15); "More bitter than death is a woman: she is all traps, her hands are fetters and her heart is snares" (7:26), and yet, "Enjoy life with a woman whom you love" (huh? 9:9). More generally, time itself is full of opposing actions: "There is a time to give birth[33] and a time to die, a time to plant and a time to uproot what is planted" (etc., 3:1–11). Such contradictions are apparently not the result of sloppiness, but rather reflect the author's attempt to record, and honor, the contradictory things that he has concluded at various stages of life. To him well applies the French saying *Il se contredit pour avoir tout dit,* "He contradicts himself in order to have said everything."

Rewriting Biblical Stories

One last phenomenon belongs in this chapter, although it is as difficult to pin down as some of the material already seen. In general, in any case, Second Temple period texts seem to show an interest in the role that individual people may play in determining their own destiny.* The roots of this interest may go back as early as Ezekiel's stress (examined above) on the way that a person's turning aside from sin may stave off the divine punishment that he himself deserved. Much later, as we have seen, Ben Sira argued that the source of human sinfulness was not some external "spirit" dispatched by a wicked angel, but:

> God created mankind in the beginning, and gave him over to the power of his own disposition.
> If you wish, you will keep a commandment, and faithfully do God's will.
> If you trust in Him, you too may live.
> Fire and water are set before you; extend your hand to whichever you choose.
> Life and death are before a person: whichever he chooses will be given to him. (Sir 15:14–17)

But this same interest in the human side of things finds one of its most dramatic expressions in the way later authors sometimes retold earlier biblical stories in their own words. For example, the *Book of Jubilees* goes over many of the narratives in the book of Genesis; often, the author changes the story so as to have it fit with his own ideology and/or the interpretive traditions he has inherited. But sometimes, he seems to change the narrative in order to flesh out the character of one or another figure mentioned in the narrative. This is perhaps most clearly shown in the person of Isaac's wife Rebekah.

It may be said of the portrayal of Rebekah in Genesis what was said earlier of the portrayal of Abraham and his descendants; in fact, of most of the bib-

---

* Some examples have been seen already, in chapter 3.

lical prophets as well: she is a kind of literary cipher, barely mentioned and utterly lacking in any kind of characterization or personal depth. The author of *Jubilees* seems determined to set things aright.[34] In his retelling, Rebekah suddenly becomes a real person,[35] a mother who, when her time has come to die, does all she can to prevent her two sons — who have long been on bad terms — from descending into actual violence. She first goes to her husband Isaac and asks him to make Esau swear that he will not harm Jacob (*Jub* 35:9–17). Of course, there is not a word of any of this in Genesis. But the author of *Jubilees* apparently felt that Rebekah-the-person, foreseeing her own death, ought to have done something to smooth things over between her two sons. In the process, she and her two sons become real people, whereas in Genesis they were little more than etiological stick figures, Jacob representing the future people of Israel and Esau the people of Edom, while Rebekah was no more than the biologically necessary mother of both.[36]

In fact, *Jubilees'* author was not content with merely having Rebekah ask her husband to restrain Esau. She herself then goes to speak to Esau directly:

> Then Rebekah sent and summoned Esau. When he had come to her, she said to him: "I have a request that I wish to make of you, my son. Say that you will do it, my son." He said: "I will do whatever you tell me; I will not refuse your request." She said to him: "I ask of you that on the day I die you bring me and bury me next to your father's mother Sarah; and that you and Jacob love one another, so that neither [of you] will seek anything bad for his brother, but that you will only love one another. Then you will be prosperous, my sons, and be honored on the earth. No enemy [of yours] will triumph over you. You will become a blessing and a [source of] kindness in the eyes of all who love you." And he said: "I will do everything that you have told me." (*Jub* 35:18–21)

Even recognizing the concern of *Jubilees'* author to portray Rebekah as a real-life mother, we might think that the above conversation with Esau would have ended the matter (especially since, in the end, Esau goes back on his promise — *Jub* 37:7–9). But for *Jubilees,* even this is not enough. So Rebekah then goes to Jacob, her other son, to make sure that he is onboard with this new era of fraternal good will:

> Then she summoned Jacob in Esau's presence and gave him orders in keeping with what she had said to Esau. He said, "I will do whatever pleases you. Trust me that nothing bad towards Esau will come from me or my sons. I

> will seek only to love him." She and her sons ate and drank that night. She died that very night, at the age of three jubilees, one week, and one year [= 155 years]. Her two sons Esau and Jacob buried her in the Cave of Machpelah, next to their father's mother Sarah. (*Jub* 35:25–27)

The transformation of Rebekah in the *Book of Jubilees* is certainly striking, but hardly unique. Take, for another example, the story of Abraham's near-sacrifice of his son Isaac. We have already seen that the biblical account tells us very little about Abraham's reaction to this demand of God's; he gets up *early* in the morning, apparently a token of his unquestioning obedience to God, and sets out on a journey to kill his son.

But what of Isaac? He is about to become the actual victim, yet the narrative tells us nothing of his reaction to these events. Even if his father had kept him in the dark until almost the very end (Gen 22:7–8), Abraham ultimately did tie Isaac up and hoist him onto the altar (22:9): surely some words had to have been exchanged at that moment, if not before. And why didn't Isaac try to resist? We don't know how old he was, but he was apparently old enough to carry the load of firewood on his own (22:6); let us stipulate that he was at least a young teenager. That would mean that Abraham was 112 years old (or more) at the time of these events (Gen 21:5). Surely the young teenager could outrun his aging dad once he understood what was afoot — unless, of course, he had willingly accepted being sacrificed. Whatever the case, the Bible's schematic narrative offers no answers; apparently, Abraham was the only important figure in the story. Isaac was just a prop.

When it comes to the Second Temple period retellings of this story, the situation changes dramatically. Now Isaac is indeed a real person, the Bible's first willing martyr:

> And as he [Abraham] was setting out, he said to his son, "Behold now, my son, I am going to offer you as a burnt offering and I am returning you into the hands of Him who gave you to me." Then the son said to the father, "Hear me, father. If [ordinarily] a lamb of the flocks is accepted as a sacrifice to the Lord with a sweet savor, and if [whole] flocks have been set aside for slaughter [to atone] for human iniquity, while man, on the contrary, has been designated to inherit this world — why should you now be saying to me, 'Come and inherit eternal life and time without measure'? Why if not that I was indeed born in this world *in order to* be offered as a sacrifice to Him who made me? In fact, this [sacrifice] will be [the mark of] my blessedness over other men — for no such thing will ever be [again] — and in me

> the generations will be proclaimed and through me nations will understand how God made a human soul worthy for sacrifice. (Pseudo-Philo, *Book of Biblical Antiquities* 32:3)[37]

Josephus retells the crucial exchange between father and son in even greater detail. Here both Abraham and Isaac appear in their human glory:

> But after the altar had been prepared and he had put the firewood on it and everything was ready, he said to his son: "My child, in thousands of prayers I begged God for you to be born, and once you had entered this world, I spared nothing to lavish on your upbringing. I could think of nothing that would give me greater happiness than to see you grow to manhood, and at my death to bequeath to you my whole estate. But since it was by God's will that I became your father, and now it seems best to Him that I give you up, accept bravely this act of consecration. [After all,] I am giving you up to God; He is the one who is demanding this homage in return for the favors that He has granted me as my support and ally . . ."
>
> Isaac, being the son of such a father, could hardly *not* be brave of heart; and he did indeed accept these words with joy. He said that if he resisted the decision of God and of his father and did not willingly surrender to the will of both, he ought never to have been born in the first place; [in fact,] even if this were his father's decision alone, it would have been unworthy on his part to disobey—whereupon he rushed to the altar to be slaughtered. The whole thing would have indeed been carried out, if God had not stood in the way, calling Abraham by name and forbidding him to slay the boy. (Josephus, *Jewish Antiquities,* 1: 228–33)

Many such instances, whereby a biblical cipher is retrofitted with human character, can be found in Second Temple period writings. But let one more example serve for many, the elaboration of Joseph's entanglement with the wife of his master Potiphar after Joseph has been sold as a slave. Potiphar's wife is attracted to the handsome young man, and the Genesis account does not mince words in relating what happened between them.

> After a time, [Potiphar's] wife cast her eyes on Joseph and said, "Lie with me." But he refused. He said to his master's wife, "Look, with me here, my master gives no thought to anything in this house, and everything that he owns he has entrusted to me. There is no one more important in this household than me, and he has held back nothing from me—except of course for

> you, being his wife. So how could I do this great evil and sin against God?" Although she kept speaking to Joseph [like this] day after day, he did not pay her mind, to lie with her or even to be around her. Then, on a certain day, he went to the house to do his work, but none of the household was there in the house. She grabbed him by his garment and said, "Lie with me," but he left his garment in her hand and got away and fled outside. (Gen 39:7–12)

Here, we are actually allowed to hear Joseph thinking out loud — quite rare in biblical narrative — in fact, in this long speech, it seems Joseph may even be seriously weighing the proposal for a minute or two (as if he were saying, "Look, your husband trusts me implicitly, and none of the household staff would dare report on me, I *am* the chief slave, so maybe . . ."), before deciding that he really ought to refuse and not "do this great evil and sin against God."

We thus get a sustained look at Joseph — and this really ought to be enough. But what about Potiphar's wife? A reteller of these same events could easily have turned her into a stock character, the unattractive harpy, or simpler still, she could have been utterly neglected, as in the biblical story. But the author of the *Testaments of the Twelve Patriarchs* took the trouble of detailing her thoughts and deeds, as seen by Joseph himself:

> How often did she flatter me, calling me a holy man, praising my self-restraint with deceitful words in the presence of her husband, but wishing only to trap me when we were alone! In public, she would praise me as showing self-restraint, but in secret she would say to me: "Don't worry about my husband — he is already convinced of your self-restraint! Even if someone were to tell him about [the two of] us, he wouldn't believe it." Amidst all these things I lay down on the ground in sackcloth and I beseeched God, so that the Lord might save me from the Egyptian woman.
>
> When she in no way succeeded, she again came to me under the pretext of [wanting] instruction, "to learn the word of God." And she said to me: "If you want me to abandon the idols [that I worship,] then sleep with me, and I will persuade the Egyptian [Potiphar] to give up idols, [so that] we both will walk in the law of your Lord." And I said to her, "The Lord does not accept any who [would] worship Him in impurity, nor is He pleased by those who commit adultery." At this she remained silent, wishing [only] to carry her desires to their conclusion. For my part, I increased my fasting and prayer, so that the Lord would save me from her.

Here, it would seem, it is Joseph who is close to being a cliché: pious in the extreme, he is beyond all temptation. She, on the other hand, is realistic even in her desperation. Her attempts to seduce Joseph know no bounds, and they go on for pages and pages. She threatens to kill her husband so that she can marry Joseph legally, then tries to work some sorcery by tampering with Joseph's food; after this, she resorts to a little piety of her own, promising to convert to the religion of Israel if only Joseph will submit. This is followed by a period of piteous weeping and groaning, leading eventually to her threatened suicide — all to no avail.

> But realizing that the Spirit of Beliar was tormenting her, I prayed to the Lord [on her behalf. Then] I said to her, "Why are you so disturbed and upset? [Are you] blinded by sins? Remember that if you kill yourself, Setho, your husband's concubine — your rival! — will beat your children and destroy your memorial from the earth."[38] Then she said to me: "So you do love me! It is enough for me [to know] that you care about my life and my children's. I can still expect that my desire [for you] will be fulfilled."

The account of her tormented, unrequited love goes on, as mentioned, for pages and pages — even after, in keeping with the biblical account, she finally accuses Joseph of attempted rape and has him imprisoned. But this, according to the author of the *Testaments*, was just another stratagem, since Joseph's imprisonment would give her unobstructed access to him in his cell:[39]

> How often, despite her being ill [i.e., lovesick], did she used to come down to [my cell] at midnight to hear my voice as I prayed! But whenever I heard her groan, I would stay still. For when I was in her house, she used to bare her arms and breasts and legs to get me to lie with her — and she was very beautiful, splendidly adorned in order to seduce me — but the Lord saved me from her exertions.

Such novelization of various schematic biblical figures may simply represent the adoption of the conventions of Greek romances and other genres by later Jewish writers. But the broader question that this raises is: Why? It is easy to imagine a pious critic in antiquity rebuking the author of the *Testaments* or anyone else who sought to Hellenize biblical narratives:[40] "How dare you act as if this biblical tale was anything remotely resembling a Greek novella? It is sacred Scripture, as far from such literature as Jerusalem is from

Athens." If such reproaches were made, however, they apparently did not stop the author of the *Testaments* from doing what he did. Nor did they impede the Jew who recast Joseph's encounter with his future bride Aseneth in the Hellenistic novella *Joseph and Aseneth,* nor the writer who sought to explore Eve's inner motives in the Garden of Eden in the *Life of Adam and Eve.* So perhaps all of these were a reflection of some great sea change, something like a new understanding of the human being as having "inner depths" that had previously gone unrecognized.

Or perhaps not. In fact, as I have been suggesting, everything surveyed in the present chapter may rightly be explained on other, more limited grounds. The rejection of vicarious and transgenerational punishment may have been no more than a reflection of a very local shift in human judicial norms. Jeremiah's laments — in fact, Jeremiah's generally painful depiction of himself as a struggling, vulnerable prophet — seems to have been altogether sui generis, not comparable to the presentation of any other prophet, earlier or later. Job and Koheleth are both protestors against the standards of conventional wisdom — this may be part of the reason for their authors' very human portrayal of both. And as just suggested, the "novelization" of biblical figures, especially women, in Second Temple times may simply be evidence of one relatively small change in the "representation of reality in Western literature" (as Eric Auerbach subtitled his famous work, *Mimesis*). Perhaps more damning than any of these arguments is the ineluctable fact that they are all based on *texts,* things that were written down and copied and recast and recopied. We don't really know much about scribal culture before the Babylonian exile (and not all that much about what followed the return from exile), nor is it easy to guess why many of these texts were written down in the first place. As a general principle, it is probably safe to say that most of them were written down for one purpose and ended up being preserved in the Bible for quite another.

And yet, surveying what seem to be some of the oldest texts in the Hebrew Bible and comparing them to others that are clearly later, a real difference is evident. Most of the stories of the patriarchs in Genesis, along with those of Deborah or Gideon or Samson or the concubine at Gibeah (all in the book of Judges), seem to exist in a different *world of assumptions* from that underlying the portrayal of the various ideas and figures surveyed in the present chapter. Was this a strictly literary change, or is it attesting to something far broader if harder to pin down, a different sense of what it means to be a person, indeed, that elusive item, the individual?

15

HUMANS IN SEARCH

Psalms that establish contact; Divine remoteness and the heavenly temple; Retrofitted with virtue; The Song of Songs and the yearning for God

The Second Temple period's greater focus on a single human life (as suggested by various texts mentioned in the last chapter) was accompanied by another change. A number of texts from this period seem to highlight God's remoteness. Now, instead of God intervening in human affairs by stepping across the dividing line that separated ordinary from extraordinary reality, it was human beings who were suddenly "in search of God," a God who was frequently depicted as remote and out of reach. Were these two phenomena related?

Since the late nineteenth century, scholars have divided the book of Psalms into various subcategories. Apart from the psalms of petition examined above, there are psalms of praise (in general) and psalms of thanksgiving (for a specific act of intervention, or thanksgiving offered time and again at various festivals or other ritual occasions). In addition, there are "enthronement psalms," proclaiming God as king at one or another hypothetical celebration, psalms recited by or on behalf of individuals upon payment of a vow or in search of divine approval, plus "Zion hymns," pilgrimage psalms or "psalms of ascents," and so forth. Almost all of these psalms have a presumed place in which they were sung or recited: the Israelite temple(s) as well as, at least for a time, "high places" or other sacred sites.

Placeless, Occasionless Psalms

But then, toward the end of the biblical period, come a number of psalms that are apparently placeless and occasionless, psalms that seem neither to be asking for something specific nor offering heartfelt thanks for a particular act of divine intervention, nor praising God in connection with some festival or rite.[1] They offer no particular reason for being recited. They also consistently speak in the first person singular, "I," "me," or "my soul" (*nafshi*). Attaching a date to a particular psalm has always been a somewhat risky business; many scholars are content to label psalms as pre-exilic or post-exilic and leave it at that. (Sometimes a historic reference will support a more specific dating. Psalm 137 begins, "By the rivers of Babylon we sat down and wept," an obvious reference to the Babylonian exile, hence its dating as "exilic or early post-exilic.") But these placeless and occasionless psalms are often dated late not because of some historical reference, but because of the specific words they use, words that seem not to have existed in earlier Hebrew texts (in some cases because they were borrowed from Aramaic in post-exilic times), or lexical items that seem to have taken on a different meaning in later times, or formulations that seem to have been gradually modified over time. A good example is Psalm 145:

A [psalm of] praise, of David*

1 I will exalt You, O God and King, and bless Your name forever and ever.
2 Let me bless You every day, and praise Your name forever and ever.
3 Great is the LORD, and much to be praised; His greatness is unfathomable.
4 For ages and ages Your deeds will be hymned, and Your mighty acts recounted.
5 I will speak of the splendor of Your glorious majesty and of Your wondrous acts.
6 Let the might of Your fearsome deeds be told, and let me recount Your greatness.
7 Let the fame of Your beneficence be told, and Your righteousness be sung.

* The apparent attribution to David (or: the Davidic collection of psalms) is not taken by most scholars as an actual indication of its origin, but a late editor's addition. Such attributions continued to be added in the Septuagint translations of the Psalms as well as in noncanonical works.

8 The LORD is gracious and merciful, slow to anger and abounding in kindness.
9 The LORD is good to everyone, and His mercy extends over all the living.
10 Let all whom You made give You thanks, O LORD, and let Your faithful ones bless You.
11 They will speak of Your glorious kingship and tell of Your powers,
12 Making known to all people Your mighty deeds, and the glorious splendor of Your kingship.
13 Your kingship is an everlasting kingship, and Your dominion will last for all generations.
14 The LORD upholds all who stumble, and makes all who are bent stand straight.
15 The eyes of all look to You in hope, and You give them their food in its time,
16 Opening Your hand and feeding every living thing its needs.
17 The LORD is just in all His ways, and kindly in all that He does.
18 The LORD is close to all who cry out to Him, to all who cry out to Him faithfully.
19 He fulfills the desire of all who worship Him; He hears their plea and saves them.
20 The LORD watches over all who love Him, but all the wicked He will destroy.
21 Let my mouth speak the praise of the LORD, and all flesh bless His holy name forever and ever.

The linguistic arguments suggesting a late dating for this psalm are many.[2] While most of the indications of lateness would pass the nonspecialist by, such lexical items as the word translated "hymned" in verse 4, the references to God's "kingship" in verses 11 through 13, the particular formulations "everlasting" (literally, "in all ages") and "for all generations" (more literally, "in each and every generation") in verse 13, and the word for "stand straight" in verse 14 (apparently an Aramaism) all suggest a rather late date of composition.[3]

But what is particularly interesting about this psalm is precisely its placeless and occasionless quality. There is no mention of a temple or other holy spot where the psalm is to be recited; there are no other people in the background. In fact, the psalmist seems altogether alone: for the most part it is just God and "I." As for its being occasioned by some specific thing that happened or some particular celebration, the psalmist rules this out from the start: "Let me bless You *every day*," the second line says. In fact, if this psalm has an overall theme or subject (not all psalms do), it would seem to be the act of praising God itself. This is what the psalmist talks about in each of the first seven verses, and then returns to this subject again in verses 10–12 and yet again in verse 21. Between these verses, the psalmist seems to be taking his own advice, repeatedly praising God's goodness and mercy. Note also that the psalmist doesn't seem to be expecting any kind of answer. In fact, despite God's being repeatedly addressed as "You," He seems quite distant in this psalm. His greatness is "unfathomable." His "kingship" — no matter how His control of things may be obscured from time to time — will always exist: "Your dominion will last for all generations."[4]

Considering all this, praising God seems to be not only the subject, but the psalmist's whole reason (one might even say, his pretext) for opening his mouth in the first place. "Praising You," he says, "is what I wish to do now — after all, doing so altogether befits Your greatness, and it is what everyone else does, or at least should do [vv. 1–7]. So I will recite these verses, which have conveniently been composed in alphabetical order, in fact I wish to do so every day, as a gesture of devotion and piety."[5]

Psalm 145 is not quite unique in its offering of placeless and occasionless praise to God, though it is certainly a relatively rare sort of psalm.[6] But one might include under the same rubric another alphabetical psalm with signs of lateness, Psalm 34, which begins,

> Let me bless the Lord at any time, let praise of Him be forever in my mouth.
> Let my soul glorify the Lord, so that the lowly may hear and be glad.
> Exalt the Lord and with me, let us praise His name together. (34:1–3)

Here again is the theme of perpetual praise ("at any time," which can also mean "at all times").

Another example — if anything, more obviously placeless and occasionless — has already been discussed: Psalm 119. The mere recitation of this huge, 176-verse litany must have been thought to be a kind of offering, and it has the same solitary feel as Psalm 145: the psalmist is alone, endlessly reiterating in different combinations his praise of God (here along with his requests for enlightenment, understanding, and secret knowledge from the Torah).* What is striking in both psalms is the writers' evident taking the initiative,

---

* Note, however, that the psalm offers no clue as to what this enlightenment or secret knowledge might consist of or come in answer to.

seeking out God at no special time or place and with no special need or request, offering praise along some pretty standard lines, as if merely repeating these things constituted a readily available reason for addressing Him. A dotted line connects these three psalms to a few others in the book of Psalms (certainly 103, 104, 139, 146, and perhaps some others) that are also placeless and occasionless (and apparently late),[7] and thence to the *Thanksgiving Hymns* from the Dead Sea Scrolls, with their repeated offerings of thanks that also sound like pretexts — for having been saved from apparently typological enemies, or for God's having "revealed the ways of truth and the works of evil" (col 5:20), "placed me by the source of streams in a dry land" (col 16:5), and repeatedly for "not rejecting me," "purifying me," "having made known to me the secret counsel of truth," and the like.

It is difficult not to contrast all this with relations between man and God in an earlier day, when He was said to buttonhole Moses or Jeremiah or Jonah. Then it was indeed "God in search of man," a God who calls out from the middle of a burning bush, or who picks up Ezekiel from over here and drops him down over there. But after a while, all this stopped happening, and I believe that this is what those placeless, occasionless psalms are all about. The balance had somehow shifted; now it was the human who was searching, reaching out to a remote and hard-to-imagine deity through prayers of praise.

Heavenly Travelers

This new phenomenon, people being "in search of God," is manifest most strikingly in those human beings who actually ascended into heaven in order to stand before God's heavenly throne. Of course, from time immemorial, people had imagined what it would be like to ascend to heaven and look around. The earliest written account of such an ascent goes back to ancient Sumer, in the late third or early second millennium BCE, and peoples in the ancient Near East and elsewhere continued to explore the possibilities of this genre in the centuries that followed. It should be mentioned that heaven in those days didn't mean the limitless reaches of outer space, as it does today. Rather, it was the "upper shelf," that sky-blue expanse just above the lowest clouds and a little higher than the highest mountain peak. If one could only get up there, one could commune directly with the gods or the angels and find out what they were planning, or gain some other form of hidden knowledge, or request a special favor, or stay there permanently and become immortal.[8]

Yet it is striking that the Hebrew Bible itself contains only one heavenly ascent,[9] the famous account of how a chariot of fire came sweeping down and picked up the prophet Elijah:

> Now when the LORD was about to carry Elijah up to heaven by a whirlwind, Elijah and Elisha [his prophet-apprentice] were on their way from Gilgal. Elijah said to Elisha, "Stay here; the LORD is sending me to Bethel." But Elisha said, "As the LORD lives, and as you yourself live, I will not leave you." So they went down to Bethel. The company of prophets who were in Bethel came out to Elisha and said to him, "Do you know that today the LORD is taking your master away from you?" And he said, "Yes, I know; keep silent." . . .
>
> They were walking and talking as they went, when a chariot of fire and fiery horses separated the two of them, and Elijah *ascended in a whirlwind into heaven.* Elisha kept watching and cried out, "Father, O father! The chariots of Israel and its horsemen!" (2 Kgs 2:1–12)

In its larger context, this account seems designed to assert that Elisha was indeed a fit successor to Elijah, and almost his prophetic equal. (In the continuation of this passage, Elisha quite literally picks up Elijah's prophetic mantle, a symbol of his succession.) But as for Elijah, his ascent into heaven puts the final seal of divine approval on his life's work. This prophet and miracle worker did not die like an ordinary human being, this text says; he ascended bodily into the upper realms on a chariot of fire.

That this is the only account in the Hebrew Bible of a heavenly ascent seems significant in light of what happened in the late- and post-biblical period. Suddenly, anonymous writers began to imagine all sorts of other heavenly voyagers.[10] For the most part, they chose figures known from the Bible itself who, for one reason or another, might be likely candidates for such a heavenly ascent — such as the antediluvian Enoch. The book of Genesis had related his death in somewhat ambiguous terms:

> And Enoch lived sixty-five years and he became the father of Methuselah. And Enoch *walked with God* after he became the father of Methuselah for three hundred years; and he fathered sons and daughters. And all the days of Enoch were three hundred and sixty-five years. And Enoch *walked with God;* and he was not, for God *had taken him.* (Gen 5:21–24)

Enoch must have been a particularly righteous fellow if the passage mentions that he "walked with God," not once but twice. (The same phrase was used only once for the righteous Noah, Gen 6:9.) But why, among all the other ancestors mentioned in the genealogical list of this chapter, was Enoch the only one of whom it is *not* said, "and he died"? Ancient interpreters came to believe that Enoch didn't die. If the text said that God had "taken him," this may not have been a euphemism for death; it may have meant that God took him up bodily into heaven while Enoch was still alive, and that he continued to live a blessed existence up there ever after, on that sky-blue upper shelf.

A number of distinct compositions of the Second Temple period thus matter-of-factly relate that Enoch traveled to heaven:

> [Enoch says:] And the vision appeared to me as follows: the winds caused me to fly and hastened me and *lifted me into heaven.* (*1 En* 14:8; also 4Q204 col 6:21)

> Few on earth were created like Enoch, and he was *likewise taken within.* (Sir 49:14)*

> He [Enoch] lived three hundred and sixty-five years and then *returned to divinity,* which is why nothing is recorded of his death. (Josephus, *Ant.* 1:85; cf. 9:28)

> By faith was *Enoch taken up* so that he should not see death; and [this is what is meant by] "he was not found because God had taken him." (Heb 11:5)

The first mention of Enoch's heavenly ascent cited above comes from the "Book of the Watchers" section of *1 Enoch,* currently chapters 14–16 of *1 Enoch.* A more detailed version of his ascent is found in the "Similitudes" section of that same work (first century CE), chapters 37–71. Another, quite separate, Enoch pseudepigraphon, *2 Enoch* (or *Slavonic Apocalypse*) from the first century CE contains a far more extensive tour of heaven, in which Enoch learns not only secrets of the heavens themselves, but how the wicked are punished for their sins, the location of paradise, and the answer to various questions arising out of Scripture.

Jacob's son Levi was another biblical figure who was retroactively pro-

---

* "Taken within" seems to mean taken bodily inside heaven. Ben Sira says "likewise" because he had earlier mentioned Elijah's ascent into heaven (Sir 48:9–10).

moted to heavenly traveler by an anonymous, Second Temple–period author.[11] In the section devoted to Levi in the *Testaments of the Twelve Patriarchs,* Levi reports:

> And I was grieved for the race of the sons of men . . . and I prayed to the Lord to be saved. Then sleep fell upon me, and I saw a high mountain, and I was on it.[12] And behold, the skies were opened and an angel of the Lord said to me: "Levi, enter." And I entered the first heaven I saw there a great [body of] water, suspended. And I saw a second heaven and more luminous and brighter, and the height of it was boundless. And I said to the angel: "Why is this so?" And the angel said to me: "Do not marvel over this, for you will see another heaven, brighter still and beyond compare, when you get there. You will stand close to the Lord, and you will be His servant, and you will announce His secrets to men . . . And your livelihood will be from the Lord's portion, and He shall be your field, vineyard, fruits, silver, gold." (T. Levi 2:4–12)

The angel is apparently referring to the future selection of Levi's descendants to serve in the temple of Jerusalem. Notice, however, that this text is also interested in revealing what it's like up in heaven. There are apparently three heavens, or rather, three layers of heaven, as the angel goes on to explain:

> Hear, then, is [what I have to say] about the heavens that have been shown to you. The lowest one is, by that very fact, gloomy-looking to you, since [as the lowest] it looks out on all the sins of men; and it has fire, snow, ice, ready for the day of the judgment in God's righteous meting out of justice, for in it are all the Spirits of [various] afflictions [used] as punishments for the wicked.
>
> And in the second [level of heaven] are the forces of the armies [of angels], which are arrayed for the Day of Judgment, to punish the Spirits of deceit and of Beliar.
>
> And in the highest heaven resides the Great Glory, in the holy of holies, far above all [other] holiness. In it [i.e., the highest heaven], next [in rank] to Him, are the angels of the Lord's Presence, who serve and make atonement before the Lord for all the unwitting sins of the righteous, offering to the Lord a sweet savor, a reasonable and bloodless sacrifice.
>
> And in the lower heavens are the angels who carry the answers [*better:* repentances] to the angels of the Lord's Presence. And in the one next to these are thrones and dominions, by whom praises are always [i.e., contin-

ually] offered to God. And when the Lord looks out on us, we all tremble —indeed, the heavens and the earth and the abysses [themselves] tremble at the presence of His majesty. But humans do not perceive these things and [so] sin and provoke the Most High. (T. Levi 3:1–3:10)

The Temple in the Sky

While the apparent purpose of this visionary trip to heaven (from which Levi returns to earth alive) is to validate his descendants' appointment to serve in Israel's earthly temple, it is significant that his angelic guide takes the time to explain heaven to him as well. God was not just "up there," somewhere; this text, along with other Second Temple writings, has a definite picture of what goes on there. God presides over a temple in heaven.[13] He sits enthroned and surrounded by angels; these are frequently depicted as *fiery* angels (in part because of a certain reference in Ps 104:4); indeed, the whole scene is often alive with bright flames.[14] By common accord, heaven consisted of different levels. The above passage seems to maintain that there are three such levels, corresponding to the three ranks of angels assigned to each. But other texts maintain that there were actually seven levels (perhaps corresponding to the seven planets, as well as to the sanctity of the number 7)—whence our expression "seventh heaven," meaning heaven's highest level.

These same themes were taken up by other heavenly travelers. Here is Abraham in the *Apocalypse of Abraham* (possibly composed in the first or second century CE):

> And it came to pass that when the sun was setting, and behold, a smoke like that of a furnace, and the angels who had the divided parts of the sacrifice ascended from the top of the furnace of smoke. And the angel took me with his right hand . . . And *we ascended* like great winds to the heaven that was fixed on the expanses. And I saw on the sky, on the height we had ascended, a strong light that cannot be described. And behold, in this light a fire was kindled [and there was] a crowd of many people in the likeness of men. They were all changing in appearance and likeness, running and being transformed and bowing and shouting in a language the words of which I did not know.
>
> And I said to the angel, "Where, then, have you brought me now? For now I can no longer see, because I am weakened and my spirit is departing from me." And he said to me, "Remain with me, do not fear! He whom you

> will see going before both of us in a great sound of holiness is the Eternal One who had loved you, whom himself you will not see . . ." (*Apoc. Abr.*, 15:1–16:2)

The text goes on to describe a multilayered heaven (this time, there are seven layers — or perhaps eight) and the different sorts of angels who serve before God's heavenly throne.

Baruch, Jeremiah's scribe, was also promoted retroactively to heavenly traveler in another late Second Temple period text (*3 Baruch*). His heavenly ascent includes a vision of things mentioned in the Bible:

> And again the angel of hosts said to me, "Come and I will show you greater mysteries." And I said, "I pray you, show me what those men are." And he said to me, "These are the ones who built the tower of the war against God, and the Lord removed them." And taking me, the angel of the Lord led me to a second heaven. And he showed me there a door similar to the first. And he said, "Let us enter through it."
>
> And we entered, flying about the distance of sixty days' journey. And he showed me there also a plain, and it was full of men, and their appearance was like (that) of dogs, and their feet (like those) of deer. And I asked the angel, "I pray you, sir, tell me who these are." And he said, "These are the ones who plotted to build the tower. These whom you see forced many men and women to make bricks. Among them one woman was making bricks in the time of her delivery; they did not permit her to be released, but while making bricks she gave birth. And she carried her child in her cloak and continued making bricks. And appearing to them, the Lord changed their languages by that time they had built the tower 463 cubits (high). And taking an auger, they attempted to pierce the heaven, saying, 'Let us see whether the heaven is (made) of clay or copper or iron.' Seeing these things, God did not permit them (to continue), but struck them with blindness and with confusion of tongues, and he made them be as you see . . ." (*3 Bar* 2:6–3:8)

Here again the heavenly traveler not only sees heaven but is also made privy to heaven's secrets. This time, however, those secrets include additional information about things related in the Bible. The angel thus shows Baruch the full punishment God imposed on the builders of the tower of Babel, while also explaining the true nature of their crimes (not mentioned in Genesis). He goes on to explain what really happened in the Garden of Eden, and other biblical narratives.

This hardly exhausts the list of heavenly travelers,[15] and it is noteworthy that the New Testament includes the heavenly ascent of Jesus (Luke 24:51; Acts 1:9) and of John of Patmos (starting in Rev 4:1), as well as Paul's oblique account of his own ascent (2 Cor 11:30–12:7).

A World of Mystery

As mentioned earlier, heavenly ascents are found in numerous texts in ancient Near Eastern writings, as well as in those of Greco-Roman literature, including such compositions as the proem of Parmenides's poem *On Nature* (late sixth or early fifth century BCE), the "Myth of Er" in Plato's *Republic* (10.614–21), and Cicero's *Somnium Scipionis.* Even within the Jewish and Christian orbit, the different accounts of ascents serve varied purposes.[16] But the particularly striking element in most of the Jewish and Christian material is precisely their common assumption that just above the clouds is a mysterious world not normally accessible, but one that has been revealed to the heavenly traveler.[17] "Up there," the traveler can observe the movement of the stars and the geography of heaven, as well as — in some of the texts seen above — be informed about the orderliness of the universe and of biblical history, which, taking the long view, will ultimately reveal God's utter control of reality.

This sort of revelation is quite different from those of earlier biblical texts. In the prophetic books, for example, God is generally represented as speaking to prophets here on earth — in fact, they usually seem to have no need to travel anywhere.[18] Moreover, the messages that they receive are generally not about anything secret. God tells them what to say to someone else — to fellow Israelites, to kings and queens, or to foreign nations. Moreover, His messages generally relate to what is happening now or about to happen in the near future. But the heavenly travelers whom we have surveyed enter a world of secrets: the layout of heaven, the ways of divine justice, the secret meaning of biblical texts. If they speak of the future, it is usually the distant future. In all these senses, these various ascents to heaven seem to be the most vivid representation of how humans came to be "in search of God." They expect and want to find Him up there *since He is no longer down here,* and they all end up having their wish granted, taking in a breathtaking vista of God's own throne room on high, indeed, seeing God Himself.

Much of the same sort of information, minus the breathtaking vistas, is imparted in the various other Second Temple narratives, in which a figure from the Hebrew Bible meets up with an angel here on earth. The angel answers the same sort of difficult questions as were posed by the heavenly travelers, questions about God's control of things on earth, divine justice, the future of Israel, the resurrection of the dead, and so forth. So in a sense, these angel interviews are the complement of the heavenly ascents — in this case, a denizen of heaven comes down to human beings to converse with them on earth. Here, for example, is part of the extended series of questions and answers between the angel Uriel and Ezra in *4 Ezra*, an apocryphal book composed sometime in the last decades of the first century CE. After a brief review of biblical history, from the creation of Adam to the time of David and the building of the Jerusalem temple, Ezra asks God (via Uriel) how He could have allowed His temple in Jerusalem to fall into the hands of the Babylonians and be destroyed:

> [Ezra says:] And so it was that You handed over Your city to Your enemies.
>
> But then I thought: "Are the deeds of those who inhabit Babylon any better [than Israel's]? Is that why it has gained dominion over Zion?" For when I came here [to Babylon], I saw ungodly deeds without number, and my soul has seen many sinners during these thirty years. And my heart failed me, because I saw how You have put up with those who sin, and [how You] have spared those who act wickedly. You have destroyed Your own people and protected Your enemies! And You have not shown to anyone how Your way may be comprehended. Are the deeds of Babylon better than those of Zion? Or has some other nation recognized You besides Israel?

Ezra's angelic interlocutor Uriel doesn't really have a good answer. All he can come up with is the usual, "You're just a human being — what can you understand?" (see Job chapters 39–42). "Go weigh for me the weight of fire," he says, "or measure for me a blast of wind, or call back for me a day that is past." But Ezra is not giving up.

> [Ezra replies:] I wasn't asking about the ways above, but about those things that we experience every day. Why has Israel been given over to the Gentiles in disgrace? Why have the people whom You loved been given over to godless tribes, while the Torah of our ancestors has been made invalid and the written covenants no longer exist? We pass from this world like locusts, and our life is like a mist, and we are not worthy to obtain mercy. But what will He do for His own name, by which we are called? These are the things that I am asking about. (*4 Ezra* 4:23–25)

This back-and-forth goes on for pages, and the challenging questions are hardly unique to *4 Ezra*. (Scholars have long noted the striking similarity between *4 Ezra* and another pseudepigraphic text, *2 Baruch*, from the same period.) And, as already noted, the same sorts of probing questions are asked by some of the heavenly travelers seen above. The reason is that underlying both the heavenly ascents and the angel interviews is (among other things) a basic unease with the "messiness of history," a feeling that God may have abandoned His people. If this was the problem, then the solution must be somewhere "up there," in the secrets of heaven that only a few privileged humans have been allowed to glimpse, or "down here," where an angel has consented to answer the questions of a virtuous sage.

Yet it is also noteworthy that Ezra's words cited above are not just, or even principally, concerned with the nation of Israel. Even in the above passage, his complaint about Israel's fate strikes an oddly individualistic note: "We [present-day Israelites] pass from this world like locusts, and our life is like a mist, and we are not worthy to obtain mercy." In a similar vein, Ezra elsewhere asks about the fate of individuals after their death. Will their souls, "after they have been separated from their bodies," be judged entirely on their own merits, or as part of some larger collectivity?

> [Ezra says:] If I have found favor in your eyes, show further to me, your servant, whether on the day of judgment the righteous will be able to intercede for the ungodly or entreat the Most High for them — fathers for sons or sons for fathers, brothers for brothers, relatives for kinsmen or friends for friends. (*4 Ezra* 7:102)

In other words, can a particular individual who has not led a particularly virtuous life be saved by the intervention of his super-righteous friends or family members? The angel's answer is a definite no: "Everyone shall bear his own righteousness or unrighteousness." Later, the angel elaborates:

> The Most High made this world for the sake of many, but the world to come for the sake of few . . . Just as, if you were to ask the earth, it would tell you that it provides very much clay, from which earthenware is made, but only a little dust from which gold comes; so in the course of the present world many have been created, but few shall be saved [for the next world]. (*4 Ezra* 8:1–3)

As one scholar recently observed, "The emphasis is not on nations, but on individuals."[19] If so, then here is another bit of evidence of a broader shift toward the individual in early post-biblical times.

The Song of Songs

One of the strangest books in the Hebrew Bible is the Song of Songs (also called the Song of Solomon or Canticles). On the face of it, it seems to be about two young lovers who are absolutely infatuated with each other. They both seem to be from the north country, and she in particular has a kind of rustic, peasant diction that is quite different from standard Hebrew. This notwithstanding, the language of the book overall is so lush and imaginative, so full of unforgettable turns of phrase, that it might rightly be called the most beautiful poem in the whole Bible.

A lot of the song has to do with the pair's physical beauty, and the poet does not shy away from eroticism, though sometimes lightly veiling his descriptions in easily deciphered metaphor:

> You are so beautiful, my darling—your eyes like doves behind a veil . . .
> Your lips are like a crimson thread—it's so sweet to watch them speaking!
> Your neck is like the Tower of David, decked with a thousand shields, the bucklers of his champions.
> Your two breasts are twin fawns born to a gazelle, grazing among the lilies.
> When daylight starts to fade and the shadows disappear,
> I'll go off to Spice Mountain, to the fragrant hill.
> Every bit of you is beautiful, there's not one thing that's not. (Song 4:1–7)
>
> Your lips drip with nectar, O my bride;* honey and milk underneath your tongue,
> and the scent of your clothes is like a scent drifting in from Lebanon.
> But a locked-up garden is my love, a locked-up fountain, a sealed-up spring.
> Your body is the ripest orchard—all the choicest fruits:
> With henna and nard, nard and saffron, reeds and cinnamon perfume,
> myrrh and aloes and all the best of spices—
> A garden spring, a well of running water, oozing down from Lebanon. (Song 4:11–15)

* A term of affection, sometimes "my sister, my bride"; strictly speaking, neither phrase indicates that the couple is married.

What is this book doing in the Bible? The question has been asked more than once, and the simple answer is that at a certain point it came to be read as an allegory: The "he" in the poem was understood to be God, the "she" was the people of Israel, and the love they shared was the historic bond that joined God with His people. (Later, early Christians revised the allegorical message, but only slightly: it became Christ's love for the Church.) How did this idea get started? No one knows for sure,[20] but soon the allegorical reading had squeezed out the erotic one entirely, and what was left was a pure paean of love, the desire for the human having melted utterly into the desire for God.

But if we look deeply into the words of this poem, something striking emerges. Suspended over the breathless phrases of earthly love hangs a certain sadness. There is so much yearning! The two are together for a while, but then they have to part (2:16–17). She looks and looks for him, but he keeps fading away.

> One night, when I was in my bed, I looked for my true love—looked for him but couldn't find him.
> So let me search the town, its streets and squares, looking for my dear—
> I looked for him but couldn't find him.
> The town watchmen saw me on their rounds—Have you seen my own true love?
> No sooner did I leave them than I found my own true love.
> I've got him now and won't let go . . . (Song 3:1–4)

If this allegorical reading ever got started, was it not because there was something essential, something so true about what it said? "Where has your love gone off to?" her friends ask her. "Where has he gone away?"(6:1). Wasn't this just the way God was sometimes? The Bible says as much. "Why should the nations ask, 'Where is your God?'" (Ps 115:2); "When I call out, oh answer me, my God" (Ps 4:2); "I called out with all my heart; answer me, O Lord" (Ps 119:145).

Back in the Song, the lovesick woman says, "If only you were my brother, the child of my own mother, then I could throw my arms around you, kiss you in the street, and no one would say a thing" (8:1). But of course she can't. And the poem's ending certainly isn't happy: reunited for a time, now once again they must go their separate ways. "Run my love! Run like a deer, or like a mountain stag on the sweet-smelling hills" (8:14). In terms of the allegory, this is Israel telling God, "Begone!" The thought is so terrible that Jewish custom requires that the public recitation of the Song not end on the last verse; instead, the verse just before it is recited again after it: "As for you, my darling, lingering down in the gardens, friends are listening for your voice. Let them hear you!"

It is far from clear *when* people began to hear this song in the new, allegorical way, but it certainly was toward the end of the biblical period, or shortly thereafter. According to rabbinic tradition, people were still arguing about it in the first century CE:

> All the sacred writings are canonical. [Reporting another tradition on the topic,] Rabbi Judah said: "The Song of Songs is canonical, but the status of Ecclesiastes is contested." Rabbi Yose said: "Ecclesiastes is not canonical and the status of the Song is contested . . ." Rabbi Akiba said: "Heaven forbid! No one ever contested the fact that the Song is canonical. For the whole world altogether is not as worthy as the day on which the Song of Songs was given to Israel. If all the sacred writings are holy, then the Song of Songs is the Holy of Holies." (Mishnah *Yadayim* 3:5)

The Song of Songs may thus take its place beside the texts mentioned earlier in this chapter, Psalm 145, Psalm 119, and some of the other psalms mentioned, the various accounts of heavenly ascents or of earthly conversations and debates with angels, plus the Qumran *Thanksgiving Hymns* and later Jewish and then Christian prayers. All of these, along with the allegorizing of the Song of Songs, are the product of a time when humans began to be "in search of God."

I do not wish this assertion to imply that in earlier times people enjoyed a free and easy intercourse with the divine. Certainly not! Rather, in an earlier day, to encounter God seems to have been a fearsome thing that most people happily avoided. Israel's God was, like any deity, overwhelming. He was "out there," an undeniable, powerful presence. He was also present (or could be) in His sanctuary, but people were generally content in the knowledge that the professionals, the priests, were doing all they could to keep Him satisfied, or at least at bay. They would provide all the divine-human contact that was needed, offering up animal sacrifices every day and otherwise tending to the needs of God's "house" on earth, His earthly temple(s) and sacred spots.

Under special circumstances, of course, an individual person might deploy all the means available to bring about a specific divine intervention, crying out to a sluggish God and begging Him to cross over the curtain for just a few moments in order to heal an illness or smite an enemy, vowing whatever one could (and being sure to pay off the vow) if only He would intervene. But for the most part, there was no apparent need to *reach out* to God for its own sake, to establish contact, as it were. And having said all this, I should add that, beyond the few schematic observations just offered, I am not sure that we can ever really see the world in the same way as an ancient Israelite did; they were not "primitives," as some scholars have implied, but they did have a sense of self that was different from ours, as I have tried to argue. At any rate, as the late biblical period comes into sight we seem to be in more familiar territory. We understand what it is to yearn for God, to pray to God, and to search for the secrets of heaven.

16

OUTSIDE THE TEMPLE

Prayers to be said every day; The increasing importance of sacred texts; Ancient biblical interpretation

Throughout the ancient Near East and beyond, the temple was the meeting place of gods and human beings. For countless centuries, people had offered sacrifices to their gods and lifted their voices in praise or supplication. This was true of ancient Israel as well. But as early as the fifth or fourth century BCE, *part of Israel's religious life seems to have reached beyond the temple, spiritually as well as geographically. What changed?*

Israel, like other ancient Near Eastern peoples, had temples, but these were not exactly places of worship in the modern sense. Rather, as we have seen, they were conceived as the earthly residences of the deity, and ordinary people could not usually approach their most sacred realms. Of course, an ancient Israelite could, and did, bring a sacrifice in the temple to repay a vow, for example, or as a voluntary act of piety; nevertheless, the temple remained principally the province of the priests and others who served there.[1]

This is not to say, however, that people did not turn to God from other locations. Spontaneous prayers had always been, according to biblical narrative, offered up at any time and from any place — even from the belly of a big fish! — and did not require any particular expertise.[2] But these spontaneous expressions were for the most part what one scholar has defined as *circumstantial* prayers, "uttered by the individual or the community in specific circumstances that have arisen: a plea spoken in times of suffering or misfortune, thanks or praise in times of salvation or celebration, a blessing spoken in certain circumstances of daily life or on festive occasions."[3]

As the Second Temple period progressed, however, regular and nonspontaneous prayer seems to have gained in importance.[4] We have already seen that the placeless and occasionless psalms in the book of Psalms suggest the existence of worship outside of the temple, whether by individuals or groups. One such psalm is quite explicit:

> I call out to You, LORD, listen to my prayer; hear my voice as I call to You.
> Let my prayer be to You *like an offering of incense, my upraised hands like an evening sacrifice.*
> O LORD, put a guard at my mouth, to watch at the door of my lips.
> (Ps 141:1–3)

The highlighted phrases suggest that the speaker is *not* inside the temple when incense is offered by the community with the evening sacrifice; rather, his or her prayer is being presented as a substitute. Equally important, what the psalmist is asking for in the third line is not God's granting of a onetime request, but a piece of *ongoing,* divinely given help. To put that line a bit differently: "Please, God, prevent me from saying things that will get me into trouble," presumably not on any specific occasion, but constantly.

The book of Ben Sira, written in the early second century BCE, offers further evidence of the role of prayer in everyday life.[5] In addition to heeding the advice of one's friends and one's own heart, Ben Sira says, "pray to God, for He will faithfully direct your steps" (37:15). He seems to be referring to seeking God's counsel through individual prayer, in an act that would not necessarily involve a trip to the Jerusalem temple but could be performed anywhere. Elsewhere, Ben Sira stresses the importance of prayer in recovery from illness: "My son, when you are ill do not delay, but pray to the LORD and He will heal you" (38:10). ("Do not delay" may again mean "do not wait to go to the temple.") At another point in his book, Ben Sira presents his own prayer for divine help in controlling his speech, one that in fact begins by elaborating on the verse from Psalm 141 seen above:

> Who will set a guard over my mouth, and wisdom's seal over my lips,
> So that I will not falter because of them, and my own tongue will not destroy me?
> O God, my Father and Master of my life, do not let me fall victim to these.
> Who [but You] will hold a lash to keep my thoughts in check, and [set] a punishing rod over my heart,
> One that will not spare me when I do wrong, and will not overlook my sins?

> [This may] keep my transgressions from multiplying, and my sins from growing greater,
> Lest I fall before my adversary, and my enemy rejoice over me.
> O God, my Father and Master of my life, do not abandon me to their designs.
> Save me from haughtiness; keep wantonness far from my mind.
> Let no wanton desires rule my flesh, nor strong passions take control of me.
> (Sir 22:27–23:6)[6]

This is another inward-looking prayer, like the placeless, occasionless psalms seen in the last chapter, and while it evokes Psalm 141, Ben Sira no longer needs, as the psalmist did, to suggest that "my prayer" may indeed be a fit substitute for the incense and grain offerings that take place in the temple. As one scholar writes about (admittedly) a later class of Hebrew prayers: "Finally, the prayer ritual can be seen as a form of sacrifice itself."[7]

Praying Regularly

Eventually, a wholly new practice took hold: the establishment of statutory prayers that were to be said regularly at certain fixed times outside the temple.[8] A biblical example of this practice is found in the book of Daniel, whose composition is usually dated to the middle of the second century BCE.

> Now Daniel, once he learned that the decree had been written, [nevertheless] went to his house, which had windows in its upper floor facing Jerusalem; *three times a day* he would get down on his knees and pray and offer praise before his God, *as he had always done.* (Dan 6:11)

The stressed words make it clear that these were regular prayers not prompted by any particular occasion.

The Dead Sea Scrolls similarly include prayers that are to be recited each day, morning and evening.[9] The most detailed prayers of this sort are the *Words of the Luminaries*, whose very name[10] suggests their connection to what might be seen as the most ordinary of circumstances, the rising of the sun at dawn, and its setting at evening. Another, very fragmentary set of prayers from Qumran likewise highlights the same, everyday event:

> And when the sun [goes forth] to illuminate the eart[h], let them bless . . .

> When the sun goe[s f]orth over the [earth, let them bless and utter these words: Blessed is the God of Israel,] who has renewed our joy with the light of day . . . (4Q503 Daily Prayers, frag 33–35, col 1–2)[11]

In his account of the Essene sect of Judaism, Josephus offers a description of practices similar to those suggested by these Qumran texts and their focus on the morning sun:

> Their reverence toward God is somewhat idiosyncratic. Before the rising of the sun, they speak nothing of everyday matters, but offer certain prayers handed down from their ancestors [and addressed] to it [i.e., the sun], as if beseeching it to rise . . . (*Jewish War* 2:128–131)[12]

Noteworthy as well is Philo's description of the regular, communal prayers of a Jewish community called the Therapeutai, a group which he describes as "philosophers" who "spend their time pursuing solitude in gardens or solitary fields."

> Twice each day they pray, at dawn and in the evening. At sunrise they pray for a fine, bright day, "fine" and "bright" in the true sense of the heavenly daylight which they pray may fill their minds. At sunset they ask that the soul may be wholly relieved from the press of the senses and the objects of sense and, sitting where she [the soul] is consistory and council chamber to herself, pursue the quest of truth . . .
>
> They stand with their faces and whole body turned to the east and when they see the sun rising they stretch their hands up to heaven and pray for bright days and knowledge of the truth and the power of keen-sighted thinking. After the prayers they depart each to his private sanctuary. (*De vita contemplativa* 27, 89)[13]

The fact that both the Qumran community and the Therapeutai were at some distance from the Jerusalem temple (indeed, the Qumranites had apparently foresworn the temple service entirely)[14] may seem to explain the institution of these prayers; they were a substitution for the morning and evening *tamid* sacrifices offered in Jerusalem. But if so, why is it that none of the above-cited sources mentions the distance from Jerusalem as the raison d'être for these prayers—indeed, none of them makes any mention of the *tamid* sacrifices! It would seem that the idea of fixed, statutory prayers substituting for these sacrifices required no explanation. But I suspect that an Israelite from five or six hundred years earlier would indeed have been puzzled by such regular, routine praying. "What's the point?" he would ask. What changed during the intervening centuries?[15]

The Ascendency of Prayer

This question inevitably leads us back to the themes highlighted in the foregoing chapters. If prayer from places outside the Jerusalem temple apparently became a regular practice for some, then one might consider the rise of monotheism and its depiction of God as one possible cause. A remote, huge, heavenly-enthroned (and earth-overshadowing) God does not fit well with the idea of His hearing prayers from within a certain earthly sanctuary in one specific spot on earth.[16] Couldn't He receive prayers equally from anywhere, directly or with the help of angelic intermediaries? In fact, Second Temple texts frequently explain that God's angels tirelessly patrol the earth and report back to Him on people's doings.[17] These same angels were sometimes specifically said to carry people's prayers all the way up to the heavenly throne[18] — so what good was an earthly temple at all?* In addition, the growing interiority in what some psalms report or ask for — requests for God's ongoing guidance or others that might likewise seem inappropriate to the public nature of temple worship — may also have played a role. Ben Sira's plea for God to put "a guard over my mouth, and wisdom's seal over my lips," along with his hope for ongoing advice and help from God, may also be connected to the gradual emergence of the *nefesh* (or *ruaḥ,* or *neshamah*) as a person's inner, divinely given presence in the late- and post-biblical self. All this in turn may be related to various manifestations seen earlier of the "elusive individual" in Israelite religion and the very posture of people now "in search of God."**

Apart from these considerations, however, one might point to a certain intellectual disenchantment with sacrificial worship as favoring the creation

---

* Of course, people continued to frequent the Jerusalem temple (and others), not only because of its traditional role in collective worship, but because of the vibrancy of the sacrificial cult in general and the fact that sacrifices on the part of an individual were still a powerful mark of devotion. On top of all this was a political consideration: the priesthood, indissolubly connected to temple worship, also ran Judea's affairs throughout the Second Temple period.

** As with the "elusive individual," I am excluding here any evidence from psalms and prayers themselves because of the circular-argument problem of nontemple prayers. Was God really persuaded by animal carcasses burnt on an altar? Certainly some people continued to answer in the affirmative. Recall that even in the fourth century CE, the Roman philosopher Sallust opined, "Prayer without sacrifice is just words." In other quarters, however, the whole necessity of the sacrificial cult was under attack. In earlier times, to be sure, prophets had intoned against the reliance on sacrifices as a way of gaining divine favor. Consider God's words to Isaiah:

> "Why should I have all these sacrifices?" says the LORD.
> "I have had more than enough of burnt offerings, of rams and the suet of fatlings, and bulls' blood.
> I take no pleasure in lambs and he-goats . . .
> Stop your wrongdoing; learn to do good. Seek out justice." (Isa 1:11, 16–17)

Or Amos's sarcastic invitation:

> Come to Bethel for sins, to Gilgal for sins galore!
> But bring your offerings every morning, and a tithe every three days;
> Send up a thanksgiving and shout: "Freewill sacrifice!"—let people know!—
> for such is your devotion, Israel, says the LORD. (Amos 4:4–5)

But here and elsewhere in early times, it is the people's lack of devotion that the prophets attack. The act of sacrificing itself is not being called into question. Later, however, a psalmist could presume a definite divine preference:

> O Master, open my lips, so that my mouth may utter Your praises.
> For if You desired a sacrifice, I would surely give it; but it is not a burnt offering that will please You.
> God's [true] sacrifices are a broken spirit, a broken and shattered heart; God will not reject these. (Ps 51:17–19)

Now, the cleansing power of sacrificial blood no longer seemed persuasive. When Levi toured the heavens in the late-biblical "Testament of Levi," he reached the highest part of heaven and God's heavenly throne:

> [An angelic guide explains:] Next to Him are the angels of the Lord's Presence, who serve and make atonement before the Lord for all the unwitting sins of the righteous, offering to the Lord a sweet savor, a *reasonable and bloodless sacrifice.* (T Levi 3:5–6)[19]

The author of the New Testament Letter to the Hebrews likewise saw the role of blood in effecting divine forgiveness as a thing whose time had come and gone:

> For when every commandment had been told to all the people by Moses in accordance with the Torah, he took the blood of calves and goats, with water and scarlet wool and hyssop, and sprinkled both the scroll [of laws, Exod 24:8] itself and all the people, saying, "This is the blood of the covenant that God has ordained for you." And in the same way he sprinkled with the blood both the tent and all the vessels used in worship. Indeed, under the Torah almost everything is purified with blood, and without the shedding of blood there is no forgiveness of sins. (Heb 9:19–22)

But all this blood, the letter continues, is ultimately ineffective, "for it is impossible for the blood of bulls and goats to take away sins" (10:4). While this assertion in Hebrews was tied specifically to the message of the early Christian movement, it seems unlikely to have come out of nowhere. No doubt others were asking about the necessity of sacrificial animals in general.

Beyond all these, one final factor stands out. The very idea of fixed, statutory prayer returns us to the "establish contact" aspect of people being in search of God. After all, statutory prayers are not usually uttered because the person praying needs something in particular or wishes to acknowledge receipt of a specific divine favor. To say certain fixed, unchanging words to God at the crack of dawn or at sunset is a way of affirming contact each day and thereby seeking God's favor. Of course, the communal dimension of a fixed liturgy is highly important as well; people who pray together in a fixed ritual also reaffirm their connection with each other and with the ideas and practices that they share.[20] But this hardly eliminates the *vertical* connection to God. Mere contact, in other words, is an underlying theme of obligatory, fixed prayer, and this theme is inevitably, if paradoxically, tied to that of divine remoteness: "I will turn to You on a regular basis in a prayer that is essentially disinterested and which, therefore, expects no immediate answer."[21] Rather, like the dove released by Noah after the flood, the people who sent forth those fixed prayers hoped, and believed, that they were not sent off in vain but would somehow find their intended goal even though unacknowledged. And such fixed prayers did not cease at the end of the Second Temple period. Various forms of both Judaism and Christianity came to establish fixed, obligatory prayer as a central form of piety.

Songs of the Heavenly Temple

This is not to say that Second Temple period prayers were all of the "establish contact" variety. We have already seen the unique character of the *Thanksgiving Hymns,* with their urgent and otherworldly quality. Alongside these, the Qumran caves have also yielded prayers that seem intended simply to imitate the style and substance of our canonical psalms, adopting whole phrases as well as the pseudepigraphic attributions and grammatical features characteristic of our canonical Psalter.[22] And in addition to these are a series of altogether unique hymns, called *Songs of the Sabbath Sacrifice.*[23] They describe, in breathless enthusiasm, God's great temple in heaven and the angels who serve in it, sometimes addressing them directly, as in this (unfortunately very fragmentary) opening hymn:

> [O you angels,] praise [the God of . . .], the God of the holiest of holy ones (i.e., the God of the angels who serve in His heavenly temple), and [rejoice] in the Godliness of His kingship, for He [has appointed (?)] the holiest of the holy ones of eternity, and they have become His priests . . . serving before Him in His glorious inner sanctum. (4Q400 col 1:1–4)

For all its lacunae, this passage makes it clear that what is being described is indeed the heavenly temple, akin to the heavenly temple that had been glimpsed by Enoch, Abraham, Levi, and others in their ascents to heaven. Here, the analogy with the earthly Jerusalem temple is explicit: Just as God chose priests to serve before Him on earth eternally (in the sense that the earthly priesthood was held to be hereditary, passed on from generation to generation), so He appointed the very holiest of His angels to serve before Him forever in His temple just above the clouds.

Following this hymn are others — thirteen in all — that detail such things as the praises and blessings that are offered in various parts of heaven and the different names and classes of angels serving there. It is hard to be certain, but the *Songs of the Sabbath Sacrifice* seem to presume a series of seven different levels in heaven; on the highest level is the central throne room inhabited by God Himself. In this respect, too, these compositions are similar to those apocalyptic ascents to heaven seen earlier, except that here there is no angelic interpreter explaining heaven to the earthly visitor. Instead, the *Songs* just describe what a human visitor might see on his or her own ascent to heaven.

But what did the real-life singers of these *Songs* think they were doing by singing them?[24] Did they suppose they were speaking directly to the angels surrounding God's throne, as implied in the fragmentary opening hymn cited above? Clearly, they were not just describing what the heavenly temple was like; they seem to have been suggesting some sort of connection or proximity between those angels and themselves. Unfortunately, the *Songs of the Sabbath Sacrifice* never quite articulate the nature of this connection, at least not in the surviving fragments. Some scholars hold that by singing these hymns, the human beings at Qumran (and quite possibly elsewhere) actually believed that they were somehow participating in the heavenly service on high. Other scholars hesitate, arguing that these songs suggest only a correspondence to, but not necessarily an actual participation in, that heavenly service.[25]

Whichever the case, it is certainly noteworthy that slightly later worshipers, both Jewish and Christian, did explicitly assert a connection between their own prayers and the words of praise sung by angels surrounding the heavenly throne. Recalling that the prophet Isaiah had reported hearing the angels cry out, "Holy, holy, holy is the LORD of Hosts, the whole world is full of His glory" (Isa 6:3), later liturgists urged their congregations to take up this refrain in their own praise of God:

> Let us sanctify Your name in the world [that is, down here on earth] in the same manner as they [i.e., the angels] sanctify it in highest heaven, as was written by Your prophet, "Holy, holy, holy is the LORD of Hosts, the whole world is full of His glory." (Jewish *Kedushah*)

> And therefore let us, along with the angels and archangels, with thrones and dominions and with the whole host of the heavenly multitude, sing a hymn to Your glory, endlessly saying: "Holy, holy, holy is the Lord God Sabaoth; the heavens and the earth are full of Your glory, Hosanna in the highest! Blessed is he who comes in the name of the Lord. Hosanna in the highest." (*Preface to the Eucharist* in the traditional Latin Mass)

In sum: these different sorts of prayers suggest that prayer itself was coming to occupy an increasingly important role in Second Temple period piety (as well as pointing to some striking continuities between such worship in the closing centuries BCE and that of Jews and early Christians in the two or three centuries that followed). Prayer was now in its ascendancy. Of course, the offering of animal sacrifices in the Jerusalem temple continued until its destruction in the great revolt against Rome in 66–70 BCE. But the loss of their temple did not exactly catch the Jews flatfooted. They already had in place a developing supplement or alternative. Taking as their motto a somewhat cryptic verse in Hos 14:3, now understood as "Let us substitute for [sacrificial] bulls the offerings of our lips," later rabbinic authorities quite consciously equated prayer with actual sacrifice.[26] But quite apart from prayer itself, there was another form of piety, equally important and equally new, emerging in the Second Temple period: the recitation and study of sacred texts.

The Rise of Scripture

The writings that make up our Bible belong to different times, stretching over a period of centuries. But as time went on, these writings came to play an increasingly important role. They were preserved and often revised in the process, studied and compared with one another. One text in particular was deemed preeminent, the Torah or Pentateuch, comprising the first five books of the Bible, Genesis through Deuteronomy. From an early period, the Torah seems to have functioned as *the* sacred text par excellence.[27]

One early depiction of this Torah's importance is found in the book of Nehemiah, which recounts a great public reading convened by Ezra, spiritual leader of the reestablished Jewish community in Jerusalem:

> In the seventh month . . . the whole people were gathered as one man to the square opposite the Water Gate, and they asked Ezra to bring the scroll of the Torah of Moses that the LORD had commanded to Israel. On the first day of the seventh month, Ezra the Priest brought the Torah before the assembly, men and women and all who could listen and understand it. He read from it, [standing] in front of the square that is in front of the Water Gate, to the men and women and those who could understand, from first light to midday; and the ears of all the people were [given] to the scroll of the Torah. (Neh 8:1–3)

Scholars suspect that this public reading of the Torah[28] is a somewhat idealized event, but a few important themes are nonetheless worthy of mention. First, it is highly significant that the people are represented here as requesting this reading. Whether this is exactly what happened or not, the idea that ordinary Judeans would feel the need to know what the Torah says was probably not anachronistic. They or their immediate ancestors had been conquered and forcibly exiled, and the Judeans were no doubt eager not to repeat the experience. If, as certainly some of them believed, the exile had come about as punishment for Israel's failure to keep its part of the covenant and the Torah's laws on which it was conditioned, then it was imperative that they now master those laws in order to avoid any repeat disaster. Indeed, the book of Jeremiah had spoken of God creating a "new covenant" with Israel (Jer 31:31), whereby everyone will know the Torah; this assembly and public reading may be seen as part of such a program's idealized fulfillment.

The passage further reports that this public reading was made not for the men alone, but for women and "all who could listen and understand it," presumably children above a certain age. Here is a sweeping inclusiveness: *everyone* ought to know the Torah's laws—that is, the Torah was not a text for rulers or judges alone. And whether or not it is probable that this mass of humanity stood quietly "from first light to midday" to hear the Torah's words, this very assertion may reflect what was already a widespread commitment, even if idealized, to running things in keeping with the Torah's words. Finally, this passage goes on to list a group of people who, during this public reading or thereafter, "helped the people to understand the Torah, while the people remained standing" (Neh 8:7). Here is a glimpse of a new sort of figure, the interpreter of Scripture, whose role will be of great importance. Here, the interpreters "read from the scroll of God's Torah, translating [presumably from Hebrew to Aramaic] and giving its meaning, so that they [the people] understood the reading" (Neh 8:8). The message is unmistakable: if this Torah is to function as the central text for the community, then it must truly be the community's common property, known and understood by all.

The Torah Supreme

It is sometimes said that democracy started off as a system of government, a way for a society to select its leaders and run its affairs, but that in America it eventually became something more like a national ideology of equality, espoused (or at least given lip service) by all and expressed in hundreds of little ways in daily life quite apart from government. Somewhat analogously, the Torah began as a collection of narratives and laws, but it soon became much more than that. In the early second century BCE, Ben Sira described it as nothing less than the embodiment of divine wisdom—the set of principles by which God governed the world—so that if you wished to know what God wanted of you, or to explain His ways with the world, you needed to go no further than this book. At one point, Ben Sira explained how this came to be:

[Wisdom speaks:] I came forth from the mouth of the Most High,
and covered the earth like a mist.
I dwelt in the highest heavens, and my throne was in a pillar of cloud.
Alone I compassed the vault of heaven and traversed the depths of the abyss.
Over waves of the sea, over all the earth, and over every people and nation I have held sway.
Among all these I sought a resting-place; in whose territory should I abide?
Then the Creator of all things gave me a command, and my Creator chose the place for my tent.
He said, "Make your dwelling in Jacob, and in Israel receive your inheritance."

Divine wisdom, in other words, had always existed in heaven; it "came forth" from God's own mouth. But at a certain point, Wisdom began to look for a dwelling place on earth, and God told her to make Israel her home. Once transplanted in Israel's territory, she grew like a great tree:

I took root in an honored people, in the portion of the Lord, his heritage.
I grew tall like a cedar in Lebanon, and like a cypress on the heights of Hermon.
I grew as great as a palm tree in Ein-gedi, and like rose-bushes in Jericho;
like a fair olive tree in the field, and like a plane tree beside water I grew tall.

Lest there be any doubt about who this "Wisdom" figure truly was, Ben Sira then makes the matter triumphantly clear:

All this is the book of the covenant of the Most High God,
the Torah that Moses commanded us, as an inheritance for the congregations of Jacob. (Sir 24:3–8, 12–14, 23)

In other words, the Torah was not just a collection of laws and stories; it was nothing less than the written embodiment of all of divine wisdom.

Something similar was said at the same time, or perhaps even a bit earlier than Ben Sira, by the anonymous author of *1 Baruch,* a book included among the biblical Apocrypha:

No one knows the way to her [i.e., Wisdom], or is concerned about the path to her.
But the One who knows all things knows her, He found her by His understanding.
The One who prepared the earth for all time filled it with four-footed creatures;

> the One who sends forth the light, and it goes;
> He called it, and it obeyed him, trembling; the stars shone in their watches, and were glad;
> He called them, and they said, "Here we are!" They shone with gladness for Him who made them.
> This is our God; no other can be compared to Him.
> He found the whole way to knowledge, and gave her [Wisdom] to His servant Jacob, and to Israel, whom He loved.
> Afterwards she appeared on earth and lived with humankind.
> She is the book of the commandments of God, the Torah that endures forever.
> All who hold her fast will live, and those who forsake her will die.
> Turn, O Jacob, and take her; walk toward the shining of her light.
> Do not give your glory to another, or your advantages to an alien people.
> Happy are we, O Israel, for we know what is pleasing to God.

This last line is perhaps the most significant. Once the Torah, the "book of the commandments of God," had been given over to the people of Israel, they no longer had to worry about what God might want them to do, because now "we *know* what is pleasing to God." Now there would be no more guesswork. A path had been given for every man, woman, and child to follow — the laws of the Torah.

God Speaks from the Page

Along with the Torah came books that recounted Israel's history after the death of Moses, as well as the collected writings of various prophets and sages. Many of these texts went back to the distant past; indeed, parts of some were apparently preserved from at least the eighth century BCE (and a number of items arguably date from one or two centuries before that, or even earlier), although no one is sure exactly how they were preserved, or what the people doing the preserving thought they were doing. Indeed, where all these texts originated and how and by whom, as well as how they came repeatedly to be revised and edited, has been the subject of a great deal of research over the last two centuries.[29]

Little by little, a specific group of these texts gradually crystallized, joined with the Torah as part of Israel's sacred library. The Dead Sea Scrolls offer scholars a glimpse of this process in the making. The fragments of different scrolls found at Qumran represent some eight hundred documents. A little more than a quarter of these consist of bits and pieces of various books that are considered part of the Hebrew canon: thirty-six copies of parts of our book of Psalms, twenty-nine pieces of Deuteronomy, seventeen Exodus manuscripts, and so forth. It is striking that every book of the Hebrew Bible is represented among these fragments except for the book of Esther. (Was its omission the result of an intentional decision to exclude that book, or was the absence of a single fragment simply a matter of chance? No one knows.)[30] Whatever the case, the fact that nearly all the books of the future canonical Bible were attested in the Qumran caves suggests that, by sometime in the late second century BCE, there may have been some widespread agreement on their importance and perhaps their sanctity.[31]

Was this the first suggestion that a kind of proto-Bible existed? The problem is that those caves also contained other material — multiple copies of *1 Enoch* and *Jubilees,* for example, as well as numerous sectarian texts, including hymns, prayers, legal writings, and others that seem to reflect specifically the beliefs and practices of the Qumranites themselves and (perhaps) the larger movement to which they belonged. Some of these other books are cited in the group's writings as authoritative, as Scripture. So we have little indication that the idea of a widely recognized, defined canon existed; it rather seems that a somewhat more fluid collection of texts was held to be authoritative for the Qumran sect, but one that was not identical with the proto-Bible (or Bibles) of other communities.

Eventually, however, the establishment of a delineated biblical canon was accomplished.[32] Various writings from the late- or post–Second Temple period bear witness to the emergence of such a Bible. The book of Ben Sira, composed in the early second century BCE, ends with a catalogue of biblical heroes, and these are all found in our canonical Bible; indeed, they are presented basically in the order in which they appear in the Jewish biblical canon. Ben Sira's grandson translated his grandfather's book into Greek and, in a preface, refers to "the Torah and the Prophets and the others that followed them," "the Torah and the Prophets and the other books," and so on. While "the Torah and the Prophets" seems to refer to a fixed group — remember that prophecy was later held in some circles to have ceased with Haggai, Zechariah, and Malachi, all of whom were connected to the period following the return from exile — the "other books" sounds deliberately vague.[33] (Perhaps Ben Sira's grandson was hoping his own distinguished ancestor's book would forever be included among these "others.") Ultimately, however, even these "other books" came to be specified by name, until all these *ins* were in and everything else was out; the Hebrew Bible was now complete.*

The emergence of the Bible says a lot about Israel's religion in the Second Temple period. There may still have been prophets around, but now, God spoke principally through the written word. His voice was heard — constantly — from the pages of the Torah and the other books. Indeed, the career of the Bible paralleled, in a subtle way, the rise of fixed, statutory prayer seen above. The two bespeak a common mentality. For, just as statutory prayers were instituted as a kind of regular, daily connection joining human beings to God via the fixed words and fixed times of these prayers' recitation, so the emergence of a certified body of sacred texts created a similarly ongoing, daily connection in the opposite direction, joining God to His worshipers via the fixed words of His books. In both cases, what had once been spontaneous and undefined (prayers spoken at any time and saying almost anything; God speaking to humans whatever and whenever He saw fit) had now hardened into something regular, dependable, and unchanging. To modern ears, "hardening" may sound bad, but for ancient worshipers, it was surely a positive development precisely because of its fixed character. Those who recited statutory prayers at sunrise or sunset were not, as we have seen, necessarily seeking an answer; rather, their prayers were a way of establishing contact, a reaching out to bring near the universal, and therefore potentially distant, God. Similarly, God no longer manifested Himself in some dazzling, supernatural theophany (such as that at Mount Sinai), but He was nonetheless brought close simply because there was now a Torah scroll, or a whole Bible, in the room. Of course, His "presence" was not of the sort of thing we usually mean by this term; but He was present, speaking aloud, in the text — and in particular in the Torah's commandments, whereby God's voice was directed to everyone in the room.[34] This is what *1 Baruch* meant by saying, "Happy are we, O Israel, for we know what is pleasing to God." What was pleasing to God were the things that He had commanded Israel to do, and in carrying out those commandments, Israel's connection to the universal God was firmly established, day after day.

---

* Scholars like to point out that the Greek name eventually conferred on this collection was *ta biblía*, "the books" — in the neuter plural. Eventually, however, the same word came to be thought of as a Latin feminine singular, "the Book," as if the whole collection were really a single, unitary composition, which is in fact how it came to be treated.

A More Perfect Bible

There remained the problem of *how* the Bible was to be read. It was made up of texts composed at various points in Israel's long history, texts that likewise seemed to reflect the different points of view of various sectors of Israelite society (the priesthood, the royal court, prophetic schools or guilds, and so forth). These two basic facts inevitably meant that the sacred texts from Israel's illustrious past were full of contradictions, which could only lead to confusion. Did God favor transgenerational and collective punishment, or was each person punished for his or her sins? (We have seen passages that support both positions.) Did God descend onto Mount Sinai to deliver the Ten Commandments, as some passages asserted (Exod 19:20, 24:9, 34:5), or did He remain in heaven the whole time (Exod 20:19, Deut 4:36)? The answer certainly had implications for God's very nature—was He truly corporeal, moving around the earth, or was He an essentially heavenly deity who ruled by remote control? There were numerous questions about specific religious practices. What exactly did the Torah intend by forbidding "work" on the Sabbath? And how in practice was someone to observe such a broad commandment as "You shall love your neighbor like yourself" (Lev 19:18)? It was the task of Scripture's ancient interpreters to find answers to such questions.

These text scholars were a varied group, or group of groups. In some sense such scholars had been around almost as long as the biblical texts they were interpreting. Modern research has highlighted the fact that virtually every book of the Hebrew Bible is the product of multiple acts of supplementation and rearrangement and further editing; all of these revisions constituted a kind of reinterpretation of the earlier versions, subtly (or not so subtly) changing the meaning for later readers. But even after the texts themselves had been revised for the last time (indeed, well before that time), ancient interpreters were busy *explaining* the meaning of the texts—often transforming them to fit current reality and current needs. Their work thus came to constitute what might be called the great Interpretive Revolution of the closing three centuries BCE and on into the first century or so CE.

For the most part we do not know the names of these ancient interpreters, but by studying the earliest traces of their activity—particularly in the Dead Sea Scrolls and the bits of interpretation that have survived in the biblical Apocrypha and pseudepigrapha—scholars have learned much about their interpretive methods and the great influence they had on what became the Bible. One thing is clear: they had a definite program. Although the texts that they were interpreting had, in most cases, been around for centuries and often talked about people or events from the still more distant past, it was the interpreters' goal to read them not as ancient history, but as fundamentally *relevant* writings addressed to people in the interpreters' own day, as well as embodying some of the interpreters' key beliefs and concerns. This meant first of all resolving any apparent contradictions within the corpus so as to give the texts a single, unitary message applicable to the present. In addition, the goal of relevance often meant transforming these ancient writings into *lessons* for the present day; for example, turning texts that had no apparent interest in ethical instruction into lessons of morality. Thus, the accounts of Israel's remote ancestors narrated in the book of Genesis were reinterpreted so as to become stories with a message: Noah, Abraham, Jacob, and the others were argued to be models of ethical behavior (which, at first glance, they certainly were not). The Torah's laws underwent similar modification, making them applicable to current-day society and appropriate to later standards of behavior. The Bible's famous dictate of "an eye for an eye" was thus explained by interpreters to mean that, while a person who knocked out someone's eye had to provide the victim with monetary compensation, he was not to be punished by having his own eye knocked out. In other words, the true meaning of "an eye for an eye," these interpreters said, was "*not* an eye for an eye."

Changes in the apparent meaning of the Torah's words were not always so radical, but they were widespread: it is no exaggeration to say that nearly every page of the Torah included at least one verse that had been radically recast by ancient interpreters. And while their activity was at first focused primarily on the Pentateuch, the words of prophets from centuries past were similarly reinterpreted—often so as to highlight their eternal teachings about the ways of God with mankind, or sometimes to turn them into cryptic messages about events in the interpreters' own time (another way of making ancient texts relevant to today).[35]

But wasn't this what prophecy had always been about? Yes and no. As we have seen, earlier biblical prophets were often involved in the events of their own day, discoursing with the powers-that-be on various matters. Nathan rebuked King David after his sin with Bathsheba, Elijah reproved King Ahab, Isaiah offered advice to King Ahaz about the Assyrian crisis, Jeremiah took on King Jehoiakim, and so forth. By the time of the ancient interpreters, however, those events were long past. Instead, such episodes were reread as ethical instruction; what counted was not how they influenced the events of the day, but the eternal moral lessons that they embodied or included.[36] By the same token, the historical narratives from the book of Joshua through 2 Kings were read not so much as history as they were lessons in morality.[37]

In keeping with this, the prophets themselves underwent a subtle modification. As one scholar has noted:

> In general it is fair to say that Christians seem to have been interested in the prophets as *people,* in what they did and suffered in the name of God, rather than as names of books or rather featureless recipients of oracles—a tendency shared with Josephus and Philo. This produces some surprising judgments on who are the "major" prophets. Habakkuk, to us a shadowy figure, was evidently a focus of some interest . . . We know, of course, from the evidence of Qumran that Habakkuk's book was a focus of much interest around the turn of the era. Daniel, too, enjoyed a much higher status than he now has in mainstream Judaism or Christianity; as with Habakkuk and Jonah, this may reflect that there were more *stories* about him in Scripture than about some other prophets.[38]

This is of course an important observation for the present study, one more indication of the way in which the "elusive individual" came to change the way in which people read Scripture. At the same time, this way of reading is also a manifestation of ancient interpreters' concern for making the past relevant to the present, *our* present. Looking for lessons in ethical instruction in accounts of the distant past, to be acted on by each individual, is rather like pinning down divine commandments to specific acts—again, to be performed by each individual.

A text discovered among the Dead Sea Scrolls tells us something about the importance of studying the interpretation of Scripture in the life of their religious community.

> And wherever ten men [of the community council] shall be assembled, let there not be lacking someone *interpreting* the Torah day and night, continuously in shifts, one after another. And let the Many be sure [to devote] a third of every night of the year to reading together from the book and to *interpreting* the law and blessing together. (1QS *Community Rule* col 6:6–8)

A Special Style of Interpretation

How did the ancient interpreters manage to make such dramatic changes in the text's apparent meaning? In part, it had to do with their specific style of interpreting. However radical were the "improvements" that interpreters introduced, they always had a particular scriptural hook on which to hang their reinterpretations and could thus claim that they were merely making explicit what Scripture had *always* meant:

- The fact that Adam didn't die as soon as he ate the forbidden fruit—although God had said that he would "surely die *on the day*" in which he ate it—indicated that God never meant that Adam would instantly fall over dead. Instead, what He was saying was that Adam, although originally created to be immortal, would become mortal if he ate the fruit and so eventually die, which he did (at the age of 930). This narrative thus became an explanation of human mortality—passed on from Adam and Eve to all their descendants—and an object lesson in the importance of heeding God's commands.
- The Torah says *twice* that Abraham and Isaac "walked together" (Gen 22:6 and 22:8) on their way to where Isaac was to be sacrificed. The first mention meant that they walked together physically, but the second indicated something else entirely: Isaac now understood that he was to be a human sacrifice offered up to God (although Abraham had never mentioned that fact explicitly), and he voluntarily accepted this role, demonstrating his willingness to be a martyr for his religion.
- In the first two of the Ten Commandments, God speaks in the first person, "I," but after that He is suddenly in the third person, "the Lord your God." The reason is that God spoke only the first two commandments directly to the people of Israel; the others He spoke to Moses, who then repeated them to the people. Why this change? Interpreters explained that ordinary human beings cannot stand to hear God's voice directly—hence the need for Moses and later prophets to act as intermediaries, their words preserved in sacred Scripture.

But the interpreters' success also had to do with how Scripture was passed along, and who was doing the passing. In the ancient world, books were an expensive artifact; ordinary people did not possess them. If they knew Scripture at all, it was because they had learned it by heart in school, and this rote learning probably included not only memorizing the actual words of the text, but learning their standard interpretation as well. Such standard interpretations came from the ancient interpreters—some of whom were doubtless leaders of different groups or factions. They were the experts.

It is also likely that many of these interpreters were wealthy men, people who could devote substantial time to studying the interpretations of their predecessors and transmitting their own refinements. As Ben Sira opined in the early second century BCE: "[Only] someone who has little daily occupation can be a sage," adding somewhat snootily:

> How can a plowman become a sage, or someone whose glory's in a goad's straight shaft—
> Someone who drives an ox in the furrows, and whose sole conversation is with his own cattle? (Sir 38:24–25)

Relatively few people enjoyed a way of life that allowed them the time to look deeply into Scripture and thus become interpreters; but this very circumstance meant that those who did constituted a small and prestigious company. Everyone else looked to them to explain the sacred words of bygone times. Once introduced, their interpretations were passed on from teacher to pupil and from the old to the young; eventually, they were also written down (which is how we know them), incorporated into the writings of ancient sages and translators, inserted into retellings of biblical stories, into liturgical poems and legal compendia, and alluded to in passing in all manner of other compositions. Thanks to all these, the creations of these ancient interpreters came to be understood as simply *what the text* really *means.*

These two activities—statutory, fixed prayers and the reading and interpreting of Scripture—could be carried on anywhere, and they ultimately became *the* central acts of piety in the period before and just after the start of the Common Era. But they also tell us something striking about the changing encounter with God during this period. Prayers that were recited each day at fixed times and without any specific request or expectation of an answer—such prayers give expression to the growing distance between God and the individual supplicant.[39] Similarly, God's voice, in bygone days heard firsthand by His prophets, has been increasingly displaced by the written word: His book was right here, while His presence remained elusive and difficult to conceive.[40]

Important as these aspects of prayer and Scripture may be, they were far from all that was new in the religion of late Second Temple times. To help fill out the encounter between God and humans in this period, one further development must be considered.

17

PERSONAL RELIGION

Laws for each individual; The fate of a person's soul; Perceiving the divine order

The origin of the word "religion" is somewhat obscure; one theory connects it to the Latin verb ligere, *"to bind or hold fast." True or not, this etymology well captures the spirit of religious observance in Second Temple times. Individuals sought to bind themselves to God by performing specific acts and practices enjoined in the Torah. At the same time, however, they could not but wonder at God's apparent indifference to the fate of His own, chosen people. When would He restore them to their former greatness?*

Go back far enough in biblical history and there is little of what could be called personal religion. Sacrifices were offered on behalf of the community in the temples and "high places" that dotted the Israelite landscape; festivals were celebrated as a group activity; clans, tribes, and the nation as a whole turned to God in gratitude or supplication. But gradually all this began to change. The book of Deuteronomy in particular seems to include numerous duties incumbent on each person, starting with the obligation to "love the Lord your God with all your heart and all your soul and all your might" (Deut 6:5) and going on to list quite a few specific, concrete acts for each person to perform.[1] In post-exilic times, the "religion of laws" came to focus increasingly on *each person* carrying out such duties.

Keeping the Sabbath

The Sabbath is certainly a venerable institution, enshrined in the Ten Commandments:

> Remember the Sabbath day, to keep it holy. You may work for six days and perform all your labor, but the seventh day is the Sabbath of the LORD your God: you may not do any work—you or your son or your daughter, your male or female slave, your livestock or the foreigner within your city gates. (Exod 20:8–10; cf. Deut 5:12–14)

But what exactly constituted "work"? Did this mean not performing one's own profession*—so that, for example, a farmer wasn't allowed to farm, but he could still fix his leaky roof on the Sabbath, while a roofer could still tend his vegetable garden? Or did practicing *anyone's* profession (perhaps implied by the phrase "*all* your labor") constitute forbidden work? At one point the Torah commands: "Six days shall you work, but on the seventh day you shall rest; in plowing time and in harvest time you shall rest" (Exod 34:21). Was the mention of these agricultural seasons intended in a general sense ("no matter how pressing the need for intensive labor might be"), or was it a clue as to the specific sort of work forbidden to everyone? Exodus 35:3 added, "You shall not kindle a fire in all your habitations on the Sabbath day." Did "kindle" mean having any fire at all, even if it was burning before the Sabbath started, or did this word merely refer to starting up a fire once the Sabbath had begun?

For a time, such questions do not appear to have troubled ancient Israelites; indeed, we have seen that such post-Sinai figures as Gideon, Deborah, Samson, and the other heroes of the book of Judges are never even said to have kept the Sabbath; the same is true of David, Solomon, and subsequent Israelite kings and prophets. Still more basically, it is not clear from some biblical texts if observance of the Sabbath was conceived to be the duty of each person individually or if it was a general requirement incumbent on, and enforced by, society as a whole.[2]

In Second Temple times, the Sabbath was unambiguously to be observed by each and every individual, and this very fact was in keeping with the broad changes traced in the previous chapters. The book of Jeremiah had looked forward to a day when "no longer will one person teach another, [not

* "Profession" seems to be the sense of Hebrew *melakhah,* as in Jonah 1:8.

even] one man teach his brother, saying 'This [is how] to obey the LORD' " (Jer 31:34). That day was now here. Each person was deemed responsible to observe the various Sabbath restrictions, and ancient interpreters offered their aid by pinning down all the specifics required by the Torah's general statements, occasionally supplementing them with altogether new prohibitions of their own. The *Book of Jubilees* thus went out of its way to list a few kinds of work forbidden on the Sabbath which were never mentioned in the Torah:

> [The angel of the Presence says to Moses:] Command the Israelites to observe this day [i.e., the Sabbath] so that they keep it holy and not do any work on it and not defile it, for it is holier than all [other] days . . . So make it known and tell the Israelites the commandments of this day so that they rest on it and not neglect it through the error of their minds, lest they do [any] work on it — [the day] on which they should not be found *pursuing their own desires,* [namely] *preparing on it anything that is to be eaten or drunk, or drawing water,* or *carrying in or out of the gates anything that can be carried,* and let them not *carry in or take out anything from house to house on this day,* such that they could not have prepared for themselves at home during the six days of the week; since it is more holy and blessed than any day of the jubilee of jubilees. We [angels] rested on it in heaven before any creature on earth was commanded to rest on it on the earth. (2:26–30)

The italicized items are not found among the Sabbath prohibitions of the Pentateuch. Some do echo things mentioned elsewhere in Scripture (Isa 58:13–14; Jer 17:21–22), while other items are altogether new. This passage in *Jubilees* was in turn supplemented by still more prohibitions listed at the very end of the book (*Jub* 50:6–13), apparently an interpolation by some later writer.[3]

The Dead Sea Scrolls contain further references to Sabbath prohibitions beyond these,[4] and rabbinic Judaism was to go still farther:

> There are 39 general categories* of work [forbidden on the Sabbath]: [With regard to grain in the field:] planting, and plowing, and harvesting, and binding sheaves; [once the grain is harvested,] threshing, and winnowing; getting rid of foreign material [from the grain], grinding, and sifting, and

* Literally, "fathers," whose "offspring" consist of various further elaborations and subtypes.

> kneading, and baking; [with regard to wool:] shearing the wool, washing it white, and shaking it [to separate the strands], and dyeing it, and spinning, and weaving, and arranging the threads, and setting the warp and the weft, and weaving two threads, and cutting two threads; [with regard to sewing:] tying [any knot], and untying, and sewing two stitches, and ripping in order to [subsequently] sew two stitches; [with regard to animals:] hunting a deer; slaughtering it, and skinning it, salting it, and curing the skin, and scraping it down, and cutting it; [with regard to writing:] writing two or more letters; and scraping down [the parchment] for the purpose of writing two or more letters; [with regard to construction:] building, and tearing down; [with regard to fire:] extinguishing, and lighting; [also:] striking something with a hammer; carrying something from one property to another. (Mishnah *Shabbat* 7:2)

All these particulars (and they are only "general categories," with many offshoots for each category) were deemed to be observed by each individual, hence the necessity of specifying exactly what each person could—and mostly, could not—do.

Loving Your Neighbor

The Torah appears to obligate individual people in numerous other matters whose precise sense seemed to require further specification. How exactly—to take a somewhat different case—could one begin to enumerate all the possible permutations of such a sweeping commandment as the Torah's "You shall love your neighbor like yourself" (Lev 19:18)? Does this mean that if I win the lottery, the Torah requires me to share the money with my neighbor, and if so, is it supposed to be a fifty-fifty split? Where does "love of neighbor" end? Some ancient interpreters seemed to go rather far in interpreting the extent of this commandment:

> And among yourselves, my sons, be *loving of your brothers as a man loves himself,* with each man seeking for his brother what is good for him, and acting together on the earth, and loving each other as themselves.[5] (*Jub* 36:4)

> You shall love your neighbor even above your own soul [life]. ([early Christian] *Letter of Barnabas* 19:5)

On the other hand, the Dead Sea Scrolls community appears to have endorsed a far more restrictive reading, as if this law applied only to members of their own group, that is, "And you shall love [only] your-neighbor-who-is-like-yourself."[6] A somewhat middle ground was endorsed elsewhere:

> Love your neighbor: for what is hateful to you yourself, do not do to him. (A rabbinic *targum* [translation into Aramaic] of Lev 19:18)

The famous parable of the good Samaritan was specifically addressed to the same question: Who am I required to "love"—anyone, even one of those hated Northerners, the Samaritans? Are they really my *neighbors*? (See Luke 10:25–29.)

Saying the Shema

Another act of personal piety was deduced from a passage in the Torah that likewise brought with it a number of questions:

> Hear this, O Israel: The LORD is our God, the LORD alone; [thus,] you shall love the LORD your God with your whole [i.e., undivided] heart and self and might. Let these things that I am commanding you this day stay in your mind. And you shall impress them on your children and think about them, whether you are at home or on a journey, when you lie down and when you get up. Bind them as a sign on your hand and as frontlets between your eyes, and write them on the doorposts of your house and your gates. (Deut 6:4–9)

Read without presupposition, this appears to be a commandment to keep in mind the various matters ("these things that I am commanding you this day") that Moses had been, and would be, transmitting to the people of Israel in the book of Deuteronomy. The items mentioned—teaching these things to your children, thinking about them at home or away, from the time you get up in the morning until you go to bed at night,[7] keeping them as close to yourself as physical ornaments—seem all to be in the nature of illustrations of how important this commandment is. It is unlikely that any person, ancient or modern, could actually keep thinking of "these things"—apparently, the whole book of Deuteronomy—nonstop all day. Rather, this passage was simply an expansive exhortation to keep in mind the wholehearted devotion to Israel's God and His laws. Likewise, some scholars have argued that "Bind them as a sign on your hand and as frontlets between your eyes" was not intended to be carried out physically, but was merely a metaphor of closeness, as similar expressions from the Bible seem to demonstrate.[8]

Ancient interpreters sought to convert this whole exhortation into a series of specific acts of personal piety. If it refers to keeping in mind "these things that I am commanding you this day," interpreters understood this to mean the specific act of reciting certain *words** — not the words of the whole book of Deuteronomy every day, since that would have seemed highly unlikely — but specifically the words just preceding this sentence, namely, "Hear this, O Israel: The LORD is our God, the LORD alone; and [therefore] you shall love the LORD your God with your whole [i.e., undivided] heart and being and might." But even if the text intended for people to recite only this sentence, should people recite it all the time, like some sort of mantra? Instead, interpreters understood the reference to "when you lie down and when you get up" not as a merism ("all the time"),[9] but as a specification of precisely *when* this commandment is to be carried out: twice a day, upon going to bed and again upon rising:

> "He also commanded that on going to bed and rising, men should *meditate on the ordinances of God.*" (*Letter of Aristeas* [late 2nd or early 1st cen. BCE], 160)

> "With the entrance of day and of night, I shall *enter into the covenant of God,* and with the going out of evening and of morning, *I shall speak His laws* . . . Before I move my hands and feet, I will *bless His name;* I will *praise Him* before I *go out or enter, or sit or rise,* and while I lie on the couch of my bed I will *extol Him;* I will *bless Him* with the offering that comes from my lips in the company of men." (1Q*Community Rule* col 10:10–14)

> Two times each day, at dawn and when it is time to go to sleep, let everyone acknowledge to God the gifts that He has bestowed upon them through their deliverance from the land of Egypt, the offering of thanks being by its nature praiseworthy, and something that is done both in response to past favors and so as to invite future ones. (Josephus, *Ant.* 4:212)

In these various examples (as well as others),[10] there is a marked desire to specify and pin things down, to take what looks like a broad assertion and

---

* Remember that Hebrew *devarim,* "things," can also mean "words."

connect it to specific acts: *these* are the things that constitute work that you cannot do on the Sabbath, *these* are the people you are obligated to love like yourself, *this* is precisely what such love should consist of, and *these* are the words you must recite each day, morning and evening. Such acts of specification in turn bespeak the same mentality mentioned earlier: fixed prayers at fixed times, a fixed collection of sacred texts, further specified by their fixed interpretation. This very fixity created a solid structure of religious dos and don'ts for each person to follow. And surely the "each person" part is highly significant. The universal God, who was in charge of the fate of nations, was also keeping track of individuals, since He ultimately was to judge each person.

Life After Death

This concern with the fate of individuals was also expressed in an intensified concern with the afterlife evidenced in late Second Temple times. No doubt many people believed—as they do today—that death was simply the end of the road. There was little in the Hebrew Bible itself to counter this idea; as Job asserts, "A man lies down never to rise . . . if a man dies, can he live again?" (14:12, 14). But we have seen above that Plato and later Greek sources had posited a soul altogether distinct from the body, so that a person's soul could conceivably survive the body's death and continue to exist in eternity. Perhaps under Greek influence, the idea of some sort of life-after-death came to be important for Jews as well in later biblical times. The biblical book of Ecclesiastes concludes:

> The end of the matter, when all has been heard: Fear God and keep His commandments, for this is the whole of human life. For God will pass judgment on every person[11] with regard to everything hidden, whether good or bad. (Eccles 12:13–14)

For the most part, Jewish sources speak not of a Greek-style, immaterial and imperishable soul living forever after death, but of the dead being physically *resurrected,* brought back to life at some time in the future.

> Many of those that sleep in the dust of the earth will awake, some to eternal life, others to reproaches [and] eternal abhorrence. And the knowl-

> edgeable will shine as the brightness of the firmament, and those who lead the many to righteousness will be like the stars forever and ever. (Dan 12:2–3)

This famous passage does not merely say that the dead will be resurrected; it says that what happens after they are resurrected will depend on what sort of people they were during their lifetimes. (Similarly, the Ecclesiastes verse cited above says that God will pass judgment "with regard to everything hidden, whether good or bad.") Some people will be given eternal life, but others will awaken to "eternal abhorrence." Here then is another important milestone in the career of the "elusive individual." Each person will be judged on an individual basis and will be rewarded or punished in kind. Something similar is suggested by the *Book of Jubilees,* a slightly earlier contemporary of the book of Daniel:

> [*The angel of the Presence describes the righteous in time to come:*] They will complete their days in peace and happiness and they will live without any [satanic] Accuser or evil mishap, for all their lifetimes will be lifetimes of blessing and health. Then God will *restore His servants, and they will arise and enjoy great peace.* He will *strike down His enemies* and the righteous will look on and give thanks and rejoice forever and ever in happiness. They will see all the punishments and curses [that will befall] their enemies. While the bones [of the righteous] will rest in the earth, *their spirits will have great joy,* and they will know that the Lord is one who executes judgment but shows kindness to hundreds and thousands and to all who love Him. (*Jub* 23:29–31)

This individualized resurrection was not, however, the only scenario.[12] Other Jewish sources presume a collective resurrection, with no account taken of individual merits and demerits:

> [God said to the Israelites in the time of Joshua:] I will plant you like a desirable vine and tend to you like a loving flock; and I will command the rain and the dew, and they will be abundant for you during your lifetime. But also *at the end, the lot of each one of you* will be eternal life, for you and your offspring, and I will take your souls and store them in peace, until the allotted to the world will be complete. (Pseudo-Philo, *Book of Biblical Antiquities* 23:12–13)

> *All Israel* will have their lot in the world to come, as it is written, "And your people are all of them righteous, they will inherit the land for all time; [they are] the shoot that I planted, My handiwork in which I glory." [Isa 60:21] (Mishnah *Sanhedrin* 10:1)

The idea of a bodily resurrection, presumed in the above-cited Dan 12:2–3, *Jub* 23:29–31, and elsewhere, did not have an easy reception. Everyone knew that bodies begin to decay immediately after death, so that soon all that remains in the ground is the person's skeleton. How could God restore all that has decayed—wasn't it gone forever?[13] Some Jewish sources therefore seem to hesitate between the two scenarios: the imperishable and eternal (Greek-style) soul, and that other notion, the bodily resurrection of the dead:

> Do not dig up the graves of the departed, nor expose to the sun what must not be seen, lest you stir up divine anger.
> It is not good to dissolve the human frame, for we hope that the remains of the departed will soon come to light (again)
> out of the earth, and afterward they will become as gods. For the souls remain unharmed among the deceased.
> For the spirit is a loan of God to mortals, and (is in His) image.
> For we have a body made out of earth, and when afterward we are resolved again into earth
> we are mere dust; but [by] then the air has received our spirit . . .
> We humans do not live a long time, but only for a season.
> But our soul is immortal and lives ageless forever. (*Sayings of Pseudo-Phocylides* 100–115)

The New Testament reports that Paul encountered some incredulity in Athens when he spoke of bodily resurrection:

> [Paul told the assembled:] "While God has overlooked the times of human ignorance, now He commands all people everywhere to repent, because He has fixed a day on which He will have the world judged in righteousness by a man whom He has appointed, and of this He has given assurance to all by *raising him from the dead.*" When they heard of the resurrection of the dead, some scoffed; but others said, "We will hear you again about this." (Acts 17:30–32)

The Kingship of God

One further manifestation of the changing character of Judaism in this period may be mentioned here. It is familiar to many Christians in John the Baptist's call: "Repent, for the kingdom of Heaven is at hand" (Matt 3:2). In truth, this well known verse contains a somewhat misleading translation of the Hebrew *malkhut shamayim.* Toward the end of the biblical period, the word "Heaven" in Hebrew (*shamayim*) was often used as a way of avoiding saying "God," just as we say in English, "*Heaven knows* when my refund will arrive," which really means, "God only knows." As for "kingdom" (*malkhut*), a better translation would be "king*ship,*" because the kingdom of Heaven was not originally some mysterious *place;* this phrase meant, quite simply, God's making apparent His role as king and ruler over the world. This is what John the Baptist was referring to by saying, "Repent, for the kingdom of heaven is at hand": soon enough, God will reassert His kingship, His power over the world, so repent before it's too late. (This statement is paralleled in Mark 1:14, but with a significant change: "The time is fulfilled and *the kingdom of God* is at hand; repent and believe in the good news.")

But why should God's kingship be "at hand," that is, be *about to* come into effect? Isn't His rule over all of reality already a fact now?[14] This was the whole point of John the Baptist's words. Toward the end of the biblical period, many Jews (like John) believed that God's kingship had somehow been temporarily put on hold, or at least hidden from view. In fact, an anonymous contemporary of John's said almost the same thing, foreseeing a time when

> His kingdom will appear throughout His whole creation;
> that is when the Devil will meet his end,
> and sorrow will be led away with him. (*Testament of Moses* 10:1)

Here too, God's kingship is slated to *appear;* for the present, it would seem, His kingship has been hidden. But when His kingship does return, the Devil and human suffering will come to an end. Such were the hopes and dreams of many Jews in first-century Judea.[15]

Taking a step backwards, one cannot but be struck by how things had changed. Now, it was the imminent *reassertion* of God's kingship that people spoke of (including John the Baptist and the writers of the New Testament). But previously, the central claim of monotheism had been that God is and always has been the controller of all reality; He is, quite simply, the ruler of heaven and earth.[16] A substantial group of psalms, known to scholars as the "enthronement psalms," celebrate God's kingship in the here-and-now: "The LORD is king! Let the earth rejoice" (Ps 97:1), "The LORD is king, let the nations tremble" (Ps 99:1), and so forth.[17] Moreover, the idea of God's control of the world underlies much of the Bible's recounting of Israel's history. Even the Assyrians' capture and exile of Israel's northern tribes (the "ten lost tribes") and, later on, the fall of Jerusalem to the Babylonians—even these cataclysmic events could be, and were, fitted to the paradigm of a single divine power's control of all. The explanation, simply put, was that God had been angry with His people and had punished them, first the Northerners, then the Judeans.

Following this, however, history seemed to have bogged down, as one occupying foreign power replaced another in running the land of Judea. The Persians, who had replaced the Babylonians in ruling Israel's territory, were in turn conquered by Alexander the Great in 332 BCE, and the Greeks took over the Jewish homeland along with the rest of the region. One of Alexander's generals, Ptolemy I, became the ruler of Egypt and outlying areas (including Judea) in 323 BCE. Judea continued to be governed by the Egyptian Ptolemies for a time, until they were ousted from Judea by the Hellenizing Seleucids, headquartered in Syria, just before the start of the second century BCE. True, the revolt of the (Jewish) Maccabees, starting in 166 BCE, provided the Jews with a brief taste of political independence, but this hardly led to a restoration of Israel's long-lost empire and was short-lived. A century later, in 63 BCE, the Romans became the next occupying power to take over Judea.

The Romans were not particularly nice rulers, and they controlled much of everyday life in the Jewish homeland; directly or through their appointees, they decided affairs of state as well as micromanaging more local matters. If God had long ago determined Israel to be His own people, how could anyone account for the fact that this people was now being kicked around by the imperial army of a foreign power, indeed, by a nation that worshiped false gods, while our God stood on the sidelines? One could, of course, adopt the approach of *The Book of Jubilees* and say that all these ups and downs were simply the manipulations of the God of *longue durée:* "Don't get lost in the moment," was the message of *Jubilees'* chronology, "God calculates time in multiples of the forty-nine-year jubilees." In this same spirit, we saw that Psalm 145 asserts: "Your kingship (*malkhut*) is an everlasting kingship, and your rule [exists] in every age" (Ps 145:13).[18] God is always in charge, so no need to worry about the temporary fluctuations of history. But as time went on and the Romans still weren't leaving, many Jews became impatient. "Why doesn't He do something?" they asked. One answer, now provided with increasing urgency, was that He was indeed about to act: "the kingdom of Heaven is at hand," or rather, "God's kingship is about to be revealed."

Two millennia later, this is still the rub of monotheism. In fact, "Why doesn't He do something?" is a question implicit in the very idea of one God alone ruling an inevitably imperfect world. The death of a single infant, in fact, the merest hangnail on a righteous man's finger, might theoretically elicit the same question. But finding an answer becomes most urgent when this question is asked of the great events on the world stage, evil that affects not just a single individual or family, but whole populations. For modern Jews the question of course posed itself most directly with the events of World War II; one out of every three Jews in the world was killed by the Nazi extermination machine. A few decades later, the angry philosopher of Judaism, Israeli professor Yeshayahu Leibowitz, was to say what many Jews thought: "God doesn't save. He didn't save in the Holocaust, and He doesn't save now." Leibowitz was a religious Jew, careful to keep the commandments of the Torah, but his God had no discernible connection to the events of this world. When a person complained to Leibowitz that he had lost his belief in God after the Holocaust, Leibowitz is said to have replied, "Then you never believed in Him in the first place."

Our interest here is in the end of the biblical period and the time when God's kingship (that is, the "kingdom of Heaven") had become a phrase on everyone's lips. Things *must* be about to change; God's kingship will once again be made manifest. Mankind's (or at least Judaism's) search for God was at last to reach its positive conclusion.

The Messiah

It should be noted that, throughout the biblical period, major shifts in human affairs were generally conceived to be the result of, or to pass through, *people,* and to move from the top down. Thus, only an actual king chosen by God, and not any abstract entity like "the balance of power," "the economy," or "improved international relations," could bring about real change in the Jews' fortunes. So it was that hopes for the return of the "kingship of God" came to focus on an expected human ruler whose reign would usher in the new reality. Our word *messiah* comes from an elegant Hebrew synonym for the word "king": the *mashiaḥ*, "the anointed one," was so called because kings were anointed by pouring fragrant oil on their heads to mark the start of their reign. During the last century BCE, expectations of the coming of such a future king had reached a fever pitch, at least in some segments of Jewish society. Among these expectants were the followers of Jesus of Nazareth. Surely he could bring about the departure of the Romans from Judea and inaugurate the return of God's kingship on earth. As his followers increased, so did the hope that the time was truly at hand. And then it all collapsed. Jesus was killed in the cruel form of execution practiced by the Romans, live crucifixion.[19] Some of his followers must have despaired, assuming that his death proved that their messianic hopes had been in vain. Others, however, went on to create a new form of Judaism centered on the figure of the murdered Christ* (which only later became a separate religion, Christianity).

In the meantime, other Jews still hoped for the return of God's kingship, and some of them were responsible for fomenting an outright revolt against the Romans. The Great Revolt (66–70 CE), as it is called, ended in catastrophic failure; when it was over, the Jerusalem Temple, the great, throbbing heart of Jewish piety, lay in ruins, and the attempt to throw off Roman rule had been utterly defeated (save for a few mountaintop pockets of resistance, which were wiped out in the course of the next three years). Even this, however, did not put an end to messianic hopes: it was not until another major attempt to oust Roman power, led by Simeon bar Kosiba (Bar Kokhba) in 132–35 CE, had been routed and the Jews exiled from Jerusalem that the revolutionary fervor began to die down.

Acceptance of God's Kingship

And what of the kingship of God? In rabbinic writings of the second century CE and later, the kingship of God was still sometimes evoked in the old sense, as something that will appear imminently:

> From your place, O King, *appear* and rule over us, for we are waiting for You. When will you rule [again] in Zion? Soon, in our time, and forevermore will You dwell . . . And our eyes will behold *Your kingship*, as is said

* The Greek *christos*, "anointed one," was the standard translation of the Hebrew *mashiaḥ*.

> in the songs [celebrating] Your might, transmitted by David your righteous king, "The Lord will rule forever, your God, O Zion, from age to age, Hallelujah!" (Jewish *Kedushah* prayer, the last line a quote from Ps. 146:10)

The Kaddish prayer, from late rabbinic times, likewise preserves the same expectation: "Let the great name [of God] be magnified and sanctified in the world that He created according to His own will, *and let Him establish His kingship . . .*"[20]

But in some rabbinic texts, the kingship of God acquires a new sense: it refers to an *internal recognition* of what is not obvious to the eyes. Thus, a Mishnaic text explains, in the daily recitation of the Shema, the worshiper is first to concentrate and "accept God's kingship," that is, concentrate and accept the *idea* of God's sovereignty (despite what sometimes might appear); only then, having recognized His kingship, can the worshiper accept the "yoke of the commandments," the duty to keep the things commanded in the Torah that were ordained by this God.

> Why do the verses [of the Shema], beginning "Hear O Israel" [Deut 6:4–9], come before those that begin "And if you obey fully My commandments . . ." [Deut 11:13–21]? So that one may accept upon oneself the kingship of God (*malkhut shamayim*) first and after that accept upon oneself the yoke of the commandments.[21]

Here there is no apocalyptic event in the future that will reveal God's utter control of reality to the world at large. Instead, God's kingship is something that one must "accept upon oneself"—mentally. This act of acceptance is, as it were, a bit of enabling legislation that will allow a person to keep all of God's commandments faithfully, since without the belief that God is indeed in charge, what reason would a person have to abide by all the Torah's dos and don'ts?

Christianity, too, saw a shift in the meaning of the Kingdom of Heaven. In some early texts, its revelation is still a yearned-for event. Thus, the Lord's Prayer says, "May Your kingdom [that is, Your kingship] come and Your will be done on earth, as it is [already being done] in heaven" (Matt 6:10 and parallels).[22] In fact, the arrival of God's kingdom is not far in the future:

> And he said to them: "Truly I tell you, there are some people standing here who will not taste death before they see that the kingdom of God has come —with force!" (Mark 9:1; cf. Matt 16:28, Luke 9:27)

Elsewhere, however, God's kingship seems to have become — very much as in the later rabbinic texts cited above — something internalized, realized through a mental act:

> Once he [Jesus] was asked by the Pharisees when the kingdom of God was coming, and he answered, "The kingdom of God is not coming with things that can be observed; they will not say, 'Look! Here it is!' or 'There it is!' For the kingdom of God is within you." (Luke 17:20–21)

An interesting parallel to this passage exists in the noncanonical Gospel of Thomas, discovered in Egypt in 1945:

> His disciples said to him, "When will [God's] imperial reign come?" [He answered:] "It will not come by watching for it. It will not be said, 'Look here!' or 'Look there!' Rather, the Father's imperial rule is spread out upon the earth, and people don't see it." (*Thom.* 113:4)

In either of these passages, as well as in numerous others in early Christian writings, the old sense of the "kingship of God" has been transformed, spiritualized. It no longer belongs to the reality just outside your window. It is not "with things that can be observed"; "people don't see it."[23]

And so, Jews of various allegiances (including those who, in later times, would call themselves Christians) fell into a state of cautious expectation. The Messiah would come, or would come again, at some point in the near future; in the meantime God's kingship would remain asserted but not always evident. He was increasingly (to borrow a phrase from Isa 45:15) a kind of *Deus absconditus*, a God who, though hidden for the present, would eventually save Israel. In the meantime, He seemed to be content to control things from a distance.

There is much more to the religion of the Second Temple period than the specific items mentioned here, but I have highlighted these in particular both for what they show about our subject overall and for what they imply about the religions of Judaism and Christianity in somewhat later times. This was a period when, as we have seen, the fate of individual human beings seems to have gained new attention. This attention was expressed in late biblical psalms and still later statutory prayers, as well as in practices such as the daily recitation of the Shema and individual adherence to divine laws. God was watching you and, presumably, rewarding you individually for carrying out his commandments.[24] At the same time, many of the writings of this period stress the great distance between God and humans. He presides in highest heaven, surrounded by angels and enthroned on the uppermost of three, or seven, celestial layers, while humans dwell way down below. So people pray to Him regularly without any specific request, but merely to "establish contact" and so gain His favor. Moving in the opposite direction, God no longer speaks principally to humans through the intermediation of His prophets, but via the words of His book, which had become a detailed guide for living one's life. Indeed, keeping God's laws in all their particulars (particulars that were often dependent on the elaborations introduced by ancient interpreters) became the central act of Jewish religiosity.

Prayer and other routine acts of devotion were never all there was to Second Temple religion; the whole idea of *encountering* God has always raised untrammeled possibilities, and in Second Temple times these sometimes led, as we have seen, to visions of humans ascending to heaven or questioning angels face-to-face down here. But for the most part, the humble acts of turning to God in prayer at regular intervals and seeking to live in consonance with Scripture were indeed a way of *binding* one's daily life to God, and their very fixity was, I believe, their most enduring legacy to later ages. The reason, I think, is that these two postures — the prayerful supplicant and the obedient servant — embody a specific way of fitting into the world, one that holds human beings to their fundamental smallness vis-à-vis the divine.

"But how different," one might say, "is this way of encountering God from those of an earlier day!" So it may seem; certainly in this later disposition, much of the initiative in the divine-human encounter has passed from God to human beings. Yet what I have been suggesting is that this change (expressed in the dozens of little modifications and innovations chronicled above) ultimately had everything to do with the human beings — with their desire to encounter and truly *know* the divine, and along with this, their ongoing ability to adapt their apprehension of God to their own changing sense of what a human being is and does. Moreover, I have tried to suggest here and there in this survey that, viewed in its full perspective, the gap separating earlier apprehensions of the divine from later ones, while certainly not illusory, is not so great as it might first appear.

18

SOME CONCLUSIONS

This book began with a question: What was the "lived reality" of ancient Israelites' encounters with God, when God was said to have appeared to Abraham and spoken directly to Moses and other prophets — and why has this reality disappeared for most people nowadays? The answer lies, I believe, in the various forms of encountering God surveyed in the preceding chapters, from earliest times to the Second Temple period and beyond.

One thing about those early encounters should be obvious. Although they are narrated in the Bible as actual events — God "appeared" to Abraham, "spoke to Moses," and so forth — they take place in a reality different from our ordinary one; they occur "in a different register," as I put it once or twice. The tricky thing that these biblical narratives seek to represent is what that other register is like. So they start off by describing things as if they were taking place in the ordinary world: Abraham and Sarah "see" three men, Jacob physically wrestles with a "man" all night long, Manoah's wife meets someone "like a prophet," and so forth. At the same time, these people are clearly *in a fog:* the most obviously strange things pass them right by. Then the illusion that all this is happening in the ordinary world dissolves, and the people are left in that "different register," in which God speaks to them directly.

In some passages this other reality is simply assumed. At Mount Sinai, Moses and the seventy elders "saw the God of Israel," no further qualification needed, nor even any suggestion that this was some kind of special seeing. In a way, this is reminiscent of what was glimpsed of Mesopotamian religion and the "fog of divine beings." Everyone knew, apparently, that an *ilu* was not a single god-in-a-body as we might imagine in ordinary reality, but merely an earthly embodiment of a powerful being who simultaneously existed in various other places on earth as well as in some heavenly body, a star or planet or whole constellation, and perhaps as well in some other, utterly nonphysical manifestations. In this other reality, an onlooker could actually notice slight changes in the expression of Marduk's cultic statue as it was paraded by; it was not a statue at all, but Marduk himself. Indeed, once the craftsmen had finished fashioning that statue, they could symbolically deny what they had just done and proclaim, "This god was born in heaven."

I suggested (although there is obviously no evidence to back this up) that the "fog of divine beings" in ancient times goes back to a still-earlier stage, a time when humans first began to contemplate their own existence as something separate, but only barely so, from everything else. The undifferentiated Outside was all around them; in fact, it could sometimes move freely *into* them, despite their separateness. In every way, it utterly overshadowed their own little selves. The gods, indeed, the whole enchanted world that was this separate, *other* reality, thus represent a later stage, when that Outside had subdivided into distinct *causers*, residents of the "upper shelf" of powerful beings who make things happen. Their existence was as obvious to humans as the things that the gods controlled or inhabited (rain or drought, fertility or barrenness, sun and moon and stars); but unlike these, the gods themselves existed in a state of being that was axiomatically *not* ordinary. The deity whose huge stride was represented by the footprints on the steps of the temple at 'Ain Dara could also exist in a spindly little statue of the same god kept inside, while Ba'al (and perhaps YHWH as well) might somehow be both here and somewhere else. This extraordinary reality apparently did not require, as it does today, some special introduction or explanation: it had always been there, an aspect of existence just on the other side of the curtain. When Joshua, Samuel, and the others realized that they were encountering God, they were "surprised but not flabbergasted." Such things did happen. Indeed, God not only crossed that curtain from time to time; He could also hear the cries of human beings calling to Him from their side. Sometimes He conspicuously, almost visibly, came to their rescue.

And then things began to change. It did not happen all at once, but gradually Israel's embodied God became the "the appearance of the likeness of the presence of the LORD" (Ezek 1: 28). His body was now seen — but barely seen — through a much acknowledged screen of as-it-weres. Heaven had always been His abode, but now He took up permanent residence there, managing things on earth by remote control ("Let there be light") or through an army of helpers. He who had once buttonholed prophets in the street now remained at a distance. His spokesmen, the angels, came down to earth to speak with prophets on His behalf (but it used to be the prophets themselves who were His spokesmen!), while He remained on high. Nevertheless, a few privileged visionaries had actually ascended to a place above the clouds and saw Him enthroned there, surrounded by a flaming entourage of angels. The visionaries came back and told of what they had seen, revealing the secrets of heaven's various layers.

These *all* were actual encounters, the first and the last in the same degree. But clearly, something had been happening inside the human beings to change things. People had once feared any direct encounter with God; now they reached out to Him in regular, statutory prayers that asked for nothing more than some sort of remote contact, not even seeking confirmation that He was listening. At the same time, in certain late psalms as well as in prayers from Qumran, supplicants probed their own "inner depths" or begged God for mystical enlightenment, sometimes thanking Him as well for protection from enemies altogether phantasmagorical. To be sure, this hardly meant that the people as a whole had entered a state of passive self-reflection. In late Second Temple times, Israel yearned for nothing less than the total reestablishment of God's kingship on earth, presumably to be brought about by an earthly king who would retake control and fix all that had gone awry. But then, with time, the very nature of God's kingship came to be redefined. It became at times a way of seeing, something like the visionary state of old, which now allowed people to peer through the veil of apparent reality and glimpse God's rule behind and through it.

What brought about this gradual but thoroughgoing change in human beings' encounters with the divine? So many things had happened, people's whole way of life had so drastically changed in the course of ten centuries, that it may seem altogether inadequate to refer, as I have, to people's changing sense of self, as if this really clarified anything. Surely something, or rather, a lot of specific somethings, had come along and changed things: technological innovations that made possible new forms of existence;[1] Israel's geopolitical reality,[2] which brought with it (and not always in friendly fashion) the steady introduction of foreign practices and new ideas;[3] various political and social changes;[4] as well as a host of internally generated changes of various sorts, some of which were altogether nonmaterial, emerging from deep inside and taking wing.[5] No doubt it was all of these that changed Israel's apprehension of its God. (In mentioning these I am also rejecting by implication what some others have proposed: I don't believe this gradual shift was the result of a few significant individuals coming along simultaneously in the space of a few centuries,[6] nor of some fundamental change in the functioning of the bicameral brain.[7])

But to say, "These numerous changes came about and as a result people began conceiving of God in a different way" is likewise incomplete, precisely because it skips over the all-important mediating factor dismissed in the previous paragraph. It was not the material conditions of daily life or mere geopolitics that alone altered Israel's encounter with God; what was changing along with these — over a period of centuries — was a set of unspoken assumptions about what the self consists of and how it fits into the world. So it was in a substantially reconfigured self (and the self, it should be recalled, is always a human construct) that humans encountered God anew in the late- and post-biblical era. The evidence is in the very texts examined in the previous chapters.

Before leaving this topic, however, I wish to stress again that this sense of self is not a little detail housed somewhere in the brain, a *thing* that can be identified and moved beyond. To contemplate our sense of self in any true fashion is ultimately to bump up against our inability to know what it's like to be a bat, or to be anything substantially different from what we are. Everyone fits into the world in some way or other, but the way a particular person or society does so seems at a certain point to close off the possibility of truly entering a very different way of fitting in. Here, for example, is Clifford Geertz's description of the Balinese trance, a regular feature of certain public ceremonies:

> The Balinese fall into extreme dissociated states in which they perform all sorts of spectacular activities — biting off the heads of living chickens, stabbing themselves with daggers, throwing themselves wildly about, speaking in tongues, performing miraculous feats of equilibration, mimicking sexual intercourse, eating feces, and so on — rather more easily and much more suddenly than most of us fall asleep. Trance states are a crucial part of every ceremony. In some, fifty or sixty people may fall, one after the other ("like a string of firecrackers going off," as one observer puts it), emerging anywhere from five minutes to several hours later, totally unaware of what they have been doing and convinced, despite the amnesia, that they have had the most extraordinary and deeply satisfying experience a man can have.

Do we really have any sense of what it feels like to be a Balinese celebrant for having had him so described? Geertz goes on to ask this question in somewhat different terms:

> What does one learn about human nature from this sort of thing and from the thousand similarly peculiar things anthropologists discover, investigate, and describe? That the Balinese are peculiar sorts of beings, South Sea Martians? That they are just the same as we are at base, but with some peculiar, but really incidental, customs we do not happen to have gone in for? That they are innately gifted or even instinctively driven in certain directions rather than others? Or that human nature does not exist and men are pure and simply what their culture makes of them? It is among such interpretations as these, all unsatisfactory, that anthropology has attempted to find its way to a more viable concept of man . . . To entertain the idea that the diversity of custom across time and over space is not a mere matter of garb and appearance, of stage settings and comedic masques, is to entertain also the idea that humanity is as various *in its essence* as it is in its expression.[8]

Geertz's reflections are those of an anthropologist. He does not consider what has seemed to me the great unknown underlying any sense of self, the actual mechanics (though I'm not happy with this word, I can't think of another) involved in our conceiving of ourselves and so fitting into the world, a subject which inevitably must lead to the "mystery of cognition" and, even by omission, to whatever is involved in people's encountering the divine. I am not sure one can say much more than this. Perhaps the one thing that might be added here has been said once or twice already, that the wavelengths of reflected light are indeed "out there," but they need a brain to become the colors that we see, truly see.

The Great Shift

The changes traced over the preceding pages were certainly far-reaching, but it is important to point out that they were, in the broad perspective, *transformations* rather than wholly new departures. Indeed, we have seen that a transformation on one side of the human encounter with God has often been accompanied by a parallel one on the other side. Thus, as God came to be conceived as increasingly distant and abstract, the human *nefesh* went from being a general form of self-reference, "me," to being a special, separate entity inside the human body, an entity uniquely attached to God, and thence to being God's own property inside us, to be reclaimed after our body's demise. The same process has continued into more recent times. Our modern, sealed-off individualism has emerged in part thanks to the reconfiguring of what was once the semipermeable mind, and our complicated modern psyche has been purchased for a sky emptied of angels. To understand this is to realize that the basic elements of the human encounter with the divine are still with us, even as its reality is sometimes denied. Indeed, the particular difficulty of many modern Westerners is to find a way of conceiving of something for which they no longer have a name; adrift in today's version of the self, they cannot imagine trying to see beyond it in order to address an unknown You.

I was well into the writing of this book when a journal kept by the American writer Flannery O'Connor turned up among her papers and was published posthumously in 2013. O'Connor was a deeply religious Catholic throughout her short life (she died at the age of 39). Her journal is addressed to God—it's what is called a prayer journal—and the opening page, written when she was 20, has been much on my mind since its publication. Here is what she wrote:

> Dear God, I cannot love Thee the way I want to. You are the slim crescent of a moon that I see and my self is the earth's shadow that keeps me from seeing all the moon. The crescent is very beautiful and perhaps that is all one like I am should or could see; but what I am afraid of, dear God, is that my self shadow will grow so large that it blocks the whole moon, and that I will judge myself by the shadow that is nothing.
>
> I do not know you God because I am in the way. Please help me to push myself aside.

The image is striking: God is like the moon whose full being is partially obscured by the earth's shadow, so that all that is left is one glimmering crescent. That crescent is very beautiful, and like many religious people, O'Connor would like to see—to know—more. But the problem, she says, is "my self." How fine of her to start by separating those two words, as if to make clear that it is not her very existence, not "myself," that keeps getting in the way, but rather the thing that we carry around in our heads, that bulky and clumsy imagination of who we are that we call our "self." This self is like the earth's shadow, she says, gradually encroaching on the moon's disk; what she fears is that it will ultimately block off the moon's light entirely, so that "I will judge myself by the shadow that is nothing," that is, I will think that all I am is that shadow-self. Her respelling "myself" in this sentence may just be accidental—this is a private diary, after all, and she was a pretty erratic speller — but I would like to think she meant it to say that there really is more to us ("myself") than that bulky, God-blocking shadow ("my self shadow"). But like it or not, that self is still a lot of what we have become — it's what the modern world has made of us — so "Please help me to push myself aside."

There is little to be added to this twenty-year-old's diagnosis, but I should like to end by suggesting that her prayer — "Please help me to push myself aside" — in fact invokes an age-old theme. Going about in our sumptuous capacities as human beings and in a world of our own making has long made it difficult to see anything else; what is human in us inevitably leads us to try to apprehend God in ways consistent with our way of being.

The Bible says something similar, I think, in describing a brief exchange between King David and the prophet Nathan. David, having completed construction of a magnificent palace for himself in Jerusalem, is suddenly struck by the incongruity of God still dwelling in a flimsy tent, the tabernacle:

> The king said to the prophet Nathan, "Here I am living in a palace made of cedar wood, while the Ark of God resides in a tent!" Nathan said to the king, "Whatever it is that is in your heart, go and do it, since the LORD is with you." But that very night, the word of the LORD came to Nathan, saying: "Go and say to My servant David, 'Thus says the LORD: Are you proposing to build Me a house to dwell in? I have not dwelt in a house from the time that I led the people of Israel out of Egypt until this very day, but I have forever been going about in tent and tabernacle.'" (2 Sam 7:1–6)

God has no need of a kingly palace — this is a strictly human demand. But what sort of a palace is it to be? Since the time of King David (in fact, starting well before then), the divine accommodations have kept changing. And it's not over yet.

ACKNOWLEDGMENTS

Behind these pages stand conversations (and a few arguments) with friends and colleagues, stretching over at least the last decade. I wish here to acknowledge my debt to, among others, Gary Anderson, John Barton, Ellen Birnbaum, Marc Brettler, John Collins, Devorah Dimant, Ed Greenstein, Theodore Gross, William Hallo, Matthias Henze, Avi Hurvitz, Jan Joosten, Menahem Kister, Jacob Klein, David Lambert, Jon Levenson, Bernard Levinson, Peter Machinist, Pinchas Mandel, Chaim Milikowsky, Greg Nagy, Hindy Najman, Judith Newman, Carol Newsom, Bill Propp, Elisha Qimron, Lawrence Rhu, Ishay Rosen-Zvi, Lawrence Schiffman, Baruch Schwartz, Michael Segal, Bernard Septimus, Aharon Shemesh, Ben Sommer, Michael Stone, Guy Stroumsa, Loren Stuckenbruck, Eibert Tigchelaar, Robert R. Wilson, and Ziony Zevit. Despite this lengthy list, I may have inadvertently left out the names of at least a few other scholars, for which I apologize. More significantly, I must stress that at least some of the foregoing will likely find in this book ideas or arguments with which they disagree; in mentioning them, I do not wish to imply otherwise. Equally important, I alone am responsible for any errors of fact or expression in this book.

I am indebted once again to my friend and publisher (a rare combination in my experience), Bruce Nichols of Houghton Mifflin Harcourt, as well as to Larry Cooper for his production help, and to Melissa Dobson for her careful copyediting. Above all, I am grateful to the members of my own family for their insights and their patience.

NOTES

In writing this book, I have drawn liberally on the work of contemporary scholars. These notes are intended to express my thanks for, and my debt to, their research, and in some cases as well to take up issues still under discussion. But these notes are mostly intended for specialists. While I do hope that non-specialists may likewise find some of them of interest, I wish to assure all readers that I have quite consciously arranged things so as to leave out nothing essential from the body of the book.

FOREWORD

1. See Gen 15:6, Num 20:12, Deut 9:23, 2 Kings 17:14, Isa 7:9, etc. Some have argued that the phrase *'ein elohim* in Ps 10:4, 14:1, and 53:1 strictly means "God does not exist"; see Barr (1961), 62. However, it is God's presence, rather than existence, that is being denied: NJPS therefore translates, "God does not care," while NRSV Study Edition explains, "The fool denies not God's existence, but divine governance of the world and attention to humankind." Only toward the end of biblical times did faith in God's very existence begin to emerge as a central item; those who did not perceive God's presence on their own were now urged to believe, in any case, to "have faith." Faith was a little click in the brain, a conscious, willful act that opened a door. The early Christian writer Tertullian probably did not utter the words often attributed to him, *Credo quia absurdum est* ("I believe because it is absurd"), but this well captures the flavor of having faith in the context of the early Roman encounter with Christian teachings. (Tertullian did say something rather similar in his *On the Flesh of Christ,* 5:4: "The son of God died: this is altogether believable, because it is absurd." See on this Ruel (1982). Belief existed in spite of what seemed to be true. And so it often is today. That little click, more difficult than ever to achieve in today's world, is absolutely crucial. But it should leave one wondering: Why is it absent from most of the Bible and the religions of the ancient Near East?
2. One might say more generally that biblical texts give the impression that ordinary people in biblical times "experienced" God's presence in their lives, but useful here is Nathan Rotenstreich's distinction between two German words for experience, *Erlebnis* and *Erfahrung*: the former "connotes more than experience in the limited sense. It is an impression absorbed or integrated in the texture of our existence. Sometimes it con-

notes an event solely or particularly significant for ourselves, thus becoming part of our broader existence. Thus, *Erlebnis* connotes more an internalization of an occurrence, while *Erfahrung* connotes more the encounter with something that we undergo, that we experience" (Rotenstreich [1998], 18). If so, what I intend to say is that for most ancient Israelites God's existence was a matter of *Erlebnis,* although, as we shall see, for some it was indeed an *Erfahrung.*

1. SEEING BIBLICALLY

1. Hermann Gunkel first identified this genre in *The Legends of Genesis* (1901); see Garsiel (1991).
2. To be sure, not every divine encounter is so marked, nor are these expressions limited to divine encounters. In particular, to "lift up one's eyes and see" can either be used to stress that the thing seen came in a divine vision (Gen 24:18; Josh 5:13; Isa 40:26, 49:18, 51:6, 60:4; Jer 13:20; Ezek 8:5; Zech 2:1, 5; 5:1, 5; 5:9; 6:1; 9:6; Dan 8:3, 10:5; 1 Chr 21:16) or, for example, to suggest that the thing was seen from afar (Gen 13:10, 14; 22:4; 24:63–64; 31:10, 12; 33:1, 5; 37:25; Num 24:2; Deut 3:27; 1 Sam 6:13; 2 Sam 13:34, 18:24; Ps 121:1; Job 2:12). But I don't think that the latter usage detracts from the former. "Looking up," then "seeing," then "beholding" is a rather strongly marked way of saying that this was an unusual sight.
3. On this element in the stories of Gideon and of Manoah and his wife, see below; also Tobit 12:9, Sir 16:27.
4. Strange to tell, this point has been lost on some modern scholars, who fail to follow the text's clear hints that what is being narrated is a divine vision. Even Esther Hamori's otherwise excellent study asserts: "There are several texts in which an angel clearly has physical human form, not in a dream or a vision, but on earth, most notably in Gen 18–19 [the encounter between Abraham and the three strangers], Judges 6 and 13, and Joshua 5 . . . The anthropomorphic realism in Genesis [18] is equally stark. It is only the other two figures who are called angels": Hamori (2010), 96. See also M. Smith (2015), who (wrongly, I believe) assimilates the waking vision of Gen 18 to the depiction of God in Gen 2–3, where God is indeed represented as having a physical body ordinarily visible to Adam and Eve.
5. In this case, there is no specific indication of when Abraham caught on. After Sarah's laughter, "The LORD said to Abraham, 'Why did Sarah laugh?'" The mention of "the LORD" may once again be intended to indicate *to the reader* who was speaking, or it may represent the fact that she has just caught on. However, the fact that Abraham goes on to escort the three men on their journey indicates that he is still in a fog. Cf. the discussion in Savran (2005), 79, 135.
6. A somewhat ambiguous affirmation, since Hebrew *mar'eh,* "sight," sometimes specifically refers to such a vision; note in particular Num 12:8.
7. I examined some of these in Kugel (2003), 5–36, though readers may notice that I have somewhat modified my understanding of these passages in the present study.
8. Ibid.
9. Cf. Isa 7:11.
10. In fact, the text never says he is anything other than that — but of course, ancient readers would have no doubt that he was a divine being, even without the help of Hos 12:4–5: "In his strength he fought with God, he fought with an angel and prevailed." Rather than

understanding this all-night wrestling match as a vision, some scholars have identified Jacob's opponent as a demon, who "really" attacked him: see on this Köckert (2003). A lot hangs on what "really" means, as we shall see.

11. It is only toward the end of the biblical period that angels become independent divine beings with names: see Dan 10:13, 21, etc.; *1 Enoch*, ch. 6 and thereafter.
12. This has led some to lump such angelic appearances together as a "type scene." On this phenomenon: Arend (1933) and, with respect to the Bible, Alter (1978) and (1981). There can be no doubt that literary conventions characterized ancient Israel's writings as much as they do all literatures, but the label "type scene" can nevertheless be misleading. In the biblical context, it can conveniently put aside questions of the historical or redactional relationship of two similar accounts, sometimes for plainly apologetic purpose. More important, in the present case it can leave the impression that these are merely literary manipulations, rather than following their cues to uncover the reality being addressed.
13. See Sommer (2009), 1–11. However, as Sommer goes on to argue, divine bodies were different from human bodies in several important respects: they were apparently made of different material, or no material at all; sometimes (but not always) they were much bigger than human bodies; most important, they could be conceived of as being present in more than one place at a time (pp. 12–57). Even this, however, does not quite cover all the biblical evidence; the true nature of an "angel" in the passages examined in the present chapter argues a somewhat different understanding of God's *apparent* physicality. The very vision of a humanlike "body" is clearly an illusion in these passages, one that fades away into disembodied speech. So while God can and does manifest Himself elsewhere in embodied form, and numerous texts speak of God's eyes, ears, hands, forearms, feet, and so forth, this embodiment is crucially undercut — it is not *just* a body, or it is only a body by analogy. This stands in contrast to, for example, the physical attributes of Ugaritic deities (who are *not* encountered in visions), who have "limbs, vertebrae, a spine, a back, a pelvis, lungs, a breast, a chest, collar bones and shoulder blades," though they can also fly, eat, and drink more than men, "and are simply not chained to the anthropomorphic shape": Korpel (1990), 89–90.
14. At other times, God's body is hidden in a cloud or by fire, or otherwise occulted: Exod 3:2; 13:21; 14:19, 24; 16:10; 19:9, 18; 24:16; 34:5; Num 12:5, 14:14; Deut 4:24, 9:3, 31:15; etc.; on rare occasions He is just "seen" (Exod 24:10).
15. In fact, sleep researchers know that eyes do actually move behind closed eyelids during sleep, as if actually seeing. This is rapid eye movement (REM) sleep, first identified by Nathaniel Kleitman and Eugene Aserinsky; see Aserinsky and Kleitman (1953). Most vivid dreams reported by subjects occur during REM sleep.
16. Kugel (1998a), 362–63.
17. Modern scholars suggest that the text's mention of Jacob just "happening" on the place, along with his setting up a pillar to mark the spot and his naming it Bethel, constitutes a blatant case of protesting too much. Bethel, it seems, was originally the site of a Canaanite temple, complete with its holy pillar (*maṣṣebah*). See Kugel (2007a), 150–51.
18. See above, note 12.
19. Note the nuanced discussion in Sommer (2009), 30–36.
20. Burkert (1985), 186–88. He writes: "In epic, encounters between gods and men are among the standard scenes; and yet, Homer employs them with marked reserve . . . In order to speak to a human being, a god will usually assume the shape of some friend; it is only the outcome, the turn of events, which gives evidence of the fact that a Stronger One was at

work here. Occasionally, the gods will reveal themselves by some token. Aphrodite who comes to Helen as an aged woman is recognized by her beautiful throat, her desirable breasts, and her sparkling eyes; Achilles recognizes Athena at once by the terrifying light in her eyes. After she has lain with Anchises, Aphrodite rises from the couch and reveals herself in all her immortal beauty, which shines forth from her cheeks; her head reaches to the roof of her chamber; Anchises is terror-stricken and hides his face" (p. 187). See also R. Fox (1986): "In epic poems, the gods mixed with men by daylight, [either] gods in disguise . . . or gods made manifest by signs of their power . . . There was no end to the gods' human disguises, as old men and women, heralds, and frequently, young and beautiful people . . . Did the gods also appear as animals? Occasionally, Homer's gods appeared 'like birds,' but there is no episode when a god turns completely into a bird . . . Essentially anthropomorphic, the gods stalked the world as mortals, disguising themselves so well that people could never be totally sure that a stranger was all that he seemed" (pp. 104–6).

21. I use this word throughout *not* in the sense of something false, but what one scholar has defined as "a sensory experience, which occurs in the absence of corresponding external stimulation of the relevant sensory organ, [yet] has a sufficient sense of reality to resemble a veridical perception, over which the subject does not feel s/he has direct and voluntary control and which occurs in the awake state." See A. S. David (2004).
22. Lindblom (1962), 173–74.

2. JOSEPH AND HIS BROTHERS

1. Sometimes actions are attributed to two different "causers," a divine one and a human. See Seeligmann (1963), 385–411. In legal matters, David Daube has subtly distinguished between different concepts of human causality in biblical law, and these might profitably be applied to shades of divine causality: Daube (1961); see also Daube (2008).
2. See the brief but seminal essay of von Rad, "The Joseph Narrative and Ancient Wisdom" (1953), included in von Rad (1968), 292–300. The subject has been taken up by other scholars, sometimes in disagreement: see Crenshaw (1969) and Crenshaw (1998), 29–30; Redford (1970); Coats (1973); Wessels (1984); and M. Fox (2001).
3. In this sense, Israelite *wisdom* has been compared to the Egyptian concept of *ma'at,* the divinely established order. "Maat is right order in nature and society, as established by the act of creation," Morentz (1992), 113. See also Volten (1992) and Würthwein (1976). For a dissenting view: M. Fox (1995); also, M. Fox (1992). Other scholars have rightly stressed the connection between Israelite *ḥokhmah* and creation: Zimmerli (1976). The point, however, is the underlying set of rules that were established at the creation.
4. See on this Alter (1981), 216.
5. The story similarly has Reuben tell Joseph (whom he believes to be an Egyptian official): "We are all of us sons of one man . . . We, your servants, are twelve brothers, the sons of one man in the land of Canaan" (Gen 42:12–13). Reuben doesn't realize how true his words are. Including Joseph, to whom he is talking, they are indeed twelve brothers, all of them the sons of Jacob. See *Genesis Rabba,* 42:7.
6. See on this Segal (2011).
7. See Dimant (1993) and Werman (2006).
8. Ancient interpreters supposed that the only reason Joseph was not executed—since

that would normally have been the fate of a slave who attempts to rape his mistress—was that there was irrefutable evidence of his innocence. See Kugel (1990a), 64, n. 47.

9. Repeated in Gen 41:28 and 32.
10. This is of course quite a different statement from that of the book of Judges, "the spirit of the LORD came over [him]" (3:10, 11:29, etc.), or Ezekiel's "the spirit of the LORD entered into me" (Ezek 2:2, 3:24). Here, the spirit is permanently in residence in Joseph's brain. John Levison has put the matter clearly: this phrase in regard to Joseph "would suggest spiritual vitality but no special endowment, giftedness without a definitive moment in which that gift was imparted . . . Pharaoh attributes Joseph's ability to interpret dreams to the divine character of the spirit within him—not the divine spirit that has come upon him": Levison (2009), 39, 49; see also below, chapter 11.
11. Auerbach (1957), 9.
12. Kugel (1998a), 308–9.

3. THE LAST WILLS OF JACOB'S SONS

1. See Flusser (1966); Baumgarten (1985–86); Maurer (2003) in Schiffman et al. (2003); Alexander (1999); Eshel (1999), 295–324; and below, note 5.
2. In Greek, ὁ ἄρχων τῆς πλάνης.
3. This phrase is a reflection of Lev 19:17, "You shall not hate your brother in your heart," where hatred *in the heart* means concealed hatred. Instead of hating in secret, Lev 19:17 continues, "you shall surely reprove your fellow and bear no sin because of him." Further: Kugel (1987).
4. On the whole question of *Jubilees'* position on the origin of evil in the world, see Segal (2007), 97–269. On this passage in particular, pp. 150–63, 169–80, 265–66. My aim in the present chapter is to focus on the attribution of human evildoing to internal and/or external sources; for that reason, I have not dealt specifically with Gen 6:1–4 and the Watchers narrative of *1 Enoch* or *Jubilees*, nor, by the same token, with the interpretation of the Garden of Eden narrative in Gen 2–3, but many of the studies cited below have. See also Stone (1999) and, briefly, Stone (2011), 51–58. Note also Kugel (2013b).
5. See on this prayer Segal (2007), 259–62, and Kister (2010), which argues that this prayer was borrowed from an earlier source. On "evil spirits who rule the thoughts of people's minds," see below.
6. See also the *Aramaic Levi Document,* among the Dead Sea Scrolls, 3:6–10: "[Levi prays:] O Lord, let the holy spirit be shown to me, and give me sage counsel, and wisdom and knowledge and strength, in order to do what pleases You and [so] to find mercy before You, to praise/sing Your words within me [and do] what is pleasing and good before You. *Let no satan rule over me,* making me stray [πλανῆσαί με] from Your path, and have mercy on me, O Lord, and bring me close to be Your servant and to minister to You properly." Similarly: "And Uriel said to me, 'There stand the angels who mingled with the women [i.e., the Watchers]. And *their spirits—having assumed many forms—bring destruction on men and lead them astray* to sacrifice to demons as to gods until the day of the great judgment, in which they will be judged with finality'" (*1 En* 19:1).
7. On the phrase "rule over me" see Greenfield (1992). "Satan" here and elsewhere appears to be a common (rather than proper) noun: Greenfield, Stone, and Eshel (2004), 129–30.
8. First published in Sanders (1965), 76–79. Further examples of Qumran apotropaic

prayers: 4Q510 frag 1, 4Q444 *4QIncantation*, 4Q510 *4QSongs of the Sage[a]*, possibly also 6Q18 *6QHymn* and 1QH[a] *Thanksgiving Hymns* frag 4; all of these are discussed in Eshel (1999), 69–88. Kister (2010) suggests that "evil inclination" here and (presumably) in *Jub* 12:20 is related to the meaning of this term in rabbinic writings; cf. Rosen-Zvi (2011), 47.

9. A vast scholarly literature has been devoted to examining this passage. See among many others: DiLella (1966), 121–25; Hadot (1970), 91–103; G. Meier (1971); Crenshaw (1975), 48–51; S.G.H. Cohen (1984), 89; B. Wright (1989); Winston (1989); Wischmeier (1999); Reiterer (1999); Mattila (2000); Aitkin (2002); Gilbert (2002); Ruger (1970); Beentjes (2002).

10. Though even presented in the clearest terms, these two poles are sometimes of ambiguous intention. Rosen-Zvi (2011) argues that an earlier, "biblical" view that basically attributed human evildoing to human agency (a proposition that I wish, however, to explore further below) came to be complicated by, or even pushed aside by, Persian demonological accounts for evil's origin (which then caused the human *yetzer* to be represented as a demon or otherwise external being), along with Greek ideas that sought a complex (Platonic- or Stoic-influenced) "anthropological" (i.e., rooted in the human self; see below, note 18) explanation for evildoing. Rosen-Zvi ultimately sees in the rabbinic *yetzer* an attempt to acknowledge these independent sources of sin without, however, renouncing human responsibility. Note also the recent doctoral dissertation of Miryam Brand (2011), which (somewhat similar to Bruno Snell discussed below) seeks to connect the preference of internal or external sources of sin to the literary genre and purpose of the texts involved; the external-source approach is sometimes associated with the angelology and demonology prominent in late biblical and other Second Temple period writings, while the internal-source approach may have been influenced by Greek ideas about the role of conflicting components within the human "inside."

11. Cf. Segal (2007), 251–56.

12. It may be that *Jubilees* here is contrasting the fate of Israel-the-nation, which will be the object of Belial's "bringing charges" against them on high, to the acts of individual Israelites "go[ing] along in the error of their minds," perhaps suggesting that these individuals' actions are what will ultimately lead Belial to accuse the nation as a whole. (Note that throughout, "Beliar" is a variant form of "Belial.")

13. Note the comparison of this passage to two other Qumran prayers as well as b. *Berakhot* 16b and 60b in Nitzan (1996), 250–52.

14. Even in the latter case, however, it is not clear that this is altogether an internal event. Even the passage cited earlier from the "Testament of Asher" — an apparently clear example of the "internally generated" explanation for human evil — seems a little less clear in its larger context: "There are two ways, of good and of evil, and along with them two impulses within our breasts that differentiate them. Thus, if the soul chooses the good [impulse], everything it does will be [done] in righteousness, and [even] if it sins, it will repent right away. For when a person's thoughts are set on righteous things and he rejects wickedness, he immediately overthrows what is evil and uproots the sin. But if [the person's soul] opts for the [evil] impulse, then its every action will be in wickedness, and, having driven away the good, [it] will take hold of the bad; *it will eventually be ruled by Beliar. [Then,] even if [the person] does something good, he [Beliar] will convert it into something bad.* For, should it [the soul] start to do something good, he [Beliar] arranges

for the upshot of the action to work evil for him, for the [evil] impulse's storage chamber is now filled with the poison of an evil Spirit" (T. Asher 1:5–9).

Here, an initially independent, internal choice ultimately leads to the soul being taken over entirely by an outside actor: that is, having opted for the bad, the soul "will eventually be ruled by Beliar. [Then,] even if [the person] does something good, he [Beliar] will convert it into something bad" and so forth. What is more, the passage asserts that the evil impulse has a little warehouse, a "storage chamber," inside the person that can be filled with poison from an apparently *external* evil spirit.

15. Note the discussion of *leb ra'* in Najman (2014), 73–93. Various senses of "spirit" in classical, biblical, and extrabiblical sources are surveyed in Levison (1997) and (2009). Note in the latter the Stoic *pneuma:* "By the first century C.E., one of the foundational conceptions of of Stoicism was that *pneuma* pervades a living and rational cosmos . . . This distinctive view of the cosmos as pervaded by *pneuma* drew its inspiration, by way of analogy, from Stoic anthropology . . . In this way, the view that *pneuma* unifies both cosmos and psyche would become regnant in Stoic thought" (137–40).

16. Perhaps the most discussed instance of this ambiguity is the famous "Two Spirits" passage of the *Serekh ha-Yahad* (1QS *Community Rule* III:13–IV:26). Among many recent treatments: Lange (1995), 121–43; Metso (2007b), 26–27; Duhaime (2003), 103–31; Hempel (2010); Stuckenbruck (2011).

17. Defining the self (and, although it is different, the sense of self as well) is not a task to be disposed of in a sentence or two. My starting point—the common starting point, I believe—is the work of William James; see in particular James (1892), 151–216. Among many later treatments building on James, see Flanagan (1992), in particular 177–211. Discussion of the self and of the sense of self crosses disciplinary lines, and the focus of research, as well as the terminology, sometimes changes. Some psychologists and anthropologists thus speak of the sense of self as *self-representation,* "the individual's mental representation of his own person." See Spiro (1993), Ewing (1990); Quinn (2006). What I intend by offering the rather limited definition of "sense of self" here is to suggest the variety of ways in which this or that "defined group of people" may differ in their most basic assumptions about their own minds and how they interact with all that is not "me." Note that James's definition distinguished (here I am citing Flanagan's restatement of it) "a range of things that can be appropriated into the 'me,' into the self-conception, into the thought or set of thoughts that constitute the model of one's self. James distinguishes among a 'material me,' a 'social me,' and a 'spiritual me'": Flanagan (1992), 180.

18. Some scholars refer to this mental picture as the "anthropology" that a certain culture or society may have, including "biblical anthropology." See thus Di Vito (1999); Janowski and Liess (2009); cf. Heelas and Lock (1981). The obvious problem with this term is that it is also used to describe all sorts of other things, particularly the study of ancient or modern societies and cultures. To add to the confusion, "anthropology" itself is sometimes used in this sense as synonymous, or nearly synonymous, with "ethnology" or "ethnography," though these two more frequently refer specifically to the *reporting* aspect of social anthropology, usually accomplished by living in a given society and reporting on its members' way of life, customs, beliefs, and so forth. "In anthropology, or anyway social anthropology, what the practitioners do is ethnography . . . From one point of view, that of the textbook, doing ethnography is establishing rapport, selecting informants, transcribing texts, taking genealogies, mapping fields, keeping a diary, and so on. But it is not these things, techniques and received procedures, that define the en-

terprise. What defines it is the kind of intellectual effort it is: an elaborate venture in, to borrow a notion from Gilbert Ryle, 'thick description'": Geertz (1973), 5–6. In any case, in this book I have preferred "sense of self" over any other term to mean specifically the mental picture that a given individual or culture or society has of what a person consists of, the assumptions about what a person *is* that a defined group of people carry around in their heads, while "anthropology" herein usually refers to the study of all aspects of human existence in past or present-day societies. I use the terms "ethnography" and "ethnology" to refer specifically (when such specification is necessary) to the fieldwork and gathering of information about contemporary peoples and cultures, generally different from those of the modern West.

19. This is, in turn, part of the larger study of the whole phenomenon of consciousness. It may be pointless to single out one work or another in this huge field, especially one with so many competing approaches and theories. Nevertheless: a good introductory volume is the anthology of Block et al. (2002); note especially therein Güzeldere (2002); Dennett (2002a); and Dennett and Kinsbourne (2002). See also Dennett (1991), a fuller exposition of his "multiple drafts" model. Also: Churchland (1986) and (2002). Finally, with regard to "embodied cognition," see Lakoff and Johnson (1999) and Shapiro (2011).

20. This subject has been explored in the context of psychoanalytic theory by Heinz Kohut; see Kohut (1977) and (1978–81). Note also Ewing (1990), 261. In this connection Noam Chomsky relates: "I read my grandchildren stories. If they like a story, they want it read ten thousand times. One story that they like is about a donkey that somebody has turned into a rock. The rest of the story is about the little donkey trying to tell its parents that it's a baby donkey, although it's obviously a rock. Something or another happens at the end, and it's a baby donkey again. But every kid, no matter how young, knows that that rock is a donkey, that it's not a rock. It's a donkey because it's got psychic continuity, and so on. That can't be just developed from language, or from experience": Chomsky (2012), 27.

21. The very idea of such a clearinghouse has been rejected by Daniel Dennett and others, who refer to it as the "Cartesian theater" model of the brain's workings (because the philosopher René Descartes had hypothesized that the pineal gland was the brain's central clearinghouse; nowadays we know that the pineal gland's main function is the production of melatonin). Dennett's alternative, the "multiple drafts" model, has been put forward in his various books and essays; see Dennett (1994) and (2002a). (For the similar proposals by Kenneth Craik [1943] and William Calvin [1990], see Flanagan [1992], 41.) Nevertheless, other scholars have suggested that the prefrontal cortex may exercise such a clearinghouse role: see Kane and Engle (2002), Coolidge and Wynn (2009), 14. Yet others have suggested that this executive center is to be located in the medial temporal area, in or around the hippocampus: see Flanagan (1992), 17–18. (By now these references are probably out of date; I mention them nevertheless, if only to show that not long ago, the physical-clearinghouse question remained unresolved.)

22. Feinberg (2009), xi. Note as well the sources cited above, note 17, and Daniel Dennett's claim that the human self is, in biological terms, "just an abstraction, a principle of organization." He continues: "Like the biological self, th[e] psychological or narrative self is not a *thing* in the brain, but still a remarkably robust and almost tangible attractor of properties": (1991), 414. See also: Bennett and Hacker (2013), 241–63.

23. See among others the essays collected in van Huyssteen and Wiebe (2011), esp. 33–49, 104–22, 319–37; also Hallam (2009) and Rose (1996) and in particular Dennett (this

chap., notes 19 and 21) and Pinker (1997). I have discussed some of these in Kugel (2011a).

24. W. T. Anderson (1997), 3.
25. Markus and Kitayama (1991), 18–48.
26. General discussions of the phenomenon: Bourguignon (1976) and Lewis (1979); note in particular the sympathetic treatment by Leavitt (1993).
27. Lambek (1981), 40.
28. Messing (1958); see also Torrey (1967) and Boddy (1988) and (1989).
29. Boddy (1988); this was followed by a longer study, Boddy (1989).
30. Grisaru and Witztum (2014), 329.
31. For this reason, I feel some reservation about the excellent study of Ishay Rosen-Zvi (2011), which attributes Israelite possession to, specifically, Persian demonology.
32. See further, chapter 5.
33. These inscriptions were called *katadesma* ("binding spells") in Greek and *defixiones* ("enchantments") in Latin; see Faraone (1991), 13–14.
34. See for example Burkert (1985), 82–84.
35. See on this Bohak (2008).
36. Some sources listed in Kugel (2003), 222–23; see also Sommer (2009), 19–24 and 183–84.
37. This phenomenon has been extensively surveyed in Sommer (2009), esp. 12–57.
38. "Back then" is precisely what the French classicist Paul Veyne referred to as *in illo tempore* or *le temps des anciens,* a period disconnected in time from our own: Veyne (1988). By the same token, how can we properly appreciate the gap between the Joseph story and those other tales in Genesis if we cannot recognize how different Joseph's "sense of self" is from his bedfellows in that book?
39. For Philo's understanding of the spirit as a hypostasis or an "invading angel," see Levison (1997), esp. 27–54 and 238. One might simply attribute this to the influence of Platonic ideas, an influence reflected as well in his account of actual prophetic possession: referring to Gen 15:12, for example, Philo writes: "When the light of God shines, the human light sets; when the divine light sets, the human light rises. This is what regularly befalls the fellowship of the prophets. The mind is evicted at the arrival of the divine Spirit, but when that departs, the mind returns to its tenancy. Mortal and immortal may not share the same home" (*Heres* 264–65). But surely this is not mere lip service: note in particular Philo's description of his own experience of a kind of possession, *Migr.* 34–35.
40. Lienhardt (1961), 149–50. Note also D'Andrade (1995), 158–69.
41. Geertz (1983), 59.
42. "Porous" is a fine term for what Taylor is describing, but in this book and earlier writings I have preferred the term "semipermeable." Veterans of high school biology will recognize "semipermeable" as having been coined to describe cell structure: a semipermeable cell membrane is designed to let certain molecules or ions pass through it, but not anything else. I think this model better represents the sense of self I am describing: it recognizes that some of what the self perceives or decides is altogether autonomous, but not everything; some external things do get through. On this phenomenon in Abraham and Homer, see below.
43. Taylor (2007), 35–38.
44. Snell (1960), 31.
45. "In Homer, the narrator is wholly dependent on the Muses for his knowledge of the events of the story, but the pay-off for this subordination is omniscience (*Il.* 2:485–86).

He does not have to make inferences about the motivations of his characters in the manner of the Apollonian narrator, because he has privileged knowledge [i.e., the Muses' — JK] of the workings of their minds": Morrison (2008), 278–79.

46. Particularly helpful in conceptualizing these differences is the schematic graph developed by Andrew Lock (1981). I owe this reference to C. Newsom (2012a). See also Newsom (2012b).
47. For the origin and development of this exegetical motif see Kugel (1998a), 245–51, 259–64.
48. Note that Josephus has merged two departures — the first from Ur, the second from Harran — into one: "the Chaldeans *and the other peoples of Mesopotamia* rose against him," these "other peoples" being the inhabitants of Harran. In so doing, Josephus not only accounted for the otherwise inexplicable contretemps in Harran, but attributed both departures to a single cause, Abraham's monotheism (and not to any divine command).

4. ADAM AND EVE AND THE UNDIFFERENTIATED OUTSIDE

1. See Kugel (1998a), 98–100, 121–25.
2. A tradition reflected even in Matt 10:16, "See, I am sending you out like sheep into the midst of wolves; so be *wise as serpents* and innocent as doves." See D. Smith (2015), esp. 44–46.
3. See Exod 20:23, some Bibles 20:26; 28:42, Deut 23:15, Isa 6:2.
4. To palliate this shock, the Bible's earliest interpreters created the notion that Adam and Eve were *slightly* clothed, enveloped in "garments of light" or "garments of glory." See Kugel (1998a), 114–20, to which I should have added a reference to Ps 49:13, "A man [Heb. *adam,* understood here as the *first* man, Adam] will not long abide in *glory,*" understood as a reference to Adam's glorious clothing. Note that this verse is reflected as well in the Aramaic translation of Gen 2:24 found in *Targum Pseudo-Jonathan:* "And the two of them became wise, Adam and his wife, *and they did not abide long in their glory*"; that is, they did not continue to walk about in the near-nudity afforded by their flimsy "garments of glory."
5. For this purpose, the anthropologist Clifford Geertz's synthetic definition of religion is instructive. According to Geertz, religion is "(1) a system of symbols (2) which acts to establish powerful, pervasive and long-lasting moods and motivations in men (3) by formulating conceptions of a general order of existence and (4) clothing these conceptions with such an aura of factuality that (5) the moods and motivations seem uniquely realistic": Geertz (1973), 87–125.
6. First attested in Olduvai Gorge, Tanzania, in 1960, *Homo habilis* was distinguished from the various species of genus *Australopithecus* ("southern ape") not only by having larger brains, smaller teeth, and bigger bodies overall, but by hands better suited to toolmaking and other tasks.
7. The validity of distinguishing these two as separate species remains a disputed topic among scholars. Both have been proposed as the species of the remarkable skeleton of "Nariokotome," an approximately eleven-year-old youth who died 1.6 million years ago near the Kenyan town whose name paleoarchaeologists chose to use for the skeleton as well. The discovery was described and analyzed in Walker and Leakey (1993).

8. Based on the presence of burnt animal bones and crude hearths at *H. erectus* sites. The site at Gesher Benot Ya'akov in northern Israel, containing clearer evidence of hominin control of fire, has been dated to 790,000 years ago. Some attribute the site to *Homo heidelbergensis*, but there is no actual proof of this identification.
9. The lower jaw of *Homo heidelbergensis* was first discovered near Heidelberg, Germany, in 1908 and described by Otto Schoetensack ("Der Unterkiefer des Homo heidelbergensis aus den Sanden von Mauer bei Heidelberg") in 1908. See Coolidge and Wynn (2009), 151–79.
10. Ibid., 151.
11. This term was apparently first used by the comparatist Mircea Eliade, not, however, as an actual species in human development, but as a generalized, ideal type.
12. Neandertals have suffered from bad press over the years; nowadays the name conjures up in many readers a towering and violent ancestor whom humanity is better off without. Actually, this descendant of *Homo heidelbergensis* was rather short (five feet, six inches on average) and stocky (80 kilograms, or 176 pounds for a male); judging by cranial capacity, his brain was actually bigger than that of modern humans, though differently shaped (and crucially so). His great technological achievements include Levallois knapping (see below) and hafting (attaching a blade to a wooden handle or shaft, such as that of an ax). Though the point is contested, his anatomical remains may indicate some sustained form of speech. See on all these Coolidge and Wynn (2009), 180–206. The old picture ended with the Neandertals being driven out of Europe by *Homo sapiens*, but recent genetic research suggests that Neandertals interbred with *Homo sapiens* until relatively recent times, perhaps until around fifty thousand years ago; see Sankararaman et al. (2012).
13. Note the ingenious theory of Zevit (2013).
14. The British anthropologist Colin Turnbull studied the Mbuti (or Bambuti) pygmies of the Congo, noting that, unlike their Bantu neighbors, the Mbuti lacked any sacred hierarchy; instead, they "believe in a beneficent deity or supernatural power which they identify with the forest"; it is regarded as the source of *pepo* (life force) and of their whole existence. When evil befalls them, it is because the forest is asleep; in such cases, the noisy *molimo* ritual is employed to wake the forest up. See Turnbull (1961) and (1965).
15. As of this writing, archaeologists in Israel have announced a find in the Galilee region of modern Israel that suggests the very first humans to practice cereal cultivation may go back to around 20,000 BCE, roughly double the previous dating. See Schuster (2015).
16. Pinker (1997), 183.
17. Digestive tissue is particularly expensive in metabolic terms, but a brain consumes even more. (For example, a gram of brain tissue takes twenty times more energy to grow and maintain than a gram of tissue from the kidney, heart, or liver.) So as brain size increased, its demands had to be compensated from elsewhere: the quantity of digestive tissue decreased. See Aiello (1994) and (1995).
18. The recent discovery at the site known as Lomekwi 3, near the western shore of Lake Turkana in Kenya, may revise the chronology somewhat. Although as of this writing scholars are just beginning to investigate it, the site would appear to contain signs of stone knapping going back 3.3 million years ago, some 700,000 years earlier than the previous evidence. The identity of the hypothetical knappers is not known; see Harmand et al. (2015).
19. A recent genomic study of different populations around the world has apparently re-

vealed that all non-Africans today trace their ancestry to a single African population that emerged between fifty thousand and eighty thousand years ago. See: Simons Genome Diversity Project (2016).

20. The evidence comes again from Gesher Benot Ya'akov in northern Israel; see Alperson-Afil and Goren-Inbar, (2006); also Alperson-Afil (2000) and (2008). A 1999 study led by the British primatologist Richard Wrangham suggested that regular cooking began much earlier and is reflected even in the physiology of *H. erectus.* See Wrangham et al. (1999); but other scholars have expressed doubt, arguing that the evidence for cooking fires at such an early date is lacking.
21. Stout and Chaminade (2009). The authors conclude: "Stone tool-making is an ancient and prototypically human skill characterized by multiple levels of intentional organization. In a formal sense, it displays surprising similarities to the multi-level organization of human language. Recent functional brain imaging studies of stone tool-making similarly demonstrate overlap with neural circuits involved in language processing. These observations [are] consistent with the hypothesis that language and tool-making share key requirements for the construction of hierarchically structured action sequences and evolved together in a mutually reinforcing way."
22. Coolidge and Wynn (2009), 112.
23. Eventually, humans developed the highly sophisticated "Levallois technique" of knapping (so named because the first evidence of it was found in a Paris suburb by the same name). This technique requires first shaping the core stone into a rounded, tortoise-shell-like form, more convex at the top but rounded as well at the bottom; this core can then be used to create an especially useful chip, thicker in the middle and sharp around the edges, which might serve as a highly effective knife, scraper, or projectile. Scholars disagree about where and when this technique evolved, as well as whether its appearance in different locations bespeaks a chain of transmission or reinvention. See Adler et al. (2014).
24. Pinker (1997), 201–2.
25. Perhaps the most intriguing evidence of this interest will come from the Neolithic and Chalcolithic site of Çatal Höyük in today's Turkey, currently being excavated. See Faraone and Naiden (2012), 45.
26. In general, caves preserve things better than open-air settlements, so we are back at the common problem of "absence of evidence." Archaeologists are often in the same position as the fellow whose house key fell out of his pocket one night; he decides to concentrate his search for it under the street lamps "because those are the places that have the best lighting."
27. See Leroi-Gourhan (1993), 108; also the paper by Wunn (2001).
28. I have borrowed the phrase from Charles Taylor (2007), though in a different sense.
29. Claude Lévi-Strauss and other anthropologists have demonstrated the complex acts of classification that underlie the "science of the concrete," and even more than this, the way in which classifying moves beyond the utilitarian value of sorting things into groups to classification for its own sake. Summarizing the researches of H. C. Conklin (1954) and (1958) and R. B. Fox (1952), Lévi-Strauss wrote: "Among the Hanunóo of the Philippines, a custom as simple as that of betel chewing demands a knowledge of four varieties of areca nut and eight substitutes for them, and of five varieties of betel and five substitutes. Almost all Hanunóo activities require an intimate familiarity with local plants and a precise knowledge of plant classification. Contrary to the assumption that

subsistence level groups never use but a small segment of the local flora, ninety-three per cent of the total number of native plant types are recognized by the Hanunóo as culturally significant . . . The Hanunóo have more than a hundred and fifty terms for the parts and properties of plants. These provide categories for the identification of plants and for discussing the hundreds of characteristics which differentiate plant types and often indicate significant features of medicinal or nutritional value. Over six hundred named plants have been recorded among the Pinatubo and in addition to having an amazing knowledge of plants and their uses . . . [they] employ nearly one hundred terms in describing the parts or characteristics of plants. *Knowledge as systematically developed as this clearly cannot relate just to practical purposes*": Lévi-Strauss (1966), 2–3.

30. The understanding of causality (and what this last term specifically designates) has been the subject of much recent research. Chimpanzees have been shown to be capable of distinguishing the components of a causal sequence (actor, object, and instrument) but incapable of more complex causal reasoning. "When given information showing the inference to be unsound—physically impossible—4-year-old children abandoned the inference but younger children and chimpanzees did not": Premack and Premack (1994). It has been argued that by the age of seven months or so, infants demonstrate surprise at simple "launching" displays that seem to violate their notion of causality. See Oakes (1994); Kotovsky and Baillargeon (2000); G. E. Newman et al. (2008); Rips (2008). Citing Oakes, Rips observes: "What we do know, however, is that infants take longer than seven months to recognize causal interactions even slightly more complex than simple launching. For example, at seven months they fail to understand situations in which one object causes another to move in a path other than dead ahead, situations that adults report as causal" (p. 602).
31. Scholars have sought to connect this phenomenon to a built-in feature of the brains of various species, the so-called agency detection device (ADD) or hyperactive agent detection device (HADD); on this see next chapter.
32. Studied by N. Chagnon (1992) and J. Lizot (1985).
33. See above, note 14.

5. THE FOG OF DIVINE BEINGS

1. Scholars have long recognized that this epithet was adapted and applied to Israel's God in Ps 68:5.
2. Presumably, Hosea is claiming, because they were an illusion.
3. This seems to be the case as well with Isa 1:3, "An ox knows its owner (*qonehu*), and an ass the trough of its master (*be'alayw*)," where the two Hebrew words are intended to evoke epithets of YHWH. See the discussion in Cooper (1981) and Smith (2002), 50–55.
4. Of course, some deities were not conceived to be heavenly at all. In fact, classical studies of Greek religion have distinguished between heavenly gods and chthonic gods (deities located on or below the earth); for a time, some scholars equated the heavenly gods with originally Greek traditions and the chthonic ones with pre-Greek religion, or saw in them an ancient opposition between Indo-European deities and those of the eastern Mediterranean and beyond. See Burkert (1985), 199. In a broader perspective, however, it is clear that there have always been earthbound gods in a variety of ancient religions. This notwithstanding, it is well known that deities across the globe are often depicted as living somewhere in the skies above, frequently connected with heavenly bodies like

the sun, the moon, and various prominent planets and stars. Scholars have rightly asked how this apparently extremely ancient way of conceiving of deities got started. One possible explanation is connected to "embodied cognition," the notion that human thought is not some abstract, disembodied activity, but is shaped at every turn by the fact that the thinker has a body and therefore perceives reality in paradigms created by the very fact of his embodiment. So we move forward in searching for solutions, "progressing" (a Latinate term for moving forward) toward an answer and so forth, because this is how the human body works: it doesn't usually move backward or sideways toward a desired goal. The extent of our embodiment's role in shaping human thought goes well beyond what can be said in a sentence or two here, but in regard to the role of the "up there" in religious thought, the connection to our embodiment seems clear enough: since the gods are the powerful ones, they are naturally held to be "up," because *up* is the embodied way in which humans perceive all that is *superior* and, hence, in charge of things. See further: Lakoff and Johnson (1999), 16–44 and esp. 30–39; Shapiro (2011), 70–113. Another factor favoring a heavenly location: in Canaan as in many parts of the world, various forms of precipitation also played a vital role in survival; this obviously figured in the location of deities in the skies. Finally, note that the heavens were also thought to be the place of unchanging eternity, as opposed to "down here," where things are born, grow, and die. Hence the biblical Enoch and Elijah, both of whom were said to have entered heaven while still alive, were believed by ancient biblical interpreters to be living up there still. See Kugel (1998a), 173–74, 192–93, 813–14.

5. Burkert (1985), 12. Much later, from early Neolithic times (seventh millennium BCE), comes the evidence of the Sesklo culture in Thessaly and northern Macedonia, and that of the Anatolian town of Çatal höyük in what is now southern Turkey. In the latter site are "wall reliefs of a Great Goddess with uplifted arms and straddled legs—clearly the birth-giving mother of the animals and life itself."
6. An approximate model of a widely shared tradition of worshiping such deities is that of the *kami* of Shintoism, whose worship has survived into modern times; see Reader and Tanabe (1998).
7. These ideas are nicely surveyed in Boyer (2001), 1–31.
8. A more science-based approach leading to a similar conclusion is the recent study by the evolutionary biologist David Sloan Wilson (2003). Wilson combines his own evolutionary approach, based on the previously discredited role of group selection, with the work of anthropologists and other social scientists in order to argue that, like a biological organism, societies developed religious beliefs that select for their own smooth functioning and survival. Note the brief critique by Dennett (2006), 106.
9. Some of their efforts were reviewed briefly in Kugel (2011a); see especially pp. 209–13. An important early work not mentioned there was that of Stewart Guthrie (1993). Guthrie highlighted the brain's tendency to anthropomorphize objects—for example, to see the two headlights of a car as the "eyes" of a humanlike face—or, as his title indicates, to see human faces in the clouds. This same tendency, he argued, is reflected in the anthropomorphic features of gods and spirits: we say that they are very different from ourselves, but in fact, they are very much like us. The doctoral dissertation of Justin Barrett (1997) carried this line of inquiry further; see also Barrett (2000), 29–34. From an early stage, the philosopher and cognitive scientist Daniel Dennett has been a leading figure in the scientific exploration of religion; see among other of his writings Dennett (1987) and (2006). Another approach was put forward in Lawson and McCauley (1990),

which sought to adapt the methods and model of contemporary linguistic theory in order to deduce a kind of generative grammar of religious ritual, or what it called the "universal principles of religious ritual structure"—see pp. 84–169, esp. 121–36—but this approach has met with little approval. Two other highly significant contributions should be mentioned here: Boyer (2001) and Atran (2002). Shortly after these appeared another excellent work of synthesis, Tremlin (2006). (Somewhat more polemical are various popular books by Richard Dawkins, Christopher Hitchins, and others written during this same period.) See also below.

10. It was Justin Barrett who introduced the name hyperactive (or hypersensitive) agent detection device (HADD). See previous note.

11. The term was apparently introduced by Premack and Woodruff (1978). This is what Dennett (above, n. 8) referred to as the "intentional stance," our tendency to attribute intentionality to animals and even inanimate objects that are perceived to move. Our capacity to imagine the thoughts of others may be inborn, but it is only developed after a certain age. This was illustrated by the "Smarties task"; children are shown a box that looks as if it contains candy (in the original experiment, the candy involved was *Smarties*). The box is then opened and instead it turns out to contain pencils. The box is then closed again and the children are asked what other children, who haven't seen the open box, will think it contains. Up to age four or so, the children will say pencils, while after that age they will say candy. See further, Kugel (2011a), 211–12 and sources cited there. The interaction of theory of mind (ToM) with the HADD is nicely explained in Tremlin (2006), 79–81.

12. The term "exaptation" was originally coined by Gould and Vrba (1982). It referred to features in evolutionary development that were originally designed to accomplish one purpose but ended up being *exapted* for another: for example, evolutionary biologists theorize that feathers were originally evolved for the regulation of body heat, only later evolving for display purposes, and finally so as to enable birds to fly. By analogy, the attribution of conscious agency to heavenly or terrestrial bodies may be an exaptation of an altogether helpful feature of human evolution, the so-called hyperactive agent detection device (HADD).

13. "Spandrel" is a term from architecture. It refers to a byproduct of some intended design feature: the classic example is the "dead space" underneath a set of stairs in a house. Such a spandrel can end up being used for some other purpose—a set of shelves or closet space underneath the stairs—but these uses are secondary to the main purpose, creating a set of steps leading to the upper floor. Similarly, it is claimed, a design feature of the brain such as the HADD, which originally evolved to help humans to survive, may have led to a secondary effect, the belief in the existence of unseen agents who control aspects of human existence. See Atran (2002), 43–50; also Tremlin (2006), 75–86.

14. This claim is associated with the work of Eugene D'Aquili and Andrew Newberg (2001). Using brain imaging techniques, the pair sought to demonstrate that "spiritual experience, at its very root, is intimately interwoven with human biology. *That biology, in some way, compels the spiritual urge*" (p. 8). In a sense this was nothing new; the connection of religious feeling with the onset of epileptic seizures has long been observed and was mentioned in William James's seminal work, *The Varieties of Religious Experience.* See Kugel (2011a) and sources cited there, pp. 60–61 and 214. In the 1990s V. S. Ramachandran sought to demonstrate that patients with temporal lobe epilepsy (TLE) are particularly sensitive to religious symbols and ideas. Subsequent experiments with nonepileptic

volunteers have produced similar results by using an oscillating magnetic field to excite temporal lobe neurons. Researchers on religion and TLE have focused in particular on the onset stage of the seizure, known to researchers as the "aura." This stage may last up to several hours, during which the seizure is relatively contained in one part of the brain and in which patients sometimes report intense religious feelings. (The seizure then gradually spreads to other parts of the brain, resulting in loss of consciousness, muscle contractions, and other classic symptoms of epilepsy.) These phenomena were studied in Persinger (1983); note also Churchland (2002), 381–89. Psychologists as well have sought to connect the worship of divine agents to recent experimental results with children; see Keleman (2004); also Bloom (2007).

15. Cf. Tremlin (2006), 143: "People have minds that easily and quite naturally entertain religious concepts."
16. See Dennett (2006), 116–25; also Pascal Boyer's discussion of "counterintuitive mentation" in Boyer (2001), 51–91 and *passim;* Atran (2002), 83–113; Tremlin (2006), 86–106.
17. This is too broad a subject to take on properly here, but I will mention what seem to me to be three specific shortcomings: (1) To focus on the HADD-inspired imagining of specific agents is to define religious consciousness too narrowly. In the terms that I have been using, it is to begin with the hidden causers, which is to say, it begins too late, "after the Garden." Surely it was those millennia of contemplating the *undifferentiated* Outside that were crucial in creating the basic sense of self characteristic of *Homo religiosus,* including his semipermeable mind—long before any human being began to differentiate individual gods and goddesses. (On this and the following point, see below, note 25) (2) Equating religion with the belief in humanoid deities is also far too narrow and, as just suggested, too late as well. (3) The equation HADD + ToM = belief in divine beings is altogether mechanical; it takes no account of the broader environment that was the "enchanted world"—most particularly, the still vivid sense of a living, breathing world all around that persisted long after the age of gods. All these, I think, are related to a more basic shortcoming mentioned earlier, the lack of religious imagination among those conducting the research.
18. Malinowski worked principally in the Trobriand Islands, starting with *Argonauts of the Western Pacific: An Account of Native Enterprise and Adventure in the Archipelagoes of Melanesian New Guinea* (1922) and followed by a long series of books and essays. See in particular the collection Malinowski (1954).
19. See especially his *The Mind of Primitive Man* (1937) and *Race, Language and Culture* (1940).
20. In particular Evans-Pritchard (1937) and (1956); see also my brief discussion, Kugel (2011a), 124–26, 161–65.
21. A student of Evans-Pritchard; see Lienhardt (1961).
22. Among many: Lévi-Strauss (1955, *Tristes Tropiques*); (1964, *The Raw and the Cooked*); (1966, *The Savage Mind*).
23. In particular the essays collected in Geertz (1973), esp. 87–125, 170–89; and in the present context, Geertz (2000), 167–86.
24. Worthy of mention here is the work of Susanne K. Langer, whose interest in religion is well known (she described religion as nothing less than the "most typical and fundamental edifice of the human mind": Langer (1942), 33. This book (often unacknowledged) opened the way to the whole modern approach to religion as symbol-making,

reflecting the universal human tendency to create meaning out of the raw data of the senses through language and other means.

25. The Egyptologist Jan Assmann has well captured the distinction between the first deities to emerge from the great Outside (which he calls "tribal" deities) and the much later stage represented by the polytheism of the ancient Near East and Egypt. "The polytheistic religions of the ancient Near East and Ancient Egypt represent highly developed cultural achievements that are inseparably linked to the political organization of the early state and are not to be found in tribal societies. Tribal religions are characterized by their *scarcely humanized and only weakly articulated and differentiated concepts of the divine,* which is worshiped in the form of ancestral spirits, and which is adored without any ritual worship in the form of a very remote high god . . . The great achievement of polytheism is the articulation of a common semantic universe. The gods are given a semantic dimension by means of mythical narratives and theocosmological speculation. It is this semantic dimension that makes the[ir] names translatable. Tribal religions are ethnocentric. The powers that are worshiped by one tribe are different from the powers worshiped by another tribe. By contrast, the highly differentiated members of polytheistic pantheons lend themselves easily to cross-cultural translation or 'interpretation'": Assmann (1997), 45.
26. Burkert (1985), 10.
27. The plurality of religious ideas and practices even within Iron Age Israel has been studied in, among other works, Z. Zevit's wide-ranging survey of the archaeological and textual evidence: see Zevit (2001); the plural "religions" in his title well reflects not only the broad variety of religious practices, but the plurality of sources on which his study draws.
28. See for example Burkert (1985), 82–84.
29. Foster (1995), 55.
30. Ibid., 57.
31. See on this M. Smith (2002); Sommer (2009), 188–89, n. 79.
32. Mark Smith correctly points out that these two verses are redactional, "dating probably to the second half of the monarchy," while the reference to Ba'al in Jud 6 "appears to be older, as it is integrated into the fabric of the story": Smith (2002), 12–13.
33. Cited in Baines (2000), 33.
34. Cited in Sommer (2009), 16. This and subsequent examples are all drawn from Sommer, 13–37.
35. Ba'al-Shamēm is literally the "Ba'al of heaven," Ba'al-Malagē is apparently the syncretistic association of Ba'al with the tutelary Phoenician god of Tyre, Melqart ("king of the city"), while Ba'al-Ṣaphon is identified with the sacred Mount Saphon (modern Jebel al-Aqra', on the Syrian Turkish border). See further on this Sommer (2009), 24–25 and 188 n. 79, as well as Parpola and Parpola (1988) cited in Sommer (2009), 13–37.
36. Porter (2000), 243–44.
37. See on the same topic Pongratz-Leisten (n.d.), 6.
38. Porter (2000), 247–48.
39. Foster (1995), 713–14.
40. As several scholars have pointed out: Porter (2000), 249–50; Pongratz-Leisten (n.d.), 6; Sommer (2009), 16.
41. Sommer (2009), 15, citing Kinsley, "*Avatāras,*" in M. Eliade et al., *Encyclopedia of Religion,* vol. 2 (New York: Macmillan, 1987) 14–15.

42. Final publication of the excavation was reported in Meshel (2012).
43. This is indeed the God of much of the Hebrew Bible, if not necessarily that of the above-cited inscriptional evidence ("YHWH of Teman" etc.). In the Bible, God is *not* omnipresent, but neither is He openly asserted to be present in two places at once. Instead, as we have already seen, He appears, delivers a message or does something else, and then disappears. He *goes down* from heaven to inspect the tower of Babel (Gen 11:5) or to find out what the inhabitants of Sodom are up to (Gen 18:21). He moves from place to place. Whatever its original meaning, the description of God in Deut 33:2 was certainly included there as a description of a sequence of actions, tracing His path into Canaan: "The LORD went forth from Sinai; He shone upon them from Seir; He appeared from Mount Paran; He entered from Ribbebot-kodesh." This certainly accords with the narrative tradition: He was on Mount Sinai, but after some persuading, agreed to go along with the Israelites to Canaan (Exod 33:12–17), where He ultimately takes residence on another mountain, Zion. On what is called the Zion (or Zion-Sebaoth) theology, see Levenson (1985), 97–137.

6. ETERNITY IN ANCIENT TEMPLES

1. Some have pointed to the Turkish site Göbekli Tepe in southeastern Anatolia, not far from the Syrian border, as giving the earliest evidence in the ancient Near East of a temple-like structure, going back to the tenth–eighth millennia BCE. At the same time, many scholars theorize that the earliest Mesopotamian shrines and temples might have been constructed of wood and reeds, perishable materials that would disappear without leaving a trace and thus might date back to far earlier times.
2. Was the ark basically a container of objects sacred to God, like the two tablets of the Ten Commandments, or was it actually a kind of throne, the very throne that an invisible God would occupy when He spoke to Moses and his successors? On this, earlier scholars disagreed; see Haran (1985), 246–48. But the disagreement was in the biblical sources themselves: Deuteronomy and the texts that its theology influenced basically maintained the "container" position, while priestly texts adopted and adapted the "throne" position. For a clear presentation of the evidence: Sommer (2009), esp. 58–79.
3. "Mystery" is only part of what *mysterium* designates, as Otto was well aware: it was also the hidden teachings or sacred rites that stood at the heart of ancient Greco-Roman religion, the thing that a *mystagogus* could impart to the initiate. As for *tremendum*, it means "to be trembled at." The point is thus that the prospect of truly encountering the divine is one that simultaneously attracts and terrifies.
4. On this psalm: Sommer (2015).
5. In fact, our use of "temple" has a slightly prejudicial side to it: it usually designates the house of worship of people other than the majority. Thus, in English-speaking countries, Christians go to church; Jews, Buddhists, Hindus, and other people have temples, whereas logically, their places of worship might likewise be called churches. In France, where most of the population is — if only nominally — Roman Catholic, non-Catholic Christians, a tiny minority in France, are said to worship in a *temple protestant*.
6. See L. Levine (2000), who briefly considers the idea that the city gates may have served as a kind of forerunner of the synagogue (pp. 25–28), along with various other early datings of the synagogue (pp. 38–44) before getting to more solid evidence from pre-70 CE Judea (pp. 45–80). The role of the synagogue in Second Temple Judaism is connected to

the practice of obligatory communal prayer, on which there remains considerable disagreement. One recent, thoughtful review of the evidence is that of Penner (2012), 3–72.

7. These generalizations require some nuances. To begin with, the very category of priest covers a broad variety of temple personnel, so much so that the scholarly use of "priest" itself has been questioned. For example, one recent study that focuses on sixth-century Babylon distinguishes four main groups of priest-like functionaries: *caterers* (a category that included "brewers, bakers, butchers, milkmen, fishermen, oxherds, oil pressers, orchard keepers, and table setters"); *artisans* (including reed-workers, potters, weavers, washermen, goldsmiths, jewelers, and carpenters); *ritual and prayer specialists* (singers, lamentation priests, acrobats, exorcists, and temple-enterers); and *other officials* who, while not participating directly in cultic worship, were responsible for its smooth running (measurers, scribes, gatekeepers, and barbers). See Waerzeggers (2011). Moreover, the whole matter of cultic purity involved not only the absence of bodily impurities, but was related as well to the person's descent (as in Leviticus, so too in Babylon, the "priesthood" was hereditary) and possession of a prebend (a share of a particular area of the cult). "Qualification depended on the candidate's physical, mental, social, and legal status. Most requirements derived from purity concerns and involved the requirement of being whole, without blemish. Physically, the candidate had to be well-formed, showing no bodily defects, no signs of skin disease or illness. Mentally, he was expected to be devoted to his lord, not prone to criminal behaviour. Socially, the candidate had to descend from a consecrated priest. Purity of descent applied to all sons born within their father's marriage, so the emphasis was on the mother's virginity at marriage, not on her own descent, which was irrelevant. The fourth rule of admission was of a different nature as it did not relate to the candidate's purity but to his legal status. Even before considering ritual qualifications, the experts checked whether the candidate was the owner of the relevant prebend. For instance, if the candidate applied for a position in the bakers' division, he had to be in possession of a baker's prebend. Concretely, this meant that the candidate was the legal successor of a retiring or deceased priest who owned that share before him. It was a custom in Neo-Babylonian temples for the retiring priest to introduce the young man personally to the temple board (*kiništu*) and propose his nomination. In normal circumstances, sons followed in the footsteps of their fathers, but it was not uncommon for an older priest to adopt his successor at a young age and introduce him to the craft": ibid., 66.

8. These statues have not survived, probably because the basic shape was carved out of altogether perishable wood, while precious metals and jewelry were looted; we do, however, have descriptions of the process of the god's manufacture; see below.

9. Of course there were others, at such places as Shiloh, Bethel, Dan, Beersheba, and into relatively late times, Elephantine in Egypt.

10. As biblical scholars know, the picture here is rather more complex. Priestly sources indeed maintain that God has a *kabod*, a visible body, and that this body can be seen in the temple: nevertheless, the fact that it appears enthroned above the wings of the cherubim in what is otherwise an empty space would seem to imply that P's God has something less than an ongoing, *physical* presence (otherwise, why not a real throne on which the embodied God might sit in permanence?). This notwithstanding, as we shall see, this priestly model of the deity and his temple does owe much to the old Mesopotamian one. (Later, in the priestly book of Ezekiel, God's *kabod* departs its home for a throne-chariot that follows Israel into exile.) Deuteronomy, by contrast, locates God permanently in

heaven; the temple is merely the place where God has "caused His name to dwell." The precise significance of this repeated phrase in D is never made explicit; I find it difficult to believe that Deuteronomy's "name theology" was merely the result of a misinterpretation of the Akkadian cognate *šumšu šakān,* which refers to the erection of a "display monument" marking a victory as well as a claim to the land on which the monument was erected. See Kugel (2007a), 727, n. 2. But the significance of God's *šem* ("name") in D is unspecified. It may not quite be a hypostasis of God (see Sommer [2009], 66), but God's *šem* "connects heaven and earth" (ibid., 63), so that its presence in the temple refers to something real that simultaneously happens above—a bit like the later notion, attested in the late Second Temple period and for some time thereafter, that there exist two corresponding sanctuaries, a heavenly and earthly one. See Kugel (1998a), 712–17, 730–31. Apart from P and D, and more significant for the present study, is the older conception of a God whose presence is intermittent and fleeting, the God who appears, delivers a message, and disappears. Sommer points out that this conception is found most explicitly in passages attributed to E, but as we have seen (chapter 1), this conception is found as well in J.

11. Haran (1985), 175–81.
12. Note that while the Aaronid priests were permitted to touch the sacred objects of the tabernacle, their fellow tribesmen, the Levites, were not; indeed, at the time of breaking camp to move to another location, the "sons of Aaron" were ordered to cover all the sacred objects and temple appurtenances with cloths or skins before the Levites (in this case, the Kohathites) could enter and carry off the appurtenances (Num 4:15); apparently, the covers were designed to prevent the Levites from even *seeing* the holy objects.
13. See Israel Knohl on the Priestly Torah (PT): "The cultic system of the PT takes place in a sacred sphere far removed from the masses. Barriers are maintained through taboos prohibiting the people from entering the area of intense and contagious holiness in the Tabernacle. Furthermore, PT assigns the people no role in the erection of the Tent of meeting . . . No outsider's eye may witness the mysterious ceremony in the depth of the holy, and only vague bits of information on the cultic system filter out of Priestly circles": Knohl (1995), 152–53.
14. Pollock (1999).
15. Oppenheim (1977), 183.
16. As is said explicitly in the Bible, e.g., Num 28:2, "My sacrifice, [that is,] My *food as a fiery offering,* My sweet savor—be sure to offer it to Me in its proper time."
17. For the common reference to sacrifices as "gifts" (e.g., Lev 23:38, Num 18:29, Deut 16:17, Ezek 20:26, 31, 39; Hos 8:13), as well as the dual sense of *minḥah,* see Anderson (1987), 31–33.
18. Called by W. Burkert (1985), p. 58, the "shared guilt which creates solidarity" in the sacrificing community. For this shared aspect note again Hos 8:13.
19. See Vernant and Detienne (1989).
20. This approach, associated primarily with René Girard, has lately been justly criticized; see Klawans (2006), 22–27.
21. In Ovid's words, *animam pro anima,* taking "a soul for a soul." See Burkert (1996), 54.
22. See Kugel (1998a), 149–51, 158–59.
23. Sallust, *On the Gods and the World,* chap. 16.
24. The dimensions of the *mishkan* were not, as was once claimed, simply those of the Jerusalem temple divided in half; see Friedman (1980).

25. Cross (1998), 84–95.
26. Cited in Sommer (2009), 14.
27. See Walker and Dick (1999), 55–121.
28. See Sommer (2009), 19.
29. Kugel (2003), 82–85, and sources cited on 222–23.
30. Ibid., 82–85.
31. The temple, dated to between the tenth and eighth centuries BCE, was unearthed at in modern Syria starting in 1956. See J. Monson (2000).
32. Hallo (1981), 25.
33. F. O'Connor (1979), 125.
34. As is well known, Jereboam simultaneously set up two golden calves as divine thrones, one in Bethel and the other in Dan (1 Kings 12:29). Clearly, both were conceived as alternative worship sites to the Jerusalem temple; presumably, the deity could be present at all three (perhaps simultaneously, although this is not explicit). Quite apart from these, however, were other sanctuaries and "high places" that existed at various times, including the temple used by Jewish mercenaries in Elephantine (Egypt) in the fifth century BCE.
35. The question of the antiquity of aniconism was raised by S. Mowinckel (1930); with regard to the explicit prohibition in the Decalogue, see Zimmerli (1930) and Dohmen (1985). Christoph Dohmen, like his predecessors, holds this commandment to be essentially Deuteronomic, although he finds an earlier allusion to such a prohibition in Exod 20:23. T. Mettinger (1995) rejects the antiquity of this verse on source-critical grounds (p. 138). Moreover, a late dating of this prohibition is at odds with the recent work of Othmar Keel and Christoph Uehlinger; see further Kugel (2003), 217–34.
36. The evidence for this assertion is reviewed in Kugel (2003), 217–19.
37. Often cited in this connection is Pausanias, a Greek travel writer/geographer of the second century CE: "At a more remote period all the Greeks alike worshipped uncarved stones instead of images of the gods" (*Description of Greece* 7:22.4). Cf. Walter Burkert: "In many places the most important gods of the Mycenean period, Zeus and Poseidon, did without cult image and temple down into classical times; it is possible that Indo-Europeans used no images of the gods": Burkert (1985), 88.
38. See Gaifman (2008). This is particularly the case with the sacred stones called *baetyli* or *betyls*, as Gaifman shows.
39. Ibid.
40. The term comes from Mettinger (1995). On such empty-space aniconism in Israel, see also the two golden calves established at Bethel and Dan (1 Kings 12:28–30), which many scholars see as the equivalent of the empty space iconography of the outstretched wings of the cherubim in the Jerusalem temple. A Greek example of "empty-throne aniconism" is the double rock-cut seat of Zeus and Hekate at Chalke, on which again see Gaifman (2008).
41. The notion of such a cherub (apparently a kind of gryphon) throne is found in texts of different dates, but the priestly picture in Exodus 25 "does not describe a throne [*pace* Haran (1985), 251, 254]. There is no seat, no armrests, no footstool; the creatures do not stand side-by-side, but face each other . . . There is no way this can be envisioned as a throne": Propp (2006), 390. Similarly, Jacob Milgrom writes: "Indeed, that the cherubim are winged means that the divine seat is in reality a chariot: His dominion is the world, and only when He wishes to manifest Himself to Israel does He condense His presence

upon the Ark-cherubim inside the Holy of Holies . . . He summons Moses to receive His commands (e.g., Exod 25:20, Lev 1:1). Another tradition informs us that even when Moses enters the Tent on his own initiative for oracular purposes, there is no guarantee that the Lord will answer him or even that He is there. Only the descent of the pillar of cloud at the entrance to the Tent indicates that the Lord is present and is ready for an audience (Exod 33:8–9)": Milgrom (1990), 375.

42. Sommer draws a sharp contrast between the views of E and P: "The tabernacle is described in P as the site of an unceasing and ever accessible theophany . . . The differences between E's conception of the tent and P's are readily evident. E's 'tent of meeting' (*ohel mo'ed*); E never calls it the 'tabernacle' or 'tent of the pact') was located outside the Israelites' camp, indeed, at some distance from it . . . God did not dwell in E's tent but popped in on appropriate occasions to reveal Himself to Moses or to other Israelites" (pp. 81–82). I believe this contrast is too sharp. If, indeed, P's God is, as Sommer writes, a "non-fluid" and fully embodied God, it is hard to see how He could be located "permanently" in the tabernacle (p. 76), "dwelling there without interruption for centuries" (90). If His presence there was indeed "an unceasing and ever accessible theophany," why don't we hear of Him being endlessly encountered by humans? What would be the point of such a nonfluid, fully embodied deity just hanging around back there, behind a curtain and perched (somehow!) on the outspread wings of two cherubs? (See previous note.) Instead, P's view seems to identify the holy of holies as God's home base, where He indeed reveals Himself to humans on specific occasions, but He cannot be stuck there without interruption forever. Perhaps it would be more useful to say that P himself does not like to depict God as *doing* things, and sometimes even not as *saying* things; see Knohl (1995), 128–52. But even P does not maintain that his God is endlessly present in the sanctuary. He *appears* there (cf. Ps 94:1); where He is the rest of the time we don't know.

43. In saying this, I realize that in speaking of "the conception of things," I am really referring only to what is presented in biblical texts, and even these, as scholars know well, do not speak with one voice: P's conception of the sanctuary and its functions are at odds with those attributed to E (and J), P differs with H, and all these clash with D and the texts influenced by his/their school. These differences have been explored in some detail by, among others, Weinfeld (1992a), Knohl (1995), and Sommer (2009). I believe the intermittently appearing God is a notion that underlies *all* Pentateuchal sources although, in the case of P, the immanence of God's presence is stressed (not surprisingly for a priestly source).

44. An incident not usually associated with this theme is found in 1 Kgs 12:32–13:1–2. Jeroboam, having established the priests who are to serve at the temple at Bethel, ascends the altar to offer a sacrifice. Suddenly, a "man of God" (a Northern expression meaning a prophet) cries out, "O altar, altar! Thus says the Lord . . ." But if God were present in this sanctuary, what need was there of a prophet to address the altar? Let God Himself shoot fire onto the altar, as in Lev 9:24. "O altar, altar!" means that the golden calf, meant as an empty-space icon, was unoccupied at the time.

45. Apart from the visual appearances of God studied above, note that He appears *visually* in front of the whole people of Israel at Mount Sinai, albeit surrounded by a "thick cloud" (Exod 19:9); He also is said to have appeared to David (2 Chron 3:1), to Solomon at Gibeon (1 Kings 3:5), as well as to prophets like Isaiah (Isa 6:1), Jeremiah (Jer 31:2), Amos (Amos 9:1), and others. "The Lord appeared to Abram," the book of Genesis reports in yet another place, "and he built an altar to the Lord who appeared to him"

(Gen 12:7). "God Almighty appeared to me in Luz in the land of Canaan," Jacob reports, "and He blessed me" (Gen 48:3). The psalmist says, "My soul thirsts for the living God, for the time when I may go and see God's face" (Ps 42:2). When Moses expresses doubts about the Israelites' willingness to follow him, he says, "They will not believe me or do what I say. Instead they will say, 'The LORD did not *appear to you.*'" Later, Moses says, "You, O LORD, are in the midst of this people, and You are seen by them eye to eye . . . In a pillar of cloud You go before them by day, and in a pillar of fire by night" (Num 14:14). These are but a few more visual appearances.

7. IMAGINING PROPHECY

1. Lawlor (2004).
2. This is sometimes part of a related theme, that the prophets were essentially social reformers (in turn related to the "low Christology" theme of Jesus as a social reformer). This understanding of the social side of prophecy has a rich history, going back more than a century; see for example Stiblitz (1898); note the survey of Bruce Malchow (1996).
3. Divine inspiration here (and perhaps in Hebrew Scripture as well) is tied to oral composition: the poet spontaneously re-creates his text with each recital. This was demonstrated in the researches of Milman Parry and set out by his student Albert Lord; see Lord (1990). Note also Nagy (1990a). Particularly helpful in our present context is Nagy's brief survey of various Greek terms related to prophecy: see Nagy (1990b).
4. Indeed, poetic inspiration has never really died, though it has changed. Reformulated as the Holy Spirit, the poetic muse was reborn (or still alive?) in Milton's proem to *Paradise Lost.*

   Of man's first disobedience, and the fruit
   Of that forbidden tree, whose mortal taste
   Brought death into the world, and all our woe,
   With loss of Eden, till one greater man
   Restore us, and regain the blissful seat,
   Sing, heavenly muse, that on the secret top
   Of Oreb, or of Sinai, didst inspire
   That shepherd, who first taught the chosen seed. (1:1–8)

   The muse who inspired "that shepherd," Moses, to recount the fall of man in Gen 2–3 is, for Milton, none other than the Holy Spirit, as he goes on to relate:

   And chiefly thou O spirit, that dost prefer
   Before all temples the upright heart and pure,
   Instruct me, for thou knowest; thou from the first
   Wast present, and with mighty wings outspread
   Dove-like satst brooding on the vast abyss. (1:17–21)

   For Milton, the visitations of his muse were apparently a reality: she would reportedly communicate with him at night, and he would wake up early the next morning, ready to dictate dozens of verses to his amanuensis. At the beginning of Book 9 of *Paradise Lost,* he promises to write something no less heroic than a classical Greek and Latin epic,

   If answerable style I can obtaine

Of my Celestial Patroness, who deignes
Her nightly visitation unimplor'd,
And dictates to me slumb'ring, or inspires
Easie my unpremeditated Verse. (9:20–24)

How striking, then, is the reformulation of the muse's invocation in the prologue of Wordsworth's *The Prelude* two centuries later, her inspiration now reconceived as a "half-conscious" visitant blown into his room from the fields and originating, just perhaps, from something like heaven:

Oh there is blessing in this gentle breeze,
A visitant that while it fans my cheek
Doth seem half-conscious of the joy it brings
From the green fields, and from yon azure sky. (1:1–4)

See further Rhu (1990). Among contemporary poets, the clearest example of an undisguisedly inspired poet might be James Merrill, who recounts at length the role of a kind of divination in his *The Changing Light at Sandover.* See Hammer (2015), 194–206 and *passim.*

5. The idea that biblical prophets were "divine poets" had its own, interesting history even before Robert Lowth popularized this notion in the eighteenth century; see Kugel (1981) and Kugel (1990d), 1–25, esp. 21–23.
6. On the relation of such theoretical statements to those of various poets, see Murray (1981).
7. Plato, *Ion* (534), in Jowett (1931) vol. 1, 501–2; cf. Plato's distinction between *mantis,* "seer," and *prophētēs,* "declarer" in *Timaeus* 71e-72b. Here, Nagy argues, the mantis is "one who speaks from an altered mental state, let us call it *inspiration,* while the *prophētēs* does not": see Nagy (1990b), esp. 61.
8. A possible exception may be found in the reference to a "band of prophets," in 1 Sam 10:10 and in its doublet in 1 Sam 19:20, but it is far from clear why this collective existed or what its function was. The similar term "sons of prophets" is, in the words of one scholar, "restricted to Ephraimite narratives describing prophetic activity in Israel during the reigns of Ahab, Azariah, and Joram (1 Kgs 20:35; 2 Kgs 2:3, 5, 7, 15; 4:1, 38; 5:22; 6:1, 9:1). The title thus seems to have been employed for a relatively brief period of time (ca. 869–842 BCE) and is particularly identified with the activities of Elisha": R. R. Wilson (1980), 140–41. Apart from these, biblical prophets were all apparently loners.
9. Exception made for Ezekiel's admirers in the passage just cited.
10. In ancient Greece, this function was closer to that of the *theōros,* a term that designated someone assigned to go to Delphi and consult the oracle there; he was a bit like a biblical prophet in that the oracle "confer[red] an inner vision upon the *theōros,* the one who consult[ed] him . . . To be a *theōros,* as Theognis declares, you may not change for your audience one iota of what the god had imparted to you, just as whoever consults an oracle must report to the community exactly what the priestess has said": see Nagy (1990b), 62, 64.
11. Note in this connection Philo's description of the biblical prophet, based almost entirely on Plato's description of the poet in *Ion* (cited above): "For a prophet, being a spokesman, has no utterance of his own, but all his utterance came from elsewhere, the echoes of Another's voice . . . For when the light of God shines, the human light sets; when the divine light sets, the human light dawns and rises. This is what regularly befalls the fel-

lowship of the prophets. The mind is evicted at the arrival of the divine Spirit, but when that departs the mind returns to its tenancy. Mortal and immortal may not share the same home": *Quis haeris* 259, 263–65. For later Jewish understandings of the prophetic office: Cooper (1990).

12. Though even this qualification must be further qualified, since ancient Greek and Latin lyrics did sometimes take on contemporary political figures or themes, though hardly in the manner of Israel's prophets; much later, the hexametric Sibylline oracles present a true fusion of biblical and classical models. See Collins (1983).
13. A few prophets also seem to have been ecstatics, falling into trances, unable to control their movements, gyrating, stripping off their clothes, and the like, acts somewhat paralleled by the poetic fury of ancient Greek poets or, later, the Sibyls. See on these Lindblom (1962), 47–65.
14. Scholars have remarked on the prevalence of miracle stories with regard to northern prophets, Elijah and Elisha in particular; they can heal the sick (2 Kings 5:1–14), revive the dead (1 Kings 17:17–24; 2 Kings 4:17–37), or merely cause an ax head that had fallen into a river to float to the surface (2 Kings 6:6). On the overall differences between prophets in the North and in the South, see Wilson (1980), 135–296. Note also that some northern texts represent prophets as ecstatics, though this hardly distinguishes them from certain Greek poets and the Sibyls.
15. Nor, it should be stressed, did all prophets answer to the same job description: prophecy in the north was different from prophecy in the south, and the institution itself clearly evolved over time. Among other studies: R. R. Wilson (1980).
16. The eighth- or early-seventh-century Deir 'Alla inscription, discovered in 1967, speaks of a "seer of the gods" named Balaam son of Be'or, suggesting that the real or fictional figure in the biblical account was known outside the biblical orbit. See Vuilleumier (1966); Hackett (1984), Hoftijzer and Van der Kooij (1991), Dijkstra (1995).
17. On the prophetic "oracle against the nations" genre: Christensen (1975), 58–72; Clements (1975); Kugel (2007a), 626–28.
18. Of course, this is the editorial frame of the Balaam periscope. For the historical background, see Kugel (2007a), 338–40.
19. This is the translation suggested by Jonathan Stökl in his nuanced discussion of the term in Stökl (2012), 38–43; the book as a whole examines in detail the terminology applied to prophet-like figures in Old Babylonian and Neo-Assyrian inscriptions as well as in biblical texts.
20. On these see Durand (1988), 386–96; Huffmon (2000), 47–70.
21. I refer here to the *book* of Jeremiah because, in fact, we have no way of knowing what, if anything in that book (which itself exists in different recensions), might actually have been spoken by the prophet himself, if such a prophet existed. What we have at best is someone else's accounts of this prophet's words; as one scholar has noted, "a written prophecy is always a scribal work, and it is ultimately beyond our knowledge to determine to what extent the scribe would, or could, transmit the exact wording of the prophecy": Nissinen (2004), p. 29. Scholars have long hypothesized that, following the putative appearance of an early collection of Jeremianic sayings, a subsequent Deuteronomic revision of various parts of the book was made; some even now speak of a secondary revision thereof, that is, a "Deutero-Deuteronomic" editor putting his own spin on the book. See most recently Stipp (2016), Kratz (2016), along with the other contributions in Najman and Schmid (2016). My references elsewhere to Jeremiah the man should

be understood in this light: they really refer to the Jeremiah presented in this biblical book. The paradox of this prophet was thus summed up nicely by the Assyriologist and biblicist Herbert Huffmon: "Jeremiah is the most accessible of the prophets; Jeremiah is the most hidden of the prophets": Huffmon (1999), p. 261. Having stated this qualification, however, I should add that in the present context the matter of authorship (that is, our ability or inability to attribute this or that statement to the historical Jeremiah) is somewhat less crucial than it might be elsewhere. The important thing here is to examine carefully what the text says in order to understand what it can tell us about the very nature of prophecy as it was conceived at the end of the First Temple period (the early sixth century BCE), or not long thereafter. What did it mean then for a prophet to deliver a message that, he said, God had put in his mouth?

22. I am guilty of free translations throughout this chapter, but "obey" here is not one of them; scholars have long recognized that *da'at* is sometimes used in the sense of "be loyal to": see Huffmon, (1966).
23. On these and other findings see I. E. Sommer et al. (2010).
24. Bentall and Slade (1985).
25. Sommer et al. (2010).
26. Beavan, Read, and Cartwright (2011).
27. See further: Corstens et al. (2014); also Thomas et al. (2014).
28. Luhrmann et al. (2014).
29. It is striking that the authors of this study went on specifically to single out the very different sense of self prevailing in the three locales as responsible for the different ways in which voice hearing was treated: "Outside Western culture people are more likely to imagine [a person's] mind and self as interwoven with others. These are, of course, social expectations, or cultural 'invitations'—ways in which other people expect people like themselves to behave. Actual people do not always follow social norms. Nonetheless, the more 'independent' emphasis of what we typically call the 'West' and the more interdependent emphasis of other societies has been demonstrated ethnographically and experimentally many times in many places—among them India and Africa . . ." The passage continues: "For instance, the anthropologist McKim Marriott wanted to be so clear about how much Hindus conceive themselves to be made through relationships, compared with Westerners, that he called the Hindu person a 'dividual.' His observations have been supported by other anthropologists of South Asia and certainly in south India, and his term 'dividual' was picked up to describe other forms of non-Western personhood. The psychologist Glenn Adams has shown experimentally that Ghanaians understand themselves as intrinsically connected through relationships. The African philosopher John Mbiti remarks: 'only in terms of other people does the [African] individual become conscious of his own being.'" Further, see Markus and Mullally (1997); Nisbett (2004); Marriot (1976); Miller (2007); Trawick (1992); Strathern (1988); Ma and Schoeneman (1997); Mbiti (1969).
30. Note that a related study of visual and auditory hallucinations supports the same general conclusion, that while such hallucinations are apparently a widespread phenomenon evidenced in at least some segment of different populations, the hallucinations themselves are conditioned and shaped by the society in which they occur. In some environments, people are more likely to believe that they will be addressed by disembodied voices, and they react to the intruding voice less negatively than in other societies. In the words of this study: "Thus, we can speak of the 'cultural conditioning' of hallucination ex-

perience ... What visionaries see and hear, when they do so, and how the experience impacts their bodies, especially when onlookers are present, all evolve over time, an indication that the visions are quite vulnerable to expectations and suggestion": Laroi et al. (2014) .

31. See in particular the work of H. Huffmon and the collection of articles in his honor in Kaltner and Stulman (2004).
32. Wilson (1980), 51–52.
33. Overholt (1989), 22.
34. Ibid., 23. Overholt went on to suggest an ongoing dynamic between deity, prophet, and audience: (1) revelation from the deity leads to (2) a proclamation by the prophet, which is met by (3) the reaction of his audience, which may or may not confirm the would-be prophet's standing; on the basis of this confirmation, the prophet may (and often does) communicate his/her (4) feedback to the source of revelation, that is, the deity; there may then come (5) additional revelations (since prophets are often active over a period of time), which lead to (6) additional proclamations, and (7) supernatural confirmations — miracles or confirming signs. Finally, a prophet may sometimes have or acquire (8) disciples as a result of his or her prophetic activity. See Overholt (1989), 24–25.
35. As scholars have long noted, Jeremiah's speech at the Jerusalem temple is, according to this third-person account of it (Jer 26:4–6), much shorter than the version of this speech in Jer 7:3–15. Is the shorter version a summation of a well known event, or is the longer version a later elaboration?
36. Although his listeners' response, "Why have you prophesied in the name of the LORD ..." would seem once again to indicate that a prophet's rephrasing of the divine message, prophesying "in the name of the LORD," was what a prophet actually did.
37. See: Caroll (1981), 107–30, and Caroll (1986), 71–96; Polk (1984); Diamond (1987); K. M. O'Connor (1988).
38. Scholars see this image as connected to the one cited earlier, in the book's opening account of Jeremiah's being chosen as a prophet: "Then the LORD put out His hand and touched me on the mouth, and the LORD said to me, 'Now I have put My word in your mouth'" (Jer 1:9).
39. On the textual problems associated with this passage: Bezzel (2009), 48–73.
40. This is a notoriously difficult verse. The traditional text has Jeremiah being "a shepherd after You," but this makes little sense; among other things, when used metaphorically, "shepherd" is traditionally said of kings — there is no other place in the Bible in which a prophet is so described. See on this Stulman (2005), 173. The same consonants of "from shepherd" can be equally well construed as "from evil," which seems a more likely choice. True, this still leaves the word *aḥarekha*, "after You," unaccounted for, but that word certainly does not fit any better with "shepherd."
41. Two common renderings differ sharply from mine: "Most devious is the heart; It is perverse — who can fathom it?" (NJPS); "The heart is devious above all else; it is perverse — who can understand it?" (NRSV). But *'akob* isn't necessarily devious, just convoluted, full of twists and turns — and that's Jeremiah's point: the human mind is truly unfathomable — at least to other people, but not to God. It is, by the way, the *mind* that Jeremiah is talking about; the translation "heart" is literal but misleading, since both the "heart" and "innards" — sometimes along with kidneys and intestines — in Hebrew are the functional equivalent of *mind* in English. The mind is also said here to be *anush:* again, "perverse" also seems to miss the point. Here the Hebrew term means something

like "very deep" (said elsewhere of a deep pain or wound). Finally, the parenthetical question "Who can know it?" is here, as so often, a negation, i.e., "No one can know it"; see Kugel (1981), 7. If I have preserved the interrogative form, it is only because the next words propose the answer: "I, the LORD."

42. As many scholars have suggested, this stylized dialogue may have started with Amos 8 (see below) and was created here as a way of establishing Jeremiah's credentials as a true prophet. But from the perspective of our subject, it matters little; this was one thing that came to be expected of a prophet. (See previous note.)
43. Lindblom (1962), 122–41.
44. Probably pronounced *qeṣ* in northern Israel, hence indistinguishable from the word for "end."
45. In this respect it is different from the late-biblical "Heavenly voyage," on which see Himmelfarb (1993) and below, chapter 15; these texts represent biblical figures like Abraham, Levi, Moses, and others physically entering heaven.
46. This account may have been the source of a similar passage, 1 Kings 22:19–23, though no clear conclusion can be drawn. The phrase "Who will go for *us*" seems to indicate that the setting is the divine council on high; see Mullen (1980), De Moore (1990), Handy (1994), Smith (2002), 41–53. On these narratives of prophetic visions see P. D. Miller (2000), 184–86.
47. I have left aside the question of the potential relatedness of prophets and various sorts of mental disorders, but certainly one aspect deserves mention: what Western societies generally label as psychotic or schizophrenic behavior is, while recognized as such outside the West, not necessarily dismissed as disqualifying someone from functioning as a shaman or other intermediary. On the contrary, the display of symptoms of such disorders may be construed as confirmation of the person's fitness to function in such a special role. Some societies, it seems, reserve the social niche of divine intermediary for such people, and this social encouragement and integration can in turn have a positive clinical effect on the divine intermediary. The phenomenon is documented in some detail in a book by an Israeli psychiatrist stationed in Ghana starting in 1991, where he drove from village to village to treat patients diagnosed as suffering from various psychiatric ailments, including schizophrenia. What he found was that even extreme forms of hallucinations and other ailments were not, as in the West, treated altogether negatively; in fact, they were felt to fulfill a positive role on behalf of society as a whole: "In African cultures, one can speak as well of the concept of schizophrenia as exercising a certain *function*. These cultures do not only grant legitimacy to the disease, but they also grant it a unique role, one that is quite exceptional . . . The spectrum of reported psychotic symptoms is rich and seductive. Patients see a breath-taking array of visions: a flock of antelopes goes up in flames; cobras shoot forth a river of poison; ancient warriors appear from the tribe's mythology; a shower of semen comes down like rain. Or else there is the hearing of mysterious voices: the moans of boulders as they come apart in water; seductive words whispered by invisible women; curses that spread out into the universe on the rays of the rising sun — all these are just examples gathered from the traveling clinic. This incomprehensible richness has led many Africans to believe that these symptoms actually contain fateful messages, and that mental illness itself *serves as a messenger between spiritual entities and ordinary human beings*. Hence the villagers' appreciation of their chief, who obeys these mysterious voices, ejaculates and fructifies with his seed parcels of land that lie waste, so that the cassava and corn will sprout up

again . . . From the villagers' standpoint, these strange symptoms, even if they are not normative, carry within them a mysterious coded message, perhaps comprehensible only to the gods. This notion does not, of course, nullify the pathology of schizophrenia, but it does provide it with a significance in the cultural context, and what is still more essential, it grants a unique and respected function to those stricken with the disease": Shwarzman (2007), 122.

48. Lindblom (1962), 173–74.

8. THE BOOK OF PSALMS AND SPEAKING TO GOD

1. A measure of the Psalms' early popularity is evidenced in our oldest collection of biblical and related manuscripts, the Dead Sea Scrolls, where more manuscripts have been found containing parts of the Psalms than of any other biblical book; see Flint (1997), 22. On the editing of the book of Psalms, Westermann (1981), 250–58; G. H. Wilson (1985); and more recently the essays collected in McCann (1993), esp. 100–103.
2. See Kugel (1986a).
3. Rendsburg (1990) and (2003); also Holladay (1993) H, 26–36.
4. Sarna (1979), 350–51.
5. A. Pietersma has highlighted the fact that the "David" headings in the Greek Psalter are more numerous (and often explicitly "of David" [τοῦ Δαυιδ]); see Pietersma (1980). Note also van der Kooij (2001). As is well known, some headings (for example, those of Psalm 18 or Psalm 51) actually mention the occasion on which "David" might have been moved to compose the psalm. Such headings, long believed to clinch the case for the Davidic origin of the psalms, have been demonstrated to be a late attempt to match up a verse or phrase in the psalm in question with a specific scriptural narrative in David's (or Moses's or Solomon's) life—actually, a rather early case of midrashic-style narrative expansions. See Childs (1971).
6. Briefly: Kugel (2007a), 463–65 and sources cited there.
7. See further Mowinckel (1962), 5–8.
8. Sarna (1979), 281–300.
9. On the prophetic character of the Asaphite psalms, H. Nasuti (1988); also Hilber (2005), 128–66.
10. On Psalm 29, see chapter 9.
11. See Kugel (1986a).
12. Hurvitz (1988), 42–44.
13. P. D. Miller (1983), 34.
14. On this psalm's changing meaning, Holladay (1993), 6–14.
15. Among many others: G. H. Wilson (1985); Christensen (1996); Beckwith (1999). The Qumran manuscript 11QPs[a] has played an important role in current theories; see Sanders (1967) and (2003).
16. Of course, one might look for such interaction in other parts of the Bible as well, but accounts of past events, or speeches uttered by Israel's prophets, are often designed to drive home some ideological point, telling us about God's miraculous doings or otherwise presenting some doctrine or general principle or a specific bit of teaching. But a person in trouble—even if the trouble is sometimes, as we have glimpsed, framed in general terms designed for reuse—ultimately wants one thing, God's intervention on his or her behalf. The words of these psalms may exaggerate the speaker's own needs

or flatter the deity to whom they are addressed; still, examined carefully, they have a straightforward and single-minded purpose — getting divine help right now — of a sort not usually found in other sorts of compositions.

17. Further: Kugel (2007a), 243–49, 528.
18. There too, when He was there, He was literally on the other side of the curtain (Exod 26:31–33 etc.).
19. For a fuller discussion of this phenomenon, see Kugel (2003), 109–36.
20. Ibid., 120–25.
21. Ibid.
22. See Knohl (1995), 148–49. Speaking of P's conception of God, Knohl writes: "Such a conception leaves no room for petitional prayer, in which humans request fulfillment of their needs from God; nor does it allow a role for songs of praise in which humans thank God and recount God's wonders and mercies. The structural model of prayer, a direct address by humans to their God, as well as the frequency of anthropomorphic images in the language of prayer and song, is at odds with [P's] aim in emphasizing God's loftiness."
23. For a précis of prayer in Hinduism, see Dhavamony (1982), 204–42. Prayer in Buddhism is notoriously different from the Western tradition, but see Kapstein (2007) on the Prayer of Great Power, "recited daily by tens of thousands of Tibetans"; Lopez (2007) (on the *triskhandaka,* the three-part liturgy, of Mahayana Buddhism and its later transmission), 133–38; and Gyatso (2010), 231–33. Other studies: Headley (1966); in general: Dupré (1975), esp. 250–51. Though not a systematic survey of different societies, many cross-cultural examples are found in Zaleski and Zaleski (2005).
24. The supplicant is *always* humble, even if he himself happens to be a king; after all, there is no point in asking for divine help if one does not need it. Since the nineteenth century some scholars have suggested that petitionary psalms were intended for those who could not afford to bring sacrificial animals to the temple: see Rahlfs (1891). But this is quite wrongheaded. The whole idea that "prayer was the poor man's version of temple-worship; since he could not afford the only proper tender of homage to God — animal sacrifice — he offered a prayer in its stead" is still cited, but not for praise, by Greenberg (1983a), 42.
25. This is generally true of deities in the ancient Near East — in Egypt, Mesopotamia, Ugarit, and elsewhere. On the interrelatedness of divine and earthly kings, see Eaton (1986).
26. The kingship of the gods is certainly an ancient theme; Thorkild Jacobsen located its Mesopotamian emergence in the third millennium BCE, replacing the fourth-millennium "gods as providers" metaphor: Jacobsen (1976). (Note, however, A. Leo Oppenheim's sharp critique: Oppenheim [1977], 171–83.) For human and divine kingship in ancient Egypt, still valuable is Frankfort (1948). To be sure, kingship has long been held to be somewhat attenuated in ancient Israel, but this applies principally to the "law of the king" in Deut 17:14–20 and its offshoots; see Nicholson (1967), 49–50. On divine kingship in Israel: Brettler (1989); M. S. Smith (2002), esp. 22–26, 55–60; Kratz (2015).
27. Greenberg (1983a), 17.
28. Robert North rightly explained references to a person's "heart" alone (*leb* in biblical Hebrew) not as a precise reference to that particular organ, but as "a vaguely known or confused jumble of organs, somewhere in the area of the heart or stomach": see North (1993), 596.
29. Many modern adherents of Judaism and Christianity may find this notion difficult to

swallow, since divine omnipresence is a fundamental belief in both religions. But biblical scholars have long been aware of the evidence confuting divine omnipresence (as also divine omniscience): God walks about in the Garden of Eden (Gen 3:8)—walking is not something you do if you are omnipresent; He likewise "goes down" from heaven to inspect the tower of Babel (Gen 11:5) and the people of Sodom (18:21). In many biblical texts God is said to "dwell" in heaven, "sitting" on a heavenly throne, which He sometimes leaves to fly away on a "swift cloud" (Isa. 19:1) or on the winds (Ps 104:3). As for divine omniscience, He certainly can find things out—among other ways, by entering our semipermeable minds—but this is different from knowing everything all the time. Sometimes, in fact, He consults human beings directly: He asks Adam where he is (Gen 3:9), Cain where his brother Abel is (Gen 4:9), and Balaam who the people with him are (Num 22:9). See further: Carasik (2000).

30. A more precise instance: the above-cited (late, Deuteronomistic) description of Solomon's temple and its transmission of requests to God on high might be compared to the much earlier temple (or temples) of the Mesopotamian goddess Ishtar, who resides simultaneously down here and up there. See above, chapter 5.
31. Or is even this simply a product of the Jamesian (he coined the phrase) stream of consciousness? Cf. Flanagan (1992), 178: "There is an important sense in which consciousness is a unity. Furthermore, this unity is in need of an explanation. But the explanation that turns on the 'I' fosters an illusion. The illusion is that there are two things: on one side, a self, an ego, an 'I' that organizes experience, originates action, and accounts for our unchanging identity as persons and, on the other side, the stream of experience . . . The better view is that what there is, and all there is, is the stream of experience . . . 'Ridiculous! What accounts for my ongoing sense that I am the same person over time?' I hear you say. What accounts for your ongoing sense of self [is] the fact that you are constituted by a unique and distinctive stream, that thought can create complex models of the course of the stream in which it occurs, and that you are an insensitive detector of the great changes that accrue to you over time and thus miss how much you do in fact change over time. We are egoless [he means: we lack a self] . . . Egolessness is such a chilling thought, but we shall see that it needn't be."
32. Churchland (2002), 61.
33. The oft-cited case of Phineas Gage, a railroad worker whose personality radically changed after an injury to his prefrontal cortex in 1848, was an early piece of evidence in the association of specific areas of the brain with different functions; see Macmillan (2000). Particularly significant was the connection of specific brain injuries with various speech difficulties; see Pinker (2000), 318–24.
34. The latter position is well stated by Colin McGinn: "We know that brains are the *de facto* causal basis of consciousness, but we have, it seems, no understanding whatever of how this can be. It strikes us as miraculous, eerie, even faintly comic. Somehow, we feel the water of the physical brain is turned into the wine of consciousness, but we draw a total blank on the nature of this conversion": McGinn (2002b), 529.
35. Gerald Edelman has attempted to reconstruct a process of natural selection that would result in the emergence of a primitive sense of self out of a fundamental distinction between self and "nonself," that is, everything outside of the single creature; see Edelman (1987). Note in this connection Flanagan (1992), 50–51: "Consciousness emerged with the development of segregated neural equipment subserving, on the one hand, internal hedonic regulation and, on the other hand, information processing about the

state of the external world . . . There is evidence that the dorsal parietal region of the cortex is essential to concern for the wellbeing of the self. Lesions in these areas result in a loss of self-concern. Conversely, lesions in ventral (temporal) regions of the cortex diminish attention to and awareness of the external world. The frontal lobes meanwhile, are thought to be especially important in the maintenance of the hedonic self/nonself memory system . . . [Edelman's theory] about the emergence of consciousness about self and nonself is [thus] credible. Perhaps it is true. Some sort of sensitivity to the boundaries of the self is a necessary condition for survival." Cf. Dennett (1989): "The origin of complex life forms on this planet was also the birth of the most primitive sort of self, whatever sort of self is implied by the self-regard that prevents the lobster, when hungry, from eating itself."

36. One exponent of this view is P. S. Churchland: "In assuming that neuroscience can reveal the physical mechanisms subserving psychological functions, I am assuming that it is indeed the brain that performs those functions — that capacities of the human mind are in fact capacities of the human brain": Churchland (2002b), 127. At greater length Churchland (1986) and (2002a), esp. 43–50. Contrast Flanagan (1992), 2, and Dennett (2002a) as well as Dennett (1991) and Dennett and Kinsbourne (2002). "Let me pose an analogy: you go to the racetrack and watch three horses, Able, Baker, and Charlie, gallop around the track. At pole 97, Able leads by a neck, at pole 98, Baker, at pole 99, Charlie, but then Able takes the lead again, and then Baker and Charlie run neck and neck for a while, and then, eventually, all the horses slow down to a walk and are led to the stable. You recount all this to a friend, who asks 'Who won the race?' and you say, well, because there was no finish line, there's no telling. It wasn't a real race, you see, with a real finish line": Dennett (1994), 56–57.

37. This name (actually, "new mysterians" at first) was put forward somewhat whimsically in 1991 by Flanagan in imitation of the name of the rock group Question Mark and the Mysterians, though the name itself also suggests Noam Chomsky's distinction between *problems,* which appear to be solvable even if unsolved at present, and *mysteries,* which appear to be unsolvable; consciousness would, for Chomsky, belong in the latter category. (This in turn sounds like the medieval distinction between *mirabilia,* things that inspired wonder because they were not yet understood, and *miracula,* things that were beyond nature and hence must have been performed only by God; see Bynum [2005], 91, and sources cited on pp. 231–32.) On Thomas Nagel as a mysterian, see below. Steven Pinker has likewise endorsed a mysterian position, while also arguing that consciousness is too broad a term, only part of which appears unsolvable: self-knowledge, access to information, and sentience are all part of what people mean by consciousness, but the first two have nothing mysterious about them and even "have obvious analogues in machines." It is sentience that is unsolvable; Pinker (1997), 131–48.

38. See previous note. Indeed, numerous scholars have expressed reservations about the utility of the term "consciousness." On "Quining consciousness," Flanagan (1992), 21–34.

39. Another aspect of our inability to step outside of ourselves is the extent to which the very terms by which we perceive and seek to understand things are tied to our own embodiment, the physical conditions (and limitations) of our bodies that shape our apprehension of the world. These have been explored by (among others) Lakoff and Johnson (1999). A synthetic examination of the arguments: Shapiro (2011).

40. Nagel (2002). See also Nagel (2012).

41. Though, as Nagel observes, "if one travels too far down the phylogenetic tree, people gradually lose their faith that there is experience there at all": Nagel (2002), 319.
42. Nagel writes: "I am not adverting here to the alleged privacy of experience to its possessor. The point of view in question is not one accessible only to a single individual. Rather, it is a *type.* It is often possible to take up a point of view other than one's own, so the comprehension of such facts is not limited to one's own case . . . [However,] the more different from oneself the other experiencer is, the less success one can expect with this enterprise . . . This bears directly on the mind-body problem. For if the facts of experience—facts about what it is like *for* the experiencing organism—are accessible only from one point of view, then it is a mystery how the true character of experiences could be revealed in the physical operation of that organism. The latter is a domain of objective facts *par excellence*—the kind that can be observed and understood from many points of view and by individuals with differing perceptual systems . . . [But] what would be left of what it is like to be a bat if one removed the viewpoint of the bat?" —Nagel (2002), 522.
43. A measured introduction to the use and misuse of positron emission tomography (PET) in imaging various brain states: Dumit (2004). Unfortunately for our subject, the book deals with imaging brains as they experience ecstasy the drug but not ecstasy the religious state of mind.
44. To carry the color perception analogy further, one might note that "color perception originates in different levels of activity in the three kinds of [color-sensitive] cones" in our eyes, but those cones do not simply transmit their information on an on-or-off basis; rather, "color perception originates in different levels of activity in the three kinds of cones. Each experience of a particular color or shade is subserved by a unique ratio of activity in the three cone types and by the complex pattern of neural activity it gives rise to . . . The essential feature of the receptor cells is that they can vary across a fine-grained continuum in their degree of activation. It is the ratio across receptor cells . . . that determines what is experienced": Flanagan (1992), 52.

9. TO MONOTHEISM . . . AND BEYOND

1. In an influential article, Sigmund Mowinckel argued that the prohibition of graven images in the Decalogue was a later insertion, and that the text read far more smoothly without it; Mowinckel (1937), 218–35.
2. There is a vast scholarly literature on aniconic and semianiconic worship. Particularly significant has been the work of Triggve Mettinger; see Mettinger (1994) and (1995). For some further bibliography, Kugel (2003), 217–34.
3. Despite his later reputation as the "first monotheist" in Judaism and Islam; see Levenson (2012).
4. As is well known, Kaufmann (1960) (originally four volumes in Hebrew, abridged to one volume by M. Greenberg) attributed a fundamentally monotheistic view to Israelite religion virtually *ab initio.* A survey of recent works reacting to his scholarship would certainly include many more than the following studies, which are, however, of interest to what follows herein: B. Halpern (2009), incorporating his "Brisker Pipes Than Poetry," first published in Neusner et al. (1978), 77–115; clearly, I cannot accept his conclusion that what separated "monotheism of earliest Israel" from its later manifestation

was its "unselfconsciousness" (p. 55). Note also B. Sommer (2009), which, with many new insights and access to new data, seems to uphold something akin to Kaufmann's early monotheism. Understandably, earlier works of "continental" scholarship, such as Eichrodt (1961), 1:220–27, and Ringgren (1961), do not mention Kaufmann, no doubt because his work was then available only in modern Hebrew; cf. Albertz (1994) and the various essays in Kratz and Spiekermann (2010) and various other studies cited below.

5. Many scholars have argued that YHWH was originally a warrior deity (Exod 15:1–3); see von Rad (1958); Cross (1966) and (1998), 91–111, 158–63; Longman (1995), 31–47, 86–87; Miller (2000), 8–9; Kang (1989). Moreover, Ba'al himself had strong associations with warfare, as Cross and others have stressed; see the brief review in M. Smith (2002), 49–55.
6. Mazar (1985); Finkelstein (1988), 237–59; Dever (2003), 76–78, 102–3.
7. Various scholars have sharpened this point; see Albright (1968), and his students Cross (1973), Freedman (1987), and P. D. Miller (2000), esp. 24–28; also McCarter (1987), Olyan (1988), Dearman (1993), and numerous others. For a summary of the arguments, see Kugel (2007a), 420–32.
8. This may seem belied by the fact (seen above) that it was Hosea who favored monolatry and the king, Ahab, who didn't; but his religious junta of YHWH and Ba'al was clearly what the existing religious establishment ("prophets of Ba'al") wanted, and most likely most of his subjects as well.
9. See the pioneering collection in Porter (2000), parts of which are cited below.
10. Cf. Sommer (2009), 145.
11. The subject has been studied extensively in Hornung (1982); see esp. 49–60.; also Baines (2000), 9–78.
12. For Assyrian evidence see the essays by S. Parpola and B. N. Porter in Porter (2000).
13. See Burkert (1996), 17; Vernel (2000); for this theme in later times: Grant (1986).
14. Cf. Burkert (1996), 80–97.
15. This last is suggested by Burkert (1985), 125–27, but apparently based on his connection of this same root with *dies* etc., "day." In general, etymology is, I admit, a notoriously treacherous basis for drawing conclusions; still, these "generic" god names do give one pause.
16. This psalm has been studied by many scholars since Morgenstern (1939). For further bibliography and discussion, see Kugel (2003), 121–24, and (2007a), 545–46.
17. See on this Olyan (2012).
18. On the four archangels in *1 Enoch* 9–10 and in the Qumran War Scroll (Michael, Sariel, Raphael, and Gabriel), and then seven, see Nickelsburg (2001), 207 and sources cited there. He notes that these four were later augmented to seven through the addition of Uriel, Reuel, and Remiel in *1 Enoch* 20–36, 81. See also: Olyan (1993).
19. Sommer (2009), 145–74. One later version of this approach is embodied in the first-century Jewish composition (written in Greek) called the *Wisdom of Solomon*, though included in some Bibles as, simply, [the *Book of*] *Wisdom*. In it, God is basically a heavenly deity, whereas Wisdom (Greek *Sophia*), a "benevolent spirit" (1:6), is everywhere on earth, where she plays a somewhat ambiguous role. At times she can be just ordinary wisdom in our sense, entering the soul of Moses (10:16) or other humans and guiding their actions. But elsewhere she is much more than this: "She reaches mightily from one end of the earth to the other, and she orders all things well" (8:1; cf. Prov 8:22). Since

God remains in highest heaven, it is left to Wisdom to intervene in earthly affairs. Like many a female in such a marriage, she is charged with cleaning up all the little human messes, steering Noah in his ark during the flood, rescuing Lot from the fires of Sodom, guiding Jacob on his way to visit his uncle Laban, and many more (see Wisd chap. 10). In depicting these things, the anonymous author incorporates numerous earlier midrashic motifs: Enns (1997). In this sense, *Wisdom of Solomon* may serve as a model for the wider point to be made below: divine omnipotence, omniscience, and omnipresence may be Greek formulations, but they are simply part of a long process of development within Judaism itself. At the same time, the path from the grammatically female *sophia* (or the grammatically female *ḥokhmah* in Hebrew) as described in Prov 8:22 led the way to her transformation into grammatically male *logos,* identified as Christ in Jn 1:1–14 and its recasting of Gen 1. Further: G. Anderson (1990).

20. Shaked (1994) has argued that this oft-stated view is in need of modification. On dualism at Qumran, see two recent collection of essays: Xeravits (2010) and Lange et al. (2011). On this combat in a rabbinic context: Rosen-Zvi (2011).
21. See van der Toorn et al. (1998).
22. On *Jubilees*' "Ten Percent Solution," see Kugel (2012a), 82–84.
23. See for all of these, Kugel (1998a), 76–77; Kaduri (2015).
24. For Moses's veil, see Kugel (1998a), 737–38. William Propp treats at length this passage's suggestion that Moses's face *qaran 'or* after meeting with God, suggesting that this phrase may originally have meant that the skin of his face became hardened and disfigured like a blacksmith's. See Propp (2006), 622–23. For the tradition that Moses's face grew horns, see Mellinkoff (1970).
25. Most recently: De Vries (2016), 124, 130–31. This passage is also a good illustration of the *vayyomer . . . vayyomer* feature of direct dialogue in the Bible and rabbinic writings: see Septimus (2004).
26. The *textus receptus* has the plural form *mar'ot,* though other text traditions assume the singular *mar'it;* the frequent confusion of the letters *yodh* and *waw* is well known. Cf. Greenberg (1983a), 37–59.
27. Later, Ezekiel reports: "I was sitting in my house, and the elders of Judah were sitting in front of me, and there the hand of the Lord God fell upon me. As I looked, behold the likeness of the appearance of a man, from the appearance of His loins downward was fire and from His loins upwards, was the appearance of brightness like the color of amber. He stretched out the form of a hand and He took me by the hair of my head" (8:1–3). Note that in the version cited above, the word "man" appears in the Septuagint text, while the MT has "fire."
28. Surveyed in light of Mesopotamian scribal practices by van der Toorn (2007).
29. It may be difficult to part from the standard translation, "And God saw that it was good," but this seems to be in error. The phrase *ra'ah ki tob* is an intensification of the more common *ra'ah tob,* which means "was pleased" in a number of different contexts; see further Kugel (1980).
30. "The notion of such a cherub throne (the cherubim being apparently a kind of gryphon) is found in texts of different dates, but the priestly picture in Exodus 25 does not describe a throne (*pace* Haran, 1978:251, 254). There is no seat, no armrests, no footstool; the creatures do not stand side-by-side, but face each other . . . There is no way this can be envisioned as a throne." Propp (2006), 390.

31. This is not to say that divine hugeness was an Israelite creation invented ad hoc to account for His taking over the whole world; as we have seen, inter alia, the god of the temple at 'Ain Dara was huge, judging by his footsteps. See M. Smith (2015), 478–81.
32. See the discussion in Frankfort and Frankfort (1949), 3–30.
33. True, Jephthah may have come close to pitting YHWH against Chemosh (Jud 11:23–24), but here too, there is no direct conflict between two deities. Note also the speech of the Rabshakeh in 2 Kgs 18, esp. vv. 32–33.
34. Cross (1997), 58.
35. Of course, as we have seen, God can penetrate the human mind and find out things, but this is different from omniscience in the sense of knowing all things all the time. See Carasik (2000).
36. The huge God of 2nd Isaiah, for whom the skies themselves are simply His chair and earth His footstool, will obviously lack the fine motor control required to intervene directly into human affairs—so in this sense, He may be very close to the omnipresent deity of postbiblical times. But He still does have a body; typologically, He is closest to the unseen deity of Deuteronomy's revelation at Mount Sinai, or the priestly Creator in Genesis 1, whose spirit hovers over the deep, who speaks and things just happen. But neither of these can truly be said to be omnipresent; they are just unspecified.
37. This is *not* to say that the three omni's were an entirely Greek import; clearly, the groundwork for each of these had been laid even before Alexander's conquest of the ancient Near East. But the sweeping assertion of these three terms as definitional bears an altogether Hellenic character; note briefly Winston (1981), 335 n. 57.
38. Philo, *The Confusion of Tongues,* 136–37.
39. Philo, *The Sacrifices of Abel and Cain,* 67–68. Note that the same dissonance is found in the Hebrew, and inspired the brief comment in *Mekhilta deR. Ishmael* par. *Vayyissa'* (Horowitz-Rabin ed. 175): "Behold, I will stand before you there . . .": God said to him [Moses], "Wherever you find the footprint of man, there I will be [standing] before you." A remarkable point of resemblance, pointed out by D. Winston (1981), 348 n. 201.
40. See Kugel (1998a), 127–28.
41. I have tried to avoid referring to either divine "immanence" or "transcendence" in this book because neither term, despite their distinguished pedigrees, quite captures what I am trying to say here and elsewhere—in part because the terms themselves carry a significance heavily freighted with later theological preconceptions. The anthropologist Alfred Gell once wrote about Polynesian cosmology as follows: "The idea of an immanent rather than transcendent divinity was, I think, the source of certain cosmological anxieties that played an enormous part in Polynesian life. For us, the immanent *deus sive natura* of Spinoza represents an optimistic rather than pessimistic deism, a blessed relief from the angry and punishing Almighty God of traditional Christianity, set apart from His creation and judging it harshly. But that is because the idea of an immanent God was never really naturalized in Christian Europe, however much eighteenth-century intellectuals may have hankered after one. In Polynesia the situation was the precise opposite: the immanence of the Gods was the source of continuous anxiety (the proverbial hedonism of the South Sea islanders was founded on a sense of acute and abiding hysteria), and the rapidity and enthusiasm with which the Polynesians accomplished their conversion to Christianity stemmed from their untold relief upon discovering that God was, after all, transcendent, not part of this world . . . Most important, Polynesian ritual operated in precisely the inverse sense to Christian communion, i.e., the intention was

to cause the divinity to leave (some part of) the world, rather than to induce the divinity to enter (some part of) it": Gell (1995), 290–305.

42. See chap. 5, note 14.

10. A SACRED AGREEMENT AT SINAI

1. It is probably impossible to determine the very oldest biblical text that refers to God as a king, but among the oldest, Exod 15:18 or Deut 33:5 might be reasonable candidates. On God's kingship in the Psalms, Brettler (1989), esp. 2–26. As we have seen, this is hardly the only representation of God in early biblical times. Indeed, the Divine Warrior does not necessarily contradict the Divine King—the two coexist in Exod 15 (15:3 and 18 respectively); Ps 68 seems to embody the progression from victorious warrior (8–24) to exalted king (25–36). The former is certainly the controlling image of the ancient hymn of Habakkuk 3. Beyond these biblical examples is the broad spectrum of connections between gods and kingship among Israel's neighbors. Note also Henri Frankfort's observation: "The ancient Near East considered kingship the very basis of civilization. Only savages could live without a king. Security, peace, and justice could not prevail without a ruler to champion them. If ever a political institution functioned with the assent of the governed, it was the monarchy which built the pyramids with forced labor and drained the Assyrian peasantry by ceaseless wars": Frankfort (1948), 3.
2. See Roth (1997).
3. Noth (1967), 14.
4. The scholarly writings on this passage are understandably vast. See among many the classic studies Zenger (1977); Toeg (1977); Dozeman (1989); B. Schwartz (1996).
5. See Greenberg (1950); and further Reiner (1984), 244, in particular entry 3 "treasured possession of Divine Name$_3$"; Alalakh's goddess adopted the king as her *sikiltu;* see also Weinfeld (1970), 195, n. 103, and Weinfeld (1972), 226, n. 22, and recently Bloch (2013).
6. These were discussed by Korošec (1931), building on the two-volume study by Friedrich (1926–30). Akkadian treaties had been published somewhat earlier in Weidner (1923).
7. See on this Altman (2004). Note that the historical prologue is typical of the second-millennium treaties but *virtually absent from* the first-millennium Assyrian vassal treaties to which the Hittite treaties have been compared.
8. Cited in Beckman (1999), 60–61.
9. Ibid., 65, slightly reworded for clarity.
10. In later, Assyrian suzerain treaties, the vassal is required to "love" the suzerain; on this language, see Moran (1963).
11. Early examples include Mendenhall (1955), Beyerlin (1965), Zimmerli (1965). Their arguments were challenged early on, in particular by Perlitt (1969). The virtual absence of any reference to a great covenant between God and Israel from the eighth-century prophets would suggest that the concept was unknown until relatively late. The Assyrian vassal treaties of the eighth and ninth centuries BCE bring us closer to ancient Israel, but those treaties have a far simpler form, one that might be found in almost any age or location. See McCarthy (1978); Clements (1975). For a recent review of the question see Weeks (2004), 5–12.
12. As almost always, scholars are confronted by the problem discussed earlier as "absence of evidence is not evidence of absence"; again, see Weeks (2004), 5–12.
13. A number of recently discovered inscriptions (some mentioned in chapter 5) seem to

connect Israel's God with various sites to the south of ancient Canaan. He is thus recorded as "YHWH of Teman" (the "southland," here, probably, Edom) on a clay water jar discovered at Kuntillat Ajrud, in the eastern part of the Sinai desert not far from the current Israeli-Egyptian border. Final publication of the excavation was reported in Meshel (2012).The writing has been dated to the eighth century BCE. Another inscription at the same site likewise reads "YHWH of Teman." Two Nubian temple inscriptions from the second half of the second millennium refer to nomads in the region of Seir (again, to Israel's south) as the "Shashu (š3św, that is, Bedouins) of YHWH." These inscriptions are particularly important because, apart from them, there is little evidence that this particular God was known elsewhere. As Pharaoh says after Moses first mentions God's name to him: "Who is this YHWH, that I should obey Him and let Israel go? I never heard of YHWH" (Exod 5:2). The recent discovery of these southern inscriptions has revived interest in the nineteenth-century "Midianite (or Kenite) Hypothesis," which held that Israel's God was originally located far to the south of ancient Canaan. For a brief review of the arguments: Kugel (2007a), 63–66.

14. The divine stipulation that in accepting God's covenant Israel would become a "nation of priests" deserves mention here. Surely this phrase did not mean that everyone would henceforth be a priest, barging into sanctuaries at will and offering their own sacrifices. Nor did it likely mean that the king at any time would have to come from priestly stock; the notion that the high priest was also ex officio a kind of king only appeared much, much later, at the end of the second century BCE. Besides, the whole idea of this passage and God's subsequent issuing of the Ten Commandments is that *He* will be the people's king and the people will be his faithful subjects. Rather, this passage seems to be saying that by taking on the obligations of God's covenant — the Ten Commandments and, eventually, the other laws that follow in the Torah — the people would somehow be *like* priests in a temple or other sanctuary, those who are allowed to come close to the deity. Note the wording "you shall be *to Me* a kingdom of priests." The phrase "to Me" seems to imply some sort of qualification: you will be priests *as far as I am concerned* — not the kind of priests who officiate in a temple, but somehow the equivalent, a whole kingdom of people who are closely connected to Me. Scholars are divided as to when this passage was written, and this is, as almost always, an important matter. F. M. Cross called Exod 19:3–6 the "archaic, poetic (liturgical) prologue" of this section, citing Moran (1962); see Cross (1973), 84n. But early or late, this passage's suggestion that by "keeping My covenant" Israel will become God's "treasured people" — this was a theme with enormous ramifications for the later development of Israel's religion, as we shall see.

15. Much later, toward the end of the biblical period, such omissions bothered the author of the book of *Jubilees*, and he consciously set out to correct them — but there is scant evidence that such things bothered anyone before his time. Kugel (2007a), 41–42, 58, 65–66, 69–70, etc.

16. To be sure, the "period of the Judges" is a later construct: it means "the time before there was an established sequence of kings," a period which actually stretched back from Saul and David to time immemorial. Cf. H. Frankfort cited above, note 1.

17. Evocation of a binding, legal connection between God and Israel may, in a way, have seemed to undercut the living prophet's own authority: why should he need to evoke an ancient covenant or its stipulations when he himself has, as it were, the last word? So, for example, when the daughters of Zelophehad tell Moses that the existing laws of inheritance treat them unfairly, Moses, as a prophet, could "bring their case before the

Lord" and have the law changed (Num 27:1–11). At the same time, any society needs established rules and norms of behavior, and the existence of sophisticated legal codes in the ancient Near East that predate Israel's own existence by a wide margin suggests that such rules — indeed, many of the same rules that are found in Mesopotamian law codes — must have been promulgated in Israel from an early period. With regard to the Ten Commandments in particular, however, it may well be that they started off not as the stipulations of a great divine-human covenant, but (as Cross has suggested) as a set of simple rules agreed upon by the inhabitants of various separate highland sites at the very dawn of Israel's history — the sort of rules that would allow these isolated settlements to intermarry and cooperate in other minimal ways while maintaining their fierce independence; see below, note 20. Only later were these rules recast as a great covenant. In addition, scholars have recently emphasized that laws in the ancient Near East had more of an exemplary than a strictly prescriptive character: the biblical and ancient Near Eastern lists of laws were more in the nature of "legal treatises" rather than actual law codes in our sense. Individual laws were thus examples to be elaborated on, or departed from, by actual judges — and the laws themselves were often left uncited in narrative. This certainly seems to be the case with the famous judgment of Solomon (1 Kgs 3:16–27): underlying his apparently irrational proposal to cut the baby in half is the unstated legal principle that disputed property whose true ownership cannot be proven is to be divided by the disputants (cf. M. *Baba Meṣi'a* 1:1). But with time, citing the authority of the law came to be more frequent. See Jackson (2000), 287–97.

18. Could the Torah's laws be described as another form of *encounter* between God and Israel? At first the answer might seem to be a straightforward No. Once a set of laws has been promulgated and accepted, there is no implied encounter between the lawgiver and the people; he or she is basically out of the picture. But such a notion fails to take into account the ramifications of a *divinely* given set of laws. In an entirely human legal system, disobeying the law is a crime. In biblical law, by contrast, disobeying the law is a sin. Of course, if applied to Israelite law in its early stages, such a distinction would probably have seemed entirely theoretical: a thief is a thief, and whether his crime is committed against the deity or against the crown probably made little difference to him or to his judges in ancient times. But eventually, as we shall see, obeying God's laws came to be conceived as a kind of encounter, that is, a way of coming close to God. In this respect, the whole career of divine law is an important part of the fundamental change which lies at the heart of this book. Note in this connection Nickelsburg (2001), *1 Enoch 1:* "[In the Enochic corpus,] sin is a violation of the divine King's sovereignty through the worship of other divine beings, a transgression of the divinely created cosmic order, or disobedience of the laws that regulate the human conduct toward God and one's fellow human beings . . . The Enochic corpus explains the origins and presence of sin and evil on earth in two ways: (1) sin and evil are the function of a primordial heavenly revolt whose results continue to victimize the human race; (2) responsibility for sin and evil lies with the human beings who transgress God's law" (p. 46). By the same token, obeying the law in a human legal system is usually just a matter of staying out of trouble, or at best good citizenship. By contrast, consciously carrying out a law given by God is (or can be construed as) a way of doing His bidding, following His instructions and so acting as His faithful subject. Either way, the laws of the Pentateuch implied an automatic and *ongoing* connection between God and the human beings charged with

obeying them. Beyond this, however, is the more specific matter of enforcement. Some transgressions listed in the Torah could be found out and punished by human courts, but others could not. Who is going to enforce a commandment such as "You shall not hate your brother in your heart" (Lev 19:17)? The phrase "in your heart" means secretly, holding the hatred inside without telling anyone: see Kugel (1987). If so, then the very existence of this law implies that some non-human — God or one of His angels — must somehow always be watching in order to properly reward or punish those who keep or violate it. The same applies to "And you shall love your neighbor like yourself" (Lev 19:18) and many other biblical statutes. Indeed, a number of infractions are specifically punishable by extirpation, a punishment that presumably could be carried out only by God. See Milgrom (1990), 405–8.

19. An important proviso, since this and much of the book is attributed by scholars to later hands: a relatively early Deuteronomic compilation, followed by further additions (including a putative Deutero-Deuteronomic editing). See chapter 7, note 21.
20. Some scholars have suggested that the Ten Commandments actually began not as part of a great covenant between God and Israel, but as a code of conduct agreed upon by the inhabitants of various separate, hilltop settlements that constituted the first "Israelite" populations in Canaan. This code of conduct was only subsequently adopted (and revised) to fill an entirely different purpose, to be the covenant stipulations of an agreement binding Israel's tribes with the God YHWH. See further Cross (1998), 33, and Kugel (2007a), 721 n. 5.
21. Neither of these terms means, strictly speaking, a legal code alone; see Urbach (1987), 286–95. Moreover, what the term *torah* designated in post-exilic is a moving target; see Achenbach (2007), Kugel (1986b).
22. Interpreters concluded that He had given Israel no fewer than 613 different commandments in the Torah, though they differed on exactly which commandments to include in this total. For the biblical source of this exact number: Kugel (1998a), 637–38, 677.

11. THE EMERGENCE OF THE BIBLICAL SOUL

1. See in this connection: Clifford (2004); M. Fox (1999); see also "Solomon's Riddles," in Kugel (1999), 160–80. For the explicit connection of *mashal* ("proverb") with *ḥidah* ("riddle"), see Ezek 17:2, Hab 2:6, Ps 49:5, 78:2; Prov 1:6. Many previous writers have sought to catalogue the different forms and functions of biblical proverbs, inter alia: von Rad (1972) 25–40; Scott, (1971), 59–71.
2. See Ulmer (2009), 102–3.
3. To repeat: "The notion of such a cherub (apparently a kind of gryphon) throne is found in texts of different dates, but the priestly picture in Exodus 25 does not describe a throne (*pace* Haran, 1978:251, 254). There is no seat, no armrests, no footstool; the creatures do not stand side-by-side, but face each other . . . There is no way this can be envisioned as a throne." Propp (2006), 390.
4. This might mean (and sometimes did) that an omnipresent deity is by definition everywhere including every person's insides; some early postbiblical texts suggest, however, that "omnipresent" meant spread out all over the *outside* world. An omnipresent God was, at least for a time, all around, but this "everywhere" did not necessarily include a person's insides. (For examples, see below). In fact, this may be what the words of Prov 20:27 are trying to explain.

5. See also such uses as Isa 2:22 "breath" and Ps 150:6 "everyone that breathes" in the NRSV and NJPS translations of *neshamah.*
6. This understanding was first put forward by Dürr (1925) in the wake of earlier research by P. Dhorme (1920), esp. 482–83.
7. I should make it clear that I do not take this and other expressions as indicating that ancient Semites and other peoples had no notion of a unitary mind or of the individual as such, nor that ancient Israelite thinking was itself fundamentally different from ours (as argued by, for example, Boman [1970]) nor yet that ancient minds were structurally different from ours, as argued by Jaynes (1976), discussed below (chap. 18, note 7). Di Vito (1999) similarly asserts that "in the OT [i.e., Hebrew Bible], human faculties and bodily organs enjoy a measure of independence that is simply difficult to grasp today," illustrating this phenomenon with an array of biblical examples (p. 227) and concluding: "In short, the biblical character presents itself to us more as parts than as a whole" (pp. 227–28). Michael Carasik is perhaps the most recent scholar to debunk such notions: Carasik (2006), 2–9.
8. Krüger (2009). My thanks to Carol Newsom for this reference.
9. I have insisted on this point because it is still being missed by some contemporary scholars; they readily assert that the biblical soul was different from the Greek soul—the biblical soul was not separate from, nor opposed to, the body as the Greek soul was. But it is important for what follows in this chapter to take the next step and admit that in fact there simply is no reason to define *nefesh, ruaḥ,* or *neshamah* in most usages as any kind of soul at all. While he does not quite get to this point, Jacob Licht's survey of the subject is excellent: s.v. "nefesh" in Mazar et al. (1968), 898–904.
10. The "upon" (*'al*) in these expressions seems designed to imply that while the spirit empowers or impels the person to do things that he or she was previously unable to do, the spirit remains an external controller; see Newsom (2012a), 11.
11. This of course does not mean that ancient Israelites themselves conceived of a *ruaḥ* being responsible for such transformations "in those earlier days" but not later on; clearly, the books of Judges, Samuel, and Kings are the product of a great literary project, the Deuteronomistic history, which combined various oral and written source material culled from here and there and then reworked it (several times, in fact) into our present biblical text.
12. Note also the apparently independent "spirit of whoredom" in Hos 4:12, 5:4, or the "spirit of jealousy" that enters the mind of the suspicious husband in Num 5:14.
13. Levison (2009) poses the question clearly (pp. 11–12): "What is the relationship between the spirit that human beings possess by dint of birth—the life principle or breath within—and the spirit [of God —JK] that exhibits awesome effects?" Levison's answer, which he calls an "unapologetically alternative point of view," is that the distinction of the two is an "artificial, anachronistic, and decidedly unnecessary division that serves to obscure the relationship that exists in Israelite literature between God's initial gift of the spirit and a subsequent endowment of the spirit." I'm afraid I can't agree; see below.
14. Robert Di Vito writes: "One of the most striking manifestations of the modern sense of inwardness is the conviction that every person has 'inner depths,' which mark that person as unique . . . This conviction is completely foreign to the thought world of the OT, where identity is given with one's social role and the status it offers, whether one is a lay person or a cleric, a master or a slave, rich or poor. In a way foreign to modernity, one simply is one's social role in the OT": di Vito (1999). His point about socially defined

identity is important, but perhaps too sweeping, as we shall see below; "inner depths" is precisely what we encounter in some (especially later) biblical texts. On the social construction of identity in general: Berger and Luckman (1967); also Lieu (2004).

15. Reading *aḥuzot,* as suggested by the Old Greek and Syriac translations.
16. Reminiscent of God's promise of a "new heart and a new spirit" in Ezek 11:19, replacing the "heart of stone" with a "heart of flesh"; cf. Ezek 36:26–27.
17. This is S. Mowinckel's category of "non-cultic poems," including alphabetical acrostics, which he holds in rather low esteem: Mowinckel (1962), vol. 2, 111–12. The "anytime, anywhere" character of these psalms is well exemplified in Ps 34:2, "Let me bless the Lord at all times, let His praise be in My mouth continuously," or the opening of Ps 145: "O King, my God, let me exalt You, and bless Your name forever and ever; Let me bless You every day, and praise Your name forever and ever" (145:1–2), discussed below in greater detail, chapter 15. Note that this wording later gave rise to the midrashic assurance that anyone who recites this psalm once a day (subsequently revised to three times a day) is guaranteed a portion in the world to come. This promise is actually a reinterpretation of the psalm's second line as: "If I bless You every day, then I will praise Your name forever and ever [that is, in the world to come]." By the time of the Babylonian Talmud, the origin of this midrash was no longer recognized; see b. *Ber.* 4b. On prayer without ceasing: 1 Thess. 5:17, Rom 12:12, and the later Christian *laus perennis.*
18. Note Pss 34 and 145, mentioned in the preceding note, are likewise alphabetical acrostics, and this may be one of several indications (along with syntax, lexis, ideology) that these psalms, along with Ps 119, belong to the latest stage of biblical psalm composition; on the date of Ps 119, see Hurvitz (1972), 131–51; cf. Freedman (1999), 29; Prinsloo (2003), 422; Reynolds (2010), 50–51.
19. I must acknowledge here that some Jewish communities do make a practice of reciting Ps 119 in synagogue toward the end of Shabbat (usually with different members of the congregation taking turns reading stanzas), but the purpose is clearly to fill up the time between the afternoon and evening prayers.
20. Among other views, see those of J. D. Levenson (1987).
21. Sh. Holtz, "Seeking Torah, Seeking God," on the website TheTorah.com.
22. In fact, see Kugel (1999a), 239–70.
23. Ps 119 is widely recognized as a late biblical psalm; see the discussion by A. Hurvitz (1972), 131–51. If so, its chronological closeness to the Qumran *Hodayot* may help explain their shared focus on "me."
24. A group within the *Thanksgiving Hymns,* namely, those found in 1QH[a] columns 10–17, have been argued to refer to (and indeed, to be spoken by) a specific, historical figure, the "Teacher of Righteousness" who is mentioned elsewhere in the Qumran corpus. In particular, the speaker of 1QH[a] 12:9–10 says of his enemies: "They do not take account of me, though You show Your strength in me, for they *drive me away from my land* like a bird from her nest." This seems to tally with *Pesher Habakkuk,* which at one point refers to the Teacher of Righteousness having been driven into exile: "Its interpretation concerns the Wicked Priest who pursued the Teacher of Righteousness to swallow him up with the fury of his anger in the place of his exile." The idea that this subgroup from within the *Thanksgiving Hymns* were spoken by, or referred to, the Teacher of Righteousness was first proposed by G. Jeremias (1963) and has attracted a number of supporters; see recently M. O. Wise (2010). For our purposes, it makes little difference if the "I" of these hymns is the Teacher's or not (or if, originally having come from the Teacher,

these hymns became part of the liturgy of the Qumran community) — it is, in any case, indisputably "all about me." In this connection, see the various articles by C. Newsom: (1992), (2012a), and (2012b); as well as Newsom (2004). Note also Harkins (2012).

25. The numbering of lines in the *Thanksgiving Hymns* follows that of Stegemann and Schuller (2009), which usually differs by a few lines from the edition of Garcia Martinez and Tigchelaar (1997) and other preliminary editions.
26. See further on starkness: Kugel (2003), 137–68 and (2007a), 89–114.
27. For this and other reasons, I am skeptical about the claim that this and others of the *Hymns* refer specifically to the life of the Teacher of Righteousness; see above, n. 24.
28. Newsom notes the frequency of reference to God's having *placed the spirit within me* (Hodayot 4:29, 5:36; 8:29; 20:15; 21:34); see Newsom (2012b), 349.
29. This assertion must be qualified somewhat: while the inward explanation grew to wide acceptance, the "outside source" understanding was far from dead. Surely any reader of the New Testament, or of post-biblical Jewish and Christian writings, knows that Satan was still an exterior, dynamic power who could gain control of a human being from the outside. Indeed, in rabbinic writings the altogether interior *yetzer* (*ha-'ra*) came to be re-personified and exteriorized, as Rosen-Zvi has demonstrated: see Rosen-Zvi (2011) and n. 34 below. Even today, Satan is still very much alive: many contemporary Christians in the modern West will still insist that the Devil made them do this or that. Let one pungent example stand for many: the hit record of the Louvin Brothers (a gospel duo that clearly influenced the ultimately better known Everly Brothers) entitled "Satan Is Real" (1958). The chorus is as follows:

    Satan is real, working in spirit,
    You can see him and hear him in this world every day.
    Satan is real, working with power,
    He can tempt you and lead you astray.

    In between choruses, a man relates his sad story in church. He once had a happy home and was "loved and respected by my family," indeed, "looked upon as a leader in my community." But then "Satan came into my life. I grew selfish and un-neighborly. My friends turned against me, and finally, my home was broken apart. My children took their paths into a world of sin. So yes, preacher, it is sweet to know that God is real and that in Him all things are possible, and we know that Heaven is a real place, where joy shall never end. But sinner friend, if you're here today, Satan is real too, and hell is a real place, a place of everlasting punishment."
30. Defined as "soul, spirit, strong feeling, strength, desire, inclination" etc. For all these, Liddell and Scott (1953), 810.
31. Dodds (1951), 138–39.
32. "Homer's conception of *thymos, noos,* and *psyche* still depended to a large extent on an analogy with physical organs . . . The first writer to feature the new concept of the soul is [the sixth century philosopher] Heraclitus. He calls the soul of living man *psyche;* in his view man consists of body and soul, and the soul is endowed with qualities which differ radically from those of the body and the physical organs . . . Heraclitus says (fr. 45) 'You could not find the ends of the soul though you travelled every road, so deep is its *logos.*' This notion of the depth or profundity of the soul is not unfamiliar to us, but it involves a dimension which is foreign to a physical organ or its function." Snell (1960), 16–18.
33. Apart from *Phaedo,* the Platonic dialogue *Phaedrus* is likewise well known for its de-

piction of the immortal soul as a charioteer and two winged horses. Further: Werner (2012), 59–64.

34. It is not at all clear that the rabbinic *yetzer* (inclination to evil) is the product of Greek ideas of the "lower" (specifically sexual) impulses. After a thorough search of the rabbinic material, I. Rosen-Zvi has concluded that the rabbinic *yetzer* is far closer to Persian demonology: "The *yetzer,* as shown above, is never identified with the body, and is not modeled on the body-soul dichotomy. Rather, it creates multiplicity in one's heart and therefore must be cut off ('circumcised') in order to allow people to become 'single-minded' in the service of God . . . The *yetzer* is anything but an integral part of the 'self.' The rabbis took pains time and again to distinguish 'me' from 'my *yetzer.*' . . . In fact, the *yetzer* discourse seems to be an important tool of constructing the very notion of 'self' in rabbinic literature — the true 'me,' set against other parts in 'me' that are nonetheless not really 'me.' In this sense the *yetzer* is a result of a double, and somewhat contradictory, motion; the source of evil was inserted into humans (unlike ancient demonology) but remained a separate agent (in stark contrast to the biblical monism), . . . thus creating both duplication and hierarchy in the person." Rosen-Zvi (2011), 129.
35. J. Barr (1993) sought to argue the case for the opposition of soul and body within the Hebrew Bible, but the evidence is unconvincing.
36. Among others, see Kugel (1989).
37. See above, note 34.
38. Shaked, (1984), vol. 1, 308–25; Garcia Martinez (2003), 37–49.
39. See on this Feldman et al. (2013), vol. 2, 1697–1703.
40. Cf. 2 Bar 42:8, *1 En* 51:1, Sib Or. 1:82, etc.
41. See below and *4 Ezra* 4:41, 7:32, 7:85, 7:95, 101; also. 2 Bar 21:23; Ps.-Philo 32:13 as well as Stone (1990), 96, 99.
42. Barresi and Marten (2013), 51.
43. Dan Zahavi, citing Miri Albahari in Zahavi (2011), 316–35.

12. REMEMBERING GOD

1. It would be tedious to list all the different explanations that have been offered; see briefly Milgrom (1990) 448–49. Also: Propp (1988); Helfgot (1993); Beck (2003).
2. To be sure, this looks like a classic "doublet" of Source Criticism, that is, two versions of the same "water in the wilderness" story, the first as told by E and the second by P: see Friedman (1989), 189, 251, 253. This notwithstanding, there is an obvious difference between the two versions — the first altogether positive, the second quite the opposite (at least insofar as vv. 12–13 are concerned); it would probably be more accurate to say that in its final form, the second version is quite consciously contrasting its version to the first and thereby offering its own justification for Moses's having died before the entry into Canaan.
3. Hebrew *he'emin b-* generally has the sense of "put one's trust in," "believe in." But while this is the usual sense of the *hiph'il* form of this verb, here it refers to *showing* one's trust and thereby *causing* someone else to believe. This is made clear in the continuation of this sentence, "Since you did not show your trust in Me, *sanctifying Me in the Israelites' sight . . .*" A similar usage occurs with the *hiph'il* form *hbyn:* while it usually refers to the verb's subject understanding something, it sometimes refers to the subject causing someone else to understand, thus Neh 8:7 "The Levites who were explaining (*hmbynym*)

the Torah to the people" (cf. Neh 8:9, Ezr 8:16). Similarly in our passage, Moses's fault was that he did not *he'emin b-* in the sense of causing others to put their trust in, or believe in, God.

4. O'Connor (1979); also Longman (1990).
5. Presumably the name of his mother.
6. That is, I was their exclusive support. Text from Donner and Röllig (1962), 4–5. For aspects of this translation, see the review of scholarship and translations cited in Green (2010), 136–54.
7. Miller (1974), 12.
8. Among others, see: Deut 8:19; Jud 3:7; 1 Sam 12:9; Isa 17:10, 51:13; Jer 3:21, 13:25, 23:27; Ezek 22:12, 23:35.
9. Particularly revealing is Ps 44:14, "If we forgot the name of our God and spread out hands to a foreign god . . ." Taken at face value, this would suggest that the poor Israelites (apparently during the Babylonian exile) just couldn't remember the name of their God, so they started worshiping some other deity. Obviously, the "forgetting" here refers to willful abandonment embodied in the act specified, worshiping a foreign god. (This verse was later interpreted as referring to a god whose *name* was Zar ["foreign"].) See further Kugel (1990a), 195–97.
10. Greenfield (1969).
11. See also Kugel (1986a).
12. Claus Westermann has put the case nicely: "Lamentation has no meaning in and of itself. That it functions as an appeal is evident in its structure. What the lament is concerned with is not a description of one's own suffering or with self-pity, but with the removal of suffering itself": Westermann (1981), 266.
13. Mark the Deacon (2000), 65.
14. The latter form perhaps was preferred by students of Virgil, where the phrase is found in the *Aeneid* 1:303.
15. Ruchames (1971).
16. Along with its opposite, *à Dieu ne plaise* (that is, "May this *not* happen").
17. Rabelais (2009), 256.
18. Two landmark studies: Watts (1992) and Weitzman (1997).
19. Initially, the expectation was that praise to God on such occasions was to be *sung*, as these inserted songs attest. See further Kugel (1982a) and (2000). Scholars generally agree that these songs are *later* insertions of thanksgiving into the biblical narrative; see e.g., Watts (1992) 11, 47, 69, 85, 118, 141, 143. One exception, I believe, is Jonah's prayer from the belly of the whale, where this psalm seems to have created the preceding narrative of Jonah's attempted flight to Tarshish. That is, the core story began in what is now chapter 3; to it was added the (already extant) psalm that is now chapter 2 along with the flight narrative to provide a narrative context for the prayer. See further Kugel (2007a), 630–31.
20. As many scholars have argued; see Kugel (2007a), 392–96.
21. Ibid.
22. Cross and Freedman (1955); also Cross (1973), 112–44; cf. Wolters (1990).
23. Watts (1992) and Weitzman (1997).
24. Ibid.
25. Cf. Joel 2:26.
26. It seems likely that in this case, as so often in *Jubilees*, a particular event in the life of one

of Israel's forefathers is being presented as a precedent for what was later to become a commandment of the Torah, in this case, that of Deut 8:10. In other words, even at this early date, what might otherwise be seen as a generalized biblical encomium of the land of Israel was already being understood by the author of *Jubilees* as requiring a specific, external act to be performed after eating a festive meal (cf. *Jub* 2:21). Such a hypothesis is backed up by some of *Jubilees'* contemporaries, for example, Ben Sira's assertion: "Like a sealing-clasp on a purse of gold, so is the praise of God after a wine feast" (35:5 [ms. B]). Here, "sealing-clasp" is meant to imply the act of *sealing* or ending the evening with praise. From only a slightly later period, several texts found among the Dead Sea Scrolls — 4QDeut[n], the so-called "All Souls Deuteronomy," 4QDeut[j], and 4Q434a — suggest that the same passage ending in Deut 8:10 was being copied for liturgical use, in all likelihood as part of a fixed practice of reciting a blessing after the meal.

27. On 4Q434a see Weinfeld (1992a) and Davila (2000), 172–76. See also White (1990). Not all have found this identification convincing: Kimelman (1993); Falk (1999) 3:865.
28. See John 6:23; Acts 27:35; cf. 1 Tim 4:3–5; Rom 14:6; 1 Cor 10:30.
29. M. *Berakhot* 6–7 and thereafter.

13. THE END OF PROPHECY?

1. Among recent studies, see Jassen (2007); for a list of scholars, starting with J. Wellhausen, who have maintained that prophecy "declined" in Second Temple times, see pp. 11–12 nn. 25 and 26.
2. Nissinen (2006).
3. M. Henze rightly remarks that this passage (and the same may be said of Pr Azar 15) should not be taken as an assertion that prophecy had ceased to exist forever: "This would make little sense, given that Baruch is depicted throughout 2 Bar as the latter-day prophet par excellence . . . Rather, Baruch stresses in his epistle that there are no longer prophets in Israel who are righteous and therefore can serve as intermediaries between the people and God": Henze (2011), 363n.
4. Milikowsky (2013), vol. 1, 321–22; vol. 2, 520–21.
5. On this wording see Lieberman (1973), 736.
6. Aune (1983), 103–7; Petersen (1988), 65–71 and (2000), 33–44; Sommer (1996).
7. Josephus mentions the prophetic powers of various Essenes: Judah (*B.J.* 1:78–80 and *A.J.* 13:311–13), Menahem (*A.J.* 15:373–79), and Simon (*B.J.* 2:112–13, *A.J.* 17:345–48). About the Essene visionaries he notes in general that "seldom, if ever, do they err in their predictions" (*B.J.* 2:159). Along with this, however, Josephus's brief history of Jewish Scriptures in *Apion* 1:40–41 asserts that "from Artaxerxes to our own time, the complete history has been written, but it has not been deemed worthy of equal credit . . . because of the failure of the exact succession of the prophets." On all these Feldman (1990), 386–422; and Gray (1991), 35–69, 92–110; cf. Schwartz (1990), 6–7. Several scholars have noted that Josephus (almost) consistently refers to biblical prophets as *prophētēs* while using the term *mantis* (diviner, soothsayer) to designate prophet-like figures of his own day. This includes Josephus himself: despite his own professed abilities, Josephus never calls himself a *prophētēs*. See Aune (1983), 139.
8. See *A.J.* 13:282–83, 299, 322.
9. But see above, note 7.
10. "Flavius" being Vespasian's ancestral name. On Josephus the prophet: Gray (1991), 35–69.

11. Aune (1983), 147; Levison (2006).
12. On this there is an extensive literature; inter alia Bowley (1998), 2:354–78; Barton (2007); Jassen (2007); Brooke (2006) and (2009).
13. Various prophets are mentioned in the New Testament, such as those in the Gospel of Luke: Zechariah (John's father) and his wife, Elizabeth (in Luke 1:41–2, 67), Simeon (Luke 2:26–32) and Anna (Luke 2:36), as well as the prophets mentioned in Acts: Barnabas, Simeon, Lucius of Cyrene (Acts 13:1–2); Philip's unmarried daughters (Acts 21:9); Agabus (11:27 and 21:10–12); Judas and Silas (Acts 15:32); as well as the mention of anonymous prophets in Eph 2:20, 3:5, 4:11; Jas 5:10; 1 Pet 1:10; and John of Patmos in Rev. In addition, John the Baptist is frequently presented as a prophetic figure (see Matt 11:10, 14:5, 17:14; Luke 7:26–28), as of course are both Paul and Jesus. Moses's reference to a "prophet like me" came to be interpreted as the prediction of a specific future prophet; see Kugel (1998), 832–34, 870–71, and (1990c); Rowland (2010), 410–28; as well as Aune (1983).
14. Prophecy is frequently presented as a common phenomenon, hence the concern with false prophets, e.g., *Didache* 3–12; See in general Aune (1983), and on the *Didache* passage 208–9, 225–6.
15. E.g., Justin Martyr, *Dial.* 82:1; Origen, *Cels.* 7:8; Athanasius, *Inc.* 39–40; Augustine, *Civ.*, 17:24.
16. See the extensive review of scholarship in Cook (2011), 10–42.
17. See Urbach (1946), 1–17.
18. Cross (1973), 219–29; 343–46.
19. Aune (1983), 104 and 374–75 n. 11.
20. Among many: Hanson (1979); S. J. D. Cohen (1987), 195–201; Jassen (2007).
21. "Revelation by an angel equally is typical of the works produced in our period, but again it is important not to draw the wrong conclusions from this. It is widely held that Judaism began to take an interest in angels and other mediating figures as its theology developed in an increasingly 'transcendent' direction. Whereas the prophets had felt that God spoke to them directly, 'apocalyptists' could not approach so closely to the divine presence, and so thought of angelic guides and interpreters. As a statement about the development of theological assumptions in post-exilic Judaism this is quite possibly correct. But it does not follow that writers in our period were aware that they differed from the predecessors in this regard. Many probably held, as did Philo, that it was through an angel that God had spoken to the patriarchs, and believed, with St Paul, that angels had been involved in the transmission of the Law to Moses; small wonder, if the prophets, too, had received their revelation at the hand of angels": J. Barton (2007), 122–23.
22. Readers familiar with Ezekiel will know that his book is full of all manner of strange visions, including the humanlike figure in Ezek 8:1–3. Many scholars have suggested that this passage, along with Ezek 40:3–4, may have served as the inspiration for Zechariah's angelic intermediary. Note in this connection Tollington (1993), 97–100, and in particular the comparison of Zechariah's *angelus interpres* with the angel/God in Jacob's dream in Gen 31:10–13.
23. The same year is cited in Hag 1:15, and cf. Ezra ch. 5–6.
24. Kugel (1998a), 173–79, 191–93.
25. See on this Najman (2014), 130–36.
26. It is true that a book often connected with *4 Ezra, 2 Baruch (Syriac Apocalypse),* does present its hero in direct conversation with God; in this respect this apocalypse is significantly different from many of its contemporaries.

27. By a virtually universal scholarly consensus, Zech 1–8 is quite separate from chapters 9–14 (themselves a composite unit); see Meyers and Meyers (1993), 15.
28. This resembles, but also contrasts with, those earlier prophetic visions in which God asks "What do you see, Amos/Jeremiah?" where it is God who explains the prophet's vision.
29. Aune (1983), 113–14.
30. For this point see Najman (2010) 124–26, and (2003), 60–67.
31. "Perhaps the most well-known characterization of the prophets in the Dead Sea Scrolls is as foretellers of future events": A. P. Jassen (2007), 29. He cites examples from 1QpHab *Pesher Habakkuk* 2:5–10. It may be that Greek oracles had some influence in turning things in this direction: see Aune (1983), 52–57.
32. On this translation see Kugel (1998a), 818.
33. "To warn one's own generation of coming disaster or to assure them of divine aid was, it was felt, an important task, but not one that necessarily required supernatural inspiration, whereas to possess accurate knowledge of events that were far distant (whether past or future) was explicable only as a divine gift. It is very unusual to find the prediction of an imminent event by a contemporary described as 'prophecy' in postexilic literature": J. Barton (2007), 180.
34. See further Kugel (1990d), 45–55.
35. Kugel (1998a), 173–78, 191–3.
36. See Najman (2010), 39–71; and (2003), 60–63.
37. Michael Stone has argued convincingly that behind the phenomenon of pseudepigraphy may lurk the latter-day recipient of what he/she experienced as true revelation. See his "Apocalyptic — Vision or Hallucination?" reprinted in Stone (1991).
38. This may be related to the observation that "Christians seem to have been interested in the prophets as *people,* in what they did and suffered in the name of God, rather than as the names of books or as rather featureless recipients of oracles — a tendency shared with Josephus and Philo": J. Barton (2007), 99. On the whole phenomenon of pseudepigraphy, see Stone (1991) and (2006); Najman (2003), 1–40; Bernstein (1997).
39. Kugel and Greer (1986), 40–51.
40. Scholars regard our biblical book of Daniel as a composite: the courtier tales found in chaps. 1–6 are succeeded by the apocalyptic visions of chaps. 7–12. The linguistic division (chaps. 1:2:4a and 8–12 are written in Hebrew, while 2:4b–7:28 are in Aramaic) has been variously explained, perhaps most plausibly as an attempt to bridge the two genre divisions. Further: Collins (1994). The theme of four empires (though not necessarily Daniel's four) is found in later Jewish writings of the period. Rome is the fourth empire in *4 Ezra* 12:11–36 and *2 Baruch* 39:2–6; see Stone (1990), 361–66. Compare the four periods spoken of in *1 En* 89–90; also, 4Q552 and 553 (*Four Kingdoms ar*). On this theme in general: Flusser (1988), 317–44, and Lucas (1988), 185–202. For the four empires in the Slavonic "Ladder of Jacob," Kugel (1995a), 209–27.
41. On the origins and interrelationship of Daniel's visions, Collins (1994); also, Fröhlich (1996), 11–48.
42. This overall topic has been treated in connection with various biblical prophets, starting with Ezekiel: E. F. Davis (1989); Schaper (2006).
43. For a comparative study of the question: Heszer (2001).
44. Ezekiel's eating the scroll has been widely discussed; note in particular E. F. Davis (1987).
45. See this assessment of the incident in Schaper (2006), 76–77: "The prophet's sole task

is to relate the written word of God. There is not even an oral revelation which is then put in writing to serve as the basis for the prophet's recitation. Rather, the divine word is from the start encountered by the prophet in its written form. Only after its consumption will it be transformed into an oral 'text' . . . Ezekiel's commission thus encapsulates the 'death' of ('classic') prophecy as Israel/Judah knew it. The overpowering importance of the written text, as opposed to the aural/oral revelation of the divine word, mirrors the situation in late pre-exilic and exilic society and the increasing importance of texts in that society. Whereas many scholars date the 'death' or 'eclipse' of prophecy (one should rather say of 'classic' prophetic literature) in the late Persian period, it was in fact the exilic period that its death knell began to ring."

46. For the same nuance of "indictment" see Lev 5:1, 1 Kgs 8:31, Prov 29:24. Note also that in Num 5:11–30, an *'alah* is first written down on and then dipped into the "bitter waters of condemnation" that the accused women will subsequently drink. This written indictment is thus put to the test by having the woman drink the "waters of condemnation." Similarly, Zechariah's giant scroll goes "across the whole land" searching out anyone to whom the scroll's indictment applies: those who are found to match the charges of this heaven-sent indictment will be immediately punished.
47. Indeed, even before the post-exilic period, writing was on its way to overtaking living prophets as the preferred expression of the divine will. Thus, in a passage from 2 Kgs 22 treated above (chap. 10), the Bible reports that when King Josiah was read the laws contained in a newly discovered scroll in the Jerusalem temple, he immediately ordered the high priest to "inquire of the LORD on my behalf, and on behalf of the people, and on behalf of all of Judah, concerning the words of this scroll that has been found. For great indeed must be the wrath of the LORD that has been kindled against us, because our fathers did not obey the words of this scroll to do all that has been prescribed for us" (2 Kgs 22:13). The scroll is described as one of legal instruction (*torah*), which many scholars have identified as consisting of (roughly) the central legal core of the book of Deuteronomy. Thus Josiah, according to this account, understood at once that his people's failure to adhere to this legal code may have already spelled disaster for "all of Judah" and its people, even if they knew nothing of its existence.
48. One recent study concludes that "it is highly unlikely that as much as 10 percent of the Jewish population was literate" in the third century and early second century BCE, and that "certainly no more than a few hundred at a time" could write: S. Schwartz (1990), 10–11. Similarly Schams (1998); Heszer (2001), 34–35; and Horsley (2007): "a tiny elite" was literate, p. 91. Others have pulled in the opposite direction: Demsky (2012) argues for the existence of widespread literacy in pre-exilic times, "granting to the Kingdom of Judah of the eighth to sixth centuries BCE the title of a 'society of literacy'" (p. 323).
49. Said in reference to *Jubilees* in Najman (2003), 62.
50. Jassen has summarized the point well: "The Second Temple period witnessed a dramatic shift in the conceptualization of the revelatory experience. Evidence throughout the Second Temple period testifies to the emerging understanding of the prophet not merely as one who receives the oral word of God, but rather one whose prophetic character is thoroughly *literary.* Divine revelation for such a 'prophet' is experienced through the reading, writing, and interpretation of Scripture. This development can already be witnessed among various biblical prophets, in particular Ezekiel and Deutero-Isaiah": Jassen (2007), 203.

51. This was the assessment of Robert Lowth, who proclaimed Isaiah "the most perfect model" of a poetic prophet, "at once elegant and sublime, forcible and ornamented": Kugel (1981), 282.
52. B. Sommer (1998); see also Wiley (1997).
53. Echoed later in the *Book of Jubilees* (1:29), which John most likely knew.
54. Later in the same chapter, John's prophecy turns to chap. 60 of Isaiah: "And the City has *no need of sun or moon to shine on it,* for *the glory of God is its light,* and its lamp is the Lamb. *The nations will walk by its light, and the kings of the earth* will bring their glory into it. *Its gates will never be shut by day, and there will be no night* there. People will bring into it *the glory and the honor of nations.*" The phrase "no need of sun or moon to shine on it" alludes to Isa 60:19, "The sun will no longer be a light during the day, nor will the moon's gleam shine for you." Next, "the glory of God is its light," refers to the continuation of this same verse in Isaiah, "for the LORD will be your eternal light, and your God will be your adornment." "The nations will walk by its light, and the kings of the earth will bring their glory" reprises Isa 60:3, "And nations will come to your light, and kings to the gleam of your glory." "Its gates will never be shut by day, and there will be no night there" cites Isa 60:11, "And your gates will be forever open, day and night they will not be closed" and "Your sun will set no more, and your moon will not wane, but the LORD will be an eternal light, and the days of your mourning will end." Revelation's "People will bring into it the glory and the honor of nations" alludes to Isa 60:13, "The glory of Lebanon will come to you."
55. As related to me years ago by my late teacher Victor Erlich (I hope I have remembered the details correctly); cf. Hazlitt (1933), 277.
56. Among many studies: Dimant (1993), 57–76, and Werman (2006). Note Eshel and Eshel (2008), 13–27.
57. See Dimant (1993), 57–76. There was some dispute in Second Temple times about the length of a jubilee; because of the apparent disagreement of this verse with the mention of the "fiftieth year" in Lev 25:10, some held that a jubilee lasts fifty years.
58. Such as 4Q387 *Apocryphon of Jeremiah C*^{b} col 2:3–4 or 11Q13 *Melchizedek* col 2:7.
59. Particularly important in the biblical realm is the research carried out by Hindy Najman; see Najman (2003), esp. 3–40, as well as the subsequent essays collected in Najman (2010), in particular chaps. 1–3 and 6. Also: Reed (2008), 467–90.
60. Again, Stone (2011), 90–109.

14. THE ELUSIVE INDIVIDUAL

1. Among many studies that have wrestled with the intractable: Jacobsen (1976), 147–64, esp. 150; Johnson (2006); Starr (1986); E. Stern (2006); Rüpke (2013); Brakke et al. (2005); Berquist (2007); Lipschits et al. (2011); Yacoub (2007), 19–27; C. Morris (1972); Bynum (1980); Duby and Braunstein (1998); Weiger (1979); Renaut (1997); N. Z. Davis (1986), 53–63; Banani and Vryonis (1977); Shulman and Stroumsa (2002); Olyan (2005).
2. A number of recent works have especially helped me in writing this chapter, including Olyan (2005) and the other essays contained in Brakke et al. (2005), the various contributions in Lipschits et al. (2011), and most recently the monograph of Susan Niditch (2015).
3. On this much researched question, see in particular Fishbane (1985), 335–50; Kaminsky (1995); Levinson (2010), 57–88.

4. In discussing the case of Achan, Robert Di Vito contrasts the sense of self it implies with our own, modern one: "Over against the relative atomism, self-sufficiency, and disengagement of the modern self—which demands recognition as an individual even in the context of family—the ancient Israelite stands at the center of ever-widening circles of relation defined by kinship, beginning with the 'family' . . . Personally, socially, economically, and legally the individual Israelite was embedded in the family and enmeshed in obligations of kinship extending even beyond the father's household": Di Vito (1999), 221, 224.
5. Note that Achan is called Achor in the Septuagint and 1 Chron 2:7. But in biblical name etymologies, a similarity of two consonants is in any case often deemed sufficient. See Zakovitch (1980).
6. This identification of the immediate, patriarchal family as the significant unit may have found architectural expression in the early Israelite hilltop settlements in Canaan; see Stager (1985).
7. I have argued elsewhere that this tale was originally set in the period of the Judges and transferred from there to Genesis in order to account for the (otherwise unjustified) charge in Gen 49:5–7 that Simeon and Levi had used their "tools of violence" to murder. See Kugel (2007a), 169–75.
8. David Lambert has argued that such gestures are significantly not those of "repentance," a later phenomenon; see Lambert (2016a).
9. See further 2 Kgs 9:23–26 and Weinfeld (1972), 318. For a counterargument, Levinson (2010), 74, n. 19.
10. Two further examples: the slaughter of all of Nob (1 Sam 22:19) and that of Saul's sons (2 Sam 21:7–9). See the overall discussions in: Robinson (1964), 25–44; Wolff (1974); Rogerson (1989). Note also Mauss (1985).
11. Indeed, some scholars have suggested that "those who hate Me" in this passage may be a later qualification of an originally simpler assertion that God in general punishes to the third and fourth generations. See Weinfeld (1972), 318.
12. Fishbane (1985), 342–50, goes on to examine the various biblical instances of rewordings and modifications of this passage intended to soften the promised punishment. These are numerous: see in particular Num 14:18; Jer 18:7–8; Joel 2:12–14; Jonah 3:9; Mic 7:18–20; and various psalms (though among those listed by Fishbane, only Pss 78:38, 86:5, 99:8, 111:1, and 145:8–9, seem relevant to the afterlife of Exod 34:6–7). To these might be added Pss 86:15, 103:7–10, 112:4, as well as Neh 9:17, 31; and 2 Chr 30:9. In addition, notice should be taken of the rich continuation of this theme in various biblical apocrypha and pseudepigrapha: see Kugel (1998a), 723–27, 739–41, to which should now be added 4Q504 *Words of the Luminaries* frag 6:10–14.
13. Note that this verse is cited in 2 Kgs 14:6: "But he [Amaziah] did not put to death the children of the assassins, in accordance with what is written in the Torah of Moses, where the LORD commanded, 'Fathers shall not be put to death for sons, nor sons be put to death for fathers; but a person shall be put to death only for his own offense.'"
14. Cf. Jer 31:29–30: "In that time, people will no longer say, 'The fathers ate unripe grapes, but it is the children's teeth that ache.' Because each person will die for his own sin: anyone who eats unripe grapes will have aching teeth." Many scholars see this as a redactional addition.
15. Again, see Lambert (2016a), 85–89.
16. See further Ezek 33:12–20.

17. See Mauss (1985), 3. (Note that his use of "sense of self" is quite different from that of the present study—he uses this phrase to refer to a universal and unchanging entity, otherwise called the *moi* in his taxonomy.)
18. As previously noted, this subject, *our* subject, is sometimes treated under the rubric of the "anthropology" of ancient Israel, as, for example, Di Vito's study (chapter 3, note 18). But sometimes this same term is used to designate the academic study of peoples and cultures, past and present. Thus, for example, H. W. Wolff's classic study (Wolff 1974) has almost nothing to say about our subject, nor, for that matter, does Rogerson (1989), excellent as these works may be. A useful attempt at the taxonomy of self-reflection is Carasik (2006), an important book for our subject in general, even though I hope I have disproved the author's stated premise that the human mind is fundamentally the same in all human populations (p. 9, citing D. E. Brown [1991]), leading to a chronological blurring of the material he has assembled. Whatever one might conclude about the "human mind," the sense of self has certainly changed within the biblical period.
19. Kugel (2007a), 492. An excellent sorting of the literary and historical reality: Halpern (2001).
20. Robert Di Vito (1999) dismisses from the Bible as a whole any consideration of a person's "inner depths" (231–34), and he is certainly right about such early texts, "where identity is given with one's social role and the status it offers, whether one is a lay person or a cleric, a master or a slave, rich or poor. In a way foreign to modernity, one simply is one's social role in the OT." But my point here is precisely that this seems to have changed as time went on through the Second Temple period.
21. Cf. R. Graves (1925).
22. The overlapping vocabulary of the two itself seems to argue for direct influence; see B. Sommer (1998).
23. Or even: the way that later writers conceived of these prophets and their self-presentation.
24. Two recent overviews: S. Weeks (2010), 9–47, and the recent introduction and selected translations in Shupak (2016), esp. 30–51. See also Kugel (1997a).
25. I mean by this the speakers of the various subsections of the biblical book of Proverbs. Nonetheless, Job's starting point is, in a broader perspective, hardly unique: he seems to be connected to the ancient Mesopotamian "righteous sufferer," a figure going back to the Sumerian composition entitled "Man and His God," whose connection to Job was, I believe, first argued by S. N. Kramer in 1954; see Kramer (1959), 114–18. A bit more convincingly, the Akkadian poem *Ludlul bēl nēmeqi* ("I will praise the lord of wisdom") has been compared to Job, along with the "Babylonian Theodicy." For translations: "Poem of the Righteous Sufferer with His God" in Foster (1995), 305–25; W. G. Lambert (1996), 63–89. The matter of literary genre has been taken up (and sometimes questioned) by subsequent scholars; note in particular Jacob Klein's recent study (Klein 2006), 123–44. For all Job's possible generic links to these earlier compositions, he is nearly unique in the Israelite context, though Klein has suggested that the Mesopotamian sufferer (Akk. *eṭlu*) is actually rather similar to the *gever* who is the speaker of Lamentations 3. See further Kugel (2015b).
26. See on this G. Anderson (1991), esp. 84–87; Olyan (2004); D. Lambert (2015).
27. Among others, Davila (1990).
28. Further arguments for this dating: Kugel (1989).
29. Ullendorf (1962).

30. Worthy of mention here is Machinist (1995). P. Machinist seeks to argue that Koheleth's ideas are "the product of systematic, conscious, abstract reasoning" (167): "What is significant in Qohelet is not simply the concern with the subject matter on which human reason focuses and the conclusions which it yields, but an awareness of, a reflection on, the reasoning process itself" (173). I believe this is slightly off the mark, insofar as it fails to mention the *how* of Koheleth's reasoning. His conclusions arise out of a sustained contemplation of his own life, that is, out of his own intellectual autobiography: "First I thought this, then I realized this, after that this thought occurred to me," and so forth. This is the book's most striking feature. Moreover, I believe that Machinist's assessment of the book as a "still early, incomplete exposure to Greek tradition" would require some evidence of this exposure to escape the circularity of its claim.
31. Longman (1990).
32. Further: Kugel (1999a) and (2007a), 511–14. On the root *sh-b-ḥ* in "I *rate* the dead," see Kugel (1999a), 339–40.
33. On the translation "giving birth" rather than "to be born," see Kugel (1999a), 312–13.
34. It may be that this is part of an overall effort on the part of *Jubilees'* author to fill out the personality and role of various women; see on this Halpern-Amaru (1999); also Van der Horst (1998), 73–92; Rosen-Zvi (2006). (He notes on p. 88, however, that "we cannot exclude the possibility of two competing ideologies combined here"; no, indeed.) See more generally, William Loader's ongoing study of attitudes toward sexuality in Second Temple writings, including *Jubilees*: Loader (2007). A review essay by Endres (2015) refers to "the centrality of Rebekah in *Jubilees*."
35. Note that *Jubilees* devotes almost as little to Rebekah's reaction to the events of Gen 29 as the original Genesis narrative. But on the eve of her death, we see a real person.
36. Kugel (2007a), 143–46.
37. On this translation: Kugel (1998a), 323.
38. On this sentence, see Kugel (2010d). Note also that "memorial" here corresponds to Heb *zekher*, that is, "name."
39. On this motif of Potiphar's wife having her "own little private dungeon in the basement," see Kugel (1990a), 51–55.
40. This subject is explored in a series of studies by Louis Feldman, some of which are contained in Feldman (1998a) and (1998b). The great theme of both is indeed the Hellenization of biblical figures, though both books sometimes skip the role of traditional exegetical motifs in shaping Josephus's picture of his heroes and heroines.

15. HUMANS IN SEARCH

1. These overlap to some extent with the category of "learned psalmody," a term introduced by Gunkel's student Sigmund Mowinckel; see Mowinckel (1962), 104–25.
2. Individual lexical items have been thoroughly investigated by Avi Hurvitz (1972), 70–107.
3. In addition, it should be mentioned that this psalm is composed as an alphabetical acrostic, that is, each new line begins with the letter of the alphabet following the first letter of the previous verse. Alphabetical acrostics could, and no doubt were, composed in various periods and for a number of different purposes, but one particular use stands out: arranging successive lines in alphabetical order could help people learn, and then remember, the composition by heart. To accomplish such a purpose, however, the person involved would have to first be able to recite the letters of the alphabet in order;

while we take this simple ability for granted, in times when reading and writing were still specialized skills, an alphabetical acrostic could be of little help to the unlearned. True, it has become a mantra of modern scholarship that this mnemonic purpose is to be judged insignificant or even discounted entirely, but this conclusion seems to me highly unlikely (especially when put forward by scholars who, in my own unofficial survey, have never undertaken to learn a single psalm in Hebrew by heart). In any case, few would argue that the four alphabetical acrostics of Lamentations are pre-exilic, since they all seem to be about the Babylonian conquest of Jerusalem and thus belong, at the earliest, to the first half of the sixth century BCE. Various lexical items in the alphabetical Prov 30:10–31 point to a late date: *shalal* in the sense of "wealth," *ṭeref* in the sense of "food" (also found in another alphabetical composition, Ps 111:5 and Ps 119). See Hurvitz (1972), 130–52.

4. In his only reference to Ps 145, S. Mowinckel fixed on v. 13, asserting that "the idea of His 'eternal kingdom' has more of the character of a rationalized general tenet": Mowinckel (1962), 1:187.
5. Not very long after, *laus perennis* did indeed become a form of piety, in keeping with the New Testament urging, "pray without ceasing" (1 Thess 5:17).
6. The great Psalms classifier Hermann Gunkel listed Psalm 145 along with twenty-five other psalms as belonging to the literary genre (*Gattung*) of "hymn," but within this overall category, the placeless and occasionless psalms seem to constitute a separate (and very small) subcategory.
7. Among the canonical psalms mentioned by Gunkel, there are, apart from lexical and syntactic indications, other signs of lateness: note that Ps 103:7 asserts that God "made known His ways to Moses"; God is said to be "gracious and merciful" in Ps 111:4 as in 145:8, both echoing Exod 34:6 while changing the word order; see on this Hurvitz (1972), 104–6; also Fishbane (1985) as well as the divine near-omnipresence found in Ps 139.
8. See Niditch (2010). For a broad survey of motives and motifs: A. Y. Collins (2012), 553–72.
9. To be sure, Isa 6 contains a description of the heavenly throne, but it gives no account of how Isaiah saw it or of any "tour of heaven," such as the ones mentioned below. The same is true of Micaiah's vision in 1 Kgs 22:19–23. Note that "one like a human being coming with the clouds of heaven" is presented to God in Dan 7:11–14, but this figure is certainly a supernatural being.
10. The subject has been examined several times since the influential essay of W. Bossuet, "Die Himmelsreise der Seele," *ARW* 4 (1901), 136–69, 229–73. See Himmelfarb (1993), Niditch (2010).
11. The scriptural warrant for this heavenly ascent is found in Mal 2:5–8. See further: Kugel (1993). The urtext of this section is the *Aramaic Levi Document* (*ALD*), which, in somewhat fragmentary form, seems to have included an account of Levi's ascent: "Then I was shown visions [. . .] in the vision of visions, and I saw the heaven[s . . .] beneath me, high until it reached the heaven[s . . . opened] the gates of heaven to me, and an angel [. . .] (4:4–6)" See further, Greenfield, Stone, and Eshel (2004), 66. The *ALD*, I believe, is actually a composite text commissioned by the Hasmonean priests to legitimate their claims to political and spiritual leadership of Judah; the composite was basically made of two separate pieces of writing, "Levi's Apocalypse" (consisting of T Levi 2:3–5:3) and "Levi's Priestly Initiation" (corresponding to T Levi chap. 8–9). See Kugel (2006a), 115–68.
12. Translation here follows the version in Feldman et al. (2013), 1725.

13. The heavenly temple may, or may not, be related to the earthly temple in Jerusalem. Hindy Najman has insightfully distinguished four sorts of relationships between the earthly and heavenly shrines, as follows: (1) the earthly temple is said to represent the entire cosmos, while its Holy of Holies represents the heavens themselves or some feature thereof, or an idea of the cosmos or the heavens (she identifies this first category in the writings of Philo and Josephus); (2) the earthly temple corresponds to a heavenly temple in which angels serve before God (a rabbinic conception); (3) those who participate in the earthly temple service or in prayer can, under certain conditions, participate in the angelic service in the heavenly temple, which is conceived to be in operation in the skies (also found in rabbinic sources and underlying such Qumran texts as the *Songs of the Sabbath Sacrifice,* as well as the Jewish *Kedushah* and the Christian *Trisagion/Tersanctus)*; (4) a heavenly temple, prepared before creation in Eden, will ultimately be revealed on earth: "This can be described as an edenic and paradigm of the ultimate heavenly temple" (found in "Testament of Levi," *4 Ezra, 2 Baruch,* NT book of Revelation and Hebrews, etc.). Further: Najman (2014), esp. 116–23; Himmelfarb (1993).
14. Kugel (2015a).
15. Second Temple writers came to include Moses among those who ascended to heaven: see Kugel (1998a), 635–36. Note that some exegetes associated the tower of Babel with an attempt to invade heaven: ibid., pp. 228–29, 238–40.
16. See A. Y. Collins (2012).
17. I hesitate to use the word "mysterious," since it might seem to imply a close proximity to the "mystery religions" in the Greco-Roman orbit. These, however, were generally of a different character, though I would not deny the possibility, or even probability, of some crossover or influence. In general, however, the *mustērion* of Greco-Roman religions concerned religious ritual and esoteric practices shared by their members, who were often sworn to secrecy. The heavenly ascents discussed above were, beyond their particulars, an assertion that God is indeed enthroned in heaven and that He has in fact been approached by this or that biblical hero.
18. For Isaiah, see this chap., n. 9. There are a few partial exceptions — Balaam has to walk an apparently short distance away from Balak's altar in order to meet God (Num 23:3, etc.); Ezekiel is dragged from place to place, and so forth — but in general, prophetic revelations come to pre-exilic prophets where they are.
19. Najman (2014), 133.
20. But see Kugel (1999a), 271–78, and (2007a), 514–17.

16. OUTSIDE THE TEMPLE

1. According to the Pentateuch, only those who had inherited the right from birth — that is, the temple priests and Levites — were allowed to officiate in the temple. People would, of course, flock to Jerusalem from all over the country for the annual pilgrimage festivals, but again, apart from the paschal sacrifice slaughtered for home consumption, the direct service of God was in the hands of the priests. But "according to the Pentateuch" is an important qualifier here, as many writers have shown; the archaeological record and even passages within the Hebrew Bible itself sometimes tell a very different story. On so-called "popular religion" (that is, "what people really did" as opposed to what Scripture says they did), see below, note 3. For some extrabiblical evidence from earlier times, see Gnuse (1997), Zevit (2001), Dever (2005), Lemche (2008), Meyers (2010); specifically for

the post-exilic period, Albertz and Becking (2003), Olyan (2005), E. Stern (2006). As for communal worship outside of the temple, no one knows when, or where, the first synagogue (in the sense of a noncultic "house of worship") was created, but see the review of evidence of the ancient synagogue's development in Levine (2000) esp. 45–80. The oldest *buildings* identified as ancient synagogues in ancient Israel go back only to the first or second centuries BCE, but it is certainly possible that people gathered for worship and study well before that time. In any case, one fact is certainly striking: evidence from various quarters attests to the emergence of the synagogue as an institution even before the destruction of the Jerusalem temple in 70 of the Common Era. This evidence is significant for our subject precisely because it points to the growing importance of prayer and study even before animal sacrifices had ceased.

2. Greenberg (1983a); on the interaction of spontaneity and prescription, see pp. 38–57.
3. Nitzan (1996), 27. To such circumstantial prayers are to be added various other forms of worship that may have taken place in the home or at other gathering places from earliest times, including (though certainly not limited to) acts of worship connected to weddings, healing rituals, burials, rites of mourning, and so forth. The Bible, as well as extrabiblical sources and the archaeological record, all offer ample evidence of some of these; still, it is often difficult to know what to make of such evidence. Does the discovery of a statuette in an excavated site indicate the existence of regular worship there — and if so, is it to be connected to the existence of Laban's *teraphim* (Gen 31:19, etc.) or Micah's apparently family-centered "house of God," equipped with its own ephod and *teraphim* (Jud 17:5)? Can one go further and say, on the basis of such evidence, that identifying Second Temple practices that took place outside the temple were really nothing new? The same question might be asked of the role of vows: while they certainly were a form of "personal" piety, the vowing of sacrifices and the like was practiced throughout the ancient Near East from earliest times; see Niditch (2015), 72–78; note Pagolu (1998), 193–212. All this is in turn connected to a broader issue, the difference between "official" and "popular" religion, whose very opposition is nowadays increasingly rejected as an oversimplification. As Francesca Stavrakopoulou recently observed, "Concepts of popular religion are of most relevance to religions in which a prevailing and culturally accredited dominant source of religious legitimation" is aligned with personal or institutional elites — and ancient Israel largely fails to meet this description. See Stavrakopoulou and Barton (2010), p. 50; cf. Niditch (2010), in the same volume, p. 11. Note in this connection the collection of essays of Albertz (2014), as well as the previous, coauthored volume, Albertz and Schmitt (2012), where the authors argue that ritual objects in the home, the practice of home-based healing rites, and similar phenomena had always existed in the eastern Mediterranean littoral. See further: Keel and Uehlinger (1998).
4. Such prayers thus tend to have an obvious literary character; for one such manifestation, the "scripturalization" of Second Temple period prayers, see Newman (1999).
5. On Ben Sira and prayer, see Reif (2002).
6. Text based on the proposed Hebrew retroversion of Segal (1972), 136–37. See also Reif (2006), 33–70.
7. Swartz (2012).
8. Or perhaps even inside the temple: on the Jerusalem temple's *proseuche* ("chapel," "prayer room") see Schiffman (1991), 166. Fleischer (1990) held that fixed, statutory prayer in Judaism came about as a result of the destruction of the Jerusalem temple in 70 of the Common Era. Another opinion: Heinemann (1964), 17–22, as well as the essays

collected posthumously in Heinemann (1981), 3–73. The question has been revisited by various scholars, including Chazon (2012) and (1992). Note also Schuller (2006).

9. See 1Q9:26–10:1–8, which specifies fixed prayers to be said each day, morning and evening, as well as at the *tequfot,* the beginnings of months, festivals, New Year, and so forth. In general see Falk (1998) and (1999); Davila (2000), 203–38; the essays collected in Chazon (2003); Schuller (1994); Penner et al. (2012). On *berakhot* at Qumran: Schuller (1990); Nitzan (1996), 87–103. Moshe Weinfeld has explored connections between prayers at Qumran and in rabbinic Judaism: Weinfeld (1992a).

10. "Prayers of the Heavenly Lights" would probably have been a more accurate translation of *dibrei hamme'orot,* but this was not to be. In any case, the Hebrew title appears on the back of the first column of 4Q504 and, as Esther Chazon explains further, "probably relates to the work's liturgical function as prayers for the days of the week, with *hamme'orot,* 'luminaries,' serving as a term for the day, the unit of time for which these prayers were designated (compare Gen 1:14–18)": Chazon (2006). These prayers, as well as those designated "festival prayers" (4Q509+505), follow a complex pattern, which integrated daily praise and petition with reflections on events recounted in Scripture — this last an example of what had already become a conventional feature of late biblical prayers. On this phenomenon: Newman (1999). See also Chazon (1992); also Davila (2000), 239–66.

11. This scroll (4Q503) contains a series of such prayers of praise. There is no clear proof that these were sectarian prayers, though they do show a kinship with other prayers found at Qumran that have been so identified. It seems that they were apparently intended to be recited by the community as a whole, marking the onset of daybreak and evening. In this they have a clear continuation in rabbinic Judaism, which had its own fixed prayers for morning and evening.

12. That the prayers are addressed *to* the sun (instead of to its Creator) is apparently what Josephus means by describing this prayer as "idiosyncratic" (ἰδίως), but it seems most unlikely that this is an instance of real sun-worship; cf. the prayer of the Therapeutai below. Another opinion: Jonquière (2007), 54–55.

13. Scholars have rightly concluded that this is an idealized picture, but it is probably not made up out of whole cloth. Certainly the idea of fixed prayers at daybreak and sunset was hardly Philo's invention. See the sources cited in this chap., nn. 8–10.

14. "Apparently," because, as Martin Goodman has pointed out, the Qumran texts that we possess seem to stop just short of saying so explicitly: Goodman (2010), 82. Halakhic and political considerations were certainly connected to the Qumranites' disdain, as was the moral corruption of the priesthood; see Regev (n.d.).

15. Of course, it might be suggested that there was no change at all. After all, quite a few psalms in the Psalter simply say, "Praise God" (Hallelujah) without telling us where or why; perhaps they too were designed to be uttered each day at daybreak or sunset. But if so, why is there no mention of sunrise or sunset in the psalms in question? Why no mention of the establishment of such daily praises elsewhere — in, for example, mention of songs and prayers in the temple service (see, for example, 1 Chron 6 or 16)?

16. In fact, the whole idea of this huge deity was hard to reconcile with the idea of a temple; see again, Isa 66:1. It is certainly true that the footprints on the steps of the 'Ain Dara temple (above, chap. 6) seem to pertain to a deity considerably larger than the overall structure, but this still falls short of the conception of a world-bestriding *only* God whom no physical structure could contain. Perhaps more to the point are the poly-

morphous *ilus* of Mesopotamia, but it is precisely the underlying concept of a polymorphous god, one who is present here but also there, and also in the stars, that ruled out any theoretical contradiction between an earthly temple and a heavenly deity. This was certainly true in Israel as well. Israel's God had always been presented as enthroned on high (Ps 29, etc.); moreover, some of those biblical texts generally recognized as among the most ancient also evoke His interventions from the heavens (Deut 33:26, Jud 5:20, Hab 3:3–6). Nor did more abstract theologies alter this way of thinking (e.g., Deut 26:15). The rabbinic solution to this quandary was the Shekhinah, a kind of concentrated, embodied divine presence found on earth while God Himself dwelt in heaven: see Urbach (1987), 37–65, a figure in some ways comparable to that of interventionist Wisdom in the *Wisdom of Solomon*.

17. Kugel (1998a), 75–77.
18. On their carrying Israel's "repentances" on high: Kugel (2010c). See also T Levi 3:5. Guy Stroumsa has observed that throughout the Mediterranean world, "the end of animal sacrifice gave rise to new forms of worship, with a concern for personal salvation, scriptural study, rituals like praying and fasting, and the rise of religious communities and monasticism": Stroumsa (2012), 85.
19. Had the text said merely "bloodless," this might be attributed to the sanctuary's location (in heaven); but "reasonable and bloodless" seems to evidence the apparent assessment of *bloody* sacrifices as irrational.
20. See on this Gerhards (2007), 27–28.
21. It might be argued that offering the regular *tamid* sacrifice twice a day in the temple (Exod 29:38–42 and Num 28:3–8) was likewise a way of establishing contact. But such a claim disregards the very nature of the temple, which was, and always had been, conceived as the deity's own home. What need was there to establish contact? On the contrary, the *tamid* sacrifice can be offered nowhere except within the temple, where its lambs' carcasses are deemed to be no less than "My food" (Num 28:2), and the smoke rising from the altar provided a "pleasing odor" (Exod 29:41, Num 28:2) for a deity who must not be far off. There is a world of difference between these temple-bound sacrifices and words whispered into the wind from nowhere in particular and asking for nothing, not even acknowledgment.
22. On 4Q380-301, see Schuller (1986), 21–60.
23. First published by Newsom (1985). An overview and survey of current scholarship is found in Davila (2000), 83–167.
24. Again, see Newsom (2004).
25. See the discussion in Newsom (1985), 65–67.
26. As Rabbi Joshua ben Levi is reported to have said, "Statutory prayers were established in correspondence to the [morning and evening] *tamid* sacrifices [in the temple]." Jerusalem Talmud *Berakhot* chap. 3 *halakhah* 6; Babylonian Talmud *Berakhot* 26b.
27. See the various essays collected in Watts (2001). I still find the opening essay, Peter Frei's reconstruction of the process, basically convincing; his critics in the other essays offer some probing questions, but in the end the role of Persian authorization seems basically sound. See now the further refinements of Knoppers and Levinson (2007); also, Carr (2005), (2011a), and (2011b). From this last: "Ultimately, this debate appears unresolvable with the data present at our disposal" (p. 218); however, Carr properly distinguishes between Persian sponsorship and Jewish *claims* of Persian sponsorship, as well as expressing doubts that such matters truly were ever handled at the highest level of the

Persian bureaucracy, Persian sponsorship probably being executed, in this as in other matters, "at a resolutely local level" (219).

28. Apparently, though not irrefutably, nearly identical to our Pentateuch. See Rubenstein (1995).
29. With regard to the Pentateuch itself, see the recent studies collected in Gertz et al. (2016), the product of a yearlong study group at the Institute for Advanced Studies, Hebrew University of Jerusalem. The resulting essays still reflect fundamental (and irreconcilable) disagreements about the Pentateuch's formation.
30. A highly fragmentary text has been argued to be an ancestor of the book of Esther, but the relationship is distant at best. On 4Q550 *Proto-Esther* see Milik (1992), White-Crawford (1994), Wechsler (2000).
31. Among many recent treatments, Lim (2010), esp. 314–19.
32. Exactly when and why this idea began to take hold has been the subject of some debate. Scholars used to focus on its very last stage, the moment of the "canonization of Scripture," which was treated as a specific event in history: according to this approach, the Hebrew Bible (more or less as we know it) was created when an authoritative group of Jews got together at Jamnia (Yavneh) in the late first century CE and, reviewing various candidates for inclusion in the biblical canon, established what the Bible's final contents should be. For some time, that "moment" was identified as the "Council of Jamnia [Yavneh]," ca. 90 CE, but this hypothesis has been largely abandoned; see., e.g., Lewis (1964), J. Barton (2007), 23–34. In truth, there is no evidence of such an event.
33. Note that this three-part division is reflected in other texts as well: Philo of Alexandria refers to the "laws and oracles delivered through the mouth of prophets," which would include the five books of Moses (i.e., Torah) as well as the later historical and prophetic books as well as "psalms and anything else which fosters and perfects knowledge and piety" (*Vita Contemplativa* 25). In the New Testament, Luke 24:44 refers to "the law of Moses, the Prophets, and the Psalms," and so on. While many scholars agree that "The Torah and the Prophets" (the latter including the historical books from Joshua to 1 and 2 Kings) was a widely recognized designation by the end of the second century BCE, the third category remained fluid for a few more centuries. The complicated issues of the growth of the canon and the idea of a Bible are well summarized in Stone (2011), 122–50.
34. Indeed, as K. van der Toorn has pointed out, to this day the Torah scroll in synagogues is treated in ways reminiscent of the adulation given to cult statues in ancient Mesopotamia: bowing down as the "god" passed by, touching the hem of one's garment (*talleth*) to the god's garment, and so forth. Van der Toorn (1997), 229–48.
35. The Qumran caves were thus found to contain a particular type of commentary called *pesher*, whereby the commentator seeks to connect the events of his own time to the words of prophets who had prophesied hundreds of years earlier: there is a *pesher* to Habakkuk, a *pesher* to Zephaniah, a *pesher* to Psalms, and so forth. This sort of interpretation is likewise exemplified in passages not specifically identified as *pesher*, such as the "midrash of the Well" (CD 6:3–10), explaining an incident in the book of Numbers, when the Israelites are reported to have sung a somewhat cryptic song after discovering a well in the wilderness: "Spring up, O well—they sang about it—The well that the chieftains dug, which the nobles of the people unearthed, With the scepter, with their staves" (Num 21:17–18). To the Qumran sectarians, these words could be understood to refer to an event in their own recent history, when their community was founded: "The *well* is the Torah, and *those who dug it* are those of Israel who returned [in penance]

and left the land of Judah to dwell in the land of Damascus. God called them all *princes* because they beseeched Him and because their glory was never gainsaid by any man's mouth. The *Scepter* refers to the expounder of the Torah . . . and the *nobles of the people* are those who came to dig the well with the *staves* with which the *Scepter* had decreed to walk about with" (*Damascus Document,* 6:3–10). For this translation, see Kugel (1998a), 818. Each of the italicized words — the well, the diggers, the princes, the scepter, and the staves — is being interpreted to refer to a specific element in the community's founding, whose leaders dug out (correctly exposited) the Torah, following the teachings of their leader, the "Scepter" aka the "expounder of the Torah." See further the pioneering studies Finkel (1963), Rabinowitz (1973), Horgan (1979), and Brooke (1985). More recently: Kister (1992), Mandel (2001), and Horgan (2002).

36. See further: von Rad (1968), 267–280; he cites 2 Chron 15:2–7, 19:6, 32:7–8, 30:6–9. Note also R. A. Mason (1984), and J. Barton (2007), esp. 154–78. Among Barton's examples: 1 Chron 15:2–7.
37. Again, Barton (2007), 156: "The Former Prophets or 'Deuteronomistic History' was probably understood in this way well before the New Testament era, as Martin Noth has observed: 'When this [sc. the post-exilic] community preserved and maintained the ancient narrative tradition of the history of Israel along with it [sc. the Law], it was understood as a collection of historical examples of the attitude of man to the law and its consequences.'"
38. Barton (2007), 99.
39. To be sure, these were not the only sorts of prayers recited during this period. But the Qumran *Songs of the Sabbath Sacrifice* may likewise be seen to highlight the distance separating humanity from God: it is no longer we humans who encounter Him in the earthly temple, offering sacrificial animals as a "pleasing scent" to a deity who can't be far off. Rather, the temple service has been transposed to somewhere above the clouds, and at best we humans can only aspire to be symbolically joined to this heavenly worship by singing "Holy, holy, holy." The Qumran *Thanksgiving Hymns* illuminate another aspect of this distance. They seem to be inward-looking spiritual exercises (again, reminiscent of Ps 119) whose focus is strikingly on the self of the individual supplicant. This subject has been explored at length by Carol Newsom; see Newsom (2004), 191–286.
40. The fact that human interpreters felt free to modify the meaning of a scriptural verse might seem to contradict the equation of Scripture with God's presence, but it is well to remember what Scripture had become. Its actual words were (or were becoming) unchangeable. "Interpreters" of an earlier day could simply tamper with the text itself, inserting words, sentences, or even whole chapters on their own initiative. Now it was necessary to claim that the interpreter's changed meanings were in fact the text's *original* meanings — and to justify these new meanings by hanging them on some clever hook from within the Bible's own words.

17. PERSONAL RELIGION

1. Indeed, the prominence of the individual seems to arrive more or less simultaneously in Deuteronomy and the book of Ezekiel; see B. Levinson (2010), 64–67, 72–74, 79–81.
2. See the recent survey of such questions in H. MacKay (2001), 11–20.
3. Ravid (2000).
4. Too many to list here; see the pioneering work of Schiffman (1975), 77–133.

5. These words, spoken by Isaac to Jacob and Esau, might therefore appear to be restricted to these two siblings; but the plural "be loving of your *brothers*" along with the phrases "as a man *loves himself*" and "loving each other *as themselves*," identify this passage as an allusion to Lev 19:18.
6. At Qumran as elsewhere, Lev 19:18 was read in the light of the preceding prohibition of Lev 19:17, "You shall not hate your brother in your heart." Further: Kugel (1987).
7. These two are now widely recognized as a *merism*, the naming of two extremes so as to include everything inside them, just as "night and day" means "all the time." See Honeyman (1952).
8. Some Jews (notably some Karaites, who flourished in medieval and early modern times; apparently the Samaritans as well, and probably some Jews in more ancient days) thus maintained that this commandment does not involve actually tying anything to one's arm or head. Rather, exponents of this position argue, its aim is to instruct Jews to hold the Torah's words dear, binding them close, as it were, to one's head and heart. And the exponents do have a point. One of the four verses, Deut 11:18, says more specifically: "You shall put these words of Mine on your heart and on your soul; and you shall tie them for a sign upon your arm, and they shall be as *ṭoṭafot* between your eyes." The second part of the sentence seems to be a metaphorical reiteration of the first part: "Don't ever let these words of Mine be far from you! Tie them to yourself, keep them forever close!" Such a reading is supported by other verses in the Bible. Prov 6:20–21 says, "My son, keep your father's commandment and do not neglect your mother's teachings; *tie them upon your heart* forever and *bind them around your neck*." This certainly does not seem to be a reference to *tefillin;* is it not simply the case that the parents' teachings are to be cherished and held close, and for that reason are compared to some sort of ornament worn close to the body? The lovesick maiden of the Song of Songs similarly says to her beloved, "Set me as a signet upon your hand, as a signet on your arm" (8:6), once again in the sense of, "Don't forget me, not for one minute!" Once again, an external ornament is invoked to signify metaphorical closeness. Another passage in Proverbs reads: "My son, do not forget my teaching, and may your heart keep my commandments . . . bind them around your neck, write them on the writing tablet of your heart" (3:1–3). Just as there does not seem to be any *physical* writing tablet on a person's heart, so the previous "bind them around your neck" ought likewise to be seen as figurative speech, a metaphor for keeping the parent's words constantly in mind. So, all in all, it might seem that the whole idea of binding the *tefillin* to one's arm and head is a kind of literalization, turning an originally metaphorical commandment into a physical act. These have been studied recently in Cohn (1998), 55–87. The earliest material evidence of *tefillin* is found among the Dead Sea Scrolls and was first discussed by Haberman (1954), cf. Yadin (1969). The Qumran *tefillin* arguably go back to the second century. In all, remnants of approximately forty-five separate parchment slips traced to Qumran have been identified as belonging to *tefillin* or *mezuzot,* as well as around twenty-five *tefillin* boxes (*battim*); see the discussion and sources cited in Cohn (1998), 55–79. The literary evidence for *tefillin* is somewhat ambiguous: see the Septuagint translation of Exod 13; *Letter of Aristeas* 157–158; Philo, *SpecLeg* 137–42; Josephus, *Jewish Antiquities* 4:213. Cohn expresses doubt that these literary sources refer to physical *tefillin,* but the issue remains controversial. Philo's understanding of this commandment as referring to *tefillin* is maintained in N. G. Cohen (1995), 144–55. On who actually wore *tefillin:* S. Stern (1994); S. J. D. Cohen (1999), 106–24.

9. See above, note 7.
10. See further Kugel (2008a).
11. Usually translated as "every deed," but *ma'aseh* also means "person" or "offspring," especially in late- (and post-) biblical Hebrew, e.g., Prov 31:31 (surely this ideal wife is not being praised by inanimate objects, but by her sons "at the gates," that is, the most honored place in the town).
12. Note that some writings seem to suggest that martyrs in particular will merit resurrection, perhaps because their lives were cut short. Such was the case with one martyr's death as recounted in 2 Maccabees: "A certain Razis, one of the elders of Jerusalem, was denounced to Nicanor as a man who loved his compatriots and was very well thought of and for his goodwill was called father of the Jews. Being surrounded, Razis fell upon his own sword, preferring to die nobly rather than to fall into the hands of sinners and suffer outrages unworthy of his noble birth. But in the heat of the struggle he did not hit exactly, and the crowd was now rushing in through the doors. He courageously ran up on the wall, and bravely threw himself down into the crowd. But as they quickly drew back, a space opened and he fell in the middle of the empty space. Still alive and aflame with anger, he rose, and though his blood gushed forth and his wounds were severe he ran through the crowd; and standing upon a steep rock, with his blood now completely drained from him, he tore out his entrails, took them in both hands, and hurled them at the crowd, *calling upon the Lord of life and spirit to give them back to him again.* Such was the manner of his death": (2 Macc 14:37–46). Similarly: "With these words the mother of the seven [future martyrs] exhorted each of them and persuaded them to die rather than transgress the commandment of God, and they knew full well themselves that those who die for the sake of God *live unto God,* as do Abraham and Isaac and Jacob and all the patriarchs" (4 Macc 16:25).
13. Ezekiel's vision of the valley of dry bones (Ezek 37:1–10) certainly suggested such a thing was possible, though some people objected; see below.
14. Such was certainly the understanding of God/the gods in an earlier day. Henri Frankfort put it well: "The ancient Near East considered kingship the very basis of civilization. Only savages could live without a king. Security, peace, and justice could not prevail without a ruler to champion them": Frankfort (1948), p. 3; cf. Th. Jacobsen (1976), 78–91. The idea that God/the gods were divine rulers sometimes led to the depiction of the earthly king as a priest-like figure: for Assyria and the national deity Aššur, see recently Pongratz-Leisten (2015) and Karlsson (2016), esp. 93–103; Brettler (1989).
15. This is of course related to the broader theme of apocalyptic eschatology, but to do more than merely evoke this subject in the present context would lead us far astray. Among numerous studies, see the excellent overview and history of scholarship by Knibb (1992); in addition, the numerous studies by John Collins, including Collins (1979), (1991), and (1995).
16. And even before that, the ruler of His land. This theme is connected to that of the divine council; see Kugel (2003), 122–24, 235–36, and (2007a), 545–46, and sources cited there.
17. Again, Brettler (1989). As for the apologetic motif of God's *everlasting* kingship in Dan 3:33, etc., note also Tobit 13:1: "Blessed be the living God, whose kingdom is for all ages" (text following 4Q200 6:5). Here we are back at the *longue durée* of *Jubilees.*
18. The same assertion appears in Aramaic in Dan 3:33 and cf. 4:31. Note that *malkhut* came to be favored in late biblical Hebrew over the related terms *mamlakhah* and *melukhah*

used in standard biblical Hebrew. Of the ninety-one occurrences of the word *malkhut* in the Hebrew Bible, all but five appear in late biblical texts. In general, the nominalizing suffix *-ut*, while present in many Semitic languages in different periods, became increasingly common in late biblical Hebrew and Mishnaic Hebrew; see Kutscher (1982), 81, 84, and Rabin (1991), 11.

19. This subject has been researched by numerous scholars, among them Hengel (1977), R. Brown (1994) and (1998), J. P. Meier (2009); note also Joseph Fitzmyer (2007), who takes up, among other thngs, Israel Knohl's controversial thesis: Knohl (2000).
20. A number of rabbinic texts also use the phrase to refer to the somewhat exceptional revelation of God in physical form: "Your children, O Lord, beheld Your kingship on the shores of the Red Sea . . ." based on the midash in Mekhilta deR. Ishmael *zeh eli.*
21. Mishnah *Berakhot* 2:2. On the version "accept the kingship of God" (and not "the yoke of God's kingship"), see Frankel (2014).
22. The views attributed to Jesus in the Gospels have been much discussed: see in particular the parables in Matt 13:24–50; 18:23–25; 20:1–16; 22:1–14; 25:1–13; Mark 4:26–34. In some of these as well as elsewhere, God's kingship is asserted to be already here, although Matt 5:10 remains somewhat ambiguous: "Blessed are those who are persecuted for righteousness' sake, for theirs is the kingdom of heaven"; cf. Matt 12:28. Elsewhere, however, the revelation of God's kingship is still an event in the future; Matt 8:11–12, Luke 13:28–29; Mark 9:1 (= Matt 16:28, Luke 9:27).
23. Similarly, a number of Dead Sea Scrolls texts assert that God's kingdom is in heaven, only visible, apparently, to those who ascend on high: 4Q286 *Blessings*, frag 7 col 1:6; 4Q287 *Blessings* frag 2:11; 4Q299 *Mysteries* frag 9:3; 4Q400 *ShirShabb*[a] 1:3; 2:4, etc.
24. Even if some rabbinic sages urged people not to be like servants who serve their master on condition of being rewarded (m. *Abot* 1:3), the expectation of individual reward and punishment was a fundamental of rabbinic theology. Further: Urbach (1975), 402–4, 436–44.

18. SOME CONCLUSIONS

1. Starting with terrace farming, iron farming tools, and a more effective waterproof plaster to line cisterns; see Kugel (2007a), 383–84.
2. That is, its situation at the crossroads of three continents, combined with its relatively small population (due to the paucity of natural sources of drinking water), leaving it open to relatively easy conquest by its strong and irrigation-rich neighbors.
3. In Israel's case, the rise and fall of successive empires, bringing about the region's exposure to new ideas in cycles of conquest or domination by Hittites, Egyptians, Aegeans, Babylonians, Assyrians, Neo-Babylonians, Persians, and Greeks.
4. Most conspicuously, the reversion of David's united monarchy into the divided polities of Israel and Judah, followed by the Babylonian exile and the post-exilic priestly state of Judah.
5. The late-biblical soul might be one example.
6. The German (later Swiss) philosopher and psychiatrist Karl Jaspers (1883–1969) argued that the period from the eighth to the third centuries BCE was a pivotal one in human history, a time in which great thinkers somehow appeared more or less simultaneously in different places across the globe and in relatively short order changed the whole nature of human thought: Confucius and Lao-tzu in China, Gautama Buddha in India,

Zarathustra in Persia, Homer and the early philosophers in Greece, as well as Israel's great prophets from the eighth to the sixth centuries. Jaspers called this period the Axial Age, and while his characterization of it, along with his inclusion of six rather different centuries (just look at the biblical evidence!) as constituting a single period, has not gone unopposed by other thinkers, his idea has continued to inspire studies in disparate domains. See the survey by Eisenstadt (1986), also Assmann (2014). It must be noted that, from the standpoint of the present study, the very period Jaspers identified in ancient Israel is hardly altogether "axial," since—to the extent that we can even attach approximate dates to biblical texts that were constantly revised and re-edited—the Axial Age ends up including both the old, pre-axial sort of thinking Jaspers describes alongside the very different outlook that gradually replaced it.

7. Here I am referring to the explanation offered by Julian Jaynes (1920–1997), for many years a professor of psychology at Princeton University; unlike Jaspers, Jaynes had a definite theory as to what brought about the great shift he charted in the history of human thought, presented in Jaynes (1976). Jaynes's evidence of such a change in ancient thought comes primarily from Homer's *Iliad.* Like Bruno Snell before him (see above, chapter 1), Jaynes was struck by the absence of words describing consciousness or ordinary mental acts in Homer's Greek: "There is in general no consciousness in the Iliad. I am saying 'in general' because I shall mention some exceptions later. And in general therefore, no words for consciousness or mental acts . . . There is also no concept of will or word for it, the concept developing curiously late in Greek thought." "The characters of the Iliad," Jaynes observed, "do not sit down and think out what to do. They have no conscious minds such as we say we have, and certainly no introspections. It is impossible for us with our subjectivity to appreciate what it was like": Jaynes (1976), 69–70, 72.

Note that this claim is sometimes made of biblical Hebrew as well. The misuse of such lexical arguments—as in, for example, Boman (1970)—was properly criticized by James Barr; see Barr (1961) and other works, but his critique has had a chilling effect on the broader examination of biblical representations (or lack thereof) of thinking in general, and in particular of the "inner depths" (discussed in chapters 11 and 14). See recently D. Lambert (2016b); also Carasik (2006).

Jaynes's observations about Homer open the way to his overall thesis, namely, that human brains in ancient times functioned quite differently from our brains nowadays. His argument is, above all, physiological. Human brains consist of left and right hemispheres; most of the brain's important functions are represented, at least in part, in both hemispheres, so that "if one side is injured, the other side can compensate." The exception is our capacity for speech, which in most brains is located exclusively on the left side, in Broca's area and Wernicke's area. This is particularly surprising since, in physiological terms, "the neurological structure necessary for language exists in the right hemisphere as well as the left . . . In a child, a major lesion of Wernicke's area on the left hemisphere, or of the underlying thalamus which connects it to the brainstem, produces transfer of the whole speech mechanism to the right hemisphere" (pp. 102–3).

Jaynes therefore sought to argue that the now-dormant right hemispheric area corresponding to Wernicke's area in the left was, in ancient times, altogether active. "The language of men was involved with only one hemisphere in order to leave the other free for the language of the gods." That is, for centuries the right hemisphere was abuzz with orders emanating from various deities, until its speech center eventually shut down, leaving only the human speech emanating from the left hemisphere. Such was the beginning of modern human consciousness.

This bold hypothesis has naturally been met by a number of obvious questions. What initiated the change described by Jaynes, and what caused human brains in various locations all across the globe to undergo it more or less simultaneously, all of them losing their right hemisphere's capacity for speech? And how could such a fundamental change take place in what amounts to an evolutionary nanosecond: this right-brain speech center was still active in the time of Homer (or, in biblical terms, the time of the eighth-century prophet Amos) but then came to be utterly shut down only a few centuries later (in biblical terms, in the time of the fourth- or third-century author of Ecclesiastes). Note that Jaynes specifically contrasts Amos and Ecclesiastes in this connection, p. 296.

Moreover, in many societies nowadays (as we have seen), prophet-like figures continue to receive messages from the gods; were they exempted from this otherwise widespread change in brain function, and is this exemption attested as well in other aspects of their ordinary mental life? In this connection, scholars have also been disturbed by the general absence of reference in Jaynes's book to the work of anthropologists and ethnographers focusing on civilizations far distant from those of both ancient Greece and modern Europe and America. Even if one narrows the focus to theistic religions alone, God/the gods manifest themselves in different ways among different peoples — and divine speech or visual hallucinations are apparently not a sine qua non. Finally, any student of non-Western religions knows that the gods are usually part of an entire ecosystem of thought; presumed divine speech may have been the Prime Mover in the creation of such systems, but this remains to be proven. Considered together, these arguments have caused some scholars to back off from Jaynes's neurologically based approach. But even if his theory has thus far failed to win the day, we are still left with his opening set of observations, paralleled by those of Bruno Snell discussed earlier, as well as by those of Jaspers and other thinkers (though not quite lining up chronologically with them). Despite their differences, such scholars agree that some sort of fundamental change did occur within a few centuries somewhere in the first millennium BCE — as indeed the various biblical texts surveyed herein also seem to indicate. But how is this change to be understood?

8. Geertz (1973), 36–37. Geertz does not connect these unfathomable states to what might be called the Balinese sense of self; he prefers speaking of "human nature" in the above passage, or, in a passage cited earlier, in chapter 3, "the concept of person" or "selfhood." Here is the latter passage (Geertz [1983], 59) in its entirety:

> The concept of person is, in fact, an excellent vehicle by means of which to examine this whole question of how to go about poking into another people's turn of mind. In the first place, some sort of concept of this kind . . . exists in recognizable form among all social groups. The notions of what persons *are* may be, from our point of view, sometimes more than a little odd. They may be conceived to dart about nervously at night shaped like fireflies. Essential elements of their psyches, like hatred, may be thought to be lodged in granular black bodies within their livers, discoverable upon autopsy. They may share their fates with *Doppelgänger* beasts, so that when the beast sickens or dies they sicken or die too. But at least some conception of what a human individual is,

as opposed to a rock, an animal, a rainstorm, or a god, is, so far as I can see, universal.

Yet, at the same time, as these offhand examples suggest, the actual conceptions involved vary from one group to the next, and often quite sharply. The Western conception of the person as a bounded, unique, more or less integrated motivational and cognitive universe, a dynamic center of awareness, emotion, judgment, and action organized into a distinctive whole and set contrastively both against other such wholes and against its social and natural background, is, however incorrigible it may seem to us, a rather peculiar idea within the context of the world's cultures. Rather than attempting to place the experience of others within the framework of such a conception, which is what the extolled "empathy" in fact usually comes down to, understanding them demands setting that conception aside and seeing their experiences within the framework of their own idea of what selfhood is. And for Java, Bali, and Morocco, at least, that idea differs markedly not only from our own but, no less dramatically and no less instructively, from one to the other.

WORKS CITED

Achenbach, R. 2007. "The Pentateuch, the Prophets, and the Torah in the Fifth and Fourth Centuries BCE." In Lipschits et al. (2011), 253–74.

Adams, G. 2005. "The Cultural Grounding of Personal Relationship: Enemyship in North American and West African Worlds." *Journal of Personality and Social Psychology* 88: 948–68.

Adler, D. S., et al. 2014. "Early Levallois Technology and the Lower to Middle Paleolithic Transition in the Southern Caucasus." *Science* 26: 1609–13.

Aiello, L. 1994. "The Expensive Tissue Hypothesis: Co-evolution of the Brain and the Digestive System in Humans and Other Primates." *International Journal of Anthropology* 9: 166–95.

———. 1995: "The Expensive-Tissue Hypothesis: The Brain and the Digestive System in Human and Primate Evolution." *Current Anthropology* 36: 199–221.

Aitkin, J. 2002. "Divine Will and Providence." In Egger-Wenzel (2002), 282–301.

Albertz, R. 1994. A History of Israelite Religion in the Old Testament Period. Louisville, KY: Westminster/John Knox Press.

———. 2008: "Family Religion in Ancient Israel and Its Surrounds." In *Household and Family Religion*, ed. J. Bodel and S. Olyan, 89–112. Oxford: Blackwell.

———, ed. 2014. *Family and Household Religion.* Winona Lake, IN: Eisenbrauns.

Albertz, R., and B. Becking, eds. 2003. *Yahwism After the Exile: Perspectives on Israelite Religion in the Persian Era.* Assen: Van Gorcum.

Albertz, R., and R. Schmitt. 2012: *Family and Household Religion in Ancient Israel and the Levant.* Winona Lake, IN: Eisenbrauns.

Albright, W. F. 1968. *Yahweh and the Gods of Canaan: A Historical Analysis of Two Contrasting Faiths.* Garden City, NY: Doubleday.

Alexander, P. S. 1999. "The Demonology of the Dead Sea Scrolls." In Flint and VanderKam (1999), 2:331–53.

Alperson-Afil, N. 2008. "Continual Fire-Making by Hominins at Gesher Benot Ya'aqov, Israel." *Quaternary Science Reviews* 27: 1733–39.

Alperson-Afil, N., and N. Goren-Inbar. 2006. "Out of Africa and into Eurasia with Controlled Use of Fire: The Evidence from Benot Ya'aqov, Israel." *Archaeology, Ethnology and Anthropology of Eurasia* 4:28, 63–78.

Alter, Robert. 1978. "Biblical Type Scenes and the Uses of Convention." *Critical Inquiry* 5: 355–68.

———. 1981. *The Art of Biblical Narrative.* New York: Basic Books.

Altman, A. 2004. *The Historical Prologue of the Hittite Vassal Treaties.* Ramat Gan, Israel: Bar-Ilan University Press.

Anderson, G. 1987. *Sacrifice and Offerings in Ancient Israel: Studies in Their Social and Political Importance.* Atlanta: Scholars Press, 1987.

———. 1990. "The Interpretation of Gen. 1:1 in the Targums." *Catholic Biblical Quarterly* 52: 21–29.

———. 1991. *A Time to Mourn, a Time to Dance.* University Park: Pennsylvania State University Press.

Anderson, G., and J. S. Kaminsky. 2013. *The Call of Abraham: Essays on the Election of Israel in Honor of Jon D. Levenson.* Notre Dame, IN: Notre Dame University Press.

Anderson, Walter T. 1997. *The Future of the Self: Inventing the Postmodern Person.* New York: Penguin Putnam.

Arend, W. 1933. *Die Typische Szenen bei Homer.* Berlin: Weidmann, 1933.

Aserinsky, E., and N. Kleitman. 1953. "Regularly Occurring Periods of Eye Motility, and Concomitant Phenomena, During Sleep." *Science* 118: 273–74.

Assmann, J. 1997. *Moses the Egyptian.* Cambridge, MA: Harvard University Press.

———. 2014. "Ancient Egypt and the Theory of the Axial Age." In his *From Akhenaten to Moses: Ancient Egypt and Religious Change.* Cairo: American University in Cairo Press.

Atran, S. 2002. *In Gods We Trust: The Evolutionary Landscape of Religion.* New York: Oxford University Press.

Auerbach, E. 1957. "Odysseus' Scar." In his *Mimesis: The Representation of Reality in Western Literature,* 1–20. Garden City, NY: Doubleday Anchor Books.

Aune, D. 1983. *Prophecy in Early Christianity and the Ancient Mediterranean World.* Grand Rapids, MI: Eerdmans.

Baines, J. 2000. "Egyptian Deities in Context." In Porter (2000), 9–78.

Banani, A., and S. Vryonis. 1977. *Individualism and Conformity in Classical Islam.* Wiesbaden: Harrassowitz.

Barr, J. 1961. *Semantics of Biblical Language.* London: Oxford University Press.

———. 1993. *The Garden of Eden and the Hope of Immortality.* Minneapolis: SCM Press.

Barresi, J., and R. Marten. 2013. "History as Prologue: Western Theories of the Self." In *The Oxford Handbook of the Self,* edited by S. Gallagher, 33–56. Oxford: Oxford University Press.

Barrett, J. 1997. "Anthropomorphism, Intentional Agents, and Conceptualizing God." PhD diss., Cornell University.

———. 2000. "Exploring the Natural Foundations of Religion." *Trends in Cognitive Sciences* 4: 29–34.

Barton, J. 2007. *Oracles of God: Perceptions of Ancient Prophecy in Israel After the Exile.* New York: Oxford University Press.

Baumgarten, J. M. 1985–86: "The Qumran Songs Against Demons." *Tarbiz* 55: 441–22.

Beavan, V., J. Read, and C. Cartwright. 2011. "The Prevalence of Voice-Hearers in the General Population: A Literature Review." *Journal of Mental Health* 20: 281–92.

Beck, J. 2003. "Why Did Moses Strike Out?: The Narrative-Geographical Shaping of Moses' Disqualification in Numbers 20:1–13." *Westminster Theological Journal* 65: 135–48.

Beckman, G. 1999. *Hittite Diplomatic Texts.* Atlanta: Scholars Press.

Beckwith, R. T. 1999. "The Early History of the Psalter." *Tyndale Bulletin* 46: 1–27.

Beentjes, P. C. 2002. "Theodicy in the Wisdom of Ben Sira." In *Theodicy in the World of the Bible,* edited by A. Laato et al., 509–24. Leiden: Brill.

Bennett, M. R., and P. M. S. Hacker. 2013: *The History of Cognitive Neuroscience.* Chichester, UK: Wiley-Blackwell.

Bentall, R. P., and P. D. Slade. 1985. "Reality Testing and Auditory Hallucinations: A Signal Detection Analysis." *British Journal of Clinical Psychology* 24: 159–69.

Berger, P. L., and T. Luckman. 1967. *The Social Construction of Reality.* Garden City, NY: Doubleday.

Bernstein, M. 1997. "Pseudepigraphy in the Qumran Scrolls." In *Pseudepigraphic Perspectives,* edited by E. Chazon et al., 1–26. Leiden: Brill.

Berquist, J. L. 2007. "Psalms, Postcolonialism, and the Construction of the Self." In *Approaching Yehud: New Approaches to the Study of the Persian Period,* edited by J. L. Berquist, 195–202. Atlanta: Society of Biblical Literature.

Beyerlin, W. 1965. *Origins and History of the Oldest Sinaitic Traditions.* Translated by S. Rudman. Oxford: Blackwell.

Bezzel, H. 2009. "The Suffering of the Elect: Variations on a Theological Problem in Jer 15:10–21." In *Prophecy in the Book of Jeremiah,* ed. H. M. Barstad and R. Kratz, 48–73. Berlin: De Gruyter.

Block, N., et al. 2002. *The Nature of Consciousness: Philosophical Debates.* Cambridge, MA: MIT Press.

Bloch, Y. 2013. "Sĕgullâ — A Re-examination of the Meaning of the Term Based on Two Assyrian Documents from the Thirteenth Century BCE." (Hebrew) *Shenaton* 21: 111–40.

Bloom, P. 2007. "Religion Is Natural." *Developmental Science* 10: 147–51.

Boddy, J. 1988. "Spirits and Selves in Northern Sudan: The Cultural Therapeutics of Possession and Trance." *American Ethnologist* 15: 4–27.

———. 1989. *Wombs and Alien Spirits: Women, Men and the Zar Cult in Northern Sudan.* Madison: University of Wisconsin Press.

Bohak, G. 2008. *Ancient Jewish Magic: A History.* Cambridge: Cambridge University Press.

Boman, Th. 1970. *Hebrew Thought Compared with Greek.* New York: Norton.

Bourguignon, E. 1976. *Possession.* San Francisco: Chandler and Sharp.

Bowley, J. E. 1998. "Prophets and Prophecy at Qumran." In *The Dead Sea Scrolls After Fifty Years,* edited by P. Flint and J. C. VanderKam, 354–78. Leiden: Brill.

Boyer, P. 2001. *Religion Explained: The Evolutionary Origins of Religious Thought.* New York: Basic Books.

Brakke, D., et al. 2005. *Religion and Self in Antiquity.* Bloomington: Indiana University Press.

Brand, M. 2011. "'At the Entrance Sin Is Crouching': The Source of Sin and Its Nature as Portrayed in Second Temple Literature." PhD diss., New York University.

Brettler, M. 1989. *God Is King: Understanding an Israelite Metaphor.* Sheffield: Sheffield Academic.

Brooke, G. J. 1985. *Exegesis at Qumran.* Sheffield: JSOT Press.

———. 2006. "Prophecy and Prophets in the Dead Sea Scrolls." In Floyd and Haak (2006), 151–65.

———. 2009. "Prophets and Prophecy in the Qumran Scrolls and the New Testament." In *Text, Thought, and Practice in Qumran and Early Christianity,* edited by R. A. Clements et al., 31–48. Leiden: Brill.

Brooke, G. J., et al. 2008. *Significance of Sinai: Traditions About Sinai and Divine Revelation.* Leiden: Brill.

Brown, D. E. 1991. *Human Universals.* Philadelphia: Temple University Press.

Brown, R. 1994 and 1998. *The Death of the Messiah: From Gethsemane to the Grave.* Vols 1 and 2. New Haven: Yale University Press.
Burkert, W. 1985. *Greek Religion: Archaic and Classical.* Oxford: Blackwell.
———. 1996. *Creation of the Sacred.* Cambridge, MA: Harvard University Press.
Bynum, C. 1980. "Did the Twelfth Century Discover the Individual?" *Journal of Ecclesiastical History* 31: 1–17.
———. 2005. *Metamorphosis and Identity.* New York: Zone Books.
Calduch-Benages, N., and J. Vermeylen, eds. 1999. *Treasures of Wisdom: Studies in Ben Sira and the Book of Wisdom: Festschrift M. Gilbert.* Leuven: Leuven University Press.
Carasik, M. 2000: "The Limits of Omniscience." *Journal of Biblical Literature* 119: 221–32.
———. 2006. *Theologies of the Mind in Biblical Israel.* New York: Peter Lang.
Caroll, R. P. 1981. *From Chaos to Covenant: Uses of Prophecy in the Book of Jeremiah.* London, SCM Press.
———. 1986. *Jeremiah: A Commentary.* Louisville, KY: Westminster John Knox Press.
Carr, D. M. 2005. *Writing on the Tablet of the Heart: Origins of Scripture and Literature.* New York: Oxford University Press.
———. 2011a. *The Formation of the Hebrew Bible: A New Reconstruction.* New York: Oxford University Press.
———. 2011b. "The Rise of the Torah." In Knoppers and Levinson (2007), 53–56.
Chagnon, N. 1992. *Yanomamo.* 4th ed. New York: Harcourt Brace.
Chazon, E. 1992. "Is *Divrei ha-Me'orot* a Sectarian Prayer?" In *The Dead Sea Scrolls: Forty Years of Research,* edited by D. Dimant et al., 3–17. Jerusalem: Magnes.
———, ed. 2003. *Liturgical Perspectives: Prayer and Poetry in Light of the Dead Sea Scrolls.* Leiden: Brill.
———. 2006. "Scripture and Prayer in the 'Words of the Luminaries.'" In *Prayers That Cite Scripture,* edited by J. Kugel, 25–41. Cambridge, MA: Harvard Center for Jewish Studies.
———. 2012: "Liturgy Before and After the Temple's Destruction." In *Was 70 CE a Watershed in Jewish History?,* edited by D. R. Schwartz and Z. Weiss, 371–392. Leiden: Brill.
Childs, B. 1971. "Psalm Titles and Midrashic Exegesis." *Journal of Semitic Studies* 16: 137–50.
Chomsky, N. 2012. *The Science of Language: Interviews with James McGilvray.* New York: Cambridge University Press.
Christensen, D. L. 1975. *Transformation of the War Oracle in Old Testament Prophecy: Studies in the Oracles Against the Nations.* Missoula, MT: Scholars Press.
———. 1996. "The Book of Psalms Within the Canonical Process in Ancient Israel." *Journal of the Evangelical Theological Society* 39: 421–32.
Churchland, P. S. 1986. *Neurophilosophy: Toward a Unified Science of the Mind-Brain.* Cambridge, MA: MIT Press.
———. 2002a. *Brain-Wise: Studies in Neurophilosophy.* Cambridge, MA: MIT Press.
———. 2002b. "Can Neurobiology Teach Us Anything About Consciousness?" In Block et al. (2002), 127–40.
Clements, R. E. 1975. *Prophecy and Tradition.* Oxford: Blackwell.
Clifford, R. J. 1971. "The Tent of El and the Israelite Tent of Meeting." *Catholic Biblical Quarterly* 33: 221–27.
———. 2004. "Your Attention Please!: Heeding the Proverbs." *Journal for the Study of the Old Testament* 29: 155–63.
Coats, G. 1973. "The Joseph Story and Ancient Wisdom: A Reappraisal." *Catholic Biblical Quarterly* 35: 285–97.

Cohen, N. G. 1995. *Philo Judaeus: His Universe of Discourse.* Berlin: Peter Lang.
Cohen, S. G. H. 1984. *The Struggle in Man Between Good and Evil.* Kampen: Kok.
Cohen, S. J. D. 1987. *From the Maccabees to the Mishnah.* Philadelphia: Westminster.
———. 1999. *The Beginnings of Jewishness.* Berkeley: University of California Press.
Cohn, Y. B. 1998. *Tangled Up in Text: Tefillin and the Ancient World.* Providence, RI: Brown University Press.
Collins, A. Y. 2012. "Ascents to Heaven in Antiquity: Toward a Typology." In *A Teacher for All Generations: Essays in Honor of James C. VanderKam,* edited by E. F. Mason et al., 553–72. Leiden: Brill.
Collins, J. J. 1979. *Apocalypse: The Morphology of a Genre.* Missoula, MT: Scholars Press.
———. 1983. "Sibylline Oracles." In *Old Testament Pseudepigrapha,* edited by J. Charlesworth, 1: 354–61. Garden City, NY: Doubleday.
———. 1991: "Genre, Ideology, and Social Movements in Jewish Apocalypticism." In *Mysteries and Revelations,* edited by J. J. Collins and J. Charlesworth, 11–32. Sheffield: Sheffield Academic Press.
———. 1994. *Daniel: A Commentary on the Book of Daniel.* Philadelphia: Fortress.
———. 1995. *The Scepter and the Star: The Messiahs of the Dead Sea Scrolls and Other Ancient Literature.* New York: Doubleday.
Collins, J. J., and D. C. Harlow, eds. 2010. *The Dictionary of Early Judaism.* Grand Rapids, MI: Eerdmans.
Conklin, H. C. 1954. "The Relation of Hanunóo Culture to the Plant World." PhD diss., Yale University.
———. 1958. "Betel Chewing Among the Hanunóo." *Proceedings of the 4th Fareastern Prehistoric Congress.* Quezon City: Nat. Res. Council of the Philippines.
Cook, L. S. 2011. *The Question of the Cessation of Prophecy in Ancient Judaism.* Tübingen: Mohr Siebeck.
Coolidge, F. L., and T. Wynn. 2009. *The Rise of Homo Sapiens: The Evolution of Modern Thinking.* Chichester: Wiley-Blackwell.
Cooper, A. 1981. "Divine Names and Epithets in the Ugaritic Texts." *Ras Shamra Parallels* 3 (Rome, Pontifical Biblical Institute): 431–41.
———. 1990. "Imagining Prophecy." In Kugel (1990d), 26–44.
Corstens, D., et al. 2014. "Emerging Perspectives from the Hearing Voices Movement: Implications for Research and Practice." *Schizophrenia Bulletin* 40, Supp. 4: 285–94.
Crenshaw, J. L. 1969. "Method in Determining Wisdom Influence upon 'Historical' Literature.'" *Journal of Biblical Literature* 88, 129–42.
———. 1975. "The Problem of Theodicy in Sirach." *Journal of Biblical Literature* 94: 48–51.
———. 1976. *Studies in Ancient Israelite Wisdom.* New York: Ktav.
———. 1998. *Old Testament Wisdom: An Introduction.* Rev. ed. Louisville: Westminster John Knox.
Cross, F. M. 1966. *The Divine Warrior in Israel's Early Cult.* Cambridge, MA: Harvard University Press.
———. 1973. *Canaanite Myth and Hebrew Epic: Essays in the History of the Religion of Israel.* Cambridge, MA: Harvard University Press.
———. 1998. *From Epic to Canon: History and Literature in Ancient Israel.* Baltimore: Johns Hopkins University Press.
Cross, F. M., and D. N. Freedman. 1955. "The Song of Miriam." *Journal of Near Eastern Studies* 14: 237–50.

D'Andrade, R. 1995. *Cognitive Anthropology.* Cambridge: Cambridge University Press.
D'Aquili, E., and A. Newberg. 2001. *Why God Won't Go Away.* New York: Ballantine.
Daube, D. 1961. "Direct and Indirect Causation in Biblical Law." *Vetus Testamentum* 11: 246–69.
———. 2008: *The Deed and the Doer in the Bible: David Daube's Gifford Lectures.* Compiled by Calum Carmichael. West Conshohocken, PA: Templeton Foundation Press.
David, A. S. 2004. "The Cognitive Neuropsychiatry of Auditory Verbal Hallucinations: An Overview." *Cognitive Neuropsychiatry* 9: 107–23.
David, N., et al., eds. 2012. *The Hebrew Bible in Light of the Dead Sea Scrolls.* (Forschungen zur Religion und Literature des Alten und Neuen Testaments 239.) Göttingen: Vandenhoeck & Ruprecht.
Davila, J. 1990. "*Qohelet* and Northern Hebrew." *MAARAV* 5–6: 69–87.
———. 2000. *Liturgical Works.* (Eerdmans Commentaries on the Dead Sea Scrolls 6.) Grand Rapids: Eerdmans.
Davis, E. F. 1989. *Swallowing the Scroll: Textuality and the Dynamics of Discourse in Ezekiel's Prophecy.* Sheffield: Almond Press.
Davis, J. 1982. *Religious Organization and Religious Experience.* London: Academic Press.
Davis, N. Z. 1986. "Boundaries and Sense of Self in Sixteenth-Century France." In *Reconstructing Individualism: Autonomy, Individuality, and the Self in Western Thought,* edited by T. C. Heller et al., 53-63. Stanford, CA: Stanford University Press.
Dearman, A. 1993. "Baal in Israel: The Contribution of Some Place Names and Personal Names to an Understanding of Early Israelite Religion." In *History and Interpretation: Essays in Honor of John Hayes,* edited by M. P. Graham et al., 173–91. Sheffield: JSOT Press.
De Moore, J. C. 1990. *The Rise of Yahwism: The Roots of Israelite Monotheism.* Louvain: Peeters.
Demsky, A. 2012. *Literacy in Ancient Israel.* Jerusalem: Bialik Institute.
Dennett, D. 1987. *The Intentional Stance.* Cambridge, MA: MIT Press.
———. 1989. "The Origin of Selves." *Cogito* 2: 163–73.
———. 1991. *Consciousness Explained.* Boston: Little, Brown.
———. 1994. "Real Consciousness." In *Consciousness in Philosophy and Neuroscience,* edited by A. Revonsuo and M. Kamppinen, 221–36. Hillsdale, NJ: Lawrence Erlbaum.
———. 2002a. "The Cartesian Theater and 'Filling In' the Stream of Consciousness." In Block (2002), 83–88.
———. 2002b: "Quining Qualia." In Block (2002), 619–42.
———. 2006. *Breaking the Spell.* New York: Penguin.
Dennett D., and M. Kinsbourne. 2002. "Time and the Observer: The Where and When of Consciousness in the Brain." In Block (2002), 141–74.
De Troyer, K., and A. Lange, eds. 2005. *Reading the Present in the Qumran Library.* Atlanta: SBL Press.
Dever, W. 1982. "The Cult of Asherah." *Hebrew Studies* 23: 37–43.
———. 2003. *Who Were the Early Israelites and Where Did They Come From?* Grand Rapids: Eerdmans.
———. 2005. *Did God Have a Wife?: Archaeology and Folk Religion in Ancient Israel.* Grand Rapids: Eerdmans.
De Vries, P. 2016. *The Kābôd of Yhwh in the Old Testament: With Particular Reference to the Book of Ezekiel.* Leiden: Brill.
Dhavamony, M. 1982. *Classical Hinduism.* Rome: Gregorian University Press.

Dhorme, P. 1920. "l'Emploi métaphorique des noms des parties du corps." *Revue biblique* 29: 465–506.

Diamond, A. R. P. 1987. *The Confessions of Jeremiah in Context: Scenes of Prophetic Drama.* (Journal for the Study of the Old Testament Supplement Series 45.) Sheffield: JSOT Press.

Dijkstra, M. 1995. "Is Balaam Among the Prophets?" *Journal of Biblical Literature* 114: 43–64.

DiLella, A. A. 1966. *The Hebrew Text of Sirach: A Text-Critical and Historical Study.* London: Mouton.

Dimant, D. 1993. "The Seventy Weeks Chronology (Dan. 9:24–27) in the Light of New Qumranic Texts." In *The Book of Daniel in the Light of New Findings,* edited by A. S. Van der Woude, 57–76. Louvain: Peeters.

Di Vito, R. A. 1999. "Old Testament Anthropology and the Construction of Biblical Identity." *Catholic Biblical Quarterly* 61: 217–38.

Dodds, E. R. 1951. *The Greeks and the Irrational.* Berkeley: University of California Press.

Dohmen, C. 1985. *Das Bilderverbot: Seine Enstehung und seine Entwicklung im AT.* Frankfurt an Mein: Peter Hanstein Verlag.

Donner, H., and W. Röllig. 1962. *Kanaanäische und Aramäische Inscrhiften.* Wiesbaden: Harrassowitz.

Dozeman, T. 1989. *God on the Mountain.* Atlanta: Scholars Press.

Duby, G., and Ph. Braunstein. 1998. "The Emergence of the Individual." In *Representations of the Medieval World,* edited by G. Duby, 2:507–30. Cambridge, MA: Harvard University Press.

Duhaime, J. 2003. "Cohérence structurelle et tensions internes dans l'instruction sur les deux esprits (1QS III:13-IV:26)." In *Wisdom and Apocalypticism in the Dead Sea Scrolls and in the Biblical Tradition,* edited by F. Garcia-Martinez, 103–31. Leuven: Peeters.

Dumit, J. 2004. *Picturing Personhood: Brain Scans and Biomedical Identity.* Princeton, NJ: Princeton University Press.

Dupré, W. 1975. *Religion in Primitive Cultures: A Study in Ethnophilosophy.* The Hague: Mouton.

Durand, J. M. 1988. *Archives épistolaires de Mari I/I.* (Archives Royales de Mari 26.) Paris: Editions Recherche sur les civilizations.

Dürr, L. 1925. "Hebr. *nepeš = Akk. napištu.*" *Zeitschrift für die alttestamentliche Wissenschaft* 34: 262–9.

Eaton, J. H. 1986. *Kingship and the Psalms.* Sheffield: JSOT Press.

Edelman, G. M. 1987. *Neural Darwinism.* New York: Basic Books.

Egger-Wenzel, R. 2002. *Ben Sira's God.* Berlin: De Gruyter.

Eichrodt, W. 1961. *Theology of the Old Testament.* 2 vols. Philadelphia: Westminster.

Eisenstadt, S. N. 1986. *The Origins and Diversity of Axial Age Civilizations.* Albany: State University of New York Press.

Endres, J. C. 2015. "Revisiting the Rebekah of the Book of *Jubilees.*" In Mason et al. (2012), 765–82.

Enns, P. 1997. *Exodus Retold.* Atlanta: Scholars Press.

Eshel, E. 1999. "Demonology in Palestine During the Second Temple Period." PhD diss., Hebrew University.

Eshel, E., and H. Eshel. 2008. *The Dead Sea Scrolls and the Hasmonean State.* Grand Rapids: Eerdmans.

Evans-Pritchard, E. E. 1937. *Witchcraft, Oracles and Magic Among the Azande.* Oxford: Clarendon.

———. 1956. *Nuer Religion.* Oxford: Clarendon.

Ewing, K. 1990. "The Illusion of Wholeness: Culture, Self, and the Experience of Inconsistency." *Ethos* 18: 251–78.

Falk, D. 1998. *Daily, Sabbath and Festival Prayers in the Dead Sea Scrolls.* Leiden: Brill.

———. 1999. "Prayer in the Qumran Texts." In *The Cambridge History of Judaism,* edited by W. Horbury et al., 3:852–76. Cambridge: Cambridge University Press.

Faraone, C. 1991. "The Agonistic Context of Early Greek Binding Spells." In *Magika Hiera: Ancient Greek Magic and Religion,* edited by C. Faraone and D. Obbinck, 3–32. New York: Oxford University Press.

Faraone, C., and F. S. Naiden. 2012. *Greek and Roman Animal Sacrifice: Ancient Victims, Modern Observers.* New York: Cambridge University Press.

Feinberg, T. E. 2009. *From Axons to Identity.* New York: Norton.

Feldman, L. 1990. "Prophets and Prophecy in Josephus." Journal of Theological Studies 41:386–422.

Feldman, L. 1998a. *Josephus's Interpretation of the Bible.* Berkeley: University of California Press.

———. 1998b. *Studies in Josephus' Rewritten Bible.* Leiden: Brill.

Feldman, L., J. Kugel, and L. Schiffman, eds. 2013. *Outside the Bible: Ancient Jewish Writings Related to Scripture.* Philadelphia: Jewish Publication Society/University of Nebraska Press

Finkel, A. 1963. "The Pesher of Dreams and Scriptures." *Revue de Qumran* 4: 357–70.

Finkelstein, I. 1988. *The Archaeology of the Israelite Settlement.* Jerusalem: Israel Exploration Society.

Fishbane, M. 1985. *Biblical Interpretation in Ancient Israel.* Oxford: Clarendon.

Fishbane, M., and E. Tov, eds. 1992. *Sha'arei Talmon: Studies in the Bible, Qumran, and the Ancient Near East, Presented to Shemaryahu Talmon.* Winona Lake, IN: Eisenbrauns.

Fitzmyer, J. 2007. *The One Who Is to Come.* Grand Rapids: Eerdmans.

Flanagan, O. 1992. *Consciousness Reconsidered.* Cambridge, MA: MIT Press.

Fleischer, E. 1990. "On the Beginning of Obligatory Prayer." *Tarbiz* 59: 397–441.

Flint, P. W. 1997. *The Dead Sea Psalms Scrolls and the Psalter.* Leiden: Brill.

Flint, P. W., and J. VanderKam. 1999. *The Dead Sea Scrolls After Fifty Years: A Comprehensive Assessment.* Leiden: Brill.

Floyd, M. H., and R. D. Haak, eds. 2006. *Prophets, Prophecy, and Prophetic Texts in Second Temple Judaism.* New York: T&T Clark.

Flusser, D. 1966. "Qumran and Jewish Apotropaic Prayers." *Israel Exploration Journal* 16: 194–205.

———. 1988. "The Four Empires in the Fourth Sibyl and the Book of Daniel." In his *Judaism and the Origins of Christianity.* Jerusalem: Magnes.

Foster, B. 1995. *Before the Muses: Myths, Tales and Poetry of Ancient Mesopotamia.* Bethesda, MD: CDL.

Fox, M. V. 1995. "World-Order and Ma'at: A Crooked Parallel." *Journal of the Ancient Near Eastern Society (JANES)* 23: 37–48.

———, ed. 1996. *Texts, Temples, and Traditions: A Tribute to Menahem Haran.* Winona Lake, IN: Eisenbrauns.

———. 2001. "Wisdom in the Joseph Story." *Vetus Testamentum* 51: 26–41.

———. 2004. "The Rhetoric of Disjointed Proverbs." *Journal for the Study of the Old Testament* 29: 165–79.

Fox, R. B. 1952. "The Pinatubo Negritos: Their Useful Plants and Material Culture." *Philippine Journal of Science* 81: 173–414.

Fox, R. L. 1986. *Pagans and Christians.* New York: Viking.

Frankel, E. 2014. "The Acceptance of the Kingship of God." *Oqimta* 2: 1–21.

Frankfort, H. 1948. *Kingship and the Gods.* Chicago: University of Chicago Press.

Frankfort, H., and H. A. Frankfort. 1949. "Myth and Reality." In *The Intellectual Adventure of Ancient Man,* edited by H. Frankfort et al., 3–30. Chicago: University of Chicago Press.

Freedman, D. N. 1987. "Yahweh of Samaria and His Asherah." *Biblical Archaeologist* 50: 241–49.

———. 1999. *Psalm 119: The Exaltation of Torah.* Winona Lake, IN: Eisenbrauns.

Friedman, R. E. 1980. "The Tabernacle in the Temple." *Biblical Archaeologist* 43: 241–48.

———. 1989. *Who Wrote the Bible?* New York: Perennial Library Harper & Row.

———. 1995. *The Disappearance of God: A Divine Mystery.* Boston: Little Brown.

Friedrich, J. 1926–30. *Staatsverträge des Hatti-Reiches.* 2 vols. Leipzig: Hinrichs.

Fröhlich, I. 1996. *Time and Times and Half a Time: The Beginnings of Historical Consciousness.* Sheffield: Academic Press.

Gaifman, M. 2008. "The Aniconic Image of the Roman Near East." In *The Variety of Local Religious Life in the Near East in the Hellenistic and Roman Periods,* edited by T. Kaizer, 37–72. Leiden: Brill.

Garcia Martinez, F. 2003. "Iranian Influences at Qumran?" In *Apocalyptic and Eschatological Heritage,* edited by M. McNamara, 37–49. Dublin: Four Courts.

Garcia Martinez, F., and E. Tigchelaar. 1997. *The Dead Sea Scrolls Study Edition.* Leiden: Brill.

Garsiel, M. 1991. *Biblical Names: A Literary Study of Midrashic Derivations and Puns.* Ramat-Gan, Israel: Bar-Ilan University Press.

Geertz, C. 1973. *The Interpretation of Cultures.* New York: Basic Books.

———. 1983 "From the Native's Point of View: On the Nature of Anthropological Understanding." In his *Local Knowledge: Further Essays in Interpretive Anthropology,* 55–70. New York: Basic Books.

———. 1996. "Religion as a Cultural System." In *Anthropological Approaches to the Study of Religion,* edited by M. Banton, 1–46. London: Tavistock.

———. 2000. *Available Light: Anthropological Reflections on Philosophical Topics.* Princeton, NJ: Princeton University Press.

Gell, A. 1995. "Closure and Multiplication: An Essay on Polynesian Cosmology and Ritual." Reprinted in *A Reader in the Anthropology of Religion,* edited by M. Lambek, 290–305. Oxford: Blackwell, 2002.

Geller, S. A. 2004. "The Religion of the Bible." In *The Jewish Study Bible,* edited by A. Berlin and M. Z. Brettler, 2021–40. New York: Oxford University Press.

Gerhards, A. 2007. "Crossing Borders: The *Kedusha* and the *Sanctus.*" In *Jewish and Christian Liturgy and Worship: New Insights into Its History and Interaction,* edited by A. Gerhards and C. Leonhard, 27–28. Leiden: Brill.

Gertz, J. C., et al. 2016. *The Formation of the Pentateuch: Bridging the Academic Cultures of Europe, Israel, and North America.* Tübingen: Mohr Siebeck.

Gilbert, M. 2002. "God, Sin, and Mercy." In *Ben Sira's God,* edited by R. Egger-Wenzel, 118–35. Berlin: De Gruyter.

Gnuse, R. K. 1997. *No Other Gods: Emergent Monotheism in Israel.* Sheffield: Academic Press.

Goodman, M. 2010. "Constructing Ancient Judaism from the Scrolls." In *The Oxford Hand-*

book of the Dead Sea Scrolls, edited by T. H. Lim and J. J. Collins, 81–91. New York: Oxford University Press.

Goren-Inbar, N. 2000. "Pleistocene Milestones on the Out-of-Africa Corridor at Gesher Benot Ya'aqov, Israel." *Science* 289 (2000): 944–47.

Gould, S. J., and E. S. Vrba. 1982. "Exaptation—A Missing Term in the Science of Form." *Paleobiology* 8: 4–15.

Grant, R. M. 1986. *Gods and the One God.* Philadelphia: Westminster.

Graves, R. 1925. *My Head! My Head!* New York: Knopf.

Gray, R. 1991. *Prophetic Figures in Late Second Temple Jewish Palestine: The Evidence from Josephus.* New York: Oxford University Press.

Green, A., ed. 1986. *The History of Jewish Spirituality.* New York: Crossroad.

Green, D. J. 2010. *I Undertook Great Works.* Tübingen: Mohr Siebeck.

Greenberg, M. 1950. "Hebrew *sĕgullā*: Akkadian *sikiltu*." *Journal of the American Oriental Society* 71: 172–74.

———. 1983a. *Biblical Prose Prayer.* Berkeley: University of California Press.

———. 1983b. *Ezekiel 1–20.* (Anchor Bible vol 22.) Garden City, NY: Doubleday-Anchor.

Greenfield, J. 1969. "The Zakir Inscription and the *Danklied*." *World Congress of Jewish Studies* 5, no. 1: 174–91.

———. 1992. "Two Notes on the Apocryphal Psalms." In Fishbane and Tov (1992), 309–14.

Greenfield, J., M. Stone, and E. Eshel. 2004. *The Aramaic Levi Document.* Leiden: Brill.

Grisaru, N., and E. Witztum. 2014. "Possession by *Zar* Spirits Among Ethiopian Immigrants in Israel." In their *Social, Cultural, and Clinical Aspects of Ethiopian Immigrants in Israel,* 325–46. Beer-Sheva: Ben Gurion University of the Negev Press.

Gunkel, H. 1962. *The Legends of Genesis.* Translation of 1901 original. New York: Schocken.

Guthrie, S. 1993. *Faces in the Clouds: A New Theory of Religion.* New York: Oxford University Press.

Güzeldere, G. 2002. "The Many Faces of Consciousness: A Field Guide." In Block et al. (2002), 1–67.

Gyatso, K. 2010. *Modern Buddhism: The Path of Compassion and Wisdom.* Glen Spey, NY: Tharpa.

Haberman, A. M. 1954. "On the Tefillin in Ancient Times." *Eretz-Israel* 3: 174–77.

Hackett, J-A. 1984. *The Balaam Text from Deir 'Allā.* Chico, CA: Scholars Press.

Hadot, J. 1970. *Penchant mauvais et volonté libre dans la sagesse de Sirach.* Brussels: Presses Universitaires de Bruxelles.

Hallam, R. S. 2009. *Virtual Selves, Real Persons: A Dialogue Across Disciplines.* Cambridge: Cambridge University Press.

Hallo, W. W. 1981. "Letters, Prayers, and Letter Prayers." In *Proceedings of the Seventh World Congress of Jewish Studies.* Jerusalem: World Union of Jewish Studies, 1981.

Halpern, B. 2001. *David's Secret Demons: Messiah, Murderer, Traitor, King.* Grand Rapids: Eerdmans.

———. 2009. *From Gods to God: The Dynamics of Iron Age Cosmologies.* Tübingen: Mohr Siebeck.

Halpern-Amaru, B. 1999. *The Empowerment of Women in the Book of Jubilees.* Leiden: Brill.

Hammer, L. 2015. *James Merrill, Life and Art.* New York: Knopf.

Hamori, E. 2008. *"When Gods Were Men": The Embodied God in Biblical and Near Eastern Literature.* Berlin: De Gruyter.

———. 2010. “Divine Embodiment in the Hebrew Bible.” In Kamionkowsky and Wonil Kim (2010), 163–64.

Handy, L. K. 1994. *Among the Host of Heaven.* Winona Lake, IN: Eisenbrauns.

Hanson, P. D. 1979. *The Dawn of Apocalyptic.* Philadelphia: Fortress.

Haran, M. 1985. *Temples and Temple Service in Ancient Israel.* Winona Lake, IN: Eisenbrauns.

Harkins A. K. 2012. “Who Is the Teacher of the Teacher Hymns?: Reexamining the Teacher Hymns Hypothesis Fifty Years later.” In Mason et al. (2012), 449–67.

Harmand, S., et al. 2015. “3.3-Million-Year-Old Stone Tools from Lomekwi 3, West Turkana, Kenya.” *Nature* 521: 310–15.

Hartman, G., and S. Budick. 1985. *Midrash and Literature.* New Haven, CT: Yale University Press.

Hazlitt, H. 1933. *The Anatomy of Criticism: A Trialogue.* New York: Simon & Schuster.

Headley, S. C. 1966. *Vers une anthropologie de la prière. Etudes ethnolinguistiques javanaises.* Aix-en-Provence: Publications Universitaires de Provence.

Heelas P., and A. Lock. 1981. *Indigenous Psychologies: The Anthropology of the Self.* London: Academic Press.

Heinemann, J. 1964. *Prayer in the Period of the Tannaim and Amoraim.* Jerusalem: Magnes.

———. 1981. *Studies in Jewish Liturgy.* Jerusalem: Magnes.

Helfgot, N. 1993. “And Moses Struck the Rock: Numbers 20 and the Leadership of Moses.” *Tradition* 27: 51–58.

Hempel, Ch. 2010. “*The Treatise on the Two Spirits* and the Literary History of the *Rule of the Community.*” In *Dualism in Qumran,* edited by G. Xeravits, 110–13. London: T&T Clark.

Hengel, M. 1977. *Crucifixion.* Philadelphia: Fortress.

Henze, M. 2011a. *Jewish Apocalypticism in Late First-Century Israel.* Tübingen: Mohr Siebeck.

Henze, M. 2011b. *A Companion to Biblical Interpretation in Early Judaism.* Grand Rapids, MI: Eerdmans.

Heszer, C. 2001. *Jewish Literacy in Roman Palestine.* Tübingen: Mohr Siebeck.

Hilber, W. 2005. *Cultic Prophecy in the Psalms.* Berlin: De Gruyter.

Himmelfarb, M. 1993. *The Ascent to Heaven in Jewish and Christian Apocalypses.* New York: Oxford University Press.

Hoftijzer J., and G. Van der Kooij. 1991. *The Balaam Text from Deir ʿAlla Re-evaluated.* Leiden: Brill.

Holladay, W. L. 1993. *The Psalms Through Three Thousand Years: Prayerbook of a Cloud of Witnesses.* Minneapolis: Augsburg Fortress.

Honeyman, A. M. 1952. “*Merismus* in Biblical Hebrew.” *Journal of Biblical Literature* 71: 11–18.

Horgan, M. 1979. *Pesharim: Qumran Interpretation of Biblical Books.* Washington, DC: Catholic Biblical Association of America.

———. 2002. “The Habakkuk Pesher.” In *Pesharim, Other Commentaries, and Related Documents,* edited by J. H. Charlesworth, 157–85. Vol. 6B of *The Dead Sea Scrolls: Hebrew, Aramaic, and Greek Texts with English Translations.* Tübingen: Mohr Siebeck.

Hornung, E. 1982. *Conceptions of God in Ancient Egypt: The One and the Many.* Ithaca, NY: Cornell University Press.

Horsley, R. A. 2007. *Scribes, Visionaries, and the Politics of Second Temple Judea.* Louisville: Westminster John Knox.

Huffmon, H. 1959. "Covenant Lawsuit and the Prophets." *Journal of Biblical Literature* 78: 286–95.

———. 1966. "The Treaty Background of Hebrew Yāda'." *Bulletin of American Schools of Oriental Research* 181: 31–37.

———. 1999. "Jeremiah of Anathoth: A Prophet for All Israel." In *Ki Barukh Hu: Essays in Honor of Baruch Levine,* edited by R. Chazan et al. Winona Lake, IN: Eisenbrauns.

———. 2000: "A Company of Prophets: Mari, Assyria, Israel." In *Prophecy in Its Ancient Near Eastern Context,* edited by M. Nissinen, 47–70. Atlanta: Society of Biblical Literature.

Hurvitz, A. 1972. *Between Two Languages: Toward a History of Biblical Hebrew in the Second Temple Period.* Jerusalem: Mosad Bialik.

———. 1988. "Wisdom Vocabulary in the Hebrew Psalter: A Contribution to the Study of 'Wisdom Psalms.'" *Vetus Testamentum* 38: 42–64.

Jackson, B. 2000. *Studies in the Semiotics of Biblical Law.* Sheffield: Sheffield Academic Press.

Jacobsen, T. 1976. *The Treasures of Darkness: A History of Mesopotamian Religion.* New Haven, CT: Yale University Press.

James, W. 1892. *Psychology: Briefer Course.* New York: Holt.

Janowski, B., and K. Liess. 2009. *Der Mensch im Alten Israel: Neue Forshungen zur alttestmentlischen Anthropologie.* Freiberg: Herder.

Jassen, A. P. 2007. *Mediating the Divine: Prophecy and Revelation in the Dead Sea Scrolls and Second Temple Judaism.* Leiden: Brill.

Jaynes, J. 1976. *The Origins of Consciousness in the Breakdown of the Bicameral Mind.* Boston: Houghton Mifflin.

Jeremias, G. 1963. *Der Lehrer der Gerechtigkeit.* Gotingen: Vandenhoek & Ruprecht.

Johnson, A. R. 2006. *The Vitality of the Individual in the Thought of Ancient Israel.* Eugene, OR: Wipf & Stock.

Jonquière, T. 2007. *Prayer in Josephus.* Leiden: Brill.

Jowett, B. 1931. *The Dialogues of Plato.* London: Oxford University Press.

Kaduri, Y. 2015. "Windy and Fiery Angels." In *Tradition, Transmission, and Transformation from Second Temple Literature Through Judaism and Christianity in Late Antiquity,* edited by M. Kister et al., 134–149. Leiden: Brill.

Kaltner, J., and L. Stulman, eds. 2004. *Inspired Speech: Prophecy in the Ancient Near East; Essays in Honor of Herbert B. Huffmon.* London: T&T Clark.

Kaminsky, J. 1995. *Corporate Responsibility in the Hebrew Bible.* Sheffield: Sheffield Academic Press.

Kamionkowsky, S. T., and W. Kim. 2010. *Bodies, Embodiment, and Theology of the Hebrew Bible.* New York: T&T Clark.

Kane, M. J., and R. W. Engle. 2002. "The Role of Prefrontal Cortex in Working-Memory Capacity, Executive Attention, and General Fluid Intelligence: An Individual-Differences Perspective." *Psychonomic Bulletin and Review* 9: 637–71.

Kang, S. 1989. *Divine War in the Old Testament and the Ancient Near East.* (Supplement to *Zeitschrift für die alttestamentliche Wissenschaft* 177.) Berlin: De Gruyter.

Kapstein, M. 2007. "The Prayer of Great Power." In *Buddhism in Practice,* edited by D. S. Lopez, 80–87. Princeton, NJ: Princeton University Press.

Karlsson, M. 2016. *Relations of Power in Early Neo-Assyrian State Ideology.* Berlin: De Gruyter.

Kaufmann, Y. 1960. *The Religion of Israel.* Abridged by M. Greenberg. Chicago: University of Chicago.

Keel, O., and C. Uehlinger. 1998. *Gods, Goddesses, and Images of God in Ancient Israel.* Minneapolis: Fortress.

Keleman, D. 2004. "Are Children 'Intuitive Theists'? Reasoning About Purpose and Design in Nature." *Psychological Science* 15: 295–301.

Kimelman, R. 1993. "A Note of Weinfeld's Grace After Meals." *Journal of Biblical Literature* 112: 695–96.

Kister, M. 1992. "Biblical Phrases and Hidden Biblical Interpretations and Pesharim." In *The Dead Sea Scrolls: Forty Years of Research,* edited by D. Dimant and U. Rappaport, 27–39. Jerusalem: Magnes.

Kister, M. 2010. "Body and Purification from Evil: Prayer Formulae and Concepts in Second Temple Literature and Their Relationship to Later Rabbinic Literature." *Meghillot* 8–9: 243–86.

Kister, M., et al. 2015. *Proceedings of the 13th Symposium of the Orion Center for the Study of the Dead Sea Scrolls.* Leiden: Brill.

Klawans, J. 2006. *Purity, Sacrifice, and the Temple: Symbolism and Supersessionism in the Study of Ancient Judaism.* New York: Oxford.

Klein, J. 2006. "*Man and His God:* A Wisdom Poem or a Cultic Lament." In *Approaches to Sumerian Literature,* edited by P. Michalowski and N. Feldhuis, 123–44. Leiden: Brill.

Knibb, M. 1992. "Prophecy and the Emergence of the Jewish Apocalypses." In *Israel's Prophetic Tradition,* edited by R. Coggins et al., 155–80. Cambridge: Cambridge University Press.

Knohl, I. 1995. *The Sanctuary of Silence.* Minneapolis: Fortress.

———. 2000. *The Messiah Before Jesus.* Berkeley: University of California Press.

Knoppers, G., and B. Levinson. 2007. *The Pentateuch as Torah: New Models for Understanding Its Propagation and Acceptance.* Winona Lake, IN: Eisenbrauns.

Köckert, M. 2003. "War Jakobs Gegner in Gen 32:23–33 ein Dämon?" In Lange et al. (2003), 160–83.

Kohut, H. 1977. *The Restoration of the Self.* New York: International Universities Press, 1977.

———. 1978–81. *The Search for the Self: Selected Writings of Heinz Kohut 1950–1978.* Edited by Paul Ornstein. 4 vols. New York: International Universities Press.

Korošec, V. 1931. *Hethitische Staatsverträge.* Leipzig: T. Weicher.

Korpel, M. 1990. *A Rift in the Clouds — Ugaritic and Hebrew Descriptions of the Divine.* Münster: Ugarit-Verlag.

Kotovsky, L., and R. Baillargeon. 2000: "Reasoning About Collisions Involving Inert Objects in 7.5-Month-Old Infants." *Developmental Science* 3: 344–59.

Kramer, S. N. 1959. *History Begins at Sumer.* Garden City, NY: Doubleday.

Kratz, R. 2015. "From Divine Kingship to Kingdom of God: The Psalmic Tradition." In his *Historical and Biblical Israel: The History, Tradition, and Archives of Israel and Judah.* New York: Oxford University Press.

———. 2016. "Why Jeremiah?: The Invention of a Prophetic Figure." In Najman and Schmid (2016).

Kratz R., and H. Spiekermann, eds. 2010. *One God, One Cult, One Nation.* Berlin: De Gruter.

Krüger, T. 2009. "Das 'Herz' in der alttestamentlichen Anthropologie." *Anthropologiche Aufbrüche: Alttestamentliche und interdisziplinäre Zugänge zur Historischen Anthropologie,* edited by Andreas Wagner. Göttingen: Vandenhoek & Ruprecht.

Kugel, J. 1980. "Adverbial *Kî Tôb.*" *Journal of Biblical Literature* 99: 433–36.

———. 1981. *The Idea of Biblical Poetry.* New Haven, CT: Yale University Press.

———. 1982a. "Is There But One Song?" *Biblica* 63: 329–50.
———. 1982b. "On the Bible and Literary Criticism." *Prooftexts* 1: 217–36.
———. 1983. "On the Bible and Literary Criticism" (Discussion). *Prooftexts* 3: 323–32.
———. 1986a. "Topics in the History of the Spirituality of the Psalms." In Green (1986), 113–45.
———. 1986b. "Torah." In *Contemporary Jewish Religious Thought*, edited by A. Cohen and P. Mendes-Flohr, 995–1005. New York: Scribners.
———. 1987. "On Hidden Hatred and Open Reproach: Early Exegesis of Lev. 19:17." *Harvard Theological Review* 80: 43–61.
———. 1989. "Qohelet and Money." *Catholic Biblical Quarterly* 51: 32–49.
———. 1990a. *In Potiphar's House: The Interpretive Life of Biblical Texts in Early Judaism and Christianity.* San Francisco: HarperCollins.
———. 1990b. "Poets and Prophets." In Kugel (1990d), 1–25.
———. 1990c. "David the Prophet." In Kugel (1990d), 45–55.
———. 1990d. *Poetry and Prophecy.* Ithaca, NY: Cornell University Press.
———. 1992. "The Story of Dinah in the *Testament of Levi.*" *Harvard Theological Review* 85: 1–34.
———. 1993. "Levi's Elevation to the Priesthood in Second Temple Writings." *Harvard Theological Review* 86: 1–64.
———. 1994. "The *Jubilees* Apocalypse." *Dead Sea Discoveries* 1: 322–37.
———. 1995a. "The Ladder of Jacob." *Harvard Theological Review* 88: 1–24.
———. 1995b. "Reuben's Sin with Bilhah in the *Testament of Reuben.*" In Wright et al. (1995), 525–54.
———. 1996. "The Holiness of Israel and Its Land in Second Temple Times." In Fox (1996), 21–32.
———. 1997a. "Wisdom and the Anthological Temper." *Prooftexts* 17: 9–32.
———. 1997b. *The Bible as It Was.* Cambridge, MA: Harvard University Press.
———. 1998a. *Traditions of the Bible: A Guide to the Bible as It Was at the Start of the Common Era.* Cambridge, MA: Harvard University Press.
———. 1998b: "'4Q369: 'The Prayer of Enosh' and Ancient Biblical Interpretation." *Dead Sea Discoveries* 5: 119–48.
———. 1999a. *Great Poems of the Bible.* New York: Free Press.
———. 1999b. "Solomon's Riddles." In Kugel (1999a), 160–80.
———. 2000. "Biblical Apocrypha and Pseudepigrapha and the Hebrew of the Second Temple Period." In Muraoka and Elwolde (2000), 166–77.
———. 2001a. *Studies in Ancient Midrash.* Cambridge, MA: Harvard University Press.
———. 2001b. "Biblical Interpretation and the Ancient Israelite Sage." In Kugel (2001a), 1–26.
———. 2001c. "Some Instances of Biblical Exegesis in Qumran Songs and Wisdom." In Kugel (2001a), 155–69.
———. 2002. *Shem in the Tents of Eber: Studies on the Interaction of Hellenism and Judaism.* Leiden: Brill.
———. 2003. *The God of Old: Inside the Lost World of the Bible.* New York: Free Press.
———. 2005a. *Prayers That Cite Scripture.* Cambridge, MA: Harvard University Center for Jewish Studies.
———. 2005b. "The Scripturalization of Prayer." In Kugel (2005a), 1–5.
———. 2006a. *The Ladder of Jacob: Ancient Interpretations of the Biblical Story of Jacob and His Children.* Princeton, NJ: Princeton University Press.
———. 2006b: "Exegetical Notes on 4Q225." *Dead Sea Discoveries* 13: 73–98.

———. 2007a. *How to Read the Bible: A Guide to Scripture, Then and Now.* New York: Free Press.

———. 2007b. "Some Thoughts on John Barton's *Oracles of God.*" *Journal of Hebrew Scriptures* 7: 12–21.

———. 2007c. "How Old Is the Aramaic Levi Document?" *Dead Sea Discoveries* 14: 291–312.

———. 2008a. "Another View." *Biblical Archaeology Review* 34: 68–69, 84.

———. 2008b. "Some Unanticipated Consequences of the Sinai Revelation: A Religion of Laws." In Brooke et al. (2008), 1–14.

———. 2009. "On the Interpolations in the Book of Jubilees." *Revue de Qumran* 94: 215–72.

———. 2010a. "Early Jewish Biblical Interpretation." In Collins and Harlow (2010), 121–42.

———. 2010b. "Which Is Older, the Book of Jubilees or the Genesis Apocryphon?" In Roitman et al. (2010), 257–94.

———. 2010c. "Some Translation and Copying Mistakes from the Original Hebrew of the Testaments of the Twelve Patriarchs." In Metso et al. (2010), 45–56

———. 2010d "Judaism: An Odd Sort of Religion-of-Laws." Gruss Lecture, New York University Law School. Available at www.law.nyu.edu/news/ KUGEL_ GRUSS_LECTURE.

———. 2011a. *In the Valley of the Shadow: On the Foundations of Religious Belief.* New York: Free Press.

———. 2011b. "The Beginnings of Biblical Interpretation." In Henze (2011b), 3–23.

———. 2012a. *A Walk Through Jubilees: Studies in the Book of Jubilees and the World of Its Creation.* (Supplements to the *Journal for the Study of Judaism* 156.) Leiden: Brill.

———. 2012b. "Jubilees, Philo, and the Problem of Genesis." In N. David et al. (2012), 295–311.

———. 2013a: "The Testaments of the Twelve Patriarchs: A New Translation and Commentary." In Feldman et al. (2013), 1697–1856.

———. 2013b. "The Descent of the Wicked Angels and the Persistence of Evil." In Anderson and Kaminsky (2013), 210–34.

———. 2014. "Is the Book of *Jubilees* a Commentary on Genesis or an Intended Replacement?" In *Congress Volume Munich 2013*, edited by C. M. Maier, 67–91. Leiden: Brill.

———. 2015a. "Windy and Fiery Angels: Pre-rabbinic and Rabbinic Interpretations of Ps. 104:4." In Kister (2015), 134–49.

———. 2015b. "'I am the Man': The Afterlife of a Biblical Verse in Second Temple Times." In Najman and Schmid (2016).

———. 2015c. "The Compositional History of the Book of Jubilees." *Revue de Qumran* 104: 517–37.

———. 2016. "The Divine Long-Range Planner and Second Temple Wisdom." In Rey et al. (2016), 24–42.

Kugel, J., and R. Greer. 1986. *Early Biblical Interpretation.* Philadelphia: Westminster.

Kugel, J., and L. Ravid. 2002. "The Calendar of the *Book of Jubilees:* A Reexamination." Appendix to unpublished PhD diss., "Issues in the Book of Jubilees," Bar-Ilan University.

Kutscher, E. 1982. *A History of the Hebrew Language.* Jerusalem: Magnes.

Lakoff, G., and M. Johnson. 1999. *Philosophy in the Flesh: The Embodied Mind and Its Challenge to Western Thought.* New York: Basic Books.

Lambek, M. 1981. *Human Spirits: A Cultural Account of Trance in Mayotte.* New York: Cambridge University Press.

Lambert, D. 2015. "The Book of Job in Ritual Perspective." *Journal of Biblical Literature* 134: 557–75.

———. 2016a. *How Repentance Became Biblical: Judaism, Christianity, and the Interpretation of Scripture.* New York: Oxford University Press.
———. 2016b. "Refreshing Philology: James Barr, Supersessionism, and the State of Biblical Words." *Biblical Interpretation* 24: 332–56.
Lambert, W. G. 1996. *Babylonian Wisdom Literature.* 2nd ed. Winona Lake, IN: Eisenbrauns.
Lange, A. 1995. *Weisheit und Prädestination.* Leiden: Brill.
———, et al. 2003. *Die Dämonologie der israelitisch-judischen und frühchristlichen Literatur im Kontext ihrer Umwelt.* Tübingen: Mohr-Siebeck.
———, et al. 2011. *Light Against Darkness: Dualism in Ancient Mediterranean Religion and the Contemporary World.* Göttingen: Vandenhoeck & Ruprecht.
Langer, S. K. 1942. *Philosophy in a New Key: A Study in the Symbolism of Reason, Rite, and Art.* Cambridge, MA: Harvard University Press.
Laroi, F., et al. 2014. "Culture and Hallucinations, Overview and Future Directions." *Schizophrenia Journal* 40, supp. no. 4: 213–20.
Lawlor, J. I. 2004. "Word Event in Jeremiah: A Look at the Composition's 'Introductory Formulas.'" In Kaltner and Stulman (2004), 231–43.
Lawson, E. T., and R. N. McCauley. 1990. *Rethinking Religion: Connecting Cognition and Culture.* New York: Cambridge University Press.
Leavitt, J. 1993. "Are Trance and Possession Disorders?" *Transcultural Psychiatric Review* 30: 51–57.
Leclant, J., et al. 1992. *Les sagesses du proche orient ancien.* Paris: Presses Universitaires de France.
Lemche, N. P. 2008. *The Old Testament Between Theology and History: A Critical Survey.* Louisville: Westminster John Knox.
Leroi-Gourhan, A. 1993. *Gesture and Speech.* Cambridge, MA: MIT Press.
Levenson, J. D. 1985: *From Sinai to Zion.* New York: Seabury Winston, 1985.
———. 1987. "The Sources of Torah: Psalm 119 and the Modes of Revelation in Second Temple Judaism." In *Ancient Israelite Religion,* edited by P. D. Miller et al., 559–57. Philadelphia: Fortress.
———. 2012. *Inheriting Abraham: The Legacy of the Patriarch in Judaism, Christianity, and Islam.* Princeton, NJ: Princeton University Press.
Levine, L. 2000. *The Ancient Synagogue.* New Haven, CT: Yale University Press.
Levinson, B. 1992. "The Human Voice in Divine Revelation." In *Innovation in Religious Traditions: Essays in the Interpretation of Religious Change,* edited by M. A. Williams, C. Cox, and M. S. Jaffee, 35–72. Berlin: Mouton De Gruter.
———. 2010. *Legal Revision and Religious Renewal in Israel.* Cambridge: Cambridge University Press.
Levison, J. R. 1997. *The Spirit in First Century Judaism.* Leiden: Brill.
———. 2006. "Philo's Personal Experience and the Persistence of Prophecy." In Floyd and Haak (2006), 151–65.
———. 2009. *Filled with the Spirit.* Grand Rapids: Eerdmans.
Lévi-Strauss, C. 1966. *The Savage Mind.* Chicago: University of Chicago Press.
Lewis, I. M. 1979. *Ecstatic Religion: A Study of Shamanism and Spirit Possession.* London: Routledge.
Lewis, J. P. 1964. "What Do We Mean by Jabneh?" *Journal of Bible and Religion* 32: 125–32.
Liddell, H. G., and R. Scott. 1953. *A Greek-English Lexicon, Revised and Augmented by H. S. Jones.* Oxford: Clarendon.

Lieberman, S. 1973. *Tosefta Kifshuto—Nashim*. New York: Jewish Theological Seminary.

Lienhardt, G. 1961. *Divinity and Experience: The Religion of the Dinka*. Oxford: Oxford University Press.

Lieu, J. 2004. *Christian Identity in the Jewish and Greco-Roman World*. New York: Oxford University Press.

Lim, T. H. 2010. "Authoritative Scriptures and the Dead Sea Scrolls." In *The Oxford Handbook of the Dead Sea Scrolls*, edited by T. H. Lim and J. J. Collins, 302–36. New York: Oxford University Press.

Lindblom, J. 1962. *Prophecy in Ancient Israel*. Oxford: Basil Blackwell.

Lipschits, O., et al. 2011. *Judah and Judeans in the Achaemenid Period: Negotiating Identity in an International Context*. Winona Lake, IN: Eisenbrauns.

Lizot, J. 1985. *Tales of the Yanomami: Daily Life in the Venezuelan Forest*. Cambridge: Cambridge University Press.

Loader, W. 2007. *Enoch, Levi, and Jubilees on Sexuality*. Grand Rapids: Eerdmans.

Lock, A. 1981. "Universals in Human Conception." In *Indigenous Psychologies: The Anthropology of the Self*, edited by P. Heelas and A. Lock, 19–28. London: Academic Press.

Longman, T. 1990. *Fictional Akkadian Autobiography: A Generic and Comparative Study*. Winona Lake, IN: Eisenbrauns.

———. 1995. *God Is a Warrior*. Grand Rapids: Zondervan.

Lopez, D. S. 2007. "A Prayer for the Long Life of the Dalai Lama." In *Buddhism in Practice*, edited by D. S. Lopez, 133–38. Princeton NJ: Princeton University Press.

Lord, A. 1990. *The Singer of Tales*. Cambridge, MA: Harvard University Press.

Lucas, E. C. 1988. "The Origin of Daniel's Four Empires in the Fourth Sibyl and the Book of Daniel." *Tyndale Bulletin* 39: 185–202.

Luhrmann, T., et al. 2014. "Differences in Voice-Hearing Experiences of People with Psychosis in the USA, India and Ghana: Interview-Based Study." *British Journal of Psychiatry*, https://www.academia.edu/8691319/hearing_voices_in_three_different_cultures.

Ma, C., and T. J. Schoeneman. 1997. "Individualism vs. Collectivism: A Comparison of Kenyan and American Self-Concepts." *Basic and Applied Social Psychology* 19: 261–73.

Machinist, P. 1995. "Fate, *miqreh*, and Reason: Some Reflections on Qohelet and Biblical Thought." In *Solving Riddles and Untying Knots: Studies in Honor of Jonas Greenfield*, edited by Z. Zevit et al., 159–75. Winona Lake, IN: Eisenbrauns.

MacKay, H. 2001. *Sabbath and Synagogue: The Question of Sabbath Worship in Ancient Judaism*. Leiden: Brill.

Macmillan, M. B. 2000. *An Odd Kind of Fame: Stories of Phineas Gage*. Cambridge, MA: MIT Press.

Malchow, B. V. 1996. *Social Justice in the Hebrew Bible*. Wilmington, DE: Glazier, 1996.

Malinowski, B. 1954. *"Magic, Science and Religion" and Other Essays*. Garden City, NY: Anchor-Doubleday.

Mandel, P. 2001. "Midrashic Exegesis and Its Precedents in the Dead Sea Scrolls." *Dead Sea Discoveries* 8: 149–68.

Mark the Deacon. 2000. "The Life of Saint Porphyry of Gaza." Translated by Claudia Rapp. In *Medieval Hagiography: An Anthology*, edited by T. Head, 53–75. London: Routledge.

Markus, H. R., and S. Kitayama. 1991. "Cultural Variation in the Self-Concept." In *The Self: Interdisciplinary Approaches*, edited by J. Strauss and G. R. Goethals. Berlin: Springer Verlag.

Markus, H. R., and S. K. Mullally. 1997. "Diversity in Modes of Cultural Participation." In

The Conceptual Self in Context, edited by U. Neisser and D. Jopling, 13–74. Cambridge: Cambridge University Press.

Marriot, M. 1976. "Hindu Transactions: Diversity Without Dualism." In *Transaction and Meaning: Directions in the Anthropology of Exchange and Symbolic Behavior*, edited by B. Kapferer, 109–42. Philadelphia: Institute for the Study of Human Issues.

Mason, E., et al. 2012. *A Teacher for All Generations: Essays in Honor of James C. VanderKam*. Leiden: Brill.

Mason, R. A. 1984. "Some Echoes of the Preaching in the Second Temple?: Traditional Elements in Zechariah 1–8." *Zeitschrift für die alttestamentliche Wissenschaft* 96: 221–35.

Mattila, S. L. 2000. "Ben Sira and the Stoics." *Journal of Biblical Literature* 119: 473–501.

Maurer, A. 2003. "Some Remarks on 4Q510 and 511." In Schiffman et al. (2003).

Mauss, M. 1950. *Sociologie et anthropologie*. Paris: Presse Universitaire de France.

———. 1985. "A Category of the Human Mind: The Notion of Person, the Notion of Self." In *The Category of Person: Anthropology, Philosophy, History*, edited by M. Carrithers et al., 1–25. New York: Cambridge University Press.

Mazar, A. 1985. "The Israelites in Canaan in the Light of Archaeological Excavations." In *Biblical Archaeology Today*, edited by J. Aviram et al., 61–70. Jerusalem: Israel Exploration Society.

Mazar, B., et al. 1968. *Encyclopaedia Biblica* (Hebrew). Vol. 5. Jerusalem: Mosad Bialik.

Mbiti J. S. 1969. *African Religions and Philosophy*. Oxford: Heinemann Educational.

McCann, J. C. 1993. *The Shape and Shaping of the Psalter*. Sheffield: JSOT Press.

McCarter, P. K. 1987. "Aspects of the Religion of the Israelite Monarchy: Biblical and Epigraphic Data." In *Ancient Israelite Religion: Essays in Honor of Frank Moore Cross*, edited by P. D. Hanson et al., 137–55. Philadelphia: Fortress.

McCarthy, D. J. 1978. *Treaty and Covenant*. Rev. ed. Rome: PBI.

McGinn, C. 2002a. "Consciousness and Content." In Block et al. (2002), 295–308.

———. 2002b. "Can We Solve the Mind-Body Problem?" In Block et al. (2002), 529–42.

Meier, G. 1971. *Mensch und Freier Wille*. Tuebingen: Mohr.

Meier, J. P. 2009. *A Marginal Jew: Rethinking the Historical Jesus*. New Haven, CT: Yale University Press.

Mellinkoff, R. 1970. *The Horned Moses in Medieval Art and Thought*. Berkeley: University of California Press.

Mendenhall, G. 1955. *Law and Covenant in Israel and the Ancient Near East*. Pittsburgh: Presbyterian Committee of Colportage of Western Pennsylvania.

Meshel, Z. 2012. *Kuntillet ʿAjrud: An Iron Age II Religious Site on the Judah-Sinai Border*. Jerusalem: Israel Exploration Society.

Messing, S. D. 1958. "Group Therapy and Social Status in the *Zar* Cult of Ethiopia." *American Anthropologist* 60: 1120–25.

Metso, S. 2007a. *The Textual Development of the Qumran Community Rule*. Leiden: Brill.

———. 2007b. *The Serekh Texts*. London: T&T Clark.

Metso, S., et al. 2010. *The Dead Sea Scrolls: Transmission of Traditions and Production of Texts*. Leiden: Brill.

Mettinger, T. 1994. "Aniconism—A West Semitic Context for the Israelite Phenomenon." In *Ein Gott Allein?*, edited by W. Dietrich and M. A. Klopfenstein. Freiburg: Freiburg University Press.

———. 1995. *No Graven Image?: Israelite Aniconism in Its Ancient Near Eastern Context*. Stockholm: Almqvist & Wiksell.

Meyers, C. 2010. "Household Religion." In *Religious Diversity in Ancient Israel and Judah,* edited by F. Stavrakopoulou and J. Barton, 118–34. London: T&T Clark.

Meyers, C., and E. Meyers. 1993. *Zechariah 9–14.* (Anchor Bible vol. 25C.) New York: Doubleday.

Milgrom, J. 1990. *Numbers.* Philadelphia: Jewish Publication Society.

Milik, J. T. 1992. "Les modèles araméens du livre d'Esther dans la grotte 4 à Qumran." *Revue de Qumran* 15: 321–406.

Milikowsky, Ch. 2013. *Seder Olam: Critical Edition, Commentary, and Introduction.* Jerusalem: Yad Ben Zvi.

Miller, J. 2007. "Cultural Psychology of Moral Development." In *Handbook of Cultural Psychology,* edited by S. Kitayama and D. Cohen, 477–99. New York: Guilford Press.

Miller, M. 1974. "The Moabite Stone as a Memorial Stela." *Palestine Exploration Quarterly* 106: 9–18.

Miller, P. D. 1983. "Trouble and Woe: Interpreting the Biblical Laments." *Interpretation* 37: 32–45.

———. 2000. *The Religion of Ancient Israel.* Louisville: Westminster John Knox.

Monson, J. 2000. "The New 'Ain Dara Temple: Closest Solomonic Parallel." *Biblical Archaeology Review* 26: 20–35.

Moran, W. 1962. "A Kingdom of Priests." In *The Bible in Current Catholic Thought,* edited by J. L. McKenzie, 7–20. New York: Herder & Herder.

———. 1963. "The Ancient Near Eastern Background of the Love of God in Deuteronomy." *Catholic Biblical Quarterly* 25: 77–87.

Morentz, S. 1992. *Egyptian Religion.* Translated by Anne Keep. Ithaca, NY: Cornell University Press.

Morgenstern, J. 1939. "The Mythological Background of Psalm 82." *Hebrew Union College Annual* 14: 29–126.

Morris, C. 1972. *The Discovery of the Individual, 1050–1200.* London: SPCK.

Morris, T. V. 2003. "Omnipotence and Omniscience." Reprinted in *Philosophy of Religion: An Anthology,* edited by C. Taliaferro and P. J. Griffiths, 58–72. Oxford: Blackwell.

Morrison, A. D. 2008. *The Narrator in Archaic Greek and Hellenistic Poetry.* New York: Cambridge University Press.

Mowinckel, S. 1930. "Wann wurde der J-Kultus in Jerusalem offiziel bildlos?" *Acta Orientalia* 8: 257–79.

———. 1937. "Zur Geschichte der Decaloge." *Zeitschrift für die alttestamentliche Wissenschaft* 55: 218–35.

———. 1962. *The Psalms in Israel's Worship.* 2 vols. Nashville: Abingdon.

Moyise, S. 1995. *The Old Testament in the Book of Revelation.* Sheffield: Sheffield Academic Press.

———. 2002. "Intertextuality and Biblical Studies: A Review." *Verbum et Ecclesia* 23: 418–31.

Mullen, E. T. 1980. *The Assembly of the Gods.* Cambridge, MA: Harvard University Press.

Muraoka, T., and J. F. Elwolde. 2000. *Diggers at the Well: Proceedings of a Third International Symposium on the Hebrew of the Dead Sea Scrolls and Ben Sira.* Leiden: Brill.

Murray, P. 1981. "Poetic Inspiration in Early Greece." *Journal of Hellenic Studies* 101: 87–100.

Nagel, T. 2002. "What's It Like to Be a Bat?" Originally published 1974. Reprinted in Block et al. (2002), 319–27.

———. 2012. *Mind and Cosmos: Why the Materialist Neo-Darwinian Conception of Nature Is Almost Certainly False.* New York: Oxford University Press.

Nagy, G. 1990a. *Pindar's Homer: The Lyric Possession of an Epic Past.* Baltimore: Johns Hopkins University Press.

———. 1990b. "Ancient Greek Poetry, Prophecy, and Concepts of Theory." In Kugel (1990d), 56–64.

Naidoff, B. 1978. "A Man to Work the Soil: A New Interpretation of Genesis 2–3." *Journal for the Study of the Old Testament* 5: 2–14.

Najman, H. 2003. *Seconding Sinai: The Development of Mosaic Discourse in Second Temple Judaism.* Leiden: Brill.

———. 2010. *Past Renewals: Interpretive Authority, Renewed Revelation, and the Quest for Perfection in Jewish Antiquity.* (Supplements to the *Journal for the Study of Judaism* 53.) Leiden: Brill.

———. 2014. *Losing the Temple and Recovering the Future.* New York: Cambridge University Press.

Najman, H., and K. Schmid, eds. 2016. *Jeremiah's Scriptures: Production, Reception, Interaction, and Transformation.* (Supplements to the *Journal for the Study of Judaism.*) Leiden: Brill.

Nasuti, H. 1988. *Tradition History and the Psalms of Asaph.* Atlanta: Scholars Press.

Neusner, J., et al., eds. 1978. *Judaic Perspectives on Ancient Israel.* Philadelphia: Fortress.

Newman, G. E., et al. 2008. "The Origins of Causal Perception: Evidence from Postdictive Processing in Infancy." *Cognitive Psychology* 57: 262–91.

Newman, J. 1999. *Praying by the Book.* Atlanta: Scholars Press.

Newsom, C. 1985. *Songs of the Sabbath Service.* Atlanta: Scholars Press.

———. 1992. "The Case of the Blinking I: Discourse of the Self at Qumran." *Semeia* 57: 13–23.

———. 2004. *The Self as Symbolic Space: Constructing Identity and Community at Qumran.* Leiden: Brill.

———. 2012a. "Models of the Moral Self: Hebrew Bible and Second Temple Judaism." *Journal of Biblical Literature* 131: 5–25.

———. 2012b. "Flesh, Spirit, and the Indigenous Psychology of the *Hodayo.*" In *Prayer and Poetry in the Dead Sea Scrolls and Related Literature,* edited by J. Penner et al. Leiden: Brill.

Nicholson, E. W. 1967. *Deuteronomy and Tradition.* Philadelphia: Fortress.

———. 1973. *Exodus and Sinai in History and Tradition.* Oxford: Oxford University Press.

Nickelsburg, G. W. E. 2001. *1 Enoch 1.* Minneapolis: Fortress.

Niditch, S. 2010. "Experiencing the Divine: Heavenly Visits, Earthly Encounters, and the Land of the Dead." In *Religious Diversity in Ancient Israel and Judah,* edited by F. Stavrakopoulou and J. Barton, 11–22. London: T&T Clark.

———. 2015. *The Responsive Self: Personal Religion in Biblical Literature of the Neo-Babylonian and Persian Periods.* New Haven, CT: Yale University Press.

Nisbett, R. 2004. *The Geography of Thought.* New York: Free Press.

Nissinen, M. 2004. "What Is Prophecy?: An Ancient Near Eastern Perspective." In Kaltner and Stulman (2004).

———. 2006. "The Dubious Image of Prophecy." In Floyd and Haak (2006), 35–41.

Nitzan, B. 1996. *Qumran Prayer and Poetry.* Jerusalem: Mosad Bialik.

North, R. 1993. "Brain and Nerve in the Biblical Outlook." *Biblica* 74: 577–97.

Noth, M. 1967. *The Laws in the Pentateuch and Other Studies.* Philadelphia: Fortress.

Oakes, L. M. 1994. "The Development of Infants' Use of Continuity Cues in Their Perception of Causality." *Developmental Psychology* 30: 869–79.

O'Connor, F. 1979. *The Habit of Being: Letters of Flannery O'Connor.* New York: Farrar, Straus and Giroux.

O'Connor, K. M. 1988. *The Confessions of Jeremiah: Their Interpretation and Role in Chapters 1–25.* Atlanta: Scholars Press.

O'Connor, M. 1979. "The Rhetoric of the Kilamuwa Inscription." *Bulletin of the American Schools of Oriental Research* 226: 15–29.

Olyan, S. 1988. *Asherah and the Cult of YHWH.* Atlanta: Scholars Press.

———. 1993. *A Thousand Thousands Served Him: Exegesis and the Naming of Angels in Ancient Judaism.* Tübingen: Mohr.

———. 2004. *Biblical Mourning: Ritual and Social Dimensions.* New York: Oxford University Press.

———. 2005. "The Search for the Elusive Self in Texts of the Hebrew Bible." In *Religion and the Self in Antiquity,* edited by D. Brakke et al., 40–50. Bloomington: Indiana University Press.

———. 2008. "Family Religion in Israel and the Wider Levant of the First Millennium BCE." In *Household and Family Religion,* edited by J. Bodel and S. Olyan, 113–26. Oxford: Blackwell.

———. 2012. "Is Isaiah 40–55 Really Monotheistic?" *Journal of Ancient Near Eastern Religions* 12: 190–201.

Oppenheim, L. 1977. *Ancient Mesopotamia: Portrait of a Dead Civilization.* Rev. ed. completed by E. Reiner. Chicago: University of Chicago Press.

Overholt, T. 1986. *Prophecy in Cross-Cultural Perspective.* Atlanta: Society of Biblical Literature.

———. 1989. *Channels of Prophecy.* Minneapolis: Fortress.

Pagolu, A. 1998. *The Religion of the Patriarchs.* Sheffield: Sheffield Academic Press.

Parpola, S., and K. Parpola. 1988. *Neo-Syrian Treaties and Loyalty Oaths.* Helsinki: Helsinki University Press.

Penner, J. 2012. *Patterns of Daily Prayer in Second Temple Period Judaism.* Leiden: Brill.

Penner, J., et al. 2012. *Prayer and Poetry in the Dead Sea Scrolls and Related Literature.* Leiden: Brill.

Perlitt, L. 1969. *Bundestheologie im Alten Testament.* Neukirchen-Vluyn: Neukirchener Verlag.

Persinger, M. 1983. "Religious and Mystical Experiences as Artifacts of Temporal Lobe Function: A General Hypothesis." In *Perceptual and Motor Skills* 57: 1255–62.

Petersen D. 1988. "Rethinking the End of Prophecy." In *Wünschet Jerusalem Frieden: Collected Communications to the XIIth Congress of the International Organization for the Study of the Old Testament, Jerusalem 1986,* edited by M. Augustin and K. Schunck, 65–71. Frankfort am Main: Peter Lang.

———. 2000. "Defining Prophecy and Prophetic Literature." In *Prophecy in Its Ancient Near Eastern Context,* edited by M. Nissinen, 33–44. Atlanta: Society of Biblical Literature.

Pietersma, A. 1980. "David in the Greek Psalter." *Vetus Testamentum* 30: 213–26.

Pinker, S. 1997. *How the Mind Works.* New York: Norton.

———. 2000. *The Language Instinct.* New York: Harper Collins.

Polk, T. 1984. *The Prophetic Persona: Jeremiah and the Language of the Self.* (*Journal for the Study of the Old Testament,* supp. 45.) Sheffield: JSOT Press.

Pollock, S. 1999. *Ancient Mesopotamia: The Eden That Never Was.* Cambridge: Cambridge University Press.

Pongratz-Leisten, B. n.d. "Divine Agency and Astralization of Gods in Ancient Mesopotamia." Available at: http://www.academia.edu/369377/Divine_Agency_and_Astralization_of_gods_in_ Ancient_Mesopotamia.

———. 2015. *Religion and Ideology in Assyria.* Berlin: De Gruyter.

Porter, B. N., ed. 2000: *One God or Many?: Concepts of Divinity in the Ancient World.* (Transactions of the Casco Bay Assyriological Institute, vol. 1.) Bethesda, MD: CDL.

Premack, D., and A. J. Premack. 1994. "Levels of Causal Understanding in Chimpanzees and Children." *Cognition* 50: 347–62.

Premack, D., and G. Woodruff. 1978. "Does the Chimpanzee Have a Theory of Mind?" *Behavioral and Brain Science* 4: 515–26.

Prinsloo, W. 2003. "The Psalms." In *Eerdmans Commentary on the Bible,* edited by J. Dunn and J. W. Rogerson, 364–436. Grand Rapids: Eerdmans.

Propp, W. 1988. "The Rod of Aaron and the Sin of Moses." *Journal of Biblical Literature* 107: 19–26.

———. 2006. *Exodus 19–40.* (Anchor Bible.) New Haven, CT: Yale University Press.

Quinn, N. 2006. "The Self." *Anthropological Theory* 6: 362–84.

Rabelais, F. 1904. *Gargantua and Pantagruel.* Translated by T. Urquhart and P. Motteux. London: Bullen.

Rabin, Ch. 1991. *Semitic Languages.* Jerusalem: Mosad Bialik.

Rabinowitz, I. 1973. "Pesher/Pittaron: Its Biblical Meaning and Its Significance in the Qumran Literature." *Revue de Qumran* 8: 219–32.

Rahlfs, A. 1891. *'Āni und 'ānāw in den Psalmen.* Leipzig: A. Pries.

Ravid, L, 2000. "The Relationship of the Sabbath Laws in *Jubilees* 50:6–13 to the Rest of the Book." *Tarbiz* 69: 161–66.

Reader, I., and G. J. J. Tanabe. 1998. *Practically Religious: Worldly Benefits and the Common Religion of Japan.* Honolulu: University of Hawaii Press.

Redford, D. B. 1970. *A Study of the Biblical Story of Joseph (Genesis 37–50).* Leiden: Brill.

Reed, A. Yoshiko. 2008. "Pseudepigraphy, Authorship, and the Reception of 'the Bible' in Late Antiquity." In *The Reception and Interpretation of the Bible in Late Antiquity,* edited by L. DiTommaso and L. Turcescu, 467–90. Leiden: Brill.

Regev, E. n.d. "Temple and Righteousness in Qumran and Early Christianity: Tracing the Social Difference Between the Two Movements." Available at: booksandjournals.brillonline.com/content/books/10.1163/ej.9789004175242.i=326.18.

Reif, S. 2002. "Prayer in Ben Sira, Qumran, and Second Temple Judaism." In *Ben Sira's God,* edited by R. Egger-Wenzel. Berlin: De Gruyter.

———. 2006. *Problems with Prayers: Studies in the Textual History of Early Rabbinic Liturgy.* Berlin: De Gruyter.

Reiner, E., ed. 1984. *Chicago Assyriological Dictionary.* Vol. 15 ("S"). Chicago: University of Chicago.

Reiterer, F. 1999. "Die immateriallen Ebenen der Schoepfung bei Ben Sira." In Calduch-Benages and Vermeylen (1999), 91–127.

Renaut, A. 1997. *The Era of the Individual: A Contribution to a History of Subjectivity.* Princeton, NJ: Princeton University Press.

Rendsburg, G. 1990. *Linguistic Evidence for the Northern Origin of Selected Psalms.* Atlanta: Scholars Press.

———. 2003. "A Comprehensive Guide to Israelian Hebrew: Grammar and Lexicon." *Orient* 38: 5–35.

Rey, J.-S., et al. 2016. *Rethinking the Boundaries of Sapiential Traditions in Ancient Judaism.* Third International Symposium on Jewish and Christian Literature from the Hellenistic and Roman Period. Leiden, Brill.

Reynolds, K. A. 2010. *Torah as Teacher.* Leiden: Brill.

Rhu, L. 1990. "After the Middle Ages: Authority and Human Fallibility in Renaissance Epic." In Kugel (1990d), 163–84.

Ringgren, H. 1961. *Israelite Religion.* London: SPCK.

Rips, L. J. 2008. "Causal Thinking." In *Reasoning: Studies of Human Inference and Its Foundation,* edited by J. E. Adler and L. J. Rips, 597–631. Cambridge: Cambridge University Press.

Robinson, H. W. 1964. *Corporate Personality in Ancient Israel.* Philadelphia: Fortress.

Rogerson, J. W. 1989. "Anthropology and the Old Testament." In *The World of Ancient Israel,* edited by R. E. Clements, 17–37. New York: Cambridge University Press.

Roitman, A., et al. 2010. *The Dead Sea Scrolls and Contemporary Culture: Proceedings of the International Conference Held at the Israel Museum, Jerusalem (July 6–8, 2008).* Leiden: Brill.

Rollston, C. R. 2010. *Writing and Literacy in the World of Ancient Israel: Epigraphic Evidence from the Iron Age.* Atlanta: Society of Biblical Literature.

Rose, N. 1996. *Inventing Our Selves: Psychology, Power, and Personhood.* Cambridge: Cambridge University Press.

Rosen-Zvi, I. 2006. "Bilhah the Temptress: *The Testament of Reuben* and 'The Birth of Sexuality.'" *Jewish Quarterly Review* 96: 65–94.

———. 2011. *Demonic Desires:* Yetzer Hara *and the Problem of Evil in Late Antiquity.* Philadelphia: University of Pennsylvania Press.

Rotenstreich, N. 1998. *On Faith.* Edited by P. Mendes-Flohr. Chicago: University of Chicago Press.

Roth, M. 1997. *Law Collections from Mesopotamia and Asia Minor.* Atlanta: Scholars Press.

Rowland, C. 2010. "Prophecy and the New Testament." In *Prophets and Prophecy in Ancient Israel,* edited by J. Day, 410–28. New York: T&T Clark.

Rubenstein, J. L. 1995. *The History of Sukkot in the Second Temple and Rabbinic Periods.* Atlanta: Scholars Press.

Ruchames, L., ed. 1971. *A House Dividing Against Itself.* Vol. 2 of *The Letters of William Lloyd Garrison.* Cambridge, MA: Harvard University Press.

Ruel, M. 1982. "Christians as Believers." In *Religious Organization and Religious Experience,* edited by J. Davis, 9–31. London: Academic Press.

Ruger, H. P. 1970. *Text und Textform im Hebraeischen Sirach.* Berlin: De Gruyter.

Rüpke, Jörg, ed. 2013. *The Individual in the Religions of the Ancient Mediterranean.* New York: Oxford University Press.

Sanders, J. A., ed. 1965. *The Psalms Scroll of Qumran Cave 11.* (Discoveries in the Judaean Desert 4.) Oxford: Clarendon.

———, ed. 1967. *The Dead Sea Psalms Scroll.* Ithaca, NY: Cornell University Press.

———. 2003. "The Modern History of the Qumran Psalms Scroll and Canonical Criticism." In *Emanuel: Studies in the Hebrew Bible, the Septuagint, and Dead Sea Scrolls in Honor of Emanuel Tov,* edited by S. M. Paul et al., 393–411. Boston: Brill.

Sankararaman, S., et al. 2012. "The Date of Interbreeding Between Neandertals and Modern Humans." *PLoS Genetics* 8: e-1002947.

Sarna, N. 1979. "The Psalm Superscriptions and the Guilds." In *Studies in Jewish Religious*

and Intellectual History: Presented to Alexander Altmann on the Occasion of His Seventieth Birthday, edited by S. Stein and R. Loewe. Tuscaloosa: University of Alabama Press.
Savran, G. W. 2005. *Encountering the Divine: Theophany in Biblical Narrative.* New York: T&T Clark.
Schams, C. 1998. *Jewish Scribes in the Second Temple Period.* Sheffield: Sheffield Academic Press.
Schaper, J. 2006. "The Death of the Prophet: The Transition from the Spoken to the Written Word of God in the Book of Ezekiel." In Floyd and Haak (2006), 63–79.
Schiffman, L. H. 1975. *The Halakhah at Qumran.* Leiden: Brill.
———. 1991. *From Text to Tradition: A History of Second Temple and Rabbinic Judaism.* Hoboken, NJ: Ktav.
———, et al. 2003. *The Dead Sea Scrolls, 50 Years After Their Discovery: Proceedings of the Jerusalem Congress, July 20–25, 1997.* Jerusalem: Israel Exploration Society.
Schuller, E. 1986. *Non-Canonical Psalms from Qumran.* Atlanta: Scholars Press.
———. 1990. "Some Observations of Blessings on God in Texts from Qumran." In *Of Scribes and Scrolls,* edited by H. Attridge et al., 133–43. Lanham, MD: University Press of America.
———. 1994: "Prayer, Hymnic and Liturgical Texts from Qumran." In *The Community of the Renewed Covenant: The Notre Dame Symposium on the Dead Sea Scrolls,* edited by E. Ulrich and J. C. VanderKam, 153–71. Notre Dame, IN: Notre Dame University Press.
———. 2006. "Prayers and Psalms from the Pre-Maccabean Period." *Dead Sea Discoveries* 13: 306–18.
Schuster, R. 2015. "Discovery in Israel Pushes Back Dawn of Agriculture to 23,000 Years Ago." *Haaretz,* July 23.
Schwartz, B. 1996. "The Priestly Account of the Theophany and Lawgiving at Mount Sinai." In *Texts, Temples and Traditions: A Tribute to Menahem Haran,* edited by M. V. Fox et al., 103–34. Winona Lake, IN: Eisenbrauns.
Schwartz, S. 1990. *Josephus and Judean Politics.* Leiden: Brill.
Scott, R. B. Y. 1971. *The Way of Wisdom.* New York: Macmillan.
Seeligman, I. L. 1963. "Menschliches Heldentum und Göttliches Hilfe." *Theologische Zeitschrift* 19: 385–411.
Segal, M. 2007. *The Book of Jubilees: Rewritten Bible, Redaction, Ideology and Theology.* Leiden: Brill.
Segal, M. 2011. "The Chronological Conception of the Persian Period in Daniel 9." *Journal of Ancient Judaism* 2: 283–303.
Segal, M. H. 1972. *The Complete Book of Ben Sira.* Jerusalem: Bialik Institute.
Septimus, B. 2004. "Iterated Quotation Formulae in Talmudic Narrative and Exegesis." In *The Idea of Biblical Interpretation,* edited by H. Najman and J. H. Newman, 371–98. Leiden: Brill.
Shaked, S. 1984. "Iranian Influence on Judaism: First Century BCE to Second Century CE." In *Cambridge History of Judaism,* edited by W. Horbury et al., 1:308–25. Cambridge: Cambridge University Press.
———. 1994. *Dualism in Transition.* London: SOAS.
Shapiro, L. 2011. *Embodied Cognition.* Oxford: Routledge.
Shulman, D., and G Stroumsa. 2002. *Self and Self Transformation in the History of Religions.* New York: Oxford University Press.

Shupak, N. 2016. *"No Man Is Born Wise": Ancient Egyptian Wisdom and Its Contact with Biblical Literature*. Jerusalem: Bialik Institute.
Shwarzman, O. 2007. *White Doctor, Black Gods*. Tel Aviv: Aryeh Nir.
Simons Genome Diversity Project. 2016. "300 Genomes from 142 Diverse Populations." *Nature* 21 (September).
Smith, D. E. 2015. "The Divining Snake: Reading Genesis 3 in the Context of Mesopotamian Ophiomancy." *Journal of Biblical Literature* 134: 31–49.
Smith, M. S. 2002. *The Early History of God: Yahweh and the Other Deities in Ancient Israel*. Grand Rapids: Eerdmans.
———. 2015. "The Three Bodies of God in the Hebrew Bible." *Journal of Biblical Literature* 134: 471–84.
Snell, B. 1960. *The Discovery of the Mind in Greek Philosophy and Literature*. New York: Harper.
Sommer, B. 1996. "Did Prophecy Cease?: Evaluating a Reevaluation." *Journal of Biblical Literature* 115: 31–47.
———. 1998. *A Prophet Reads Scripture: Allusion in Isaiah 40–66*. Palo Alto, CA: Stanford University Press.
———. 2009. *The Bodies of God and the World of Ancient Israel*. Cambridge: Cambridge University Press.
———. 2015. "Nature, Revelation, and Grace in Psalm 19: Towards a Theological Reading of Scripture." *Harvard Theological Review* 108: 376–401.
Sommer, I. E., et al. 2010. "Healthy Individuals with Auditory Verbal Hallucinations; Who Are They? Psychiatric Assessments of a Selected Sample of 103 Subjects." *Schizophrenia Bulletin* 36: 633–41.
Spiro, M. 1993. "Is the Western Conception of the Self 'Peculiar' Within the Context of the World Cultures?" *Ethos* 21: 312–28.
Stager, L. 1985. "The Archaeology of the Family in Ancient Israel." *Bulletin of the American Schools of Oriental Research* 260: 1–35.
Starr, C. 1986. *Individual and Community: The Rise of the Polis, 800-500 BC*. New York: Oxford University Press.
Stavrakopoulo, F., and J. Barton, ed. 2010. *Religious Diversity in Ancient Israel and Judah*. London: T&T Clark.
Stead, M. R. 2009. *The Intertextuality of Zechariah 1–8*. New York: T&T Clark.
Stegemann, H., and E. Schuller, eds. 2009. *1QHodayot[a]*. Translated by C. Newsom. (Discoveries in the Judean Desert 40.) Oxford: Clarendon.
Stern, E. 2006. "The Religious Revolution in Persian-Period Judah." In *Judah and the Judeans in the Persian Period*, edited by O. Lipschits and M. Oeming, 199–205. Winona Lake, IN: Eisenbrauns.
Stern, S. 1994. *Jewish Identity in Early Rabbinic Writings*. Leiden: Brill.
Stiblitz, G. 1898. "The Old Testament Prophets as Social Reformers." *Biblical World* 12: 20–28.
Stipp, H-J. 2016. "Deutero-Jeremianic Language in the Book of Jeremiah." In Najman and Schmid (2016).
Stökl, J. 2012. *Prophecy in the Ancient Near East: A Philological and Sociological Comparison*. Leiden: Brill.
Stone, M. 1990. *Fourth Ezra*. Minneapolis: Fortress.
———. 1991. *Selected Studies in Pseudepigrapha with Special Reference to the Armenian Tradition*. Leiden: Brill.

——. 1999. "The Axis of History at Qumran." In *Pseudepigraphic Perspectives: The Apocrypha and Pseudepigrapha in Light of the Dead Sea Scrolls*, edited by E. Chazon and M. Stone, 133–49. Leiden: Brill.

——. 2006. "Pseudepigraphy Reconsidered." *Review of Rabbinic Judaism* 9: 1–15.

——. 2011. *Ancient Judaism: New Visions and Views.* Grand Rapids: Eerdmans.

Stout, D., and T. Chaminade. 2009. "Making Tools and Making Sense: Complex, Intentional Behaviour in Human Evolution." Available at: http:// discovery.ucl.ac.uk/14327/1/14327.pdf.

Strathern, M. 1988. *The Gender of the Gift.* Berkeley: University of California Press.

Stroumsa, G. 2012. *The End of Sacrifice: Religious Transformations in Late Antiquity.* Chicago: University of Chicago Press.

Stuckenbruck, L. 2011. "The Interiorization of Dualism Within the Human Being in Second Temple Judaism: The Treatise of the Two Spirits in Its Tradition-Historical Context." In *Light Against Darkness: Dualism in Ancient Mediterranean Religion and the Contemporary World*, edited by A. Lange et al., 145–68. Göttingen: Vandenhoeck & Ruprecht.

Stulman, L. 2005. *Jeremiah.* Nashville: Abingdon.

Swartz, M. 2012. "Liturgy, Poetry, and the Persistence of Sacrifices." In *Was 70 CE a Watershed in Jewish History?*, edited by D. R. Schwartz and Z. Weiss, 393–412. Leiden: Brill.

Taylor, C. 1989. *Sources of the Self: The Making of the Modern Identity.* New York: Cambridge University Press.

——. 2007: *A Secular Age.* Cambridge, MA: Harvard University Press.

Thomas, N., et al. 2014. "Psychological Therapies for Auditory Hallucinations (Voices): Current Status and Key Directions for Future Research." *Schizophrenia Bulletin* 40, supp. 4: 202–12.

Toeg, A. 1977. *The Giving of the Torah at Mount Sinai.* Jerusalem: Magnes.

Tollington, J. E. 1993. *Tradition and Innovation in Haggai and Zechariah 1–8.* Sheffield: JSOT Press.

Torrey, E. F. 1967. "The *Zar* Cult in Ethiopia." *International Journal of Social Psychiatry* 13: 216–23.

Trawick, M. 1992. *Notes on Love in a Tamil Culture.* Berkeley: University of California Press.

Tremlin, T. 2006. *Minds and Gods: The Cognitive Foundations of Religion.* New York: Oxford University Press.

Turnbull, C. 1961. *The Forest People.* New York: Simon & Schuster.

——. 1965. *Wayward Servants.* Garden City, NY: American Museum of Natural History.

Ullendorf, E. 1962. "The Meaning of qhlt." *Vetus Testamentum* 2: 215.

Ulmer, R., ed. 2009. *Pesiqta Rabbati: A Synoptic Edition.* Lanham, MD: University Press of America.

Urbach, E. E. 1946. "When Did Prophecy Cease?" *Tarbiz* 17: 1–17.

——. 1975. *The Sages.* Cambridge, MA: Harvard University Press.

Van der Horst, P. W. 1998. *Hellenism-Judaism-Christianity: Essays on Their Interaction.* Louvain: Peeters.

Van der Kooij, A. 2001. "The Septuagint Psalms and the First Book of Maccabees." In *The Old Greek Psalter: Studies in Honour of Albert Pietersma*, edited by R. J. Hiebert, 229–47. Sheffield: Sheffield Academic Press.

Van der Toorn, K., ed. 1997. "The Iconic Book: Analogies Between the Babylonian Cult of Images and the Veneration of the Torah." In *The Image and the Book: Iconic Cults, Ani-*

conism, and the Rise of Book Religion in Ancient Israel and the Near East, edited by K. Van der Toorn. Leuven: Peeters.

———, et al. 1998. *A Dictionary of Deities and Demons in the Bible.* Leiden: Brill.

———. 2007. *Scribal Culture and the Making of the Hebrew Bible.* Cambridge, MA: Harvard University Press.

Van Huyssteen, J. W., and E. P. Wiebe. 2011. *In Search of Self: Interdisciplinary Perspectives on Personhood.* Grand Rapids: Eerdmans.

Vernant, J-P., and M. Detienne. 1989. *Cuisine of Sacrifice Among the Greeks.* Chicago: University of Chicago Press.

Vernel, H. S. 2000. "Thrice One: Three Greek Experiments in Oneness." In Porter (2000), 79–164.

Veyne, P. 1988. *Did the Greeks Believe in Their Myths?: An Essay on the Constitutive Imagination.* Chicago: University of Chicago Press.

Volten, A. 1992. "Der Begriff der Maat in den ägyptische Weisheitstexten." In Leclant (1992), 77–102.

Von Rad, G. 1958. *Holy War in Ancient Israel.* Grand Rapids: Eerdmans.

———. 1968. *The Problem of the Hexateuch.* London: SCM Press.

———. 1972. *Wisdom in Israel.* Nashville: Abingdon.

Vuilleumier, R. 1966. "Bileam zwischen Bibel und Deir 'Alla." *Theologische Zeitschrift* 52: 150–63.

Waerzeggers, C. 2011. "The Babylonian Priesthood in the Long Sixth Century BC." *Bulletin of the Institute of Classical Studies* 54, no. 2: 59–70.

Walker, A., and R. Leakey. 1993. *The Nariokotome Homo Erectus Skeleton.* Netherlands: Springer.

Walker, C., and M. B. Dick. 1999. "The Induction of the Cult Image in Ancient Mesopotamia: The Mesopotamian *mīs-pî* Ritual." In *Born in Heaven: The Making of the Cult Image in the Ancient Near East,* edited by M. B. Dick. Winona Lake, IN: Eisenbrauns.

Walton, J. H. 2006. *Ancient Near Eastern Thought and the Old Testament.* Grand Rapids: Baker Academic.

Watts, J. W. 1992. *Psalm and Story: Inset Hymns in Hebrew Narrative.* Sheffield: JSOT Press.

———. 2001. *Persia and Torah: The Theory of Imperial Authorization of the Pentateuch.* Atlanta: Scholars Press.

Wechsler, M. G. 2000. "Two Para-Biblical Novellae from Qumran Cave 4: A Reevaluation." *Dead Sea Discoveries* 7: 130–72.

Weeks, N. 2004. *Admonition and Curse: The Ancient Near Eastern Treaty/Covenant Form as a Problem in Inter-Cultural Relationships.* London: T&T Clark.

Weeks, S. 2010. *An Introduction to the Study of Wisdom Literature.* London: T&T Clark.

Weidner, E. F. 1923. *Politische Dokumente aus Kleinasien.* Hildesheim: Olms.

Weiger, J. G. 1979. *The Individuated Self: Cervantes and the Emergence of the Individual.* Columbus: Ohio University Press.

Weinfeld, M. 1970. "The Covenant of Grant in the Old Testament and in the Ancient Near East." *Journal of the American Oriental Society* 90: 184–203.

———. 1972. *Deuteronomy and the Deuteronomic School.* Oxford: Clarendon.

———. 1992a. "Prayer and Liturgical Practice in the Qumran Sect." In *The Dead Sea Scrolls: Forty Years of Research,* edited by D. Dimant et al., 241–58. Leiden: Brill.

———. 1992b. "Grace After Meals in Qumran." *Journal of Biblical Literature* 111: 427–40.

Weitzman, S. 1997. *Song and Story in Biblical Narrative.* Bloomington: Indiana University Press.

Werman, C. 2006. "Epochs and End-Time: The 490-Year Scheme in Second Temple Literature." *Dead Sea Discoveries* 13: 229–55.

Werner, D. S. 2012. *Myth and Philosophy in Plato's* Phaedrus. Cambridge: Cambridge University Press.

Wessels, J. P. H. 1984. "The Joseph Story as a Wisdom Novelette." *Old Testament Essays* (NS) 2: 39–60.

Westermann, C. 1981. *Praise and Lament in the Psalms.* Atlanta: John Knox.

White, S. A. 1990. "4QDt^n: Biblical Manuscript or Excerpted Text?" In *Of Scribes and Scrolls: Studies on the Hebrew Bible, Intertestamental Judaism, and Christian Origins,* edited by H. W. Attridge et al., 13–20. Lanham, MD: University Press of America.

White-Crawford, S. 1994. "Has Esther Been Found at Qumran?" *Revue de Qumran* 17: 306–25.

Wiley, P. T. 1997. *Remember the Former Things: The Recollection of Previous Texts in Isaiah 40–55.* Atlanta: Scholars Press.

Wilson, D. S. 2003. *Darwin's Cathedral: Evolution, Religion, and the Nature of Society.* Chicago: University of Chicago Press.

Wilson, G. H. 1985. *The Editing of the Hebrew Psalter.* Chico, CA: Scholars Press.

Wilson, R. R. 1980. *Prophecy and Society in Ancient Israel.* Philadelphia: Fortress.

Winston, D. 1981. *Philo of Alexandria: The Contemplative Life, the Giants, and Selections.* Ramsey, NJ: Paulist Press.

———. 1989. "Theodicy in Ben Sira and Stoic Philosophy." In *Of Scholars, Savants and Their Texts: Studies in Philosophy and Religious Thought; Essays in Honor of Arthur Hyman,* edited by R. Link-Salinger, 239–49. Berlin: Peter Lang.

Wischmeier, O. 1999. "Gut und Böse: Antithetisches Denken im NT und bei Jesus ben Sirach." In Calduch-Benages and Vermeylen (1999), 129–36.

Wise, M. O. 2010. "The Origins and History of the Teacher's Movement." In *The Oxford Handbook of the Dead Sea Scrolls,* edited by T. H. Lim and J. J. Collins, 92–122. New York: Oxford University Press.

Wolff, H. W. 1974. *Anthropology of the Old Testament.* London: SCM.

Wolters, A. 1990. "Not Rescue but Destruction: Rereading Exod. 15:8." *Catholic Biblical Quarterly* 52: 223–41.

Wrangham, R., et al. 1999. "The Raw and the Stolen: Cooking and the Ecology of Human Origins." *Current Anthropology* 40: 567–94.

Wright, B. 1989. *No Small Difference.* Atlanta: Scholars Press.

Wright, D., D. N. Freedman, and A. Hurvitz. 1995. *Pomegranates and Golden Bells: Studies in Biblical, Jewish, and Near Eastern Ritual, Law, and Literature in Honor of Jacob Milgrom.* Winona Lake, IN: Eisenbrauns.

Wunn, I. 2001. "Cave Bear Worship in the Paleolithic." *Cadernos Lab. Xeolóxico de Laxe* 26: 457–63.

Würthwein, E. 1976. "Egyptian Wisdom and the Old Testament." In Crenshaw (1976), 113–33.

Xeravits, G. G. 2010. *Dualism at Qumran.* London: T&T Clark.

Yacoub, Y. 2007. "The Dignity of the Individuals and Peoples: The Contribution of Mesopotamia and the Syriac Heritage." *Diogenes* 215: 19–37.

Yadin, Y. 1969. "Tefillin (Phylacteries) from Qumran." *Eretz Yisrael* 9: 60–85.

Zahavi, D. 2011. "Unity of Consciousness and the Problem of Self." In *Oxford Handbook of the Self*, edited by S. Gallagher, 316–35. Oxford: Oxford University Press.

Zakovitch, Y. 1980. "A Study of Precise and Partial Name Derivations in Biblical Etymology." *Journal for the Study of the Old Testament* 15: 31–50.

Zaleski, P., and C. Zaleski. 2005. *Prayer: A History.* Boston: Houghton Mifflin Harcourt.

Zenger, E. 1977. *Die Sinaitheophanie: Untersuchungen zum jahwistischen und elohistischen Geschichtswerk.* (Forschung zum Bibel 3.) Wurzburg: EchterVerlag.

Zevit, Z. 2001. *The Religions of Israel: A Synthesis of Parallactic Approaches.* New York: Continuum.

———. 2013. *What Really Happened in the Garden of Eden.* New Haven, CT: Yale University Press.

Zimmerli, W. 1930. "Das Zweite Gebot." In *Festschrift Alfred Bertholet*, edited by W. Baumgartner et al., 550–63. Tübingen: Mohr-Siebeck.

———. 1965. *The Law and the Prophets.* Oxford: Oxford University Press.

———. 1976. "The Place and Limit of the Wisdom in the Framework of the Old Testament Theology." In Crenshaw (1976), 314–26.

SUBJECT INDEX

VERSES CITED